Doctor In Jeopardy

The shocking first inside look into Medicine's dark secrets -
Bad Faith Peer Review and the Conspiracy of Silence

—Ralph J. Miller, Sr., M. D.

Original Unabridged Edition

Doctor In Jeopardy

The shocking first inside look into Medicine's dark secrets -
Bad Faith Peer Review and the Conspiracy of Silence.

by Ralph J. Miller, Sr., M.D.

Published by Aesculapius Publishing
P. O. Box 427
Indiana, PA 15701

http://www.bookmasters.com/marktplc/00345.htm

All Rights Reserved
© Copyright 1998 by Aesculapius Publishing
First Printing 1999

ISBN 0-9669724-0-6

Library of Congress Catalog Card Number 99-94770

*TO MY FAMILY
AND
ANNETTE*

*WITHOUT THEM THIS
WOULD NEVER
HAVE BEEN
POSSIBLE*

— *The Author*

DOCTOR IN JEOPARDY

Chapter One
  A Surgeon's Nightmare
Chapter Two
  The Wartime Campus
Chapter Three
  War Games
Chapter Four
  Portsmouth
Chapter Five
  Jacksonville
Chapter Six
  A Return To The Pitt Campus
Chapter Seven
  Washington, D.C.
Chapter Eight
  Internship
Chapter Nine
  Residency
Chapter Ten
  Indiana - The Early Years
Chapter Eleven
  The Later Years
Chapter Twelve
  The Medical Center
Chapter Thirteen
  The Kangaroo Court
Chapter Fourteen
  The Pennsylvania Courts
Chapter Fifteen
  The Citizens Committee
Chapter Sixteen
  The Federal Courts - The Twelve Year Odyssey
Chapter Seventeen
  The Depositions
Chapter Eighteen
  The Postal Inspection Service
Chapter Nineteen
  The Trial That Never Was
Chapter Twenty
  The Aftermath

PREFACE

Human egotism probably reaches a new level when an inexperienced writer launches into a novel or life story without possessing more than an average degree of literary craftsmanship.

These misguided efforts generally draw to them the vacuum of response that is due; and if such is the fate of this effort, so be it.

The difference here, however, lies in the fact that there is a story that needs to be told - not so much for the writer, as for the professions and for those professionals who will follow. Perhaps, more importantly, the story is for those who are dependent upon them.

The veneer of civilization, at times, wears thin indeed. Our bulwark against a return to barbarism appears, at times, to depend upon an ineffective, disrespected, outlandish system of law, populated by a probable majority of incompetents, who collectively staff what is euphemistically known as the American System of Justice. Similarly, and shoulder to shoulder with the creatures in judicial robes, are the men in white, who have forgotten, or who never really realized the enormity of their responsibility and the potential for their talents to ease the onslaught of human disease and suffering.

An observation of the indifference of those who have pilfered their professions, and an unavoidable truth that the future lies in the hands of a privileged and talented few, prompts the telling of this tale.

The story attempts to relate the best and the worst of two noble professions - Medicine and Law, and the extent to which the knaves within those professions can overshadow and dominate the faint-of-heart and those not willing to be involved.

Law and Medicine have no monopoly on influence, creativity or intelligence, despite the God-like auras emanating from some of our courthouse chambers and doctors' offices. Compared to many of our gifted scholars, statesmen and scientists, many of the braggarts and self-proclaimed spokesmen of our professions seem to be doing so with puny intellects.

Nevertheless, despite enormous erosions of respect for those professionals; physicians and lawyers will continue to hold great potential to influence the outcome of things and to do what is right. This will not occur while the least talented of the lawyers are able to climb their way onto the hardwood perches we have fashioned for them in courtrooms, or while the least talented or misdirected of physicians become our medical politicians and speak for the rest of us. Unfortunately, the professional spokesmen, too often, are recruited from the ranks of mediocrity; and therein lies our story. It is a story of bullies and it is a story of American health care.

Major urban health centers get the headlines, but the overwhelming bulk of health care in America is provided in smaller communities and in community hospitals. Too often, the community hospital is controlled by a group with no concept of hospital or health care management, and with no real sense of obligation to the community it serves. At this point, the door is open for self-interest and abuse.

Paramount to the desire to tell an almost unbelievable tale, there is also the need to uncover a desperate attempt that has been used to conceal the truth of a threat to all American physicians - Bad Faith Peer Review. The story corrects misinformation circulated by and to the news media over a period of time, and which has allowed the misinformed to pass judgement. In the atmosphere of secrecy, there is little chance for truth; and little defense against malicious gossip.

<u>Doctor in Jeopardy</u> is a first - an inside look at a hospital's Peer Review activities gone amuck.

<u>Doctor in Jeopardy</u> is the story of a successful surgeon who was the victim of an inconceivable Peer Review trial, and his subsequent battle within the Pennsylvania and the Federal Court systems, looking for justice.

The story is a chilling revelation of those in Medicine and Law who are willing to undermine the esteem of their chosen professions for money. A few of the names have been changed, but the story is true.

The facts are supported by extensive public documentation now that the Federal and State Courts have unsealed the records at the insistence of the Author.

Modesty often precludes the use of the first person and the substitution of fictitious characters in the telling of a story. After much serious introspection and soul searching, it is evident that would be inadequate in this case - it would be a retreat.

The story is personal; and it must be told as such.

It is the story of a community hospital that lost its soul.

Chapter 1

"You gain strength, courage and confidence by every experience in which you really stop to look fear in the face. You are able to say to yourself, I have lived through this horror. I can take the next thing that comes along. You must do the thing you cannot do."

— Anna Eleanor Roosevelt

A Surgeon's Nightmare

Standing at the scrub sink, mechanically brushing each finger, in turn, even in the middle of the night, wasn't unique. We had done it dozens of times. But, this time, as I watched the nurses through the glass O. R. window; as they positioned and prepped the patient; it was all I could do to keep emotion under control.

I had roused my gynecologist friend from sleep to assist in an effort to stop horrendous bleeding. I needed the best help I could get. Earlier, I had summoned my former Chief from Pittsburgh's Medical Center to come and perform the emergency surgery. The State Police were waiting on Route 22 at New Alexandria to intercept him and escort him to Indiana Hospital. But, he was still an hour away. The lab had called donors for additional transfusions; and the O. R. crew and anesthetist had been summoned. The patient had hemorrhaged several times over the past two or three weeks after prostatic surgery and had responded to transfusions and temporizing. But, this time, transfusions and efforts to stop the bleeding were not affecting the impending shock.

When I reached the patient's bedside, after midnight, he was clammy and restless, with pure blood clogging his drainage tubes. His pressure was low and was falling. The urgency was apparent.

We began wheeling the white tubular hospital bed from the patient's tiny room; and to everyone's horror, found that the bed would not fit through the doorway. The Hospital had attached heavy side rails to the antique bed, without thought; and without knowing that patients would be trapped in that room by the added hardware.

As if we didn't have enough on our hands, I found myself under the bed with a pipe wrench unbolting the hardware from the bed. On the trip down the long green-tiled hallway to the O. R., we passed the Hospital Lab. Logan Bence, the Chief Technician, opened the door and advised, "We have four donors for you. Lots of luck, Buddy." That was one of the most thoughtful remarks I had ever heard. It was certainly appreciated.

John and I were silent as we scrubbed - there was only the splashing of water on the stainless steel of the sink. Mariah, at the head of the table, finished fastening the cardiograph leads to the patient's chest; and after checking the intravenous line, began fastening a mask to the patient's face with those black rubber straps. She was whispering to the patient and then looked around for an O.K. to start the anesthesia. I nodded, hoping that the police had found Doctor Kuehn and that he would arrive in time.

The nightmare had begun some weeks earlier when the patient had travelled to Albany for prostatic surgery by the renowned urologic surgeon of the day, Doctor William Milner and his assistant, Bill Crafton. There was hemorrhage following the transurethral procedure, delaying hospital discharge for a week or more. Each time the hemorrhage was controlled, everyone breathed easier; only to be horrified by renewed bleeding days or weeks later.

John and I took towels from Peggy, our faithful scrub nurse, and dried off before stepping into our dull, green gowns and dusting our hands with powder, before pushing into the rubber gloves.

As I began draping the patient with sterile towels, the patient threw up stomach contents into his mask; our hearts stopped. This can be a catastrophic event, particularly with a patient heading into shock.

Mariah instantly removed the mask and suctioned out the patient's throat before he could aspirate. After a few breathtaking minutes, with the mask back in place and the patient breathing normally, it appeared that things were under control. She peered over her gauze mask and quietly whispered, "O.K.". She was a saint!

I kept looking out toward the scrub sinks for Doctor Kuehn. He wasn't there yet. It was frighteningly clear that we couldn't wait.

John looked across the table and, as our eyes met, he whispered, "Go ahead, Ralph, I'll help." As I gingerly picked up a scalpel from Peggy's tray, I fought back emotions of an intensity never before experienced. With some success, I blocked out those emotions and began to feel a strange sense of tranquility and confidence. I knew I could proceed with what I had to do; even though the patient was my father.

John, as ever, was an excellent assistant; and I found myself describing the anatomy we were encountering. Within seconds, we had identified the urinary bladder and had plunged a scalpel into its wall, releasing a gush of fluid and livery blood clots.

As we deftly explored the area where Crafton had resected the prostate at the bladder's base, we could see the culprit. It was a large artery pumping away at the bladder neck where the resection had been done, leaving a gaping defect and the exposed artery. An index finder, applying pressure, quickly shut off the pumper; and after several minutes Mariah nodded and advised that the pressure was beginning to stabilize.

Peggy passed the needle holder with an atraumatic needle and chromic suture; and for the first time, I glanced away and saw Dr. Kuehn at the scrub sink. He didn't waste much time scrubbing and came to the side of the table quickly. Without the need for an explanation, he plunged a finger into the resected area at the base of the bladder and quipped, "Crafton certainly took a chunk out of there, didn't he?"

I handed the needle holder to him but he quickly pushed my hand away and advised, "Go ahead, you're doing fine. I'll give you some exposure."

The man had always demonstrated his strength with a sincere sense of humility. That gesture only enhanced his already sizable stature.

We placed two "figure of eight" sutures around the bleeding vessel and the damaged bladder neck and confirmed that the vessel was well secured. We agreed on further safety by packing the damaged area with a long length of narrow surgical gauze. We then closed the bladder and overlying structures; after confirming that we had been successful in repairing the damage.

Sometime during the skin closure and the taping of protective gauze dressings, I noticed that Dr. Kuehn had left the table. He had quietly slipped out and headed back to Pittsburgh. He had left the dressing room by the time we looked for him.

John and I helped lift our patient onto a stretcher, and after a final check that things were under control; fired our gloves and gowns into a hamper. There was none of the usual banter that usually follows the tension of a difficult case. There was an unusual silence, except for a few whispers.

I never knew whether the others felt it; but there was a presence in that room that night. I had never been one to believe in such things; but something of great strength and encouragement was there and helped our little team do their best.

John and I stepped out of the O.R. double doors and washed the powder from our hands at the sinks. John tried to catch my eye but I couldn't look at him. "Ralph", he said quietly, "I couldn't have done that." Without looking, I could only mumble, "I can't ever thank you enough."

I followed the bed back to that little room, and after checking the drainage and vital signs; headed down the hallway to the sun porch looking out over the Hospital's winding driveway. The sun was just beginning to come up between the maples lining the drive; and I found myself almost too drained to think.

Sandra Hood, a night supervisor, appeared behind me and asked quietly, "Can I get you a cup of coffee?" She noted the tears welling up and I broke into uncontrollable sobbing - I just could not control myself. She quickly spun around and left, and I was again alone, staring at that beautiful sunrise.

My thoughts were in a muddle. I couldn't get the events of Albany out of my mind. I had taken Dad to Albany so that he could have the best in surgery. Bill Crafton had squandered my trust in him. In the O.R., he had shown-off trying to impress everyone with how fast he could do the procedure. I was remembering how difficult it was, later that day, to get him back to the hospital to help his bleeding patient. How could he be so arrogant when he held a life in his hands? I was beginning to wonder who we could trust.

The idealistic belief of being part of a profession of idealists, dedicated to excellence, had been slowly tempered over the past few years. But, the experience with a show-off surgeon and a hospital with beds that trapped patients was bringing reality to mind with a crashing crescendo.

Probably, for the first time, I was tempering my vision of the future with a questioning of the past; and how I had arrived at that community hospital in the foothills of the Alleghenys.

It must have all begun on that June day on the University of Pittsburgh Campus.

Chapter 2

*"Education is not something to prepare you for life;
it is a continuous part of life."*

— *Henry Ford*

THE WARTIME CAMPUS

I suppose Pitt was always a part of the family. Dad had graduated from the University of Pittsburgh School of Dentistry in the class of '19 - an impressive year indeed. The immortal Jock Southerland, Katie Easterday, Tommy Davies and other football greats studied to become dentists while members of the great teams of Pop Warner, the famous coach. Jock was older than the rest, who had entered the School directly from high school. He had been a policeman in Sewickly for some time, and went on to coach more great football teams with stars like Marshall Goldberg, Curley Stebbens and Bill Dadio. He was one of the first to take a team to Pasadena's Rose Bowl. The family would bump into Dad's colleagues every so often; and I always got a great kick out of listening to Dr. Southerland's Scottish accent. He was always Dr. Southerland to his players - "Jock", to everyone else. These men were giants at the time; but in later years, I would marvel that these men of average physical stature, especially Davies, were so outstanding in their sport.

The early Pitt teams played at Forbes Field - home of the Pirates, on the other side of Forbes Avenue, looking out into Panther Hollow and Schenley Park. Later, the giant oval of Pitt's Stadium had been carved into the hillside overlooking the lower Pitt Campus. The Pitt fans still know it as "cardiac hill" - because of the steep climb up DeSoto Street, past

Western State Institute and Childrens Hospital. There was an added challenge from Gate 2 through the interior of the Stadium to the seats.

Grade school kids could get their tickets for home games for a quarter and join that hooting grade school crowd of youngsters in section 13 near the far end zone. The "82 Lincoln", one of the bulky, orange, clanking iron street cars, would carry excited kids from the East End Lincoln Avenue district down Fifth Avenue, past the Cathedral of Learning. After another two blocks, we would be at the bottom of DeSoto Street. The ride was a series of grinding, noisy stops and even noisier, grinding starts, lasting an hour or more. Those slippery, woven-cane seats, the slotted wooden-slat floors and the dirty glass windows that wouldn't open, never took away from the excitement of it all. The conductor would be in his shiny, worn, navy blue uniform with that distinctive cap, featuring a short, black beak and an unimpressive silver emblem above. He would pull the rope hanging from the ceiling, to register each fare on a meter for all to see. There was all sorts of clanking : the coins going into the steel and glass fare box; the overhead loud "ding" with each pull of the overhead cord and the loud "clang" after each stomp on a brass knob projecting from the floor at the conductor's feet. That would be the conductor impatiently trying to move traffic ahead.

Joining the mob marching up DeSoto Street, past the vendors, the college pennants, the lapel ornaments, the chrysanthemums and newsboys hocking special football editions of the Pittsburgh Press and the Sun-Telegraph was as much fun as watching a game.

The Boy Scout ushers would find our seats in the stadium; and like all the rest of the kids, we would be in our seat for a few moments and then probably visit a dozen other seats before the game ended.

Never to be forgotten was the game with Nebraska, when temporary bleachers were built onto the Stadium's track to accommodate the largest crowd in Pitt football history. We would never forget Curly Stebbens' ninety one yard kick-off return and the Pitt Panther. Imagine being able to run down the steps of the aisle to the first row and actually touch the man in a Panther suit; even peer into the open jaws of that panther head, confirming that there really was a man in there!

There was never doubt that Pitt would be the next step after high school; and there was never any thought that a college education would require any more effort or performance than Wilkinsburg High; when a book was never taken home and where the favorite course was wood shop.

That dreary, overcast Sunday afternoon, after tinkering with a neighborhood kid's chemistry set, would change all that. As I walked home, kicking loose gravel on the wet asphalt of Orlando Drive, I wondered what that radio announcement meant. I would ask the folks where Pearl Harbor was.

Within weeks, the high school principal would announce at Assembly, that anyone planning to enter college would be excused for the rest of the senior year and could return for graduation with the class in June. The sudden, unexpected transition from high school antics and a thoughtless existence into academia left some of us unprepared and confused.

Somehow the entrance requirements for "Pre-Med" had been met - even the two years of Latin.

In an effort to squeeze by that required second year, I had been tutored in the hated subject by Mrs. Patterson, a retired Latin teacher. My visits to her North Avenue apartment for an hour after school, I'm afraid, seriously threatened the poor woman's sanity.

The poor soul, at times, would feel that she was making some real progress when I would make some bone-headed mistake in declining a verb or translating a passage. She would loose all composure and pound her manicured fists on the card table where we worked, shouting, "No, No, No!" I still see the pencils and books bouncing from the surface of the table as she vented her frustration.

Years later, she would inquire, at a Garden Club function, as to the whereabouts of her less-than-favorite student. She would stare in disbelief on learning that he was a medical student.

The Mrs. Pattersons are the real unsung heroes of the academic world. What greater calling is there than that of motivating and teaching disinterested juveniles, who will eventually be called upon to play a role in our Society?

The first stroll into Pitt's Cathedral had been on an overcast, cold, January day. The "75 Wilkinsburg" stopped in front of the Pittsburgh Athletic Club, on the corner of Fifth and the Boulevard. After crossing Fifth, I walked toward the entrance of the Cathedral along the wide flagstone walk, gazing upward at the structure jutting into the overcast, as I entered the three story high, cavernous Commons Room. The day had arrived all too suddenly, and rather than being one of excitement, was one of quiet apprehension.

At the far corners of that huge interior were large fireplaces devouring tree-sized logs and shedding the only real sense of warmth under those high vaulted stone ceilings. The large, wrought-iron chandeliers suspended by iron chains from the vaulted ceilings, gave a quiet, cool glow, reflecting from the frugal oak tables and benches and the polished flagstone floors. A few young faces were enjoying the warmth of the fireplaces, while others, seated at the tables and the matching hard benches, were quietly reading or chatting. The scene unmistakedly provoked a sense of respect, if not reverence.

The Nationality Rooms surrounding the main hall, on all four sides and up a few steps from the main hall, overlooked the Commons Room through arches bridged by wrought-iron railings. Occasionally, one of the room's heavy plank doors would swing open on its wrought-iron hinges, to reveal the elegance of a classroom constructed and furnished in the tradition of the country it represented. Would it be possible that I would one day have a class in one of these rooms?

Tradition had it that the "Tuck Shops" on a lower level of the Cathedral were "tucked" into unused space as an afterthought. As I walked past the cafeteria line of the Red Tuck Shop, named for the scarlet vinyl of the booths, and past the baby-blue booths of the larger Blue Shop, there was a sense of being a total stranger and being totally out of place. I wondered if I could - or wanted to be - part of that scene. The girls seemed so mature and the groups so confident, as they mingled around the booths. I felt insignificant and unprepared for this.

An express elevator ride to the twenty-sixth floor and an aerial view of Pittsburgh's Oakland district, Forbes Field, just across Forbes Avenue, downtown Pittsburgh, the flashing Iron City Beer sign on Mt. Washington in the distance and the towering six J&L blast furnaces in the Mon Valley, ended the day.

On the street car ride home, the Registrar's booklets outlining the courses for "Pre-Med" heightened, not only a sense of new experiences, but also more of the uneasiness. Reminiscing, one can now only recognize how immature we were at the time and how that immaturity on being dragged from childhood would affect the rest of our lives.

Registration was held in the Commons Room with absolutey no respect for its Gothic elegance. The heavy oak tables and benches were replaced by long rows of tables - simply wide boards on wooden "horses" covered with brown wrapping paper, and with instruction cards suspended from overhead wires.

The lighting was irreverently supplemented by "floods" jutting from the iron railings separating the main hall from the second floor corridors and classrooms. The quiet elegance of the place had been replaced by a babbling cauldron of humanity: faculty behind the long tables, piled high with schedules and books, and on the other side, students frantically trying to match schedules and courses.

By surviving that experience, I found myself enrolled in the Pre-Med sciences, and . . .the Reserve Officers Training Corps.

It was a surprise to learn how much free time there was between classes; and no one around to see what was done with the free time. I soon found that there was a choice. One could lounge in the Tuck Shop drinking Coke or the time could be spent in study.

There were a number of quiet corners in different libraries and halls. Spending evenings in study still didn't appeal; so that I found myself quietly alone and reading between classes. The science courses were tedious, but there were interesting long hours in the laboratories of Alumni Hall - a long, narrow, yellow brick building, high on the bluff overlooking the Cathedral and lower Campus. The architecture of those buildings on the hill was part of an earlier scheme of the University to have the hill become a replica of the Acropolis.

The building was filled with labs, each with rows of wooden cabinets, topped with slabs of polished slate and wooden racks running along their lengths and loaded with glass-stoppered bottles, each holding a variety of chemicals. Each station had a sink, lined with slate with a tarnished goose-neck faucet.

During lab sessions, four or five experimenters would stand along either side of the counter, facing each other, separated by the racks of reagents. We would distill, and percolate and boil and compound; recording the results in our lab manuals. By the end of those Freshman Labs, enthusiasm for the marvels of Chemistry would wane.

Red McGeary was the Pre-Med across from me. We would exchange wisecracks and the latest information on the girls in the class across those reagent bottles. His snickering and witty reflections on the nonsense of boiling all that stuff, made the lab a lot more tolerable. Spring had arrived and the large casement lab windows were open, looking out over the steep, grassy slope, dotted with dandelions, falling away to the brick paving of Alumni Drive. The window to my left was a mere two feet from the ground and I felt a craving to just bolt out and sprint down that bank. As I looked over to McGeary, I could tell he was thinking the same thing. We got to discussing the potentials and the chemical properties of potassium chlorate, powdered carbon and powdered magnesium. We had seen the properties of these substances in some of our experiments and determined that we could make some dandy smoke bombs from just the right combination. There were some large gelatin capsules in the lower cabinet, and we found ourselves compounding the mixture and pouring it into a number of those capsules. I recall lighting the rounded end of one of the capsules, watching it smoulder and then giving it a toss out the open window and over the bank. There was a flash of bright light followed by a large puff of dense, white smoke. As the puff grew into a small cloud and drifted down toward the lower campus, my red-headed friend and I stood in amazement.

A few of the "scientists" from other sections of the lab gathered around us in a quest for scientific knowledge. "How did we do it?" "Would we do it again?" Several repeat launchings demonstrated reproducible results. Each flash would be followed by a dense white cloud that would slowly rise and then drift off. Someone reflected that Doctor Silverman's office was just two floors up. We decided to avoid detection and put all of the fixings into one last shot. We loaded a larger capsule, and after we lit the smooth end in a Bunsen burner, gave it a mighty heave. It was a beautiful result. There was a bright flash and another, even larger, puff of white smoke. For some reason, we didn't get the same exclamations of amazement from our scientific friends. There were no oohs or aahs - just silence. As I turned around, everyone was back at his bench and busily at work. In their place, at the doorway, stood Doctor Silverman, Professor of Chemistry. He didn't say a word and never changed his expression which appeared to be unbridled amazement. He slowly turned and disappeared, as I busied myself with the rest of the day's experiments. I often wondered what he had been thinking.

Making gym classes at Treese Gym and other buildings on that hill above Pitt Stadium in the short time between classes at the Cathedral and those on the hill, just about made track stars of all of us. But, I was setting no records with my efforts on the Pitt track team, which was struggling along after the team's coach joined the Navy. On a late summer afternoon a few of us were socializing outside the entrance to Thaw Hall, when one of the group mentioned that there was a notice in the Pitt News for try-outs for the cheerleading squad. The squad was a varsity sport, at the time, and a spot with the squad was somewhat of an honor. McGeary mentioned that Miller should try out for that; and I began to think, once again, that it might be something worthwhile. Try-outs were held; and I found myself part of that all-male group and leading cheers on Saturday afternoons in front of the student section of home games and a few away games. The Pitt band always sent a drum and trumpet section through the gates at the end of the stadium to herald the band - at the time, one of the largest in the country. I had convinced the squad that we could make a grand entrance by running through the gates and through the drum and trumpet section, and after a sharp turn to the left, whip up the student sections into a frenzy of cheers. On that Saturday afternoon, we did that with the sharp turn toward the student section, but my ensuing hand spring was altered by a bit of wet turf and I found myself flat on my back before a few thousand boisterous students. It was not one of life's most thrilling moments.

Of a lot more significance was the part-time job at Western State - the psychiatric hospital on the Pitt Campus. Ed Ochs, another Pre-Med, told of openings for part-time attendants at the Hospital just below Pitt Stadium. The openings were brought on by the wartime shortage of regulars. Ed was an easy going, likable kid, whose pals had dubbed him, "Hose Nose", even though he was a good-looking kid. So, Ed and I met with Miss Harden, the Hospital's Administrator, and were hired for late afternoon and weekend shifts. We had no way of knowing how unusual an experience that would be. "Western State" - actually the "Western State Psychiatric Institute"- was the large, yellow brick structure, affiliated with the University, in the shadow of Pitt Stadium. The elevator banks arose from a small, marble lobby facing the street entrance and the flight of granite steps. Ed and I were met in the lobby by a tall, muscular man of about fifty, in a white uniform accentuated by a thick, gold chain looped into a side pocket. He used his keys on the chain to summon the elevator and explained that it was the access to the "secure" floors. We had learned that the third and fourth floors were controlled with tight security. We stepped off on the fourth floor, and our guard explained that this was the "secure" floor for violent men, with the third floor being home for the most severely disturbed women. The striking design of the building was evident. A central hallway ran the entire length of the building, joining sun porches on each end. "You probably notice how long the hallway is", our guide noticed. "This is so we can keep an eye on things from any spot on the floor." We were introduced to the Head Nurse, manning a small, glass-enclosed station, after the glass panelled door was unlocked. She was immaculate in her highly starched white uniform and cap and her pristine complexion was accentuated by gold spectacles and tight blond curls. She softly spoke of her duties in taking care of the patients, and gave us pass keys and chains for passage through the units. We would find her words of caution to be grossly understated; "You know, we have patients here who can become acute and you should be cautious not to leave yourself vulnerable. It is best for you to work in pairs and not be too far apart at any one time."

We found that there were, indeed, such things as padded cells and straight-jackets. On our first tour through the ward, we glanced into one of the "safe rooms" through a small rectangle of safety glass and saw a hairy, bearded man attempting to crawl up the walls, which had been covered with tufted canvas not unlike gym mats. He was naked and had shredded his pajamas into fine tatters, which were strewn about the dull tile floor. A solitary outside window was covered with a tightly woven steel screen. The nude body was thick with matted, black hair, plastered with the poor man's excretions, which were also smeared on the walls and into the fine squares of the window screen. His body was covered with dime-sized scabs, which had been produced by self-mutilation. Dull roars increasing to hoarse screams came from that troubled throat. At one point, as I stared through the fine octagons of wire in the safety glass, he came to the door and our eyes met. That look was unforgettable and beyond description. I was reminded of burning coals in that exchange of glances; but mixed with rage, was unmistakable, exquisite pain. Ochs tried to be nonchalant after his turn to view his first contact with insanity; but he stepped back, looked at me and blurted, "Jesus."

The patient was named Santilla, a U. S. Army Sergeant. We were to learn that he had been sent to Western State as part of a psychiatric research program conducted by the University for the Army. Santilla had gone berserk during the stress of service and was considered uncontrollable during his episodes of rage. At other times, he appeared to be near-normal.

I couldn't help but muse, for the first time, on the fine line that separated Santilla and probably the rest of us from some distant ancestor. In reflecting, I think of the helplessness of psychiatry, such a short time ago, to treat and manage mental disease. We were to learn that standard treatments with hydrotherapy, barbiturates and bromide were largely ineffective in that wide range of illnesses lumped together as schizophrenia. It would be years before the new drugs - the Phenothiazines and the Benzodiazepines - the psychotropic drugs - would make the padded rooms, the straight-jackets and the hydrotherapy rooms obsolete.

Mr. Medley was my favorite of the patients. He was a diminutive, little man - white-haired, mild-mannered and non-communicative. He had a ruddy complexion and a cherubic, pink face. Dressed in his standard blue robe and slippers, he would walk the length of that endless hallway hour after hour. The rhythmic slap of his slippers on the tile would be punctuated at each overhead light. With his hands tightly clasped in prayer, except for the index fingers, he would pause briefly under each light, raise his hands in a salute to the light and recite, "Take me, My Lord, just as I am" or, "Oh Lord, Oh Lord, take me just as I am." No one was quite sure whether Mr. Medley had been a minister or just thought that he was one of the Clergy.

Belcher was a tall, muscular, handsome, young guy who quietly kept to himself and who always appeared jovial and cooperative. His records revealed a medical discharge from the Army for homosexual behavior. Ed had little doubt about the accuracy of that, and often complained that Belcher was overly friendly. After awhile, the amorous attractions to Ed became a little less discrete - usually at bath time. Ed and I would lead groups of patients to the showers and help them bathe and dry before returning them to their rooms. There he would be -Belcher - with nothing on but a smile, waiting for his shower. As Ochs would hand him a towel to cover his muscular frame, he would routinely drawl an obscene offer.

One story on the ward was too bizarre to believe. A patient whose name has been lost with time, and who carried a diagnosis of catatonic schizophrenia, spent his entire life in typical catatonic fashion - completely immobilized, day after day, lying flat on his back in bed. He would allow the nurses to tube-feed him three times a day. But, we would never hear a word from him or detect any sign of movement; as we would pass the rubber tube down his throat and pour the liquid diet into his stomach. Even though the eyes were open, they simply stared ahead, never focusing, never indicating any recognition. The story had it that the patient would come out of his trance once a year - early on each Easter Sunday.

I was there on Easter Sunday and it happened. He was seen sitting on the side of the bed; walking down the hall; speaking to a few of us and then returning to his bed. I was amazed. To this day, I don't understand how he ever knew it was Easter; and I wonder, more so, about what modern medication could now do for him and those so unfortunate to be like him.

At the time, there was too much bravado to admit that we were afraid of any of the patients. But, it was obvious that Ochs and I were more than a little fearful of another "schizophrenic" - a small, Chinese boy of about twenty, with a frozen, cruel scowl and a gaze that never indicated that anything was ever seen or noticed. Ed would talk about the boy's great strength despite his slight build, but I was never quite a believer. The Chinese boy was one of the patients prescribed hydrotherapy; and I got my first view of the therapy unit late one afternoon while relieving Ed. I escorted our little friend to the hydrotherapy department on an upper floor; always keeping him at arm's length and in front of me. The hydrotherapy room was a large, white-tiled room, fitted with a line of several large, porcelain tubs and a parallel row of stainless steel tables. Our patient slipped out of his pajamas without incident and allowed the nurses to put him in one of the tubs. A canvas cover was then snapped across the top, allowing his head to protrude, while he relaxed in the warmth of the water-filled tub. After an hour in the relaxing, warm water, the patients would be released from their tubs and stretched out on one of the tables which had been prepared with a series of overlapping cold, wet sheets, alternately, one side at a time. The cold sheets would be folded across the unclad body until the patient, in his frigid cocoon, was unable to move. This was called the cold-pack, and the interior of the pack apparently gained warmth by the time the sheets were unfolded. After another hour, there would be a supposedly sedated patient.

    On this occasion, I helped my Oriental friend off the table, keeping a respectful distance; and was holding his sheet in front of him, as he dried. Without a flicker in those deep, wicked, little eyes, I was the sudden recipient of a body blow through the sheet that left me on one knee and windless. After that, I managed to keep my distance from that character. My stomach knotted when I saw him. He really had me snake-bit.

    It wasn't too long after that event, that Ed and I were on duty together on a late afternoon shift. Things had been quiet and the dinner trays had been returned with a welcome lull before evening showers. I was casually talking with one of the patients, on one of the sun porches at the end of that long, long hallway. Ochs was at the far end of the hall, walking toward the opposite sun porch. I stood frozen, as a figure leaped from one of the doorways, knocking Ed to the floor and entangling him in a choking grip. After I collected myself, I set off on a sprint to get Ed free of that strangle-hold. I now recognized it was was being administered by my Chinese acquaintance.

    I was a track team hopeful at the time and wasn't gaining any wide recognition for speed. Nevertheless, I think my sprint down that hallway might have been a world mark; as I plowed into the back of that little attacker. Ed obviously couldn't breathe and I was approaching panic by my failure to break that unbelievably strong death-grip around Ed's neck. In desperation, I got an arm around the attacker's neck and squeezed like I didn't know I could. It seemed like a week before that arm loosened around Och's neck and he began gulping air. There were soon a few gurgles from my little friend and he went limp. I couldn't believe the little fellow's strength.

Ed recovered quickly, and together, we carried the patient to a quiet room where he was later sedated and strapped into a restraining jacket. I had always been skeptical of stories of padded cells, straight-jackets and the "superhuman" strength exhibited by the insane. But, as I recall, that stint at Western State changed all that. I now realized that, as a teenager, I had participated in the era of insane asylums before the age of mind-altering drug therapy.

We were too dazzled, at the time, by our sudden entry into the hospital scene, to empathize with the patients. Looking back, it is now impossible to overlook the intense pain inflicted by mental illness - not only upon the insane themselves but upon those close to them.

The years since, with their myriad of patient experiences, have underlined the thin line separating the minor peculiarities of human behavior, we see in ourselves and in those around us daily, from true illness. A compassionate physician can be expected to believe, "But, for the grace of God, there go I."

There were too many distractions on that war-time campus for the plight of Mr. Medley, Santilla, Belcher and the other tortured souls of that place to impact in a meaningful way; but, it was a beginning.

The football season with its fun weekends was over and the daily routine of lectures and the science labs were becoming less interesting and more of a chore. The whole atmosphere of the campus was becoming military, with more and more Army Air Force Cadets occupying the upper floors of the Cathedral. News of the Atlantic and Pacific wars dominated much of campus thinking, and I was having trouble with Organic Chemistry. The first semester had been manageable, but the second had seen growth in the complexity of the subject, requiring longer and longer hours, just to stay abreast. Many of the Freshman buddies had joined the Navy and Army college programs and had accelerated their careers. But, for some reason, I simply expected to be drafted into the Army. The campus life was becoming pointless.

The Wilkinsburg draft board was housed in a dreary second floor suite above Hays' Stationery Store on Wood Street. Over the final month, I would find myself, on the way home, climbing those concrete steps to the short hallway above and entering the ribbed glass door reading, "Draft Board #13." Miss Martin, a gray-haired, middle-aged lady with bifocals, ran the place from a small desk facing the door in the front room. She would routinely scan a list and, without looking up, simply advise, "No, you're not on the list."

On that late afternoon in November, the "75 Wilkinsburg" rolled along Trenton Avenue; and I recall staring absent-mindedly through the narrow parallel rods outside the streetcar's windows at the dull, soot-darkened apartments lining Trenton Avenue. There had been a November snow and little streams of blackened water ran down the curbs into the sewers.

I jumped off before the car made its turn and avoided a series of puddles to reach the tunnel under the Pennsylvania tracks leading to Wood Street.

I expected the draft board to be closed, and took the steps two at a time. But, the door was unlocked. The office was darkened except for a desk lamp with a green glass shade. Miss Martin was writing on pages before her and quietly put them in a desk drawer when she saw me. After apologizing for the intrusion, I made the usual inquiry. She tilted her head back, and for the first time, with a direct gaze advised, "You will be inducted on the third of next month."

Chapter 3

"Older men declare war. But, it is the youth that must fight and die, and it is the youth who must inherit the tribulations, the sorrow and the triumphs that are the aftermaths of war."

— *Republican National Convention*

WAR GAMES

The notice in the mail was in a plain, official looking envelope with unimpressive black lettering in the corner reading: "Selective Service, Draft Board #13", with a Wood Street address. The message was on a sloppily mimeographed page with my name and address filling out the blanks. The message began, "Greeting", and in official language, related that I had been selected by my fellow citizens to serve the Country. The time and place of induction were typed into another space near the end of the message.

Induction was to be at the Old Post Office building in Pittsburgh, a large, square, limestone structure, its exterior blackened and streaked by the passage of steam locomotives, only a few yards away. From there, the silver rails of the Pennsylvania Line emerged from the sheds over its loading platforms at the Pennsylvania Station and headed east toward the Ohio River; squeezing between the Post Office and Bigelow Boulevard. Printed signs on the walls of the Grant Street Lobby of the Post office gave directions to the induction area on the fourth floor. Beyond a frosted glass and walnut door was the room filled with folding wooden chairs, facing a tattered desk, which, in turn, stood beneath a portrait of Franklin Delano Roosevelt. On the President's right was a large flag, edged with gold fringe; and posted on the wall to the President's left was a poster with a stern

Uncle Sam pointing a finger and captioned, "Uncle Sam Wants You". An Army private motioned me to the desk and went through a routine of checking name and birth certificate in an exaggerated official manner. All the time, I couldn't help glancing at the poster. Uncle Sam seemed to catch one's attention. My thoughts reflected on the message, "He wants you" and I found myself thinking, "He sure as hell does."

Gradually, the room filled with a mixture of men and boys all wearing clothing and expressions reflecting a serious lack of enthusiasm for the occasion. But for me, it was all a big adventure. The uncertainty, the expectations, the military, all combined to create a feeling of great expectations as I sat with the growing group. A moderately built, pleasant looking fellow in a plaid shirt and leather jacket sat on the folding chair to my left, and gave a half-hearted "Hi". He had no more notion of what came next or where we were headed than I did; but he seemed almost fatherly as he talked about his family and his feelings at leaving his wife and children. He talked with a cockey self-assertion and with a slight suggestion of a dialect. His manner reflected warmth and it was clear that his feelings at the moment were far different from mine. We shook hands and he said to call him "DiBlasi". As he talked abut his young son and daughter and his wife I couldn't imagine what an old man in his forties was doing in the draft. As he talked and gave reassurance, I noticed more and more old fellows filling the chairs and I became impressed with the character of the man on my left. I noticed his crisp features and olive complexion, his neatly trimmed black mustache; and I thought I noticed his eyes beginning to water a little.

As they called our names, we would be led into a series of adjoining rooms, each starkly furnished with nothing more than a wooden table or two and a few folding chairs. A fat little fellow in khaki commanded each of us to strip down to our shorts and put our belongings in one of the wicker baskets on a counter at the far wall. Then the physical examination was begun. There were two or three men in business suits holding stethoscopes, which they appeared to use as symbols of their authority; but even without them, we knew they were the doctors.

After we were handed a bottle to fill and complied with instructions for this filling, the bottles were placed in a long line on a narrow shelf outside a small, square porthole leading into another small room. A peak through that square aperture revealed a young man in khaki obviously performing tests on the amber specimens. We found ourselves walking back and forth in front of a line of doctors and young men in khaki. They kept looking at our feet, and I had the feeling that I was about to be rejected for flat feet; so, as I walked past a doctor with curly hair and a distinct New York accent, I tried to arch my feet a little. It would be terrible to get turned down and go back home a 4-F. "What the hell are you doing?" he snapped, and I abandoned my efforts to hide my lack of arches.

We then formed another line in an adjoining room, standing shoulder to shoulder, while two of the doctors gave a brief listen to our chests, front and back, and would mutter, "O. K", after each examination. This must be it. The whole thing took less than ten minutes. Was I in or was I going to be turned down? Then, the curly haired fellow with the sharp accent, stethoscope dangling from his neck, accosted each of us. As he faced each of us, he would command, "Drop your shorts, turn your head to the left and cough, turn your head to the right and cough." With each head turn, he would thrust his finger, like a javelin, into our lower parts. The first thrust caught me by surprise and I found myself headed for the ceiling. When he repeated the maneuver on the other side, I stoically bit my tongue with determination and merely stood on tiptoe. He approached a fat kid, next in line and I couldn't help but wonder how this would turn out. As the kid's shorts fluttered to his ankles, that educated finger shot into the kid's left groin like lightning. The kid let out a loud scream followed by convulsive giggling, while grabbing the examiner's arm in the process. With each try, the giggling and the bouncing of fatty flesh became more pronounced, putting the whole room into gales of laughter. Finally, the red-faced examiner moved on down the line barking, "Drop your shorts, turn your head to the left and cough, turn your head to the right and cough."

One at a time, the inductees would be directed into the room of folding wooden chairs where we had first assembled. As the room again filled, we all noticed the absence of three or four faces that had been with us. A brief glance through a partially opened door in the far corner caught this little group passing en route to an exit leading to the stairway. Whispers raced around the room between the men, now all seated on the folding chairs. This small group had been rejected and were returning home.

The room was strangely silent with us all expectant of what might follow. Again, on my left, was DeBlasi, who knowingly announced that we would soon be inducted but would have a few days before leaving for Army basic training. He firmly predicted we would be on the way to a southern Army camp within a week and confided that Fort Bragg was the most likely destination. Under all the certainty that DeBlasi exuded, there was a hint of trepidation and a trace of uncertainty. He was mature; he was the father of a family and had become accustomed to his fatherly role.

Our speculations were suddenly ended when a tall, skinny, pasty-faced Corporal, sporting a shock of red hair angling across his forehead, commanded us to attention. There was a noisy shuffling of feet and scraping of those folding chairs across those floor boards as a moderately built officer entered and rigidly turned to face us. What a contrast. His olive coat and light beige trousers were beautifully pressed at just the right places. His plain, brown shoes were polished into mirrors and his captain's bars and battle ribbons accentuated his appearance to all of us dressed like beggars by comparison. There we stood - in sloppy informality with our baggy pants, unshined shoes and worn jackets. We were obviously creating a sense of disdain with the officer - a symbol of military pride.

His disregard for us was poorly concealed as we found ourselves standing there with our right hands raised, repeating an oath of allegiance to our country, and anticipating our fate.

After the oath, the captain sharply turned again and marched off as suddenly as he had entered. With a disinterested monotone, the Corporal advised us that we would be called, one by one, to receive our orders in one of the adjoining rooms. He confided that most of us would not report back for a week or more but that some would be leaving within twenty-four hours. We would be given the time and place and would present ourselves with simple clothing that could be mailed back home and were to bring no jewelry or equipment. But, we would be allowed a small container of toilet items. We were warned not to attempt to bring a camera, a radio, or any significant amounts of money.

We seemed to be called alphabetically, and in short order, DeBlasi was called and ushered into another room. Everyone before him had gone into the room and had not returned. We reasoned that they had been dismissed and were leaving by the back entrance. As DeBlasi left, he shook hands and speculated that maybe we would be together at Fort Bragg. He disappeared into the next room and I began to notice the empty chairs. Little by little, the room emptied until, "Miller, R. J." was barked out by the Corporal. I found myself being ushered into one of the large rooms of desks manned by men in khaki and civilian clerks. I stood before a battered wooden desk behind which sat an older plump man in khaki with a series of chevrons on each sleeve. He was ruddy complexioned and had a bulbous nose over a pleasant grin. He gave a jolly "Hello" and handed me a small brown envelope which he said contained my orders. He seemed relaxed and allowed me to scan the contents of the envelope - a single, unofficial white card reading: "Miller, R. J. U.S.N.I 9867001." On the next line it read: "Report Pennsylvania R.R. Station Gate E, December 11, 1943, 6:30 P.M., departure 7:30 P.M.". The sergeant obligingly looked at the card to determine for me which Army camp would be my likely destination. "Why son", he said quietly, "You're in the Navy. Your group will be heading for Newport, Rhode Island."

Dad and his friend, Frank, were joking back and forth as Frank drove us to the station in his old black Willies. The Pennsylvania Station, an imposing, ornate structure of seven or eight stories, was not brightly lighted inside. Its reddish exterior had been blackened by years of Pittsburgh's soot and steam locomotives passing through. Its exterior now dimly reflected the bright lights of the street lamps lining the long, oval concourse leading into the sheltered marquee. The entire drive was clogged with wartime traffic. The cars, buses and cabs were disgorging families there to meet a serviceman and families who were staying with servicemen until the last minute before they would board a train and leave. Men in khaki and navy blue were everywhere. Some were frantically rushing to meet a schedule, while others were sitting with families on the stark, slatted benches inside the massive interior. The high, arched ceiling reflected the buzz of dozens of conversations, but no laughter. There would be an occasional shout of delight from a friend or relative first sighting a loved one, but the mood was urgent and somber. For me, the minutes were filled with anticipation of the great things ahead. The surprise of being Navy and not Army had passed and the excitement of entering a new life almost eclipsed the pangs of uncertainty at leaving home. Dad and Frank made an effort to keep things light with their usual banter. But, it was apparent that, even to an eighteen year old, immature for his age, that Dad was concerned. Much later his words, "You'll never know until you are a parent", would echo back to remind me of the anguish the folks would live with over the coming few years.

As we approached Gate E, the group heading for Newport was assembling under the direction of a salty looking character in a Navy pea jacket and bell bottoms. The rakish angle and the crush of his white hat distinguished him from Navy recruits, who all wore their hats like pot lids. He quietly checked off names and cautioned us to stay in the immediate area until train time. Frank reached into one of his coat pockets and produced a shining, bright silver dollar. "Here you are tenderfoot", he said,

"Put this in your pocket and keep it with you." Dad looked pleased as the good luck piece was stored in a pants pocket. Then, a familiar face appeared. "DeBlasi, what are you doing here?" A good-hearted chuckle followed our recollection of our former certainty of heading south to an Army post. Now we were finding ourselves boarding a train for a Navy base to the north.

DeBlasi shook hands with Dad and Frank with a warm friendliness, and related that Newport was a naval training station, probably the oldest in the Country. He said that we would be there by late afternoon the following day. Our speculation on what lay ahead was interrupted by a firm command for the group for Newport to assemble at the gate. There must have been thirty of us, but scarcely two or three of my age. It was obvious that the draft had reached into families to take husbands and fathers.

A final handshake with Frank and Dad and we found ourselves moving through the iron gate onto the wooden slatted platform between waiting trains extending out into the night. Bare bulbs swinging from circles of white porcelain hanging from the overhead canopies of the platform illuminated the sides of the dull, maroon passenger cars. Their rows of rivets cast little shadows contrasting with the bright gold Pennsylvania R. R. lettering above the windows. Wisps of steam hissed from the couplings between the cars and red-capped porters were maneuvering large, crate-like motorized baggage carts up and down the platform. They stood on a little step on the front of the wagons loaded with luggage and directed the wagons with a single long rod at their side. They would whir by with the solid rubber tires thumping across the planking of the platform.

Our train was on the right and seemed to be a mile long. After we had passed the large, black, hissing engine, we walked and walked. Finally, we found ourselves stepping up on the rusting, iron steps of an ancient car with a weathered, gray wood planking exterior and no markings. In place of windows, were four or five circles of glass on each side, with no other view. The interior walls were lined with unfinished, rough wood planking and the floor was a close match, save for the grime that had been ground into the grained surfaces over a period of years.

"God Almighty, they got us in a cattle car", bellowed a husky voice from the rear, as we maneuvered single file between the seats to the front of the car. They had bolted old wooden benches, with a semblance of leather upholstery to the planking, to serve as seats. The leather was of an indescribable dark color and was cracked in enough places so that the seats were a combination of a concrete bench and a bed of nails. Without much thought, I found myself throwing my handbag on a bare, iron rack over the windows and sat in one of the first seats next to a pleasant looking gray-haired man, who sat quietly alone. He was staring at the tiers of plain boards on the wall directly ahead of him. His short, gray hair and boyish complexion competed with silver rimmed glasses for clues to his age. He must have been the only one in the group wearing a white shirt and striped tie with a little silver bar under the knot of his tie joining the two triangles of the collar. A matching tie bar with a smartly tailored jacket completed his neatness. The neatness was matched by his sharp conversation and his accurate description of our route to Philadelphia and transfer to trains headed for Boston and Providence. At the offer of a cigarette, I began to feel more mature by the minute. Not knowing how to turn down the offer in a manly or sophisticated way, I merely responded by shaking my head with a mumble, "No thanks." As he delicately opened the cellophane of a pack of Lucky Strikes with the red circle logo, I noticed his beautifully manicured nails, polished to a bright sheen and tipping off delicate white fingers. He delicately tapped the pack against the side of his open left hand, moving three or four cigarettes out of the pack and then, delicately slipped one into the corner of his mouth with one smooth gesture. Another quick one-handed move produced a bright flame and an instantaneous puff of smoke, followed by deliberate inhaling and a sophisticated, almost theatrical, blowing of smoke rings. A porter bellowed, "Yaaboard" outside, and there was a slamming of outside doors muting the outside bustle of escaping steam and traffic along the platform.

There were a series of thuds, starting at a distance and rapidly approaching our car with a backward jolt, when the slack in the coupling between our car and the next was eliminated. There was a muffled blast from the stack of the locomotive far to the rear and we backed out of the station. The lurch of our start had knocked the ash from my companion's cigarette and, as he brushed his left sleeve, he announced, "Here we go." One of the portholes over our left shoulder revealed our motion as the lights of the train shed would slowly appear and move off into the distance, creating momentary bursts of light. The increasing tempo of the puffs of the engine far back, created a crescendo, then a pause, then a crescendo, until there was a rhythmic, even tempo with the flashes of light disappearing into the distance.

As we headed east, our speed gradually increased, as I stood and gazed out one of the porthole windows into the darkness. I suddenly realized we were rushing past the Wilkinsburg Station. I had never seen the home town station from a train. I caught only a brief glance of the station's white, glazed tile stairway, leading down to the street level. The red and gold station sign and the stark, bare lights of the platform eerily faded into the distance. It was a sobering site as I mused on when I would see those lights again.

The crossing of the Alleghenies was another new experience. By the time we reached the famous Horseshoe Curve, we were all grimy from the soot creeping into that less than luxurious car. A porter in a white starched jacket came through the car with a basket of sandwiches and soft drinks. We could look out into the darkness and see the lighted cars at the tail end of our train across that mountain chasm, which appeared to be moving in the opposite direction from us. After a long descent to the outskirts of Harrisburg, our cars were coupled to an electric engine that raced us to the Philadelphia Station and a government sponsored breakfast at the Pennsylvania Station lunch counter.

Our efforts to scrub off some of the grime of that cattle car in the restroom were a little less than effective. It was a real luxury, after a two hour wait, to board a Pullman and head for Boston and Providence in comfort.

At Providence, gray Navy buses waited. The journey ended when the buses crossed the narrow, white wooden-railed bridge onto the Island and past the guard station with its sign reading in gold letters, "United States Naval Training Station, Newport, Rhode Island."

Without a pause, we joined other dull, gray Navy buses unloading recruits and were herded into a long, low, gray frame building. Without delay, we were given cardboard boxes for our "civies", which were stuffed into the boxes and addressed, without thinking that it may not be a pleasant piece of mail for our families.

Summer uniforms, winter uniforms, underwear, gloves and overcoats were shoved over counters and stuffed into our canvas sea bags. Finally, a mattress, a canvas hammock and blankets were thrown at us. We were shown how to fold and secure the hammock around the sea bag to make a large, solid bundle.

With these hoisted to our shoulders, we were led to the next building where a line of men in white coats - I hesitate to call them barbers - sheared our skulls like a herd of sheep. The average "hair cut", reducing us to "Skin Head" status, never lasted more than a couple of minutes. It was probably successful in eliminating any trace of individuality.

The bags and hammocks were lugged to a two story, gray wooden barracks, many blocks away, after passing row upon row of those dull buildings and several gigantic "Quonset Hut" drill halls. Everywhere there were recruits in navy blue stocking caps, gloves, pea jackets and bell bottoms, tightly bound with khaki leggings. They were marching and going through the "Manual-of-Arms." The leggings were apparently why we were called "boots."

The barrack was a frigid delight. Each floor was a totally empty wooden shell. Within minutes, we had reluctantly learned to string the hammocks between the beams under the direction of our muscular, wrinkled Company Commander. He was a second class petty officer, I think - a Bosn's mate - who made no attempt at diplomacy or proper English. The long red hash marks on his left sleeve, from many years of service, would suggest little regard for his recruits or his duty assignment. He barked that we were Company 913 and that he would be our Commander for the next seven weeks. Our hopes that someone would turn on some heat in the barrack was ill-founded.

No one knew, at the time, but the shortage of oil to heat barracks was due, in part, to the massive toll of freighters in our shipping lanes off the east coast being sunk by German subs.

The mid-December temperature on that island in the Atlantic was below zero on that bright December day, with a view of white caps rolling in from the Atlantic, accentuating the numbing cold. The massive Quonset Hut drill halls and the rows of gray, unheated barracks gave a stark, immaculate sense of order to the place. It turned out to be the locus of the most intense experience in self discipline I had yet experienced. I still recall the drills with a Garand rifle on the snow-swept drill fields jutting into the Atlantic and the rowing drills in a dory on those icy waves. Two fingers of the right hand would be routinely frozen stiff for hours, from holding the rifle at "parade rest." Whole hands would suffer from gripping those frigid oars. Returning to those icy barracks would do little to help.

The days at the rifle range, the evacuation drills of forced jumps from high towers into the swimming pools, aircraft spotting classes and the daily runs on those brutal obstacle courses before dawn - dubbed "happy hour" - began to give us all the reality of it all. These were not games. It began to register that there was a real possibility that some of us would not survive at all.

We knew little then about the war on the coast. The Navy's response to the havoc being wrought by the Nazi subs on our shipping was to send hastily constructed aircraft carriers to patrol the coast and the north Atlantic. It was an attempt to launch planes from their decks to depth charge the subs out of existence. The "carriers', however, were converted cargo ships that had been known as "Liberty Ships." Their superstructures were replaced by teak-wood decks. It was amazing that planes could conceivably land and take off from those tiny, pitching landing strips, which were unstable, rolling bowling alleys - even in the best of conditions.

The Franklin, one of those converted vessels, was being outfitted in a nearby port. Company 913 and a majority of that last battalion from Newport, were to join that Ship's Company. Later that year, we heard the report that the subs had sunk the Franklin off the Atlantic coast, with few survivors.

As I look back on that early experience, I again realize how immature some of us were when confronted with living in close quarters with the mixture of older men and a few young boys. It seemed that manliness was to be demonstrated by the volume of profanity uttered or by bloated descriptions of previous sexual conquest; or by cursing the circumstances that brought us all together there. Brutality among some of our elders began to emerge. Gang rule on the second tier of the barracks began to rear its ugly head when few of the men half-drowned one of the younger kids in the shower while scrubbing him with a stiff-bristled G.I. brush. It was on the pretext of his poor hygiene. The sadistic Navy Company Commander occasionally entertained all by forcing his Company "goat" to stand with a heavy rifle over his head until his arms were ready to drop off.

The sinking, dismal, sick feeling each dawn when that blaring loud speaker over our heads would announce, "Now drop your jocks and grab your socks", would herald another fun-packed day. The nights in those canvas hammocks were an experience in trying to sleep with one's feet in the air or one's knees under his chin. The blasting loud speaker was, to a degree, a relief from that torture rack. We learned that we were part of that historic last battalion to be issued hammocks by the U. S. Navy and to go through "boot camp" at Newport. They were apparently bringing to an end all the injuries to sailors who had been falling out of those canvas cocoons.

We were looking forward to that day about two weeks away when the daily ritual would come to an end and we would "ship out." Out of the blue, came the surprise at roll call in the early dawn. That tough, rock-hard

Company Commander, with his own brand of raspy voice, was calling roll call with a responding "Yo" from the troops. After my name was barked, he shouted, "You're ordered to report to the Officer of the Day." Even though at attention, we exchanged glances. My heart sank.

The young "j.g." at battalion headquarters housed in another of the drab gray buildings ordered, "Pack your gear, you're going to the Naval Hospital; you're in the Hospital Corps."

As the Navy bus pulled over the bridge heading for the Newport Naval Hospital, I glanced back at the scene behind. Looking, perhaps for the last time, across that dreary windswept island with its drab barracks and drill halls, I couldn't help wonder the fate of the other members of Company 913 and whether our paths would ever cross again.

The Naval Hospital at Newport was small, with only a few immaculate colonial-style brick buildings. I didn't know that my duty there was temporary. I don't recall any duty assignment; and within a few days, I had been given orders to report to the U. S. Naval Hospital, Portsmouth, Virginia.

Before leaving, I had talked with anyone who would listen, to gain insight into a way to serve in the Hospital's Operating Room. A noontime discussion with a young Pharmacist's Mate revealed that he, indeed, worked in the Hospital's O. R. Here was a break, I thought. With great authority though, he advised, "There isn't a chance you could work in an operating room, since you wear glasses. We have to be able to distinguish sutures of difference colors and that requires keen eyesight."

The Pullman trip south away from frigid Rhode Island was uneventful. The Pennsylvania line ended in Norfolk's dirtier than average Pennsylvania Station - not unlike a long, gray warehouse. I was sent down to the wharf to pick up my "gear" - that tightly-wrapped bundle of canvas and rope. The waterfront shed was on pilings jutting out into the Elizabeth River as part of downtown Norfolk's shabby waterfront. I wasn't due at the Portsmouth ferry for a couple of hours, so it seemed appropriate to nap for awhile on a large coil of hemp hawser.

The Portsmouth Ferry would bump into the Norfolk dock; its gates would be lowered and twenty or thirty cars would roll off and on into downtown Norfolk. After a few minutes, the Portsmouth-bound cars from Norfolk would roll in and fill the deck. The ride across the Elizabeth lasted only fifteen minutes or so and a Navy bus was waiting for the trip to the Hospital. Surprisingly, the trip ended in a quiet, residential section of town. The only sign that the Hospital was a military base were the Navy people passing through the large, brick pillars and iron gates of its entrance, stopping first for identification by Marine guards.

Chapter 4

"Sometime they'll give a war and nobody will come."

— *Carl Sandberg*

Portsmouth

The Hospital's personnel officer quickly dashed all hopes of an assignment to the Hospital's operating room. He curtly advised that only Pharmacist's Mates in the operating room training program worked in the operating room and that the training courses were filled for the foreseeable future. I was humiliated to find myself assigned to the Hospital's Library under the supervision of an aging civil service employee, Miss Craigie.

Miss Craigie was a quiet, kind old soul, whose thick lenses hid her deepset, almost sad blue eyes. She never said anything of a personal nature to us and my library shipmates, and I mistakenly deduced that she was oblivious to our antics. Russo and I were instantly kindred spirits in our frustration at pushing book carts though the Hospital wards and replacing books on shelves in the Library. How could we ever go home on leave and tell people that we were working in a library? The third member of the library squad was Gilcash, a tall, skinny, stooped-shouldered kid, whose octagonal lensed spectacles gave him an appearance of an age he would not reach for some time. Russo and I delighted in ribbing Gilcash about this Maine accent and old man demeanor. He never really minded, and would advise with his words of wisdom designed to help us improve our outlook on life. What more could we do to cope with a life of humiliation?

Quite by contrast, a system called "section watch" required us all to be on call every second or third night. With regularity, we would be assigned to a special watch during nighttime hours to sit with critically ill patients. At the time, sailors who had contracted pneumonia while on North Atlantic patrols were reaching the hospital wards near death. Cases of empyema - collections of pus between the outer surface of the lungs and the chest wall - were common. It was a frightening experience to fight sleep under the threat of court-marshal for sleeping on duty when we were assigned to a special watch for these patients. At the same time, we listened to the terrible troubled breathing of those desperately sick souls. Those were the days of oxygen tents before the era of antibiotics. The stench from the putrid discharges from the surgically draining wounds was overwhelming, despite our efforts to keep large chest dressings fresh. It was common practice to remove sections of rib to allow drainage of those infected fluids. I can't forget the first experience in that little dimly-lit room, of removing a dressing and watching a lung expand and contract through a two inch gash in the sailor's chest.

Permission to attend autopsies was almost routine, and as we sat on the second row of seats above the autopsy table, we were horrified to see the pathologist make a long incision across the cadaver's entire scalp, reflect the entire scalp over the face and saw off the top of the skull. Within moments, the brain was on a maple cutting board and was being sliced into half inch sections. There, near the center, was a globular golf ball shaped cavity filled with the thick, greenish, sickly, foul fluid we had all come to recognize so well - putrid pus.

It would be another year or more before the first precious vials of penicillin would reach the wards and put an end to much of the misery and sepsis of those wards. It now seems sinful that we allowed this gift to make it through commerce and to find its way into toothpaste and skin creams and to be given, for a price, in the treatment of carelessly made diagnoses such as "walking pneumonia."

We all had great regard for the "old salts" who had come to the hospital for intensive training in the Independent Duty School. It was at about this time that a Pharmacist's Mate on a Navy submarine, miles from any medical help, had fashioned a mask for anesthesia from a coffee strainer and gauze and had anesthetized a ship-mate with a can of ether. He had then performed an appendectomy saving the man's life. These men, with the diagonal red hash marks on their left sleeve, were a tough breed and we all secretly wanted to be like them.

The Independent Duty School was housed in three story yellow brick building down near the river. The commander of the School was the Chief Warrant Officer who had come through the ranks as a Pharmacist's Mate and was uniformly despised by his subordinates. Stories abounded of the unwarranted, strict discipline and petty rules that he enforced. That sort of thing was tolerated by recruits, but his charges now were a seasoned bunch who had seen their share of war and real trouble. They had no respect for that kind of discipline.

One of the salty students was notorious around the base. His name has faded from memory; but I see him yet as a medium height sinewy figure with a wiry, purposeful gait, with arms swinging and displaying the red stripes for many years of service and his rank of Pharmacist's Mate, first class. Rumor had it that he had been a Chief Pharmacist's Mate on one or more occasions, only to be broken down in rank for his hell-raising escapades. I watched him once or twice during brief encounters and could see the devilment in those eyes hidden behind that deeply furrowed, tanned countenance.

Looking back, I wonder if those eyes didn't reveal a strength and character that, by far, outweighed the petty mandates sometimes passed on by his superiors.

Unfortunately for our hero, the architecture of the building housing the Independent Duty School included, not only tiers of bunks at each end of the third floor in dormitories, but found the Commanding Officer's room and the "head "- the Navy term for bathroom - side by side at the top of the third floor steps. It may have been inevitable, but the scuttlebutt was to persist and was not to be discounted.

After a night of our comrade's socializing in the bars and tattoo parlors along Norfolk's wharf and Granby Street, he had found his way to the School, climbed the stairs and headed for the head. Instead, he was in the Commander's room by mistake. He can't be faulted for thinking he was standing over the long porcelain trough of the head. In the darkness, as luck would have it, he had unbuttoned those thirteen buttons of his bell-bottom trousers and relieved himself onto the Commander, comatose in his own bunk.

The day's humiliation - having to push a library cart through the hospital wards, and arranging books on the library shelves seemed endless. The only real contact with the practice of Medicine were the eight hour midnight watches we would draw. Sitting at a critically ill sailor's bedside all night, after a long day, was less than fun. I recall dozing off, on occasion; but somehow, never caught the discipline threatened for anyone caught sleeping on watch. That was offset by the Base Commander, however - a Captain Lindall. Early one spring morning, Miss Craigie needed a message presented to the mighty man personally and I had the misfortune to be the messenger. The Commander's office was just off the pristine, white lobby of the original ancient wing of the Hospital. That wing was fronted by an expansive entrance through a line of stone columns facing the Elizabeth River. The wing was topped, three or four stories above, by a glistening white dome known to have been the original operating theater of the Hospital. The elegant charm of that facade belied its age, the entrance to the nation's oldest Naval Hospital. As I made my way across the large, black and white squares of the lobby floor, I noted the heavy walnut door of the Commander's office ajar, and without hesitation, approached the large matching desk at the far end of the room, came to attention and gave a smart salute. He was middle-aged and distinguished in his navy blue and gold braid. Those stripes on his sleeve seemed to run almost to his elbow. Instead of a return salute, there was an icy stare from behind those rimless glasses, followed by a shouted order to a Pharmacist's Mate stationed on duty just outside the door. "Put this man on report, he's out of uniform. Look at those white socks!"

    I found myself at sick call, white socks and all, with those infected feet as a reminder of the cold showers in the barracks at Newport. The young Navy Doctor agreed that white socks would be best to help clear the athlete's foot, but his note to the Captain brought the reply, "Tell him to wear black socks over the white ones." The Captain's award of thirty hours extra duty eliminated liberty time in Norfolk for a month or so and added extra all-night watches for awhile. But, this was a minor distraction compared to the daily routine of pushing a book cart through the wards. I did begin, though, to listen with more understanding to the barrack's stories of that Navy Doctor who had become a commanding officer and his "chicken shit" attitude toward the enlisted men. No one seemed to question how a doctor could get that way.

    The extra duty didn't last forever and the ventures into downtown Norfolk resumed. The Portsmouth ferry ran from the end of Portsmouth's main street across the Elizabeth and stopped just short of an arcade of small shops leading out to Norfolk's notorious Granby Street. In groups of two or three, we would take in the sights of the tattoo parlors and bars along the famous avenue which paralled the long sheds and piers of the wharf jutting out into the Elizabeth. The Pennsylvania Station, several blocks away, was a grimy, ornate supplement to the piers and the downtown buildings which were not much different. Watching "beered up" young kids become manly and "salty" as objects of the artistry of the tattoo shops, and having a beer at one of the street's dives, was just about all there was to do. On occasion, we would decide to take an hour long, jarring ride on a dilapidated trolley to the amusement park at Ocean View. One of my salty buddies initiated me into the art of cigarette smoking on the way across on the ferry, and the resultant nausea and lightheadedness that prevented any serious interest in the tobacco habit.

The barker in front of the Gaiety Theater in Ocean View Park was something to remember. In a whining monotone he would groan on repeatedly, "Step right up boys; see a red hot, racy girl show." The girl show, featuring headliners like Ann Corio and Georgia Southern, seemed to eclipse some of the sad, worn-out skits of the burlesque comics and the awkward, amateurish routines of the chorus line. Occasionally, one of the girls in the chorus would sport a noticeable abdominal scar and this would do little to add to the ecstasy of the performance. On occasion, some poor soul would be met by a chorus of boos and shouts of "Put it on" as she disrobed on her way to stardom. But the popcorn and the Hershey bars, huckstered on the inside and which were supposed to include an "erotic" gift, were really not too bad. So, too, were the six or seven piece off-beat, off-key bands belting out Lady of Spain or Sweet Georgia Brown, as the girls went through their bumps and grinds.

Other than a movie on base, Grandby Street and Ocean View park were <u>the</u> entertainment. There was unanimous consent that Norfolk epitomized the "ass hole" of the world. I never saw the signs reportedly posted by the natives which were said to read, "Dogs and Sailors Keep Off the Grass"; but the message was subliminal everywhere.

Her name was Nancy and her Dad was a welder at the Navy Yard; and "Why didn't I come out and visit on my next liberty?" Sounded like a good idea. Nancy seemed awfully mature for a high school senior and had a certain way about her when she used her shoulder-length hair and her soft voice, along with the Virginia drawl, to draw attention. She gained enough attention from me to travel the Portsmouth Ferry and the "Toonnerville Trolley" out to her home on Sewell's Point. After that two hour journey, the hours must have slipped by unnoticed, so that I would miss the last transportation back to base. It was in the wee hours when we said good night and I departed from the Goral's little white cottage on Sewell's Point Road and started the long walk back to the main trolley line.

In later weeks, I introduced Nancy to one of my buddies before going home for a short leave and found, on returning, that Nancy was then the girlfriend of my good old buddy. The heartbreak was momentary but the events of that early morning walk along Sewell's Point Road were destined to help shape a lifetime.

The traffic had dwindled after the midnight Navy Yard's change of shift was over and I found it impossible to flag a ride back to town. I was disgusted and almost resigned to a long, monotonous walk back to civilization and an early arrival, just in time for another inspiring day at the Library. I recall trudging along through the roadside gravel never expecting the scene that was occurring another half mile ahead. A loud crash and a series of flashing headlights signaled an accident. Arriving out of breath, I found a scene beyond anything yet imagined. A middle-aged shipyard worker had pulled part-way off the road to change a tire, and in the darkness, four naval officers, returning from a night on the town, had slammed into the parked car - pinning the victim between the bumpers of the two cars. The man was conscious and screamed for help as the four officers in their "summer whites" moved aimlessly around the poor man, whose legs were almost amputated and were lying at grotesque angles on the pavement. One of the young officers, obviously having partied a little too much, spotted the red cross on my sleeve and slurred, "For God's sake, help us."

Two belts were commandeered, and with the help of a couple of screw drivers from the victim's crumpled car trunk, we were able to fashion tourniquets to avoid more hemorrhage into that ugly pool of blood that was expanding over the asphalt and gravel. The front of the officers' damaged car sent the headlights into crazy angles, but there was enough light to determine that our patient, in severe shock, was rapidly losing consciousness. A civilian ambulance of uncertain vintage finally appeared. We were able to lift the victim onto a stretcher and into the dark interior of the ambulance with the help of a few bystanders. Without a second thought, I leaped in with the stretcher and we took off for parts unknown. I probably had some idea of what medieval medicine had been like, but the scene we were about to enter, more likely resembled the Stone Age.

The rickety ambulance backed into a darkened below-ground entrance marked, "Emergency", and I was told that we were at St. Something-or-other. Without waiting, I grabbed a stretcher, and with volunteers from the front of the ambulance, we wheeled our patient into a small, dimly-lit room containing not much more than a white tubular steel table and a few enameled white cabinets. A nun with a large, black hood, framed in white, made an appearance as another sleepy-eyed volunteer - he must have been an orderly - helped cut away the poor man's khaki work pants. The nun nearly fainted as she viewed the tangled mass of flesh and blood. We agreed to try to find some blood replacement and to find a doctor. As I recall, we were able to start some blood after and hour or so. I still recall talking with the man's wife and young daughters as he was taken to an operating room on an upper level on a floppy-wheeled stretcher. We were told that a doctor was on the way. I recall squeezing the half-conscious man's arm and giving incredulous reassurance. There was a similar wave of doubt in trying to give a degree of hope to the white-faced wife and the two teenage daughters.

As I walked out of that dismal scene and up the sloping driveway through those old iron fences and out into the street, it suddenly occurred that the sunlight streaming through the iron fence signaled a new day and that my liberty expired at 0-eight hundred.

It seemed like hours, as I crossed one intersection after another of Norfolk's back streets, until I found a bus loaded with people in work clothes holding lunch pails and headed for the Navy Yard. Instinctively I moved to the back of the bus past filled seats and took a seat in the rear, surrounded by curious glances from the people occupying the rear of the bus.

The ferry seemed to take much longer than usual to fill its deck with cars, and the trip across the river was agonizingly slow. It became obvious that I would be A.W.O.L.

The Marine Corporal at the Hospital's gate looked at my liberty pass with great authority, and with great superiority, told me to report to the Master-of-Arms. We really hated those overbearing "gyrenes." The Master-of-Arms was a Navy petty officer who matter-of-factly, and without questions, took my liberty pass and advised that I could have it back again after serving thirty hours extra duty. There went another month or so of liberty and some more sleepless nights.

"Jesus, Miller, your ass is in a sling", advised Russo as I arrived late for another fun-filled day, pushing the library cart and stacking books. Miss Cragie, without a bit of emotion, or even a gesture, assigned me to help Russo return to the shelves a load of books that Gilcash had just returned. Russo's quizzing, as we stood side by side sliding books into place, betrayed his greater-than-average curiosity. I wondered whether playing it cool, giving little information, would lead old Russo to conclude that I was being a gentleman of the world by not discussing a romantic interlude. It seemed like a good idea; but by the time Gilcash returned from lunch and Russo and I headed for the chow line in the main building, he had wheedled the whole story. I had lost the opportunity to be a sex symbol.

So, to make a miserable day and a miserable experience worse, we stopped at the Admissions Station on the way to the main building. Our buddy Hatcher was on duty and let us use the phone, protesting all the way, that it was against orders. The operator at St. Something Hospital finally put me through to a nursing supervisor. She very quietly related that my patient had died in the operating room at seven o'clock A.M.

Three or four days later, Russo and I were needling Gilcash in a far corner of the library, while he was throwing it back at us for not having reached a high enough level in civilization to appreciate his Maine culture. We were all laughing at his good natured rebuttal and thought we were in for it as Miss Craigie approached. "Mr. Miller, could I see you at my desk?" "Mr. Miller", she continued, "you've been reassigned." She said, "Please report to the Personnel Office." My thoughts, as I slowly made my way past the rows of white, one story pavilions, housing the long-term recovery units, were simply focused on how much worse things could get. How long would the war last? How many months, how many days, before I could get back home - get back to school? I knew we never paid much attention to miss Craigie and never included her in our discussions. After all, she was sort of a robot without much interest in anything or any one. But why would she be so upset because I was late just once?

The Lieutenant came up to the front counter, weaving his way through the rows of desks manned by WAVE secretaries. The WAVES and a few civilian girls were busily shuffling papers and I realized that each shuffled paper belonged to a sailor coming onto base or being sent somewhere. Think of the effect these people were having on other people's lives. Where was I being sent, simply because I was AWOL for a couple of hours?

The Lieutenant carried a file and I noticed my serial number and name on the jacket. He shuffled through the papers for a minute and then made an entry on the top page. "Miller, you've been accepted for the Operating Room course. The next class will start in twelve weeks in the O.R. In the meantime, you report to Lieutenant Powell in Central Supply. You'll be there until it's time for you to report to the Operating Room. By the way, your extra duty has been reduced to fifteen hours and you can work that off for Lieutenant Powell." I was in too much of a hurry to report to Lieutenant Powell to recover from all of this, . . . and in too much of hurry to get as far away as possible from the Library. But, why didn't they give some encouragement when I first asked about O. R. school?

The Sunday morning routine was to call home "collect" whenever I could get to a phone. No one knows, until they are a parent, the fears that parents face when their progeny are facing the threats of harm during a global war. The calls home were always reassuring and we always talked about the good days ahead when the war would be over. On that Sunday morning, my intended humor was relayed to Mom. "Collect call from Yersun", voiced by the operator momentarily confused her. "Oh!", she giggled, "That must be <u>Your Son</u>." "Yes, indeed", came the reply. "Good morning", I chirped, anxious with my news that would reassure the folks that it would at least six months before overseas duty. "Guess what?", I quizzed. "Yes, I know", Mom interrupted. "You got what you were hoping for." "How did you know?" "I got the nicest note from Miss Craigie", Mom gushed. "She told me about the accident and how proud I should be. She knows how discontented you were and wanted you to have a chance to become what you want." That was why she had interceded with the Commanding Officer and the Personnel Office.

It would be a week or two before I would take time from the new routine to think about the Library and Miss Craigie. I was still doing night duty to work off the fifteen hours, but strolled down to that little Library one afternoon. Gilcash was loading well-worn mysteries and paperbacks into his cart and gave me his usual formal, "Good afternoon." "Where's Russo?" I quizzed. "Shipped out -yesterday -for NOB - expects destroyer duty."

Miss Craigie looked up from her writing and may have given a slight smile. One of the nurses had volunteered a tale that a tragedy in the librarian's young life had destroyed marriage plans. Perhaps so. She and I were still formal and brief, but when I thanked her, she looked right at me through those thick lenses, probably for the first time; and I thought I saw her eyes moisten a little.

It's remarkable what a little time does for insight. As pen meets paper after all this time, I find myself thinking about how nice it would have been for Gilcash, Russo and me to take Miss Cragie out for dinner sometime.

Lieutenant Powell's Central Supply was housed in the large, white dome perched atop the old building. Along with the stone columns flanking the main entrance, the dome was a landmark for the river traffic.

On entering the big dome, now divided into separate areas and cubicles, one entered another era. The dome was circled by skylights and below them were large, porcelain scrub sinks with thick elbow-controlled spigots. The white glazed tile walls were reminders of the surgery that had been done there in the years past. We were in another era where natural light was needed for surgery and when white tile was the only possible choice for an area that had to be spotlessly clean. Standing on the octagons of white floor tile were a row of autoclaves, each occasionally giving off a hiss accompanied by a small jet of steam.

Like any school kid, I had learned about the antiseptic era and the work of Lord Lister who had sprayed operating rooms with carbolic acid, destroying bacteria; but reportedly affecting the health of operating room personnel. Pasteur had previously demonstrated the role of microbes in the French wine industry and of the role of those microscopic organisms in the ravaging of European populations at the time. Koch had been the pioneer who had further defined the role of microscopic pathogens in the production of infection.

At this point, however, I hadn't heard of Ignaz Semmelweis, an Austrian physician who was drummed out of the practice of medicine when he had the audacity to claim that infection may be the cause of "childbed fever" taking the lives of newborn infants and their mothers. I hadn't heard the stories, but Semmelweis was driven from his profession and his sanity by colleagues who rejected his advice to wash their hands before delivering babies and before caring for the mothers. I had no idea, at the time, and didn't foresee, the role that Dr. Semmelweis would play in my life many years hence.

Lieutenant Powell explained that Central Supply processed all the sterile goods and intravenous fluids for the Hospital. It was becoming clear that sterile meant the absence of disease-producing bacteria and that the practice of asepsis - the destruction of sepsis-producing bacteria - had replaced the carbolic acid days and the antiseptics used by Lister. Instead, the Department was producing fluids and dressings that would simply prevent the access of bacteria to patients. Although we had heard of Dr. Fleming and the mold he had discovered that could destroy infection, we were again told that penicillin would go to the armed forces first, but was still a year or more away.

Days that followed were anything but dull. The nurses of Central Supply were a good group and down-to-earth. There were little or no officer-enlisted men barriers. Lieutenant Powell assumed one of the toughest, most crucial jobs in the department. She took charge of preparing the intravenous solutions and the equipment used to administer the fluids. We worked together well, and in return, she became a built-in teacher. Her nurses cap, with its two full stripes of gold braid, were the only reminder of her rank. She would routinely wrap a large square of muslin around her waist as an apron , and would go about her work; rhythmically moving about the white-tiled part of the old operating theater that was her small factory.

The four steam autoclaves along the wall radiated heat as they cycled through the sterilization of bottles of solution and tubing. The solutions, I learned, were either salt water or sugar water and were created by carefully weighing quantities of salt and sugar on a delicate scale and dissolving the crystals with carefully measured volumes of distilled water. The water came from a steam-operated still on the wall opposite the autoclaves. It became clear that these solutions, administered slowly into a critical patient's veins, could tide the patient over until able to take nourishment by mouth.

The solutions were mixed in quart-sized Fenwall bottles - thick-walled glass containers with rubber stoppers - which could withstand the steam pressure released into the autoclave chambers where they would be loaded for sterilization. Pressure would build after the doors were sealed by several turns of a large hand-wheel on the autoclave door. After the heat and pressure were maintained for a period designed to destroy all microbes, the steam would be exhausted and the chambers cooled. After partial cooling, a steel cap would be locked into place through a rubber ring on each bottle. When the bottles were cooled, we would test the seal by bumping the cap with a fist. A distinct thud on the opposite end of the bottle - the water hammer effect - signaled that we had a good seal as well as the assurance which was provided by the circular revolving chart over each autoclave. These charts would make a record documenting that the proper temperature had been maintained long enough to assure sterility of the solutions.

While the mixing and sterilization were proceeding, four-foot lengths of amber rubber tubing, used to deliver the solutions, were being prepared. My mentor had explained that, untreated, the rubber tubing would release substances into a patient's blood stream creating a severe reaction, including a marked fever. She called it a pyrogenic reaction. As a precaution, we would connect several lengths of tubing together with glass connectors and run a bicarbonate solution through these long coils for hours at a time. We would then flush the tubing for additional hours with distilled water before sterilization in the steam chambers.

It wouldn't be difficult to forget those earlier days of intravenous therapy when we delivered either salt water or sugar water through crude rubber tubing. Today's packaged plastic bags of delicately balanced electrolyte solutions with disposable plastic tubing and drip chambers have become commonplace. The trade names of Baxter and Travenol are so much a part of our everyday lives, that the Fenwall bottles and rubber tubing have become all but forgotten. Someone has said that all progress depends upon each succeeding generation standing upon the shoulders of those who have gone before. Nowhere is this more true than in the practice of Medicine.

A side alcove of Central Supply had a low ceiling and a long, white wooden table with matching benches facing a series of low windows overlooking the Hospital Compound. Anyone in Central Supply, not busy, was expected to sit and fold "four-by-fours" - four inch squares of gauze used as surgical sponges and dressings. Large bundles of gauze would first be rolled and laid out flat, to be cut into manageable squares with an electric machine with a spinning steel blade. We would then sit, by the hour, folding large squares into small squares, making certain that all raw edges were concealed on the inside of the finished square. It is unlikely that anyone opening a plastic packet of gauze today would realize, or even care, that things weren't always in the pre-packaged era.

In place of those night-long watches at the bedsides of critical patients, extra hour duty became nighttime shifts, every third or fourth night, in Central Supply or in the Admitting Unit, through which all new patients passed. Every new patient passing through processing needed completion of endless sheaves of paper followed by the ritual of submitting a blood sample for VD testing.

Carla, a Lieutenant, junior grade from Brooklyn and I had finished the routine of Central Supply for the night. We were having a Coke and sharing thoughts about anything and everything; trying to cope with boredom, when I mentioned some hesitation at jabbing sailors with a needle for a blood sample over in Admitting. She always came across as a competent, well-muscled lady and talked just a little bit that way. I had thought that she was really tough when she insisted that I practice venipuncture on her. I recall sitting opposite her in one of the supply rooms jabbing away at her forearm, with her calmly directing the procedure and without wincing once. After that, venipuncture at Admissions was a routine procedure. That was a good thing, because sailors fresh from sea duty were less than tolerant with a Pharmacist's Mate poking needles into their arms.

We were allowed to sleep in a small room in Admissions and would be available for any emergency admission. Hatcher was on with us this particular night. Hatcher was bright and had been yanked out of college along with the rest of us. Hatcher also had decided that he would proceed during his military service at half speed. He would shuffle along slowly, taking in the world around him, earning the nickname, "Stepenfetchit." Hatcher just stayed in bed when the aged patient came in a little after midnight. The doctor on call, a young J. G., gave a few perfunctory resuscitation efforts, but it had been obvious that the poor soul had gone to his reward before ever reaching the Hospital. The consensus was quickly formed that Hatcher should help prepare the body for the morgue, and without ceremony, Hatcher was roused from dreamland. Mechanically, he dressed and walked out into the admitting area in a daze. Someone handed him a stainless steel urinal and pointed toward the deceased. "Give that patient the "duck" and help him relieve himself", someone said. The "duck" was the Navy term for a urinal. With absolutely no respect for the deceased, our group was in an adjoining room chuckling, as the half-comatose Hatcher positioned the stainless steel vessel, and in his Alabama drawl, encouraged the deceased to relieve himself.

The six months in the Operating Room began with a surprise at the informality and yet the no-nonsense efficiency of the place. What a contrast to Saint Somebody's. The long, light green- tiled corridor on the third floor of the new wing was spotless and glistening. It took little time to realize why it was that way. We were constantly mopping with disinfectant or wiping down tiled walls with alcohol sponges. Between cases, instruments were scrubbed and lightly oiled. Containers were scrubbed and bloodied linens were soaked and sent to the laundry. At the end of the day's schedule, instruments and equipment were wrapped in muslin covers and autoclaved for the next day's schedule. The nurses worked right with us and were not only, without exception, top professionals; but they became friendly and great teachers. There was little question that they were the top of their profession from across the country. Likewise, the surgeons were fresh from civilian practice or Navy college programs and were good at their work and were striving to become better at their specialties. There was a distinction though. There was an aloofness that went with their gold-braid, and unlike the nurses, their relationships with the

Corpsmen was without any sign of friendship or comradery; their relationship with us was often condescending.

Gradually, we were allowed to "scrub" - that is, go through the ritual of using a disinfectant soap and a bristled brush to surgically clean one's hands and forearms. Each finger of each hand was scrubbed in turn, and then the scrubbing moved up to each elbow for ten to fifteen minutes in preparing for a case. That first case began by standing beside the "scrub nurse" and watching her keep her instrument tray in order and pass instruments to the surgeon. "You must flex your wrist and slap the end of the instrument into the surgeon's glove so that he knows he has the instrument", we were always advised. The names of the instruments were a mixture of slang and medical ego. While a hemostat used to clamp bleeding vessels was either a "curve" or a "straight", many instruments carried the name of a surgeon-innovator. A "Kocher" was a heavy hemostat with a notched end for locking tissues into its grip, while a curved "Mayo" was a heavy, curved hemostatic clamp and a "Metzenbaum" was a delicate, long-handled scissors. The instruments known as retractors were used for pulling tissues aside for better access and vision for the surgeon. These were the "Richardsons", a handled, stainless steel retractor of various sizes used for retracting abdominal muscles. The "Penningtons" were smaller versions of the "Richardsons" and the "Deavers" were the intern-hated ribbons of stainless steel formed into S curves. They were thought by many to be fiendishly designed to bite into the hands of surgical assistants and occasionally into a patient's liver or spleen. No awards have been given for the surgical assistants who have held those instruments of torture - sometimes for hours on end; but I felt privileged when I was first asked to hold a "Deaver" and be part of the team.

It would be some years before innovative surgeons and instrument companies would, together, design and produce self-retaining retractors - the instruments that would maintain retraction after being properly placed within an incisional area without abusing the assistant assigned to the procedure.

It came as a shocker. Colona, a tall, lanky kid from New York, who had completed the O. R. training, had been seriously wounded on Iwo Jima. A growing number of "O. R. Techs" were being assigned to the Marine Corps to help set up mobile operating rooms in front line casualty stations in the Pacific. Colona's letter from a West Coast Naval Hospital described a neck wound from one of the small-caliber rifles the Japs were using. His jaw had been shattered but he was keeping high hopes that all would be well. He described that the Japs were using Corpsmen's Red Cross arm bands as targets and advised us to be "just one of the troops" when we found ourselves in a combat situation. The letter brought a real sense of reality to those of us still able to sleep in a bunk at night and to go through a chow line three times a day.

Not all casualties were across the ocean. Late one evening, three or four of us were putting up instruments and linen packs for the next day's cases, when we got word that an emergency would be hitting the operating room within minutes. The casualty was a young sailor from one of the ships in the harbor. When the stretcher arrived at the far end of the long O. R. corridor, we saw that the patient was a young fellow with his right arm lying useless and almost detached - held in place only by blood-soaked dressings. He had been working in the ship's laundry and had thrust his arm into a spinning dryer to slow the spinning. The machine literally tore his arm off. The surgeons had no choice but to amputate the poor kid's arm.

It seemed to be a tradition that liberty for the sailors in port was not successful without the consumption of large volumes of alcohol. The Shore Patrol - the Navy's Military Police - with their canvas leggings and S. P. arm bands, strolled through the streets at night, brandishing their three foot "billy clubs" and keeping order. But it was beyond them to clap any but the drunkest of sailors into the "brig."

We had heard that a celebrating naval Captain had overdone his shore leave a bit and had fallen off the Portsmouth ferry. He had been sucked under the vessel and one of the screws had badly lacerated one of his legs. The Hospital surgeons had been doing everything possible to save the leg, but shortly after eating chow one humid summer evening, we were alerted to set up for surgery. The O. R. schedule listed an amputation. I wasn't part of the team for the procedure but was working in the autoclave room and trying not to notice the rotten, penetrating odor of gangrene coming down the hallway from the O. R. One of the nurses ordered me to bring a cart and a container to the O. R. door. The door opened and the circulating nurse dropped the leg, wrapped in surgical towels, into the container. Clapping the lid on the container didn't help. I had never smelled anything remotely approaching that horrid, penetrating odor before. The three story ride in that small elevator to street level, with just the canister and me, was torture.

I was trying to contain wave after wave of nausea and began to gag as the doors opened. There was some relief as I pushed the cart through the back entrance into the twilight, but as I approached the entrance to the morgue incinerator, I found myself jackknifed over a privet hedge, losing my supper.

On other nights, duty was actually pleasant. Lieutenant junior grade Naomi Porter was fun to work with. She was a little plump and very pretty. There was very little demand during those evening hours manning the first aid station in one of the outpatient pavilions. We had plenty of time to exchange stories and talked about our hopes for a life after the war. She had a quiet manner and seemed to enjoy teaching the art of bandaging. When business lagged, she would demonstrate the procedure for stabilizing a fractured arm or leg and she felt secure being Navy and trying to help; while her fiance' served in Europe. She gave me her picture when she shipped out to a hospital ship in the harbor and we promised to write. We never did; but I still hope that she found her way back to Cincinnati and had fourteen kids.

The activity around the Navy Yard and at N. O. B., the Naval Operations Base, had been feverish for months. No one was surprised when General Eisenhower announced that American, British and Canadian troops had landed in Normandy. And, . . . no one knew, at the time, of the terrible risk of the operation or of the horrendous casualties.

The scope of it all began to dawn when a few of us were ordered to report for temporary duty to staff the hospital train carrying the first D-Day casualties from Norfolk to the Bethesda Naval Hospital..

The train must have been half a mile long; made up of dark olive-drab Pullman cars, each with a red cross on a square white background on its midsection.

The patients were transported from the hospital ship in the harbor to the train by both sleek, gray Navy ambulances and bulky, square khaki-colored Army vehicles.

Each car had rows of stretchers, each holding a surviving sailor on each side in three tiers. Some of the wounds we saw and tended seemed almost minor but others left us aghast.

I will always remember the face of a handsome dark-haired Bosn's Mate who had been on the bridge of the Texas as it bombarded the Normandy coast. On the slow swaying ride to Bethesda, he described that a German shell had exploded just beneath the deck of the bridge, driving the deck upward with unbelievable force. His legs had been rammed upward, literally compressing them like accordions. The heavy, convoluted dressings left little doubt of the deformities. I found myself doubting that he would ever walk again.

The six months of training had been over for about a week when the order to report to the Personnel Office came. The young WAVE in the office advised that my orders had been cut and I was to pick up travel orders at 0-seven hundred the next day. The destination was the Marine base, Camp LeJeune, North Carolina. There was little time to contemplate the destination, but those who professed to know, advised that Colona and the others shipped to LeJeune found themselves in the Fleet Marine Force. The Navy Hospital Corps was supplying the medical teams to the Marine Corps, and Corpsmen assigned to the Corps switched their Navy blues for Marine Corps khaki and Marine Corps insignia. The base was said to be in the town of Jacksonville, North Carolina.

U.S. Naval Hospital — Portsmouth, Virginia
Official U.S. Navy Photographby Dan C. Gay

U.S. Naval Hospital — Camp LeJeune, New River, North Carolina
Official U.S. Navy photograph

Chapter 5

"It is well that war is so terrible, or we should grow fond of it."

— Robert E. Lee

JACKSONVILLE

The Trailways bus pulled into the terminal. The driver announced, without fanfare, "Jacksonville." As I peered out the side window there was little in sight. The highway through town was asphalt, but it seemed that most of the area was just sunbaked dust. The town of Jacksonville seemed to boast three buildings. We were at the terminal, a drab, concrete block building, and I could see another similar structure with a large, red and white ABC sign and what appeared to be a small motel set back from the street. I later learned that the ABC sign signaled the area's liquor store. So there we had it, Jacksonville was a bus depot, a small run-down motel and a liquor store. It certainly seemed adequate for the necessities of life, but a Las Vegas or a Big Apple it was not.

The interior of the depot was as drab as the exterior, with a few long, dirty wooden benches, and for the first time, I saw the duplicate faciilties reflecting life in the South. There were four restroom doors with black and white overhead signs reading, "Men White; Women White; Men Colored; Women Colored", and on the wall opposite these doors were two porcelain drinking fountains marked "White" and "Colored."

The small, olive-drab Marine bus passed through the main gates and wound its way for several miles past several regimental clusters of red brick two-story structures, and then along a scenic, winding route paralleling the North Carolina coast. The swamps leading down to the shore were populated by tall, closely growing pines and live oaks with Spanish moss dangling from their lower branches. By this time, I knew that the destination was the Base Hospital.

We stopped at a small, white guard hut at the entrance to the Hospital grounds and were cleared by a Navy guard before proceeding on to a colonial structure of the same design as the Marine buildings we had passed. The Petty Officer assigned a dormatory bunk and a locker and I was on my way to report to the Hospital Operating room.

As the elevator doors opened to the Operating Rooms, I could see that the operating suite was entered through a double set of panelled glass doors. Just inside and on the right was the Supervisor's office. On her desk was a name plate - Lieutenant Ann Boyle. There she was, immaculate in her starched, white uniform and white nurses cap with the braid of a full lieutenant. She was thin and immediately reflected a no-nonsense manner. The fiery, red hair and freckled complexion were striking as she arose and said she had been expecting me. "You'll be on the starboard watch under Gillingham", she advised. "Come on, I'll show you around." It was a modest operating unit in size - three operating rooms and a large central supply room with autoclaves and steel-topped work tables. The day's schedule had been completed and the Lieutenant went through the introductions to the crew, who were in the central supply cleaning and packing instruments for the next day's schedule. The nurses, the WAVES and Corpsmen all wore dull-green scrub suits and paused only momentarily for introductions. Poncho was a short, muscular, black-haired fellow with a distinct Brooklyn accent who briefly acknowleged the introduction and confirmed that I would be on "starboard." The Lieutenant explained that Poncho had been the Senior Corpsman for two years or more and was in charge of enlisted men and women and would be assigning me my duties.

Most of the surgery was routine, but the casualties that arrived from maneuvers held off the Carolina coast were shocking. There was never much advance warning, but emergency surgery for high explosive injuries of young Marines was far from rare. One of the first assignments was to assist the orthopedic surgeons who had attempted to piece together the limbs of a group of Marines who had wandered into high explosives on reaching shore in a landing craft. I was beginning to see the less than glamorous side in the life of a military surgeon.

The base had its own recreation. There was a small marina just off the swamps that were universally termed the "boondocks" and a movie theater along with a non-commissioned officers club for each regiment on the main base. The clubs were affectionately known as "Slop Chutes", with a menu of one item - a bottled beer with an unusual label depicting a king on a large, gold throne and the trade name of Barbarosa. The taste of this wartime substitute for a quality brew was as distinct as the label. We all would, from time to time, endure the after effects of a little too much Barbarosa.

There were long hours on watch in the O. R., when all work had been cleared, and the favorite sport involved squirting a sleeping buddy on a stretcher discreetly pulled off into an alcove. There was some talent required to arc the stream from a twenty cc. syringe into an arc which would end hitting the sleeping victim twenty feet or so away. The Senior Corpsman, Poncho, was on the other watch with his own crew, but we began to hear stories of Poncho attacking his subordinates with strangling neck holds in the event that something rubbed him the wrong way. This was eventually reported to the Master-at-Arms and the bully Poncho was shortly thereafter on his way to sea duty. On the day of Poncho's departure Lieutenant Boyle's approach was direct. "Miller", she said, "You're now the Senior Corpsman. You know what needs to be done and what I expect." Over the next year or so things on starboard watch didn't change, but hopefully, port watch relaxed a little without the threat of Poncho's bullying.

We began to experiment a little on those long evening and weekend hours. After the instruments were clean and "picked" for the next day, we would have little sessions naming the instruments lining the rows of glass shelves in the instrument room and experimenting with the Berman Locator - an electronic machine for locating metal buried in tissues. It took a degree of practice to direct the probe of the machine toward a sliver of metal that we would pierce into a potato or a ball of putty. The machine sounded a high pitched whine when the probe approaced metal, and the closer to the metal, the louder the machine would squeal. The machine was designed to locate shrapnel and would be used on occasion when the casualties from maneuvers would arrive without much notice.

Years later, similar technology would create a whole new advance in medicine - the use of ultrasound to look into the body's interior non-invasively and spot such foreign objects.

Then again there was the weekly ritual of pouring the O. R.'s allotment of ethyl alcohol into a gallon jug that we all knew was for the celebration of V-J Day. Those three ounces, grudgingy provided by the Hospital Pharmacy each week would, eventually, add up to a quart or more. The liquid was affectionately known as "torpedo juice." We learned that the name came from torpedo-boat crews where this highly purified alcohol was used as torpedo fuel.

Not all the Marines were of the male variety. The troops affectionately and irreverently called the lady Marines "BAM'S." Everyone knew these were the initials for "broad-ass Marines." The name was used generally and not disrespectively. These ladies did a great service filling stateside jobs, thereby relieving men for overseas duty. Some of them also matched their male counterparts in hell raising.

One lady Corporal was actually notorious for her after-hours excursions with the boys. Legend had it that her capacity for Barbarosa exceeded that of any of the men in the Regiment. One of the favorite sports around the area surrounding the base included high speed motorcycle rides with the riders well lubricted with Barbarosa. The inevitable happened. Our heroine and her Marine companion crashed their cycle during a midnight ride and were brought to the Hospital near death. The O. R. crew and surgeons worked through the night and well into the next morning's hours performing orthopedic procedures to salvage the fractured limbs of this pair. They both left the Operating Room, late that morning, in orthopedic beds, with arms and legs elevated into awkward positions, with all sorts of pulleys and ropes.

Weeks later, one of the corpsmen from the young woman's ward was in charge of delivering the bed and our heroine to the operating room for an adjustment of some of the orthopedic hardware. There was a wait of an hour or more, with surgeons, nurses and corpsmen waiting for the celebrity. Lieutenant Boyle, after several calls, determined that the bed, the patient and her companion corpsman were in the elevator which was then located between the second and third floors. Someone determined that it was an emergency and that the elevator was stuck between floors. To the surprise of all, the emergency squad found the bed, its notorious occupant, and her dedicated corpsman unharmed and perhaps very content, without any explanation as to why they had stopped the elevator between floors. There was instantaneous speculation across the Base; but as I recall, very little divergence of opinion as to the activities within that elevator between floors two and three. There was also a degree of admiration that an orthopedic bed, with all its appliances, wouldn't be allowed to interfere with true love.

The Marine Corps wisely recognized the advantages of keeping the men on base rather than on the narrow, winding highways in that isolated area of North Carolina. The "Slop Chutes" and movie theaters were a limited answer. A little closer to civilized existence though, were the two golf courses where the officers and enlisted men were treated somewhat as equals. Officers played with officers and enlisted men with enlisted men, but the courses were open to all.

Saturday afternoon would see a small crowd of khaki uniforms ringing the first tee of the smaller nine hole course with a very limited amount of conversation; considering it was supposed to be recreation. On that one weekend afternoon, as we all stood around the tee, a foursome of Marine lieutenants was teeing off, and one by one, belted out beautiful drives for the admiration of the enlisted men surrounding the tee. Then the fourth, a particularly muscular, tanned authoritative fellow in a tight tee shirt stepped up, teed up the ball, took a couple of gigantic practice swings and then smacked the pellet with a resounding dull thud. The ball took off like a rocket; but about fifty yards from the tee, it took a nose drive and buried itself in the fairway turf. No one moved a muscle as the overpowered athlete stomped off the tee, snapping for all to hear, "goddamn wartime balls." We were only "swabies" so we stood there with grins from ear to ear, accompanied by a few knowing winks; but the other Marines never showed a trace of amusement. Never again did I question Marine Corps discipline. That is, until later, when the story circulated that a Marine at Camp Pendelton had taken a pot-shot at the Camp's bugler during reveille.

Getting off the base on weekends presented enough transportation difficulties that we usually settled for a round of golf on one of the base courses or a sun bath. One Saturday though, found three of us thumbing rides down the North Carolina coast toward Carolina Beach.

The last available room at the ramshackle old frame hotel at the beach was at least six feet square and had an elegant hundred-watt bare bulb hanging by a braided wire over the brass bed.

The beach was beautiful and the water warm, but my sophisticated buddies insisted on Coke as a mixer for our bottle of rum - the only drink on the shelves of the ABC store. They explained that Rum and Coke was really a "Cuba Libra", an elegant, sought-after nectar.

That night saw little sleep - some of us were sunburned - all were nauseated from that cheap rum.

But the real damper on any future excursions to that beach came a week or two later. We heard that a young Marine had been attacked by a shark while swimming there. A friend at the Hospital Morgue obligingly pulled back the black oilskin cover over that young body one noontime.

The gash across the upper thigh had to be a foot long and had just about severed the entire leg. Swimming off the coast had lost a great deal of its appeal.

It was becoming evident that much of the actual activity across the base was part of a massive build-up, quite possibly to be a direct invasion of Japan itself. There was a distinct concern of all those who would be part of that invasion. The men of the First Division were the veterans of Guadalcanal, who had seen half of their numbers lost in the stinking South Pacific tropics. They were a somber lot, exhibiting a great degree of discipline and restraint, and generally accepted the likelihood that they would again head for the Pacific. Their ear infections and "jungle rot" - a fungus skin infection without any really effective treatment, would evoke the most emotional language these veterans could muster. On the other hand, the Fifth Division was being formed with eighteen and nineteen year old recruits who were out to lick the world. If they couldn't find Japs, they were willing to take on the Navy. We all speculated though, which of us would be wearing khaki and red cross arm bands and go with a Hospital Corps unit.

It came suddenly, dramatically and unexpectedly on that August morning. "The Bomb" was something that we really hadn't heard of, except for the nation's fear that such a thing was being developed in Germany with "heavy water" from a large electrical installation somewhere in Norway.

We all knew, without doubt, that the end was in sight and our thoughts turned to returning home rather than Pacific duty. Gabriel Heater was the foremost news commentator of the day and his routine, reassuring opening on evenings at seven would be, "Ah, there's good news tonight", from that tiny radio on the dormitory radiator. But, from that day on, the tiny radio took on a new dimension of reality. It suddenly became apparent, in a few days, that the war was indeed over. My jug of torpedo juice suddenly was coveted by the O. R. crowd. Out came the half-filllled jug from the locked scrub sink cabinet. Someone had a buddy in the hospital kitchen and he appeared with bottles of orange juice, pretty much determining that the victory celebration would be with "screwdrivers".

There were hoots and hollers coming from all ends of the Corps Quarters as we sat on our bunks sipping the juice and complementing each other all around. Guys that never cared much for each other shook hands and speculated on how long it would take for discharge. Someone spilled a little of the juice on the asphalt tile floor and we all thought it was hilarious when someone with a lighter lit the little puddle and we watched it burn with a little blue flame.

Somehow, we ended up in Jay Beres's room. Jay was part of the hospital brass and welcomed the partying into his quarters. Partiers were coming and going - mainly through the door. That is, until Derik, one of the younger of the O. R. gang, banged on the outside window. The next thing we knew, he was shoving a lady Marine through the window and then followed her. With that unorthodox entrance, Derik and the lady named Doris joined the V-J day revelry.

Derik, sometime later, wanted the O. R. keys; and there didn't seem to be anything wrong with him scouting for more torpedo juice. But, when someone noticed that Derik and Doris hadn't returned to the party, it became urgent to find Derik and the keys.

As expected, the French doors into the O. R. suite were unlocked and the O. R. was in total darkness as our little search party proceeded down the hallway to the operating rooms. "Wonder if he's really here", someone whispered. Someone said they heard a noise in Room Three, and without a second thought, flipped the switch for the circular operating light over the table. There was Derik and Doris, sharing the operating table. All I recall, is that the search party dispersed with participants banging on each other and laughing with repeated references to the emergency operation in Room Three.

Lieutenant Boyle and I had a good relationship and an underlying friendship. There was no familiarity, but we truly worked well together with mutual respect. There was never any doubt that I was held responsible for anything that went wrong in the Operating Room, however.

"Miller, I need to see you in my office", she greeted me the next dawn. She seated herself in her starched whites and looked as stern as possible as she stared right through me. "Who was in here last night?", she inquired. "I don't know, Lieutenant", I lied. Without taking her eyes from mine, she said, "Miss Tulley found a rubber article in the nurses commode this morning and is quite upset." I was speechless. If it had only been someone other than the prissy Miss Tulley. "If you find out anything about this let me know." "Yes Maam", I replied. I wondered if the Lieutenant had cut it short and had dismissed me rather than lose her composure over the distress of our Miss Tulley.

Derik suddenly became more manageable and devoted to his work. I never had a moment's problem with him; and as far as I knew, the nurses never heard a word from the V-J day O. R. search party.

The casualties from maneuvers seemed to suddenly stop and the orthopedic surgeons seemed to be doing more of the procedures they would be doing when they returned to their civilian practices. Commander Crosby was said to be from Hartford and had a favorite operation to correct recurrent shoulder dislocations. It was called the Nikola procedure and Crosby would get almost ecstatic in his enthusiasm in stringing a biceps tendon through a hole he would drill in the head of the humerus. Marines were being shipped in from all over to have the Commander do his thing. But the "scuttlebut" soon got around that, after Crosby's operation "you couldn't lift your arm above your shoulder." Some of his prospective patients wisely decided to tough it out and would leave the hospital without having surgery.

One morning, during a grafting procedure, the Commander was using a small electric circular saw to cut a wedge of bone from a Marine's tibia, for grafting. The rapidly spinning saw would be irrigated by an assistant who would gradually drip a saline solution from a syringe to irrigate the saw blade. On this occasion, the salt water was being thrown into the air and was dripping off the operating room light and back into the operating area, contaminating everything. Crosby was beside himself. "Dr. Crosby, the saw blade is on backwards", I offered without much thought. The enraged Crosby raised the heavy instrument and threw it across the room with a clatter that brought Lieutenant Boyle into the room. "No Goddamn Corpsman is going to tell me how to operate!", he shouted at her.

Ater lunch, Lieutenant Boyle quietly suggested that I step down to the ward and apologize to the Commander. His "Come on in" was friendly enough as I gave a hestitating knock on his door. He actualy seemed tranquil, seated behind his desk, with all that gold braid showing, as he put his elbows on the desk. After the apology, Crosby relaxed and was almost kittenish with his tranquil, rambling explanation of how he really didn't have anything against Corpsmen. I was encourgaged to tell him of hopes for a career in Medicine as he rambled on. He seemed to be a little glassey-eyed as he stared past me and then I noticed it. A small can of ether with its distinctive gold seal - the Squibb trademark - was sitting on his blotter. Without a thought, and without missing a word, he uncorked the little can and began taking deep whiffs of the vapor through first one nostril and then the other, while compressing the other side of his nose with his thumb. I didn't know too much about glue-sniffing at the time, but I knew we had been missing ether from the O. R. for some time. As I passed the

Lieutenant's office, I briefly stuck my head in; as she looked up from scheudlilng the next day's cases. "I think I know where our ether has been going." "Yes, I know", she said. Nothing more was ever said.

The boondocks of that coastal area are a series of swamps extending out into the New River for a number of miles before it empties into the Atlantic. The base had a few boat docks at the river edge, not far from the Hospital Compound. A short road led to the docks through the "boonies"; but otherwise, the swamps were waste-deep water, made almost impenetrable by a tangle of trees, roots, hanging vines and mosses. All sorts of wildlife could be expected there, along with an occasional alligator.

The Hospital's chain-link fence extended well into the swamps, preventing any access to the hospital grounds unless someone would be foolish enough to brave the "boonies." A few of us were just that foolish and lived to remember it. It wasn't hard to slip out onto the main base, but coming in after hours could bring down the "wrath of God."

A few of us had decided to try an escape from Navy "chow" at a small place outside the base without the formality of being granted liberty. We were too late returning to enter through the gate and climbing the fence topped by barbed wire was too risky. So, the plan was an excursion through the swamp with an end-run around the fence. We got away with that wade through the waist-high water - or did we?

Everyone seemed in good spirits the next morning. As I recall it was a Sunday. But, I looked like an over-ripe tomato. It was an interesting way to learn that part of the subtropical flora was poison ivy. I had the ability, while on intravenous fluids over the next few days, to ruminate on that information.

The announcement of a point system for discharge began to emerge for the Navy and a recent promotion had made life a little more relaxed. The date for discharge from the Navy was only a few months away and we all looked forward to that little embroidered insignia over our left pocket ("the ruptured duck") that would denote us as Navy "veterans."

The order finally came to head back to Norfolk's Receiving Station for a few weeks to await discharge. Lieutenant Boyle never said much about the orders, but shortly before I left for Norfolk, she advised that I could have stayed and been discharged from LeJune if I had asked her to use her influence. But I was happy to move closer to Pennsylvania, and besides, the orders were already cut.

The Receiving Station was a return to the more realistic Navy life of bunk beds and barracks; the living first found at Boot Camp and being the standard for most other Navy bases. The barracks were dismal, but I found myself assigned to the base's dispensary for those weeks awaiting discharge.

Richard Foster was the M. D. in command of the dispensary and we struck up a friendship that would go on after we returned to civilian life. Here was another fine teacher. We would hold sick call together and he often turned the minor surgery over to me. He would go on to a residency and surgical practice in Fort Lauderdale and I would become more convinced that I wanted a surgical career.

Close to the Receiving Station was the P.O.W. Camp. A hundred or more German prisoners were held there; and we provided the medical care for them. Their cooks were probably former chefs and their meals were uncharacteristically good. We found ourselves enjoying their cuisine from time to time; but the Germans were exceptionally aloof. It became apparent that they were in fear of their lives at the hands of Americans - especially that someone would poison their food.

The Compound had its own Army vehicles and no apparent system for their use. On a few occasions, I would be seen driving an "ammunition carrier" through downtown Norfolk. No one ever said a word.

The day finally arrived and as Dick Foster and I shook hands. We agreed that we would meet in Florida and compare notes. We later did, while I was a surgical resident, and he was a successful surgeon in Fort Lauderdale.

Two days at the Bainbridge, Maryland Discharge Center and I was thumbing a ride on the Pennsylvania Trunpike, excited to be returning to the Cathedral and Campus life.

Chapter 6

"I am convinced that it is of primordial importance to learn more every year than the year before. After all, what is education but a process by which a person begins to learn how to learn?"

— *Peter Ustinov*

A RETURN TO THE PITT CAMPUS

The pin oaks dotting the wide expanse of lawn surrounding the Cathedral of Learning were coming into full leaf as Chick and I strolled down ODK walk toward Heinz Chapel. Noonday sun, on that day in early June, cast a shadow from the Gothic architecture of the Cathedral, rising twenty-six stories above us, across the flagstone walk; and sent shimmering reflections from the oaks's waxy new leaves. We chuckled a little at the names of the outstanding student leaders chiseled into the borderstone of the walk. Neither of us were much interested in Campus politics or the scholastic effort that was behind the honor of having one's name chiseled into the walk for all eternity. Chick had had a long recovery in Naval Hospitals, repairing his leg wounds. He would, on occasion, describe hitting the beach at Saipan- deathly sick and retching from the rough ride to shore in a small landing craft, with the reeking odor of fuel oil. He would describe "hitting the beach", only to experience the searing pain from an exploding shell within a few hundred feet of the shoreline. Chick's goal, at the present, was to be a big-time fraternity man, offering the benefit of his charms to the co-eds. He was doing just that when we had met, a little earlier, in the Blue Tuck Shop on one of the lower levels of the Cathedral. The large, semi-circular, blue vinyl booths of the Shop, rimmed with modernistic oak, were the gathering points for the sororities. Chick had been giving the Tri-Delts the benefit of his cherubic crewcut countenance and charm when we decided to take in one of Mrs. Dougherty's lunches at the Delt House. The bulky, square red-brick residence of another era at 4712 Bayard, was part of Pitt's Fraternity Row, several blocks away.

We reached the end of the long, flagstone walk leading into the limestone steps of the elegant Heinz Chapel, with its towering spire and heavy plank and wrought-iron doors; and took the walk to the left and headed down Fifth Avenue toward Bayard Street.

The instant friendship with the jolly, round-faced, round-eyed Chick had apparently been jelled by the catalyst of our mutual hedonistic pursuit of all that life had to offer. We both felt it time to spread our wings, without an excess of enthusiasm or time for academics. Our accomplishments in academia were mediocre, but the fraternity beer busts were more than an adequate compensation. There had been less than full attention paid to what might follow the rah-rah college years. I guess I just assumed that a career in Medicine would follow. Actually, there was no doubt about it - it was just what I intended to do.

There was never too much serious talk between us - there didn't seem to be time for it. The joking, devil-may-care attitude seemed to be all around us. The irreverent students had created an epithet for the elegant Gothic skyscraper school house - "Bowman's Erection" - in honor of the former University Chancellor who had championed its construction. There were though, some veteran students older than we, and some who were married with families. They were intent on improving their lives with the help of the G. I. Bill, granting them a chance for a college degree or even a chance for a professional school. We all knew the chances - probably one in twenty - of finding a spot in medical school, and of those chosen, a number would never graduate. The older returning vets were serious and their no-nonsense approach made them tough competitors; although that never seemed to register with those of us who thought that this was fun time. We believed in the axiom, "Work hard, play hard", with accent on the play part.

The fraternity connection had been almost by accident. On returning home, the previous summer, I had jumped right into summer science courses with considerable more success than before the Navy years, even though the football season that year had left little spare time. I got back into the Varsity Cheerleading Squad again hoping to win a varsity letter - that was apparently important at the time. As Head Cheerleader for the

University, there were the road trips throughout the mid-west and through the east as Pitt met many of the Big Ten teams of the time. I found myself leading pep rallies and becoming less introverted than the kid who had been uncomfortable walking through the Tuck Shops a few years earlier.

One of the guys on the Cheerleading Squad who was headed for law school invited me to the Delt House and I entered the next pledge class, although there had never been great enthusiasm for fraternaties or the fraternity system. There was always an awareness of a fair amount of showing-off by the fraternity crowd and I wasn't at all certain that I wanted to be a part of that scene. Nevertheless, the experience led to life-long friendships and seriously set the course for the years to come.

Norman MacLeod was perhaps the best-known alumnus of the national fraternity and was often called "Mr. Delta Tau Delta." He was modest, and his soft spoken manner gave scarcely a hint of Scotch ancestry. The manner had served him well as the founder of a major advertising firm as well as a Trustee of the University. As a bachelor, he had devoted a substantial part of his life to the Fraternity and the numbers of successful friends he had made through the years.

On an earlier fall afternoon, I had lagged behind in the Chemistry Lab to finish a troublesome organic chemistry experiment in Alumni Hall, an elongated buff brick structure overlooking the Cathedral and the lower Pitt Campus. I was late and had missed Mrs. Dougherty's supper at the House, but had hopes of finding a few left-overs. The falling dried leaves along Bigelow Boulevard and Bayard Street crunched noisily as I kicked through their accumulations on the walk. I hurried toward the House and went into the front parlor, absent-mindedly dropping off an armload of chemistry manuals on a side table.

The antiquated oak sliding doors leading into the dining room were still open and the room, with its two long, narrow tables and white cloths spotted from the evening meal were empty; except for a middle-aged man facing the far windows. Mrs. Dougherty and her helper, Ruby, were out in the kitchen clearing up the last of the dishes; and without too much resistance, yielded to a little sweet-talk and offered to heat up a little supper. Mrs. Dougherty advised that I could go out to the dining room and join Mr. MacLeod. In an almost courtly manner, he reached across the table with a firm handshake and offered, "I'm Norm MacLeod, and I can use some company." In the hour or so we spent together during that dinner hour, I realized that this was a man truly interested in other people, although I have never been able to recall much of the conversation that evening. I do recall though, his interest in my hopes for a career in Medicine.

Some years later, Norm, in the course of a conversation, related that, during that first meeting, he had noted an unusual determination and decided then to do whatever he could to help me enter Medical School. That was, indeed, a turning point in a young undisciplined life; even though I was having a great deal of difficulty putting in the required hours in the science labs up on that hill.

"Want to pick up a shift tonight?", Chick quizzed. "Why not?", I shot back as we crossed Fifth Avenue, in front of the towering limestone columns of the Mellon Institute. A few of the fraternity brothers had found that they could make good money by working a weekly shift or two at Jones & Laughlin's ore trestle on the northern bank of the Monongahela, just below the Oakland district. The J&L Mill stretched along both banks of the Mon River for at least a mile. Across the river on the South Side, were the finishing mills where the raw pig iron was refined in open hearth furnaces and Bessemer converters, lighting Pittsburgh's night skies with brilliant showers of sparks and flaming gases. Rail cars of Minnesota iron ore from Ashtabula, coal from western Pennsylvania mines, and limestone, would be backed onto the ore trestle and unloaded. The cars' hopper doors would be opened, dropping the cargo down through grates into cavernous steel bins below. Little cars would then carry the raw materials up the sides of the towering blast furnaces between the trestle and the river and dump their loads into the tops of those giant furnaces. The continuous process produced molten iron which was periodically tapped from the bases of the monsters and transported across the J&L bridge in cigar-shaped rail cars to the South Side.

We were called Trestlemen and it was our job to empty the ore cars, which had arrived from Lake Erie. In the summer, the ore was a dull, red mud and could be pried from the cars without too much difficulty, once the hopper doors were opened. In the winter, the ore would be transformed into a solid, frozen mass after its transport through the Great Lakes and a long wait at the loading docks at Ashtabula. We revelled in our body-building work of climbing into the cars and prying the ore lose with heavy, seven foot steel bars; or pounding the sides of the hoppers with sixteen-pound sledges. One of our fraternity work pals was dubbed "Muscle Mel", when he remarked, during one night shift, that the work was "good for the pectorals."

On one afternoon, Chick and I appeared for a shift and were assigned to unload a box car of eighty pound sacks of lime. Each sack was to be hoisted to a shoulder and carried a few hundred feet down a plank walkway, repeatedly, for eight hours; which had a tendency to impart a real respect for the previously unrecognized size of a box car's interior. When we finished the shift at midnight, we had emptied exactly half of the car. On our drive back to Oakland, Chick announced, "I am never going to do that again. If I starve, I'll never do that again."

The next afternoon, we reported to the Foreman and he, matter-of-factly advised, "You boys can go down and finish that car you worked last night."

Later, we were transferred to the mill's labor gang and probably saw every nook and cranny and every bend in every steam line in that sprawling plant. That work has to be the hottest, dirtiest, employment on earth. At times we would be transported to a shut-down open-hearth furnace on the South Side, and before the furnace even cooled, we were assigned to "clean out the checkers." We found the checkers to be a series of brick catacombs, under the elongated bowl of an open hearth, which would accumulate "flu dust" during the operation of the furnace.

With steel wheelbarrows and steel shovels, we would venture into the passages of the checkers and shovel and haul the heavy soot to a waiting truck outside. "The dust is mostly iron and weighs a ton", advised one of the old hands. Those passages were so hot that our crews were able to work only twenty minutes with an intervening rest period of twenty minutes. We were forced to strap two inch thick wooden soles onto our shoes, to avoid being burned.

Just before that last summer vacation, at a fraternity house sports night, Rip Loughrey, a jolly alumnus with a grin from ear to ear and ready laugh, showed up at the House. He was now the Superintendent of the Jones & Laughlin South Side Works and was amused that we had been working for him and that we would be working full time during the summer. Rip liked to relate how he had broken the immortal Jock Sutherland's leg during a wrestling match as an undergraduate. "Well now, you boys need to come over and see me. We need some relief cranemen for the summer." Believe it or not, he was serious and later hired both Chick and me to learn to operate the giant cranes at the South Side plant.

It was an exciting summer. I was transferred from crane to crane, as the regular operators took vacations. Some of the cranes lifted hot steel from one end of the mill to the other. The most interesting was the two-block long crane that used a five ton steel magnet to lift scrap iron from gondola cars far below. The crane would lift and then drop the scrap into truck-sized iron tubs. They would, in turn, be lifted by the charging machines, carrying the scrap into the searing heat of the open-hearth furnaces.

Rip's office was built on steel girders straddling the rail system that brought in the scrap, and on one fateful afternoon, I was operating the crane next to his office. That crane was fitted with a large, clamshell bucket that would be lowered into a gondola loaded with limestone, sixty feet or more below. When the massive jaws closed, the bucket would gobble up a few tons of limestone, which in turn, would be lifted one or more stories and out onto the open hearth charging machines. The crane was the terror of the mill's cranesmen. We were told that there was too little clearance on the crane for an automatic safety; that on most cranes, prevented the "block" from contacting the main beam. The crane's motors were powerful and could snap the cables suspending the load if the block was allowed to contact the beam. It happened. After lowering the clamshell and scooping a full load of stone; I had not fully centered the lift control, and almost imperceptively, the crane's motors continued to lift the load against the huge beam of the crane. I was occupied with sending the load out to the waiting chargers. The cable snapped and the entire block, with twisted steel cable, and the bucket with its load, plummeted downward and landed precisely in the center of a box car. I don't believe I'll ever forget that scene. I hadn't seen a box car bent into a U-shape before. I also won't forget the look on Rip's face as he dashed to his window and looked down at the demolished box car.

The crane incident known as "running up the blocks", became a source of humor for some time and I would be the source of a few jollies during our work excursions into one or more of the South Side bars. The mill workers were a tough bunch - they had to be - and they enjoyed quenching their thirst before leaving the South Side. The work was grueling, whether it was in the searing heat in front of the open-hearths, or in the winter chill of the ore trestle. But we found these men to be responsible and intelligent along with their toughness. There were also those who would blow their Friday pay check in the bars in one evening.

The most unforgettable character on the ore trestle was "Crazy Mike." Mike was a toothless, ragged fixture of the ore trestle. His English was either limited or absent, but he was predictable. He would confront any new arrival on the trestle with his standard, "You Scotch-Irish?" The regulars would explain that Mike despised the Scotch-Irish, so, of course, there were no Scotch-Irish on the trestle. In the winter, the charcoal braziers along the trestle were a minor source of heat and would be a target for any trestleman's throat-clearing expectorations and tobacco juice. Any direct hit on the steel plate covering the brazier would, of course, sizzle away for awhile; but Mike never seemed to notice. He always arrived at work with a large shopping bag stuffed with links of salami and thick-crusted bread. He would be seen producing a rusty blade from his pocket and slicing sections of salami and bread, which were then grilled on the sputum-spattered steel covering the brazier. We often reflected on the merits of heat sterilization and whether Mike knew of this.

One of the South Side bars had a polished brass trough running between the dark, walnut panels of the bar and the long, polished brass foot rail. A small stream of water played into the trough at its far end and slowly ran into a drain at its other end. The general impression was that the trough was for extinguishing cigarettes; but on occasion, we would note one of the patrons using the trough to avoid a trip to the restroom.

On that day in June, after we had passed Heinz Chapel; our pace quickened as we turned onto Bayard and looked forward to lunch. A group of the brothers graced the porch steps of the Delt House, the bulky square red brick structure of another era. There were a few good-natured barbs as we walked through the crowd of jokers and Chick, as always, was able to dish it back at them with enthusiasm.

The panelled, white front door was ajar, and as we walked down the front hall, one of the pledges whispered, "Norm McLeod was here and he is looking for you." No sooner had he finished when Norm appeared, coming down the curving, ornate oak staircase, passing the large, stained glass window at the head of the steps. "Hi there", he beamed, as he shook hands with us. "I thought I might find you here. I have news."

Chick went on to find a spot in the dining room and we could hear him give his exaggerated call to Ruby, Mrs. Dougherty's young, good-looking helper. "Rooby" he shouted, with giggles from the rest of the lunch crowd.

I could tell that Norm was just about bursting, as he shook hands again with, "Congratulations." He handed me a small, unimpressive envelope from Leland Parr, PhD., Director of the Department of Bacteriology, George Washington University School of Medicine. The envelope held a brief, friendly note, noting that Ralph Miller had been accepted into the next class at the George Washington University School of Medicine, pending successful completion of the current term. I, of course, was elated, but somehow, a sense of seriousness took over and I decided I didn't need lunch.

Norm excused himself for an early afternoon appointment and I told Chick I would meet him later for our evening shift at J&L.

I found myself heading back to the Cathedral, passing Heinz Hall and heading for the reference library on the eighth floor. My favorite spot was a comfortable, dark-green leather chair in a quiet corner, secluded by stacks of ancient, little-used volumes.

I found my thoughts wandering; but they kept returning to the realization that the fun-filled existence was over. I began, at that point, to realize a responsibility to do well and to wonder if I could handle the challenge ahead. The sense of cockey self-assurance that had produced a less than outstanding academic record seemed to be fading. It was obvious that I had a lot of catching up to do. It was probably well that I didn't know, at that time, that I would be the first of seven young men from the Delt House to be accepted for careers in medicine by Leland Parr, George Washington's Chairman of the Medical School's Admission Committee.

I had always been impressed by the admonition, "Be careful what you wish for; you may get it", and I began to look back on the sequence of events that led to a determination for a career in Medicine. The determination had probably begun to crystallize at the time of that fateful letter from the Wilkinsburg draft board and during those earlier careers that brought to a halt the early experience with the "Pre-Med" program on the Pitt Campus.

Chapter 7

"The direction in which education starts a man will determine his future life."

— Plato

WASHINGTON, D. C.

That last summer of devil-may-care attitudes came to an end in a rush. Full time and double-shifts at the mill had helped with the payments for a new Buick convertible. It was a gorgeous pale-green boat with a light tan top and the distinctive four round ports on the front fenders. Rather than relief at leaving the status of Craneman at Jones & Laughlin, there was a sense of loss when we punched out of the Southside Works and headed down Carson Street to the new car. Chick was dumped off at the Fraternity House and I had to hustle to make the Saturday night date with Margie. God love her; she knew, as I did, that the fun times were over. We had talked and agreed, that there was nothing much ahead but four years or more of confinement with books. I had never before been more serious about an undertaking than doing well in Medical School; but despite all that, I was badly underestimating what lay ahead.

Margie's smart alec little brother made a cute comment without moving his feet from the porch railing. Margie looked awfully nice in her low-cut white summer dress and we hustled down to the car to avoid more remarks from her smart-mouthed sibling. Margie wanted to hear the band at Ginny Lou's - a non-descript roadhouse out route 51 in Pittsburgh's South Hills. I didn't object; after all, it was our last night out. The ride down the parkway and across the Liberty Bridge and through the tunnels was quiet. I guess we were both thinking that we really didn't know what lay ahead. But whatever it was ; it would be different.

Margie gave some excuse for bypassing the dance floor and bandstand after we walked through the canopied entrance to Ginny Lou's. We took the back steps that led into a large party room, and as we opened the door, there was the whole gang assembled. In unison, glasses of beer were hoisted with an ungodly, "Surprise!".

It was a great evening. That dingy party-room shook with giggles and guffaws as we retold old jokes and relived many of the crazy antics of the past couple of years, into the wee hours. We parted that night, with a few hugs and a few hand-shakes; but no goodbyes. We didn't seem to give much thought as to how our paths may cross or perhaps never cross again - or whether the romances in that room would continue through life or come to an end. It would take awhile for the reality of the real world to settle in.

I found that the antique oak desk from my bedroom would fit, upside down, into the back seat of the convertible, if I put the top down. The car was all packed the next day - a Sunday. And, after one of Mom's famous roast beef dinners, it was time to take off for Washington. There were certainly mixed emotions, as I looked ahead with great anticipation and thought about Margie's wet eyes and the look on the folks' faces as I headed for the Turnpike entrance. It seemed we were always saying goodbye. The route was along the Turnpike to Breezewood, and then those winding roads through the Maryland countryside to D. C. The thoughts were mixed - sadness at leaving all that life behind, mixed with the exhilaration of realizing that this was it - this was the beginning of the real thing.

The little rented room on Butterworth Place, just a few blocks from Wisconsin Avenue, was pleasant and bright, but with just enough room for the antique desk and a bed. The bus to downtown Washington was only three blocks away. I began to learn Washington's systematic system of street names: the first alphabet, as it was known, named streets merely with letters, and the second alphabet named streets with their first letter being a progression of the alphabet with names of two syllables and the third alphabet similarly used names with three syllables.

The George Washington University School of Medicine was housed in an old, almost ancient, dull, four story red brick building near the intersection of 14th. and H Streets - just across from the New York Avenue Church. The polished brass plate to the left of the front entrance was the only bright spot of the whole building. The first floor was about as lackluster as a place could be. A dull terrazzo floor, cracked in many places, led to the worn, black slate steps at the far end of the entrance hall. The steps were flanked by black wrought iron railings capped with well-worn varnished wood railings leading to the second floor. An antique elevator with noisy doors of latticed black iron was at the far end of the hall to the right of the stairway. The walls of brick showed the effect of many layers of paint applied over the years. Their uninspiring beige was chipped in spots revealing the underlying colors of years gone by. The Dean's Office on the left of the hall was no more remarkable. The doors that were always closed were covered with the same dull beige and had a polished brass knob that could have served well for a bathroom door. The outstanding features of that hallway were the large glass frames hanging on those dull brick walls; each with the class photographs of the students who had graduated in years gone by. How many times we would stop and look at some of those goofy photos and remark, "If they could get through this place - so could we."

The tiered amphitheater, a half-flight up and straight ahead from the first floor hallway, was as ancient as the rest of the building. The curved tiers of wooden floors and desk chairs looked down on a long blackboard behind a long slate topped chemistry counter at the lower level.

The upper floors matched everything below. There were well-worn floors of cupped maple boards, enameled black iron railings, dull beige brick walls and half-illuminated glass spheres suspended from the ceilings. The Pathology Museum, on the second floor, housed the shelved glass-fronted cabinets holding hundreds of glass urns filled with the pickled remains of stillborn babies and abnormal human organs - all medical curiosities. The Physiology Lab on the third floor shared the floor with a tiered classroom while the entire fourth floor housed the large anatomy classroom and the Anatomy Lab. The Lab was a large, brightly lit room surrounded by windows and filled with tubular steel-legged tables, enameled white and topped with stainless steel. Each held a shriveled cadaver covered with a grimy, yellow oilskin.

George Washington School of Medicine had established a reputation for training physicians from the entire country, and our class of something more than a hundred, had representatives from most of the States.

At once, it became obvious that the group was more than competitive; they were neurotically competitive. I guess it was a natural reaction, because we all knew that as many as a third of our group would not survive and enter the second year. I was not interested in competing, only in staying.

Some of the personalities were, to say the least, unusual. There was very little friendly association and only limited friendships. The personalities ranged from a few introverted types who would rarely be seen to speak, to a loud bully who had been a George Washington football lineman. He enjoyed inviting a few naive classmates to the G. W. Gym on Saturday afternoons for "a little basketball." He inevitably ended up wresting less muscular victims on the mats choking them half to death. I couldn't help wonder how some of our classmates would fare when they were dealing with patients and what kind of physicians they would become.

An exception to the humorless, competitive class were Woody and John. The three of us shared a small, unpretentious apartment in a mediocre Washington suburb for the better part of that first year after I had left the seclusion of that Butterworth Place prison. We usually cooked an evening meal together, so that we could quickly get to the books. I still recall John's paper-thin curled pork chops and those greasy French fries. Study would start about six and last for several hours. John and Woody would hit the hay at eleven or twelve and I would be trying to cram in some more information until two or later. They would often go out to one of Washington's State Dances on Saturday night, while I would use the time to catch up with the rest of the class.

I learned that I had not mastered the art of study. But, it would gradually dawn that success in that first year was dependent, not necessarily on common good judgement or reason, but on the ability to memorize data for the short term and regurgitate it onto paper.

Anatomy was taught by an immaculately dressed Italian-American professor named Calibrese. Calibrese was called Doctor Calibrese, but it was common knowledge that he had never attended medical school and did not have a doctorate in anatomy. He was authoritative, but pleasant and usually down-to-earth. I liked him, although his lectures were not helpful; and we found that digging around in a mummified corpse gave little help in learning true human anatomy. We named our cadaver Ernest so that we could claim were working in dead earnest.

The professor had, for years, stood behind his lectern and recited anatomy with long descriptions of this nerve crossing that vessel and that muscle attaching to that tendon after crossing something-or other, ad infinitum.

We all, at first, marveled at his brilliance in memorizing so much; but we always wondered why he insisted on not allowing us to raise our heads while he was lecturing. If a rapid writer raised his head, he would be told to keep his head down. It all led to a dramatic revelation; one of our classmates had been rummaging through a used-book store, on a weekend trip to New York; and had come upon a small paper-backed British anatomy volume. As he scanned the pages, he realized he had a copy of Calibrese's lectures. Some of the class pointed out errors in the ancient text, repeated verbatim by the learned professor. He had obviously, over the years, pocketed that small text and had been reading from it without detection.

I had tried, without much success, to learn anatomy with an overly detailed study of Gray's Anatomy, but finally decided to do what everyone else had been doing - memorizing Calibrese's lectures. There was a great deal of merriment in our little dissection group when my mid-term average rose from the low forties to the top grade in the class on the final exam. That exam was related to lower body parts and our group speculated on my future speciality. They were right; but that year of anatomy was hardly worth the long hours that we had all put in.

Calibrese became the butt of clandestine ridicule and humor, so often lacking with that class. A red-headed kid named Greene would imitate those lectures in a rendition with that high pitched voice. He had us all holding our sides with his imitation of Calibrese's claim to be a consultant helping the Air Force design seats for fighter pilots. I truly believe that if Calibrese had ever learned of that class's knowledge of his deception, none of them would have reached the sophomore year.

In later years, Joan and I, on our honeymoon, would visit the Professor and would have a pleasant reunion; but there was no discussion of anatomy.

Doctor Leese headed the Physiology Department and was a modest man with glasses, usually having slipped down his nose, and a brown, uncontrolled mustache. He would roam through the Physiology Lab in his shirt sleeves, with his shirt bulging in a ballooned circle over his belt and threatening to come out altogether. He was a good teacher, but his expertise hit its zenith with his annual course-ending lecture on sexuality - which was always played to a packed house.

The Bacteriology lab was on the second floor of a small wing of the main building. The professor, Doctor Leland Parr, was also the Chairman of the Admissions Committee. I felt a degree of indebtedness to him for the opportunity to be there, after my less than resplendent college performance. He was a quiet, bespectacled, white-haired little man who would quietly conduct our lab sessions. We would culture bacteria and identify them with a series of incubation and tests in glass tubes designed to identify their species. Much of that tedious testing has given way to our modern, more rapid identification systems.

The Biochemistry lectures were given in the large amphitheater, a short flight up from the first floor hallway. The complexity of the body's enzyme systems were regularly outlined on that long blackboard by the professor, a tall, lanky man, or his assistant - Mary Margaret Mills, a gorgeous statuesque self-assured blonde. Mary Margaret was just as nice as she was pretty.

Her boss was not quite so compassionate. Before some of his lectures he would excoriate one of our students who had divorced a wife shortly before entering Medical School. We would, of course, have to sit through the man's moral views on divorce.

Neuroanatomy was a bitch. The intricacies of the nervous system were, at first, incomprehensible. The professor was a Colonel from the staff of Walter Reed Hospital. He was egotistical and so rigid and so military that it's a wonder he didn't snap in-half. During a question and answer session one early afternoon, I heard my name called and he aimed his pointer at a chart of a brain and asked what it was. He bristled when he misinterpreted my answer as flippant and made a note in his little note book. Calibrese later told me that the Colonel said, "That man is going to show me something before he passes this course." I knew then, that it would take an added effort to ever get past this gentleman.

That first year really was terrible. The Navy years had at least provided almost enough sleep. But, the sleep deprivation from studying half the night made it tough to keep an optimistic outlook. By Christmas that first year, I was flunking the three major subjects and not by a few points, but by a lot.

Chuck Vivian was one of the earthy classmates who had been raised on a cattle ranch in Montana and was one of the top students in the class. He came home along to Pennsylvania on that first Christmas and proved to be a real friend.

On our trip through the Maryland countryside he convinced me that memorization of some isolated material was the only thing needed to pass those courses. I began to see that I was trying to absorb too much detail, too thoroughly; which may have been next to impossible. Most everyone else had resigned themselves to this fact of life; for example, memorizing Calibrese's lectures that really gave little insight into real anatomy.

That Christmas was not as bright as it could have been. I spent a good part of it with my nose in the books. But, it turned out to be the beginning of the turn-around.

The sleepless nights weren't any easier, but little by little, the subjects began to make more sense. Mary Margaret Mills, the lovely teacher with a really bright mind, was helpful by volunteering a few minutes after classes to do a little tutoring. It was encouraging when she advised that my questions were beginning to show more understanding.

My old friend and sponsor, Norm, called one evening. He was in Washington on business and suggested our having dinner together the next day. I, of course, told him I had to study but he insisted and we went to Mrs. K's, a well-known suburban restaurant. He knew a couple of hours wouldn't hurt and I was back at the books as soon as I dropped him off. In a couple of days I got a thoughtful and a deeply appreciated letter. He was concerned with my despair over poor grades, but convincingly wrote that he was absolutely convinced I would be one of the ones to succeed. Those thoughts were appreciated, not only at the time, but for years to come.

The week of final exams was a stressful period for everyone - not just the average students - but for everyone. It was particularly troublesome for those of us who were on the brink of not making it. We were responsible for everything that had been taught over the entire year. Notes and texts for that entire year had to be revisited and again memorized.

We were all frantic to see the list of those who had made it. When the list was finally posted, there was a rush to see who the survivors were. A number of our classmates had already dropped out during the year and a few more would not be allowed to return. All in all, about a third of that class would not be seen again.

Woody and John ran into the little hamburger shop a block or so from the school and shook hands with congratulations. I didn't finish lunch but raced back to school. I had to see that list, of course. And there it was, my name with an average above seventy in all subjects except neuroanatomy. The "Colonel" had given me an "incomplete" grade and I would have to "show him something" before I would be allowed to enter the second year.

Not knowing what the rigid Colonel would ask, I spent much of the summer vacation sunbathing in our back yard and memorizing two authoritative neuroanatomy texts. It was in late August when I drove up the long, winding drive to Walter Reed Hospital. The Neurology department was one of the colonial style buildings separated from the main Hospital. A receptionist showed me to a basement level room that was obviously a classroom with a few tables and a projection screen. In about twenty minutes the Colonel entered from a far door and was carrying a porcelain tray. He put the tray on the table in true military fashion and removed the cloth cover, exposing a human brain. "We're here to test your knowledge of neuroanatomy", he announced. He proceeded to cut the brain into half inch sections, exposing one small structure after another, and asking what each was. His stern demeanor lessened a little and there was obviously surprise as the answers came without hesitation. There was almost a hint of attempted friendliness. I wasn't feeling friendly myself, however - only relief. After the brain lay in small pieces, he said, "Well, you certainly have mastered the subject. I'll notify the school." With that, we both rose, shook hands and with a simple "Thanks", I headed out. I didn't know, at the time, just how valuable that summer study course would become, when I would later meet and work with one of the country's outstanding neurosurgeons.

G. W. was pioneering a new curriculum with their second year medical students being sent to district hospitals while still in their Sophomore year - a much earlier entry into clinical medicine than other schools at the time. There were still enough science classes, that late evening study was still the rule. But, everyone's confidence level was a little higher and thoughts were directed more toward concerns in dealing with real patients. However, there would still be another "weeding-out" process. A few more of our class would be dropping out. Others would be determining that they would spend their careers in research labs or in specialties which didn't require direct contact with patients.

During that first part of the year, we had all been assembling the equipment that was required for our clinical experience. We were required to have a professional handbag, a stethoscope, a blood pressure cuff, an ophthalmoscope and tongue blades.

The physical diagnosis course was probably the most interesting thing we had done to date. For the first time, most of our instructors were physicians rather than PhD's, and we were generally in awe at their expertise. We would check each others blood pressure, listen to chests, look down throats and check out eyes and ears with great interest. We were told that, "it would all come together" with all that science blending with the study of disease. Eventually, it began to do just that.

The pathology course was like a whole new world opening up. We would be amazed as we stared into microscopes and saw the effects of disease on the body's tissues. The autopsies we witnessed were even more dramatic.

Often we would be summoned for an afternoon or a weekend autopsy at Gallenger, the District's public hospital. Most of the patients were charity cases and certainly were at the lower end of the economic ladder. Often they had diseases that had been allowed to run their course for years without treatment.

On one Saturday afternoon we were called to Gallenger's Morgue and about ten of us entered the plain steel door of the plain, one story red brick building which led to a short flight of steps up to a higher level. We were seated on benches around a rectangular railing which surrounded an opening in the floor, directly over the autopsy table. As we sat and looked directly down over the railing, we were looking at the corpse of a young girl. The Pathologist and his assistant were beginning the "postmortem" and the Pathologist was dictating a description of the body into a small microphone that hung from a cord over the table. The assistant was directing a spray of water over the body. As the history was dictated, we leaned that the young girl, aged eighteen, had died after treatment for colonic cancer. We were amazed at such a young death from cancer.

The Pathologist took up a large scalpel and made a deep "Y" incision from each shoulder area downward and inward, meeting at the center of the lower chest and then extending in the midline through the abdomen. The Assistant, without a word, with a long handled instrument, cut each rib, in turn, at the sides of the chest; while the Pathologist extended the lower incision and opened the abdomen.

The odor was not pleasant - particularly for those who had never experienced one of these procedures. The assistant's water-spray, rinsing blood from the corpse and allowing it to run off into a drain in the stainless steel table top helped only a little.

We, at once, were becoming aware of the ravages of cancer. The entire abdomen was matted into one mass by countless deposits of yellow, ugly looking tissue. The loops of bowel were plastered together, so that the entire mass was lifted out after it had been cut away from the inner walls of the abdomen. The liver was similar. Its outer surface was studded with irregular projections of the same ugly tissue.

The entire front of the rib cage was lifted away, exposing the interior of the thorax. The heart and lungs appeared normal as they were explored, but the Pathologist, who was lecturing details as he proceeded, pointed out the nodular surface of the lung, indicating more spread of the disease.

The fine dissection of the organs was less dramatic, and our group began an attempt to relax. There were several conversations which were beginning to become louder, and finally the loud talk was mingled with some inappropriate laughter. Finally, the Pathologist put down his instruments and looked upward into each of the faces in turn. "Each and every one of you would be well advised to stop this disrespect right now", he quietly said, . . . "If you have this little respect for those of us doing this work or for the human body, you probably have very little respect for yourselves. I wonder how you think you can become physicians."

There wasn't another word spoken until we were dismissed sometime later.

Gallenger wasn't always that dismal though. The young residents who took us on "rounds" were impressive. Without exception, we would be impressed on rounds, when we would surround a patient's bed and watch the meticulous examination and quizzing of a patient. More impressive was the residents' ability to interact with the patients. Joviality and a little optimistic humor seemed to have a real therapeutic effect. Some of the comments from our group revealed a real concern that they would have difficulty being as relaxed and effective with patients. The faculty members - often young physicians in private practice - were equally impressive with their knowledge and their willingness to share it. These people were truly practicing the philanthropy of Medicine.

One of the widely celebrated visiting specialists was a Doctor Freeman, who had developed his famous "ice-pick" operation. At the time, it had been found that much aberrant social behavior originated in the frontal lobes of the brain. It was believed that separating those lobes from the rest of the brain could have a calming effect on violent criminals, sociopaths and many poor souls who had been found to be incurable by other treatments.

Neurosurgeons were entering the skull and surgically cutting the connections between the frontal lobes and the remainder of the brain. Often, there would be some improvement in violence and severe, disabling psychoses. But, the patients would also experience some significant reasoning and judgmental loss.

Doctor Freeman had devised a procedure that advanced a long, thin stainless steel rod through the top of the orbit, above each eye, into those areas that carried the connections between the frontal lobes and the rest of the brain. Limited motion of those steel probes, when in place, would sever those pathways - eliminating the need for an open surgical procedure.

We watched Doctor Freeman do the procedure on two anesthetized patients one morning - poking long spikes into patients' brains through their eye sockets; and found that this procedure had little appeal.

Things had eased just a little - enough, at least, to allow an occasional weekend off. On one occasion, there was a trip to Philadelphia to enjoy a group of the Fraternity Gang for the Pitt-Penn game. That crowd hadn't slowed down much and it was great to raise a little hell even if only briefly.

On another weekend, I had been able to join Norm and his friend, Branch Rickey, for a ride from Washington to the University of Delaware, where Rickey was to speak at the installation of a new fraternity chapter. Rickey was abrupt and gravelly voiced. But, during our trip, I learned that he was deeply religious and principled. Although he had become legendary for bringing Jackie Robinson to the Dodgers while he was the General Manager, we talked only a little about baseball. It was apparent that the man had a keen intellect - particularly as it applied to the sport. We talked at length about the challenges of Medicine and he confided with some of his medical problems. His cigars were overpowering. But then, to a great degree, so was his personality. He had us promise to join him at Forbes Field for some of the Pirate home games since he had become the Pirate General Manager.

After returning to Pittsburgh, those evenings with Rickey in his box overlooking home plate were memorable. Passing through the Field's Press entrance, there would be a climb through a rickety back stairway twisting through a series of steel girders into the equally rickety box, down a couple of steps from a small landing above the box.

The box looked out over home plate and the manicured diamond and outfield ending with the scoreboard and that famous brick wall with Panther Hollow and Carnegie Tech in the distance.

Newspapermen pecked away at their typewriters in the box to the left, separated by a grimy green board partition, while Bob Prince, the sportscaster, blabbed into his microphone in the booth to the right. Prince never seemed to require a pause for a breath.

George Sissler, a coach and one of baseball's greats, usually sat next to Rickey and it was amazing to hear these men analyze plays and the players' performances.

On one occasion Rickey, without restraint, voiced his annoyance with one of the visiting players - Ted Kluszweski - a Cincinnati star. Kluszewski always appeared with the sleeves cut from his uniform. Rickey opined that he disliked the muscle flexions while at bat for the entertainment of the girls in the audience ... and, "if that young man was ever on one of my teams he would leave the sleeves on his uniform like anyone else!"

Well, Kluszewski was traded to Pittsburgh...and continued to star with his sleeveless uniform. Pittsburgh kids dubbed him "Big Klu" and were often seen with their sleeves missing. "Big Klu" became a favorite baseball card celebrity.

Was this a harbinger of the more recent entry of musclemen into the game?

Toward the end of the year, we were introduced to psychiatry. There were a series of lectures detailing mental illness and we then were given an opportunity to interact with a series of mental patients.

St. Elizabeth was the large mental hospital for the District. It housed not only patients undergoing intensive psychotherapy, but had a large, well-guarded fenced-in unit housing the criminally insane. Some of those inmates had been known nationally for their horrendous crimes.

We never got near the criminal unit, but our psychiatrist-teacher would meet with us in small groups and would have the attendants bring in patients affected with various mental disorders. I remember the young girl who represented a manic-depressive disorder, now called bipolar disorder. It was a pitiful experience. She conversed with our group and appeared perfectly sane. But, she would go over a short period of time, from a "high" or euphoria, into a terrible depressed state. We would later see and attempt to talk with "schizophrenics" and those suffering from the dementia of tertiary syphilis.

Early treatment and prevention of syphilis was not yet effective and discussion of the disease was taboo until Dr. Perron wrote his classical book, Shadow on The Land. It helped bring discussion, and thereby rational treatment, into the open. My friend Norm was to be instrumental in bringing Dr. Perron to Pitt to establish and to head the new Graduate

School of Public Health. Yet, we were seeing patients who had contracted the disease years earlier and who were showing the effects of the third stage of the disease - an attack on the central nervous system. The brains of these poor people would be affected with the disease's organisms - spirochetes - and would develop the dementia known as General Paresis. Often, the spinal cord would be attacked with the resulting paralysis and loss of coordination known as Tabes Dorsalis.

It had been found that some of these patients, who had developed an unrelated fever on occasion, would improve somewhat. So, St. Elizabeth's physicians were producing high fevers in some patients by actually giving them malaria, under some limited control, for a period of time. These patients were very, very sick while undergoing this "cure."

That was probably the beginning of a realization of the very thin line separating us all from the abnormalities of those neuroses and psychoses. The disagreement in diagnoses among some of our learned teachers taught that there was much we didn't know about mental disease, and quite probably, that we knew very little.

The "Moment of Truth" came upon us before we knew it. Our small group reported to one of Gallenger's medical wards where the nurses gave us white jackets for the first time and amazingly called us "Doctor." I didn't know about anyone else, but I felt embarrassed. There we were with our white jackets, clutching those obviously brand-new black leather bags, trying to look like doctors.

Our physician-teacher assigned each pair of us to a patient and instructed us to do a complete "history and physical", which we would then reduce to writing. There was hesitation, as we all stood around trying to get up the courage to go out on that ward. My partner advised that I was to go first and was to do the interview and exam. I swear, that as our phalanx of white jackets hit the ward, I saw the patients cringe and pull away. I swear they were thinking "Here we go again."

My patient was a younger man who didn't appear too sick; and after we had shaken hands and introduced ourselves, it really became a relaxed and rewarding experience. We kept it informal, and the encounter became a lesson with my first patient. There was no need for pretense; only a need for directness and honesty - perhaps mixed with a little friendliness. Our patient, during the exam, allowed as to how we were the third group to have examined him that week. Nevertheless, he was pleased to help. That first history and exam went well. I remember being a little pleased with myself - after all, hadn't all those sleepless nights been a preparation for this?

When all the groups got together at the School the next morning, the stories flew. It seemed that the stories centered on how great everything went or what a disaster the experience had been - both obvious exaggerations. But, a section of our class had been on the same ward the day before, and that section included a couple of characters who were a little more adept with the use of the King's English than with the finer points of physical examination. They had jointly examined a very large lady and apparently had made quite an impression. When two of our guys approached her, she quickly said that she didn't need an examination; she had been examined by a couple of "specialists" the day before.

I suppose the closest I'll ever come to celebrity status happened on a Saturday morning near the end of the second year. A little bit behind schedule for an eight-thirty class, I was driving a little faster than usual down the street that butts directly into Pennsylvania Avenue directly in front of the White House. I had found a parking garage a couple of blocks away with affordable weekend rates. I was going to zip through that yellow light with a left turn onto Pennsylvania, when a group of five or six well-dressed men briskly stepped off the curb and marched directly into my path. There was a screech of rubber. But the little militaristic group never broke step. The look I got from the bespectacled, dapper fellow in the gray fedora could have melted lead. By the time the group stepped up onto the opposite curb, I realized how close I had come to running down Harry Truman and the Secret Service. On a later Saturday afternoon, while shopping with a friend on one of the lower Washington streets, a pleasant looking plump lady, in a beautiful fur coat, stepped out of a limousine and attempted to step up the double curb. We were absorbed by the window display of a leather shop as we walked along and I bumped into the nice lady and caused her to back down onto the street. After an apology and a little help back up onto the sidewalk, we went on. After a minute or so my friend asked, "Didn't you know who that was? That was Bess", she said. I remember hoping that the Trumans didn't think I had a grudge against them.

All that was coming to a close. I had come to love the beauty of the Capitol even though most of what I had seen was only in passing. But, Pitt Med School had accepted me back for the final two years . . . and that's where my heart was.

The School required us all to pass the first two parts of the "National Board" exams before we would be allowed to enter the last two years of school - the clinical years. Most of us passed the first part, a written exam, and it had become apparent that the curriculum at G. W. had been tough enough that anyone who got through these courses would find the National Boards reasonable. It was said that the school took great pride in the percentage of its students who passed the "Boards" - particularly when it was compared with its rival, Georgetown. The completion of all three parts of the "Boards" allowed physicians to be licensed to practice in most any state.

The two years confinement at George Washington made the summer break before heading to the Pitt Campus again a real Utopia. I spent a good part of the time in seclusion on a few wooded acres along Crooked Creek. It was a wilderness and the days were spent in hard labor; hauling rocks from the creek and surrounding woods and building the huge fireplace and stone chimney, that would become the centerpiece of the large rustic room. It was a great relief from academia. It would be the start of a get-away home for the family.

By the time the calloused hands of a stone mason had replaced the previous soft palms, it was time to think about getting back to business.

First, there was the return trip to the Pitt Campus and Med School to take the National Board Exam. The exam took a whole day, but was reasonable; and I began to see the value of the sacrifice of those earlier two years. I took the opportunity to see the Medical Center where I would spend many of the upcoming years. The exam was given in a third floor classroom of Falk Clinic fronting on Fifth Avenue. The driveway off Fifth, past Falk Clinic, led to the entrance of Childrens Hospital; and towering above, was the limestone expanse and angular walls and towers of the Center - housing the Eye and Ear, Presbyterian and Women's Hospitals. Women's looked across DeSoto Street upon the Western State Psychiatric Institute where we, as teenagers, had first experienced the ghastliness of mental disease. Just above, at the head of DeSoto, was the famous Pitt Stadium. It always would bring back memories of the antics of those earlier football seasons and earlier days in the kid's section.

The class schedule revealed that there was little classroom space for Med Students in their clinical years. Most of the classes were held in the hospitals and were scheduled at Falk Clinic, Presbyterian, Eye and Ear, Mercy, Allegheny General, Women's and McGee.

It didn't take long to discover that my classmates were an entirely different breed than the introverted, grimly competitive bunch at G. W. I found myself surrounded and becoming part of a group of characters. We all were serious about our goals, but appreciated a good laugh and a break from the routine from time to time.

Our little crowd would occasionally bum a sandwich at Fred Obley's house on DeSoto Street, just below the Stadium, before heading down the Boulevard to Mercy's marble amphitheater for Dr. Bracken's Wednesday afternoon lecture. Fred was one of the few married guys and "Mrs. Fred" was always a willing and cheerful hostess for the grubbers. Fred was always the organizer, whether the event would be a stag party at the Amen Corner in the downtown William Penn or an impromptu beer-bust. He was the manager of the scoreboard at Forbes Field and had to be there for all home games. We always wondered when he found time to study.

Mercy's amphitheater was a circular marble arena bounded by a chest-high marble balustrade. Behind, were several circular tiers of wooden seats, with each rising steeply above that in front, with each seat occupied by a student peering down into the arena. Dr. Bracken was a tall, thin, balding and bespectacled soft-spoken man whose subject was Pathology. He had a collection of aluminum trays with a layer of beeswax on the bottoms and would regularly adorn each tray with a chunk of formaldehyde-drenched human tissue. The trays would be passed, row by row, through the amphitheater's rows of students to illustrate the day's subject. At times, it would take an extreme effort to retain one's lunch as the reeking trays were passed from hand to hand. Large slices of liver, sections of brain, and occasionally a pickled human heart, would pass across a tier and then upward to make the curved course of the next row.

At Fred's house, the decision was made one noontime. We decided to garnish one of the specimens a little. As we sat in an upper tier, it was interesting to watch the reactions as Dr. Bracken's leathery slice of liver was seen, ensconced on a large slice of Jewish rye, topped by a tomato slice and flanked by a dill pickle and an olive.

Dr. Bracken's true test came at a later time when, during one of his lectures, strange, rhythmic sounds were heard from an unoccupied section of the upper tier. We all seemed a little oblivious to the noise until it began reaching a crescendo of deep-toned rumblings and intermittent whistles.

Bracken finally exploded. The Mercy Hospital's Chief of Pathology was heard to announce in a shaking voice, "I don't know who is making that racket, but if it doesn't stop, the whole bunch of you are going to get thrown out of here." There was brief silence but then the cacophony continued.

Suddenly, one of the guys in a lower row raced up the steps to the upper tier, and the next thing we saw, was a classmate sit upright and rub his eyes - unceremoniously awakened from his noontime nap.

The ultimate in self control was required to maintain consciousness during Dr. Mabon's Public Health after-lunch lecture. All the shades would be drawn in that second floor Falk Clinic classroom and the lecturer would stand in front of the darkened audience, pressing a button that would change the images projected onto a large screen beside him. There was no way to absorb the information represented by one graph after another that he would project. We would just sit and stare ahead.

On this occasion, someone whispered that Jack Wagner had substituted one of Mabon's slides. The drapes were drawn; the lights were doused; and on came the lantern show. Mabon began by pressing the button; and in place of one of the graphs illustrating the declining incidence of pellagra, the screen reflected a well endowed statuesque blonde, nude against a brilliant red background.

After the howls and giggles quieted, Mabon gained near-immortality when he quietly said, "Could you sharpen that a little?"

Another lecturer was one of Mercy Hospital's surgeons who had all the personality characteristics of a Storm Trooper. He was so authoritative, as he bragged about his surgical prowess, and so intimidating as he scanned each face in the audience, during a middling presentation; that everyone was afraid to breathe. At a dinner table one evening, we were allowed to sit with the "Great One", while he reminded us that students were to be seen and not heard.

Others were great teachers and were more realistic, treating us as colleagues. Doctor Stevenson, a pediatrician, gave us great insight into the diagnosis of pediatric disorders, and more importantly, the practical approach in dealing with kids and their distraught mothers.

There was, at one time, a major flap, when a group of our class protested having to drive across town to hear a surgical lecture once a week by one of the Hospital's greats. The surgeon was always late and his twenty minute discourse on his accomplishments were voiced by many to be worthless expenditure of their finances and time. That was probably his last series of student lectures.

The O. B. stint at McGee Women's Hospital was a live-in experience for about three weeks. Anyone who lived through the experience was understandably qualified to deliver babies. The residents in charge were astute and thorough, and the volume of deliveries taking place was assurance that we would leave with a mass of experience. It would be a major part of the training for those of us who would enter general practice and be required to practice obstetrics.

We were called for deliveries day and night over those three weeks. Our living quarters were on a basement level. Somehow, the deliveries of some sort of glass bottles took place through the corridor outside our room. It was the decided impression of those of us, who tried to catch a few winks in that room, that the bottles were fiendishly arranged on some sort of a cart in order to give the highest decibel level as they jingled against each other. It was suspected that the cart had square wheels.

The time restraints of those final two years of school were serious enough. But, there was beginning to be a realization that we would, in the not too distant future, have to plan our course for a lifetime. We could take a year's rotating internship at a hospital and later enter practice or go on for additional training for a speciality in an approved residency program. A residency program had its pitfalls, just as with everything else we had done to date. Residency programs generally accepted several physicians, and over a period of four or five years, would eliminate all but one or two of the residents who would then become "Chief Residents." Generally, only Chief Residents would be eligible for Speciality Board Certification after competing in one of these "pyramid programs." Certification often was necessary for appointment to the staff of a good hospital.

It was becoming apparent that a years's internship would qualify us for treating head colds and directing normal deliveries; but in order to provide the most sophisticated care, one would have to spend added years to learn those skills. It was becoming more and more evident that the "jacks-of-all-trades" would be "masters-of-none."

I was beginning also to see an unsettling occurrence. A group that I had lunch with from time to time were becoming truly good friends; but two of the guys, always together, were arousing the suspicions of our group. One came from a well-to-do family; his father was a surgeon. In a word, Charlie was badly spoiled. His buddy, another Charlie, was from a modest, working-class background. But we began to notice that the Charlies would sit in a back row together during examinations and would combine their knowledge. At first, I couldn't believe that anyone who had survived what we had, and who aspired to be part of a great profession, would stoop to cheating while the rest of us were playing it straight.

But, I did become a believer. During a difficult Obstetrics exam, I found myself in the next to last row, directly in front of the Charlies. There was a constant conversation between them as they completed their exams. I admit to being more than a little annoyed. I finally turned and told my friends to stop or there would be trouble. They stopped, and I had lost two friends. I suppose I was very regretfully beginning to lose some idealism. When we talked about the two of them during bull sessions from time to time, I would suggest that people like that eventually get caught and pay the price. "No", someone would say, "They are clever and don't get caught, and often go on to the top." I was to learn that my Med school colleagues were right.

The Med School and the Law School were competitive in their devilment in the off-hours. Our bunch had little beer parties when we would let off steam and goad each other; and there would be an occasional class function. But the Law School parties were always well organized and just as hilarious.

There was little time for socializing in that final year of school, but the invitations to some of the Law School parties gave an insight into the differences in outlooks between the professions; and we were forging bonds that would endure over our lifetimes. One of the Law school parties was held at a large, suburban night club, and at that party, Jerry Weaver - one of my friend Ralph's circle - was part of a parody - poking fun at the Law school's assistant Dean, Charles Nutting. I had already been taken aback when the Dean of the Law school had entered with a girlfriend rather than the spouse. That was one hell of a step socially, at the time, and he got away with it. He played the piano and had a great time - never losing an ounce of respect or affection that his students held for him.

Jerry Weaver's skit was a riot. The Assistant Law School Dean was a very bald, reserve Army Colonel. He often showed up for his Law School lectures in the full uniform of a "Bird Colonel." Jerry and his group appeared in Army officer's uniforms with Jerry in the lead, in his smartly pressed olive drab. . . and with an oscillating Christmas tree canary on each shoulder. As the little canaries vibrated back and forth on each shoulder on their coil-spring legs, Jerry and his group rendered a highly altered version of a well known radio hair tonic commercial at the time - "Use Wildroot Cream Oil, Charlie." By the second stanza, we were all (including Charlie) convulsing. Nutting and his wife stood up and applauded the little group. If Dean Nutting had been a Med School professor the response may have been a little different. Doctors take themselves much more seriously. Some physicians are acutely defensive by any imagined assault on their fragile egos.

Any other response at the time may not have been gracious, but I was learning that lawyers are another breed. As my good friend Clara, Ralph's wife, has said, "They think differently."

Physicians by nature, and perhaps by selection, are different. The give and take of lawyers is not understood by them and grudges are held for a lifetime.

The lawyers, on one hand will fight each other aggressively, and then, at the end of the day, decide to go out and have a beer together. There are, of course, the brutal, aggressive unprincipled members of their profession who will attempt to destroy the competition . . . for a price, and with the goal of winning at any cost. But I believe the balance, to a great degree, is in favor of the gentlemen.

During that final year of Med School, we were feeling relief from some of the pressures of the previous years. The class was divided into clinical groups of four as we circulated through Pittsburgh's hospital wards. Ralph Morrison, Bertie Most and a fellow named Medwid were my partners in that undistinguished group.

On one afternoon at Presbyterian Hospital, heart patients were wheeled into a small meeting room on the first floor. One at a time, we would listen to their chests as our instructor would explain the sounds we were expected to hear. Medwid was the last to listen to the sound of a loud mitral murmur of a pathetic young man bearing the severe cardiac damage of earlier rheumatic fever.

Medwid listened, and in amazement announced loudly, "It sounds like a freight train." We all were a little stunned by his insensitivity.

During our trips through the clinics of Pittsburgh Hospitals, we were privileged to see the other half of society. During an afternoon at Mercy's Clinic, I was assigned an elderly man who was a known diabetic. He complained of foot trouble. He obligingly took off a shoe and was obviously missing two of his toes. Shockingly, the two toes had remained in the shoe.

On another afternoon, I saw a little two year old lady with a running nose and cough. She was given a prescription for a cough remedy. But, before she could leave, an older sister, herself no more than ten, entered in a fit of temper. I still remember her tight red, white and blue shiny shorts. In short order, she castigated me in unlady-like terms, expressing displeasure for my G.D. wooden bench that caused her to get a splinter in her posterior parts; (she didn't say posterior parts). The splinter was removed without incident.

The afternoon "clinic" at St. Francis was just about completed when a bedraggled old fellow appeared, complaining of an ear ache. We hadn't had much experience looking into ears, but I borrowed an otoscope and looked into the offending ear. It seemed like the ear was looking back. The ear canal was crawling with maggots. The problem was one of the hazards of sleeping on a park bench.

The final exams of the final year weren't bad and much of the class looked forward to the trip to Indianapolis - sponsored by the Eli Lilly Company. The pharmaceutical company would bus the Senior Class to their home headquarters to watch drug production. The class would be wined and dined, hear a sex lecture by the famous Dr. Kinsey at the University, and see the time-trials for the upcoming Memorial Day classic at the Speedway.

A few of the boys had made less than complimentary remarks about the hotel, and in particular, the room furnishings, during one of the all-night parties. One early morning, during that trip, there was a considerable discussion among the hotel's management. No one ever was able to give a satisfactory explanation as to how a sofa and two or three overstuffed chairs got to the bottom of an elevator shaft.

The trip, though was a great experience and we returned to Pittsburgh to face the uncertainties of Internship.

Chapter 8

"Education has for its object the foundation of character."

— *Herbert Spencer*

INTERNSHIP

St. Margaret Hospital had an excellent reputation. Its Medical Staff was considered tops. The Hospital wasn't large and was crowded into a steep Pittsburgh hillside section of town, originally populated by Polish immigrants. The small, immaculate, well-kept houses lined the streets side-by-side, without any sign of front lawns. An occasional small passage between two of the houses would lead to a tiny back yard and an occasional tiny garden. A new wing of the Hospital was about to open, but the bulk of the structure loomed as a grimy, red brick square without ornamentation; blackened by years of smoke and soot from Lawrenceville's steel plants. The towering slate roof sloped into copper gutters, green with age, surrounding the upper floors.

The attic-like intern quarters were several small rooms crowded into the top floor of the old building and would have been appropriate for a monastery. I was assigned to a cubbyhole, just adequate to accommodate a bed, a chair and a telephone stand. But, compared to the Navy barracks and the rooming houses from the prior years, this was luxury.

The salary was less than modest, but we had free access to the dining room and free laundry. Much was made of these perks, but it soon became apparent that the Hospital, through the system requiring a year's internship as a prerequisite for a medical license, was able to attract slave labor. The situation was compounded by a less than full complement of interns for that year.

There were three of us, dictating that we would be on call every third night. Call, it turned out, meant a sleepless night, two or more times a week. It was considered a ritual or initiation; but what it really was, was a system for hospitals to provide staffing at a minimum cost. The system was bound to change in time; but for that year, we were trapped and we were to become exhausted.

The Hospital had no emergency physicians and no laboratory people at night; so that we found ourselves starting intravenous lines, seeing emergency patients, delivering babies, doing emergency laboratory studies, cross-matching blood and being at the beck and call of the Nursing Supervisor. Mrs. Harden was a stern, no-nonsense supervisor and was competent to handle many situations; and generally did her best not to arouse the guy on call. But one or two of her replacements would have us running all night.

On one occasion, Norm Azen, one of our trio, fell into bed, after a long evening of service. He had apparently just nodded off and was more or less "non compos mentis." When our beloved substitute supervisor aroused him in the wee hours with a request to come down and discuss a patient's progress with the family, Norm was quoted as saying, "Give them a quarter grain of morphine and I'll see them in the morning."

The staff of obstetrics was a jovial, closely-knit group who showed a real interest in teaching and who felt a responsibility to help us gain something from that year of servitude. They would sit in a tiny room drinking coffee while waiting for a delivery, and would routinely welcome us to join. I think we all gained a great deal of confidence in dealing with those mothers in labor, and occasionally, delivering the baby on our own, and by associating with the obstetricians.

Assistants for surgery were in short supply and we would quite often be called upon to assist one of the surgeons with a major case. A few of these men were excellent technicians and just being with them during a procedure was an enviable experience . . . even after being up all night.

It was a major event when we heard that a pneumonectomy - that is, the removal of a diseased lung - was going to be done. It was a first for the Hospital - a truly major event. Without question, I would give my eye teeth to be in the room to watch. The surgeon, Bill Ford, a young thoracic surgeon - not long out of residency - appeared soon after the noon hour. I intercepted him on his way to the dressing room, and with some hesitation asked, "Dr. Ford, is there any chance I could watch your case?" "Hell", he replied, "You're going to assist me; get dressed." In all the surgeons I've known and have been with, Bill was the coolest and most casual. He was an excellent technician and it is still a wonder to me that he did his first major procedure in Pittsburgh with an intern as an assistant.

The procedure went well, but just as the patient was moved onto a stretcher, he developed a sudden pulmonary collapse and went into shock. Another real professional, Bill Stewart, the anesthesiologist, immediately diagnosed the problem - a tension pneumothorax. Air was being trapped in the empty space after removal of the lung and was compressing the remaining lung, preventing adequate air exchange. In an instant, Bill plunged a large needle into the chest and sucked out the trapped air with a large syringe. The patient rebounded and made a full recovery.

A few of these experiences probably made the sleepless nights somewhat worthwhile. I was grasping the value of an expert anesthesiologist to a surgeon. Together, as a team. they can accomplish results not possible without that teamwork. I hadn't begun to think of the possibility of doing major surgery without the help of men like Bill Stewart. It would be some time before I would learn the tribulations of doing major surgery without the expertise of men like Bill.

Doing laboratory work at night was not something we relished. If a "stat" lab study was ordered by one of the Medical Staff after hours, we would hear the ring of the wretched black phone next to our ear. Doing a blood count or cross-matching a unit of blood was tedious enough in the daytime, let alone after being hustled out of bed.

Dr. Mason, the Hospital's Pathologist, was a red-headed stickler for detail. But that detail was always accomplished before the cocktail hour. He was probably oblivious to the dangers to patients having interns do laboratory work at night. He summoned me to his office on one occasion and thoroughly dressed me down for mis-matching a unit of blood the previous night.

While I was on the two month laboratory service with the man, I was assisting him on a routine autopsy. There was little or no teaching from him - just instructions to do some of the more unpleasant tasks over a decaying, odorous corpse. The entire bowel, twenty feet or more, was generally removed in one mass, and as routine, I was handed the mass and put it into a knee level porcelain sink. That twisted mass was floating appropriately as I returned to the stainless steel table to help complete the "post-mortem." Near the conclusion of the autopsy, I was ordered to "run the bowel." That was a somewhat tedious procedure using surgical scissors to open the entire length of the organ to eliminate the possibility of any abnormal findings on the interior. When I returned to the sink for that unpleasant task, the whole mass was gone. Somehow, it had slid down the porcelain neck of that sink and had disappeared. The Good Doctor came over to the sink, stared into it, in disbelief, and simply raised his head and looked at the ceiling. His ruddy complexion became even ruddier.

At the early morning ritual of breakfast, a few hours later, my companions in servitude entered into extensive speculation as to how far down the Allegheny River that particular object had traveled.

During internship, the service on surgery was, without a doubt, the most demanding. Yet, it was a step toward what I wanted to do. Dr. Watson, probably the leading surgeon at the hospital, readily admitted to being a Mayo graduate and so obviously superior to us mortals, that one, at times, felt almost compelled to grovel at his feet. He was an excellent surgeon and the unspoken law demanded that we scrub with him, when he did a case, in preference to the other surgeons. "Jungle Jim" would have our back-breaking help pulling those finger-numbing surgical retractors for hours, and then would allow the scrub nurse to "close" the incision. It was the ultimate insult and it left little doubt of our status.

Not all experiences during that year were wonderful excursions into the glamourous world of surgery. At a fraternity gathering, I was introduced to "Hack" O'Connor, one of Pittsburgh's outstanding surgeons. He was a big, likeable, gregarious fellow. He invited me to assist him at his hospital the following morning - a Saturday. The patient was scheduled for the removal of a cancerous lung. I had never seen a pneumonectomy, let alone assist at one; so that there was no hesitation to accept the offer.

In the early Saturday hours, the dressing, the scrub, the patient prep with my congenial host was routine. When the procedure started, I had trouble believing what I was seeing. The surgeon attacked the body with a frenzy I had never seen in an operating room. I think we would expect to see better technique in a butcher shop. I was glad to get out of there and couldn't help wonder how my host had acquired the moniker, "Hack."

On the way to the surgeon's lounge, we passed another operating room and a friendly nurse advised that Dr. Brickmore was dong an intracranial procedure - I think for a brain tumor.

I quietly slipped in and watched the procedure unnoticed. That is, I watched very briefly. While he operated, the highly respected neurosurgeon was having a tantrum and his language was reminiscent of the communications we would hear at some of the waterfront bars we visited during those Navy days. Most of the fury was directed at the man's scrub nurse. I was humiliated for her and couldn't believe a professional could be treated that way; or in fact, put up with it. I slipped out as quietly as I had entered, with the very obvious conclusion that I could do better than what I had seen that day.

During that surgical stint, Annie McElroy and I developed a real personality conflict; and we really did not like each other. Ann was the chief anesthetist, and I wondered where she got off being so bossy. After a few weeks of back-and-forth snipping and snapping, I found myself alone in the Blood Bank one evening. I had just finished drawing a unit of blood and was cleaning up. In comes Ann. It was the first time I had seen her without that ugly O. R. hat and green scrubs. Her hair was hanging loosely to her shoulders and her natural beauty was obvious. She never wore makeup and she was older by a few years, and very self-assured. Her starched, white uniform made her as bright as a new penny. She was almost antiseptic. She jumped up on the vinyl covered table that I had just wiped, lit two cigarettes at once, handed one to me, and with a direct gaze, said quietly, "I think we should be friends."

In an effort to look sophisticated, or unsurprised or something, I took the cigarette, and for a non-smoker, managed to take a few drags without choking. We seemed to agree on the friendship thing and were fast friends for years after that.

During that internship year, and on a few occasions during residency, we would join a few doctor friends and visit the Bachelor's Club in New Kensington. We were always hosted by the congenial barber, Jubie, who not only did barbering at the front entrance of the bank, located over the Club, but was apparently the Club's manager. The Club was apparently the front for the Western Pennsylvania underworld until, some years later when the Appalachian meeting of the eastern Mafia chieftains was raided by the Feds in upper New York State.

July 1 was the end of that year when the new group of idealistic victims reported to start their year of servitude and set us free. A number of the Medical Staff jovially shook hands; wished us well and gave a "Thank you for a good job." A few others simply went about their rounds without knowing that anything was happening. Miss Ludwig, the highly starched, rigid and very prissy nurse Administrator, gave us a handshake; and for the first time, I thought I saw the semblance of a smile as she sent us off.

A few months later, we heard that she had come upon one of the new interns, late at night, perilously traveling that ancient copper rain gutter, from the interns' quarters on the third floor, to the Student Nurses' quarters at the other end of the building. We heard (and could readily conceive) the uproar when the intern's lawyer was called in to do battle with Miss Ludwig and her Hospital Lawyer.

What was all the fuss about? We veterans knew that the kid was just taking the shortcut into the lady's chamber to share a late evening coke and sandwich.

Chapter 9

"No physician, insofar as he is a physician, considers his own good in what he prescribes, but the good of his patient; for the true physician is also a ruler having the human body as a subject, and is not a mere moneymaker."

— *Plato*

RESIDENCY

Internship at St. Margaret's solidified the decision to enter the specialty of Urology. Urologists appeared to be a jovial, well-rounded bunch and the specialty combined the practices of Medicine and Surgery. Urology appeared to be a distinct challenge. The choice of residency and finding the best of the country's programs appeared to narrow down to a practical choice between the Mayo Clinic or other quality programs and Pittsburgh's Medical Center. The choice was easy. There had been enough time away from home; and training under the well-known Conrad Kuehn at the Veteran's Hospital and the Medical Center in Pittsburgh gave the advantage of enough hands-on experience. His men left residency with the competency to enter solo practice, not being restricted to a group practice. Mayo residents were reported, at the time, to receive limited hands-on experience during their residency.

On the negative side, was the tight control of hospital appointments in Western Pennsylvania. The residents who had gone ahead in Pittsburgh had left their residency training capable, but unable to overcome the monopoly of well-entrenched specialists in a number of specialties. There was an elderly czar controlling plastic surgery, one in neurosurgery, and another brother group controlling orthopedic surgery. Urology was no exception. The specialty first evolved in Pittsburgh as elsewhere, with "clap doctors" who specialized in treating venereal disease - predominantly syphilis and gonorrhea.

The venereal clinics at the time, featured heavy metal injections, designed to kill the spirochete of syphilis; and one of the drugs at the time was popularly called Dr. Ehrlich's magic bullet. It was an arsenic compound called Salvarsan, which was injected into the muscles of the patients, over a period of time; eventually and hopefully, eradicating the disease. Then there were the irrigations of the lower urinary tract of men for gonorrhea, which was the only treatment available to control the purulent discharges of "the clap". The discovery of penicillin by Sir Alexander Fleming changed things overnight.

Hugh Hampton Young, of John Hopkins, has been credited with being the Father of Urology in America and was one of those who pioneered Urology as a respected surgical specialty. Urology was moving from the treatment of venereal disease to the surgical and medical treatment of diseases of the urinary system and of the genital system in men.

For centuries, men had treated prostatic disease, which obstructed the lower urinary system, with self-catheterization. Men would often carry hollow silver or rubber tubes with them - sometimes in their hat band - to drain their bladders from time to time. The practice invariably led to infection, and sometimes, sepsis and death.

The early urological surgeons learned that they could surgically place a tube in the bladder through the lower abdomen, relieving obstruction and sepsis, and later reopen the incision and remove the obstructing prostatic tissue. The mortality rate was high in this type of surgery, before transfusions and antibiotics; but it was lower than the death rate from sepsis.

Dr. Anderson of Pittsburgh was one of the early urologists, and not only helped advance the new specialty; but was astute in forming an association that would be successful in nearly monopolizing the practice of Urology in Western Pennsylvania.

Anderson's group formed when urologic instruments were becoming available. A German immigrant named Wapler was a genius at optics and was successful in fashioning a tiny lens system that could be inserted into the lower urinary system. Along with a tiny incandescent bulb, the instrument allowed visualization of the interior of the urinary bladder and the channel to the exterior - the urethra. Later, the passage of tiny hollow tubes to the kidneys through the urinary bladder allowed visualization of the upper part of the urinary system with the use of x-ray techniques. Wapler formed the pioneering company of urologic instrumentation - the American Cystoscope Makers, Inc. A member of Anderson's group, Dr. James Lee, became adept at the use of the resectoscope - an instrument using the same visual system with the addition of an electrically energized loop that could cut away the obstructing prostate without an open surgical incision. Lee and Anderson expanded their group and pretty well staffed not only the Urology services in Pittsburgh's Medical Center, then at Presbyterian Hospital; but eventually at many of the outlying community hospitals in Western Pennsylvania. The hospitals often were served by men who Lee trained and who would travel from hospital to hospital performing surgery, and often leaving the patients in the care of family physicians or a general surgeon. This was the era of the itinerant urologist, which carried , along with it, questionable pre and post operative surgical care at some of those institutions.

Dr. Kuehn, my mentor, came to Pittsburgh with his wife Ruth, who was installed as the new Dean of Pittsburgh's School of Nursing. She was a personable lady, persistent and dedicated to advancing the role of nurses away from immediate patient care and more into administrative positions. Dr. Kuehn, on the other hand, found himself in a community where the practice of Urology was controlled by a handful of men. The opportunity of being appointed to the Medical Staff of any city hospital was virtually non-existent. He had a short stint with the group at the city's Mercy Hospital and reportedly left after he appeared in the operating room one day to care for one of his patients, and was told that the senior member did all the surgery. To his credit, he became Chief of Urology at Pittsburgh's Veteran's Hospital and established an outstanding residency program. His residents, over the years, would establish departments across the country, and some of us would begin to challenge Dr. Lee's monopoly.

My first meeting with Dr. Kuehn was at the Veteran's Hospital in a spacious, park-like setting in the prestigious Fox Chapel section of Pittsburgh. He met me, dressed in a faded, threadbare scrub suit and his matching manner was similarly relaxed and informal. I was to learn that he would daily rifle through the pile of scrub suits in the surgical lounge to find the most tattered and faded for himself. We never knew whether this was a "sack cloth and ashes" routine or whether he was calling attention to the quality of operating room attire. He was obviously bright and deeply introspective. I knew, at once, that if selected, I would be working under a complex personality, but I sensed that he would be a fair and skillful teacher.

The end of internship arrived on a Sunday morning, and I reported to the Veteran's Hospital on a Monday morning, in early July. As instructed, I spoke with the telephone operator in the hospital's modest front lobby and in a very few minutes or so, a short, rather rotund gent in a green scrub suit and white jacket came through the swinging doors at the far end of the lobby.

"Doctor Miller? Hi, I'm Bert Neft." He wore glasses and was a little balding. He explained that he was Senior Resident on my service and would show me around. He explained that our ward was Four West and we headed upward to the West Wing of the fourth floor. The halls were plain, with highly polished, dull square-tiled floors and equally uninspiring beige walls. A few patients in pajamas and navy blue bath robes shuffled through the halls. We stopped briefly at the Chief Surgeon's office and I was introduced to a pleasant, dark-haired lady who was the Chief's Secretary. She advised, that after I got settled, I could drop back and sign some papers.

We strolled down that long hallway lined with patient's rooms on either side and made a left turn into Four West. Bert opened a door on the right explaining that this was the Resident's Office where we did physical exams and dictated our records. He demonstrated how to use the wax cylinder of the Dictaphone and suggested that I come along to meet the Resident Staff.

I was unaware that I was about to experience one of life's unforgettable moments. Just before we reached the glass-enclosed nursing station on the right, Bert paused before an open door. A secretary was at a desk facing the left wall and was typing away at break-neck speed. Bert was obviously watching me for a reaction. I tried not to gaze, but the girl was strikingly thin with long, dark hair to her shoulders. She had a beautiful complexion and a very ample figure. She was obviously more than just attractive. Bert said, "B. J., this is Dr. Miller." Without altering her typing for an instant, she turned her head toward, us for a second, and gave a quick downward nod. "This is B. J. Hindman", he explained. "Our Ward Secretary." Another brief turn and downward nod. "If you need any help with dictation or lab work, see B. J.", he continued. Again, a brief head turn and a nod. "If you need a clean lab coat, see B. J.". A turn and a nod.

"If you need laid, see B. J." A final head turn and nod without a moment's pause in the furious pace of typing.

Bill Palmer, Chief Resident, and the other residents were making rounds on the surgical patients. We shook hands, in turn, and they continued their rounds, pushing the stainless steel chart rack from bed to bed, examining patients and writing progress notes. It was obvious I was with a group of characters who I'd be with for two years of general surgery. I got the impression I'd fit right in.

The resident staff worked under the direction of full time surgeons such as Jim Altenhoff, the Chief, and a cadre of prominent local consultants who would visit on a regular basis to consult with the resident staff or assist in difficult surgery.

My first assignment was with Carl Blake on proctology. Our consultants were Dr. Mechling and Dr. Zimmerman, the team of foremost Proctologists in the area. They were excellent and patient teachers. They would assist and teach while we did simple hemorrhoid surgery or the excision of congenital cysts in the sacral area. I was amazed the first time we opened one of those cysts and saw the contents of hair and skin and even rudimentary teeth, as well as bone parts - which were actually the distorted beginnings of another human body.

At times Dr. Zimmerman would take charge of a procedure, and if a resident would get his hands in the way, he could expect a rap on the knuckles and an admonition, "Only Zimmie cuts the meat."

Sigmoidoscopy is the procedure for examination of the lower bowel through a hollow, stainless steel tube with a small incandescent light on the tip. Early on, we were entrusted with doing these procedures, which entailed a bit of sacrifice by our patients. The procedure is never pleasant for a patient, but when it is performed by a novice surgeon, it can be more than just a little troublesome for some poor patient.

I still recall the ruddy-faced gentleman who was sent to my little clinic on the fourth floor for sigmoidoscopy. To this day, I remember his name . . . Dugan. He had been experiencing some lower bowel complaints and willingly pulled up his bath robe and positioned himself, face down and jack-knifed, on that leather-covered examining table; with his bottom pointed skyward. The scope was inserted without a problem, and after a little suctioning, I had a clear view of the lower bowel and moved the instrument gently upward into the sigmoid colon. There, for the first time, I saw a sigmoid polyp - a reddish sphere of flesh a little larger than a marble, hanging from the bowel by a slender whitish stock. Enthused at the prospect of curing a potentially dangerous lesion, I had the scrub nurse attach a long cautery rod to the Bovie unit to the right of the table. It looked like such a simple move to just zap that narrow base, have the polyp fall down, remove it and send it to the lab.

The first step went as planned. I touched the cautery tip to the base of the narrow stock, pressed the power pedal of the cautery and watched the sparking and a little smoke as the polyp dropped. I pivoted a little to pick up a bayonet forceps to lift out the loose tissue, but as I turned back, I found the opening of the scope to be gushing bright red blood. It was the first experience of real fright during surgery. With difficulty, I put aside the urge to just drop everything and run. It was a terrible sensation. I couldn't recall ever being frightened like that, but later learned that surgeons describe that type of situation as the loose sphincter syndrome - trying to put a humorous twist on the stress that surgeons sometimes feel.

I kept packing cotton sponges into the bleeding area, without effect. The instrument continued to spout blood and drain onto the drapes, forming a puddle on the white tile floor and splashing onto my lap. Larger sponges slowed the flow; which only returned in full force after they were gently pulled away. The patient was becoming uncomfortable and I was out of ideas.

Les Dunmire, the Senior Resident on the other Service, responded to our call and greeted the scene with a big grin. He always had an intentionally high pitched drawl, and on this occasion, looked at the scene and came out with, "Way-ell, what do we have here?" We removed all the bloody packing from the poor man and gradually cleared out the clots with suction; so we could see the small artery pumping away. Les carefully took a chromic gut suture on a tiny needle from the scrub nurse and skillfully sewed a circle of gut around the pumper and then tightened the circle with a long needle holder. To my relief, the hemorrhage dramatically stopped.

Les was probably the prime humorist of our group and made the most of that experience. As he would tell the story, over and over, he would describe entering the scene with Miller frantically stuffing items into a patient's rectum. Eventually, he would describe that Miller had stripped the room of all loose items to insert and was looking at the porcelain sink in a way to see if it could be used.

Lester was a born comedian and he could have us holding our sides laughing at some of his tales. Actually, some of the comments he would put into his discharge summaries were attention-getting. On one occasion, he described a patient's hospital admission with life-threatening wounds with the opening quote, "The patient was entered into hospital admission following a slight altercation with his father-in-law."

It was traditional to throw a party for the Chief Resident, as he left residency to enter practice, and on one of those occasions, Lester was giving all present the benefit of his tales at an Italian restaurant on Oakland's's Center Avenue.

One of his favorite tales was the earlier experience with the bleeding polyp. We were all in high spirits and enjoying ourselves to the fullest, when someone mentioned that our ward secretary, B. J., lived in an apartment just across Center Avenue. Lester, as I recall, was the first to opine that it would be sinful not to visit her since we were in the neighborhood.

As I recall, there were three of us merrily crossing Center Avenue, and we found our way to B. J.'s third floor apartment without hesitation. Lester pounded on her door and the door opened with the entire doorway filled with a gigantic bearded guy who barked, "Wattayawant?"

For the first time in memory, Lester was at a loss for words and stuttered something to the effect that we had just wanted to say "Hello". But, on second thought, would return some other time more convenient. The retreat back across Center Avenue was punctuated with hoots and laughter which continued as we rejoined the party. This time, Lester was the butt of the jokes.

Beacher, one of the residents from another service, was occasionally guilty of some thoughtless behavior and could raise the ire of a coworker. We had all learned that B. J. was quite capable of coming out of her office, and with a piercing yell, slightly salted with a Brooklyn accent, call a culprit to task. Such was the case one early evening, when she caught Beacher dangling one of her Dictaphones as he rolled it down the hallway, rhythmically bouncing its wheels on the tile. Beacher, however, was somewhat oblivious to any injury and survived her heated admonition. He, however, must have been permanently impressed by his relationship with our Chief, Bill Palmer. Beacher had been doing rectal exams on a group of patients and had been using the rubber gloves which were kept in plastic bags in the lower drawers of the stainless steel chart racks. We used those gloves on rounds. Rather than put his dirty gloves in the supply room for cleaning, Beacher apparently returned them to one of the bags after turning them inside out.

Palmer, on rounds with the rest of the group, had needed a glove, and on using one of Beacher's discards, had noticed those gooey messes on the end of his fingers after he had put on one of them. I guess Palmer's excoriation of Beacher surpassed B. J.'s earlier recommendations.

My first impression of that group proved to be accurate. They were a group of characters, who mixed humor with a real desire to succeed - and succeed they did. They've gone on to successful careers.

A friendship with B.J. revealed, in the later years of residency, that she was a sensitive and strong personality, whose rough exterior hid some early devastating lifetime events. She was truly a handsome lady.

After standing at the operating table as a "second or third assist", and doing some excisions and biopsies, there was advancement to doing hernia repair and being the "first assistant" at major abdominal surgery. It was at that point in time that some residents decide upon another line of work. While it became apparent that dexterity had a great deal to do with surgical proficiency, the real quality for a surgeon was the self-discipline that allowed a cool, effective performance during extremely stressful experiences.

As part of the surgical experience, we would spend a few months on the plastic surgery service. The senior resident, Dwight Hanna, was a meticulous surgeon and his teaching led to an invaluable sense of precision when performing delicate surgery and respect for the delicate handling of tissue. The plastic people taught the value in the use of tiny needles, tiny instruments and precision in suturing.

The consultant for the plastic surgeons was a Dr. Wise, who liked to be called "Willy"; and "Willy" wanted to be one of the boys. "Willy", however, one of the monopoly of plastic surgeons in Pittsburgh, was a duplicitous soul. He would regularly give a failing evaluation to the resident coming under his authority. He came close to ending the surgical careers of a few who had rotated through the plastic service, until the people in charge of the Residents' destiny began to ignore "Willy's" evaluations. We all did become a little cautious around "Willy" and became aware that some unusual personalities could find their way into positions of authority. One of the senior residents confided one day of the emotional turmoil he experienced after "Willy's report threatened his hopes of a career in surgery.

As quite a contrast, was the relationship with Peter Lindstrohm. The well known physician was the head of Neurosurgery and was known to be a brilliant surgeon. I had developed a degree of confidence in neuroanatomy from the experience in Medical School with that rigid military instructor and looked forward to a few months with Lindstrohm.

Lindstrohm's reputation wasn't overstated. He was indeed brilliant. He was another who had hoped to establish a practice in neurosurgery at a major Pittsburgh hospital; but had run into the neurosurgical monopoly of Western Pennsylvania. Peter and I gradually became friends in the early weeks with him, when I was his junior resident. He had my respect and I felt it to be a real privilege to be with him. But that also meant dealing with a top flight egomaniac. He was truly another character who felt the need to demonstrate his superiority - both mentally and physically, over his residents. One of the Senior Residents warned me when he learned I was headed for Peter's service. He advised that every Resident had to go with this tall, gaunt Swede to the Hospital Gym for a session of physical combat.

After an x-ray review one morning, I became amazed at the man's knowledge of neuroanatomy. He had taken a brain, and with a long, thin knife, sectioned a brain into half-inch slices and rapidly pointed out the origins of the cranial nerves, the various motor and sensory areas, the hollow drainage system and blood supply of the brain. I was transfixed by the man's knowledge when he concluded by . "...and now my friend, we will go over to the gym", with that unmistakable Swedish accent. The Senior Resident who had warned of the required physical encounter confided that, when his time had come for a wrestle with the Chief, he was determined to win, even if it meant developing a hernia. However, he lost.

We arm-wrestled and it wasn't even a contest. We lifted weights, did push ups, and squeezed hand exercises as he unquestionably demonstrated his strength. That tall, lean frame was stronger than his appearance would suggest. As I crawled away from that gym, I mentioned that I really preferred running for exercise. "Ah, my friend, we will have to run sometime." The time came soon.

One evening after work, we played a few sets of tennis at Frick Park, and were preparing to leave when "Mr. Physical Prowess" noticed a jogging trail. "Ah, my friend, we must run a mile." And that we did. After the first half mile or so, I passed him and could hear that labored breathing behind. I think he would have killed himself trying, if he thought he could win. The Chief finally dropped back and I stood waiting for him at the finish line with an unapologetic big grin. As he puffed up to the finish line, he stuck out his hand and exclaimed, "Ah, my friend, that was good." We worked together a number of months after that, but he never suggested another run.

The rotation through Neurosurgery was completed and I was looking forward to several months with the Hospital Pathologists. Work in the pathology department and laboratory - the study of the effects of disease on the body's tissues - was totally unlike life on the surgical wards. The work was unlike working with patients and nurses. The Pathologists were certainly a different bunch. The atmosphere was academic and serious, with none of the jovial interplay that identified the surgical groups. Nevertheless, the Pathologists, in their seriousness and efficiency, were an indispensable part of the medical team. Their analyses of tissues, supplied by the Surgeons, or obtained from autopsies, invariably led to a better understanding of a patient's demise; or aided critically in the clinical management of patients. After seven weeks on Pathology, I was entrusted to carefully slice representative pieces of tissue specimens that were supplied by the Surgeons and enclose them in small, metal capsules with multiple perforations, making them sort of a strainer. The capsules would then be mechanically dipped into one solution after another with a large, rotating, automatic machine called the " Tissuematon." This process fixed the tissues into a firm mass that allowed the technicians then, to slice the tissue into microscopically thin slices that would be stained and mounted onto glass slides to be reviewed by the Pathologists. The Pathologists were highly skilled professionals, and could, with great accuracy, review those slides under the microscope and come up with almost infallibly accurate diagnoses. When in doubt, they conferred.

One of the Pathologists was a very bright, attractive lady who was married to one of my old fraternity brothers. Jeanne was unusually bright in a very practical way. She had a serious approach and asked me to help with autopsies, on occasion. She was another excellent teacher and knew that I was eager to absorb as much information, during those months, as possible. After a few autopsies together, she offered to call when there was a nighttime or a weekend post-mortem. During the time we shared call, I began to gain a great deal of confidence through her teaching. She knew anatomy and pathology and was a joy to work with.

The Pathologists would meet regularly and we would all discuss each autopsy performed. I always felt a little privileged to be included. As that stint was coming to an end, Bill Altenhoff called me to his office and asked if I'd like to spend more time on neurosurgery. Dr. Lindstrohm had requested that I come back as his Senior Resident. I was anxious to start the final two years on Urology, but was enthused to go back with that great teacher.

That was an exciting few months. Lindstrohm was a tough taskmaster and egocentric, but had become a good friend. There were long hours in the operating room. The cranial procedures would sometimes last most of a day, and it would be grueling to stand for that period of time delicately creating a path through brain tissues to explore a brain tumor or a bleeding vessel. The procedures would begin with reflection of an entire scalp. Then a Gigli saw - a wire with sharp edges - was used to cut the skull between burr holes drilled into the skull. Then, lifting a bone flap, allowing access to the brain was, in itself, tedious and time consuming.

The results with neurological procedures were not often spectacular, and often not even good. Tumors were often not resectable, and when we would send a biopsy to the lab for a quick analysis - a frozen section - and have a diagnosis of malignancy returned, it would often be futile to continue the procedure. We would close the patient's head and hope that radiation would help somewhat.

Lindstrohm not only reveled in demonstrating his surgical skill, but was just the same with his skiing prowess. On our trips to Seven Springs, he would ski as naturally as walking. I would tell him that Swedes were probably born with skis on. On one occasion, I tried to keep up with him and took a disastrous spill. I tore the left knee badly, and the next morning, a Sunday, Carl Blake suggested a cast. He covered the leg with stockinette, (a tubular gauze) and saturated it with tincture of benzoin before wrapping on the plaster. The benzoin created a terrible itching sensation, and early the next morning, an orderly and I sawed the damn thing off. (The cast, not the leg). For weeks, Blake would remind me that I was walking like a peg-leg.

Lindstrohm was not a generally warm personality and routinely kept people at arms-length. He routinely declined invitations and just about never mingled with his peers. He was probably not at all pleased with his celebrity status. There were those who considered this snobbishness, but there was much more to it than that. The man was hurting.

Over weeks and months, he would reveal that under Sweden's socialized system, he became a dentist and became interested in dental research and invented a series of devices used in dental prosthetics. His young wife was interested in acting and was offered a role on the Broadway stage. She gained enough success that she was able to support him throughout the University of Rochester Medical School. When her carer took her to Hollywood, he entered a neurosurgical residency at Ceders of Lebanon Hospital. His young daughter was named Pia. He revealed that this was meant to symbolize Peter and Ingrid always. By the time the father and daughter came to Pittsburgh and rented the house on Fifth Avenue, it was evident that this wasn't to be and Pia was renamed "Jenny."

More of the delicate procedures were being entrusted to residents, and I found myself doing the angiography, which entailed the precarious injection of dye into patients' carotid arteries to outline the vessels of the brain with a rapid series of x-ray films. Spinal surgery was just as demanding, and if we hadn't meticulously performed a procedure we would expect the Chief to peer over our shoulder with a sharp, "Vat are you doing?", or , "You are making hoom-burg." Rightfully, there was no room for error.

Early one afternoon, I knocked on the Chief's office door and reported the results of a myelogram I had just completed. He took off his reading glasses and showed no surprise at the report, but softly answered, "My friend, what is the matter with you?" "Nothing at all." I answered. "Oh yes", he said, "Come in; sit down." I was taken aback, but closed the door and sat on the chair beside his desk. The shaded florescent bulbs of his desk lamp reflected on those stony features showing a concern and a depth that I hadn't seen before. "What is the trouble, my friend; there is something wrong. What is it?" He explained that I hadn't been myself for a few days and I expressed surprise that he would notice.

I fumbled through an explanation that I had parted company with a girl I had dated for a few years, after we both had decided that our friendship would not lead to a permanent commitment.

"Yes, I know," he said. "I do know." He leaned back in his chair and began a melancholy chronicle of the loss of his famous wife. "She was beautiful", he said. "Of all those actresses out there, she was the most beautiful - whether she was on the commode or on the stage."

As he reflected on his early life with Ingrid in Sweden, he returned to the later years and bluntly said, "But, she was so impressionable; she was influenced by those people out there. She was influenced by all of them - one after another."

I was surprised to be sitting there and listening to my friend who often went to great lengths to appear as "Mr. Cool" or "Mr. Tough Guy." But I could sense that this man whom I respected greatly needed a friend. I sat back, and we talked for much of that afternoon.

"You know," he said, "that place is prostitution . . .everyone out there is a prostitute and will do anything with anyone to get what they want." He talked about the personalities he and Ingrid had socialized with in Hollywood and his disgust with the whole scene, leading to his flight, along with Jenny, to Pittsburgh. It was interesting to hear about the weaknesses and antics of people like Daryl Zanuck and Jennifer Jones, even though I was never much of a celebrity worshipper. But, I had always been in awe of some of the successes of some very average humans. Perhaps even Ingrid Bergman.

I had never seen Peter as relaxed, as I slid forward on my chair to leave. He concluded, "After she left for Italy, I never heard from her again. After she tied up with Rosellini I never heard a word." "Not one?", I asked. "Not one," he said. "No letters, no calls, nothing."

Peter and Jenny spent some vacation days with us at Crooked Creek. They would totally unwind and run around in tattered bathing trunks and sandals. Jenny loved to swing from the rope hanging from a large sycamore, arched out over the creek, and tramp in the mud along the shore. In other ways she was the most mature and sophisticated sixteen year old I had ever known.

The first day of the two years on Urology service was a milestone. It was the final phase of a long, long education. The Hospital in Fox Chapel had closed and the new Veteran's Hospital, high on the hill above the Pitt Campus and the Pitt Stadium, had opened.

Dr. Kuehn's office on the fifth floor overlooked the Oakland district and the Pitt Campus, stretching along between Fifth and Forbes Avenue. In the foreground was an aerial look into Pitt Stadium flanked by Western State Hospital. The view always brought back thoughts of those college days and the quarter-mile laps I had taken around the Stadium track; and the time I had spent with those poor demented patients we had tried to help at Western State. To the right and left of the Stadium were those early buff brick halls that were fashioned to blend into the hillside as a replica of the Acropolis. But, the majesty of the Gothic Cathedral of Learning testified to the abandonment of the Acropolis scheme of the latter part of the previous century. The red brick center field wall and the green outfield of Forbes Field could be seen to the right of the Panther Hollow Bridge, with the Carnegie Institute and Carnegie Tech in the distance. Over Forbes Field, one could see the Mon Valley, and I could just catch sight of the tops of those six gray towers of the J & L blast furnaces in the valley, with thoughts of those nights on the labor gang and the ore trestle in that valley. Just beyond the Stadium were the gray limestone hospitals of the Medical Center.

Dr. Kuehn and I gazed out on the scene for a few minutes as he casually explained my duties. He knew I had spent an extra year in the surgical specialties and with the Pathologists. He appeared pleased that the ultimate in recognition of competence - certification by the American Board of Urology - would soon require four years of residency training rather than three.

Before we left for a tour of the Urology Ward and the G. U. Clinic, he talked about his residency at Ohio State. He described his Chief as a tyrant who reigned over the residents without concern for their feelings, treating them more as servants. He talked about Sunday mornings in Columbus, lugging a heavy Bovie unit for this chief, who apparently did Sunday morning prostate surgery at various small hospitals around the city. He looked away as he said, "I hope your residency will be different."

At a later date, he would become more than a little annoyed with me when I was reluctant to leave a critically ill patient in order to begin a clinic at Butler Veteran's Hospital. We had a heart to heart talk after that, and after hearing of my concern for the patient, he stopped gazing out over the Pitt Campus, wheeled around to face me, reached into a lower desk drawer and produced a framed photo. Obviously it was his former Chief. As he threw it onto his desk, he blurted out, "Doctor, if I'm anything like that man, you have a real problem on your hands."

We had our ups and downs over those two years, but I think we worked together with mutual respect. We would not only work together, but on a number of occasions, would learn together. I think he would actually enjoy having a student who didn't always agree; even though, on some occasions in the middle of a discussion, he would suddenly spin and leave - not to be seen for the rest of the day. Sam, my senior Resident for that first year, would remind us that, on occasion, after a surgical error, he wouldn't be spoken to for weeks at a time.

On one occasion, the Doctor turned and announced, "Dr. Miller, you are an iconoclast." I didn't know whether that was a compliment or and insult - whether it was a political or a religious designation. So, I was anxious to get to the dictionary. It turned out he was right. I truly was not an admirer of some of the traditions and the practices that were keeping young physicians in servitude over a period of years, and then, quite likely, prevented them from practicing in their own home towns.

Those two years brought about new efforts to master the techniques of Urologic Surgery. Urology was pioneering the continuing improvement in optical instruments that would, eventually, be used in other specialties. The scopes that the urologists were using to visualize the lower urinary system would be adapted, in time, to explore the digestive and respiratory systems, as well as the body cavities themselves.

One of the Urology consultants arranged to have the Chief Urology Resident spend a few months with the gynecologists at his hospital. I was the first to be sent and found myself in the new supplemental program and accepted by the gynecologists who were gentlemen, without exception. They seemed to be pleased to be in a teaching role. One of them spent an entire afternoon in the Residents' quarters making certain that I perfected the art of tying surgical knots. He wasn't satisfied until he saw the "one hand tie" and the "two hand tie" performed flawlessly, right handed and left handed.

During that stint, the presence of a pair of very unusual interns, Martini and Rostis, became unmistakable. There was general recognition of some of their wild antics. I had been given firm instructions on leaving for that tour that my presence in that new location would be scrutinized very closely to determine whether the cooperation between the two hospitals would continue. It was just as well that contact with those interns was limited.

The Residents' quarters was on the hospital's third floor and the interns were housed on the fourth. At times, it would be difficult to sleep in that third floor room - there was this strange grinding nosie overhead, which seemed to travel from one end of that hospital wing to the other.

Someone volunteered that it was Martini and Rostis roller skating in the hallway above.

I was the only surgical resident on duty that Christmas Eve. A nurse anesthetist and I were enjoying a coke and a little friendly conversation when we glanced out a window and saw a party in progress in another hospital wing, a floor or so below. Sure enough, it was Martini and Rostis chug-a-lugging with one of the hospital's head nurses. She was very attractive and mature and we were surprised she was having so much fun with those juveniles.

A few hours later, I was listening to Christmas music and feeling sorry for myself, when the hospital switchboard forwarded an urgent call from Dr. Martini.

Martini advised that he was at the Coronado Apartments with Rostis and that their "friend" had fallen and had suffered a large gash on her forehead. I had to bring a suture set and sew up the wound. "No Martini, I can't do that. I'm on call here." "You got to Ralph, we're in real trouble." "Bring her to the E.R.." "We can't, Ralph, we'll explain when you get here."

The apartment was beautiful, and the lady, almost comatose, was stretched out on the sofa holding a wash cloth on a gash over her left eye. As I turned around for a little help for the upcoming surgery, I found that the dynamic duo had split.

The suturing, without the need for anesthetic, was done without delay, and as I gathered up the instruments, I absent-mindedly set up a picture frame that had been face down on the coffee table- it held a color photo of the hospital's Chief of Staff. That was another occasion when a prompt exit was indicated.

On another occasion, arrangements were made to visit Dr. Milner and his staff in Albany. Milner was renowned as a pioneer and expert in transurethral surgery, known in the trade as TUR - (transurethral resection). The surgery was done entirely through a small instrument and had reversed the mortality and morbidity rates of the open surgery of previous years. I was permitted to scrub with the Doctor during a number of those procedures over a period of a few days. He was a master at resection and taught the fine points of that type of surgery that couldn't be gained by any amount of reading. His Chief Resident and spouse graciously insisted that I stay with them over those few days and they were, indeed, superb hosts. Discussions with them would last into the wee hours - in itself an education. The residents in that program, without exception, were a dissatisfied bunch. They resented the lack of hands-on experience and being allowed to do only "scut work." I realized that I had, indeed, chosen the correct residency program. On the final day with Dr. Milner, he asked me to sign his visitor's log and he pointed out the signatures of visitors from various points over the globe. He mused that there wasn't one signature of a Urologist near the Albany area. The log was, very obviously, documenting an existing professional jealousy within the area.

After that trip, Conrad Kuehn and I became more of a partnership, in a way. I would be entrusted with a procedure and my mentor would come into the O. R. off and on, while peering over my shoulder. We would describe little ways in which we could perfect the procedure. He often remarked that "Surgery is self-taught."

On the Resident Staff to an elegant dinner at their fashionable apartment, from time to time.

My one and only visit to that apartment wasn't exactly a social triumph. When I arrived for the gourmet dinner, the assembled group were seated around the living room, sipping wine and commenting on its quality.

I accepted a delicate glass of wine and attempted to enjoy the flavor, but it was sour - even bitter - so that I finished the glass reluctantly.

It was announced that dinner was served, and we were seated around the candle-lit dining room table. The silver and china were delicate and the atmosphere warm. I had never seen my colleagues so polite.

Halfway through the first course, I felt a sudden wave of nausea. A few deep breaths didn't help, and I found myself rushing to the bathroom, opposite and just inside the apartment door. It was terrible, throwing up and attempting to do it silently.

When I finally felt able to move, I left the bath and found my host standing at the apartment door. He handed me my hat without a word.

The next morning, my colleagues were politely silent, so I finally was forced to ask Sam, the Chief Resident, if they had heard me.

He looked at me, wide-eyed, and blurted out, "Are you kidding?"

During those years, there would be weekend surgery at Childrens Hospital. "Bud" Johnson was another excellent teacher in Pediatric Urology and one never had much doubt where they stood with him. After he had helped with a difficult major procedure on a Saturday morning, he had appeared at a urologic event in the evening. I introduced him to my bride-to-be and he acknowledged by, "Ralph did a nice job this morning; but he dragged his ass." As I say, we always knew where we stood with "Bud". He never knew that his partner, a nervous little man, always was annoyed when he was helping with a case, claiming that I "worked too fast."

On one Saturday morning, "Bud's" partner involved me in a little deception. A young boy had not done well post operatively, and when an x-ray of the child's abdomen was put up on the viewing box, the tell-tale marker of a surgical sponge near the right kidney was undeniable. The film was taken down and was never seen again.

The child was scheduled for repeat surgery, but there was a complication. The child's aunt was a nurse and wanted to be present. I was assigned to assist at the surgery and to help distract the boy's aunt, once the lost sponge was located. At the appropriate time, the Surgeon winked at me and I asked Auntie to check a drainage bottle on the floor; and as she stooped down, the sponge was removed and lost from sight forever.

The new Veteran's Hospital provided quarters for the Chief Resident. My room opened out onto a wide balcony overlooking the Stadium and Campus, but I never had time to venture out and enjoy the view. After a late supper, it was really all I could do to fall into bed.

Occasionally, I would join a group of young lawyer friends around a circular table at the "U Club" at the foot of the hill. We would argue for hours about what the Law was and what it should be. We never agreed, but there was a laugh a minute. They never hesitated to ridicule my naive belief that justice was assured in our court systems. It was probably destined that I would, eventually, learn the truth.

Jerry Weber was the comedian of the bunch. We would converse back and forth in bastardized Latin, interspersed with dirty stories from the rest of the group. At one point, Jerry announced that this wife had thrown him out of the house. In his homeless state, I offered my quarters, while I was assigned to Presbyterian Hospital for a few months. For weeks afterward, he would have us guffawing by describing late night calls to the Resident Quarters that he was occupying. He would describe the need for his presence in the O. R. for urgent surgery, and his response; with glowing accounts of him performing unbelievable surgical feats, followed by applause and adulation from all in attendance. He lived in the quarters for a few weeks, and as far as I knew, never got caught. He later went back home.

During that year, we had heard reports that it might be possible to biopsy portions of the prostate gland by inserting biopsy needles through the perineum - the lowest portion of the pelvis. I presented the possibility to Doctor Kuehn and Ed Fisher, the flamboyant Chief Pathologist at the Veteran's Hospital. I finally got clearance to attempt the procedure on cadavers.

It was quite an experience, after a death, to go down to the Hospital Morgue and wrestle with a stiffening corpse, in an effort to get a small sample of prostatic tissue. Somewhat to everyone's surprise, the attempts were successful on almost every try, and we began to use the procedure routinely prior to prostatic surgery. Ed was a master at interpreting the specimens to demonstrate or exclude cancer. We felt like pioneers when we presented our results to a joint meeting of the Pittsburgh and Cleveland Urologic Societies. We would have to smile, in later years, when a Urologist from Montefiore Hospital would present a paper at a major medical conference, describing the biopsy technique as a "new procedure."

As the years progressed, prostatic biopsy would become a standard and valuable procedure in the diagnosis of prostatic disease. The development of ultrasonographic equipment - high frequency sound - would allow urologists to obtain specimens with a greatly increased accuracy than we were able to accomplish blindly in the years before the new technology.

My oldest son would become one of those adept at blending those techniques into innovative new treatments for prostatic cancer - Cryosurgery and Brachytherapy - which would destroy prostatic cancer by freezing - or by the insertion of radioactive needles, rather than by the standard radical surgical approach.

The residents on our urology service would pass on some of Dr.Kuehn's favorite stories and some of his whimsical comments. One story involved a patient who had described a highly unusual sexual history, and as this history was related to others on the service, Dr. Kuehn had been said to exclaim, "When it comes to sex, I don't even believe myself."

On another afternoon, during an x-ray conference, he described an experience during his residency at Ohio State. His Chief was doing cystoscopy in a small, cramped cystoscopy room. The low voltage power for the cystoscope bulb came from an overhead lamp cord hanging from the ceiling, and similarly, the water supply came from a glass flask hanging next to the electrical cord. The ordinary household current was reduced to very low voltage by a rheostat at the end of the cord and small wires carried the low current from there to the cystoscope, which had been passed to the patient's bladder without incident.

The patient, a muscular young man, was tolerating the procedure well, when somehow, the water from the flask leaked onto the cord near the rheostat, allowing the full household current to surge through the cystoscope and into both the patient and the surgeon.

Dr. Kuehn described that the patient and examiner became rigid and frozen together, unable to move. Someone pulled the plug and the two were separated. Dr. Kuehn wryly concluded his story by observing, "We must have cured that fellow, he never came back."

One of the surgical consultants was an amateur pilot and would invite me for an evening flight with him, now and then. He was a good pilot and loved to skim the treetops. There was some humor around the hanger at Graham Field near Butler. It was said that some excellent pilots were trained by low-level flight, over an area nudist camp.

After some flight instruction, I began some evening solo flights around Butler. I was flying a small J-3 Piper Cub one evening, and somehow lost my bearings. The sun was dipping toward the horizon and the wire rod between the prop and the windshield indicated an almost dry gas tank.

I was frantically circling the area without much luck in identifying landmarks. The sun was just touching the horizon when I spotted a windsock next to a barn. I set the plane down on a pasture next to the barn, and the farmer came running out.

When I expressed reluctance at getting back into that plane, he advised, "If you don't get back in that plane, you'll never fly a plane again." He poured a few gallons of gas into the tank and gave the prop a hearty spin, as he advised, "Just head a little to the right of my silo there, and you'll find the field."

With his advice, I took off and found the field. The runway lights were on, and planes were circling the area looking for me; they knew I'd be out of gas.

I've advised pilot-patients on more than one occasion since then, that that was the genesis of thirteen new religions over Butler County that evening.

The last day of June that year was a warm and sunny Saturday. It marked the end of those long years of training. The new residents would arrive the next day, July 1, and I would begin private practice.

I was determined to finish my work in the clinic and leave without any undue comment or show.

We finished the last patient and I thanked the Chief for everything and said something like, "Goodbye" or "I'll be seeing you".

The Doctor followed me out into the hall and down into the stairway. As we neared the first floor, he was beside me, and looking straight ahead said, "Dr. Miller, you are simply the best, . . . but I don't know about you."

I stopped for a moment, and we looked at each other and smiled.

Chapter 10

> *"Tis common proof*
> *That lawliness is young ambition's ladder, whereto the*
> *climber - upward turns his face;*
> *But when he once attains the upmost round,*
> *he then unto the ladder he turns his back,*
> *looks in the clouds, scorning the base degrees*
> *By which he did ascend."*
> — *Shakespeare*

INDIANA, PA. - THE EARLY DAYS

During those final years in school, a friend of Dad found that I had returned to Pittsburgh and suggested that I stop by and talk with him. He suggested his office in the Highland Building in the East Liberty section of town. We met several times in his sparsely furnished office and treatment rooms. The office was dreary with a reception room shared with two internists. The dull squares of worn tile of the floor were uninspiring and the white enamel examining tables and the office's instruments were anything but modern. However, I was given what I thought was an outstanding offer.

I had intended to train as a General Surgeon, but if I accepted an internship at St. Margaret's and a residency with Dr. Kuehn or a residency at Mayo's, the Doctor would be ready to retire and turn the practice over. The medical atmosphere in Pittsburgh, at the time, prevented many young specialists from practicing in that town; but the offer - always the same - appeared "too good to be true"; and it was. After a year with the Doctor and doing most of the practice's surgery, the offer turned out to be just that. There was no plan to retire and I was looking at years of servitude.

The family commiserated for weeks and months on the deception which had cost us another year. It wasn't the frugal living, even with the two of us working and expecting our first son; it was the loss of independence for another indefinite period of time that was most disturbing. All those years had been spent preparing for a goal that had seemed to be promised, but realistically had never really been intended. I had been deceived into believing that I had bypassed the "Feudal System" of the Pittsburgh surgical specialties.

After realizing the futility of believing that I would inherit my own practice and not be an "employee", I opened my own office and talked at length with my former Chief and advisor, Dr. Kuehn.

During that first year of private practice, I had made occasional visits to Veteran's Hospital with arm loads of x-ray films. Dr. Kuehn would call the Residents in and we would go over the interesting films from patients seen during the preceding weeks. The discussions were spirited; and we all gained a great deal, I thought. I still remember the comment - "Where are you getting all these cases?"

Also, during that year, we got our first glimpse of Indiana Hospital. The Hospital always had a great potential - so I thought. After all, it was the only hospital in the county, nestled in a beautiful university community in the northern foothills of the Alleghenies, with no competition within thirty or forty miles.

My first contact with the Hospital was a shocker. It was in the late fifties, during my first years of practice in Pittsburgh.

Joan and I had stopped at my parent's house on Crooked Creek, a few miles from Indiana and then had continued on our drive east for a few quiet days at the Jersey shore. Rounding a sharp curve on the narrow crowned surface of Route 156, just west of Indiana, we came upon a two car, head-on pileup. The scene was that of mass confusion. It seemed that two elderly brothers from Pittsburgh had been headed for Pittsburgh in their rusty, old station wagon, packed with crated chickens for their poultry store in the East Liberty section of Pittsburgh. A young couple in a late model sports car had slammed into them at high speed, when they were unable to negotiate the curve. The station wagon was on its side and the sports car had come to rest at a grotesque angle in the far roadside ditch. White Leghorns, out of their crushed cages, were creating a frenzy of feathers and blood. Mangled masses of blood and feathers littered the roadway along with the twisted remains of the station wagon. The surviving fowl were either flapping pitifully along the roadway or were beginning to roost in roadside trees. Two ancient hearses, the area's only ambulances, had arrived; and one very shortly departed with the young girl from the sports car. I was to learn later that she was taken to Indiana Hospital, treated for hysteria and released. A small crowd had gathered, and together we were able to pry the elderly brothers from their crumpled quarters, crowd them into the remaining hearse and get them on their way to the Hospital. I promised the driver, a local mortician, I would follow and do what I could at the Hospital.

The Hospital was an L-shaped, drab, yellow brick structure, perched on a knoll overlooking the town of Indiana. As we sped up the maple-lined serpentine drive, I expected to spot an emergency direction sign of some sort; but instead, the hearse with its mangled cargo, backed into a lower level ornate, stone entrance with the name Mack, a hospital benefactor, chiseled into the limestone lintel.

As a few volunteers, who had followed along with us, prepared to carry the wounded brothers inside, I went ahead into the dimly-lit area furnished with a single white enameled operating table and an overhead operating light - reminiscent of the portable equipment we worked with during the war. I was greeted by an elderly nurse in an immaculate white uniform. Her starched white cap resembled a cupcake paper and the black silk cord of her glasses oscillated as she anxiously promised to get help. We lowered one patient carefully onto the table and the other onto a rickety stretcher from the far corner of the area.

As I recall, my assistant was an orderly, hastily summoned from the Men's Ward. We cut away bloody clothing, controlled some obvious bleeding and got some intravenous lines established. Getting the I.V. solutions and tubing, at that time, seemed to be like getting blood from a turnip. I can't forget being unable to start saline solution; there seemed to be a local belief that balanced solutions containing salt and other minerals would cause heart failure.

After things had stabilized a little, a gentlemanly, soft-spoken, articulate gentleman, in casual attire, appeared and identified himself as the Hospital's Chief of Staff. He casually looked over the scene and made a great effort to be gracious and to ffer profuse thanks for the help. He assured me that the Hospital's Surgeons would soon arrive and volunteered that a more formal thank-you would come my way from the County Medical Society. I didn't know, at the time, that that graciousness would later help the man achieve the Presidency of the Pennsylvania Medical Society.

Somewhat assured, somewhat credulous, I thanked the nurse and orderly friends from that little emergency team, and somewhat reluctantly, left that scene to join my anxious spouse in the driveway, for the long-overdue carefree trip to the seashore. But the monotonous nighttime miles on the Turnpike, and later, the suds and subs on the beach couldn't begin to quiet the speculation over the possible outcome for those two needy men, dependent on the archaic services of the dimly lit little corner of central Indiana County, Pennsylvania. Little did I know the impact that that little drama would have on my career and on my family.

Dad and I were buddies and we never needed urging to get in a round of weekend golf together, as time allowed. On a whim, we dropped into the almost deserted white frame club house of the local Indiana Country Club on a Saturday afternoon to find a few members enjoying themselves in the little knotty-pine bar room, just off the main dining area of the club. We walked through the large open dining area and across the hard maple dance floor, noting the massive stone fireplace at the far end of the room and the u-shaped balcony with its white balustrades circling three sides of that wide open dining area. We were greeted warmly by the members in that barroom. The next hal fhour, not only resulted in friendships that were to last for years to come; but when we left the Club that afternoon, we were experiencing, for the first time, the sincere friendliness of the Club. The friendliness, at that time, was the cornerstone of a modest nine-hole golf club with an unpretentious club house and a down-to-earth membership.

The Club's senior members gave new meaning to their roles as "characters."Arch McGrew was always in dutch for driving his golf cart onto the course's greens and "Pop" Hewitt always blamed a poor shot on his caddy.

A Sunday tradition was for the ladies to surround the number one tee after church and watch the men tee off. On another occasion, he dubbed one off the tee and then cameback and announced, "... and I did so want to hit a good one for Annie Buterbaugh."

"Turf" was the Club's mongrel mascot and his house was out a few yards and to the left of that first tee. On another Sunday, "Pop" shanked another drive, and to the amusement of the crowd, sent the ball screaming into the open door of Turf's dog house where it loudly ricocheted inside for a time.

The rounds of golf were intended to be worry-free interludes; they often weren't. Golf pro Joe, in his battered old blue pick-up, would be seen coming out to take us back to the caddy shack phone - another hospital "emergency."

There would be many fine hours on that scenic hilltop overlooking the town in the years ahead; as a welcome break from the demand of surgical practice. The occasional casual trip to Indiana for a round of golf was to change.

Some time later, very early on a summer Sunday morning, Dad and I pulled into the lower parking lot of the Club, and were carrying our clubs up to the caddie shack; when a large, pale, freckle-faced man with a shock of graying, reddish hair, approached us and asked if we could chat for a few moments. He was Gilbert Wolfenden, a former State Senator and owner of a wholesale grocery business in town. He quickly revealed that he was Chairman of the Hospital Board of Directors and that the Hospital wanted me to consider a practice at the town's Hospital. He knew that my interest in Indiana was casual, but as I was to learn, Gib usually had his way. Within the hour, he had gone up to Mary Bruno's kitchen in the clubhouse and had used her wall phone inside the swinging kitchen door and had talked with Adeline Hawxhurst, the matronly Administrator of the Hospital.

When he came back down the wide clubhouse staircase, he announced that I had been granted temporary privileges at the Hospital; and before he left, I had agreed to consider a part-time Indiana practice. There was an air of expectancy during the nine holes of golf that Sunday morning. My mind really wasn't on the game.

Here I was considering, at least a part-time lifestyle, when all along, I had planned to practice in a city hospital with an elegant lobby and an excellent medical staff. I hadn't forgotten the experience of a few months earlier in that dingy, poorly equipped Emergency Room. What I had seen there more closely resembled the St. Something or Other primitive hospital in Norfolk where we had taken the accident victim some years earlier. There were no modern intravenous fluids, or for that matter, no emergency medical help. It was not difficult to imagine what standard of care the Hospital followed.

Nevertheless, there could be excitement in facing the challenge of helping to bring up-to-date medicine to a beautiful community like Indiana. I had no delusion about the quality of care being practiced in the community; but I would gravely underestimate some of the reactions in a medical community which I would find was dedicated to the status quo.

I, of course, talked with Dr. Kuehn, after the offer to spend some time with an Indiana practice. He listened intently as I outlined the pros and cons of a part-time practice there. We had gone to a small, windowless conference room just off the large tiled lobby of the Veteran's Hospital for some privacy. I cannot forget his advice. I had received some early overtures to join a urologic group at a large Pittsburgh hospital, and without hesitation, he said, "I cannot talk about why; but never, never consider joining with that group." Knowing of the Doctor's unpleasant experience with Pittsburgh's hospitals, I hadn't considered questioning any further. Now, he continued with an uncharacteristic blunt assertion. "You, at some point, will have to make the decision whether you fight it out in Indiana or fight it out here." There was no doubt that he knew what he was talking about.

I was learning what "fighting it out" in Pittsburgh would be like. It was considered to be proper etiquette for senior physicians to blackball young physicians for membership in important societies if they were to leave the senior's employ. My former employer attempted just that; but his attempt to bar me from the American Urologic Association and to prevent my certification by the American Board of Urology backfired. My teachers, who had known the man, overturned his behind-the-scenes activities and I was successful with both organizations.

On the other hand, I trustingly never anticipated any such behavior in a lovely town like Indiana.

Within a week or so after meeting Wolfenden, I kept an appointment with Miss Hawxhurst, the Hospital's Administrator. She was a rotund, intent, bespectacled lady with a head that seemed to sit directly on her shoulders. She pleasantly invited me into her new glass-enclosed office, just off the lobby of the Hospital's newly opened diagnostic wing. As a gesture, she noticeably wagged an ample double chin to emphasize her points, and she proudly alluded to her rise from the time she was first employed by the Hospital as a young bookkeeper.

"Dr. Miller", she intoned, "you have certainly chosen an opportune time to come." With that, she launched into a description of the problems the Hospital had faced by being dependent on an itinerant Urologist. He was described as traveling from hospital to hospital doing surgery and then disappearing, leaving the patients to the care of one of his cronies, who all too often, would not be too willing or too qualified to handle postoperative problems. We had known beforehand about him. He was part of a network of Urologists who had trained under the Professor of Urology at Pittsburgh's Medical Center. In effect, the Professor's men and his former trainees, blanketed the hospitals of western Pennsylvania with itinerant urologic care; effectively excluding other young Urologists from practicing in western Pennsylvania.

As Miss Hawxhurst continued, she, in an almost melodious voice, continued to describe the itinerant Urologist and his patient care. It became obvious that she was deeply concerned by apparent neglect of patients. She emotionally began to describe afternoons of surgery, once a week, followed by a night of postoperative hemorrhage and futile calls; without being able to have the Urologist return to care for his patients. The woman seemed near desperation, but her sincerity was unmistakable. The whole scene reinforced my wonderment in the ability of men like the Professor to monopolize a medical specialty with substandard care; and at the same time, prevent newly trained and competent competitors from entering their domain.

As Miss Hawxhurst handed me an application for Medical Staff privileges, I sensed the opportunity for a real challenge. The challenge had always been to be a Staff Physician with a hospital with the largest marble lobby, but on that afternoon, the challenge of building a surgical practice, almost from scratch, in a small community hospital, with an outstanding potential, appeared as a realistic and exciting alternative.

I found myself looking ahead to being the first of a new breed of surgical specialists in a hospital holding a monopoly for an entire county. I knew the sophistication of care at this place wasn't the best, but I began thinking of the opportunity to show and to teach and to build.

Such naivete'! I never gave much thought to the significance of the itinerant Urologist and his cronies. I had no inkling of the malice and intrigue that would flow from that first small crevice in the Professor's wall around western Pennsylvania.

Despite the poor impression that the itinerant Urologist had made with the Hospital's Administrator and Board, I would find that he had substantial support from some of his cronies at the Hospital. I would learn of the unprincipled behavior of some of these: the Hospital Pathologist, the local Opthalmologist, one of the General Surgeons and two General Practitioners from outlying towns, as well as the local Urologist. What I wouldn't know was that these people would form their opinions before ever knowing me and would hold their grudges forever.

Miss Hawxhurst advised that I visit some of the town's physicians and I found myself at a later date in Dr. Bee's office, a modest little dark brown clapboard structure adjoining the porch of his frame house on Water Street. The street paralleled and was a block away from Philadelphia Street, the town's main drag. The Doctor was congenial and quite formal; but relaxed once I had reminded him of meeting in the Hospital's Emergency Room a year or so earlier. He never mentioned that he had never gotten in touch, as he had promised, after the Emergency Room tragedy; but he did confirm that one of the two victims of that crash had died at the hospital and the other, a brother, had been transferred to a Pittsburgh hospital. He discussed that there was a definite need for modern Urology at the Hospital, confirming the patient neglect over a period of years. He assured that the itinerant's local partner, who usually provided the post-operative patient care would not be harmed; noting that he had substantial income from his strip mining business. The doctor finally suggested that I visit Anna Simpson, a physician's widow who may just rent me Dr. Simpson's old office.

I visited some of the other physicians in town and continued to receive encouragement to come to the community; that is, except for the local Urologist who performed no surgery. He staunchly suggested that I take my talent elsewhere.

A noontime visit with Mrs. Simpson has to be another of those significant lifetime events. The Simpson house was a large, square turn-of-the-century red brick structure, fronted by a large, covered porch. It faced South Seventh Street and sat next to the Post Office, only a few doors from the main intersection of Philadelphia Street with South Seventh. When I got no answer at the front door, I walked around to the left into an elegant garden surrounding a small patio. It was almost like stepping into another world - perhaps an English garden or a quiet little corner in a rain forest.

There, in quiet conversation around an umbrella table, was Mrs. Simpson and two well-dressed men. Her aristocratic manner was evident at once, as she introduced me to her guests - her son John, a lawyer, and her cousin, John St. Clair, a banker. Her strength of character was unmistakable. She was to become one of our warmest friends and a most unforgettable character.

Things didn't happen all at once, but Mrs. Simpson did agree to rent Dr. Simpson's old office with its entrance off to the side of that large front porch. She would allow me to put in a partition or two, and with a telephone and answering machine I would be in business. After a little renovation of the office, I began driving up from Pittsburgh two afternoons a week, waiting for someone to call. Week after week, a young female voice would leave a message on the machine that she wanted an appointment; but there never was a number left. I was becoming desperate to see my first patient; but then it happened. She called while I was there. She was surprised that she wasn't talking to a machine and gave her name. She wanted to know if I would take care of her ingrown toenails.

But, not too long afterward, I got a call in Pittsburgh from Dr. Kellam, the Hospital's Chief of Surgery. In his gentlemanly sourthern drawl, he asked me to meet him early the next morning to see a patient. It still wasn't full light when the doctor and I wound our way from the Hospital's Medical Staff Room over to the Mack Wing. The patient's name, I still recall, was Bruno. Bruno had the misfortune of having his heavy clothing being caught in farm machinery, and as the clothing was snatched up in the machine, it took along all of the skin of his scrotum. I advised Bruno and Dr. Kellam that nature was kind to this type of injury and advised conservative care, allowing nature, in fact, to regenerate a new scrotum. After weeks of careful dressing changes, nature did her job and Bruno was discharged fully healed.

When I returned my application to Miss Hawxhurst, she asked me to sit down for a moment and said,"Doctor_____was here to see me and is terribly upset." She continued, "but he has abused us for years and we are not going to allow him to stop your coming now. Are you sure you can do things like remove kidneys and so forth?" she queried. "Yes." I replied. As we walked from the new modernistic office into the lobby, my hostess again suggested that I continue to talk with Dr. Bee and Dr. Lapsley."They are my guiding lights", she confided. "They know the situation and can advise you."

My appointment to the Medical Staff was required to be probationary for three months or so and I thought it best not to attend medical staff business meetings until my permanent appointment was confirmed.

What a surprise to learn that the Itinerant Urologist and his group had shown up at a business meeting and had made an effort to block my appointment to the Staff. Leonard Volkin, a friendly, soft-spoken nose and throater, described the meeting as a real circus. The Urologist had been joined by the unstable Hospital Pathologist and a General Practitioner-Surgeon in castigating the Hospital Administration for bringing competition into the Urologic monopoly extending across a portion of the state of

Pennsylvania. Leonard often repeated the story and would describe how he had engineered a compromise: I was to be appointed to the Associate Staff rather than the full "senior" or "active" staff - an appointment without the prestige of a "senior" staff appointment ; but with all the privileges necessary. I could have cared less and thought little more of the incident. But, despite my lack of concern, it would turn out that those people involved would never lose their envy and ill feelings. At that same time, two recent graduates from internships (General Practitioners) were added to the Medical Staff without incident. Their enmity would begin at once.

Often, during one of my afternoons in that less than elegant little office on South Seventh Street, Mrs. Simpson would call; and if I weren't busy, would then appear with milk and cookies. She was one grand person. Joan and I became very fond of her and she, more or less, introduced us to Indiana "society."

During my afternoon chats with Mrs. Simpson, it became apparent that she influenced the Hospital Board Chairman Wolfenden greatly. Anna was truly the grande dame of Indiana.

On occasion, she would kindly describe towns' leading citizens and some of its characters. Dr. Simpson had delivered the town's famous citizen - James Stewart.

There had been a funeral service at the funeral home just behind the Simpson house the day before. Anna described that the mourners had assembled in the small chapel and were listening to the strains of soft organ music. The funeral director, a large, friendly, white-haired fellow, had felt the need to visit the adjacent restroom, and apparently the room hadn't been designed with modern sound proofing. Anna, a perfect lady, was far too reserved to describe the sound effects of the funeral director's efforts; but the co-mingling of the restroom resonance with soft music apparently produced a new experience in harmonics for the assembled guests.

To my surprise, Wolfenden appeared at the office one afternoon, unannounced, and strode in with a little bluster and insincere apology. I had become more convinced that he usually got what he wanted and seldom took "no" for an answer. Anna had talked about his marrying the daughter of the owner of the local wholesale grocery business and managing the business after his career in Harrisburg politics. He appeared to have no problem or qualm in supplying the groceries for the Hospital that he controlled with an iron fist. He exchanged small talk for a few moments and then came to the point."There was a group at the Hospital that wanted to block you from full Senior Staff privileges - afraid of your competition", he said, "but, at the Board meeting last night, the Board granted you full Senior Staff privileges. We want you to seriously consider coming here full-time and help develop a first class hospital." While Wolfenden was a little overbearing, he was obviously sincere and his challenge was tempting.

After an afternoon conference with Dr. Kuehn in Pittsburgh, we began to seriously consider moving to Indiana and giving that venture our full effort. As Dr. Kuehn had put it, "You shouldn't do both; you must decide to fight it out here or fight it out there." It took some time for the wisdom of that admonition to set in. The Doctor had battled with the Pittsburgh Hospital Establishment when he came to Pittsburgh with his wife Ruth, the new Dean of the School of Nursing at Pitt. He had finally accepted the haven provided by his role as a teacher at the Veteran's Administration Hospital and I was one of a long line of residents who had benefited from his teaching and wisdom. When he said, "Fight it out here or fight it out there", he spoke from bitter experience and it was, with a limited degree of understanding, that Joan and I decided to take our brand new son and "fight it out there."

No one ever had a better friend than Anna Simpson. She was delighted to hear of our plans. She took us under her wing and continued to make an effort to introduce us around. Joan and I not only listened to her advice about local customs and people, but found ourselves being truly fond of her. We still talk about her strength of character and mannerisms. Joan had nicknamed the new baby "Boomie", and on occasion, Anna would look in while I baby sat "Boomie" at the office - him in his little wicker basket - while I kept up on my journal reading. Our favorite remembrance, to this day, is Anna inviting us to drop by some afternoon and urging, "and don't forget to bring along little "Goofy."

Things in Indiana seemed to snowball after that. Dr. Kellam had usually sent major surgical cases to Cleveland, but invited me, one morning, to see one of his "select"patients. The man had a large bladder stone, and I advised the obvious - open surgery. The Doctor and his associate, Dr. Joe Gatti, assisted the morning that we did the case, and it went well. I was understandably pleased when the Doctor came into the surgeon's lounge and blurted out, "Doctor, that was the finest piece of surgical work I think I've ever seen." Within a short time, another surgeon, Tim Kredel, advised one of the town's "prominent" families that their son should udergo major stone surgery at home rather than traveling to Cleveland. He assisted, and again, the procedure went well. I learned , later that day, that after Kredel broke scrub, he went down to the Hospital lobby and raved to the family about the fine surgery. Kredel, however, never gave personal complements.

It wasn't long before referrals began to come, not only from local physicians, but gradually from other towns and eventually from out of state. It was a chore top lease everyone, but I was trying. For awhile, it was difficult to ignore the blatant hostility of the Itinerant's group. I must have had every reason to think that everyone was truly pleased to have some early help in improving the County's Urologic care. What a ridiculous notion!

That early practice was not city oriented. Some early experiences contributed to a little humility.

During afternoon office hours an elderly fellow in a baseball cap came through the large front reception room and knocked on the inner door. When I opened the door, he announced that he wanted to use the rest room. The room was in use, but I told him I'd let him in, in a minute. When I returned to get him, he was furious - "It's too damned late", he yelled. "I already went." When I asked where he had gone he snapped, "in my hat."

At about that same period in time, a large, black sedan of an earlier era pulled up to the front curb. Two large, swarthy men came through the reception room and asked to have me look at a sick woman with them.

It took only a brief examination to determine that the feverish, pregnant young woman was very sick with a urinary infection. The men advised that they were with the carnival at the fairgrounds and reluctantly agreed to admit the young woman to the hospital.

She responded well to intravenous fluids and antibiotics after two days. When I made early morning rounds on the third day, the nurses advised that the gypsies had left during the night - taking with them the patient, the room's blankets and a brass door knob.

The Hospital Parking lot was, in itself, a status symbol. The parking lot was just to the right of that stone entrance we had entered a few years earlier, after the auto accident that first took us to the Hospital in an attempt to help those two elderly brothers from Pittsburgh. At the head of each parking spot was a galvanized pipe toped by a rectangular sign, bearing the name of a Medical Staff member. Parking in someone else's spot was comparable to armed robbery. Such an indiscretion would cause a tempest which could last for days. A review of the signs physically delineated the pecking order. The signs, after awhile, just disappeared.

Access to the Hospital was usually gained through a covered entrance leading toa short flight of steps into the hallway which, in turn, passed the nursing station of the Mack Wing. A turn to the left brought one to the sign-in panel of lights and the entrance to the Medical Staff Room. To the right of the Staff Room door was a mammoth red Coke machine, which one would learn, looked down upon many a conference between the Medical Staff politicos - who eventually would become known as "The Boys." The Medical Staff Room was unusual. It was a remnant from an earlier era. The room was dreary, even on the brightest of days. The walls were of an irregular yellowish plaster. The windows on the far wall were partially covered with heavy, reddish draperies, held back with wrought iron fixtures. The large, maroon, leather sofa at the foot of the windows left little room between it and the large oaken table which was surrounded by ornate oaken chairs. There was even less room on the other side of the table between it and dreary pine shelves holding an array of almost ancient texts and outdated periodicals. The routine would usually be to sign in at the light panel, enter the cloak room just off to the left of the Staff Room and then pick up one's mail and laboratory reports from a set of pigeon holes next to the hallway door. After one retrieved copies of lab and x-ray reports, the ritual could end with one going about one's business. Occasionally, a colleague would initiate a discussion or one would enter from the adjoining restroom still zipping up.

Adding to the somber tone of the room, were a dozen or more brass memorial plaques, just to the left of the windows, honoring physicians who had passed on. A few of us later swore that we would put codicils in our wills to prevent anyone from adding us to that morbid display.

I was beginning to learn the local rules. And. . . I was also being <u>told</u> the local rules. At one time, Miss Hawxhurst, in a friendly little chat, educated me that her sister - who was a private duty nurse, and her husband, were "very prominent in town". I suppose the message was that it would be politically proper to have her sister attend my cases and to display unflagging respect for her social prominence. I suppose I fell short of what was expected. The Administrator's sister liked to "play doctor" and I probably didn't show the proper respect for the social prominence.

On another occasion I really did put my foot in it with the Administrator. A family had asked if their "Dad" could have a little beer with his dinner after surgery. We had all seen post-operative problems with elderly men suddenly deprived of their evening libation. So I, of course, encouraged the family to let "Dad" have his dinnertime beer. I had never seen Miss Hawxhurst's chin go into such convulsion as when I responded to her summons one morning and heard, "Dr. Miller, who authorized you to have that family bring a whole case of beer through my lobby?"

One of Miss Hawxhurst's advisors was a ruddy-faced white-haired elder physician who would often station himself on the Staff Room sofa. Some of the younger G.P.'s would sit and listen to his description of home deliveries on kitchen tables and traumatic deliveries using his special technique - internal podalic version; that is, the procedure when the baby is manually turned in the birth canal and delivered feet first. Althought his traumatic maneuver was used infrequently by trained obstetricians, this practitioner used the procedure regularly. I never hung around to hear those descriptions, but over a period of several years, we would begin to see the results of traumatic or lengthy deliveries in the surrounding mining towns. There was a high local incidence of cerebral palsy and damaged extremities. Some of these deformed babies we would continue to know as adults - a living testimony to the barbaric obstetrics that was practiced by men who weren't trained to do Cesarean sections. This particular practitioner made every effort to sound gruff and tough. But, a little later, at a state medical conference, I had run into one of the Doctor's classmates. He inquired about "Old Tom". When I described Tom, he was obviously surprised. He said that he had known Tom as a red-faced kid who always threw up before examinations in Medical School.

Unfortunately, some of the next generation of G.P.'s would follow with accidents, if anything, worse than those which preceded. The newer generation of G.P.'s were allowed to use obstetrical forceps - a dangerous instrument in unskilled hands.

During one of the Staff Room discussions, a local G.P., Don Donaldson, known more for his ribald jokes than his medical skills, advised that I should stop using a stethoscope. He said that that was his job; in an effort to stop me from carefully examining my patients. He referred one of his patients, whom he had treated for years for "albumin." She turned out to have a huge renal abscess that had been growing for years and wasn't referred for surgical care until she was on the brink of death. To this day, I remember the difficulty involved in treating that poor woman. We actually had to leave instruments in her side for a period of days, after the surgery, being unable to find enough healthy tissue remaining to assure adequate blood control.

At that time, when I was attempting to please everyone - with the probable exception of myself - office hours became the scene of a chilling, lasting episode.

A middle-aged woman came into my unpretentious reception room and asked to be seen. She, somewhat hesitatingly, admitted she had no money but felt she had a serious problem. When I saw little droplets of urine falling to the floor, there was little doubt of the woman's plight. A pelvic examination was frightful. My gloved fingers slipped into a large defect - directly into the poor woman's bladder - destroyed by an extensive cervical cancer.

If possible, the woman's history was more frightful. She related that she had been treated for vaginal bleeding by her family doctor over a period of months. She hadn't ever been examined; but on each office visit sat opposite her physician at his desk as he would renew her prescription for a female hormone. These hormones in the presence of genital cancer is akin to dousing a bonfire with gasoline.

We all make mistakes; we're all human and deserve sympathetic understanding of our foibles. But, sympathy toward such horrific indifference is just not possible. I never revealed this episode - even when the physician attained the highest position in Pennsylvania Medical Politics.

Harry Jones was a G.P. from one of the surrounding towns. When he approached me, at the elevator one evening, I was caught by surprise. "Ralph", he said, "I'll do my best to send you some patients. What kind of an arrangement can we make?" "Well, Harry", I said, "I'll do my best to give them good care and I'll send you a complete report on your patient's progress." That wasn't what he wanted. I was too dumb at the time to recognize my first offer for some sort of fee splitting. One of the variants of the splitting routine was the "referring doctor routine." It was a wonderful way to reward a General Practitioner for referring a patient. It would be a request for a consultation after the patient had been admitted to the Hospital. Under the scheme, the G.P. would visit the patient before surgery, write a note that the patient was "satisfactory for surgery" and submit a bill. Often the "consultant" would visit the patient daily after surgery; often with no more than a head in the door and a "Hello", followed by a series of bills to the patient or his insurance company. I was beginning to see some of the bills local people had received after surgical procedures and that some of these bills were astronomical.

Peter Post was one of the G.P.'s who had decided to bill himself as a "Cardiologist" after an incomplete residency and failure to pass his "boards." Although his peers quietly chastised him for frightening patients into thinking they had serious heart disease that didn't exist, his real claim lay in his business acumen. He became known as "Modane", stemming from his expertise in wandering into the room of another physician's patient and ordering his favorite laxative (Modane) and then sending a bill.

Post would regularly refer patients to one of the town's General Surgeons. That was - until the Surgeon built a beautiful house just across the street from Modane's modest home, in one of the town's fancier neighborhoods - Pill Hill. The Surgeon's wife, astutely critical, left no doubt to those who would listen, that there had been a sudden loss of business from "Modane."

I would like to think that I was just a little naive or just a little too altruistic in thinking that the Medical Community was interested first and foremost with doing the best for their patients. Perhaps I wasn't naive. I guess I may have been gullible. I was beginning to experience the "round-robin" game in that little Hospital Community. Round-robin was the practice of bouncing patients around from doctor to doctor that some of the inept practitioners were using to round out their incomes and to either please the patient or fleece an insurance company.

Gradually, over time, it would become evident that there were various levels of care at the Hospital: there was the care for the well-to-do, and the care for the miners. A number of men on the Hospital Staff had been Company Docs for the surrounding small mining communities and had their little offices in these outlying towns with its rows of neatly-kept company houses. Some of these men would gradually come to town and would eventually find a place on the Hospital Staff. Some of them would return, for a time, to city hospitals for specialty training.

The older miners in the early days were always grateful for any care they would receive. Occasionally, these men and their wives would carry out the custom of kissing the Doctor's hand in concluding an office visit. I felt more than a little uncomfortable when that happened.

I felt even less comfortable when a young friend told of her grandfather being killed in a mine accident and just being dropped off at his company house by a horse-drawn wagon without any pre-warning to the family. More recently, one of the outlying Company Docs would regularly admit "important" patients through a side door, detouring his waiting room full of sick miners and their families.

I found the miners to be a solid, decent people. Their row houses, although in grimy areas with unpaved streets, were always kept up immaculately with lace curtains at the windows and flowers in the summer. They all had respect for hard work and good manners. Many of these men were not far removed in time from the memory of the European troubles that they had left behind. They had to be content with a Company House, buying their goods form the Company Store and accepting the care of the Company Docs.

In later years, it would be revealed that some hospital patients would have a notation (usually V.I.P.) on nursing rosters - signaling the need for special care. This was apparently a long-standing practice.

During those earlier years, while the practice was flourishing, it was becoming less difficult to ignore the distractions. It had become evident that the small band of the Itinerant Urologist's cronies were of a different breed. I began to see that, although we had never met prior to our move to Indiana, they had vowed, early on, to discourage me sufficiently to leave town.

I suppose that, during that period, I just wasn't aware of how much vicious activity I was ignoring. The group who were involved in the behind-the-scenes activities, would regularly hold impromptu conferences - almost always at the large red Coke machine just outside of the Medical Staff Room.

As I look back on those days, I'm surprised that I just ignored the Itinerant Urologist's crowd for as long as I did. I think I came to the conclusion that they were ananomalous gang of bullies. I think I always believed Webster's definition of bullies - "cowardly, rough fellows who intimidate smaller victims." I had never forgotten a beating I took from a neighborhood bully when a kid. Dad had said, "No son of mine is ever going to take a beating like that again." He was right. He bought a set of boxing gloves and began basement boxing lessons over a number of evenings.

On the other hand, I felt that, by ignoring the ruffians, I was probably giving the wrong impression. Shortly after entering practice my mother gave me a framed copy of a poem she had been obliged to memorize in childhood. It was Rudyard Kipling's,

"If", and it has hung opposite my desk ever since.

Over the years I would take a moment now and then to read Kipling's wisdom and reaffirm my belief in those values:

"If you can keep your head when all about you
Are losing theirs and blaming it on you;

If you can trust yourself when all men doubt you;
But make allowance for their doubting you;
If you can wait and not be tired by waiting;
Or being lied about, don't deal in lies,
Or being hated, don't give way to hating,
And yet don't look too good, nor talk too wise;
If you can dream - and not make dreams your master;
If you can think - and not make thoughts your aim;
If you can meet with triumph and disaster
And treat those two impostors just the same;
If you can bear to hear the truth you've spoken
Twisted by knaves to make a trap for fools,
Or watch the things you gave your life to broken,
And stoop and build 'em up with worn-out tools;
If you can make one heap of all your winnings
And risk it on one turn of pitch-and-toss,
And lose, and start again at your beginnings
And never breathe a word about your loss;

If you can force your heart and nerve and sinew
To serve your turn long after they are gone;
And so hold on when there is nothing in you
Except the Will which says to them: "Hold on!";
If you can talk with crowds and keep your virtue,
Or walk with kings - nor lose the common touch;
If neither foes nor loving friends can hurt you;
If all men count with you, but none too much;
If you can fill the unforgiving minute
With sixty seconds' worth of distance run -
Yours is the Earth and everything that's in it,
And - which is more - you'll be a Man my son!

— Rudyard Kipling

The admonition to "turn the other cheek" had been taught as a child, but over the years, I had begun to suspect that that advice was not meant to promote timidity but rather to advise as Kipling wrote, "on being hated, don't give way to hatred."

I was aware, all along, that if I gave way to that kind of hatred I would succumb. But, there would be a time when turning the other cheek would not be effective and could only encourage miscalculation by bullies.

The Hospital Psychiatrist was a strange member of the small opposing crowd and habitually could be seen leaning against a door jamb either alone or with a crony. I couldn't pass him without an insult. On other occasions, as we passed he would veer toward me, forcing me to step aside.

The Psychiatrist was more than strange. He was aggressively strange. I had learned to pass him and endure his insulting comments without reaction. A friendly "hello" or a "good morning" did no good.

I must have really provoked him when I began wearing a white lab coat on rounds. I thought it time to have a standard already adopted by most hospitals. There were a few comments from the nurses - usually positive. But, within a few days, my Psychiatrist friend began walking through the halls wearing a purple smock decorated with white stars and signs of the Zodiac. Without a doubt things were getting stranger and stranger.

Toward noon one morning, I left the second floor entrance to the Operating Suite and started down the hallway to the main Hospital. The corridor was not brightly lit and I saw the Psychiatrist coming at a rapid pace toward me. We were alone and I could see his bulky frame, expressionless face and black knitted eyebrows. As usual, he began to edge toward me and I slowly gave the impression that I, once again, was going to move away from his path; but at the last instant, I lowered my shoulder and gave him abody block that was quite likely a new experience for him.

He spun like a top, and on recovering, issued an onslaught of profanities that I hadn't heard since Navy days. As I recall, most of the insults delt with perverted sexual activities. For some reason, I never had another problem with him. Perhap we had found a common language.

The Itinerant Urologist's other crony, the Hospital Pathologist, was a disheveled figure. He always appeared in a black, baggy suit that appeared never to have been pressed, with a grayish shirt and a loosely hanging tie - which I believe was always the same one. Early in the day, his eyes were blearier than later and he seemd never to lift his feet. As he shuffled around, he would return any greeting with, "Wadda, ya say?"

In cases of doubt I would send pathology specimens to the University for a second opinion. When he was in error, he became apoplectic. I couldn't do anything but ignore his tirades; mistakes in diagnosis could very well threaten a patient's life.

I finally couldn't ignore that gentleman's total disregard of decency, when he would shuffle through the Operating Room in street clothes, open the Operating Room door where I was working, and cause an interruption during a delicate procedure. I wasn't rattled, but I was annoyed. Annoyed enough that I finally caught him lounging in the Medical Staff Room one morning, and with a finger in his face, outlined in firm terms what would occur if he continued contaminating the operating suite and disturbing surgery. It seems that the Itinerant Urologist's henchmen, the Psychiatrist and the Pathologist, had finally gotten the message - like any coward, they withdrew when confronted.

In those early years we were attempting to "accentuate the positive." The little Itinerant Surgeon's group had finally pretty well burned themselves out; they just couldn't sustain the energy levels required for their original hatred, and . . . they were being totally unsuccessful. On another front, people were just not buying the gossip that continued from the two young G.P.'s, one from outlying Homer City and one from Blairsville - Claude Clippins and Abdul Hankey. They had smarted by being given only "Associate Staff "privileges." As a contrast, Abdul's cousin in Indiana responded to a little kindness and occasionally helped out at surgery. I was finding that there had been a scarcity of urologic surgery in the County for years for anyone without health insurance. Some of the other surgeons apparently operated only on those able to pay, so that I found myself doing the "charity" surgery. I was happy to. It was a great experience. The men in Pittsburgh would often be surprised to see the x-rays of disease processes that had advanced so far before treatment.

On two occasions, patients were admitted after treatment by local chiropractors. Neither of these men could walk after an "adjustment." After spinal x-rays, the diagnoses were obvious - the spines were riddled with prostatic malignancy, and had collapsed during the treatments.

After high doses of female hormone - a treatment pioneered by Dr. Huggins - a Nobel Prize winner from Cleveland - both patients slowly responded and eventually walked out of the hospital. They, however, were facing many tough days ahead. They themselves had to be partly responsible for the delay in treatment.

Alex Stewart was one of the town's characters, who, if not famous, was the best known resident. His hardware store was one of the town's landmarks. One could find anything from horseshoes to shotguns there. Chairs, horse collars, sleigh bells, ropes, pulleys - all hung from the rafters of the store's high interior. There were rows of fine antique vases and candy jars which were just as likely to be given to a customer as sold. In another area there was a sort of shrine with a framed photo of his famous son and a marble based statuette - the "Oscar" his son had won.

Alex appeared unannounced during hours one afternoon and confessed that it was time to take care of his "prostrate troubles." He was, indeed, in need of care and anxiously agreed to enter the hospital in a few days.

I was making rounds on my patients on a late afternoon when Miss Hawxhurst summoned. I caught her briefly in her office, and with one of her chin waggles, she advised, "Mr. Stewart is staying in room 310 upstairs and would like to talk with you before his Dad's surgery."

Room 310 was one of the more elegant rooms on the third floor of the yet unopened new wing. I knocked and slowly opened the heavy oak door and a tall, thin gentleman rose from an opposite chair and put down his reading. "Hi, I'm Jim Stewart and I had hoped we could talk a minute about Dad's surgery."

"Sure."

We both relaxed and I couldn't help note the man's casualness and modesty. There was none of the drawl we had heard so often. He was ruddy complexioned and was almost totally bald. We discussed the upcoming surgery and I agreed to look in after the procedure the next morning.

Things went well, and after I had reported, we shook hands and he said, "Guess I'll be heading back to L.A.."

In later years, when some of our self-promoting citizens were attaching themselves to the man's fame, I could only recall the warm, self-effacing personality and wonder if he really approved of all the town's celebrity hype.

That kind of self-advancement, over the years, was to lead to numerous comments from a number of sources that the town was changing - and not for the better. I've heard, many times, questions about why such a beautiful town would tolerate some of the wild machinations, including the Hospital's policy of secrecy. One of our town's young professionals observed that "Indiana has a lot of little Donald Trumps running around."

The miner's union was a powerful influence in the County, as was the local coal company. George Mottey stopped in the office one afternoon and made an appointment. I learned, before he came back, that he was a tough, tough leader in a tough, tough organization. He was large and imposing, with somewhat coarse speech and looked a great deal younger than his age.

George related that he had had urinary bleeding for several years and had undergone transurethral surgery at the University Medical Center on three occasions, but he was still showing blood. He was admitted, and after a few studies, it was evident that only a portion of the offending prostatic enlargement had been removed. At open surgery we removed the remaining mass, the size of a small orange, with a resulting permanent cure. Deep inside the mass was the culprit - a globular cancer.

The union hierarchy attempted to depose George from his union leadership,citing poor health and I found myself in the middle of a miniature union war. My refusal to abandon George led to threats by the union hierarchy. When the skirmish reached Washington, my friends in the union health care system later revealed that the matter had been put to rest by John L. Lewis himself.

During that period I had perfected a small instrument that was manufactured by two well-known instrument manufacturers. This led to trips to Cincinnati and relationships with the engineers developing a new and innovative line of urologic equipment. As a result, we obtained some of the first models of urologic diagnostic and electronic equipment reaching market.

A new procedure was being developed using a small catheter passed througha neck vein into the right side of the heart to monitor critical patients' conditions during surgery. I recall that when the procedure was first used, I looked up to see a group ofthe Medical Staff watching through the O.R. window.

The responsibility for initiating new procedures at the Hospital consumed about all the energy there was. We had established the first artificial kidney procedure at the Hospital. The procedure known as peritoneal dialysis began to save patients in kidney failure and brought a comment from one of the Medical Staff at a nursing station one morning. "Well, we have seen another one of Dr. Miller's resurrections." The resurrection was simply the use of modern fluid and electrolyte therapy.

There was a great deal of satisfaction in treating difficult or unusual problems. The added effort was always worth it. One such unusual problem presented with an attractive and bright woman who had been annoyed with "bladder symptoms" for a period of years without response to treatment. She responded to relatively simple surgery after her problem was discovered and became somewhat of a walking advertisement for us.

Surprisingly, a call came from Washington, D. C. A woman's voice related that she had heard of that surgery through a friend and swore that she had the same long-standing symptoms, and therefore, wanted the same surgery. Our efforts to convince herof the ridiculous assumption that she, too, had such a rare problem, were unsuccessful.

Within a few days, she boarded a bus and appeared at the office. She did, in fact, have the same problem, and underwent the same surgery. Life is strange, isn't it?

During those years, we would be reminded that surgery could be hazardous. There had been an unusual number of testicular malignancies appearing on the scene. The disease usually had been thought to be a rarity - but not in Indiana County. As part of that large group of surgical patients, a young dairy farmer came to surgery with evidence that his cancer had spread throughout his abdominal cavity. We attempted to "debulk" as much of the tumor as possible, but simply were unable to remove enough to hope for reasonable results from x-ray therapy or chemotherapy. The patient died shortly after being taken off of the operating table.

I was shaken, and would have done most anything to have avoided talking with the young man's wife with such horrible news.

I reviewed the anesthesia of the case with the Professor of Anesthesiology atthe University. After reviewing the case, he said, "The man was doomed." That didn't help much.

Like mountain climbers looking for challenges, there was great satisfaction in tackling a difficult problem or, at times, sweating through a difficult problem and coming up with a good result.

Danny was a frail, forty pounds when his parents first brought him to the office. He had been born overseas. His parents were an Air Force couple and had found, shortly after Danny's birth, their infant had been born with kidney failure due to severe obstructions in his urinary system. There had been several operative procedures at military hospitals around the globe to drain each kidney through an ostomy (opening) on each side of the abdomen.

During that first hospital admission, we discussed the severe damage to both kidneys and began a series of procedures to eliminate the obstructions; and then, to reassemble the urinary tracts to a normal configuration. It was a great day when we finished the procedure to finally close the last opening for the little fellow.

The recovery of those badly damaged kidneys was in serious doubt; but Danny was born under the right star. He appeared in our reception room as a healthy teenager - he just wanted to say hello. No one can doubt the satisfaction from the kind of experience.

I was finding, though, that a great deal of nurses training was becoming necessary for my patients to receive a reasonable degree of post operative care. One Saturday we had been out for the evening and I had decided to stop by the Hospital and see a patient who had undergone extensive surgery earlier that morning. When I pulled down the bed cover, I found the patient lying in a pool of blood. She obviously hadn't been checked for hours. It was not difficult to then begin to insist on something better than that for our patients. Over a period of time, we were able to help the nurses feel that they were part of a team and to provide excellent care. I can't say that the top care was universal. Top care was provided to the patients whose physicians demanded it.

The G. P.'s in Indiana, however, were undoubtedly successful in setting the Hospital standards. The Emergency Room continued to assign Emergency Room patients to the G.P.'s who would likely retain control of the patient, and with the help of a compliant surgeon or internist, would enter into the double billing "consultation scheme" - resulting, at times, with unnecessary procedures, unnecessary hospital stays and, at times, unnecessary discomfort and risk.

Lester Lazarus, probably the only member of the species who demonstrated an absolute deficiency of modesty and good manners, appeared on the local Medical Staff directly from a general practice program and unabashedly made the prediction of his immediate financial success that actually and prophetically, was accurate. He never doubted his announcement that "Indiana was a G. P. town and would stay that way."He, of course, appealed to those who were fearful of the gradual appearance of specialists on the Medical Staff. He was able to assume control of the medical care of the area's nursing home patients - due mainly to the default of his colleagues. For years, patients' families would tell of him rousting poor old nursing home souls at two, three or four in the morning after a night on the town. Families who never heard of Lester received bills for services they never requested. The nursing home rounds were followed by Hospital rounds on patients who were given multiple medications and numerous diagnostic procedures - dear to the hearts of the Hospital Administration - grateful for the business.

All this had no adverse effect on activities at his office. Patients and some physicians would describe the dispensing of multiple medications directly. The medications often numbered ten or more. Reports from other patients described that the office nurses were staffing the "line-up" for B-12 shots which was becoming a standard of believers in the "tonic."

Most of the patients with abdominal complaints were ordered his "Blue CrossSpecial" - a somewhat complex x-ray of the urinary system and a "barium enema." This went on for years until the politically correct Hospital Radiologist finally summoned the courage to call attention to all this. During that period, Lester, perhaps subconsciously or perhaps intentionally, became the bellwether for hospital policy. The "round robin referral scheme" flourished and Lester appeared to become a frequent spokesman for the General Practitioners. The lightly suppressed inferiority complex of the G.P.'s appeared to be leading to an undue self assertion of some. Apparently, this had the affect of bringing about the formation of a national specialty board. The "Board" grandfathered the Hospital's General Practitioners with a brief written examination allowing them to be called "Board Certified Family Practitioners." This titling probably resulted in less than full respect by surgeons and medical specialists who had spent years in gaining recognition by their Specialty Boards. But, over the years, these people would be replaced by physicians well-trained in family practice residencies with standards set by a bonafide Board of Family Practice.

The General Practitioners, during that period, enjoyed the support of The Hospital - who enjoyed the revenues from hospital admissions.

Lester's loyalty didn't go unrewarded. A clandestine "investigation" was said to have taken place when a drug used in labor resulted in the death of a young mother in labor. Nothing more was heard of the incident.

Lester must have had gargantuan stamina. He had been described as appearing in a local tavern or two, at times in a huge cowboy hat and an ankle length fur coat. It was reported on one or more other occasions, that he was seen driving down the side-walks of Philadelphia Street in a golf cart in the wee hours and to later begin his day.

One of the County Commissioners learned of a suicide at the hospital. He described that a young male patient (L.B.) had been admitted through the emergency room to Lester. He described that the patient had been brought by police and had been admitted "despondent and agitated." Hospital policy allowed Lester to treat anything from ringworm to coronary occlusions. He admitted the patient, without seeing him, to a secluded room, alone, along with an order for a sleeping pill. In the early morning, he made rounds, and he and a nurse cut the young man down from the bathroom light fixture where he had hung himself. The County Coroner, shortly thereafter, related that the body had been removed from the Hospital without a report to him and that he heard of the death only after hearing Hospital gossip. But, Lester continued to be a high occupancy friend of the Hospital Administration.

The epitome of arrogance was revealed when one of the surgeons described that one of Lester's hospital order's read:" Have Dr. _____ do an appendectomy." The surgeon simply couldn't believe such a thing. There was no room for the surgeon's opinion. The surgeon couldn't believe that a physician could be so blind to professional courtesy, let alone reasonable manners.

After he had written that famous order, "Have Dr. _____ do an appendectomy", as far as I knew, the patient never underwent surgery. But; Lester continued his shenanigans.

During his tenure, he was arrested for firing buckshot into the car of a group of young people gathering fishing worms on one of the Country Club's fairways at night. The local court sentenced him to the State's Accelerated Rehabilitation Program for a year. The B-12 line and Hospital admissions continued uninterrupted.

Incredibly, before he left town, a newspaper ad carried Lester's name endorsing a local politician's bid for office.

If I ever had any residual belief that beautiful small towns held only beautiful people, that belief was totally shattered by an early church experience. Although not firmly religious, I felt good listening to Jim Rush's weekly sermons. He was intelligent and his sermons were inspirational. Some church members constantly griped about his sermons being too long. Their annoyance would continue to simmer and Jim would not bend - his mistake. But, I suspect that many of his critics found the sermons too long because they didn't really understand them.

It all came to a head at a well-attended church business meeting in the church's basement. Jim opened the meeting and suddenly released one of the worst spectacles of human vitriol I had ever witnessed. The worst harangue was from one of the town's lawyers. I sat in that audience dumbfounded that this man could put on such a display of hatred in a house of worship. Religion, I thought, was to help people be better. To top off the religious castigation, a parishioner who operated a local greenhouse got up and offered six hundred dollars to anyone who would get rid of the preacher.

Once at home, I called Jim and offered any consolation I could. He took the whole happening well, but I could imagine the hurtful experience it was for him. It was the last time I was in church and the experience became another incident in a series of incidents confirming that Indiana tolerated some unusual people and their unusual conduct. I began to think it may be something in the water.

It was well known, though, that some folks would find themselves spread over the front page of the evening paper, outlining benevolent activities, while other news-worthy matters occurring in the town never reached print.

Peter Post returned from a short residency and offered his services as a cardiologist. During those years, Post posed as a friend. He once confided that he was having a stressful problem over his envy of Lester Lazarus, the aggressive General Practitioner who had come to town and who was setting his own rules, with a great deal of success.

After a year or so, Post found himself rotating into the office of Hospital Medical Staff President. Surprisingly, I found myself his Vice-President and a member of his "Executive Committee." I credulously believed I could have some effect on the qualityof care at the Hospital and even the nasty envious atmosphere developing among the Medical Staff.

Rather than improving the atmosphere, I found myself, at one point, adding to the punitive activities. One of the Staff and his partner in general surgery were roundly disliked for their acutely greedy natures. One of them would routinely hang around the Hospital Emergency Room and would pounce on any unsuspecting patient who was admitted there, potentially needing surgical care.

One Saturday morning, Post was taking pleasure in his new authority as Medical Staff President and called an "emergency meeting" of the Executive Committee, advising that one of those surgical entrepreneurs had gotten into a shouting match with the Hospital Pathologist and needed to be disciplined; a punishment without meaning, since the partner could continue the parade of surgery. The Committee met at noon, and I found myself going along with that discipline which amounted to the culprit being sentenced to a three month suspension from the Hospital.

Over the next several weeks, I found myself more ill-at-ease with myself. I finally stopped making excuses and faced the fact that I didn't, under any circumstance, want to be part of a group of vigilantes. When the convicted bullying surgeon returned, I found him alone in the Medical Staff Room early one morning. I found it no problem to tell him that I was ashamed for having taken part in that emerging group of "Executives" and apologized for being part of his punishment. He took no solace in my apology, but questioned my right to sit in judgement of him. So did I.

Somewhat later, perhaps as a reward for my "going along", Post and a few others were in quiet discussion when I entered the Medical Staff Room. Post announced that I was going to be the next County Medical Society President. I seemed to have a knack for pricking people's cherished balloons. After all, Dr. Kuehn had properly called me an iconoclast. The little group fell silent and stared in disbelief when I unceremoniously advised that I didn't care to be the Medical Society President.

I suppose that was a defining moment for some people. It was apparent that I wasn't going to "go along to get along", as one of those gallbladder surgeons later observed.

Post and his spouse, along with another of the younger couples, seemed overtime, to intensify their climbing activities. One of the climbers, the spouse, (we'll call her "Peg") was involved in all sorts of benevolent activities. She acquired all sorts of like-minded friends and would go to great lengths to be noticed. She was a skeletal, sharp-featured lady, and as one of the doctor's wives observed, talked loudly with an attention gaining cackle. It was not unusual for the lady to spot an acquaintance across a crowded room and scream with a wave and a loud "yoo-hoo, yoo-hoo." She was one of those adept at scanning a room over someone's shoulder during an animated conversation.

The couple always appeared late at a social gathering with a loud entrance. Post with a limp wrist and over-compensating baritone and sometimes with a dangling stethoscope with the accompanying screeching, "yoo-hoo" and celebrity arm waves.

At other times Post, with stethoscope dangling, would pass by mumbling, "I'm so busy, so very busy." I never quite grasped the significance of this until a medical essayist, Bob Lanier, M. D. wrote: "I don't think physicians really have "affluenza", I don't think they're nearly as worried about the loss of income as they are subconsciously afraid of the loss of over-work and the self-esteem that goes along with it."

In those early days there was perfunctory socializing with Post and his spouse and a few other young couples who were hoping to get ahead at the Hospital, but eventually, envy would become more and more noticeable. It wasn't too pleasurable to listen to the suggestions by some of the wives as to whom we should socialize with and whom to avoid. Above all, we were never to associate with chiropractors.

By far the most popular social activity was bridge. I had never bothered to learn the game, so that I was fully capable of making some really bonehead plays during the course of an evening's bridge game. I was chastised once for "trumping my partner's ace." I think that may have been the last time we were invited for bridge.

We found ourselves enjoying the company of struggling young neighborhood couples who just enjoyed good humor without pretentiousness. Saturday nights at the inelegant Country Club always led to chuckles, guffaws, and occasionally, childish pranks.

I think we all inwardly smiled at those who thought that they had scored some sort of a social coup by "seeing and being seen" at that middling framed clubhouse in the center of a nine-hole golf course.

There was, at the time, the legend of the FFI, the "First Families of Indiana."Stories set the number of families at eleven and others claimed there were not more than eight or so. Whatever. We met them all. We attended the parties which were, without exception, catered by a middle-aged server who provided her hor-d'oeuvres. Her husband tended bar with his wide choice of booze: scotch, bourbon or gin highballs,water or ginger ale, served from his linen-draped card table. The men's conversations were unrevealing, but Joan would have all sort of information from the ladies after we got home.

One of the first persons I met in Indiana was Bill Musser. Bill was a jovial lawyer and always provided good humor.

On one occasion, I took a small group to a Pirate's home game. We stopped at a small roadside bar just outside Monroeville for a pre-game beer. I had been in the restroom, and when I joined the group at the bar the atmosphere had become sullen.There was a prompt exit and no explanation until we were back in the car. Apparently, Bill had asked the bartender "if there was any charge" and the bartender had become irate. Rather than get thrown out, the group promptly left, allowing the bartender to return to his T.V.

Bill had me join him as an expert witness in a hearing in Jefferson County to help an elderly widow collect her husband's death benefits. We were pulled over by a state policeman for speeding. I never let Bill forget that I considered him a real "mouthpiece" after I heard him talk his way out of that ticket.

Bill and his spouse Judy threw a beautiful dinner party at the old Country Club on the hill. The meal was delicious and the company congenial. After the meal, the discussions pleasantly went on for some time, until Bill went to each table and snuffed out each candle, announcing, "This here party's over." This was one of those unassuming events that made those early Indiana years so memorable.

When Administrator Hawxhurst retired, a young, energetic Administrator - one of the new breed of educated CEO's - took over. He, in a money-saving move, announced a new Emergency Room policy: We would each spend one night a month staying at the Hospital to provide what he called "emergency care." After a couple of months of bunking at the Hospital, we found that the "emergency care" was mainly for people who had sore throats or some minor complaint and could be treated during regular hours. And, there were those who found that, if they waited until nightfall, they could be treated without waiting in a doctor's office and could probably be treated for free. We were beginning to see that there were those who demanded the best and most convenient medical care and who preferred that someone else pay for it.

The resentment of most of the Medical Staff led to a showdown when the Administrator called a special meeting to discuss the Emergency room staffing problem. There was a better than average attendance at that noontime gathering in the stark basement Medical Staff dining room. The Administrator walked behind the speaker's table and quickly asked for attention. He promptly laid to rest any notion that there was to be a discussion. He authoritatively detailed his demands for the Medical Staff, created by him and his Board of Directors.

I was stunned by his arrogance - as was just about everyone there. I had made a practice of not getting into the petty arguments that took place at the noontime chow-downs, so that I rarely had anything to say. But now, I found myself on my feet as the Administrator finished his ultimatum. As I recall, I advised him of his impropriety and disrespect toward a group of professionals. I outlined the true nature of the people actually presenting at the Emergency Room and the abuse of professionals who were required to reside at the Hospital after a trying, stressful day. I think I ended with a suggestion that he draw in his horns and talk about staffing the Emergency

Room, as other hospitals did, with professional E.R. physicians. There were a few brief comments by the assembled group and he left redfaced without another word. I was more than surprised when some of the remaining "itinerant urologist faction" came up later and thanked me for a "good speech." Whether the speech was good or not, it was apparently effective. The Administrator, not long after that, moved on to another hospital job somewhere in the Great Lakes region.

At about that time, Board Chairman Wolfendon announced his retirement and his successor. The successor had served on the Hospital Board for a time and it was never known whether he was appointed by Wolfenden or was somehow elected. He had come from Philadelphia to manage the new Robertshaw - Fulton Controls Plant -a boost for the community. It was a substantial light industry and employer. It was said that the new Board Chairman had acquired his managerial job in exchange for a patent on a kitchen range control that he had, one way or another, acquired in Philadelphia. He had built a beautiful house two doors from us in our modest neighborhood. It seemed that, all at once, he took over the role of a community leader. He unabashedly formed a neighborhood committee to "oversee" neighborhood projects and to set neighborhood standards. Meetings for the neighborhood were held in members' basements and usually he would attend with a thick pile of papers and would conduct and often, dominate the meeting. Early on, I had the impression that the man just didn't care for physicians, even though a son was a Pathologist in Connecticut. That family relationship was apparently anything but close. He was, however, close to his teenage daughter. She was a tall, quiet, likeable girl, and on occasion, would baby-sit our young son. The new Board Chairman teamed up with a political crony, Bill McMasters, a County Commissioner who served as the Vice Chairman of the Hospital Board. McMasters owned a burial vault company in Blairsville. The company apparently ran itself, since Bill spent much of his time strolling along Philadelphia Street "pressing the flesh" and giving advice in a loud, rather deep voice. It was a contrast - Bill himself was short and always acted with authority; but presented a less than overwhelming appearance. He had a round face, large protruding ears and a grin that seemed to extend from ear to ear. I was always reminded of the face on the "Jolly Boy" kites we flew when we were kids. I would never suspect that this politician would some day be one of my judges and have a profound influence on my career.

I was asked by the Hospital Auxiliary to "M.C." an anniversary celebration of the Hospital Ladies Auxiliary. Even though I was not comfortable with public speaking, I agreed to serve. The audience was congenial and the program went well; but when I introduced the new Hospital Board chairman, the scowl he gave, as he approached the podium, left no doubt that we weren't friends. I truly didn't know why.

The new Board Chairman was not only the manager of the local Robertshaw Plant, but became a church leader; a member of crony Bill's Airport Authority; and was involved with a number of charities and organizations. He cultivated the publishers of the local newspaper which was accused by some as seldom publishing the real Indiana news. But, it seemed that the Chairman's picture was in the paper regularly. The paper's publisher, of course, was on the Hospital Board. Some Indiana residents would either complain of the absence of real news affecting the town's big shots or would often get the real news by reading out of town papers.

There were tales that the Chairman would routinely call in an unwanted employee at the Robertshaw Plant, and would give the victim twenty minutes to gather up his belongings and leave the plant. It was said that this usually took place on Monday mornings leading to the phrase, "the Monday morning massacres."

There would inevitably follow labor trouble, acrimony and closure of the plant ,reportedly with the loss of six hundred jobs. This allowed the Chairman full time to"supervise" the construction of a new Hospital wing - to be his memorial.

When the former Administrator left, Bill Price was hired and it appeared that finally there would be a progressive Administration at the Hospital. Bill was a reasonable,but no-nonsense administrator with an excellent background. He began to effect much ofthe needed reforms to bring the Hospital into the twentieth century. Most of the Hospital people welcomed the change and the atmosphere appeared to be changing.

Bill became a friend and we would occasionally get together over a beer and discuss all sorts of issues; but always excluded shop talk and Hospital gossip. One evening, he told Joan and me that the new Board Chairman had warned him not to associate with us. We were annoyed but not surprised. Bill chose to choose his own friends and they were numerous. He and a group of his friends included me in planning a Canadian fishing trip; but, before that needed vacation took place, Bill called the office early one afternoon. He was calling from home and revealed that the

Chairman had walked into his office that noontime and had given him twenty minutes to clear out his desk and leave. I was stupefied, but managed to ask, "Why?". "No reason was given, "Bill replied. Bill planned to go ahead with the fishing vacation; but I, with just about everyone else, felt the insecurity that surrounded the Hospital by the vicious and startling dismissal of a talented and dedicated professional who was beginning to make a difference in the quality of care provided by the institution, and to begin a new era of progress.

It seemed that everyone was looking over their shoulders and joining in the speculation. I didn't feel it a good idea to be out of town on vacation, even though I wanted to do anything possible to support my friend. Bill understood and agreed that possibly I could somehow help by staying in town and learning what I could about the secrecy that had suddenly descended.

The rumor mill exploded. Bill, it was speculated by the town gossips, was guilty of all sorts of indiscretions. None was true. No one at the time realized that Bill was the first sacrifice to the gods of secrecy, deceit and innuendo. We didn't know that we were facing a decade or more of rule by a deceitful martinet, the Chairman of the Board, and his ambitious, compliant rubber-stamp Board.

After some months, we were to learn that the Chairman had established his rule of secrecy with an evening meeting of his Board at his home - out of sight - where a unanimous vote decided to end a professional career in Indiana for the Administrator without due process or explanation.

Not surprisingly though, Bill went on to substantial success with Project Hope. He traveled the globe, on the Good Ship Hope, taking modern medical care to undeveloped countries. He could have done the same for Indiana.

Chapter 11

> *"The reasonable man adapts himself to the world; the unreasonable one persists, trying to adapt the world to himself. Therefore all progress depends on the unreasonable man."*
>
> — George Bernard Shaw

THE LATER YEARS

As surely as night follows day, the town would change. It seemed reasonable to believe that the out-of-town influences would have a positive effect on the town, and likewise, for the Hospital.

The impression of a sleepy college town that I had formed on that first mid-August visit to town had gradually changed. The main intersection of Philadelphia and South 7th. Streets, only a few feet from that first modest office, now bustled with traffic. But, the center of the town's commerce was shifting to the western side of town where new malls and offices were springing up.

Jack Smith was the husband of a patient who had undergone extensive surgery. He was grateful for her recovery and was enthusiastic about my hope for a new office on the outskirts of town. He volunteered to scout around for a site and, before too long, had talked with a dairy farmer and had negotiated for a section of farm land as the site for a new office.

Anna Simpson's stately old house near the main intersection which had housed my first office, had been leveled to become a parking lot for the Post Office. That was enough of a stimulus to try a new concept - a medical office away from the parking problems of downtown.

The Hospital people had warned that I would lose all referrals if I built a "clinic", and were apparently glued to the concept that all medical offices be crowded into a two block area of downtown.

The new office was built and became the first to demonstrate that a medical office in a less congested area could be successful. Other medical offices in outlying areas would follow, once the example had been set.

We held an open house for the county's physicians and apparently set the stage for other colleagues to follow with their own offices. I always had felt that physicians would help provide themselves some independence from Hospital domination if they owned their own offices. I remember that, at the open house, I came upon one of the G.P.'s from an outlying town measuring our treatment rooms with a tape measure.

One friend who was a Hospital Board Member, and aware of the evil of professional envy, advised, "It is a beautiful building, but you've lost all your friends". He may have been right, but the time had come to either be one's own man or to be part of a herd and slosh around in mediocrity.

The choice hadn't been difficult and the decision to lead the way with a new office led to successes and pointed the way for others to follow.

With the town undergoing a busy expansion to the west, the Hospital was undergoing its own changes - imperceptible at first, but accellerating with each passing day.

It soon became apparent that the clandestine Hospital Board meeting at the Chairman's house and the decision to dismiss the young, energetic Administrator, signaled the beginning of a vindictive, deceitful, punitive Hospital Administration with a strict policy of secrecy surrounding a growing mass of behind-the-scenes activity. All this was occurring in an institution thriving on public funds and private gifts. Nevertheless, those people in charge undoubtedly believed the Hospital to be their personal property. It was admitted by a later administration that the Hospital belonged to the community.

Historically, the Hospital had been established as a private, not-for-profit corporation and had benefited from large donations from benefactors and corporations - particularly the local coal company.

In its early years,the Hospital served the local miners and their families while enjoying support from many interests. But, each year brought more need for higher standards and for services that would satisfy a growing, more sophisticated population. In truth, the standard of care that had been provided the miners was unacceptable to many who were employed by the local University and the new faces in local commerce. Many local residents who demanded a high standard of hospital care would still travel to Cleveland, Pittsburgh, and even Rochester, Minnesota for care.

Unfortunately, there continued to evolve varying standards of care for different patients. Nurses began to talk about the notations of V.I.P. being written beside some patients' names alerting all to the need for "special" care.

A few of the former Company Docs returned after leaving general practice for specialty training. One of these physicians who moved to town and endlessly pursued socialite status, was the one who had had the side door to his office so that the 'important' people from town didn't have to wait. Traces of this attitude would continue to linger as the Hospital continued to be obsessed with tailoring its services to its patients social or economic status.

One can reasonably wonder, not only why such a mind-set would evolve, but more to the point - why would it survive; and survive it did.

In more recent years, nurses would be troubled by the standards of care or the lack of it and would describe in detail, incidents of unusual care that had troubled them. Instead of newer members of the Medical Staff, attracted by the Hospital's open door, non selective policy, the newer physicians increased the policy of medical care tailored to economic status.

One example was graphically detailed in a later affidavit; a physician who had come to town and who had established a practice of Internal Medicine, (Dr. Vader), was called at night to come to the aide of a hospital patient in severe respiratory distress. He refused to see the patient, saying he would see the man in the morning. The affidavit states, "... although upright in bed...we tried to make the patient comfortable ... was having significant breathing difficulty ... with oxygen at seven liters ... respiratory distress increased steadily ... patient's color changed markedly ... anxiety level became quite concerning ... tongue was swelling ... trouble swallowing ... vital signs were changing ... charge nurse went to desk to call doctor ... telling Doctor of patient's deteriorating status and the rapidity ... Doctor Vader became irritated and asked if patient was any one important or related to any one important in town ... present orders were to stand ... anyway, patient was an old man ... patient was fully aware and increasingly panicked ... tongue so swollen it protruded from his mouth as his throat continued to swell ... eyes bulged in terror and disbelief as we stood by unable to do anything to help ... until mercifully, he passed beyond the need for oxygen or for Doctor Vader".

After this fellow had been in town for a while longer, he quit private practice and headed a Hospital Department. Why was a professional of this caliber not only tolerated, but allowed to advise on Hospital standards?

On another occasion, the same physician was called to the Emergency Room to see a heart patient. A nurse's affidavit again described that the physician refused to see the patient unless someone met him at the door and paid him his thirty dollar fee in advance.

When this fellow came to town, I felt it would be good for the Hospital. He was the first fully qualified internist, and initially gave the impression of stability, and early on, went to some lengths to be friendly. At one point, he had admitted his father from a northern Pennsylvania hamlet to our care. He was one of a series of specialists who had left the Army disgruntled and had heard of the open policy at the local Hospital. He was candid in his disillusionment with Army medicine and I thought little of it. But it seemed a bit strange when he confided that he had fired a young lady from his office - simply because she had left a message for him using his first name. I couldn't understand the severe reaction to a minor social blunder. But, then again, I didn't think any more of it. That is, until he appeared at our office in a late afternoon several months later. He slid into the chair opposite my desk and related the circumstances of his arrival in town. He had written Peter Post; the only physician in town claiming to be an internist, and had asked for advice and help in opening a practice in town. He got no response from Post, but after persisting, finally moved to town and shared an office with Post.

On this occasion, he denounced Post, and wanted an immediate agreement to sell him property and allow him to build an office next to ours. It was difficult to understand another impulsive decision. His agitation was obvious and I felt that I was observing truly aberrant behavior.

I suppose my reluctance to join up with this fellow was obvious. At the time, he would be seen in hushed conversation with the Hospital Psychiatrist. It was at about that time that the psychiatrist had gone through the Hospital corridors in a purple smock decorated with large, white signs of the Zodiac, in response to my beginning to wear a white lab coat on rounds.

After Vader's visit to the office, my entrance into the Hospital the following morning was turbulent, to say the least. Instead of a warm "hello" from the nurses at the Nursing Station just inside the parking lot entrance, I was accosted by my visitor of the previous day. His rage was unmistakable. His eyes, framed by his thick, tortoise shell glasses, were intense. "Doctor", he said, "You just forget that I talked with you yesterday. I don't ever want to join with you out there".

"O.K.", I said, and moved around him and onto the sign-in panel. I would not be surprised in later months and years when Vader would cause me endless trouble as he gained position in the Hospital's political hierarchy - nurtured by a Hospital Administration that thrived on his brand of politics.

Vader then got a small group together and built his office a few blocks away from ours. He then, before long, lost interest in the demands of private practice; sold his office and became a Hospital employee without the need for nighttime service. We would later understand his reasons for such a drastic move to avoid night calls. He was given the reading of the Hospital's cardiograms (quite a plum) and parlayed this source of revenue into an enticement for another Army dissident to come to town and become his lackey. There was no mistaking the fact - he was clever.

This manipulative personality was successful, in great part, due to the presence of the new Administrator hired by the Board Chairman. The new Hospital Administrator first introduced himself in the parking lot early one morning. He was short, balding and his voice was intentionally low, and somewhat muffled. His handshake was weak and he demonstrated a trait of looking from side to side during a conversation. He had bounced around the northern states, serving various hospitals. His most recent position had been at Children's Hospital in Washington, D.C. It was said that he had left after a huge cost overrun and shortage during a construction project. It was apparent he would be compliant as the Board Chairman's marionette. More significantly, he would mirror the Board Chairman's cruelty with employees. It became known that he would not only enjoy the firing process, but would telephone other Hospital administrators throughout the region to blackball a fired employee.

The viciousness of these people went generally unknown for years - probably due in great part, by the veil of secrecy surrounding all Hospital business. Most of the firings left people with no defense against the almost automatic barrage of innuendo.

With the loss of the Hospital's first progressive Administrator, Bill Price, a truly bright light for the future had dimmed, and time would reveal that a vindictive personality had taken over as dictator. No one knew for sure how the transfer of authority had taken place, but the new Board Chairman gradually solidified his position, first through a compliant

Administrator, then with an equally malicious Nursing Director, and finally, an intimidated Medical staff.

The Chairmans' Hospital Board selections established a rubber-stamp outfit of climbers and seekers, in general, knowing little of health care administration. The manager of the local scientific manufacturing plant resigned from the Hospital Board shortly after the change of Chairmanship. He had learned quickly that there was no room for diversity of opinion.

The Chairman's sidekick, a local politician, who served as a County Commissioner for a time, was made the Vice Chairman. There were two women on the Board: one was a woman who ran a small chain saw business and the other a wealthy, aging widow of the owner of a large, successful manufacturing industry. Her cerebration had seen better days.

There was a general contractor and two local lawyers who, at a later date, were reported to have received substantial sums for hospital legal work. Some questioned what work had been performed. An insurance company owner resigned from the Board, denouncing the Chairman's activities. The only member of that Board who knew anything about health care was a professor from the local University who headed a health care department at the University. The editors-publishers of the local newspaper were carefully cultivated by the Hospital Board Chairman, adding to the secrecy of the Hospital operation.

Other businesses represented were a department store owner, who would declare bankruptcy, and then skip town; as well as a ne'er-do-well heir of a local industrial plant. He had been involved in a tragic scandal involving the suicide of an employee's wife. He had married his secretary and presided over the decline of his inheritance. The most controversial of all the appointed Board members was the heir to a gas well business. He reigned over an inherited fortune drilling gas wells. He had himself placed not only on the Hospital Board; but on the Boards of the local University, a private preparatory school, and the local Country Club - drilling wells on all these properties in the process. He managed to have his name put on a generating plant at the University, on brass plates in the Country Club dining room, in an alcove in a local restaurant, on a building at the private school, and finally, on the local ambulance headquarters.

A member of the ambulance Board of Directors described that this benefactor actually substituted his own name for his father's on the ambulance building. Shortly thereafter, the "benefactor" decreed that all ambulance employees use the back entrance, causing a brief turmoil. He created a greater storm when he advised university students to sell cookies to pay for their tuitions. The students dubbed him the "Cookie Monster" in the student newspaper.

The sisters who staffed the Country Club kitchen described that they had never seen anyone enjoy an experience like he did when he fired them without notice. Sadly, the police described his demise with a .357 Magnum in his shower stall.

I haven't been able to forget that afternoon in the office when this troubled fellow came in looking for a friend. He offered to pay for some friendly conversation. I misinterpreted a desperate need for help, and to this day, wish that I had done differently. Whether or not it would have made a difference, no one knows, but at least, I wish that I had tried. Maybe that would have prevented some of the harm he inflicted on a number of others.

From time to time, one would hear comments about our town. Some felt that the town tolerated activities that would, quite likely, not be tolerated elsewhere. It was a beautiful community with some wonderful people, but it seemed always to have a capacity to condone, or at least tolerate, abysmal conduct by certain of its citizens - particularly those of wealth. When I would hear stories from people who had been harmed by the town's elitist group, I would facetiously remark that I thought it was something in the water.

In the early years, the Coal Company had reigned supreme. No law suit against the Company it was said, for example, would have had a chance of success in the local Court. Litigants would, at times, ask for change of venue. The Company always filled a seat on the Hospital Board.

The true agenda of the Hospital would not be revealed for some time. It would turn out that the agenda included the construction of a new hospital building to stand as a memorial to the Board Chairman, and secondarily, the agenda included the elimination from town, those persons whom the Chairman did not admire.

The Hospital's Assistant Administrator, a young accountant acting both as the Chief Financial Officer and the Assistant Administrator, told quite a tale. In an affidavit, he told of being interrogated by the Administrator after the Board Chairman had used his position on a bank Board of Directors to rummage through the young man's financial records at the bank. He, of course, suffered those devastating innuendos when he became another victim. Not surprisingly, he is now the administrator of a West Coast hospital. We had been friends and he would merrily relate that he had been instructed by the Administrator to use his occasional coffee breaks with Dr. Miller to "learn of Dr. Miller's plans and activities; and report back."

His dismissal resulted in no break in the Administrator's espionage network, however. A new Assistant Administrator had been hired and told the same story. He was to use his friendship with Dr. Miller to learn of "Miller's plans".

As before, the system backfired. He also talked at length about the Administrator's activities and duplicity.

The Administrator's brutal delight in cruelty came into full flower with this Assistant. The Assistant's spouse had given birth to a child with severe birth defects. The birth lowered upon them the burden of constant care for the child. The Administrator recommended that the couple put their child under Dr. Miller's care, and at the same time, suggested continuation of the previous espionage. The doctor-patient relationship has continued for years, and the child is now a young woman and still requires constant care.

After some time, the pattern repeated itself. The Administrator relayed that the Board Chairman's disapproval of the Assistant's lifestyle was becoming troublesome. He had moved into the previous Assistant's modest house in a modest neighborhood. He was given his twenty minutes' notice to leave just a few days before Christmas that year. I don't think I ever felt sorrier for anyone. He was putting up a bold front, but the little family had to be devastated. I began to call a few friends in an effort to help and managed to arrange an interview for my friend that led to a new job.

I remember feeling like Scrooge visiting Bob Cratchet's house and seeing Tiny Tim, when on that Christmas Eve, I stopped by and told the little family that their Dad had been selected for the new position.

Bertha Buterbaugh was the Head Nurse on the Hospital's Women's Ward. Bertha was a frail, dark-haired lady with a steady gaze and a sharp tongue. There was never a doubt where you stood with Bertha. While she had a well-developed sense of humor, she was a dedicated professional and was good at what she did.

Somehow, Bertha and I found ourselves working together to do something about the so-called Hospital's Medical Library. For that year, I had been appointed Library Chairman and Bertha was easing off her nursing duties in anticipation of retirement. We had always worked well together and we felt a certain pleasure in throwing out the ancient, yellowing texts and the long since outdated periodicals on those tacky, dull enameled pine shelves in the Medical Staff Room. As the new volumes began to fill the shelves, we subscribed to some modern scientific journals and actually began to improve the appearance of that dingy room. The Administrator finally yielded and had some new oak shelving installed. At the end of the year there was a limited compliment or two, but aside from that, Bertha and I just quietly felt the accomplishment of a job well done. I wrote her a complimentary note praising her help with thanks for an effective effort. Bertha later told me the letter was pressed in a bible on her mantle.

As she was preparing to retire, Bertha quietly expressed her concern at the changes taking place in the Hospital's Nursing Office. The new Director of Nursing was described as a hateful, vengeful person. It had become obvious that she was an integral element in the vindictive triad, including the Administrator and Board Chairman. Bertha called the Nursing Service the Indiana Mafia and confirmed that the early morning coffee clatches in the basement cafeteria, attended by the Nursing Director and her Supervisors, were "assassination sessions". At these daily rituals, nurses and other employees of the Nursing Department could expect to be verbally dissected as a prelude to dismissal. Apparently truth was not an important element for the stories being related.

Probably not surprising, Vance Vader, one of the Army dissidents, now a Hospital department head, was ingratiating himself with the Administrator and the Nursing Director herself. Vader and the Administrator would be another duo seen conferring and would abruptly become silent when someone would come within earshot.

Vader had become President of the Medical Staff and had been part of a coup that had replaced the head of the Department of Surgery with the Opthalmologist who was adroit at politics and social elevation, but not eye surgery. One of the surgeon's wives described the new Surgery Head as "a big over-inflated balloon; and if anyone stuck a pin in him, he would deflate, and there would be a bad odor."

The Chief of Surgery's sin, leading to a nasty telephone campaign and his ouster, was that he, at the Administrator's request, had cautioned an Oriental surgeon against doing major surgery without an assistant. It's hard to imagine the dangers of such a practice, but it led to the Chief of Surgery being ousted by an indelicate and unintelligent coup.

I was so disgusted with the mess created by supposed professionals, that I decided not to serve when Vader appointed me to serve another year in the innocuous position of Library Chairman. That move, on my part, would later become one of the charges brought against me.

After the year of Vader's Presidency, it would later be revealed that the Nursing Director had instructed the Emergency Room nurses to be on the lookout for any unusual occurrence involving Dr. Miller and any such unusual occurrence was to be fully documented and reported directly to her. There were never any such occurrences, but this would be the origin of the affidavit describing Vader's refusal to see an emergency heart patient unless paid in advance.

The Emergency Room Head Nurse, who had been compiling a record as directed, described that when she was on vacation, the Nursing Director had the Maintenance Department of the Hospital pry open her desk. She described that the logs of unusual Emergency Room incidents by Vader and others were never seen again.

At the beginning of another year, I found myself appointed to the Chairmanship of the Infection Control Committee by Dr. Vader, who had been elected Staff President. The Navy years and those that followed had indelibly impressed the need for scrupulously strict sterile technique in Operating Rooms, and I had never seen a significant problem. My operating room team functioned flawlessly in protecting our patients from careless technique and infections. The Committee was required by the Medical Staff Bylaws to meet every other month; so it was a few weeks before we convened our first meeting. The Committee included the Infection Control Nurse and four or five other nurses and physicians. I learned, in a flash, as the minutes of the previous meetings were read, that these meetings had consisted only of a recitation of the list of "hospital acquired infections" that had occurred within the preceding two months. That was it. Apparently, month after month, there would be a reading of a substantial list of patients who had come to the Hospital, infection-free, and who had been given an infection during their stay. We had a dirty hospital!

Carol, the Infection Control Nurse, was a nice girl. We had known each other for several years; and we began holding short meetings to go over past records. If we had seen one, we had seen them all. At meeting after meeting of the Infection Control Committee there would be a recitation of infections - but no solutions.

After a month or so, I seemed to have gained Carol's trust. We met in the empty cafeteria in the basement floor of the Hospital and sat opposite each other at one of the long tables. She produced three pages stapled together from a manilla folder.

She somewhat reluctantly said that she had made a survey of the Operating Rooms and had prepared the report. It had been given to the Nursing Director and there it stopped. Nothing had happened. As I read those three pages, I wondered where I had been. The report detailed dozens of breaks in sterile technique, any one of which could compromise the health or the life of a surgical patient. There was no wonder that the Infection Control meetings had lists of infections every month. The report described: caps not covering hair and sideburns, anesthesia tubing used after being dragged on floor, much talking and laughing during surgical procedures, inadequate hand scrubs, dirty shoes, physicians leaving or returning for another case without clothing change, dirty nitrogen tanks, dirty x-ray equipment, and dirty wheels on stretchers. I had apparently been successful in having the nutty Pathologist stay out of the operating areas in his grimy suit, but the report described all sorts of traffic through the operating areas without precautions - orderlies with contaminated linen hampers and the Pediatrician who regularly walked through in street shoes and clothing. There was a description of people firing contaminated linen across operating rooms into hampers several feet away. I couldn't, at first, believe the later description of a surgeon operating with infected poison ivy on his forearms.

The Chief of the Surgical Department went ballistic one morning when, during surgery on a woman patient, two teenagers walked into his operating room and walked up to the ongoing surgery to observe. After the case, he fired off a firey memorandum to the Administrator, describing the incursion, and blasting the infection control lapses and the loss of privacy for the patient. The Administrator apparently wasn't too concerned, saying that the observers were the teenage son of an Executive Committee member and his girlfriend (the teenager's). The Committee member was Abdul Hankey who was always hustling about in a great hurry with a stethoscope dangling. His posture was such that the instrument would generally precede him by a foot or so.

The Chief Surgeon asked for help and I dictated a short note that the implications of lay visitors in the O.R. were serious and that "observers" were no longer allowed in the Operating Room.

The notices were put in the staff room mail boxes and the record room clerks described that Dr. Vader then went through each mail box and removed the notices.

I then had the notices mailed to the Medical Staff at their offices. Dr. Vader responded with another notice to "disregard" my notices. It appeared that we would again have visitors tramping through the sterile areas of the Operating Room.

It turned out that the Pediatrician who enjoyed walking through the Operating Room in street clothing had been the previous Chairman of the Infection Control Committee. The report compiled by the Infection Control nurse, despite all its documentation, was just the beginning. She reported one day that one of the younger surgeons had changed an infected dressing in a private room and had then gone across the hall and had changed another dressing without even an interval hand wash. An infection had developed in the second surgical wound with bacteria identical to the first.

I met briefly with the Administrator and reported the findings. He agreed to a delay of the second meeting of the Committee and to sponsor my attendance at a large Infection Control conference in Philadelphia. The conference was an eye-opener and highlighted the primitive state of infection control at our Hospital.

On returning, we met with the Hospital's Housekeeper and instituted a program for frequent cleaning and disinfection of the operating suite. The Administrator approved another trip with the Infection Control Committee to meet with a well functioning Infection Control Committee in a large Johnstown hospital.

That meeting was another revelation. The Johnstown hospital's Pathologist and the Infection Control Chairman and Nurse were knowledgable and were helpful. They graphically revealed causes of the Hospital's infection rate that had simply been reported month after month.

During that meeting, Rosemary, our Operating Room Supervisor, took the opportunity to unburden her frustrations, with trying to maintain a safe operating room area. She told of her distaste at having to be a "policeman" with a group of uncooperative physicians. We all glanced at each other when she described that her nurses were refusing to "scrub" with two of the surgeons because of the surgeons' uncontrolled body odor. The physicians from that hospital were friends and I found myself being embarrassed.

I began documenting "hospital acquired infection" with copies of records where infections had occurred and could possibly have been prevented. Suddenly the paranoia was palpable. The Administrator put a notice on the copying machine and then had it locked. He then had the record room locked after the daytime secretaries left for the day.

Dr. Vader, as Medical Staff President, seized the opportunity, and with a certified letter, fired me from the Chairmanship. This would later be one of the charges filed against me - failure to hold enough meetings of the Infection Control Committee.

Vader, however, failed to fire me from the Committee itself and I continued to attend those meetings that were then chaired by the contaminating Pediatrician - reappointed Chairman by Vader.

I recall the final meeting of the Infection Control Committee in the curtained-off meeting portion of the cafeteria. The new Chairman resorted to his old format of listing the month's infections. He asked for comments. My comment was a question: I asked if it were true that he had been walking through the Operating Room in contaminated street clothing. He admitted it and apologized. He said he would discontinue the practice. I complimented him on his frankness; but I don't think he liked the exchange. That concluded the Infection Control adventure; that is - until I found I had to defend Dr. Vader's charge of not holding enough meetings of the Committee.

There was still more than enough to do. A few of us joined with the anesthesia folks to hold classes for the Staff to teach resuscitation and I continued to teach Anatomy and Physiology to the senior nursing students.

During that period, somewhat by coincidence, I was writing on a patient's chart at the nursing station of the Mack Wing. The emergency code flashed on the paging system mounted near the ceiling on the opposite hallway. The telephone operator confirmed that the emergency was on "Mack One". I could see the activity just a few feet down the hallway and got down there in a few seconds.

The scene I came upon, to this day, approaches the inconceivable. I quickly learned that Abdul Hankey, for the second or third day in a row, had been draining a pint of blood from a frail little man in "treatment" of polycythemia. That is a condition where the body marrow manufactures too many red cells. After the poor old fellow had been drained of a large percentage of his circulating blood volume, he had lost consciousness.

There was the man lying flat on his bed and unconscious, with his chin on his chest and not breathing. He was turning blue. The side rails of the bed were up and Abdul, with a nurse, was awkwardly working over the rails to attach cardiograph leads. My God! What was he going to do with a cardiogram? He would have seen the results of a dying heart for lack of oxygen.

I put down the side-rail on my side of the bed; pulled the pillow from under the man's head; tilted his head back and pulled his tongue forward. He took a huge gasp and began breathing. I looked at Abdul, with his dangling stethoscope. He wouldn't look my way. Without a word, I left. This was the fellow who was successfully lobbying to be a "permanent" member of the Hospital Board of Directors.

I was simply dumbfounded by the incompetence that came within about thirty seconds of killing a patient.

Some weeks later, one of the surgeons and I, along with anesthetists, and recovery room nurses, were resuscitating a patient when Abdul appeared. We were too busy to greet him. He left and would later file charges against me for not utilizing his services. The shameless Lester Lazarus would rise at a noontime Medical Staff meeting and excoriate: "The physician who preferred to use only a certain type of physician in an emergency". Yes, true - it was best to use physicians who were competent when a life was at stake. Nevertheless, the failure to use Abdul became yet another charge to defend.

One of the surgeons truly despised Abdul. It was, indeed, understandably troubling to see the staff physicians Peter Post, Claude Clippins, Abdul Hankey, and the notorious Lazarus, exert such a negative influence on anything as important as a Hospital Medical Staff. But I couldn't summon the emotion needed to hate. This would certainly be disputed by the group, but my thoughts on watching this group was more of a disillusionment. The disappointment extended to the top. It took an indifferent, blatantly disinterested Administration to tolerate what was going on.

I became truly amazed when the Administration allowed Abdul to satisfy his ambition to be a permanent member of the Hospital Board of Directors. To me it was a blatant insult to have this character representing the Medical Staff. Many of us had put too much into a career and had too much respect for our profession to have reasonable standards diluted by those who were practicing beyond their competence.

Some light was shed on the question of why the Hospital Administration would have Abdul on the Hospital Board of Directors representing the Medical Staff: A local bank printed an annual report of its shareholders and listed Abdul to be holding thirty four thousand shares of the bank's stock, or 1.6 percent of all the bank's common stock. It appeared that that stock was worth well over a million. How did this fellow come up with that kind of money? This, to a degree, began to explain the interwoven relationships maintained over the years between the Hospital, the Coal

Company, the local newspaper, the banks and the local court. Some of the local townspeople believe that Indiana is just like any other small town. There are others who believe that the numerous, incestuous business relationships create a unique atmosphere that exists in very few other towns. Which group is correct?

Perhaps the answer lies with the town's most famous citizen. My short relationship with Jimmy Stewart was sufficient to reveal a modest, unassuming and truly admirable person. I had serious doubt that he would feel the need to capitalize on his fame in a small town.

Townsfolk understandably then continue to ask who is being promoted by all the Jimmy Stewart activity - Jimmy or the promoters?

We have the Jimmy Stewart Airport, the Jimmy Stewart Museum, the Jimmy Stewart statue in front of the Courthouse and, now, Wayne Avenue is Jimmy Stewart Boulevard. And, recently there is a historic marker in front of the courthouse. I suspect Mr. Stewart would have been a little embarrassed to revisit his hometown.

A somewhat cynical letter, printed in the local paper, reflected on a recently published novel describing Indiana by a former town resident. In particular, the novel describes the statue with the names of the statue committee headed by a woman politician, carved into the marble base. A local news editor was quoted as saying, "In no other place would you find the names of a committee engraved into the base of a celebrity's statue". He is very likely correct.

Jamie Flanagan was a spirited young lady who joined the Medical Staff and was building a general practice in one of the outlying areas of the county. She had a tendency to speak her mind and had been critical of some of the care her patients were receiving. This apparently led to a shouting match with the Director of Nursing, and of course, another call for the discipline waiting for anyone showing disrespect for the Hospital trinity. A disciplinary hearing was set, but Jamie beat "The Boys" to the punch. She sent a letter of resignation to the Hospital Board Chairman.

I thought her letter was a classic. She described, in her own way, that the Chairman was presiding over a backward, non-progressive hospital. The letter read:

> "My first impression of the Indiana Hospital as a regressive and overly economic institution has been reinforced with the passage of time."
>
> "The administrator and some of the supervisory personnel appear to be more interested in making noises with their

mouths than in getting a job done."

"Opportunities for continuing medical education at the Indiana Hospital are nil. The intellectual climate is stifling. I have not seen a staff or departmental meeting brought to order during my ten months here."

"The above considerations, combined with the general unfriendliness of many of the members of the medical staff, have influenced my decision to resign from the Medical Staff of the Indiana Hospital, effective immediately."

Claude Clippins had become one of the political Presidents of the noontime Staff gatherings and announced that he was instituting a "preceptor program"; young medical students would visit and join in teaching rounds with him and his colleagues. The effort was to encourage young students to return to their home town after receiving their degrees. It wasn't clear what the students would learn from Claude, but it was clear that the Medical Staff was to be assessed to pay the students (including offspring of Medical Staff members),a "stipend". One of the surgeons firmly announced that the assessment should be voluntary and some of us agreed.

It would be interesting, over time, to see more pet projects that someone else would be required to pay for. A few students, some of them sons and daughters of staff members, came for awhile during vacations. They were all good kids but none of them cared to return to practice in their home town's Hospital.

In place of Claude's mandatory assessment, I bought a needed piece of blood chemistry equipment for the Hospital. Claude's mandatory assessment was finally made voluntary and he lost interest in becoming a "professor". Later on, however, I would have to face the charge of not paying a staff assessment.

Later, the Hospital files would cough up a letter from Claude to the Dean of the University of Pittsburgh Medical School. The letter accused me of contacting the Dean to scuttle the preceptorship program. His letter said he had been accused of staffing the Program with "incompetent second rate physicians." Whether this was true or not, the Medical School Dean and I had never heard of one another.

Everyone was required to attend those staff meetings. An attendance rate of less than fifty percent would bring "discipline", but the meetings had become ridiculous charades.

At one noontime, I went through the cafeteria line, picked up a cup of coffee and teased the cashier a little - she was a patient of ours. I walked through the folding doors into the dining room section where the meetings were held. I found a seat at one of the long tables and hoped the meeting would get started on time. It did. But, the sliding doors would continue to open and close, admitting tray-carrying physicians who would shop around the small audience for a friendly seat. The reading of the minutes blended with the accompaniment of rattling knives and forks, the banging of the sliding door and the buzz of conversations. There followed a recitation of old business, none of which had direct bearing on the quality of care; and then a call for new business. I found myself asking for the floor and made a motion to adopt a resolution requiring Robert's Rules of Order as a standard for the conduct of future meetings. There seemed to be an instant lull in the cacophony. One could almost hear the wheels turning. After an instant or two, the Chairman asked for a second. There was none and the lunchtime tumult resumed.

There were some unwritten rules for those gatherings: one that was never violated dictated that a Medical Staff member would never be discussed if he were present. The circulating group running the show would never discuss anyone present. They would always manage to wait for a meeting when their target was in absentia.

By the time the disgruntled Army doctor, Vance Vader, joined the Medical Staff, the meetings included recitation of interesting cases. Lester Lazarus had demonstrated an ability to rattle off a case with some skill. Vader did the same and his cases usually described the death of a difficult case. At the time of the "preceptorship" issue, Vader felt called upon to deliver his "backbone speech." The minutes of that meeting describe Vader's warning to the assembled group that they were "heading for big trouble" if they didn't have the "backbone" to discipline anyone who didn't pay for their childrens' "stipend". He didn't mention that his daughter was one of the recipients. The charge I would face later was "failure to pay regular staff assessments", even though the levies had become voluntary.

One would think that there would be some degree of humility shown by a new arrival on the Medical Staff. Not so. A Pediatrician, who apparently had worn out his welcome at a Philadelphia area hospital immediately gave the noontime assembly, week after week, his views on any number of subjects. No one would seem to notice that this character was not making sense. His excursions through the sterile areas of the Operating Suite were similarly without reason.

The majority of new arrivals to the hospital's Medical Staff were the disgruntled Army people and foreign medical graduates. Former Army Surgeon, Hank Bailey, helped them come to town. Hank had been a Colonel in the Army Medical Corps. He returned to his hometown to begin a successful surgical practice. But, his life became a tragedy even though his presence led to the influx of other Army specialists who were learning of Indiana's open door policy.

Hank and I were friends and I assisted him at surgery from time to time. But, it began to be obvious that he was "high" at times - even when performing intricate surgery.

I got an unexpected call from an out of town psychiatrist one afternoon and learned that Hank and two of his children had been admitted to the Psychiatric Ward of a hospital for treatment of drug addiction. I did what I could to help and the family was later released. Hank and I talked out his problems from time to time but the news announced, out of the blue one evening, that Hank's wife had been found dead from a drug overdose and that Hank had been arrested and charged with homicide. I visited him at the local lockup and testified for him at trial. Not one of the Army group that he had helped come to town, nor any other physician, attended the trial. Hank was devastated by their disloyalty. His practice never recovered, after he had served his jail sentence. He shortly thereafter died from a brain tumor.

During one of our chats, Hank had described one of his Army friends, who had come to town, as being "unusual". This was the one who reflected a macho image. He was the one who had made Hospital rounds wearing leather clothing and boots. He was the one who kept vicious dogs, a firearm collection and had been featured in the local paper as a karate expert. Some of the Medical Staff began referring to him as "Dr. Karate-Chop". He would tell patients that the animal trophies in his office were his kills. Hank related that they were actually his trophies that had been given to Karate-Chop. Hank would later relate, in an affidavit, that this former friend bragged that he had killed a man in a South Philadelphia street fight.

Hank's legacy would continue to be felt. Of the Army group, Vader, and those who would listen to him, would exert their influence for some time to come.

Chapter 12

"There is nothing more difficult to take in hand, more perilous to conduct or more uncertain in its success than to take the lead in the introduction of a new order of things."

— *Machiavelli*

The Medical Center

The system based on the image of the loving family doctor was becoming a deception. The unselfish, fatherly family doctor had been replaced by a new breed of generalist, all too often dedicated to their own monetary interests and status than to the welfare of their patients. All too often, their patients without question, would trustingly follow their advice. Often, the patients' specialty care would be provided not by the most qualified, but by their physician's social or economic preferences.

The local surgeon's loss of referrals from a local generalist, after he built a new home near the generalist, was not an anomaly. It was a pattern. Envy in the medical community was intense. People who had had the benefit of the finest of educations were displaying the behavior of children in a sand box. The wives were, by no means, detached from all this.

The patients themselves were not blameless. Many knew they wanted the best in care, and of these patients, many preferred that someone else pay for it. They often would, unquestioningly, choose a hospital based on convenience or simply on the family doc's instructions. The opportunity for a "second opinion" was always there, but "second opinions" were almost a rarity. There were some patients, however, who used the privilege of self-referral to a specialist, without the family doc's approval. This, of course, led to the phrase to be used endlessly in the future:

"free choice of physician". Those patients who exercised their right of free choice would have care more likely free of political and monetary considerations.

As surely as God made little apples, there would be opposition - perhaps trouble, but I had to try. I had chosen the place. The Community had been good to us and the Community deserved the finest in health care.

It was almost an unconscious, automatic decision. I had already found that I could help young physicians come to the Community and be successful and contribute. I knew that a group of generalists and specialists working together could do much to bring up-to-date Medicine to the Community and to the Hospital.

Buttressing the notion of the need for a group practice was the vacuous, intractable mindset of the Hospital crowd to maintain the status-quo at all costs. The round-robin system allowing those with the least training and experience (and sometimes the least talent), to control the destiny of hospital patients, flew in the face of logic. A multi-specialty group practice would eliminate many of the problems of the local Hospital and help provide the community and the Hospital with efficient, reliable, multi-specialty health care.

It appeared likely that the opposition to a group practice would come through the local Medical Society. I never dreamed that a hospital claiming to be a local charity would enter into even a semblance of opposition. After all, the Hospital's Administrator, several of the Medical Staff families and several of the Hospital Board members were patients of mine.

A little research was in order. The miner's union had been an influence throughout the Appalachian region and had operated several hospitals providing care to the union members. There had been opposition to their influence throughout Western Pennsylvania and I had been caught between union factions in the past. But, through that experience, Tom Berett, the guiding light of the mine worker's health plan in the state, became a fast friend.

Tom was by no means a novice. He knew of the intrigue surrounding hospitals and physician activities. He had been in many a battle with well-entrenched health care forces. He was a little surprised when I called his Johnstown office and was more surprised when I inquired into the feasibility of a multi-specialty group practice in the County. Without hesitation, he asked if I knew a certain nursing home Administrator named Melba. I did know her. She had been a patient and I knew her to be very successful in running a quality area nursing home.

At Tom's suggestion, I contacted Melba and found her not only interested, but enthusiastic on the prospect of having highly qualified physicians practice as a group in the county. We met with Tom after a medical conference at the Chatham Center in Pittsburgh and decided to hold a meeting of local citizens, to determine interest in a group practice facility to bring improved care to the community. It was certainly a memorable evening when we met at our office with a group of local citizens. The enthusiasm of the group for our project varied from luke warm to supportive but the main attraction was a local preacher's wife. The woman was pretty - and she knew it. She would, on occasion, be seen at a speaker's table rolling her eyes with quick head turns and blinking mascara. Her teaching duties were before high school students.

In the midst of our presentation, the narcissistic lady loudly interrupted and commenced a lengthy harangue, painting our proposed project as a horrific plan to undermine the practices of the area's devoted physicians. Our efforts to answer her questions were promptly dismissed. We were not adept at either combating or lessening a challenge that was fracturing our meeting and we closed the meeting without a clear signal of where we should go from there. More accurately, we were inept at reading a clear signal of what was yet to come.

We later were told that the unusual Lester Lazarus had heard of our proposed plans and had sent the lady to torpedo the meeting. Lester, with his unbridled sense of self-fulfillment, would later be quoted as threatening to "burn down the building" if we were successful with any government grants. The preacher's wife continued in her teaching duties. But we heard later, that she and the preacher, when they separated from the town, separated from each other.

Of course there were thoughts of enlisting the help of the Hospital. It was obvious, at least to us, that a group of physicians using the Hospital would be welcome. On the other hand, it didn't make sense to trust the Hospital's administration to help in a project which they quite likely would not understand. We also didn't account for the Hospital people's insecurity which would allow them to view our plans as a threat.

Melba and I formed a partnership and decided upon a modest building to house the enterprise. It was a pre-fabricated "double-wide". I recall combining business with pleasure when a group of us drove to the Notre Dame campus for a Pitt-Notre Dame classic. We saw a prototype of the new building at the factory - not far from the Notre Dame campus.

It is strange what past events leave with us. On that trip, Tom Berett and one of the local surgeons went along. Tom was never known as a big spender, but his surgeon-roommate had elevated frugality to an art form. During the trip he had demonstrated a complete paralysis on each occasion, when a check would be presented. But, just as the trip was ending, and as we passed through the Turnpike toll booth, he sprung to the rescue with a flair. The toll was three dollars and five cents. While we all fumbled for change to go with our three "ones", he announced, "Here's the nickel." We had, all along, suspected that he had a nickel hidden somewhere.

The real challenge to opening the Center was recruitment. To the chagrin of many of "The Boys", a few years earlier, I had put an ad in the journal of the Pennsylvania Medical Society for an obstetrician. The town's only O.B. guy had become disillusioned with private practice and had left town for a job with a baby food company. There had been several responses to the ad, but very few young O.B. men were interested in a solo O.B. practice. One exception was the lumbering Fazio who had answered the ad. After his long distance response, I was not convinced that he would be an asset, but he persisted - probably because of no other offers. I did help him come to town and get started. He practiced with a mediocre style and, predictably, had become one of "The Boys."

Logically, it appeared reasonable to begin the new group practice with two or more internists. These men and women who had met the requirements for a general practice and had gone on for an additional three or more years of specialty training could, more than likely, form the core of a multi-specialty group. But, (and it's a very large but) these physicians were in demand and it proved difficult to persuade them to enter an unknown situation where they would have to build a practice from scratch. The old, self-confident desire of physicians for independence was gone, and most were looking for a ready-built practice. They were looking for regular hours, many fringes and lots of money.

One husband and wife team came to town and spent a weekend with us looking around. It was a little difficult to be enthusiastic about the Hospital situation, so I decided to take the bull by the horns and let the couple see for themselves.

Sunday mornings were a time when the Hospital Docs would gather in the Hospital Staff Room to exchange the latest gossip. On cue, the coffee urn and a large plate of cookies would be wheeled in on a stainless steel cart. I decided to take the husband and wife team to that cheery little gathering and introduce them around. In addition to the dreary little room itself, the expressions on those faces let us know that we were about as welcome as a skunk at a picnic. There were perfunctory introductions followed by a pall. Just about all conversation ceased and the young couple and I found ourselves sitting there looking at each other. I don't think our visitors sensed hostility. I think they were just amazed at that mute, brainless gathering. Yet, there was hostility there. These new people were, indeed, a threat to the old guard. In a few days, I got a well-written, thoughtful letter from my guests. They had decided to try their fortune in Williamsport, Pennsylvania.

    A change in planning was in order. A more likely nucleus for a group would be pediatricians. The local Pediatrician had encouraged Hamilton Burger to visit Indiana after they had met at an out of town meeting. The burdens of being the only pediatrician in town had forced him into a state of impending exhaustion. He would welcome the guy who, for his own reasons, was anxious to give up a practice near Philadelphia. The fellow was said to have been a Marine drill sergeant. I had known Marine drill sergeants and this man didn't look like a drill sergeant. As a matter of fact, he didn't look like a doctor. The first time I saw him was at a noontime staff meeting. He probably hadn't been in town a month when he rose and went into a rambling discourse covering a number of subjects. I had become more or less hardened to inane discussions at those noon-time meetings, but this guy was very obviously out of touch. I looked around during the speech and it appeared that no one got the same impression. He was fitting right in. Time would prove that he wouldn't restrict his eloquence to Medical Staff meetings. He would show up at all sorts of public gatherings and give one group after another his wisdom on just about any subject.

    One of the outlying school districts found itself in the midst of an epidemic of head lice. The school nurse began examining the children to stem the wild spread of the pests. The school superintendent supported her efforts but related that he had gotten a frantic phone call from the new Pediatrician, wildly decrying the school's efforts, claiming it interfered with medical care of the students. Here was a superintendent, a sensible, reasonable fellow, asking me if the pediatrician was all there. I could only agree that there was some doubt as to whether this orator was playing with a full deck. But probably, predictably, he would provide a regular noontime oration and became one of "The Boys". He saw no problem with arriving in a new locale and immediately campaigning to block any competition.

The new Pediatrician Burger's opposition to other competition was total and unrestrained. He demonstrated a complete dearth of decency and awareness of acceptable behavior. Yet he was appointed Infection Control Chairman to arrest the spread of infection in the Hospital. He would later be cited for engaging in an altercation in the Hospital parking lot. The Administrator would announce, after that episode, to all, that Burger was to be disciplined; but he never was. There was perhaps some room for understanding this fellow - after all, what kind of parent would want a child going through life with a handle like Hamilton Burger?

Our weekend entertainment of various internists, nearing completion of their residency, had been non-productive, but we had discovered that there were pediatricians finishing their training who were looking for places to practice. I had met with officers of the American Group Practice Association in Washington and representatives of several medical societies. They were helpful in providing names of qualified candidates for our venture. There were many weekend hours on the phone contacting these young, soon-to-be graduates. It was a difficult chore. I travelled to Philadelphia, Washington, Cincinnati and other towns to meet with young pediatricians who would possibly like the challenge of a new entity - a group practice with the advantages and security of a group and also the promise of independence.

A young husband and wife from Ohio State visited on a weekend and were shown around the Hospital and around town. Melba would take time to show prospective couples around town and I would show them around the Hospital and the Pediatric floor. Patsy and his wife were pleasant and both seemed impressed by the town and our new building, which was nearing completion. There was another visit with the couple a few weeks later when the couple asked for a contract. They wanted time for their lawyer to review the document. We sent along the document that we had drawn up. It detailed salary, vacation time, payment for attendance at medical meetings and what we learned was a "restrictive covenant". The covenant was generally part of any employment contract stating that if the physician left the group practice he would not compete with the group in the immediate area for a year or so. The organizations helping us get started advised this clause as a protection against a physician coming to town, accepting salary, goodwill and support in building a practice and then leaving, taking the practice with him.

Shortly after we sent the contract, Patsy began a series of letters and evening phone calls. There were all sorts of questions and it became evident that we simply weren't being trusted. As a matter of fact, distrust was so obvious I felt inept at trying to combat it. I was truly uncomfortable at trying to calm the growing apprehension. I had never given thought to the possibility that young physicians would be so demanding or so incredulous. Melba was great at finding common ground with the young doctors we were entertaining, but we were both finding it uncomfortable in consoling so many immature doubts.

During a brief golf outing at Hilton Head, I was making every attempt to forget the recruiting for a few days when the recruiting problem hit full force. When we returned to our room, after the day's golf, the red light on the phone was blinking. The operator advised that I was to call Doctor Patsy at Ohio State.

I called, and it was to answer another series of questions. I was truly uneasy. I was beginning to feel helpless. The years of training in a surgical specialty had demanded self discipline and an ability to handle difficult situations, but I was not gaining in this situation.

There was a final weekend trip to Indiana by Patsy and his wife. We reviewed his contract and he advised that he and his lawyer found it fair and generous. He would return it, signed, in a few days. After dinner at a Philadelphia Street restaurant, the couple shook hands with many thanks and left for Ohio.

In the following mid-week, a hand-addressed letter arrived from Patsy. Over three or four handwritten pages, Patsy poured out his heart. He had hoped for a practice in a beautiful town like Indiana, but, with each trip to town, he had lost trust in me. He didn't know what he was going to do but he would not be coming to Indiana. Melba and I did some serious soul-searching in trying to find an answer and struck out. We didn't have a clue as to what was going on. Patsy would go to Sunbury and start a pediatric practice in a building his mother built for him.

Within a week, the mystery was solved. One of the Hospital nurses advised that after Patsy's first visit to the pediatric wing, another nurse named Ewing had phoned Hamilton Burger with Patsy's name. Then began a series of very long evening phone calls to Patsy at Ohio State by Burger and his wife, designed to cast doubt on our integrity. The shock was not so much that these people would enter into such a dastardly enterprise, but that people like them could be persuasive. It would be only the beginning of the campaign by this buffoon and his physical therapist spouse.

The Group Practice Association had provided a list of Pediatricians who had registered with them. It was taking many weekend hours to contact these folks, but a telephone conversation was proving more enlightening and helpful than any amount of correspondence. One call to Harrisburg and the Polyclinic Hospital was most helpful. A young lady, nearing the end of her residency, was interested in practicing in a smaller community. She would visit on her next weekend off duty.

Carol was a pleasant girl with a nice smile. She was a contrast to some of the demanding young physicians and spouses we had been entertaining. We stopped off at the Country Club for a sandwich after I had shown her around the hospital and the town. There were few members around on that Saturday afternoon as we chatted in the grill room. Conversation came easily and it became apparent that Carol wanted to join with us. We showed her the new building - almost completed, and she staked out a room for her new office.

It took very little time for a contract to be signed and Carol advised that she would return it during the upcoming weekend.

We were again in the grill room on a Sunday afternoon and Carol sprung the surprise. She matter-of-factly advised that her transition to a small town practice would be much smoother if I would agree to hire one of the clerks from her residency program to be her secretary.

I was a little skeptical of the arrangement, but it seemed likely that the only way to begin staffing the practice, at this point, was to allow the two women to come together. Come together they did.

Melba helped them get settled. They settled together setting up housekeeping in a modest bungalow on one of the town's quiet side streets that Melba had helped them rent.

With a bit of advertising in the local paper and with a number of introductions, the group practice was becoming a reality. Three internist friends from Pittsburgh began building part-time practices and Carol and her secretary began seeing increasing numbers of children.

One of the internists related that he got a strange call from a Doctor Vader who said that he was the "Chief of Staff" at the Hospital and inquired about the listing we had placed in the phone directory. "Did he authorize the use of his name in the local directory?" The call ended as strangely as it began. Our internist promised to look into the matter and call back. However, he never did. He advised us that Vader would be a problem for all of us. This of course came as no news.

Once we were established, recruiting seemed to be a little easier. We got a call from a Matt McGee, in Cincinnati. He and his wife had heard of our plans and would like to visit. He did and was openly enthusiastic. Matt felt he could work well with Carol and they could provide evening and weekend coverage for each other. The original town pediatrician seemed pleased for the relief and agreed to share in the coverage.

Matt rented a large frame house in a small village near Indiana and brought Elsa and his two small children to town. Things began to look up for the group practice. The internists were making regular visits and were establishing themselves in the area and Carol and Matt were demonstrating their skills as the practices grew.

Almost overnight, clouds began to roll in. Perhaps the Pediatricians were doing too well. When I would flip my switch on the Hospital sign-in light, it would blink. This would indicate a message, and invariably, it would be Carol in pediatrics, needing to see me at once. I would find Carol in the little pediatric treatment room in tears. Here I was, due in the operating room, attempting to comfort a tearful physician. I could never quite determine what was causing the tears, but eventually it became evident that the tearful episodes were following some sort of encounter with Burger in the Department.

I did my best to reassure Carol; and then things would calm down for a few days only to recur with another tearful episode.

When Matt arrived, he had begun interviewing young women to hire as an assistant. We met after hours one late afternoon to discuss his applicants. He had narrowed the search to two girls. He openly admitted that one was well qualified but that the other was more attractive. He offered to abide by my advice but needed to have the assurance of making the decision. He decided to hire the more attractive, Thelma Lou.

Thelma Lou did well, but began bringing her young son to the office after school. He must have been a holy terror and office hours must have been in turmoil when he was there. I had my secretary go to the other building in the afternoons to help keep things in order; but now, there was conflict between Thelma Lou and the other girls.

We would learn that Carol would stay in her office while her live-in secretary saw the patients. The two of them were showing a close relationship and would regularly leave together in mid-afternoon and for long weekends early on Fridays. They were refusing to see walk-in patients.

If I felt impatient and near helplessness during the recruiting process, I felt doubly so now. I can't say that I was greatly surprised when a small note appeared. It had been carelessly left on a desk in the other building. In large imperfect scrawl, it read, "Matt, I love you". At about this time, Matt's spouse appeared at our office one afternoon and announced that Matt was leaving her and the kids. She didn't know where she would go. My God, neither did I. I called Melba in and we attempted to sort out the complexities of our fledgling group practice. Group practice? It was a love nest.

Strangely enough, the pediatricians were practicing good medicine. But this was a double edged sword. Matt reported seeing the babies with injuries caused by rough deliveries at the Hospital and had to arrange for their care in Pittsburgh's Children's Hospital. It was at that time that we first heard the whisper of an infant being decapitated during delivery.

Carol finally asked to be relieved of her contract. She and her secretary left quietly to open a practice and housekeeping together in Lebanon, Pennsylvania. In reflecting, Carol and her secretary probably never planned to stay in Indiana - they probably meant to return to their home town after saving enough to get started.

Matt gave every indication of working with us to recruit another partner. But, after he entertained a pediatrician and wife who showed an interest in the group practice, we learned that he had urged the fellow to join him after he had "jumped contract". By this time, Matt had left his wife and his kids and the local child welfare agency reported that he was not providing child support. On one occasion, he got into a street fight with Thelma Lou's husband. Without a doubt, I was becoming convinced that honest young physicians, with reasonable standards, were perhaps hard to find.

I often went to the office on Sunday mornings to catch up on reading. On that particular Sunday, there was a knock on the reception room door. It was Matt. "I want to talk to you" he said.

"O.K. sit down". He sat on a chair to one side of the reception room door and I settled onto the arm rest of the reception room sofa. We stared at each other for a moment and he opened with "I'll have to have more money". "If I don't get an increase, I'll leave".

"Don't you know you have a contract?"

"Yes, but if I break it, I'll have support", he replied.

"Who told you this, Matt?"

He shot back, "The other Pediatricians. They told me I should have twice what I'm getting".

We parted without further comment except that I expected us both to honor our contract.

Matt didn't know that the most recent Pediatrician recruit had phoned us and had advised of Matt's plans to use him to help break his contract and with the help of "The Boys". A Greensburg friend in the medical supply business had phoned also and had advised that McGee had already ordered furniture for his new office.

McGee was bright - that is, he could memorize a page in a flash and he could recite facts without a flaw. But he was without reasonable morals. Even Lester Lazarus, hardly a font of professional morality, would observe that McGee came to town for a "cheap divorce."

Within a few days, McGee's certified letter arrived announcing that he was breaking his contract unless his salary was doubled. There was simply no doubt. I just couldn't allow McGee to break his contract with the support of the Hospital group and walk away with the results of all our work in helping him succeed. It was becoming obvious that his early parentless life had left him bitter and without principle.

John DeMay, a lawyer friend in Pittsburgh, advised that our contract was valid and offered to intercede in order to avoid a head-on confrontation. His letter to McGee did no good and we decided there was no choice. DeMay went to the local Court and filed a breach of contract action. The Court determined that the contract was valid and that the restrictive covenant was reasonable. McGee was enjoined from practicing within twenty five miles of the group practice for two years.

The uproar was immediate. The local newspaper rose to the challenge. The evening paper worked me over in proud fashion. It printed "letters to the editor" castigating me for driving a dedicated healer from town. Burger and spouse sprung into action. The couple joined with a local ladies club in the fracas, and those willing dupes wrote letters, signed petitions, planned appearances at Court and we were told that they were planning a demonstration with T.V. crews at my office.

The Honorable Robert Earley, of the Court of Common Pleas folded. He reversed himself and allowed McGee to return to practice, but scheduled a hearing.

I expected the hearing to be a quiet little gathering late that afternoon. But about twenty or so of the Hospital physicians filed in and sat quietly in the Courtroom. They were obviously there to intimidate His Honor.

Earley heard testimony from the Hospital Administrator and one of the town's Pediatricians that the loss of McGee would pose a "serious and immediate threat to the health of the community". The Judge asked the Administrator, who testified of the dire need for McGee's services, why Doctor Miller could recruit pediatricians and he could not. The Administrator answered, "I don't know". After the town's Senior Pediatrician, awkwardly sitting in the witness stand testified, DeMay uncharacteristically turned and whispered, "Who is that guy? I think he is the worst witness I have ever seen". The Judge must have thought so too. He announced that our case was valid and set the date for a full hearing on the suit.

The group of McGee's supporters filed quietly and sullenly from the rear of the courtroom. DeMay and I sat quietly at the conference table as the Judge descended from his perch and left the Court. John looked pleased. He said something to the effect that he "had to laugh at that bunch of monkeys filing out of here".

Again, we were front page headlines in the evening chronicle and "The Boys" plastered the clipped stories over the Hospital staff room bulletin board.

I was making an effort to keep the uproar from the family but, Donnelly's newspaper made that impossible. Donnelly had been a friend, and during the time of our Philadelphia Street office, he and I would occasionally share a coffee break and would have spirited conversations. Joe had been a reporter, of sorts, but his status had changed dramatically when he married the daughter of one of the chronicle's owners. His friendship changed, in like fashion, when the new Chairman took over the Hospital Board and appointed Joe to that Board. It had to be, for Joe, another great step socially. For the new Hospital Board Chairman, it was the beginning of his quest for prominence as an outstanding citizen, fortified by the newspaper photos of his civic activities.

I would find that Joan would retrieve the evening paper by opening the front door and spreading the paper with her foot as it fell inside. I guess it was to ease the shock of another front page lynching by one of the paper's reporters - a young red-headed girl who seemed to enjoy her new-found importance. As hurtful as the unfairness of all that publicity was, I began to grow accustomed to it and could see why someone once proclaimed that he didn't care what they said about him, so long as they spelled his name correctly. It wasn't that simple for the family. A father certainly hopes for respect from his sons and I was being painted as a despot, threatening the health of the community.

If anyone ever doubted the damage that recklessness with the truth by a newspaper can inflict on a family, they may be inclined to read an anonymous letter I received at about that time. In a woman's handwriting it read:

"Dear Dr. Miller;

You don't know me nore (sic) do I know you only by what I hear and read in the paper. Through it all I have become very concerned about you. Your are still young and your (sic) a good doctor and so many people need you and there is a way out that will make the people highly respect you and other doctors envy you.

Find a place where you can be alone and fall on your knees and ask God to forgive you. Confess your sins and ask the Lord Jesus to apply His blood and wash you white as snow. 'Come now and let us reason together, Saith the Lord: though your Sins be as Scarlet, <u>they shall</u> be as white as snow; though they be red like crimson, <u>they shall</u> be as wool' Isaih 1"18 God loves you and if you will come clean and tell the people you are sorry God will honor you and make you a real blessing.

I am praying for you.

A Christian"

In addition, just about the most hurtful thing that I could ever remember was my younger son reporting the goading on the school bus that his father was a "quack".

I have never entertained the possibility of "Christian forgiveness" for the local newspaper's role in the "character assassination."

The new Courthouse on Philadelphia Street was a beautiful edifice of colonial red brick with large stone columns flanking the entrance. Many thought it a political boondoggle, pointing out that the old Courthouse was an elegant structure and that it could have been renovated reasonably. Some of the town's lawyers complained of the new courthouse's poor design.

For me ,on the morning of the hearing before Judge Earley, the building was lacking in any manner of beauty. DeMay and I walked up the wide, granite front steps, across the decorative, wide brick walk, up another tier of granite steps, and opened the heavy white doors into a small foyer and then the lobby. The polished terrazzo floor reflected light from the Recorder's Office on the left and the Prothonotary's Office on the right. John was carrying a large fiber envelope and pressed the elevator button on the left.

There were two colonial style court rooms on the fourth floor and we found ourselves entering the double maple doors into Judge Earley's court on the left. The hallway was mainly deserted but, as we entered, we found the entire spectator section of the court packed with women. John and I sat at one of the counsel tables in front of the elevated Judge's bench. John shook hands with McGee's new Pittsburgh lawyer; he had fired the local lawyer - apparently with rancor.

I could only marvel as I looked at that audience of young mothers, that people like Burger and Spouse, could influence so many young women.

The tipstaff gave his "hear ye, hear ye" announcement that the Court was in session. We all rose and Earley modestly allowed us to return to our seats. He called both lawyers to the bench and there was a quiet discussion among the three for a few minutes. The Judge rose and advised that Counsel was to join him in chambers.

There was a buzz from the feminine gallery and the Judge and both lawyers left through a door behind the bench and were out of sight for a time. The ladies quieted and we all sat there without looking at each other. Finally, John returned and came over to the conference table. He asked me to join them. McGee was left to sit sullenly in front of the ladies.

McGee's lawyer, the spouse of a soon-to-be federal jurist in Pittsburgh, pleasantly shook hands and advised that all concerned had agreed that the case should be settled. The pediatric practice did, indeed, belong to the Medical Center and he was advising McGee to compensate the Center for their investment - in effect, to purchase the practice. He and DeMay had agreed on a price to be paid over a period of several years. John advised that I accept, and I did. The practice was worthless without a pediatrician and it was plain that McGee could not steal the practice - even with the support of "The Boys."

We all returned to a hushed court room and took our places. The Judge announced that Doctor Miller had reasonably accepted an offer to settle and that Doctor McGee would continue his own practice in town. The courtroom burst with loud applause and a few feminine squeals. After they quieted, the Judge then asked for applause for Doctor Miller. I was dumbfounded; but on the surface it appeared as a reasonable solution. McGee was given the opportunity to purchase a practice rather than steal it.

Not many knew that this was the first round of an effort by the Hospital thugs to destroy my reputation, perhaps me, and perhaps my family.

The pleadings that McGee's lawyer had presented to the Court were typical of a lawyer's enthusiasm for overstatement of the facts. I was painted as a penny-pinching tyrant, expecting twenty-four hour toil from the Medical Center employees. John and I took it all with a liberal grain of salt, but the red-headed lady reporter dutifully reprinted all the insults on the local paper's front page.

Of great concern though, was a separate paragraph in one of the motions to the court stating, "... and Doctor Miller is in danger of losing his hospital privileges...". This was, indeed, threatening and ended any doubt about McGee's ties with "The Boys."

John petitioned the Court to expunge that remark from the court records. The Court did so, and all the records had that remark obliterated. It was obliterated from the records, but not from our minds. I was most definitely a target to be run out of town.

McGee left his wife and young children and must have been amazed when the support for his new practice didn't materialize. He finally left for Denver, with Thelma Lou and her child. As bright as he was at memorization, I suspect that, to this day, he doesn't realize how badly he was used by the Hospital gang. This time, when he left, there was no public outcry that the town was losing a devoted healer. He just simply disappeared from the scene.

We knew, by now, that there was a concerted effort to also have me leave. We also knew that I had no such plans.

Chapter 13

"Physicians without conscience is the ultimate evil"

— *Robin Cook*

THE KANGAROO COURT

It was the twelfth of February and the time, about seven P.M. The Emergency Room Physician was on the line.

"Ralph, I have an eighty-one year old gentleman here, who has been passing blood for some time, but he also has some chest congestion by x-ray and I'd like your advice. Should I admit him to your service?"

I knew Lee to be conscientious and had welcomed him as the first Emergency Room Physician employed by the Hospital. The Hospital had finally decided to staff the Emergency Room in place of demanding that the Medical Staff provide the Hospital's emergency care in their offices, without any form of compensation. Most of the "emergencies" needed only routine care.

"Lee, use your own judgement, but the urinary blood seems to be the presenting symptom".

"O.K., I've already worked him up and have written orders. There's no urgency. He has a slight fever and a few chest findings. He'll be on the third floor".

"O.K., Lee, I'll see him in the morning. Have the nurses call if there's any change".

Thus was the beginning of the opportunity that "The Boys" had been waiting for. I saw the elderly gentleman early the next morning after going over his chest x-ray with the radiologist. There was a minor chest infiltrate and a mild fever, but our major problem was the long-standing urinary blood.

After another examination and confirmation of the patient's history, I explained to the elderly gentleman that we would take a few days to clear up his pneumonitis and then investigate the source of his bleeding. Keflex was the antibiotic I ordered, as well as a culture, to determine what bacterium was present and what antibiotic would be most effective in treatment.

When the culture results came back, forty-eight hours later, the results showed that the most effective antibiotic had been ordered. The patient's temperature had dropped to normal. The patient was up and around and did look better to his family, even though they had advised that their Dad had resisted medical care for years.

The date now is February 16th. - four days after admission - about seven o'clock in the evening. Velma Marshall, a Nursing Supervisor, is on the line and advised that my postoperative patient, Reverend Englert, is "in retention" and needs a catheter. Nurse Marshall was one of the senior nurses I had held classes for, to teach the techniques of catheterization and sterile technique. It had been an effort to avoid catheterization of the Hospital's patients by orderlies who were, generally, young men without any significant training for catheterization or sterile technique.

I advised nurse Marshall that if she was unable to take care of the patient personally, I would come to the Hospital.

It is now about eight o'clock, and there is another call from nurse Marshall. She is now on the third floor and reports that my elderly patient has had a cardiac arrest. Dr. Vance Vader is there and has taken charge of the resuscitation with the help of the Anesthesia Department and several nurses and orderlies. I tell nurse Marshall I will stay on the line until she can report back. In several minutes she reports that the patient did not respond and has been "pronounced". I tell her that I will be the one to call the family. I call the oldest son of the patient and relate to his wife the disturbing news with condolences. They are not surprised, again calling attention to their Dad's long-standing refusal of medical attention. I offer any help that may be needed and advise them to call back if I can be of assistance.

It was unusual for Doctor Vader to be in the Hospital on an evening. He had gone to great lengths to avoid evening duty while in private practice - attempting to shift the care to his compliant partner. On this occasion, he had apparently been reading cardiograms, which were needed for the following morning's surgery.

At about midnight, nurse Marshall signs a log in the Hospital's Record Department and takes the deceased patient's full chart from the Department. She will later admit that it was on Doctor Vader's orders.

Two days later there was something in the air as I passed the first floor Mack nursing station on the way to check in. Mrs. Swishelm kept to her writing as I passed, without the usual greeting. A group of "The Boys" at the Coke machine hushed up as I passed; and were obviously in the process of cooking something up. There was though, a friendly wave from Mary, the cleaning lady, in her starched light green uniform, from down the hall in Men's Ward.

Hospital rounds were routine that morning and there was no surgery. I took a few charts from my stack in the record room. There was time for a little dictation before office hours. On top of the pile was the chart of my deceased patient and I noted that the resuscitation record had been added. This was routine, but I was surprised at the number of people who had been listed as present at the time of the emergency. I didn't look at the chart carefully, but I dictated a final discharge summary and went on to other charts.

In mid-afternoon, at the office, I heard our mailman talking with the girls up front as a patient was leaving. They handed me a certified letter from the Hospital. "The Boys" always attached great significance to a certified label. It was, apparently, thought to impart great authority to one of their memos.

The letter read: "As President of the Medical Staff, I have received a report questioning your management of the case of ..., case no. 320,120, with particular regard to the fact that the primary diagnosis was one of respiratory disease, the treatment of which is not encompassed by your clinical privileges. In addition, I have received a report of incidents concerning ..., case no. 320,193, and your conversations about him with Mrs. Velma Marshall, R.N.".

It was signed by Fazio, "President, Indiana Hospital Medical Staff". The first part of the letter spoke a thousand words that Fazio was going to comply with the hospital's G.P.'s, who were establishing that they were the only ones given privileges to treat anything and everything, whether they were qualified or not. Fazio himself had made the investment in a residency program following his completion of requirements to be a G.P. He was obviously selling his soul in implying that a surgeon would be unqualified to treat a pneumonitis in his patient. The second part of the notice described only a conversation with a nursing supervisor. Despite its pettiness, the reference to the conversation illustrated the midnight conference that had obviously taken place between Dr. Vader and Nursing Supervisor Velma Marshall. The notice concluded ... "The Executive Committee will meet on Saturday, February 26th. at 10:00 A.M., in the Hospital Conference Room,to consider these matters. You are, therefore, invited to attend this meeting as set forth in Section 2(A) of Article IV, Part C".

I reread those three paragraphs and knew that this one was serious. None of that group would have been considered linguists or poets, particularly Fazio. This letter was well-written and legalistic.

Good God - these people were working with a lawyer!

The obvious answer was that the Hospital Lawyer, who was one of the partners in a Pittsburgh law firm claiming to have expertise in "hospital law", had prepared the letter. A year or so earlier, the woman lawyer, hired by the Hospital, had written a new set of Medical Staff bylaws and had held an evening meeting for input by the Medical Staff.

I had missed that session, but when the draft of the new bylaws was circulated, the results were unfathomable. Not only was it difficult to understand a lawyer coming up with a set of bylaws that denied principles of Democracy, but it was equally incongruous for a Hospital's Medical Staff to agree to work under such an absurd set of rules. I had never been aware of superior intellects on that Medical Staff; but I would have thought someone would have recognized the danger in bylaws that provided for:

*any accused physician to be presumed guilty of charges unless he established his innocence;
*an accused physician would be required to present a defense before hearing any evidence against him;
*unsupported heresay evidence would be allowed as valid charges;
*the allowance of vague, unspecific charges unsupported by evidence;
*the appointment of the Hospital Lawyer as a hearing "judge."

I had earlier contacted Ms. Mattern, the Hospital lawyer, after first reading a draft of those bylaws. But, I got just about as much attention from her as when I made the motion, in a Medical Staff meeting, to conduct meetings under the generally accepted Rules of Order.

Ms. Mattern had appeared as the Hospital counsel after the new Board Chairman and his acquiescent Hospital Board had taken over. We had learned of his antipathy toward physicians and his ambition to build a new Hospital as a personal memorial, as well as his demonstrated ability to drive people from town who did not gain his favor. It was entirely possible that the Mattern bylaws were, indeed, a product of the Chairman's ambitions.

Future events would make this premise not only a possibility, but a probability.

After getting the Executive Committee's certified letter, I had shown it to my lawyer-friend, a Hospital Board member, at his Bank Building office. He read the letter carefully and advised meeting with the group and requesting them to provide specific charges or to drop the inquiry.

It was ten o'clock on a late February Saturday morning - the time set for meeting with the Medical Staff Executive Committee. I made rounds as usual and was a little late.

As I walked through the ground floor cafeteria line, I nodded to the ladies busily dropping trays of food into the steam tables for the noonday lunch crowd. The rest of the dining area and its long tables were empty. The doctors' dining area at the far end of the room was near-completely sectioned off with those large, yellow folding doors.

As I entered, I found the eight or nine member Committee seated around three tables pulled together to form a "U". No one moved. No one said a word. I had worn my overcoat and had left it on as I picked up a loose chair with one hand and set it in the open end of the "U". As I sat down, still in my overcoat, the group was giving their best effort to look serious and impressive. As I glanced around that half circle, I could see no one who merited great respect. This crowd was the distillate of the out-of-order staff meetings, the poorly functioning, or non-functioning Hospital Committees and the subpar atmosphere and services of the Hospital. There was no doubt in my mind that the meeting was a sham. In addition, I had no doubt that the patients involved in the Committee's letter had received excellent care.

The obtuse Fazio, who I had helped come to town, was apparently the Chair. He held a few pages of papers but didn't seem to know what to do. I couldn't help but notice that the group were dressed better than usual. After I had begun wearing a white lab coat on morning rounds, most of the Medical Staff had followed and usually covered up their casual attire with white coats - now being supplied by the Hospital. But today, most of the crowd wore suits with shirts and ties.

I must have stared when I looked at Bruno Hoffman, just to my left. His crew-cut and puffy countenance were unchanged, but he was in a well-pressed suit. He had always appeared much as the likeness of the posters on the walls of Navy barracks portraying German military thugs. He was one of the Army group who had followed my friend Bill to town. His appearance on the Medical Staff without even a courtesy call, had led our long-time nose and throat specialist to leave town in disgust saying that "some of the staff were sicker than their patients." On this occasion, Bruno generated the fiercest of his stares. He stared and stared. I suppose I was to have been intimidated, but I ignored him and looked at Fazio, who was having some difficulty in determining the course of the meeting.

As Fazio fumbled with his papers, he said that there had been questions about my handling of two cases, #320,120 and #320,193. He asked what I had to say in response. I advised that I could have nothing to say since I had seen no criticism. Fazio looked toward Vance Vader, sitting just to Bruno's left. Vader pulled a couple of pages from his inside coat pocket. He handed them to me and I gave the papers a cursory glance. The pages were, obviously, a critical report concerning the care of my deceased elderly patient. I refolded the papers and put them in an inner pocket and advised that I would look over the report and prepare a response. Fazio looked to his left for some sort of help and another sheaf of papers appeared. They were passed down and, again, I looked them over. They were typewritten copies of rambling notes compiled by various nurses who had been involved in the care of the second patient in question. We had known, for some time, that the Nursing Director had her nurses compile "incident reports", relating to nurses' interactions with physicians. It was called a spy system by those nurses who didn't care to join in. This was the first that I had seen such reports. Even though I didn't read all these notations carefully, I could see that it was a series of dated and timed descriptions of conversations. Just one after another of "He said this - and she said that". Again, I told the group that I would review the papers and prepare a reply.

I then turned to Bruno on my left and asked, "Do you have any charges to file?" The reply: "You never can tell". Next was Vance Vader, who had taken charge of the attempted resuscitation of my elderly patient;

had turned down another physician's help; and had watched my patient die. Within hours, he had Nurse Marshall obtain the patient's chart and wrote his "report". He was asked the same question. He replied, "Yes"; then, changed it to "No" and then, after more thought, said, "Yes" again.

I continued around the group: Vader's handmaiden, who was not taking notes, Ellis, the newly hired Emergency Room physician, Fazio, Peter Post, long time imposter as a friend, Ewalt, who had been implicated by whispers in obstetrical casualties, Abdul Hankey, (yes, his stethoscope was hanging in its usual place), and finally, the pompous Goldfarb, who had recently managed to replace the Chairman of the Surgical Department with the help of Bruno and a nasty telephone campaign. No one had a comment or charges to bring.

It was an absolute certainty that not one of that contemptible little group had the fortitude or the stomach for a one-on-one encounter. I truly would have accepted any fate rather than show respect for that mob.

I asked Fazio if there was anything further. He quickly said, "No". I advised that I had office hours and left through the double doors to the parking lot - those doors which had admitted the accident patients some years earlier.

The minutes of that meeting surfaced in a few days and were, predictably, distorted. They were signed by Garrells - Vader's associate, but were, obviously, Vader's handiwork. His aggressive, self-righteousness was all over them. Vader was clever, very clever. But, he showed now that, some of his favorite phrases in the minutes would give him away. On this occasion, he used the phrase, ... "and then he proceeded to".... It was a dead giveaway. It would be of interest, in the years to come, to see lawyers and judges quote those minutes as Gospel.

The minutes recorded that Goldfarb had moved that the Committee recommend revocation of my privileges and the motion was seconded by "my good friend", Peter Post. I really wasn't surprised at Post. I never was certain of his sincerity and there was too little character to expect loyalty.

Arthur Jacob, my lawyer, a member of the Hospital Board of Directors, and of course, the son of my old friend Anna, who had been so influential in helping the family when we came to town, was thorough and competent as my lawyer for years. But, his actions were to raise questions. Some of my closest friends suspected that he was envious of our closeness with his mother.

Jacob's office, in the modern Bank Building, was of a colonial style and rather frugal in furnishings. He worked at an antique desk and his clients would face the desk from a large, antique oak chair. Jacob looked at Vader's report detailing the death of my patient and the series of petty nurses "incidents". He looked up and said, "This is all a bucket of smoke". "You'll have no trouble in defending this." Smoke or not, Vader's report was the most degenerate, fetid set of untruths that I had ever seen. The second report of "incidents" was nothing more than a petty description of conversations.

It was obvious that this had all started on that afternoon when Vader had impulsively burst into my office, wanting to buy property so he could break his ties with Peter Post and build his own office. My lack of enthusiasm obviously triggered malice. But, the intensity of his reaction was frightening. I had learned of his family background originating in a small, northern Pennsylvania hamlet and began to wonder if there was a chance of him harming himself or someone else. One of the surgeons had described him going on a Sunday afternoon backyard rampage with a chain saw, cutting down trees that weren't his. I began wondering who would be next. Time would demonstrate just how pathologically clever this perverted personality was.

Time would also tell just how susceptible a vacuous Medical Staff would be to his baneful influence.

A lawyer acquaintance, John DeMay and I held an evening meeting in a quiet corner of the University Club library in Pittsburgh and it became obvious that the disciplinary group had completely bypassed requirements of the Medical Staff bylaws. DeMay wrote a letter to Fazio advising him of his errors and demanded a full hearing based on specific charges. This, in turn, was based on my decision that this whole matter was a sham and that my patient care was above question.

Within a few days, another certified letter from Fazio arrived and announced another meeting of the Medical Staff Executive Committee - this time, during evening hours. DeMay and I prepared a one page document in the form of a position statement advising the Committee of their violations of even their own bylaws. One of the faults was that they had never received a request for revocation of privileges that was required by the Medical Staff bylaws. We requested an impartial, ad hoc Committee to hear all charges since the present Committee had already formed an opinion. In response, we received a request for revocation of privileges authored by Vader. He had cleverly back-dated the request, so that it was appearing to have been in evidence before the Committee made their decision. But, as clever as he was, we found that he had not back-dated the letter far enough to be valid.

There was, again, full attendance by the Committee, but they sat behind one long table in the Staff dining area. DeMay and I entered and Fazio asked DeMay to leave. He did. Fazio made a short announcement concerning the nature of the meeting and, again, asked for an explanation. I walked behind the seated Committee members and gave each a copy of our written request for an impartial hearing. No one read the request and all just sat and stared. Fazio advised that if I had no explanation, then there was no further business. I left through the folding doors and picked up DeMay in the cafeteria area. He finished his coffee and mumbled, "That is some crowd."

As we left the building and circled around the Hospital to the parking lot, we passed the stone entrance into the Staff dining area. The entire Committee was still seated in the brightly lit area, and Fazio was using the wall phone behind the long table. "Probably calling Hospital Lawyer, Mattern", John advised.

The Administrator was now feeling his oats. I had gone with some friends for a round of golf at an out of town course on the previous day off. During the course of the afternoon, I had phoned each hospital station where I had patients, checking on their progress. Everything had been quiet. The Administrator now wanted me to be disciplined for placing calls through the Hospital switch board, rather than through the Emergency Room. Some of us had found that the Emergency Room would often miss or forget messages.

Another evening meeting of the Executive Committee. "The Boys" probably thought they had us on the run, but the entire scene was continuing to be one of confusion. I again sat in front of them in that cafeteria setting. There were brief questions about the Hospital call-in procedures and, I think, that they all knew that there had been many episodes of Medical Staff members being out of touch for care of their patients and that there was a long list of lost messages. My explanation of call-ins during my afternoon away seemed to satisfy some of the group; but Goldfarb, the often absent ophthalmologist, was not about to let the opportunity slip by. I was in no mood to let this hypocrite continue the quizzing. He had practiced in an outlying mining town and had closed his office to take a Pittsburgh residency in eye surgery. Many wondered how he could be in training when he was seen on the local golf course so many afternoons. On returning from residency he had instructed the Emergency Room not to call him ever after eleven o'clock P.M., and would often launch into a tirade when he was called for eye injuries. He would regularly "sign out" to an out of town ophthalmologist. People with eye injuries were often just out of luck for local help.

When this imposter blurted out, "Where were you?", I shot back, "That's none of your damned business."

Abdul, with his stethoscope dangling, observed, "That's not a proper response." It was hardly possible for that bunch to have been more inept. The meeting just ended without anything more being discussed.

A week or two passed without another word. DeMay felt we could not afford to wait for the Committee to again attack. He advised a meeting with Fazio and advised warning him that the Hospital was heading into a serious conflict that would do no one any good. He asked if I wanted to aim for a stand-off as a solution or if I wanted war. I answered quickly that I had seen the hostility of that small mob and that temporizing would lead nowhere. I was clinging to my simple belief that justice would prevail in the face of my pride in my profession and in my work. I had confidence in the integrity of some of the Hospital Board and in our courts.

My meeting with Fazio was in a small, dingy waiting room near one of the side entrances of the Hospital. It was more like a bus depot. There were two large, slatted, wooden benches and a large soft drink machine and a snack machine on the far wall. The floor was bare concrete. I stood waiting for a few minutes and Fazio shuffled in. I expected some sort of friendly greeting - after all, I was the one who had helped him come to town. I got a muffled "Hello", and we both walked over to one of the benches. As we sat, I began telling him that his group had to either come up with some specific charges or drop the matter. He said we would be hearing from the Committee within a few days; and said the Committee was going to recommend that my privileges to practice at the Hospital be revoked.

"Do you mean to tell me you've made a decision without knowing the facts?"

"Well, that's what the Committee has decided.", he mumbled.

I looked firmly into that expressionless face and said, "Fazio, you are heading into the damndest tussle of your life." "You had better reconsider your position."

"What do you want me to do?", he asked - "Resign?"

"That would be a good idea", I replied, and walked out.

On reflecting, it would be absolutely unthinkable for Fazio to resign the highest position in life that he had ever attained. I was surprised, however, even with that bunch, that they would attempt to end a successful career. It was absurd to think that even that group would vote for a sanction and then invent a crime to fit.

Jacob, my lawyer "friend", would come to the office and discuss the happenings. As no news at all, he would relate that Vader and Goldfarb were the enthusiasts for the proposed lynching. At a later time, I would tell him that I was considering a book on the unfolding affair. I can remember his reply. "It would be quite a story, but no one will believe it."

At that point, my thoughts kept returning to Goldfarb and Vader. These two, who had repeatedly and continuously failed to give sick patients help when it was needed, plainly thought they were above Hospital rules, but had the gall to appoint themselves to supervise the professional activities of others. Vader's gunbarrel vision had become pathologic. He had an unshakable, grandiose view of himself blended with a competing fragile view. It was amazing that his delusions of grandeur were accepted by some of the pawns on the Medical Staff.

Goldfarb's mindset was not as deep-seated or as elaborately protected. He was vulnerable to any imagined slight that would possibly question his self esteem. He and his spouse truly thought of themselves, in the face of their ordinary origins, as aristocrats. These people actually acted like royalty. Hospital rules, for example, were meant for the underclasses. I had never seen Goldfarb smile. One of the surgeons noted, on occasion, that the Medical Staff was afraid of him. The same was true of Vader.

I had the fortune, good or bad, to see beyond his delusions. Time after time I would wonder if these people had ever gazed upward on a clear night and pondered their relationship in such a vast universe. How could they justify their arrogance in the face of such vastness and reality? Why would they ignore so many good things in life and lead an unfulfilled existence of deceit?

As promised, a thick, certified envelope arrived at the office in a few days. The legalistic cover letter announced that the enclosed list of charges were the subject of a hearing to be held on June 6th. beginning at 10:00 A.M. Ms. Mattern, the Hospital Lawyer, would preside as the judge (hearing officer), and the Hearing Committee would be chaired by Claude Clippins. My God, Clippins, one of the Itinerant Urologist's crowd, sitting in judgement! I had only recently asked the State Society to help silence this character's fabricated attacks on my character and medical practice. The remaining seats on the so-called Hearing Committee were to be filled by a young internist associated with Vader and a staff dentist. Ye Gods! A dentist sitting in judgement of a veteran Urologic surgeon. If ever there was a stacked jury, this was it.

It didn't take a genius to foresee the unfolding scheme of things, but DeMay assured that all such violations of due process would fortify our request to a Court to intervene. We must first "exhaust all administrative remedies", he would advise. We, therefore, planned our defense in the face of Hospital Lawyer Mattern's bizarre rules. We would "make a record" in order to have a case for the Court. If DeMay had any doubts about the Hospital's lack of respect for due process, the hearings, under the guidance of that biased judge, would erase that doubt.

The four pages of charges that had been prepared by the Hospital Lawyer, were a disorderly, legalistic tangle. The description of one charge ran into another. Some of the charges were so vague as to defy interpretation.

There were paragraphs preceded by capital letters and paragraphs preceded by numbers with no obvious order. One charge simply read... "Doctor Hankey on April 8th....".

When DeMay first saw the charges, he just shook his head. We went over them and then went over them again. I recall him saying, "They're trying to make a defense impossible - multiple charges with vague meanings."

Another letter arrived advising that the Executive Committee Prosecutor would be a Pittsburgh lawyer. It meant nothing to me, but when I passed the name on to DeMay, he mused, "They are serious." DeMay's remark about the Committee's Lawyer kept running through my mind. He obviously was reflecting that this lawyer was either well known or a difficult foe or both. I made some inquiries and found that the lawyer was one of the senior partners in a large Pittsburgh firm. Nevertheless, I had confidence in DeMay. He was ethical and thorough. It appeared that the Hospital Prosecutor was hired on the advice of Ms. Mattern.

The day of the hearing was approaching and we had done our best to prepare for a defense of that four page list of charges. DeMay had tutored me in proper response from the witness chair; and both sides had provided their lists of proposed witnesses.

We met at our office early on the day of the hearing and again went over the list of charges. I offered to drive the short trip to the Hospital and

I parked just outside that well-known, ornate, stone entrance leading into the cafeteria and staff dining room. The Administrator came rushing out the double doors advising that we couldn't park there. He was really full of himself, once again. He was enjoying his new-found authority. As a surprise, he advised that the hearing was going to be in the nurses residence, across the parking lot - safely away from scrutiny.

We were directed to a small room just off the nursing residence ground level lobby. The room was oblong, and windows on the opposite wall looked out into a wooded area behind the building. An air conditioner in one of the windows was humming away and the room was reasonably cool. Against the right wall were a row of chairs and there were three long tables, two facing each other and one to the left. The Administrator advised that the first counsel table was ours and the table to the left was for the Hearing Officer and the Hearing Committee. The table opposite ours was for the Hospital Counsel. In front of that head table on its far end, was a chair where a court stenographer was now setting up her equipment. A similar chair was elevated on a small wooden platform to our left. It was obviously the witness chair. Someone had gone to a lot of trouble to have the room look like a Court.

It seemed, that all at once, the room began to fill with people entering and milling around to find their places. The Hospital lawyer, Ms. Mattern, arrived with a small briefcase and handbag. She was short, wore glasses and was dressed in a dark suit and plain white blouse. During the hearing, she would chat with the Hearing Committee, from time to time, telling of her interest in farming and her joy at driving her farm tractor. The four members of the Hearing Committee arrived - three regulars and an alternate - and were guided to their seats by "Judge" Mattern. As they seated themselves, I felt chagrined to be depending on that group to pass judgement on my career. They were: Claude Clippins, who had been antagonistic for years, a young internist (a member of Vader's group), and a dentist. The fourth member of the crew - an alternate - was one of the Staff's younger surgeons.

Everyone was seated and there was a little nervous chatter between Mattern and the Hearing Committee. The court stenographer was recording the names of everyone there, but the row of chairs along the far wall was empty, as was the opposite counsel table. It was already twenty minutes past the starting time and our first, but not last, experience with the Hospital Prosecutor's planned tardiness.

Another twenty minutes and the door behind us opened and the stocky Prosecutor entered. He was awkwardly carrying a very large leather satchel in each hand. He was out of breath and puffed his way past the witness chair and head table and deposited the satchels on the far table. He then turned to Mattern and gave an insincere apology for being late. A slim, dark-haired young lady was with him.

She and the Prosecutor sat and he began a slow, methodical positioning of the stacks of papers from the satchels onto the counsel table. He was deliberate in his slowness and was obviously putting on a show for our benefit. It would become glaringly apparent that he had been advised that I would not likely withstand a prolonged hearing. I'm sure I was to be impressed with the weight of evidence against me by that paper shuffling charade. We all sat and watched the performance: DeMay, the young woman with the "Prosecutor", "Judge" Mattern, the four young "Hearing Committee" members, and the Court Reporter, quietly waiting for something to record.

I did become concerned. What was hidden in all that paper? How brutal would this character be? When he finished his arranging and rearranging, he rose and addressed "Judge" Mattern. He gave a long explanation for his late arrival and went on at some length about his wife's undergoing surgery that day. The long discourse became an obvious ploy to elicit sympathy from all within earshot. He was loud, even though competing with the air conditioner. His shrill voice would rise every so often, to emphasize a point, turning his thought into a series of whines and non sequitors.

I glanced at DeMay for a reaction. There was none. He just sat comfortably watching the unlikely discourse. I looked at Mattern. She, likewise, just stared - occasionally carefully repositioning her cigarette lighter on the top of her pack of cigarettes. It wasn't obvious then, but it would become obvious, that the "Judge" was going to allow this guy to run the show. When he finished his final rehash of his private family matters, Mattern opened the hearing with an announcement of the purpose of the meeting. She explained that we were there to determine the validity of the Executive Committee's recommendation of the revocation of the Hospital privileges of Ralph J. Miller, M.D. This, of course, was an obvious reversal of any reasonable judicial process. The penalty had already been accessed before anyone had heard one word of testimony or had seen one page of exhibit.

I was forming a first impression of the Prosecutor. He was obviously showing off for the young woman with him. I was wondering what DeMay thought of him, but to me, he appeared to be a jerk. However, a jerk with a rigged Judge and Jury.

Mattern then read the charges with the Court Reporter making a verbatim record. A disorderly listing of supposed incidents and letters had obviously been collected by someone over a period of twelve to fifteen years. Someone had been keeping a file - similar to the Nursing Directors's "incident" file, starting at about the same time that the Chairman had taken over as the head of the Hospital Board of Directors.

Woven through the listing of twenty or more "incidents", were references claiming problems in the care of my elderly patient and the "incidents" surrounding my second patient - a clergyman. These had been the nidus of the original Executive Committee activity. We didn't know how the many other added charges had been gathered, but they were obviously set in their jumbled form by the Prosecutor. The list of charges read:

"In support of the Executive Committee's recommendation that the Medical Staff membership of Ralph J. Miller, M.D. be revoked because of serious mishandlings and/or improprieties involved in the case of patient #320,120 and patient #320,193 and because of a continuing course of serious lack of cooperation with the Hospital and the Hospital Medical Staff, evidenced by the following specific acts and omissions, all of which acts and omissions have been detrimental to the health and safety of patients, detrimental to the proper functioning of the Hospital, in derogation of the Hospital's Bylaws and standards, in violation of the Hospital's Medical Staff Rules and Regulations and/or in violation of professional ethics:

1. exhibiting disruptive, disrespectful, disparaging, insulting, intimidating, threatening, slanderous, abusive, and/or other improper conduct and behavior to:
   A. Dr. Nathan Goldfarb and the Department of Surgery. (see letter from Dr. Miller dated October 14th.)

It was obvious that the Prosecutor's penmanship was as loquacious as his speech.

The long list of adjectives (disruptive, disrespectful, etc.) had ten subparagraphs identified by letters A through J listing people who were presumably affected by that long list of descriptive adjectives. Following that, were additional wild charges numbered number one through number eleven.

"Judge" Mattern then read the rules of the Hearing:
Presumed guilt for the accused unless innocence was established; A defense presentation required before the presentation of evidence against the defendant; Admission of heresay testimony; Hospital counsel to be in charge of a hearing.

DeMay then challenged the composition of the Hearing Committee, citing their bias and unfitness. Clippins, with his longstanding hostility, the young internist controlled by Vader - the original accuser -; and finally, the unqualified dentist and the alternate Hearing Committee member whose physician father had been sued for malpractice by DeMay.

Mattern denied each and every motion to dismiss the Hearing Committee members, each time saying that they could be "objective".

Finally, DeMay moved that the hearing officer disqualify herself since she had been involved with some of the matters listed as charges. Mattern, of course, denied the motion, causing DeMay to exclaim, "Ms. Mattern, this is incredible, truly incredible."

The seven chairs along the right wall remained empty except for the occasional entrance of an Executive Committee member who would enter and watch the show for awhile from that row of chairs. I particularly noticed when one Committee member, the Emergency Room Physician, came in, slouched into a chair and crossed his legs. His blue jeans rode up exposing white hairy shins and soiled, woolen sport socks. His dirty tennis shoes didn't improve the over-all appearance.

On another occasion, Vader himself, sat in that row of chairs for a brief period. He then disappeared, not returning at any point to testify. He had begun the whole series of events with his "report", but would not testify. Why would the Prosecutor not use him as a witness? That would be learned only much later exposing unbelievable treachery.

"Judge" Mattern advised DeMay that he could begin his defense. He advised that we would cover the care of my two patients - the source of the original charges of the Committee. First, he had me take the stand, and for an hour or more, I went over the hospital course of my deceased elderly patient - pointing out the false accusations in Vader's vicious report. His report had accused me of not even notifying the family of the death and that the standard of care was below that "acceptable in any hospital". To rebut those charges, the elderly patient's family had offered to testify. They did. The patient's daughter-in-law testified that the family was satisfied with the care their father had received. But, she shocked everyone when she said that the Hospital Administrator and Dr. Vance Vader, had called her the previous evening. They had heard she would testify and tried to get her to change her testimony. She said they "tried to put words in my mouth", telling her that Doctor Miller needed to be disciplined. DeMay made certain that the witness tampering was well-documented in the record. He also entered into the record, an affidavit from the patient's son. He expressed his disgust that his father's death was being used to bring charges against a physician. We then began our rebuttal of the vague charges relating to the second patient.

I was then back on the stand discussing the series of petty incident reports compiled in the Head Nurse's office, after Vance Vader and nurse Velma Marshall joined forces on that fateful evening to create another "incident".

After presentation of the witness tampering by the Administrator and Vader, the Hearing Committee must have felt that we had spent our entire defense, but there would shortly be another surprise.

I told the story: When I had gotten the Executive Committee letter, suggesting problems with two cases, I carefully read the entire charts of both patients. The second patient (a minister) was still in the Hospital, and on an early Sunday morning, I was reading his chart at the nursing station in the Mack Wing section of the hospital. While I read, at one end of the L-shaped counter, head nurse Swishelm, was working on charts around the corner at my left elbow. I was reading the nursing notes that I had gone over briefly a few days before. I suddenly noted something strange. There appeared to be a different wording describing the patient's care on the night that nurse supervisor, Velma Marshall and Vance Vader, began their plot. I read and reread the notes of that evening, when a light flashed. The notes no longer had a few of the red ink underlines that I had noted a few days before! These notes had been altered! I turned to Mrs. Swishelm. She turned toward me, swaying the black silk cords of her glasses, as though she had been waiting for me to turn around.

"Mrs. Swishelm, what happened to the original nurses notes on this chart?"

"They were taken to the Head Nurses's office", she said, without hesitation.

"Do you mean all those nurses changed their notes?"

"Yes", she said. We looked at the altered notes and they, in turn, bore the signature of Supervisor Marshall and four of her floor nurses.

Before I left the floor that morning, Mrs. Swishelm had given me a signed statement that the five nurses had removed a full page of nursing notes from a patient's chart and had substituted altered notes.

    As I continued my testimony, DeMay displayed enlarged photos of the original page of notes and the falsified page that had been substituted. At DeMay's instruction, I pointed out to the Hearing Committee, the danger of working with people who would attempt to suborn a witness and to falsify medical records.

    Later in the Hearing, the Hospital would put the Nursing Director and Supervisor Velma Marshall on the stand as witnesses. Under DeMay's cross-examination, the Nursing Director advised that it was a policy to "recopy" notes that could be damaging to the Hospital. Even the youngest of student nurses would, undoubtedly, know that this "recopying" is akin to forgery, and is illegal.

    When DeMay cross-examined Velma Marshall, she admitted the entire scheme. He ended his cross-examination with, "Mrs. Marshall, are you ashamed of what you have done?" "No", she replied. The Prosecutor yelled at DeMay, "John!"

    As my testimony relating to the two patients ended, "Judge" Mattern advised the Prosecutor that he could cross-examine the witness. He sat motionless for a few moments. Then, once again, carefully shuffled his papers around. He then leaped forward, grabbed a chair and sat to my left, touching the witness chair. He was holding my elderly patient's chart and began a series of questions, attempting to distort and discredit my testimony. His opening questions had to do with laboratory testing of the patient's secretions. He kept referring to the patient's "spootum". I suppressed an urge to also mispronounce the word, to embarrass him, but simply answered, pronouncing the word, "sp-you-tum". The Hearing Committee smiled, but he recovered and began to bore in. It was becoming evident that he was a bully. He was using the patient's chart as an excuse to get me to read the fine print on the chart, allowing him to move in closer and closer. I allowed him to come very close by delaying my responses a little. I suddenly turned my head to the left, leaving us with our noses almost touching. We sat there like two alley cats in a staredown. It was only seconds, but it seemed like an hour. I finally rolled my eyes to look at the Committee over his shoulder. They were staring, not knowing what was next. The Prosecutor was still frozen in place. I raised an eyebrow and the Committee smiled. The Prosecutor withdrew and returned to his seat. He conducted the remainder of his cross-examination from a more respectful distance.

The Hearing Officer announced a lunch break and everyone headed for the Hospital Cafeteria, across the parking lot. I had no appetite, but sat with DeMay and my secretary at one of the long cafeteria tables. I complained to DeMay of the lawyer's tactic of pushing his nose into my face. John said, "I know, you'd like to punch him." Before I could reply, my secretary volunteered, "No, he'd like to kiss him." I told him that the thought had crossed my mind, but that this guy could, quite likely, make an ass of himself without my help. John advised that the most I could do was to tell him that it wasn't appropriate for two men to sit so close together.

As I finished a cup of coffee, my secretary nudged me, and glanced across the dining area. There was the Prosecutor, several tables away. His mannerisms had caught her attention. He was holding his fork like a hammer, with his face in his plate, and was shoveling his food in like coal into a boiler.

Humor during the hearings was almost non-existent. But, the Prosecutor, if he weren't threatening a professional career, could quite probably, in some corners, not be taken too seriously. After he had grilled me, using the deceased patient's chart, he had asked for a lunch break and had carelessly dropped the chart on a chair near our table. I put the chart with our materials and had stowed them in our car trunk for security.

DeMay reminded that it was time to meet our first witness - Doctor John Murphy, the Chief of Urology at the University of Pennsylvania. He had flown in to be our first witness and we were chatting with him beside our parked car. Suddenly, the Prosecutor came bursting out of the nursing home entrance, and approached us at full gallop. He demanded the Hospital chart. We looked at him in disbelief, as I opened the trunk and handed the chart to him. Doctor Murphy and DeMay were shaking in laughter as he trotted away with his chart.

When we reconvened, and I had again taken the stand, he started a line of questioning designed to show that I had maliciously stolen his chart. When I explained that there was no need to steal the chart; we had copies; he rephrased his questioning. Had I "noticed him approaching us in the parking lot and had I given him the chart from the trunk of car?" I confessed that he had been seen by all, sprinting across the parking lot. He then asked if I had noticed him, just prior to the lunch break, looking at Ms. Benesh. I replied that I had seen him looking at Ms. Benesh on a number of occasions during the hearing. I think the laughter from the

Hearing Panel prevented yet another charge to be added. It would have read: "Doctor Miller exhibited disruptive, threatening, intimidating etc., by stealing a patient's chart".

By the time the hearing reconvened, our scheduled witnesses for the afternoon had arrived. In addition to Doctor Murphy, there were six: the Chief of Surgery from the Hospital; Internists from Pittsburgh and Johnstown; a Urologist from Greensburg; the Chief of Pathology from Western Pennsylvania Hospital and the head of the National Medical Advisory Service, from Washington, D.C.

Doctor Murphy and those who followed, all testified that the deceased patient had been ill for some years and that they had carefully reviewed the Hospital records. They testified that the patient's demise was unpreventable and had been caused, not by a heart attack, as charged by Vader, but by a pulmonary thrombosis in the face of years of chronic pulmonary disease.

The Prosecutor cross-examined each witness with lengthy questions and interjected speeches with his high-pitched whine. DeMay called his attention to the delaying tactics. The Prosecutor was obviously trying to prevent our other witnesses from testifying. After Doctor Murphy testified, he had to rush to the airport. As we shook hands he reassured with, "I'm sure things are going to turn out fine."

The Prosecutor forcefully badgered all the witnesses, but his conflict with Doctor Katter, from Johnstown, was the most notable. Katter had, in his hand, two letters - one that he had written officially to be entered into the record, and a second which he had written to me expressing his true feelings about Vance Vader's vitriolic report. In the personal letter he described Vader's psychotic accusations as totally false and described Vader's conclusions of an electrocardiogram as patently in error. He concluded that Vader's hatred indicated he was "a dangerous man, out with an axe."

Doctor Katter, in error, gave the Prosecutor the personal letter and then quickly attempted to withdraw it, causing the Prosecutor to grab for the paper. This led to a tug-of-war for the documents, between cross-examiner and witness. DeMay couldn't control himself. He burst out laughing. It ended with both letters being entered into evidence. I couldn't help but be pleased that the description of Vader's deviant behavior was now part of the record.

The Prosecutor again accosted the witness trying to demonstrate that the witness was only a friend of mine, who had volunteered to testify.

He asked Doctor Katter, "Prior to today, how many times have you met with the Defendant, Doctor Miller?".

The witness replied, "Never". The Prosecutor was again caught short.

"How do you know Doctor Miller?", he countered.

I have sent him patients, who wanted to be under his care for a number of years." "Judge" Mattern allowed the Prosecutor to interrupt, to badger and to delay, knocking down any attempt by DeMay to object.

At one point, John passed me a note. It read: "Ralph, we're going to win this even with enemy judges." He truly believed that the irregularities of the hearing would be corrected by the State Court System. He later advised, "This will never be allowed to stand." "Get me to a judge - any judge."

The Prosecutor's witness list included a number of Medical Staff members. They, of course, would be expected to testify to the quality of care of my elderly patient. The charge related to the second patient appeared to be dropped by him after we had established the nurses' falsification of records. However, no Hospital Physician appeared to testify for the charges related to medical matters and the first patient.

The Prosecutor saw his problems. He was without witnesses to testify in support of Vader's wild accusations. Our authoritative medical witnesses had laid bare Vader's report for what it was. They had opened the door for questions about Vader's motivation and his obvious part in the conspiracy. The Prosecutor had some reason for not calling Vader himself to defend his "report". We again wondered what Vader had been doing during his fourteen minutes with our dying patient.

The following day, the Prosecutor attacked. After the lunch break, he returned to the hearing with a tall, pale, solemn-looking man, who sat with him at the counsel table. DeMay demanded to know who the man was. He was identified as a Doctor Arnold Sladen. He gave the man a grand title, but we were to learn that he was a Recovery Room Physician from Pittsburgh's Montefiore Hospital. DeMay was furious that the Prosecutor would produce a surprise witness, contrary even to those strange Hospital bylaws. This left DeMay without an opportunity to prepare a cross-examination. Mattern, of course, overruled DeMay's objection and allowed the testimony of the surprise witness.

The man testified, at length, that one of the drugs used in treatment of the patient by the respiratory therapist under my orders, could have caused a heart attack. He cited many references from the medical literature - most of which had little or no bearing on our patient. All our witnesses had agreed that Vader's description of a heart attack was in error.

We had not noticed the significance of the Prosecutor's initial questions to his witness. He had said, "How long have we known each other?" Sladen replied, "Not until last Friday when you called. I had just returned from a business trip." The answer did, indeed, go unnoticed - that is - until later, when I was given a document from the office of the Prothonotary of Allegheny County, in Pittsburgh. Its title read, "Complaint in Divorce".

Opposite the word Plaintiff, was the typed name - Arnold Sladen. Opposite the word Defendant, was the typed name - Doris Sladen. The date of the complaint was stamped near the bottom of the page, April 7th. - just a few weeks before the first day of the Hearing. The signature at the bottom of the page - by the lawyer filing the divorce complaint - the Hospital Prosecutor! This character was obviously a divorce client of the Prosecutor; and had lied. He was a perjurer!

The law requires that lawyers knowing of any perjury during a legal action, report it to the Courts. The Prosecutor never did. But he had not only known of perjury, he had helped in its commission. It was reasonable to suspect that our documentation of witness tampering, falsification of medical records and perjury would call attention to the Hospital's fabrication of charges. Only time would tell.

During several days, and sometimes evenings, the hearings extended over a several week period, because of the Prosecutor's schedule. Members of the Medical Staff Executive Committee would continue to appear in ones or twos, and after observing the show for a while from the seats along the right wall, would leave. Vader showed up once and then disappeared. Why wasn't he called to testify? His absence became more and more astounding.

DeMay and I had carefully gone over the remaining charges which presented a real smorgasbord of ambiguities which could have been fabricated only by a disorderly mind. The Prosecutor was certainly a candidate for that. His endless rambling speeches had neither beginning nor end so that the point he was trying to make would be lost in the verbiage. DeMay would object to interruptions by the Prosecutor and Ms. Mattern would routinely overrule him.

Before we began our defense of all those nebulous charges, DeMay read the list of adjectives to Mattern: disruptive, disrespectful, disparaging etc., etc. and pointed out that, when they were applied to the following list of people, they amounted to more than two hundred separate charges. She replied that the charges were perfectly clear and straight-forward. DeMay was exasperated. He had been methodical and objective to that point, but he now leaned toward me, grinding his teeth, and hissed, "That bitch!"

I took the stand again, knowing that we were in for a long, detailed defense of those absurd charges, and followed DeMay's questioning. One by one, I would counter the intent of the charge, outlining its origin and falsity, going back as far as ten or twelve years.

I eluded to the disorder of Medical Staff business meetings and my attempts to have the meetings conducted in accord with legitimate Rules of Order. I told of the problems in the Surgical Department caused by the Chairman of the Surgical Department being removed by a nasty telephone campaign when he tried to improve standards.

When I detailed all the effort that had gone into the Infection Control Committee, before Vader fired me, I think I outlined the problem of "hospital-acquired infections" which no one there previously knew existed.

Incredulously, the Prosecutor had accused me of disrespect, etc. to the nurses, who had altered and falsified nursing notes. I detailed conversations with the nurses, illustrating that the Prosecutor was turning their shameful behavior into an attack.

One of the charges was that we didn't use Abdul Hankey during a resuscitation. At the time, we were trying to save the life of a patient and certainly didn't require his incompetence. However, I just pointed out that there were seven or eight people around the patient's bed and that additional help was not needed. What did Abdul really want us to have him do?

Abdul was the center of another charge. It read:

"Doctor Hankey, in the Hospital Staff Room, about October 5th.". I explained that I had advised Hankey not to admit any more children to my care. He had gone into the room of a four year old postoperative patient on the day of surgery, and had ordered a barium enema for the little kid. I was furious and said so. I didn't need Hankey to threaten the health of any more patients. It turned out that the charge was something totally different. Hankey testified and claimed that I had bumped him in the coat room six years earlier. DeMay asked him why he had held this festering in his bosom for so long. Under cross-examination he wasn't sure whether he had been bumped and fell down on one knee or whether he had been bumped at all.

The charge that put DeMay's teeth on edge was that I "continuously failed to prepare and submit adequate patient medical records..., within fourteen days". I was one of the very few who corrected the typing on Hospital records before they were signed out. This caused a few days' delay but the records were accurate and free from typos. Mattern commented when she heard my explanation - "That is certainly a characteristic of all members of the Medical Staff." But, I would still be found guilty of that charge.

Probably the most dramatic carelessness of the Prosecutor's charges was "improperly attempting to charge a cash fee to an indigent patient and physically threatening an indigent patient."

This was the Prosecutor's most outrageous boondoggle. A few years earlier, before the Hospital hired an Emergency Room physician, the Emergency Room nurses would send patients to physicians' offices for care of minor complaints. One gentleman had appeared during afternoon office hours. The girls up front said he became abusive when they asked him how he would pay for his visit. I offered to talk with him and learned that he was the patient of a G.P. in an outlying town. But he didn't want to drive that far - the police had suspended his driver's licence. He again became agitated when I told him that he would be expected to show some responsibility, even if it would be only a few cents a month. He left in a fury and returned to the Emergency Room, where the Nursing Director had him fill out one of her "incident reports". His name was Fester Arch.

During that same period, a few years back, another patient had appeared announcing that he was from the Emergency Room. Once again, we were faced with a hostile patient when he was asked to fill out a questionnaire and was asked to be responsible for payment. He was a muscular, five feet in height and was about the same width. He was built like a Brama bull. While he was sitting across from my desk, he decided to leave. We walked down the hallway together, and when I opened the reception room door, he reached out and wrapped one of those muscular arms around my neck in a strangle-hold. I was completely off-guard and we fell to the floor together, slamming shut the reception room door in the process. I couldn't breathe and I thought I was going to black-out. In desperation, I gave him a well-placed knee to the groin. He relaxed his choke-hold and I jumped up. As I was backing up, my heel caught in the carpet, and in an instant, he was on top of me again. I truly thought I was done-for when I heard a loud, almost musical ring. Our Secretary had gone to our coffee machine in the laboratory and had picked up a Cremora jar. She gave him a resounding blow to the head (it was a family size Cremora).

He again jumped up and started for her. Almost instinctively, I rushed for a tool box in our office closet and got a claw hammer. When he saw the hammer, he made tracks through the reception room and out through the front entrance. I was truly fearful when I saw him head for the trunk of his car. A patient's husband had been in the reception room and yelled that we had to keep him from that trunk. What did he have in there?

He saw the hammer. Would I have used it? You bet.

He raced across the street, through a large parking lot and complained to a group of men that I was going to hit him. He was right. The Administrator later had recruited one of those men to testify against me at he hearing.

The girls had called the State Police and they arrived in minutes. The fellow was arrested and admitted to Torrance State Hospital (a mental institution).

Later that afternoon, Doctor Griseman, the Superintendent, called. He advised that the man had been admitted and that he had known this man for some time. The man had been admitted before after he had attacked an elderly woman - a cashier in a diner near Blairsville when she was unable to cash a five-dollar bill. During his confinement, he had attacked orderlies and nurses in his ward.

When I had finished the story of Fester Arch and the mental patient, those prize citizens sent by the Emergency Room, DeMay rose and advised that he was entering into the record the police rap sheet of Fester Arch. He advised that the sheet included convictions on burglary and assault charges on nine separate occasions. He then entered the psychiatric history and the arrest record of the mental patient.

The room fell silent. The Prosecutor sat there and stared away. He didn't look my way. The young lady with him just looked at the papers in front of him and then, for a moment, looked in my direction. I gave her a long, slow wink. She blushed and looked away and managed never to let our eyes meet again during that long ordeal. Nevertheless, my thoughts were centering on the Prosecutor - not the other participants in that travesty. How could he combine two events into a single false charge - without ever investigating those events?

I continued to have unaltered respect for my profession and many in it; and I continued to have, perhaps unjustifiable, respect for the Law. But, as I looked at the Prosecutor, I felt revulsion. How could he enter into such fraud? He and his clients were trash.

DeMay announced that that concluded the defense and I returned to my seat beside him.

The Hearing Officer, Mattern, our activist Judge, ended the session. It had been a grueling two days in that witness chair talking above that buzzing air conditioner, which wasn't doing that much to keep the room from becoming hot and humid.

DeMay zippered his brief case and we walked out side-by-side. I was not feeling at all relieved. As we walked through the lawn on our way to the parking lot, John said, "That was superb." I appreciated that encouragement but knew that we had to listen to the Prosecutor's attack of charges. John sensed that I was a little low and comforted with, "Don't you realize what an accomplishment that was to present seven outstanding physicians as witnesses?"

I was becoming more concerned at Vader's absence. "Judge" Mattern, at a later date, would offer a document to a government agency that would fall into our hands. She would be offended that charges would be leveled against the Hospital by citizens. She would state, "It has always been a firm American principle that anyone accused be given the opportunity to face his accusor."

She was correct. But, she never required Vader to appear and support his charges.

DeMay advised that if we called Vader as a witness, we would be bound to accept his testimony as truth - one of the "Rules of Procedure."

It had become obvious that the Prosecutor's plan was to delay the hearings as long as possible. He and "the Judge", of course, were being paid by the hour and wanted to keep the meter running. Again, he had obviously been told that I would, quite likely, fold my tent and leave.

In one of the intervals at the hearing, one of the surgeons caught me in the hallway and quietly told me that the Hospital Pathologist had told him of two obstetrical tragedies. The bodies of two infants had been sent to the Hospital Morgue, with the heads severed from the bodies. I just looked at him and went about my business. But, I couldn't get the matter out of mind.

I dropped into the Pathologist's office the next day and inquired about a report he had sent on one of my patients. His office was a clutter -

house plants sitting in saucers lined the window sill and his desk and table were piled high with assorted loose papers and journals. He leaned back in his chair, stroked his beard and detailed the report. That helped make a decision regarding my patient. As he finished, I asked, "Harold, is it true that two babies were sent here from O.B. in two pieces?"

"Yes, it's true."

"What do you mean?"

"Within a thirty day period", he continued, "I received two infants with heads separated from the bodies."

"You mean they were decapitated with obstetrical forceps?"

"How else?", he snapped.

I left, but I couldn't shake the image of those two little mutilated bodies.

The next morning, I went straight up to the lab and walked past the secretary into that cluttered office.

Harold was peering into his binocular scope. He turned around and invited me to sit at the only open space between the piles of papers.

"Harold, I can't forget what you told me yesterday."

"I know", he said.

"Who were the doctors?"

"Clippins and Archer."

"My God, Clippin's, the guy from Homer City is the one appointed to head the Committee sitting in judgement of me! And the other one from Clymer is on the Executive Committee!"

"I guess you know, they're trying to run me out of town."

"I know", he said.

"I don't have any plans to accomodate them."

"I guessed as much", he said.

I asked that if he were asked to testify on the deaths of those infants, what he would do. "I'd tell the truth", he said, as I left. I still couldn't forget the thought of those two infants and what those practitioners may have told the families.

When the Hearings resumed, the Prosecutor brought us up to date on his wife's postoperative progress and then began calling his witnesses. His witness list had included a number of Staff Physicians and nurses. Most of them never appeared but he made the most of those who did.

Understandably, the notorious felon, Fester Arch, was listed, but never appeared. The Prosecutor was not anxious to have that jail bird show what a mess he had made by the error of combining two unseemly characters from the Emergency Room into one ridiculous charge. Similarly, the mental patient never appeared.

He did call the Nursing Director, and discussed with her the petty conversations of some of her "incident reports". As an interesting afterthought, she said that I had touched Natalie Goss, one of her supervisors, on the tip of her nose. At his suggestion, she demonstrated touching her nose with her forefinger. At the Prosecutor's encouragement, she did it again.

DeMay interrupted. "Objection - How did she know that?" "She told me", the witness replied. "That is the worst kind of heresay", Demay yelled.

"What's not the worst kind?", the Prosecutor shot back. When DeMay cross-examined, she admitted, in detail, the alteration of the nursing notes. DeMay showed her detailed nursing rules from several Pittsburgh Hospitals prohibiting, at any time, alteration of patient records. She simply replied that Indiana Hospital regularly "recopied" nurses notes.

The Prosecutor, in order to complete the record, called Fazio to enter into the record the letters of the Executive Committee leading to the filing of charges. He was attempting to bypass the fact that the Committee had decided to revoke my privileges and then attempted to find charges that would justify that action. It had opened the way for DeMay to quiz Fazio, "How were these charges formulated?"

The inept Fazio answered, "We held meetings."
"Where?"
"In the Hospital."
"How many?"
"Several."
"When?"
"During evenings."
"Were minutes kept?"
"No."
"Who was present?"
"Executive Committee."

Then the question we had wondered about. "How did you manage to list the charges?"

The dull witness just opened up with "We would sit around and someone would say, "Remember the time he did this, and then someone else would say, remember the time he did that?"

"That's what we thought", DeMay offered.

The witness then was Nathan Goldfarb. Goldfarb and a few of the Surgical Department members had staged a coup, making Goldfarb the controversial head of the Surgical Department.

Goldfarb and his spouse had made a profession at social climbing and had been partially successful at it. They had been successful at ingratiating themselves with "important" town people. The primary targets were Hospital Board members and local judges, especially Earl Handler.

I had protested loudly when he and a few of the Surgical Department members had arranged the replacement of the Chief of Surgery. The Chairman of the Department had been the victim of a nasty telephone campaign to replace him. His sins had been attempts to correct some of the very obvious deficiencies in the Department. More recently, he had sent a memo to the Oriental surgeon, who had dangerously done a major surgical procedure without an assistant.

As Goldfarb began his testimony, it was evident that he and the Prosecutor had been working closely together. Under the Prosecutor's lead, he described that I was disruptive at Surgical Department meetings and that, "no one in the Surgical Department liked me." This dialogue dragged on and on. The people in the room were restless as DeMay cross-examined the witness. The cross-examination was short. DeMay handed him a sheaf of papers. The papers were copies of the tabulation of votes by Surgical Department members, either recommending or not recommending, their colleagues annually.

DeMay asked, "As you review those records, is it true that you and the Department members unanimously recommended Doctor Miller, based on his clinical competence, attendance at meetings, and cooperation with hospital personnel, over the past nineteen years?"

The witness answered, "Yes."

The Prosecutor took over the "redirect" and attempted to reverse that testimony. As a surprise, he announced that that concluded the Executive Committee case. Goldfarb rose, thanked the Prosecutor, and walked past very closely. Without hesitation, he turned his eyes sideways toward me, and gave me a little smug, self-satisfied smile. I couldn't believe that smug smile. It had to be disastrous to tempt fate that way. That kind of gloating had to be based on total invincibility - or something else.

Since then, I can only recall the old axiom, that "Pride goeth before a fall."

"Judge" Mattern announced that there would be a summation by the lawyers and scheduled the summation for an evening, a week or more hence.

It was a beautiful summer evening. DeMay and I were a little early for the summation and took our places at the counsel table. The court reporter made a few friendly comments, but John was quiet and sat reviewing his notes. One by one, the four members of the hearing panel and Mattern came in and sat quietly. Mattern carefully positioned her cigarettes and lighter while the members of the panel adjusted pillows which had been provided when the group had complained about the hard seats. The Prosecutor was typically late and we all sat quietly until he arrived.

As if by signal, the seven members of the Medical Staff Executive Committee filed in, and for the first time, silently filled all the chairs against the far wall. I had never seen any of them so neatly dressed. They probably felt the summation was a sort of funeral.

Mattern announced the purpose of the gathering and advised the Prosecutor to proceed.

For more than an hour, over the whine of the air conditioner, he loudly went down the long list of charges detailing the need to find me guilty of each of them.

The presentation was theatrical, even more so than the bombastic interruptions we had listened to during the hearings. As a crowing jewel, he circled in front of the Executive committee, forcefully, almost violently, pushing his nose upward, saying that that was what I had done to Nurse Goss -something that never happened.

The hearing "judge" called for a recess from that hot box. Without delay, the room quickly emptied and the Executive Committee members huddled in quiet conversation on the front lawn of the building and some of them lit up a smoke. DeMay and I took a brief stroll around the parking lot. Back in that courtroom Ms. Mattern ordered DeMay to proceed.

John began by summarizing the testimony of our respected witnesses and called attention to the lack of believable evidence for each of that long list of charges. As a closing, he looked at Vader and plainly accused Vader of cowardice to compose a hateful report of falsehoods and then retreating into the shadows, never to appear to defend his accusations and be cross-examined.

Vader and the Committee stared straight ahead, giving no recognition that they heard the accusation.

Looking back on that fetid scene, the only emotion is disgust. Four physicians at the head table with Ms. Mattern, the Hospital Prosecutor, the court reporter, the seven member Executive Committee, Demay and myself - squeezed into that psuedocourtroom. By the time the Prosecutor had exhausted his flatulence, the place was hot and humid with the aura of a lynching. Demay and I were the only ones unaware that the verdict had been established months earlier. Our evidence was so overwhelming, that we probably were justified in our optimism.

A few quiet days with the family in West Virginia was in order. The relaxation was somewhat less than complete; and was totally gone after the message from DeMay that Mattern's hearing panel gave a blanket guilty verdict of all the charges. We finished our planned stay, but I was anxious to get back to plan the appeal of that verdict to the Hospital Board of Directors.

DeMay and I prepared a thorough set of documents clearly outlining that list of charges showing little or no evidence to support those charges which the inept Fazio described as being compiled by his committee by "sitting around when somebody would say, "Remember the time he did this." and then someone would say, "Remember the time he did that."

The Hospital's letter set the appeal to be heard by a four member committee of the Hospital Board. Demay responded by advising the Board Chairman that they were again acting in disregard of their own bylaws. We were entitled to appear before the entire Board, but the letter was ignored.

The Hospital rented a conference room at the Best Western Motel and we were advised the date and time the appeal would be heard.

Demay and I arrived early, and set up a screen and a projector. DeMay felt it would be impressive to show the absurdities of Ms. Mattern's court.

While we went about our chores, the Hospital legal group and the Administrator enjoyed a supper in the far corner of the room. We mused at health care money being used to feed that group.

The room was empty except for a long table for the Board members and a few chairs. We faced our screen toward the reviewing "Committee."

The "Committee" arrived and one by one seated themselves at the head table. The Board Chairman's sidekick - the local politician, McMasters - apparently the Chairman of that "Committee", announced that the Hospital Board had appointed them to hear our appeal. He called his group the "Medical Staff Committee."

He was flanked by the woman who ran a chain saw business, the representative of the local coal company; and he announced that the fourth member of that "Committee" - the heir of a local industry - was unable to attend, but would "review the record of the appeal before voting."

The Chairman, a short fellow with a forceful, deep voice, advised the Hospital Prosecutor to proceed. His presentation was a rehash of the summation in that stuffy little "courtroom" a few weeks earlier, except that there was not a repeat of the theatrics of nose pushing at his earlier presentation.

As he concluded, the "Chairman" advised Demay to proceed. John gave a detailed description of the earlier hearings as we projected confirming documents on the screen.

As the Hospital Prosecutor spoke and even as DeMay made his presentation, one couldn't help notice the chain saw lady. She radiated importance. I don't believe I've ever seen anyone quite so full of themselves.

She was undoubtedly justified. She was sitting in judgement of a professional career.

Near the mid point of our presentation, the Chairman asked DeMay if he would shorten his review since the hour was getting late.

That, in retrospect, was the signal that we had gone through another sham hearing. They would submit their "unanimous" report to the full Hospital Board. The unanimous vote included that of the Committee member who never even made it to that hearing.

Chapter 14

> "Nobody is poor unless he stands in need of justice."
>
> —Lactantius

THE PENNSYLVANIA COURTS

When, during the Kangaroo Court, John DeMay exclaimed to the self-appointed judge, "Ms. Mattern, this is incredible, truly incredible!", he was expressing his frustration and bewilderment. He simply could not comprehend that he was part of what was happening. He had never seen such disregard of fairness and due process. When he turned to me and expressed his disgust with that "Judge", he was responding to his disbelief that a lawyer, any lawyer, could be so willing to abandon all semblance of legality, let alone justice or fair play, for a price.

He had suffered during the Hearing by being turned down by Mattern on each and every motion to have the "Court" conduct a fair hearing. He had failed to have an unbiased hearing panel - the three members of that "jury" could, in no way, be impartial. The "judge", herself, after appointing herself and using her own implausible bylaws, had denied us the right to an impartial Hearing Panel and Hearing Officer. She had demonstrated, with undeniable clarity, that she was a hired gun and would conduct a sham of a hearing with a pre-determined outcome. I would be found guilty of each of those frivolous charges.

After all, the Hospital Board Chairman had announced the outcome of the Hearing months earlier, and had his pronouncement entered into the Hospital Board minutes.

During a quiet moment between sessions of the Kangaroo Court,

John had said, "Get me to a judge, any judge. They will never get away with this". We had not found, by that time, that the Prosecutor's only expert witness had perjured himself with the Prosecutor's help. We did know, however, that Supervisor Marshall had altered and falsified hospital records; and we knew that the Administrator and Doctor Vader had attempted to suborn one of our witnesses. John felt certain that no judge would allow such behavior to stand; as well as unsupported heresay testimony and the unsupported documents presented by the Prosecutor.

At that time, we didn't know that Vader had assumed control of the resuscitation for my elderly patient and then had stood by, watching the patient die, without giving help, so that he could file charges.

We did know, following the Hearing, that there was a real doubt for a fair hearing in the local court. The town's establishment was involved with the local Court, along with the Coal Company, the banks and the Newspaper.

The County Court hadn't been known for its integrity. An earlier judge had allowed his son and son-in-law, both lawyers, to try cases before him. They compiled remarkable records until the Pennsylvania Supreme Court put an end to the family charade. In addition, the County's two Judges had been law partners prior to being elected to judgeships.

A patient and supposed friend, as a Hospital Board member and as my lawyer, would give us an honest appraisal of the local Court - so we thought.

We knew that, on more than one occasion, local citizens seeking justice would ask to have their cases transferred to another county. We wondered if we should ask for a change of venue, hoping for an honest judge.

Jacob was cordial when John DeMay and I were shown into his office on the second floor of the new Bank Building. The building stood on the site of the former Stewart Hardware and across Philadelphia Street from the new court house.

After a little small talk between the lawyers, DeMay came right to the point. "Can we get a fair hearing in the Indiana County Court?" My lawyer "friend", without hesitation, opined: "I can tell you, without doubt, that if anyone tries to influence either of our judges...they lose. The judges are both meticulously honest." It would be some time before we would discover the mendacity behind that advice. It would prove to be the most harmful bit of counsel I would ever receive. But,it would take time to realize the harm that would follow, by trusting that advice.

DeMay quickly prepared a motion for a temporary injunction against the Hospital. He explained that such an injunction is usually granted and has the effect of stopping any dispute in its tracks until the merits are argued. The next step would be to petition the court for a permanent injunction which, if granted, would prevent the Hospital from carrying out its revocation of Medical Staff privileges. There would, undoubtedly, be a hearing on that motion.

Without hesitation, Judge Robert Earley granted the injunction, and I continued in the hospital practice. The injunction stayed in place for several months. To say that the hospital atmosphere was tense during that period would be an understatement.

Nathan Goldfarb continued to conduct the Surgical Department meetings and was visibly uncomfortable with my presence. DeMay had cautioned me to say nothing. Everyone was on guard. Goldfarb had yielded to my demand that he stop acting as both Department Chairman and Department Secretary. The Department had elected a Secretary - one of the surgeons - and the Department minutes no longer read with all the personal comments and vitriol that had characterized Goldfarb's minutes.

Suddenly, we were told that Goldfarb's pal, President Judge Handler, had dismissed Judge Earley from the case and had taken over. He immediately dissolved the temporary injunction which had allowed me to practice at the Hospital. Some of the local lawyers were amazed - this was not a known practice. The local paper blasted the news across the front pages, announcing an end to my practice at the Hospital.

Judge Handler was said to be the son of a scrap dealer who had made a tidy fortune during the first world war. He was known to have a good grasp of the Law, but to harbor a great deal of intractable prejudice. However, DeMay and I were confident that the shear treachery of the hospital hearings would assure a fair judgement.

That confidence was eroded when we began hearing of attempts to influence the local judges. Weeks earlier, DeMay and I decided to drive to the Country Club as we left the courthouse. We were seeking a coffee for John and a beer for me. At the club, Judge Earley was sitting by the long row of windows of the club dining room looking out onto the long clubhouse porch and the eighteenth green. The three of us had engaged in small talk for a few minutes when John excused himself for a few minutes, leaving me alone with the Judge. At that moment, Goldfarb suddenly appeared and walked past us, not looking our way. Surprisingly, the Judge looked at me, and without restraint said, "There goes one of your detractors! He has called me twice now, advising me how to rule in your case."

The "Evening Blab" carried the injunction news on its front page almost daily. With the court hearings about to begin, the red-headed girl reporter kept repeating, on the paper's front page, that I was dismissed from the hospital due to "twenty charges, two of which involved the death of one of my patients."

It was not good publicity.

His honor, Handler, having dismissed his colleague, Judge Earley, and having dissolved Earley's injunction against the hospital, was now in control, and scheduled hearings on DeMay's petition for a permanent injunction. The final arguments by DeMay and the Hospital Lawyer were heard on June 6th.

The new County Courthouse on the town's main thoroughfare, Philadelphia Street, is a large, square, colonial structure with a geometric slate roof. The building sits back from the street and is fronted by a small, landscaped park, bisected by a flagstone walk and a series of granite steps. To the left is the bronze statue of Jimmy Stewart, signaling the county's main claim to fame. The first floor lobby is entered through large, white paneled doors. Walking to the elevators on the left, one passes the large, glass doors on each side, opening into the Prothonotary's Office and the Recorder's Office.

On the day of the hearing, DeMay and I waved to my friend, Helen, the Prothonotary, as we passed the offices and were given a rather solemn, "Good luck", as she poked her head through the slightly open glass door, while we waited for our elevator. DeMay was quiet as we rode to the courtroom areas on the fourth floor. A short walk around the corner brought us to Handler's court room, just across the hall from Earley's court. The maple double doors opened into a typical colonial interior. The room's white, enameled, wood paneling and maple trim, along with the brass chandeliers and their sparkling bulbs, gave a cheerful brightness to the place. The rows of stark maple benches for the audience were separated from the trial area by a bannister of large, white enameled panels, topped by maple rails. Matching white jury boxes flanked each side of the Judge's bench. The bench conformed with a facing of white wooden panels, elevating the bench to a level above the court floor and a little above the witness boxes. On the wall behind and above the bench in brass letters was the high sounding admonition reading: "No man is above the law; and no man is beneath it." As DeMay and I sat ourselves at the left counsel table, DeMay began carefully arranging his notes from a worn brown, leather brief case. I sat, uneasily, looking at that gold lettered phrase, "No man is above the law; and no man beneath it." I couldn't help wondering whether that applied to Judges - particularly Goldfarb's friend, Judge Handler.

Groups of twos and threes began to filter into the Court and, within a short while, the spectators benches were filled with hospital officials, a few physicians and a number of my patients. The Administrator sat in one of the benches near the rear and there seemed to be a separation between my patients on the right of the spectator area and the hospital people on the left.

Goldfarb and his wife entered and regally strolled across the aisle, separating the benches from the trial area. The girls from our office were in the front row behind the railing and I couldn't help notice their heads go together, followed by a smile. One of them had been brought up in a little mining community on the outskirts of Indiana, where Goldfarb had an office as the Company doctor, housed in one of the Company houses. She had always been aware that the miners and their families were considered second rate and were treated differently from the "important" folks. There were very few in town who failed to notice the attempted climb of the Doctor and his coiffured wife, Fluffy, on the rungs of Indiana's social and political ladder.

Despite my concern at the prospect of the upcoming argument, and a growing anxiety for my family's future, I was curious about the smiles in the front row. I later learned that one of the girls suggested that the Goldfarbs walked that way because they had "a stick up their ass." Despite the gravity of the moment, we could always count on her to tell it like it was.

As the Patrician promenade across the court room ended, Goldfarb deposited Fluffy on one of the empty spots on a front bench, and to the notice of all, walked across the trial area and seated himself on the upper level of the empty jury box. He was above the spectators but still slightly below His Honor's seat. His self-confidence was unmistakable.

I noticed one of the Medical Staff "Executives" seat himself in a front row. He had his young son with him. It was disgusting to think that a young boy would be involved. What would he think of his father's attempt to appear important and masculine?

The Hospital Attorney suddenly burst in, looking breathless, as usual, with his bulging brief case and with a young lawyer at his side. He carefully surveyed the audience and methodically laid out his notes on the opposite counsel table.

Handler's aging tipstaff barked out his notice to please rise, advising that the Court of Common Pleas of Indiana County was in session - the Honorable Earl Handler, presiding. Handler advised us all to be seated and went through a perfunctory announcement that the hearing was relative to a request for a permanent injunction against Indiana Hospital in the case of Ralph J. Miller vs. Indiana Hospital. He called DeMay and the Hospital Lawyer to the bench and there followed a muffled discussion, followed by both lawyers returning quietly to their counsel tables. He advised Demay to proceed.

John was not forceful or aggressive, but was methodical and articulate as he outlined all the intricacies of the actions by the Hospital's Medical Staff Executive Committee. He detailed the behavior of the Hospital Lawyer and the self-appointed "lawyer-judge" at the Hospital hearings. Finally, he explained, in detail, the appeal hearing before the Hospital Board's Hearing Committee, where the Board itself had repeatedly ignored their own bylaws. He then carefully outlined each of the Hospital's charges, calling attention to the rebuttal of each of the charges presented at the hospital hearing. He continually stressed that the hospital, by accepting federal funds for its programs, had subjected itself to the due process provisions of the Federal Civil Rights Acts and that the preposterous hearings at the Hospital could never meet any standard for due process. As he concluded, there was absolute silence and Handler adjourned the court for a lunch break.

When the Court reconvened, there was no loss of attendance. By the time the tipstaff announced the Court was in session, all seats were filled. The Hospital Lawyer began a two hour presentation unhindered by the need for a pause at the end of his sentences or paragraphs. He began with a glowing description of his visits to Indiana County, where he had met the County's wonderful people and had enjoyed every moment in such a beautiful community. He praised the local Hospital and its dedicated employees, its outstanding Medical Staff and its dedicated, self-sacrificing Board of Directors. He spent the next several minutes comparing the outstanding judge with the judges in his home county, whom he described as often too busy to care and be as dedicated to fairness as was Judge Handler. Handler was disinclined to interrupt such praise.

He finally brought his attention to the case and began an explanation of how troublesome it was to him to threaten a physician's career after it had taken so many trying years of sacrifice to attain a position in a community hospital. He explained that, as a defense lawyer, he had spent most of his career defending doctors and he then detailed his unbridled respect for doctors, their profession and their integrity.

In his explanation he then amazed the audience when he continued to explain his position with the statement, that, to this day, leaves those who know, incredulous. He continued:

"One of the things that I think I ought to point out at the outset of this proceedings and this summation what this is not - this for example, is not a contest or a fight or attack on Doctor Miller's right to practice Medicine. Indeed, it is not in any way an attack on his competency, his capability to practice in a highly specialized field of medicine, Urology. Indeed, I don't think anyone who has known Doctor Miller for even a short period of time would question one or two facts: one, that he is intelligent, indeed brilliant; and, two, that he is capable, capable of practicing the finest type and standard of Urological medicine in the country."

I think I was too preoccupied at the time to catch the significance of the Hospital Lawyer's remarks, but people in the courtroom remembered his "judicial admission."

The statement, now part of the public record, continues to haunt him and brand him as the Hospital's hired gun.

The rest of the Hospital Lawyer's presentation was a wandering description of me allegedly terrorizing the personnel of Indiana Hospital. He described nurses coming to him in tears in dire fear of testifying. He described the hospital's tolerance of my sins over a number of years by providing privileges each year, but finally succumbing to the final straw and needing to weed out a bad apple. His performance hit its climax when he circled the courtroom, forcefully pushing his nose toward his forehead, until his eyes seemed to bulge. He said I did that to a nurse - something that never happened. In the midst of his diatribe, a woman seated in the audience, jumped up from one of the benches and shouted at him that he was crucifying an innocent professional. Before she could continue, Handler had her ejected from the courtroom and apologized, at great lengths, to the Hospital Lawyer for disruption of his speech. That brief episode seemed to energize Handler. He had been nodding, off and on, and I had begun to wonder if he was going to fall off his perch.

We waited many weeks for Handler's opinion. During this period one day, I was at one of the local markets picking up office supplies, when one of the local ministers came up with a friendly greeting at the check-out counter.

I was carrying a plastic bag of supplies and he followed along with a friendly inquiry about Joan and the boys. I was sure he had read the local chronicle and was wondering how the family was holding up. I assured him that all was well, but he probably sensed a false bravado. I was surprised when he said that he had been in the courtroom audience during the hearings. He related that he was not at all surprised at the hospital's activities revealed at the hearings. He described the workings of the town establishment and cited the perils anyone would face if he dared to question the activities of the crowd that had taken over the Hospital. With all kindness and candor, he said that I didn't have a prayer of winning in the local Court and, almost as a second thought, he described overhearing an adamant conversation between Goldfarb and Judge Handler, about my suit before the local court. The conversation took place on a street corner in front of the courthouse. He left with the admonition that there was no way to win in the local Court. This came at a time when local dissenters, with the coal company's hiring practices, were entering suits against the company, but in other counties and were citing the slim chance of a fair hearing in the local Court on any action which involved the coal company.

I had not forgotten that Judge Early had also told me openly about Goldfarb's efforts to influence his decisions but I was shrugging it all off. I could see no way that a jurist could be blatantly in the pocket of the likes of Goldfarb, and the Hospital group.

After all, my good friend and lawyer-Hospital Board member had sworn to the unquestioned integrity of the local judges.

Handler's opinion was finally handed down and denied a permanent injunction against the Hospital. The opinion was a lengthy thirty plus pages, giving Handler's own version of the state of the law that had laid down basic requirements for hospitals to be considered "quasi public", and therefore, required to provide due process provisions to their physicians and employees. Demay had carefully argued that such protections were guaranteed following a Pittsburgh case instituted by a Doctor Adler, against Pittsburgh's Montefiore Hospital.

The Court, in that case, had established for the first time, the existence of hospitals that were "quasi public." These were hospitals that were not owned and operated by a government or a governmental agency, but which had acquired governmental funding and, therefore, were required to abide by federal standards of fairness. DeMay had documented the local hospital's receipt of Hill-Burton, Appalachian and Health, Education and Welfare grants for its new building and he had called attention to the receipt of millions from the sale of government guaranteed bonds. Handler's opinion ignored the argument and centered on a scathing description of his concept of my personality and the need for the hospital management and staff to exert the authority to preserve order and avoid the threat of malpractice. The opinion would refer to the need for the Hospital to continue to provide excellence in health care.

Unknown to us at the time, there was on file in the Prothonotary's Office, just three floors below, the records of more than sixty malpractice suits filed against the Hospital and some of its physicians over a period of several years. Handler's cynicism would eventually emerge as outright dishonesty.

After Handler's dismissal of our request for an injunction against the Hospital, DeMay assessed the chances for a reversal of Handler's decision by the Pennsylvania Superior Court. He felt that the prospects were fair that the appeal would succeed if we argued that the local Hospital was, in fact, "quasi public". That would mean that the institution's actions would be considered "state action" - a legal term indicating that the hospital had sufficiently close ties to government. Its actions, therefore, were subject to federal requirements for due process - that is, fair play. He had little doubt that this hurdle could be breached and that any judge would have little hesitation in throwing out the decision of Ms. Mattern's Hearing Committee and the opinion of the local lackey, Handler.

It was Easter Sunday. The motel was quiet and I found myself awake just as the first light was beginning to show through the curtains. The family was still asleep and the activities for parents' weekend at Franklin & Marshall wouldn't begin for hours.

Not at all unusual, I found myself thinking about our case before the state Superior Court. The Courts were beginning to recognize that physicians were in need of some sort of legal protection from predatory hospitals and vengeful physicians who were known to bring charges against a fellow physician having nothing to do with competence or quality of care.

As I turned the principles over in my mind, there didn't seem to be any question that Indiana Hospital met the requirements for federal standards for fair play. The receipt of Medicare and Medicaid funds, as well as Hill-Burton and Appalachian grants certainly characterized Indiana Hospital as a "quasi public" institution. It would be embarrassing for the Hospital to have the Kangaroo court and its actors scrutinized under standards for "due process" and "fair play."

I recalled that John DeMay had called on the previous Sunday. He had been working on our appeal to the Superior Court and was truly excited. His research had brought him to review the case of Berberian v. Lancaster Osteopathic Hospital Association. Doctor Berberain was a pioneer. He had begun caring for uncomplicated pregnancies at his private clinic. The Osteopathic Hospital had retaliated by revoking his hospital privileges. He had lost in his local Court, but the state Superior Court had reversed with the ruling that hospitals be required to closely adhere to their bylaws. Even Atorney Mattern's bylaws at Indiana didn't allow the Administrator and Vader to tamper with witnesses, or for the Hospital Lawyer's divorce client to commit perjury, or the Supervisor Marshall and her nurses to alter records.

Like a bolt from the blue, I realized that we were in Lancaster - Doctor Berberian's town. I dressed quietly and slipped out of our room and walked trough the motel's garden and pool area. I found a bank of telephones just off the deserted motel lobby, and sure enough, found Doctor Berberian listed in the directory.

Not wanting to wake the Doctor, I waited a half hour or so, and finally dialed his home number. A rather gruff, and probably sleepy voice answered. He listened as I explained our case, soon to be before the Superior Court, and he agreed to meet me at his office if I would give him time to dress and have a cup of coffee. The Clinic was in a partially remodeled, large, square house on one of Lancaster's residential streets. The Doctor answered the door wearing a blue sports shirt and plaid trousers. Without being overly gracious, he invited me to follow, and we walked through a large, front room with six or eight white enameled hospital beds. Light blankets were folded neatly at the foot of each bed, and it was apparent that the bare floor, and the room itself, were spotlessly clean.

The Doctor explained the birthing routine and the system that allowed his patients to give birth and return home within a few hours. We walked through a short hallway into a room serving as his office. His large desk was at one side of the room; and as he motioned me toward a chair at one side of the desk, I was struck that the room was more like a turn-of-the-century living area, rather than an office.

Slowly, the Doctor became more engaging, as I related the events that had taken place in Indiana County leading to the upcoming appeal to the state Superior Court. He became interested in the similarity between the controlling groups in Lancaster's Osteopathic Hospital and Indiana Hospital. It was apparent to both of us that, for years, hospital groups could band together to force their competitors from town. But, a few cases nationwide, such as the Berberian victory, were showing that the courts were beginning to show interest in improper hospital activities that could interfere with the livelihood of a physician-victim.

His one outstanding bit of advice came as a stroke of wisdom. He said, "The toughest chore you have ahead is to maintain your own self-respect." In view of the venomous tales being circulated by Goldfarb, Vader and the Hospital Lawyers, his advice was certainly fitting.

As we chatted on that Sunday morning, a friendship was formed, and we agreed to keep in touch. The Doctor posed for a snapshot on the steps of his Clinic, and as we shook hands, he said, "Call me when you win this - I'll treat you to the biggest steak dinner in town."

We filed an appeal and our brief to the Court of Appeals again outlined the violations of due process during Ms. Mattern's Kangaroo Court, including heresay testimony admitted as fact, the presumption of guilt, the need for defense to proceed first before hearing prosecution evidence, the falsification of hospital records by the Hospital, the aid to a witness's perjury by the Hospital Lawyer, the attempt of the Hospital Administrator and Vance Vader to suborn one of our witnesses and the preponderance of our evidence without the basic right provided for me to face my accuser, Vance Vader.

We began another wait for the Court to act, one of the first of the interminable waits for our justice system to function over the coming years. After several months, we were notified of a date for argument before a Superior Court panel of three judges. We were advised that the panel hearing our appeal would be: Chief Judge William Circone, a seasoned local jurist, Sydney Hoffman, a supposedly retired "Senior Judge", and a man named Weiand, who had recently been defeated in his bid for a second term on the bench. I have never been able to understand how a judge, defeated by the electorate, continues to sit and judge after his term expires. What does it take for the electorate to remove a judge? But, perhaps of even more significance, is the system where elderly judges like Hoffman pass their retirement date and continue their old routine at the same pay and with a pension without a pause. The situation became even more ludicrous after we looked into the careers of these men. Weiand had enjoyed a mediocre career before going to the Superior Court and Hoffman had been the product of a political machine ruled by a politician named Green, in Philadelphia. Pittsburgh lawyers talked about Hoffman as a real busybody on the eighth floor of the City County Building, where he ignored his "senior" status. I had seen him preside as part of a full Superior Court hearing in Philadelphia several years before. He had been seated near the far end of a wide, circular bench and sported a large bow tie - apparently his trade mark. He was not "senior" then, but had assumed a dominant role in unkindly quizzing the lawyers appearing before the Court.

My office staff had been involved in the Hospital proceedings from the beginning and were loyal. I had come to appreciate their support; I respected their appraisal of the case as it progressed; as well as their evaluation of some of the Hospital people involved.

Two of the Hospital Board members were lawyers and patients of ours, along with the Administrator at the time of the Hospital hearings. I felt there was a measure of protection by these two men, trained in the law, and in a position to review the activities of the Hospital Lawyers, who participated in the hearings.

I think we all recognized the Administrator's insecurity and devious nature early on. As a courtesy, we never charged him for our care, but I was repeatedly warned by the staff not to trust him.

The office staff went along to Pittsburgh on the day of the argument before the Superior Court. Superior Court sessions are held in a large, ornate chamber on the eighth floor of the City-County Building on Pittsburgh's Grant Street. We met DeMay in one of the anterooms adjoining the Court and quietly gave our greetings. He suggested that we go into the courtroom and wait for the Court to convene. The room was hushed and its elegance lent a cathedral-like sense of confidence and tranquility. We seated ourselves in the second row of benches on the left and, as I sat and gazed at the ornate, gilded panels on the ceiling, and the tall floor to ceiling windows flanked with elegant velvet draperies, I sensed that we had found the right place for justice, away from the pettiness and influence of the Indiana County Courthouse.

The three judges entered through a paneled walnut door behind the long, elevated walnut bench. There was a brief, perfunctory instruction by the tipstaff and we were seated after the required ritual of respectful standing. Judge Circone sat in the center with Weiand to his right, and Hoffman on his left. We listened to the arguments of two cases that were scheduled before ours. The lawyers on both sides were persuasive and well-versed on the merits of their positions. Each presentation was limited to ten minutes, giving the lawyers little leeway in making their points. We were all astonished - including DeMay - at the outright nasty, impolite, brutal interruption of the lawyers by these three robed characters. Circone made no effort to control either Weiand or Hoffman. The two lawyers were women and each, in turn, after their browbeating, returned to their seats in tears.

My staff looked at me and I looked at DeMay. He didn't return my gaze. The girls just looked astonished and then sat with their eyes lowered. Our case was called and two clerks entered from behind the bench and put stacks of papers related to our case, before each judge. DeMay quietly walked to the lectern on the left facing the bench. I felt sick. I had held out the hope that we would be given better treatment, but I felt my heart thumping and my mouth going dry as a bone. DeMay carefully and deliberately outlined the arguments for the hospital requiring it to be subject to civil rights provisions, guaranteeing fair hearings to hospital personnel. But, he was stopped abruptly by Circone, who wanted to know how old Doctor Miller was. DeMay was nearing his conclusion when Hoffman brutally and loudly interrupted DeMay's argument, opining that his arguments held no relevance. He patted the pile of records in front of him and announced that DeMay's client had had a fair hearing. There was no doubt that Hoffman had little knowledge of those documents in front of him. DeMay could do nothing but conclude and return to his seat beside us. He was unbelieving. Ms. Mattern sat on the far right of the room with a young lawyer from the Hospital's law firm. He gave a quiet and articulate presentation of the Hospital's position that it was a private institution and was not subject to legal requirements for due process. He was not questioned and he quietly sat down at the conclusion of his argument.

As we left the courtroom, DeMay had no explanation for the outrageous behavior of that Court. I would never forget the hopelessness and the disgust I felt that day as we separated. We had been subjected another "fix."

"Senior" Judge Hoffman wrote the opinion and I first learned of it when a call came from Joe Grata, a top reporter for the Pittsburgh Press. He had been working on an investigative story about Indiana Hospital when the Hospital Board Chairman and the local newspaper publisher, Donnelly, had gone to his Editor, John Troan, at the Press and had the story squelched. He was truly sorry for breaking the news that Hoffman had written the opinion and had decided that the hospital hearings were not subject to the fairness standards of the law and that the only standard required by that Court, was for the Hospital to follow its own bylaws, and, therefore, the local Court's decision stood. As DeMay and I went over that decision, it was apparent that Hoffman based his opinion on the technicality that DeMay had not entered certain documents into the record which confirmed the Hospital's acceptance of millions in federal funds. DeMay had included reference to those funds, but this was not satisfactory for Hoffman. DeMay petitioned the Court to enter those documents into the printed record but was promptly denied.

We knew then that there was a substantial chance that the Pennsylvania Supreme Court would not hear the case, but we made the necessary preparations for a further appeal. Those steps not only require the wait of many months - sometimes years - but the Courts, nevertheless, require meticulous adherence to their rules, which include elaborate printing and binding of the records supplied to them.

Our case had substantial significance in Pennsylvania for its physicians. Previous decisions had begun to recognize the need for standards for peer review proceedings at hospitals in order to protect physicians unjustly accused. The American Medical Association, for years, had described in its "Principles of Medical Ethics", the admonition:

"Due Process: The basic principles of a fair and objective hearing should always be accorded to the physician when professional conduct is being reviewed. The fundamental aspects of a fair hearing are: a listing of specific charges, adequate notice of the right to a hearing, the opportunity to be present and to rebut the evidence, and the opportunity to present a defense. These principles apply when the hearing body is a medical society tribunal or a hospital committee composed of physicians."

"These principles of fair play apply in all disciplinary hearings and to any other type of hearing in which the physician may be deprived of valuable property rights. Whenever physicians sit in judgement on physicians and whenever that judgement affects a physician's reputation, professional status, or livelihood, these principle of fair play must be observed."

The AMA's admonition continues:

"All physicians are urged to observe dilligently these fundamental safeguards of due process whenever they are called upon to serve on a committee which will pass judgement on physicians. Medical societies and hospital medical staffs are urged to review the constitution and bylaws of the society or hospital medical staff to make sure that these instruments provide for such procedural safeguards."

Like so many of its standards, the AMA over the years, had no means of implementation or enforcement of its principles. The organization scrupulously avoided any involvement in what they repeatedly referred to as local disputes. My letters to the hierarchy of the Chicago-based, East Dearborn Street institution, led only to assurances by the paper-shuffling bureaucracy that we would rely on the courts or the local Medical Society. They were unimpressed that the local Society was dominated by the same small group who were members of the Hospital Executive Committee.

The Pennsylvania Medical Society took a somewhat different view. The Society President called and listened carefully after I had sent him a letter describing the hearings at the Hospital. He felt that Indiana Hospital's problems needed to be addressed by the organized medical profession in Pennsylvania and arranged to have me meet with Barbara Starr, an executive with the state Society.

I met Miss Starr in Harrisburg on a Sunday morning over coffee and gave her copies of documents from the Hospital hearings. She had a keen intellect and I could see how she had risen to a responsible position. In disbelief, she looked over copies of the Hospital bylaws, records from the Hospital hearings and various documents which had been presented to establish innocence at the hearings. She most carefully read the transcripts of the seven physicians who had testified on my behalf. She asked to keep the transcripts and other documents and promised to get back in a short period of time, after she had had an opportunity to meet with Fred Speaker, a former Pennsylvania Attorney General, who was now counsel for the Pennsylvania Medical Society.

Barbara called several days later and scheduled a date for Speaker and her to visit Indiana. They wanted to meet with the Hospital people first and would then meet with me at the office.

After they arrived, our conversation was casual and Speaker related that he and Miss Starr had gotten very little information or cooperation at the Hospital. They had seen the Administrator and Board Chairman and reported that they had gotten no information and had gotten no indication that the Hospital people were interested in discussing peer review.

As Speaker finished a ham sandwich, he said that there was no choice but to ask the Executive Board of the State Medical society to file an amicus brief to the Appellate Court on my behalf. The brief would support our position that Pennsylvania physicians are to be guaranteed due process and a fair hearing in any matter affecting their ability to earn a livelihood. I was to learn that an 'amicus brief" (friend of the Court) could be filed with information favorable to one of the litigants in a court action.

Within days, Speaker held a telephone conference with the members of the Pennsylvania Society's Executive Board. It was reported that the Board debated the issue of entering the Society into my suit against the hospital for an hour and a half. Finally, and surprisingly, on the advice of Speaker, they voted to keep the Society out of the case. By this time, I was having less trouble believing that the Hospital's behind-the-scenes activities could be effective. We were later to receive confirmation of Doctor Goldfarb's efforts to influence the local Court and the Hospital Lawyer's illegal ex parte (behind-the-scenes) influence with the Pennsylvania Department of Health.

A number of weeks after Hoffman's decision came down, I was reading the Pennsylvania Medical Society Journal at my desk, during a noontime break. As I turned a page there was a two-page article, reviewing Hoffman's decision, and its ramification for Pennsylvania physicians. The article was authored by Speaker and was a factual review of the Hoffman opinion, but, in a final paragraph, Speaker concluded that the decision would make it simpler for hospitals to get rid of "bad physicians." DeMay dismissed the final paragraph as a slip of the pen. But I began getting calls from Pittsburgh physician friends who had trouble rationalizing Speaker's remarks. Some were furious that he would castigate one of the Society's members. One of my friends described a discussion about the article in the dining room of one of Pittsburgh's large hospitals. The diners were apparently amazed at Speaker's carelessness.

We all finally agreed that the article couldn't go unchallenged. Calls to the State Society got no attention; so a suit was filed against Speaker. We took Speaker's deposition, that is, the process of his being required to answer questions under oath with a lawyer from each side and a court stenographer present. We were hoping to find a link between Speaker and the string-pullers of the Hospital hierarchy. Speaker's experience as Pennsylvania's Attorney General for several years was apparently influencing his responses. He was obviously adept at politics and easily avoided our questions. Despite his obvious intelligence and legal skill, he could recall no one from Indiana, Pennsylvania, and claimed that he had only a slight recollection of his trip there with Barbara Starr. He had no explanation for his advice to the Governing Body of the Society to be uninvolved in my case or his abrupt turn-around from his previous desire to help.

After some months, Speaker's lawyer called and offered to settle. Speaker agreed to publish a re-traction of his previous article with an apology. The next issue of Pennsylvania Medicine printed a prominent retraction and apology on one of the front pages of the publication with copies printed in our local newspaper. The case was dismissed and we continued to wonder who influenced this man in his overnight change of direction.

<u>Dr. Harry Berberian</u> — His Lancaster clinic pioneered a new era of obstetrics without hospital admission when the local hospital retaliated by revoking his medical staff privileges. His suit against Lancaster Osteopathic Hospital Association was won; and in a landmark decision, the Pennsylvania Superior Court ruled that Pennsylvania hospitals must adhere strictly to their bylaws.

Chapter 15

"The truth is found when men are free to pursue it."

—Franklin Delano Roosevelt

THE CITIZENS COMMITTEE

There had always been rumblings about the Hospital, and the local newspaper.

People who distrusted the local hospital, would travel to out-of-town and out-of-state hospitals with established names; and there were those who were interested in unedited local news and read out-of-town papers. There were always others who feared city traffic and would trust to luck and convenience by entering the local hospital.

I had found that the deciding factor, more often than not, was the patient's physician. A hospital's success, therefore, was related to the expertise and integrity of its medical staff. I had found that patients would come from well beyond the County borders, if they believed their physician would provide excellence in services and demand excellence in their care.

But, there were also those physicians who would confuse popularity with respect, thereby clinging to the laissez faire acceptance of questionable or dangerous hospital practices. It seemed, as the years went by, that this was becoming the Hospital policy.

The new Board Chairman and his newly-hired and compliant Administrator, apparently found no problem with mediocrity, and of course, the "conspiracy of silence." Their myopic vision would become coupled with unbridled arrogance. The Administrator and the Board Chairman could hire and fire at will, and reportedly did so with impunity.

They met no resistance to their ruthless firings - always followed by inuendo and behind-the-scenes intrigue ... that is, until now.

The October Hospital Board meeting had been held, and within hours, I had learned through double agents, of that regrettable scene. The attendance of the meeting was greater than usual and reports of phone calls to members of the Board, urging their attendance to vote, began to surface. The vote was apparently the only business for that meeting, which was apparently conducted by the self-appointed "Judge" of the Kangaroo Court - Ms. Mattern.

Each Board member was presented a listing of all those "terrible charges" that were presented by the Hospital Prosecutor, at the Kangaroo Court. The lists of charges were signed by Claude Clippins, the "Hearing Committee" Chairman, the young internist and the dentist on the "Hearing Panel." Ms. Mattern was described as giving the Hospital Board members a few minutes to "look over the charges and then vote". She then made the recommendation for revocation of my Hospital privileges.

Those attending described that "all hell broke loose", when one member of the Board revolted at being asked to "pass judgement on a man's career within a few minutes of reading ridiculous charges such as "not serving on a Library Committee." There were apparently whispers from others, who agreed with him. He was the only Board Member in the health care field and the only member of the Board knowledgable of health care issues.

Lawyer Mattern, at that point, "the impartial Judge" of the Kangaroo Court insisted on an immediate vote, advising that "we can't back-down". The Administrator and the Board Chairman then joined in, insisting on an immediate vote.

The Board's Secretary - the aging dowager asked "what it was all about." Lawyer Mattern advised that "Dr. Miller "was causing confusion in the Hospital." "Well", says the lady, "that's all I need to know. Now I have something to vote on."

The Board then heard from the "Driller", who had sunk wells on the Hospital grounds. This was one of his infrequent appearances to Hospital Board meetings. He asked, "Can we be sued for this?" Lawyer Mattern was said to reply, "Yes, either in Federal or State Court, but we will win." The Driller then moved that my Hospital privileges would be revoked and he was seconded by the woman who ran a chain-saw shop.

I have always suspected that the "Driller" carried a heavy load of guilt with him until his self-destruction.

The vote was taken. Two voted against revocation; the rest followed the Hospital Lawyer's advice and voted to end my privileges at Indiana Hospital.

The next morning, I was leaving the operating room, when the Administrator handed me the large, manilla envelope. The Board Chairman had signed the letter ending my privileges at the Hospital - effective immediately. They couldn't wait for the ink to dry or for the mail.

A few days before, a well known local businessman, Bill London, had undergone a surgical procedure. I had hesitated to tell him that I couldn't continue his postoperative care so soon after surgery. I did call his spouse to give the news. She was irate. When she called back, she and a daughter, a nurse from Washington, D. C., who had been home for her Dad's surgery, had visited the Board Chairman at his home. As the Board Chairman would later describe the visit, "They raised hell." It is unlikely that he was aware, at the time, that he had overlooked the possibility that this would not be one of his routine firings. After that visit, the family did tell Bill of the recent events and he demanded to see both the Board Chairman and the Administrator in his room.

Bill was a large, white-haired impressive guy. He had a tendency to say what he meant and to mean what he said. The two men appeared in his room as directed, and Bill would later describe that he told them, "They just didn't know what they were getting into." He described that the Chairman replied, "We are prepared." But were they? Would their latest victim leave town in the midst of innuendo as others before had done, or would the Hospital's actions prove a costly misadventure? The answer would not be long in coming. Promptly, the Board Chairman would be heard to repeatedly say, "Remember, I had nothing to do with this, from beginning to end." Would events support that position or would he be branded as a liar?

My lawyer, DeMay, petitioned the local Court to extend my hospital privileges with an injunction until there could be a full hearing. Judge Earley complied, and the injunction stayed in place for several months. Despite that, a small notice of my dismissal appeared on the front page of the local paper - after it was leaked by the Administrator and a few others.

The next morning, the Korean urologist, who had been recruited by Vance Vader, caught me in the hallway and instructed me that I should refer my surgical patients to him or one of the other county urologists. He was difficult to understand, but I got the message and was, I'm afraid, too dumbfounded to give a response.

My patient, Bill, was shortly discharged to home care, but was, by no means, satisfied. He vowed to bring about a complete overhaul of the Hospital Management.

Within a few days, the local paper was deluged with letters criticizing the Hospital for "dismissing a respected veteran urologist after nineteen years of service."

Newspaper publisher Donnelly yielded, and the paper published a full page of letters, on page three, headlined, "Readers Favor Dr. Miller's Hospital Reinstatment." Donnelly had told one of the letter writers that a complete added edition of his paper would be needed if he were to print all of the letters he had received.

Bill London's two column letter led the printed letters with a firey description of the Administrator's and the Board Chairman's actions shortly after his surgery. Bill's letter continued, "After reading a list of petty charges against Dr.Miller, as published in the October 14 issue, it is quite evident that ninety percent of the charges are of a personality nature, and I for one, just don't much care if or not a doctor smiles when he operates on me! It should be noted that the other ten percent of charges listed are of a nature that can be readily refuted and proven false with affidavits from those involved."

Even though the page of "Letters to the Editor" convinced most readers that the Hospital charges were petty and false, the red-headed reporter continued her front page pasting.

Then, the unfathomable occurred. President Judge Handler (Dr. Goldfarb's pal) removed Judge Earley from our case and dissolved the injunction against the Hospital.

The front page headline was, "Dr. Miller Injunction Dismissed", and the story read,

"The Doctor's privileges were revoked by the Indiana Hospital Board of Directors on October 7, after they ruled that Miller was guilty of twenty charges, two of which involved the death of one of his patients."

The excerpts from Handler's opinion went much further. One part read, "In order to implement this (highest standards of medical care for patients), the Hospital has promulgated bylaws, Medical Staff bylaws, rules of conduct and directly regulating the practice of all professionals in the hospital."

He continued:

"The charges are not only reasonably related to the objectives of the Hospital, but go to the very heart of public interest in the manner in which the Hospital is operated. They have substance, and if established by proper evidence, are permissable grounds for the disciplinary action contemplated in this case."

The arrogance of the Hospital Board Chairman was now being matched by the Court. Handler knew of the perjury, the alteration of Hospital records, the witness tampering by the Hospital and the bias of the Hospital hearings. He was still able to dismiss the former Judge (Earley) on the case and write a dastardly set of falsehoods. Handler had to know of the number of malpractice actions that had been filed against the Hospital in the County Court. In addition to reading the transcripts of the Hospital hearings, he had to know of his doctor buddy's operating room mishaps and reputation. His opinion clearly revealed that his mind had been made up before the upcoming Court hearing. It was just as the Hospital Board Chairman had announced the outcome of the Hospital hearings before they began.

Handler's dismissal of the temporary injunction against the Hospital, the hearings before him and his refusal to grant a permanent injunction against the Hospital, continued to fuel the flames of the local uproar which was becoming more than local. It reached the pages of the Pittsburgh and other regional papers. A detailed "Letter to the Editor" appeared in the local paper criticizing the Hospital management. Only this time, the letter was signed by "The Committee of Concerned Citizens for Hospital Improvement." The group, including Bill London and Gary Buckwalter, the Chairman of the local University Physics Department, had formed a committee to look into the workings of the Hospital - until now protected by its "veil of secrecy."

Along with the bombardment I was experiencing from the local paper, there was what my friends were describing as "character assassination." "The Boys" were active in dispensing tales. They probably believed that there would be a positive efect from all their efforts. We kept hearing that I was "paranoid." We couldn't pin down the source, but it had been repeated by the Administrator although he would deny he ever heard such a thing. The source of that fabrication would later come to light strikingly.

The Board Chairman then entered the clamor publicly. Even though he continued his, "Remember, I had nothing to do with this from beginning to end", he answered the Citizens Committee letter with his own, printed in the local paper. He was now out in the open. His printed letter, in part, said, "Since the matter in question is still involved in litigation, and further, because of our concern in protecting properly confidential matters, involving patients and Dr. Miller, himself; it would be inappropriate for me to comment on the merits of this matter." He then <u>commented on the merits of the matter.</u>

His letter continued:

"However, let me assure one and all, that I am totally confident that any reasonable person, having knowledge of the facts in this matter, would reach precisely the same conclusions as did all those who have been involved in the matter to date." Here was the inuendo that had strangled all those previous victims of firings - now in the open for all to see.

At about that time, Goldfarb was going through the Hospital operating room telling people that I had put my spouse in the home for battered women.

The Chairman and Goldfarb had gone too far. For the first time, the inuendo that had forced others from the Hospital and from town had been put in print. I was determined, at some point ,to answer these people. Their treachery with people's lives had to stop. But for the time, DeMay cautioned, I had to rely on the Court and keep my silence. Also, I could not have an open association with the Citizens Committee.

The Committee held their meetings at the local Holiday Inn, and began to attract growing numbers of members who had had unpleasant experiences with the Hospital. The letters, over a period of months, began to number in the dozens. I, of course, knew the Committee's actions, and I was finding it difficult not to be openly involved. Many of my friends could have used more support; but I was forced to "grin and bear" the wild stories being circulated by the Hospital gang.

For about a year, the growing mound of evidence being collected by the Committee began to show a pattern of irregular activity by some of the Hospital people. Former Hospital employees, some former management people, and others, gave detailed financial and other critical information. They gave, not only detailed information of Hospital finances, but provided documents and suggestions for places to look for further information. Some current employees provided information of questionable activities of some of the Hospital's professionals - particularly the Medical Staff "Executive Committee" and the Nursing Department heads. These informants were frightened that they would jeopardize their own job security, but trusted the Committee never to reveal their identities. They began to describe paranoia of the Hospital Management that actually began to be the source of some humor.

At a later time, a security alarm was sounded throughout the Hospital, according to reports. A Hospital employee said that the alarm went off when someone discovered that an amateur poet had recorded, in lipstick, on an elevator wall, a poetic and unauthenticated description of the sexual activities of some of the management. I never learned whether I was being blamed for that poem, and the uproar that followed.

Many of the Citizen Committee members had known that the Hospital Administrator had been joining others in circulating the story that Miller was "paranoid." The humor was spontaneous when a high ranking member of the Hospital Administration secretly described the anxiety of the Administrator, who was learning of the detailed information that was being provided to the Committee. We were first told that the Administrator had electronic devices installed in his office to trap intruders and then rented an infrared device from the Mechanicsburg Army Depot to be installed on the Hospital roof, in order to detect Dr. Miller coming through the woods at night. For a time, it was said by some employees that people began searching the packages of evening visitors to the Hosptial.

At this point in time, I recognize that there will be those who simply will not believe that all this happened; and I can't blame them. I again think back to the afternoon when one of our patients was one of the lawyers on the Hospital Board. He agreed that we were being part of an incredible story. But, when I confided that I would some day put the story into print, he exclaimed, "It is an incredible story; but no one will believe it."

As Ripley used to say, "Believe it or not" - truth really may be stranger than fiction. The material that was being collected by the Committee shed more and more light on a strange, very strange group, who had been setting standards for a community hospital.

Dr. Goldfarb, of course, had assumed that his Surgical Department meetings would be tranquil once Miller was removed from the scene. But, not long after my absence from the Department meetings, one of the surgeons called. He described that at the Department meeting the prior evening, two of the surgeons had to be separated after they collided during a surgical fee dispute.

Finally, the "character assassination", following the tradition of inuendo, caused me to respond to the Board Chairman's distorted "Letter to the Editor." I responded with the first public challenge to the Chairman's mode of operation with a letter describing my efforts, over the years, to improve Hospital conditions. I alluded to the Hospital Lawyer's continuing assertions of my involvement with the Citizens Committee and my letter ended with, "I have, this date, written to the Committee of Concerned Citizens for Hospital Improvement, offering my services in whatever capacity I may serve."

As the suspicions of the Committee were becoming documented, the Committee members were becoming more convinced that dramatic changes at the Hospital were necessary. They wrote the Hospital Board requesting a meeting with them. The reply came from the Kangaroo Court's prosecutor. His terse reply suggested that there was no need for a meeting with a group that was under the direction and control of a "disgruntled physician who had been dismissed from the Hospital."

The Committee learned that the oversight of hospitals in Pennsylvania was provided by the Hospital Division of the Pennsylvania Department of Health, and a Chicago-based organization called the Joint Commission on Accreditation of Hospitals. The Joint Commission, for a number of years, had inspected hospitals every two or three years and then generally provided the hospital with a nice certificate for the lobby. There would then be a news conference, which would proclaim the excellence of the institution. For this, hospitals paid a fee. The organization had no enforcement authority. The Citizens Committee asked for an audience with the Commission's Inspection Team in order to present documentation of Hospital problems. The Inspection Team: a retired nurse, a retired physician, plus a retired hospital administrator came and left without meeting with the Citizens and issued a complimentary assessment of the Hospital. Soon thereafter the Citizen's Committee, through government sources, obtained a document showing that the Inspection Team had recommened correction of "fifty seven deficiencies" at the Hospital.

The Citizens Committee was learning that hospitals hiring these tired old Inspection Teams every two or three years, were becoming akin to paying the fox to watch the chicken coop.

It became obvious that the Joint Commission was another paper-shuffling bureauocracy that was dependent upon hospitals for its existence and was not likely to "bite the hand that feeds."

A decision was made by the Committee to petition the state and federal governments to conduct a bonafide inspection of the Hospital. It was summer, and with legal help, the Citizens drafted a petition that would be presented to the Pennsylvania Secretary of Health.

The petition asked for an in-depth investigation of the Hospital to determine the problems with management and the quality of care; and to take whatever steps were necesary, under the law, to correct those problems.

Over a two or three week period, the petition was circulated throughout Indiana County by several volunteers. The response was almost, without exception, overwhelming. People were more than willing to sign, and many, if not most, provided stories of problems they had experienced at the Hospital. More than seventy provided letters describing the more serious problems that they had experienced and addressed letters to the Pennsylvania Secretary of Health.

After the petition of over twelve hundred County citizens was sent to the Secretary of Health in Harrisburg, Secretary Muller's spokesman, a Bruce Reimer, told the news media that the Pennsylvania Health Department had already investigated the Hospital in the past year or two as the result of a letter of complaint sent by the Concerned Citizens Committee...to the Joint Commission on Accreditation of Hospitals. Reimer continued, that "No serious deficiencies were uncovered."

The Johnstown Tribune-Democrat headlined the story with "Indiana Hospital Probe Requested."

The Greensburg Tribune-Review, in a front page headline, announced: "Meetings Planned on Hospital Controversy."

The Pittsburgh Press had been the first to announce a meeting with Hospital officials and local politicians in Harrisburg, with the headline, "Indiana Hospital Affairs Set For High-Level Review", appearing just three days after Secretary Muller received the petition of over twelve hundred citizens.

The Press's story, with a Harrisburg dateline, began: "State Health Secretary Arnold Muller will meet Tuesday with officials from Indiana Hospital to review charges by an Indiana County citizens group that poor management and shoddy medical care plagued the facility."

The story continued: "Muller's office yesterday announced that he would meet with ... the Hospital Administrator, Hospital Board Members, and (Representative Paul Wass and state Senator Patrick Stapleton) as well as the Hospital Lawyer."

The day after that meeting in Harrisburg there appeared little doubt that the politicians were to implement the Hospital's scheme to put a quick lid on the developing events. Suspicions of cover-up were confirmed when the compliant local newspaper announced with a front page headline that read: "Hospital Charges Unsubstantiated."

The Johnstown Tribune-Democrat told the story like it was. The headline read: "Indianians' Petition Has Little Impact on State."

The story began: "The State Health Department apparently is not very impressed thus far with a citizens petition asking for an investigation of Indiana Hospital. After a meeting with Hospital officials Tuesday in Harrisburg, Dr. H. Arnold Muller, State Health Secretary, issued a statement reporting that no serious deficiencies had been found in an investigation that ended December 18 and covered a three year period or in an annual Department survey that was completed last month."

Almost condescendingly, spokesman Reimer advised, "Muller has agreed, however to meet with members of The Concerned Citizens group in Harrisburg. I think the purpose of the meeting which has been scheduled with The Committee of Concerned Citizens will be to discuss why the continuing petitions to us and the Joint Commission on Accreditation of Hospitals. Is there something we don't know about that they'd like to tell us?"

The Board Chairman and Vice Chairman were showing that, not only could they put a hold on unfavorable publicity with the Pittsburgh and local newspapers, but could get the Pennsylvania Secretary of Health to make a decision after hearing only one side of a controversy.

The Committee began to hear of the Hospital's Nursing Office comparing signatures of Hospital employees to known signers of the petition.

The local newspaper's gossip column sandwiched the following observation between its other items:

"The petitions signed by an estimated one thousand two hundred persons complaining about the operation of Indiana Hospital and subsequent stories have been given wide media attention in central and western Pennsylvania. One writer, Joe Grata, of the Pittsburgh Press, reports that the Hospital's attorney is targeting Dr. Ralph Miller, the urologist who was dismissed from the Hospital's Medical Staff three years ago, as the behind-the-scenes instigator of the petition. Comments Dr. Miller: "I intend very shortly to make a full revelation of the facts to the Indiana Gazette...".

By an unusual coincidence, the same column announced:

"There is some bad news: Robertshaw Controls Complany's announcement that it tentatively plans to phase out its Indiana Plant is a hard economic blow for the area. There has been some behind-the-scenes discussions that the announcement is geared to the recent labor dispute at the Plant."

It was well known that the Chairman of the Hospital Board, who was also the manager of the Robertshaw Plant, was at the center of the unpleasant labor vortex involving the Plant. By ominous coincidence, the problems of both locations, involving the same man, were printed side by side. What the tidbit did not include was that Reporter Joe Grata had been in town for two days interviewing the Hospital hierarchy and Citizens Committee members. He had been assigned to write an investigative story of the developing Hospital scandal. The story was suddenly squelched. We were to learn that the Hospital Board Chairman and the local paper's publisher, Donnelly, had visited John Troan, editor of the Pittsburgh Press, and influenced him to pull Grata from the story through Leo Koeberlein, an associate editor of the Paper. The Hospital Board Chairman confirmed this at deposition.

Simultaneously, Barbara Holsopple, an associate editor of The Press, was working on a story about the Citizens. She too was instructed by Koeberlein to forget the story. The veil of secrecy was falling into place.

The Hospital Attorney's attacks were becoming too much to ignore. A Pittsburgh paper printed his remark, "These people (Citizens) have to be stopped." Out of the blue, several members of the Committee received letters from him. It began to explain why an investigator, Ralph Pasant, hired by the Hospital Lawyer, had attempted to find the names of all the Committee members. Pasant was described as having visited members of the Committee at their homes, and attempted to pass himself off as an insurance agent.

The warning letter from the Hospital Lawyer was a contempable series of legalistic threats. It certainly reflected his statement to the Pittsburgh paper. We were also to learn from a Hospital Board Member that the Lawyer would attend Hospital Board meetings and harrangue Board members to file a suit against the Citizens who had dared to criticize their Hospital. The actions of the Board were certainly taking on the appearance of a business rather than a not-for-profit benevolent community health service.

The Lawyer's letter to the Citizens began: "In recent weeks it has come to the attention of the Indiana Hospital that you, either alone or in conjunction with others, including the so-called and self-designated "Committee of Concerned Citizens for Hospital Improvement" have made numerous, false and most serious statements, both written and unwritten, concerning the Indiana Hospital and various individuals associated with the Hospital which statements have been maliciously communicated to various third parties including among others, The Joint Commission of Hospital Accreditation, the U. S. Department of Health, Education and Welfare, the Pennsylvania Department of Health, as well as many private individuals."

The Lawyer had demonstrated in the courtroom that he could stretch a single sentence into a paragraph, perhaps even a chapter. But now we had evidence that he could accomplish the same feat with the written word. Literary refuse intertwined with legalistic threats continued for two pages. It was troublesome to the Citizens, without exception.

I decided to override my lawyer's advice and sent a letter to the local paper. The letter was printed and it read: "Dr. Miller Responds"

"Editor:

I am flattered that the Indiana Hospital's attorney has associated me with the Committee of Concerned Citizens working for improvement in the quality of health care at that hospital. The purpose to which that Committee is dedicated are of a humane and laudatory nature, i.e. to provide the Indiana County area residents with the most advanced medical care in a facility suitable for the preservation of health and alleviation of human suffering."

"If the Hospital Attorney's statement was intended as an accusation, then I must, in all candor, freely admit that I have joined with the Committee of Concerned Citizens and will give to that Committee all the support and advice at my command. Indeed, it was just such a wish on my part during the nineteen years that I was on the Medical Staff of the Hospital that led to the confrontation with the Hospital Management. The true nature and the depth of this confrontation has not been put before the public."

"For many years, while a member of the Hospital Medical Staff and, in particular, as Chairman of the Hospital Infection Control Committee, I brought to the attention of Hospital Management that conditions at the Hospital were not conducive to good medical care and that they presented a potential hazard to the public."

"On June 4, I wrote to the Hospital Administrator stating "the present standards for aseptic operation of the operating room at Indiana Hospital would fail to meet any of the presently recognized standards . . ." This letter produced no perceivable results. Aware that the conditions were threats to the health of the people using the Hospital facilities, and with the hope that the Chairman of the Board of the Hospital might be persuaded to react positively, I wrote to him, advising of the conditions that existed and recommended, as Chairman of the Infection Control Committee, that the deleterious conditions existing be corrected and that the quality of the Hospital's facilities be upgraded. His response was negative; he refused to recognize and remedy the problems."...

"His reaction was typified in his writing to me on December 17, when he stated:

"After reading the data attached, it is apparent that your communication is misdirected." With this one sentence, The Chairman attempted to bury the Hospital's health care problem. However, with his application of the Ostrich Principle, the problem did not go away. It was not too long after that exchange of communications and my subsequent verbal communication with Hospital Management that the Hospital was found deficient in the nature of care it provided the public by the Joint Commission on Accreditation of Hospitals. Indiana Hospital was denied full accreditation by the Commission and, in doing so, was told to remedy 57 areas in which it was lacking."

..."Instead of attacking and eliminating the problems which were depriving the public of the best in medical care, the powers that be, like the fabled king, decided to attack and eliminate the messenger who was the bearer of the bad news."

..."I have, this date, written to the Committee of Concerned Citizens for Hospital Improvement, offering my services in whatever capacity I may best serve."

Ralph J. Miller, M. D.

Indiana, Pa."

After the petition, signed by more than 1200 Indiana County residents, had been sent to the Secretary of Health, it created a flurry of front page headlines throughout Pennsylvania. Under the headline "Petition Blasts Hospital Performance", the local paper objectively described the petition stating: "More than twelve hundred Indiana County area residents have signed a petition . . . submitted to the Secretary of Health, questioning the management and performance at the Indiana Hospital . . . specific reasons listed in the petition about the quality of care at Indiana Hospital are as follows:

1. Failure of the hospital to receive full accreditation (from Joint Commission);
2. Failure of the Joint Commission to meet with the Concerned Citizens and hear their complaints regarding the Hospital . . .;
3. The large number of Indiana residents who seek medical attention outside Indiana County because of their concerns regarding poor medical attention at Indiana Hospital;
4. The purported practice of nepotism by Indiana Hospital management;
5. The fear that the hospital is not providing the best quality of medical care possible;
6. The loss in recent years of "many medical doctors who came to Indiana County to practice, but did not remain";
7. The refusal of Indiana Hospital management to meet with a group of citizens concerned with the quality of medical care . . . ;
8. The refusal of the Hospital Management to comply with a . . . request for "reasonable access to information regarding the management of Indiana Hospital" . . . in accordance with the Regulations of the Department of Health.

The Johnstown Tribune-Democrat headlined the story with "Indiana Hospital Probe Requested".

The Greensburg Tribune-Review, in a front page headline, announced: "Meetings Planned on Hospital Controversy."

August first was the day of the meeting with Muller and his staff. I had joined the Citizens and five of us traveled the turnpike to Harrisburg. The trip was anything but boring. We caught up on recent developments, and again went over our presentation to Muller. Margie, a retired head nurse, was our Chairman and the remaining three were Bill London, the retired businessman, Betty Gress, a secretary and Fern Rotigel, a housewife. Without much trouble, we found our way to the marble lobby of the Health and Welfare building and took the elevator to an upper floor.

The long hallway was empty, except for a young secretary at a lone desk near the end of the hall. As we approached, she asked if we were the Citizens group and showed us promptly into a corner conference room, just behind and to the right of her desk. She politely said we would be joined in a few minutes by the Secretary.

In front of a long row of windows on the right side of the room, was a long, walnut table facing a dozen or more straight-backed chairs on the left.

We were all a little nervous, I think. Bill and I were looking out across the Harrisburg landscape when , all of a sudden, the room seemed to be filled with people; as Secretary Muller and about four or five members of his staff entered. A stocky, dark-haired fellow with a note pad and another tall gent with a camcorder burst in. It was obviously the Harrisburg reporter of the Pittsburgh Press and his cameraman.

The cameraman began focusing on Bill, and I thought Bill was going out a window to get away from the guy. Bill did not want to be a T.V. star. That would be the source of some levity, at Bill's expense, for some time after that day.

The Health officials moved behind the long table and someone invited us to be seated. The reporter sat himself at the end of the long table and began to ask everyone's name. He wasn't just pushy - he was nasty. As he fired questions at me, it semed that he not only wasn't going to give us a break with his story, but that he may well create an unpleasant atomosphere for the meeting. We were all naively trusting in the honesty of Muller and his group.

I told the reporter that we preferred not to have the press at the meeting, but would meet with them later. When asked; he left.

As I recall, Muller's press secretary invited us to proceed. Betty had the eleven page report and a copy that she gave to Muller. She began a methodical reading of the document with explanation of the dozens of exhibits attached to it. The reading and explanation of the documents took about an hour. The row of Health Department people on the far side of the table began to cast side glances at one another. As Betty concluded, there was silence and the glances between the Health group continued. Reimer, the Press Secretary, finally broke the silence. "Well, this certainly is a different picture of the Hospital from what we were presented last week."

We had no notion of what the Hospital people and the politicians, along with the Hospital Attorney had told the assembled group the week before. But, it was very, very obvious that the group had been impressed with the complete documentation of our report.

Muller had been mute during the presentation and gave no indication he was going to break his silence. I think he was surprised enough by the presentation and documents that he just didn't know what to say.

I broke the silence again by asking the Secretary if he would come to Indiana for an open meeting where citizens could voice their concerns. He certainly lacked enthusiasm for that idea, and mumbled something to the effect that he would look into the report and documents. I was to learn later that Muller had been an Emergency Room physician in Hershey. I never learned how he landed the political appointment.

The local headline, the next day, read: "Health Secretary Hears Citizens". The text continued: "HARRISBURG - The Committee of Concerned Citizens for Hospital Improvement pressed their demands for a public hearing on practices and operations at Indiana Hospital at a meeting Friday in Harrisburg with state Health Secretary, Dr. H. Arnold Muller . . . In their written statement, the Committee noted that "it must be made absolutely certain that the present meeting is not intended to take the place of an in-depth on-site inspection of Indiana Hospital . . . and an open meeting with the Department of Health under the authority of Department of Health regulations which have the effect of law in the Commonwealth."

Department of Health spokesman, Reimer, was quoted as identifying the Committee's exhibits as "replicas of letters from patients and physicians, as well as minutes of meetings conducted at the Hospital."

The story continued: "One of the strongest charges leveled against the facility was that of nepotism by the Hospital's Administration. The petitioners' reference to nepotism at Indiana Hospital is demonstrated by the hiring of the son-in-law of the Board Chairman, as the Director of Purchasing at Indiana Hospital . . .with the suggestion that he would be given favored status for promotion as a Hospital Administrator." The son-in-law replaced the previous Director of Purchasing who was retired.

The local story continued: "The Committee's letter also criticized the Director of Nursing, who has a sister, as her assistant director of nursing, and for hiring, at one time or another, her son, a nephew and two other relatives."

The story concluded with spokesman Reimer's comment: "We felt that today's meeting certainly amplified the allegations put forth in the original petition. We obviously have a conflict of stories between what these people told us and what the Hospital officials had to say."

The front page headline and story of the Johnstown Tribune-Democrat was more graphic.

It read: "Health Secretary Hears Charges Against Hospital"; "HARRISBURG - "Charges of nepotism, intimidation, questionable health care and poor administration at the Indiana Hospital were brought into the open Friday during a two hour presentation to the Secretary of Health ... representatives presented and discussed an eleven page statement of charges ... also presented thirty one exhibits that included such things as medical staff minutes and letters from lawyers and doctors."

The story continued: "The state officials had met with Board members and Administrators of the Hospital July 15. It was apparent that the flavor of Friday's meeting with the Committee members was drastically different, however." A Health Department spokesman said, "When the Board Members came in, they presented a picture that they ran a pretty good operation and would just like to get this cloud that hangs over them removed. The picture painted in the Committee's statement was different indeed. The complaints and charges were specific, and they were backed with what the members felt were adequate supporting exhibits. They spoke of an atmosphere of intimidation and threats and said this pervades not only the Hospital, but the entire community."

"There was a charge that health care at the Hospital had deteriorated to the point that residents of the County were going to other centers ..."

"There was a charge that Emergency Room practices have been improper. The Committee said it had a notarized report that a physician (Vader) had refused emergency care to an Emergency Room patient until he was compensated in advance."

"There was a lengthy presentation on charges of nepotism."

Another headline of the Johnstown Tribune-Democrat read: "Indiana Hospital Probe Requested." The next day its headline read: "State: Specifics Needed For Probe." The story quoted Jennifer Riseon, director of the Health Department's Bureau of Quality Assurance as saying, "A public meeting was not part of the Department's routine procedure." Also quoted was Citizen's Chairman Buckwalter, who said he thought "the Hospital Administration was responsible for a poor staff attitude that "comes from the top" and ... "when you get twelve hundred signatures (on the petition), you know something's the matter."

After about three weeks, the papers announced a visit by the three Health Department personalities to Indiana Hospital. They were a physician, Jay Shue Hammon, Joyce Strouse and Mary Jane Webster, both registered nurses. The headlines and reports told the story: from the Pittsburgh Press:

"Indiana Hospital Probe Opens with Interviews." " Three Department investigators are expected to talk with dissatisfied former patients and also check into charges of nepotism at the institution. The Committee of Concerned Citizens for Hospital Improvement provided the investigators with seventy examples of alleged patient mistreatment."

Secretary Muller released a statement to the Harrisburg Bureau of The Press: "Such a visit by Health Department personnel in no way implicates the Hospital in any wrong-doing."

Muller seemed to want it both ways. The story continued: "Some of the charges leveled at the Hospital were that:

*Hospital Board Members also served on Boards of banks and other institutions doing business with the Hospital;

*Non-medical personnel (teenage son of Abdul Hankey) allowed in the operating room during surgery;

*Nepotism was prevalent in hiring practices;

*Patients often received inferior care."

The Pittsburgh Press then announced: "State Opens Indiana Hospital Probe." The story read:

"State Department investigators are scheduled to arrive ... the three investigators, who are scheduled to talk with dissatisfied former patients and check into charges of nepotism and Hospital mismanagement made by Concerned Citizens group have been provided with some seventy examples of patients disgruntled with the way they have been treated in Indiana County's only hospital."

The local paper's headline: "Investigation Of Local Hospital Slated BY P.D.H. Here Next Week."

The following story restated the outline of the petition with hundreds of signatures. But, the story went further and quoted the Hospital Board President saying, "Indiana Hospital welcomes and will fully cooperate with the survey ... the Hospital is also confident that any inquiry will further disclose that this further review of the Indiana Hospital has been occasioned by the so-called Committee of Concerned Citizens, a Committee which was instigated by and for the sole benefit of Dr. Ralph J. Miller, a physician whose staff privileges were terminated ..."

The next day, the local paper printed my response to the Board Chairman.

"Dr. Ralph J. Miller , a member of The Committee of Concerned Citizens for Hospital Improvement, issued a statement to the Gazette today attacking the Hospital Board Chairman for his remark yesterday pertaining to the state's forthcoming investigation of the facility."

Dr. Miller's statement reads: "In attempting to create a red herring, the Chairman wilfully overlooks the real issues raised by thirteen hundred citizens who have petitioned the Secretary of Health. He avoids the subject of nepotism which has resulted in the hiring of his own son-in-law to a highly paid position at the Hospital; in the hiring of five close relatives of the Director of Nursing; and to recent complaints received by the Citizens Committee, that Dr. (Vance Vader), a Hospital employee, has hired his own wife rather than other qualified nursing personnel in his own department." "In his myopia, the Chairman fixes his gaze on Dr. Miller and overlooks 1300 petitioners and seventy citizens whose descriptions of poor care were presented to the Secretary of Health."

The statement concluded with: "The Chairman must know that his Hospital hearings, which have been far more than occasional, must be fair and must provide an even break for those physicians who have been subjected to his intimidation. As one of the taxpayers indebted for some years to come, for payment of the Chairman's recent twenty four million construction, (escalated from nine million), I ask that he, in all seriousness, ask what he can do for Indiana Hospital - not what Indiana Hospital can do for his relatives."

The Pittsburgh Post Gazette featured a front page announcement on the day of the survey team's arrival. After the headline, "State Opens Indiana Hospital Probe", the Post Gazette story gave more details on the charges of nepotism. The coverage read: "Last March Dr. (Vance Vader) hired his wife as head of a stress-test lab, even though according to one former employee, other nurses at the Hospital were better qualified for the job." and, "appointment was particularly bothersome because the job was never posted officially."

The Post Gazette story continued: " ... former employees and nurses working at the Hospital called unethical a practice under which a supervisor places stars or initials V.I.P. next to the names of influential patients, signifying that they are to receive special care."

The Pittsburgh Press's headline read: "Indiana Hospital Probe Opens With Interviews."

The Health Department team arrived in town, and on the second day, they interviewed a number of citizens at the local Holiday Inn and heard stories of poor care at the Hospital.

After three days, the local headline was: "State Probe of Hospital Ends."

The story read: "Department spokesman Bruce Reimer said that the three member team was now in Harrisburg working on their report ..."

A companion story read: "Reimer added that "Muller has asked the three member team not to discuss any of their findings with anyone other than Department representatives.

Surprisingly, a few days later, Reimer told the Press: "Investigators for the State Department of Health would be returning to Indiana Hospital . . . that the three member investigating team didn't have enough time during their previous trip to gather all the necessary information to reach a decision on the facility."

In the interval between the Health Department visits, the Greensburg Tribune-Democrat editorial page carried the following:

Lifting the Pall

"State Health Secretary H. Arnold Muller, we feel is pursuing the correct course in his handling of complaints about the Indiana Hospital."

"Muller, last week, announced that he is sending a three-member team of Health Department representatives to Indiana to investigate allegations raised by members of the Citizens Committee for Hospital Improvement. The on-site visit follows up meetings in Harrisburg with members of the Hospital Administration and the Citizens Committee. Muller says that the visit will resolve questions that could not be answered by simply taking testimony."

"We agree with Muller's decision, but with one reservation. By announcing the visit so far in advance, it ensures that the Health Department team will see a facility prepared for an inspection, not necessarily one operating as it would on a day to day basis."

"An unannounced visit may have done more to anticipate criticism about the Hospital putting on a show for inspectors."

"Still, Hospital officials have said they would welcome any investigation by the Health Department and have promised to cooperate fully. We trust that their openness is genuine."

"Ever since news of the Citizen Committee's charges became public, a pall of suspicion and questioning has surrounded the Hospital and its operation. It is a pall that must be lifted, either by providing the charges against the Hospital are unfounded or - if true - by changing the conditions which gave rise to the problems."

The editorial put its literary finger directly on the problem with both the Department of Health and the Joint Commission on Accreditation of Hospitals. Hospitals would shine up for a two or three day inspection and then slide back into routine for another two or three years.

The local campus newspaper would occasionally get into the fray with students' letters to the editor. Their comments were often less restrained and more to the point than those in the local paper. Occasionally, the letters would address an issue never covered by the local paper. An example is the following:

"Hospital Lacks Psychiatrics"

"Editor, The Penn:

With fine impartiality the state department of health this summer sent a team of medical bureaucrats (a physician or two, and several registered nurses) to interview patients and others, i.e. hospital staff, and draw conclusions regarding the adequacy of medical service at Indiana Hospital. Charges of nepotism, i.e., favoring nephews, and other relatives in hiring and making appointments to the medical staff, and charge and countercharge about the adequacy of physician and nursing care have been aired in the local newspaper.

With inscrutable care not to upset anyone important, the state examiners have kept their conclusions about the sufficiency or adequacy of medical services, nursing care, diagnosis by medical doctors, and performance by physicians and specialists at Indiana Hospital secret.

NO COMMENT: REPEAT, NO COMMENT is all those interested in Indiana Hospital can learn until the state board decides to announce or publish its findings.

Even if Indiana Hospital passes with "flying colors" and is given a clean bill of health by the commonwealth team. . . the hospital still lacks psychiatric services . . .in a crisis mentioned by someone who knew, it was left up to the state police to transfer a troubled person to Kittanning. The state police have other duties. There is always the option of hanging oneself in jail or as occurred on the sixth floor of Indiana Hospital on Saturday, September 27, by a relatively young man, 37, with family responsibilities, admitted just the night before. . . How many more of these deaths do we need to convince ourselves that a bed section at Indiana Hospital for psychiatric care . . .could pay for itself?"

A concerned citizen

The Citizens Committee never learned who wrote the letter but the coroner advised that the hanging death was never reported and the story was given scant notice in the local paper. It was not the first time that students wrote letters involving Dr. Lester Lazarus.

There was silence for almost three months. Then . . . suddenly the front page of the local press exploded with the headline: "State Health Secretary Clears Hospital of Charges". No one believed the headline - particularly the hundreds of petitioners. There were questions from many as to what political strings were pulled during the period between the hospital inspections.

The story read: "Harrisburg - Indiana Hospital has been cleared by the State Health Department of a number of serious allegations leveled by the Committee of Concerned Citizens for Hospital Improvement."

"State Health Secretary Dr. H. Arnold Muller said the Department's report, based on an intensive eight day on-site investigation by three Department officials, concluded that all allegations could not be substantiated. The charges brought forth in a petition signed by 1200 county residents. . . included:

- conflict of interest involving members of the hospital board
- nepotism
- falsified records
- poor management practices
- forced signing of loyalty oaths involving hospital employees."

The article continued with: "(The Committee) further cited claims of: unauthorized teenagers entering the Operating Rooms (son of Abdul Hankey); the hiring of a private investigator by the Hospital Attorney . . . to harass Citizens Committee members; the loss of twenty or more physicians at the Hospital in the past several years; the loss of nearly one third of Indiana County obstetrical patients to other hospitals, and . . . a growing eagerness of Hospital employees to present their complaints to the Citizens Committee."

It appeared that the student letter to the editor of the campus newspaper was precisely on target when it said, "With inscrutable care not to upset anyone important", the state examiners have kept their conclusions . . . secret."

Although there was no shock that the Harrisburg people, visited by the Hospital hierarchy, their lawyer and local politicians, would attempt a cover-up, the extent of the attempt to hide the truth was shocking.

Another fallacious headline was mirrored by the Johnstown paper with the heading: "Indiana Hospital Wins Case Against Citizens."

The Citizens reacted with criticism of the Secretary who had chosen to ignore firm documentation of the Hospital Board's conflicts of interest, falsified records and poor management practices.

More surprising was the Health Department politician's attempt to bypass his Department's own demand for "corrective action" correcting the problems of:

"* non-medical personnel in operating rooms during procedures;
* a surgeon operating without an assistant;
* surgeons performing procedures for which they were not qualified;
* poor relationship of the hospital with the community;
* insufficient hospital audits and follow-up studies;
* numerous emergency room problems as described by many of the citizens interviewed during the Department "probe"."

Recommendations for correction of all these problems were in the inspection team's report and were frivolously glossed over by the illustrious State Secretary of Health.

The Citizens' criticisms of the Health Secretary's cover-up was covered by newspapers throughout the state.

Feeling the heat, the Secretary sent a letter to the Citizens. He now claimed that the effective date for the Health Department regulations prevented him from further action based on events that occurred before the regulations. He then described that federal regulations didn't take effect because of a delay in the "close-out" documents indicating completion of the federal funding for the hospital's building project. He concluded that his Department's role in Medicare regulation enforcement is very limited since the Hospital was certified by the Joint Commission.

He claimed the responsibility belonged with the federal Health Care Financing Administration. Everyone was learning that the Secretary's broken-field running was possible because of overlapping bureaucracy. In the meantime, it appeared that the Board Chairman, the Administrator, Vance Vader, Lester Lazarus and Goldfarb were able to sprint between the raindrops.

The Secretary's letter was printed in the local paper with a story that began, "In what may be the final word in the matter regarding the Indiana Hospital dispute..."

But, was it the final word?

The Citizens were beginning to see results from several Freedom of Information requests.

"FOI" requests to federal agencies, we would learn, would at times delay production of sensitive documents, but if the requests were followed up, the documents would eventually appear. The Citizens were receiving the Hospital's financial information and reports from the federal inspectors who had quietly joined the state Health Department in their return visit.

The Johnstown paper carried the following quote from the Administrator and the Chairman of the Board of Directors. They noted that they were pleased with the report issued by Dr. Muller and said, " The Board of Directors and Hospital Staff have been clearly exonerated of any mismanagement or wrongdoing".

The Administrator, et. al would learn that they were prematurely counting their chickens and gloating. It seemed to be a general trait of those who were making policy at the Hospital.

Suddenly, seven or eight of the Citizens were served notices, delivered by a Sheriff's deputy, that they were being sued by Indiana Hospital. The Hospital Lawyer had convinced the Board to try to muzzle the Citizens. As he said, in a quote to one of the Pittsburgh's newspapers: "These people have to be stopped."

This apparently raised a serious question concerning a lawyer using the Court System in an attempt to stop citizens from criticizing their only hospital.

The Tribune-Review announced: "Indiana Hospital Sues Local Group". The lead paragraph read: "Indiana Hospital has filed a libel and slander suit against members of The Committee of Concerned Citizens for Hospital Improvement in connection with a widely publicized state investigation into alleged hospital problems... The action follows by one day, the filing of a suit by Dr. Ralph Miller, an Indiana urologist suspended from the Hospital staff, in Federal District Court against the Hospital. The suit names as defendants the Hospital's Administrator, some members of the Medical Staff and State Secretary of Health, H. Arnold Muller."

Once again, the front page of the local paper heralded the Hospital suit: "Hospital Files Suit; Charges Slander, Libel". The story opened with: "Indiana Hospital countered the Concerned Citizens for Hospital Improvement yesterday with a civil suit in Indiana County charging counts of defamation and injurious falsehood and asking general and specific damages in excess of $10,000 and an equal amount for punitive and exemplary damages in each count. A few of the active Citizens were named along with "John Does number one through ten." We assumed the John Does were Committee members the Hospital hadn't heard about.

The next day, a young Sheriff's deputy came to the office with a document called a precipae. I learned that a precipae was a prelude to the filing of a suit - it apparently was intended to protect the statute of limitation which would not allow the filing of a suit after a certain date. The deputy seemed to be disappointed that we just accepted the paper with thanks. He apparently wanted some discussion that he could share at the next coffee break.

The Hospital's plan was obvious. The Lawyer would use the discovery period of the Citizens' case to gain information from the Citizens and then direct his attention to me. Discovery, we were learning, would require the Citizens, under oath, to answer written questions from the Hospital or to be called in for direct questioning by the Hospital Lawyer.

Reaction to a benevolent institution suing a group of citizens was prompt. Within a few days another Letter to the Editor of the local paper appeared. It seemed to reflect a general reaction to The Hospital Lawyer's aggressiveness. It read:

"INAPPROPRIATE TIME"

"To the Editor,

The news in today's (Wednesday) paper that Indiana Hospital is suing assorted local residents who have been vocal critics of its practices during the past several years is shocking. It would not be appropriate to comment on the merits of the case, even if I had the information, which I don't, since I've not been one of the critics.

However, it does not give me confidence in my local hospital to know that if I dislike the way it is run, I can't criticize it openly without taking the risk that I'll be sued.

A community hospital should be as open to criticism as politicians are. If it performs well, for enough people, it will overcome the criticism; there really is no other way.

Indiana Hospital's suit is ill advised, and will further polarize the community into warring camps over the matter. Whether the criticisms that have been leveled at the Hospital are true or not, the Hospital will not benefit from the further widespread publicity that will now be given them. If ever there was a time for reconciliation and repair, it is now; the lawsuit in the news, if pursued, will destroy that chance. The Hospital is embarking on a no-win course that seems unlikely to improve its image.

H.E.T.
Indiana, Pa."

It had become obvious that the Hospital, in attempting to hush the Citizens, was compounding the Hospital's bad publicity. The Lawyers had seriously underestimated the Citizens' ability to protect themselves. The longer the defamation suite dragged on, the more the Hospital and some of its actors would be subjected to scrutiny.

Friends of the Citizens Committee began to provide the Committee with revealing documents, in addition to documents that were being obtained through the Freedom of Information requests. The true nature of the Hospital's position was becoming obvious. As has been said many times, "Follow the money."

One of the early documents listed each of the two local lawyers serving on the Hospital Board as recipients of $16,500.00 each for "legal services" connected with a bond issue used to finance the construction of the new Hospital wing. A later document showed that they again each received $11,000.00 for "legal services" when the bonds were "reissued." The Committee was later informed from sources that some of those funds were returned.

Hospital management employees and former employees also described that large sums were deposited by the Hospital in a local bank - interest-free. The Hospital Board Chairman, was one of the directors of that bank.

One of the Hospital management informants described that the Director of Nursing , in addition to having five of her relatives on her Department's payroll, had purchased unneeded Hospital cabinetry without bids from her son who worked for a hospital supply firm.

The gas well driller on the Hospital Board went to great lengths to be seen as a philanthropist. Witnesses described his membership on the governing bodies of the local University, the Country Club, and a boy's prep school, in addition to his membership on the Hospital Board. Gas wells were drilled on the grounds of all of these institutions. Yes, the driller's company gained the contracts. Other witnesses described that the driller, returned some of his drilling fees to the Hospital after the news media became interested in the Hospital's Board members.

A drilling company employee described that the driller took credit for a fund presented to the family of an employee who had lost his life on a drilling rig; when actually, the fund was established by the employees' donations. This was all about the time that the university students were calling him the "cookie monster" when he advised the students to sell cookies in order to raise funds for their tuition.

During the period when it appeared that our antitrust suit in Federal Court was on the back burner, I found myself scurrying to find a defense lawyer to cope with The Hospital Lawyer's attacks. I found myself relying on a Johnstown lawyer by the name of Streaker. My first meeting with Streaker was in his office in the seedy, older section of Johnstown. The office was on the third floor of a dreary, old, stone building near the train depot. The railroad tracks ran near the building at about the second floor level and the passing trains would occasionally punctuate conversations with vibrations through the office. Streaker had a stout, middle-aged lady in a loose fitting dress, with a long string of beads hanging from her neck, usher me into his office. We passed three or four young ladies busily typing legal documents. We stepped up a step or two beyond the last typist and turned into a dim hallway, leading directly into his office. Streaker was sitting behind his desk and never bothered to rise. He was a small, medium-built fellow.

When he finally sat upward in his high-backed chair, he got right to it. "We've got a case here where Indiana Hospital said you have damaged their good name by false statements and that they intend to collect from you for the harm you've done." With his curt, sharply clipped sentences, he continued, "If you know anything about libel and slander, you know that truth is the first defense, that is, if your actions are free of malice." When I replied that I had briefly read the law relative to defamation to know that I could give as much help as possible, he snapped, "If you're so smart, tell me what assumpsit is." I didn't know assumpsit from shelled peas and I probably sat there with my mouth open. "Well, remember who the lawyer is here and you'll get along just fine. Here's a copy of the law on defamation. Take it with you and read it so that you know what's going on." Then, one by one, he went over The Hospital Lawyer's charges, asking what I knew about each allegation. He appeared to be more amazed at each allegation; particularly when I would tell him that the Committee had investigated every charge that had been presented to the Secretary of

Health and that we knew them to be true. He advised me to collect all documents which would tend to support the claim we presented to the Health Department. He advised that we would meet again before preparing his response to the Hospital's complaints.

By that time, Streaker was beginning to fidget and obviously wanted the interview to be over so he could get to some of the papers cluttering his desk top.

As a train somewhere behind us could be heard grinding to a stop at the depot, I tried to ask if we could coordinate a defense with that of the other members of the Citizens Committee. Streaker flushed and sharply rejected any hope of helping my friends defend themselves against the Hospital. As I left that office, I wondered what I had gotten into.

As agreed, I went to work studying the Pennsylvania laws governing libel - the written form of defamation and slander, the spoken form. Even though I was still feeling chastised by Streaker's admonition not to play lawyer, I couldn't see, for the life of me, how the Hospital's suit had a scrap of legitimacy to it. Everything, absolutely everything, that had been presented to the Secretary of Health, had been documented before our petition to the Department was drafted; except, the remark that one of the Citizens made to the Secretary claiming that many people felt it was more of a risk to go to the institution for care than to stay home.

The present problem was compounded by my friends' exposure to large legal fees in their defense - and that was exactly what the Hospital Lawyer was counting on.

We all met at the office one evening to formulate some sort of strategy. The number one problem was to get a lawyer for the Citizens. Dave Rotigel and his mother had been named in the suit and Dave felt that no lawyer except for a man named Garson, from Greensburg, would be able to defend the Citizens. Garson met with us and outlined the problems of having multiple clients, but would reluctantly take the case and defend the Citizens as a favor to his friend Rotigel. His favor included his fee at $150.00 per hour with no estimate of how many hours would be needed to have the Hospital back off. This was indeed troublesome. Although I knew that I could defend against the Hospital Lawyer myself, my friends were being attacked and were next to defenseless.

A friend suggested his son to defend us. He had recently graduated from Law School, had joined a law firm in Pittsburgh. The son was an affable, handsome young lawyer who had just begun to climb the ladder of success. He took the case for the remaining Citizens group and agreed to reasonable terms, although any legal fees for some of the group would be a hardship. The Citizens, of course, wanted an aggressive defense with the hope that the case could be brought to a quick end. The young lawyer provided a series of standard replies to the Hospital's suit and prepared to present his argument to the Court.

He and the Hospital Lawyer argued the early motions before Judge Earley with nothing major being accomplished except for a schedule, along which the case would proceed. The Citizens were learning that after a complaint is filed, an early motion is designed to have the case dismissed. The Citizens were learning that, unless a case is dismissed, a period of discovery follows. The period of discovery allows each side in the dispute to gain information from the opposing side. The Citizens were learning that the Court would allow "requests for admission and "document production" as methods of establishing truth rather than a more lengthy process. Often during the period of discovery, the opposing sides can present lists of questions which the opponents are required to answer under oath, (interrogatories) and quite often, the opposing sides would conduct depositions where the parties meet with lawyers and a court reporter to answer questions and make the answers part of the court records.

One of the Hospital's first moves was to request any relative documents from the Citizens, but it soon became apparent that the Hospital Lawyer wanted not only relative documents, but was looking for a mechanism to gain access to my office and rummage through my files. When the suit against the Citizens was reported in the Pittsburgh papers, we again remembered that he was quoted as saying, "These people have to be stopped." It was obvious that he would stop at nothing to destroy the group in order to get at me - hopefully with substantial information provided by the Citizens.

We were learning that there were two types of lawyer behavior. The first type would adhere to the rules, both in letter and spirit, while the second type of lawyer would bully his way to what was wanted.

We complied with document production by giving copies of the petition and exhibits which had been presented to the Secretary of Health. And, we asked for documents to be provided by the Hospital that we knew would dramatically show conditions at the Hospital and support the Citizens' claims of management problems and poor care at the Hospital.

The Citizens knew that the Joint Commission, an outfit that inspects hospitals for a fee, had found deficiencies in its last inspection of the Hospital and had not made its findings public. They had issued a glowing report to the Hospital to be used in the local media, but their full report to the Hospital might very well present a more accurate picture.

In addition to the information reaching the Committee detailing activities of the Hospital management, we knew that the Board Chairman had retired the Hospital's Director of Purchasing and had hired his son-in-law for the job, even though his relative had no experience in that field. We certainly wanted the documents related to the appointment of The Chairman's son-in-law, as well as documents which would show that the former purchasing agent had not voluntarily retired. We knew of a number of physicians who had come to the area and who had been disillusioned, so that we were interested in their resignation letters. We knew that there would be letters of complaint and many government agency documents that would support the Citizens' charges. The Hospital Lawyer did not want to supply any of these documents. These documents would demonstrate his frivolous lawsuit for what it was, ending his case and meal ticket. The result - we got no documents from the Hospital. He stonewalled for months, but without warning, a man identifying himself as an insurance agent, began appearing at the doors of the Citizens at off-hours. He was quoted as inquiring about the Committee. He began to arouse suspicion and the Committee finally identified him as an "investigator" named Ralph Passant, from the Business Information Company, an outfit hired by the Hospital Lawyer to snoop on the Citizens.

While the Lawyer was attacking, it was difficult for all of us to see the Citizens' lawyer go through perfunctory filing of papers without a truly effective defense. The young lawyer was allowing his clients to be bullied.

In the meantime, my lawyer, Streaker, was matching The Hospital's legal paper avalanche page by page, and was preparing to take depositions from a few of the Hospital people. It appeared that he may very likely be effective enough that my defense would tend to protect my friends on the Committee.

At a meeting of the Citizens with the young lawyer, he showed signs of discontent. He began more aggressive request for cash advances, presumably at the request of his law firm, and he was hesitating to aggressively oppose the Hospital Lawyer. Then the truth reared its ugly head. The Citizen's Lawyer confided to me that his law firm had six other important cases which his firm was defending. He was afraid that if he antagonized the Hospital Lawyer, it would jeopardize his firm's chances of successfully settling those cases. The Citizens were not only incredulous, but thoroughly disgusted. Most of them looked upon this young man in disbelief, but we were all to realize that there were enough of these people in the legal system to make it as flawed at it is. Needless to say, the Hospital's pressure had eliminated the Citizens' defense. The Hospital's Counsel was now ready. He promptly scheduled depositions for five of the Citizens - all of the group who had met with the Secretary of Health a year or so earlier.

    The depositions were scheduled in the office of one of the lawyers on the Hospital Board, who was now showing his true colors. He was apparently no longer my friend or even a double agent, he was firmly in with the Hospital Lawyer's attack.

    It appeared, for awhile, that the Citizens would have to undergo deposition without a lawyer to defend themselves. But, at the last minute, through friends, I was able to contact a young, inexperienced lawyer who agreed to attend the depositions and aid the Citizens. The Hospital's plan obviously was calculated to have the Citizens shift responsibility to me and then attack me with weighty ammunition. The first interview was with one of the organizers of the Citizens Committee, who was joined by the young lawyer. During The Hospital Lawyer's questioning, she was overwhelmed with his high pitched voice and bullying. She would enter an objection now and then, but was completely ignored. The questions became more obviously designed to incriminate me as the culprit behind the whole Committee. The Hospital had reluctantly admitted that I was entitled to be present at these depositions, since I was a party to the suit. But, all I could do was sit and listen to the Lawyer's abuse being passed on to my friends. His harangues dragged on for so long, that four or five Citizens were waiting in the hallway. One couple, whose son was a well-known lawyer, brought another local lawyer with them, and he began to demand that the proceedings be shortened. Before The Hospital Lawyer finished his interrogation of the first Citizen, he unbelievably, reached across the conference table, took the young lawyer's file, and went through it looking for any documents that would be of some help to him. Most lawyers would probably have relieved him of a few fingers for a move like that, but our young lawyer sat there, placidly watching him go through her papers.

    The Hospital Lawyer then introduced a tall, dark, young man he had brought with him . Together, the two speeded up the depositions and called it quits for the day. The day was to further demonstrate that the aggressive counsel was not going to allow anything to stand in the way of collecting documents that the Committee had conceded were in my possession. He had brought along a motion to compel. It was a request for the Court to order Bill London to undergo deposition even though he had recently undergone very major surgery. The court agreed to hear argument on the request, and wouldn't you know, the argument was scheduled for a day my family and I had planned to leave for a summer vacation.

I couldn't leave Bill alone with that lawyer, so we packed the car on the appointed day, hoping to leave before too late in the day and I appeared with Bill in front of the Honorable Robert Earley. The courthouse was directly across the street from the Board Member's Bank Building office. Earley was probably having a bad day. He was just a little over five feet high and now it appeared that he was about that wide. He listened to the Hospital's request that Bill be required to undergo "gentle questioning" and Bill's request that he be given a little more time to recuperate from recent major surgery. Without hesitation, Earley ordered Bill to go across the street to the Lawyer-Board Member's office and undergo deposition.

Bill was upset and a little nervous as we crossed Philadelphia Street, but I was beginning to see the chinks in the opposition's armor and was beginning to think that the Hospital Lawyer was vulnerable. I had watched him bully the decent, respectable people on the Committee, and knew full well that a confident, experienced lawyer didn't have to treat people that way. I was beginning to think that I should take him on. It was really no different than calling the bluff of a school yard bully back in grade school.

As we entered the Board Member's office, we were ushered down the hallway to the left into the conference room with its near wall lined with volumes of legal journals. Our adversary was already shedding his coat, and as he draped it across a chair back, he began to instruct the Court Reporter. He began his interrogation with the usual questions of Bill's name, address, employment, family relations and then promptly got into questions about the origin of the Citizens Committee. He wanted to know its members and its meetings, with each question directed toward an answer that would incriminate me as the sole organizer and promoter of the Committee. For some reason, he didn't notice that I had set a tape recorder on the conference table until it became necessary to change a cassette. When he noticed the recorder he said, "Is that your machine? Is that your machine?" I sat motionless and simply stared at him. With no motion from anyone, he suddenly jumped up, grabbed the recorder, and ran from the room with it. He returned, took his seat, and resumed the questioning. After I recovered from the surprise, I left the room to look for the recorder. There it was on the hallway floor. I brought it back into the conference room and continued the recording.

The interrogator became livid and raced from the room. He returned in a few minutes and seemed to have gathered himself together. He had questioned Bill for a few minutes, when the conference room door opened and an unlikely pair of humans appeared. One was the Board Member's young, overweight law partner and the other character was a frail, elderly man with a policeman's hat and a gold badge that occupied most of his left breast. Hospital Counsel barked out, "Gentlemen, we have an intruder here - an illegal intruder and he is to leave the premises, in the alternative he is to turn off his machine." I asked the Mutt and Jeff team who they were. The larger one said, "I'm Lou Kotec, a member of this law firm, and the diminutive Keystone Cop said, "I'm Stiffler - bank security - and we just want you to leave peaceable."

London spoke up and demanded that I stay, although I really couldn't imagine those two athletes evicting me from the place. Nothing would have pleased our opposition more than to have a scuffle, so I smiled at the two of them and stopped the recording.

The transcript tells the story:

Hospital Lawyer: ....Have you been recording this up until now?

Hospital Lawyer: Is this your machine? Is that your machine? Would you remove it from here at once? We'll get a ruling from the judge on the machine.

Mr. London: I insist ...

Hospital Lawyer: The machine,...I'm not insisting that he leave Mr. London, I'm insisting that that machine go out of the room and I want it out of the room right now.

At this point, the Hospital Lawyer took the recorder and left the room. He returned without the recorder.

Hospital Lawyer: If you want to leave the room to guard your machine you may.

Miller left the room and returned with the recorder which had been put on the hallway floor. He kept the recorder on his lap. The Hospital Lawyer left the room for a few minutes.

Hospital lawyer: I'll ask you some questions now specifically...Dr. Miller the machine goes out of the room and it goes out of the room <u>right now</u>! Take the machine out of the room, please.

Mr. London: I want the machine so that I...

Hospital Lawyer: Excuse me Mr. London. Excuse me Mr. London.

Would you please take the machine and go out of the room?

The Lawyer left the room for approximately ten minutes. On returning...

Hospital Lawyer: Ahh...the time ahh...should be noted, did you note about five minutes ago? Dr. Miller has refused to leave the room and I ahh...do I understand ahh...and I've also asked him to take the recorder out. He is free to stay, by my permission but he is ahh...not free to stay with his recorder on. I'd like to ask Dr. Miller if he is willing to take the recorder out of the room. Dr. Miller, are you willing to do that?

Mr. London: I prefer...

Hospital Lawyer: Sir, would Dr. Miller please answer the question. Will you take the recorder out of the room, Dr. Miller?

Hospital Lawyer: Dr. Miller?

Mr. London: No, I would rather that he would keep it.

Hospital Lawyer: Alright, second, is the recorder on at the present time?

Alright I'm asking that the recorder be turned off; in absence of the recorder being turned off, the recorder to be taken out of the room, and if that's not satisfactory, for Dr. Miller to remove himself from the room. If that doesn't take place we're going to have a court order, a sheriff remove you from the room. In the meantime, by the way, the additional time taken by this occurrence is added on this deposition. So that we will extend, and I'll take the responsibility for that, beyond the 11:30 hours, so as to make up for the lost time and any further lost time that is created by this disturbance. Mr. London, is it clear on the record that it is your desire that Dr. Miller be here, number one?

Mr. London: Yes sir.

Hospital Lawyer: Number two, is it your desire that Dr. Miller's tape recorder be here in this room?

Mr. London: It is.

Hospital Lawyer: You too will take responsibility of course. Now Mr. London, I want to ask you some specific questions at this time - concerning certain matters that have been alleged in the complaint which has been filed against you and others named in that complaint. My questions will be whether you yourself have any personal belief as to the truth of the statement that I will ask you. Do you understand that?

In approximately ten minutes two men entered the room and interrupted the deposition. The small man with a badge said:

Dr. Miller:

Hospital Lawyer: Yes, I have an intruder, a trespasser in this room. He has no legal right to be here. I will take full responsibility for his being removed from the room. I have given him as a condition for his remaining that that tape recorder that he holds on his lap either is turned off or leave the room in which case he may stay and I will now ask him again to either take that recorder ahh..put it on the table and turn it off, take it out of the room or he is to leave this room. Dr. Miller?

Miller: Could we have the two gentlemen identify themselves?

Kablack: Why I'm Wayne Kablack, I'm a partner in this law firm, as (the Hospital Lawyer) was telling me, he's correct, you don't have a legal right to be here since you're not a party.

Miller: You're one of the plaintiffs? Is that right?

Kablack: No

Miller: One of your law partners is a plaintiff?

Kablack: I'm not certain which law suit you're working on right now...

Hospital Lawyer: He's not a party...

Miller: And your name sir?

Stiffler: Bank security. My name is George Stiffler.

Miller: George Stiffler - bank security and are you under orders to come and eject me if I don't take...

Hospital Lawyer: I've given him orders and I take full responsibility for that Dr. Miller.

Stiffler: I have been asked to come in here and to ask you to please go "peacibly."

Miller: Or turn off my tape recorder?

Stiffler: Or turn off my tape recorder.

Miller: And you've gotten this order from the Hospital Lawyer?

Hospital Lawyer: that's my condition on the tape recorder.

Miller: Okay.

Recorder turned off.

The questioning resumed, and as the two would-be ejectors left the room, I turned the recorder back on. After awhile, the Hospital's Counsel said he had no more questions. We couldn't help but enjoy the moment as we left the bank building. We began to get the impression that the repeated browbeating would not be successful.

As the family headed toward the beach along the Pennsylvania Turnpike, we made a quick stop in Breezwood before heading south on the highway to Washington. I put the cassette into the car's sound system and we had entertainment for the next thirty miles or so listening to that ridiculous deposition.

After the London debacle, I finally convinced Attorney Streaker to get busy. He scheduled depositions for the Hospital's Board Chairman and Dr. Claude Clippins, Chairman of that unusual Committee at the Kangaroo Court. It was our view that the Board Chairman would be able to confirm the accuracy of most of the claims the Citizens had made about the Hospital, while Clippins was a vivid example of the things that were wrong with some of the town's medicos.

The Clippins deposition was taken in the large room at the back of our office and it was apparent, from the beginning, that Clippins was not enthusiastic. Streaker was not the most articulate or the best organized interviewer, but it was evident that he was not going to put up with the Hospital Lawyer's incessant interruptions and speeches designed to interrupt the questioning.

After about three interruptions, Streaker would announce that one more interruption would result in both lawyers going to the Judge for further instructions. Typically following an important question, the Hospital lawyer would break in with, "Pardon me." This time, he advised Clippins not to answer the question. Streaker just folded his notebook and said he would be in touch with the Judge. The Hospital Lawyer protested, implying that he may possibly allow the question if it were phrased properly. Streaker just packed his bags and left. Hospital Counsel had brought his associate for the occasion, and they both just quietly left - probably not believing what had occurred. In a few days, Streaker sent a letter advising that the Clippin's deposition had been rescheduled on order of the Judge. It appeared that Streaker and the Hospital Counsel had appeared before Judge Early and that Earley had ordered the Hospital Guy to remain silent during depositions and to allow his client to answer the questions being asked.

When Clippins appeared again, he was even less enthusiastic. As we headed back into our back room, Clippins took off his jacket and hung it across a chair back, while the lawyers seated themselves at the large, chestnut desk near the far end of the room. Clippins asked if it was all right for him to smoke and I simply said, "No."

This time, the rules had changed. The former aggressor was attempting to be congenial and cooperative and it wasn't easy for him. He still had a tendency toward rambling speeches, but the interruptions were less frequent and there were no instructions for Clippins not to answer. At one point, he interrupted the proceedings and advised that he wanted to counsel Clippins. The two of them left and headed for my office. He was intercepted by Margie, our receptionist. She advised that they would not be permitted to use my office. The two of them went into a treatment room and closed the door. Later, Margie said that she listened at the door and heard the Hospital Counsel say, "Now, how are you going to answer that one?"

After a few more introductory questions, Streaker sprung the trap. The transcript reads:

Q: "Doctor, do you know of any babies that were decapitated during delivery?"

A: "Sure."

Q: "And will you tell me abut them and how does it happen?"

Hospital Lawyer: "Excuse me. Objection. You may answer. I object, but we reserve objections. I can't imagine the relevance and materiality of the issue."

The Witness: "Fortunately it doesn't happen every day and I am not prepared to give you a lengthy dissertation on the reasons and so on. There are many books written on this subject. Dr. Kayson's Obstetrical Delivery. And if you are really interested, I think it would be a good idea, I am sure there is some out at the hospital library, and I would be glad to lend you some."

By Mr. Streaker:

Q: "Did you ever have any complications such as this when you delivered a baby?"

A: "Certainly."

Q: "In what year?"

A: "I have no idea."

Q: "Is it on record at the hospital?"

A: "Certainly."

Streaker had what he wanted and the deposition was soon completed. The two Hospital Lawyers shot uneasy glances at each other. It had been the first time that they had heard of a general practitioner pulling the head off a newborn with obstetrical forceps.

Claude Clippins was at the end of an era in Indiana County when the G.P.'s would sit in the Hospital staff room and brag about the difficult home deliveries they had accomplished. During this period, children would be seen who were suffering the results of rough deliveries. One form of injury was a partial paralysis of an upper extremity known as Erbs palsy. The practitioners had no regard for Cesarean sections. They weren't trained to perform them, so countless babies were forcibly dragged through the birth canal, and would end up with a "birth defect". How many cases of cerebral palsy in children with dysfunctional arms and legs were the result of these practitioners like Clippins and one or more of his Executive Committee colleagues? That will never be known.

Streaker took me by the arm and led me out of the room into my office. He was wide-eyed. "Can you believe that? Can you believe he admitted it?" "Yes, I can. Did you think I falsified all that?"

The Citizens Committee never learned what Clippins had told the family. The pathologist who had first described that tragedy related that, within thirty days, another member of the Medical Staff " Executive Committee" had the same sort of accident.

I recall talking with the pathologist who had told of these tragedies and observing, "and both of these people are sitting in judgement of my career." "I know", he agreed.

Streaker wasn't uneasy, Streaker was shaken. He had thrown his overcoat on the sofa in my office and had shed his overshoes at the far end of the sofa. He was gathering his papers together, and at the same time, trying to put on his coat. He began mumbling something to the effect that he had bargained with the Hospital Henchmen, that he would produce documents if he was able to take Clippins' deposition. This was the first time that I had heard of that.

"What the hell are you telling me Streaker?" I bellowed. It seems that Streaker had made this "pact with the devil". After the deposition, the Hospital Counsel believed they were to be given access to all the documents in my office. I couldn't believe this. I asked again what was going on. From Streaker I heard: "Do you recognize the trouble I caused for myself when I took that gang up to the Judge?"

Good God, I was truly distraught. As Streaker bolted down the hall with his brief case and his coat - half on and half off - I almost yelled after him the worst obscenity I could think of. I was having trouble even collecting my thoughts. I couldn't believe this was happening, and I was ashamed that I was at a loss to take control of the situation.

I finally realized that the people in my office had no right to any documents without a court order. I walked back to the big room, and with some difficulty, tried to sound authoritative and advised that was the end of the proceedings for the day and that everyone should leave. As those two tried to initiate an argument that could be recorded by the court reporter, I asked the reporter if she would fold her equipment. The two of them, after a few minutes, left and I helped the reporter, with her equipment, out to her car. The two lawyers were standing at the entrance to our building and were obviously plotting their next move.

The office staff found Streaker's overshoes in my office the next morning and they served as a source of humor for some weeks, as we would recall his emergency exit after the Clippins deposition. I hadn't thought much about it at the time, but during his hurried exit he mumbled something about not being popular with those lawyers after taking them before the Judge. The man was actually afraid of them. We eventually bundled up Streaker's rubbers in a tightly wrapped package and mailed them back to him.

We received an official looking letter from Streaker within a day or two, setting 10:00 A.M. on the following day, for the hospital attorneys to arrive at our office and go through our records. It was hard to conceive that these people would be so aggressive as to do that without a court order or that Streaker would be so overwhelmed by them.

The young lawyer attempting to help the Citizens during the depositions, had withdrawn from the case, again leaving the Citizens unprotected, and now my lawyer was caving in to those bullies. As a precaution, we gathered up several boxes of Citizens Committee correspondence and documents, and locked them in the trunk of my car. We still laugh about the events of the following day.

The Court had assured us that there would be no order for document production the next day, but sure enough, at 10:00 A.M. the next morning, there appeared the assistant to the Hospital Lawyer in the reception room with a court reporter. The recorder set up her equipment right in the reception room. The Lawyer advised that he had an order from Judge Earley. He undoubtedly had a plan, whereby he would engage us in an argument, hoping that the transcript of that argument could be read to the Judge, and, hopefully, gain sanctions against us. Our response was simple. We had canceled early morning appointments and simply ignored our guest and his court reporter. Margie, our receptionist, was busy filing patient records in the front office when the Lawyer and Court Reporter entered. She opened the sliding glass pane and the Lawyer announced that he was the Hospital Attorney, there to copy documents. She quietly advised him to have a seat and went on with her filing. Both Margie and my secretary Annette were busy around the front office for the next hour or so, and never even gave an outward glance to the reception room area. Every few minutes, the Lawyer would step up to the window and glare inward, only to be ignored. He finally thrust open the sliding window and demanded to see Dr. Miller. Annette quietly said she would tell me that he was there.

After another half hour or so, the Lawyer stood up, took the Court Reporter with him, and slammed the reception room door sufficiently to almost level the building. The girls were embracing each other and laughing, till tears came, as they watched the fellow pull out of the parking lot. That was the last we ever saw of him. In later quiet reflection, we would wonder how many people would be intimidated by the Hospital Lawyers of the world.

Not only were the Citizens again left without a lawyer, but for all practical purposes, I was left without legal help. I didn't see any way to depend on the likes of Streaker. I made a few calls to determine the name of a sturdy lawyer who would help in our defense.

On advice from friends, I contacted George Weis, one of the partners in a Pittsburgh firm. He agreed to take over for Streaker and scheduled an appointment. Before meeting with Mr. Weis, I learned that four lawyer brothers had founded the law firm. The brothers were from Pittsburgh's North Side, and the firm had an excellent reputation. George was the senior partner after his brother Joe had left private practice to join the Third Circuit Court of Appeals.

When George and I first met, he almost sullenly directed me through a maze of passages into his frugal office in one of the upper floors of the Grant Building, just across from Pittsburgh's City-County Building. He was almost surly. His ruddy, round face showed little or no reaction and absolutely no emotion. During the hour or so we were together, he methodically took notes and began his file. There was no doubt, as I left the Grant Building that evening, that George Weis was a no-nonsense professional, and that we would prevail in this attempt by the Hospital Lawyer to force me out of business.

George and I were to become fast friends and we gradually developed an efficient and effective working relationship. We even worked on his latent, but very real, sense of humor in dealing some of the Hospital characters he would encounter. We still remember George's enjoyment when we would travel to the local Ponderosa for one of their famous burgers. We also recall George's delight in pitching peanuts to our office pet German Shepherd, Heather. She became a master at grasping George's peanuts out of thin air.

After George made an appearance in the case, he set aside a day when he and I sat in my office sorting documents and collecting a file which was segregated into a single section for each of the charges the Hospital said were defamatory. For each charge, we provided records showing the Hospital Nursing Director's employee list, with the names of her relatives. We provided documentation of her purchases of hospital equipment from her son's company. We included copies of documents showing payments to Hospital lawyer-board members for work on the bond issue. Another document obtained through the Pennsylvania Department of Health and the Department of Health, Education and Welfare, described to a word, a statement of the petition to Secretary Muller. The document described "close monitoring of several Medical staff members at Indiana Hospital where infractions of rules and regulations had occurred." To illustrate the number of physicians coming and going from the Hospital, we entered employment records and letters of resignation. For the charge of poor hospital atmosphere, we included a pile of resignation letters and memos from physicians who had left the Hospital for practice elsewhere. And, finally, the section to demonstrate the quality of hospital care was filled with letters from former patients to the Citizens Committee describing everything from four hour waits in the Emergency Room, to loss of life and limb due to negligence. George was meticulously building a case. From time to time, he would momentarily break his tightlipped no comment mood and cluck a little as I would supply a document that would, in itself, clinch the truth of a specific Citizen allegation.

It became obvious that the Hospital Lawyer was doing his best to keep us from other Hospital documents, not knowing that everything that had been included as an allegation in the petition to the Department of Health had included, with the allegation, the related papers documenting the charge. Nevertheless, we were being stonewalled on efforts to see Hospital records of bank transactions and purchases to establish the connection between the illustrious Board Members and the wide- spread Hospital business. In particular, we were having difficulty in obtaining documents relating to the Indiana Hospital Coal Company.

Finally, George decided to end the frustration and scheduled depositions for The Administrator and The Board Chairman. On this occasion, George chose my office for the interrogations. Instead of using the large, back room, he sat at my desk with the Court Reporter and two of the Hospital's junior assistant lawyers on the sofa. The Administrator and the Chairman, in turn, would sit on my colonial college chair, facing the desk. George's questions were direct and well-phrased, designed to elicit the knowledge of each of the events leading to the charges leveled at The Citizens Committee. There was little that these two could remember. They answered obvious questions with generalities, but otherwise evaded and gave a number of "I don't recall's." One thing was established from the outset. George wasn't about to tolerate the tactics of that legal group. The Hospital Lawyer had influenced his underlings to interrupt the other side without putting an objection on the record - a breach of the rules of procedure. They would then proceed to make a speech that was designed to disrupt the train of thought of both questioner and deponent; and it often worked. On this occasion, the short, stocky little fellow representing the Hospital, began the routine of interruption. George paused momentarily, pointed a finger and said, "You just hold on there, if you have an objection for the record, make it and be quiet. We aren't going to have your interruptions."

We did not have any more interruptions. However, as the Administrator's interview began, Annette came back and whispered to me that there was another Hospital Lawyer in the reception room who was demanding to be let in. She asked, "Who is this self-important, pushy person?" Her diagnosis was right on target. I had encountered this person when Mr. Evans, Ralph Smith and I had gone to the Hospital Lawyer's firm. He was thin, average built fellow, with a crown of manicured, curly hair. When I was alone with documents at their firm, he had assigned a paralegal to sit with me as I recorded each document - obviously to prevent any thievery on my part. At any appearance he would make, he was just plain snotty. He had repeatedly insulted the lawyers I had been working with.

Annette and I allowed him to cool his heels for awhile in the reception room and then he came back and squeezed onto the sofa with his two colleagues. Really now, who was paying for this trio to sit there and listen to the depositions?

With less than full information attained from the depositions, George filed a motion to compel production of the Hospital documents, saying that certain documents were necessary for me and the Citizens to be able to defend ourselves. He was asking for about two hundred documents which we knew existed in Hospital files.

The main Hospital Lawyer suddenly decided he wanted to take my deposition and it was held in one of the Lawyer-Board Members's office. Because of the interrelationship with the federal suit, young Ralph Smith, who had taken over my federal suit attended, as well as George Weis. The Hospital guy, as usual was late, and made a loud entrance into the conference room. He finally began with that abrasive, nasal drawl by introducing yet another young lady as his colleague. I made no secret of the fact to Ralph and George Weis that I had total lack of respect for this fellow's conduct. I got little argument from either of them, and time has shown a general awareness of some of the actions of the Hospital's representatives.

I had felt the need to meet or match the disruptive tactics and realized that my lawyers were too professional and reserved to fully contain the unprofessional badgering. So, along came my handy tape recorder. I knew it would annoy the Hospital Lawyer and that seemed like a good idea. His tendency to grab other lawyers' papers, grab documents from witnesses and grab others' tape recorders, was evident from the start of the Hospital hearings when he grabbed a letter from Dr. Katter's hand, while Dr. Katter was testifying. It occurred again when he snatched the young lawyer's file and helped drive her from the case. That is not to mention his seizure of my tape recorder and incursion into my office to pursue my files. So, before my deposition, and as a little added development, I prepared a file in a green plastic jacket, knowing full well that that guy would be into it before the deposition was over.

At the deposition, as the inquisitor got well into his questioning, he first noticed my tape recorder and began a lengthy diatribe against it being there. We all just looked at him and he exhausted every reason, legal and otherwise, for not having it in the room. He finally paused, looked at George and said, "Give me just one good reason why that machine should be here." "Sure", replied George. "It's a free country." "O.K," said the bullying examiner, "I just wanted to know", and went on with his questioning.

Much of the time he was fishing - trying to tie me into the Citizens Committee and obviously to force me into the position of getting into a lengthy trial. I purposely made him state and re-state his questions so that there would be no room for ambiguity. He was tough, he was unprincipled and he was persistent, but he wasn't getting what he wanted. He kept eyeing the green folder and finally demanded, "What do you have there?" "Just a few notes, " I replied. "you wouldn't want these, they are just informal notes." "May I see them?" "Oh, you really wouldn't be able to understand them." "Give them to me," he again demanded. I feigned reluctance at pushing the folder across the polished walnut surface. He first encountered a post card my older son had sent me from medical school when he had learned of the Hospital's interception of my mail and of the hanky-panky of Hospital Board Members. The card was a photo of a chain gang working alongside the walls of a prison, and over three of the figures were posted the nick-names that alluded to the Lawyer, the Administrator and the Board Chairman. It took a moment for it to register, but then he described the card in great detail for the Court Reporter and the record. No one moved or said a word.

He then turned over a page in which I had written Roman numerals in a vertical column, one through twelve. After each Roman numeral, I had written a legitimate or a phony Latin phrase. Included were, E Pluribus Unum, Ex Post Facto, Semper Fedalis, Pax Vobiscum and so forth. Included opposite numeral VI was the joker - it was one of Jerry Weaver's old favorites when we were communicating across the dining table in bastardized Latin. It was, Stercus Bovinum. There was silence as our intimidating friend perused the list for what seemed to be an unusual length of time. He went over the list from top to bottom and then again and the third time. He finally snapped, "What is Stercus Bovinum?" "Oh, that's not important," I replied. With a loud voice, and a somewhat controlled exasperation, he said, "What is Stercus Bovinum?" again and, then very firmly, "What is Stercus Bovinum?" "I hesitate to say, shouldn't we move on?" "Tell me what is Stercus Bovinum!" he shrieked.... "Well, that's the Latin word for Bullshit." No one smiled, no one snickered, but he sat there for what seemed to be an unusually long time, silent. I wonder to this day if he had realized that he had been had.

Near the end of the deposition, which went on for about four hours or more; the inquisitor was visibly tired and made a slip in the way he interpreted one of my answers. He was trying to expand it into an admission on my part, that I had passed certain documents to Joe Gratta, of the Pittsburgh Press, from which he had written a front page story about the Hospital. He persisted and persisted, to no avail. I stuck to the truth, which was that Grata had produced the documents in my office. The Lawyer then threatened to keep us there all night unless I confessed to providing the documents.

Finally, George joined in and put an end to it. He said we had all been patient but that this opponent was off base and was trying to distort answers. The intimidator seemed to crumble. He reminded George of a long friendship and wanted to resolve this out of the room, "away from others." When he and George returned from their discussion out of the room, the deposition was clearly coming to a halt. One of the documents that the Lawyer found in our file was a certified copy of a complaint in divorce filed by one Arnold Sladen, against a Doris Jean Sladen, dated just a few weeks before the hearings at the Hospital. Sladen was the Hospital Lawyer's recruit and only expert witness against me at the Kangaroo Court. Sladen, in his testimony, stated that he had not known the Hospital Lawyer before the hearings, yet here was Sladen's divorce complaint signed by the Hospital Lawyer - Sladen's divorce lawyer.

    He was obviously agitated. "Where did you get this?" "From the Prothonotary of the Common Pleas Court of Allegheny County." "Who sent you to him?" "No one." "Who told you the document existed?" "I can't remember." "We are going to stay here until you tell me," He barked. I responded by, "Sir, there have been so many people, both in Pittsburgh and elsewhere who have become aware of your tactics and ethics, of what you did during the Kangaroo Court at Indiana Hospital , that literally dozens of people have volunteered to help." He exploded and threatened to see whose ethics needed review and threatened to come across the table at me. George loudly told us both to quiet down and get back to the business at hand.

    The Hospital guy seemed to be retreating. It was becoming obvious that he had encouraged a defamation suit against a group of local citizens as a ploy to stop their criticism of the Hospital - something that all of the Citizens thought was their American right. He obviously wanted to get damaging information that would allow him to put me through another trial for the entertainment of the Hospital.

    Things were quiet for a few days after that deposition until George called and said that he would be in town the following afternoon. The Judge had called for arguments on the Hospital's motion for a protective order. It was designed to keep us from access to the Hospital documents which the Hospital was attempting to protect at all costs. While George, Annette and I had a quick burger at the Ponderosa, George had even less to say than usual. He was obviously concerned that we could be denied access to the Hospital documents, moving us closer to trial. What was the Hospital hiding? Nevertheless, it was my firm conviction that our file already had enough proof to convincingly defend our actions. In fact, through various government agencies, we had, over a period of time, amassed an extensive file of financial and quality of care information that the Hospital Lawyer, at most, only suspected were in existence.

The Administrator and a few others had, for some time, whispered about Miller's paranoia. It was becoming almost comical to watch The Hospital attempt to keep a lid on my information that would find its way to the press. That was about the time we were being told of electronic equipment in the Administrator's office and on the Hospital roof.

George, between bites of his burger, commented to Annette, "They're beginning to see Ralph Miller behind every bush."

Earley's courtroom was empty except for George, the Hospital Lawyer, the Judge and me. The hearing was informal and the Judge simply held the list of the two hundred or more documents we had requested. He peered down at the two lawyers from his bench without his robes. He went through the entire list, one by one, and asked the value for each document that was to be provided, as well as the Hospital's objection to each. The list itself indicated a great deal. It was specific and left little doubt of the existence of the information the Hospital did not want to be made public. At one point, George called me up to the bench from the spectator area and inquired about a particular document. "Is this important?" he whispered. "Not very", I answered. "Then I am going to let it go", he said.

"Your Honor, we withdraw that request." It went back and forth, through the whole list, for an hour or more, and without fanfare, the Judge took the copy of the list, advised that he would issue the appropriate order, spun around and disappeared through the door behind his bench.

George was never one to express optimism ,or for that matter, to predict an outcome. But, as we drove back to the office, it was apparent that we had been granted access to the bulk of the documents we requested. There was much in those papers that the Hospital may not have been proud of.

Within a day, George's call came and announced that the Hospital had arranged another conference with the Judge in chambers. He had no notion what it was all about, but promised to stop by the office after leaving the Judge's chambers. We were just finishing afternoon hours when George appeared. He laid his brief case on my office sofa and began methodically retrieving peanuts, one-by-one, from a small, foil bag and popping them in between words. He began a factual, almost monotone description of his entering the Judge's chambers. The Hospital Lawyer was already there, talking with the Judge. Although it was beyond belief, he described that the Hospital Lawyer had pulled from his packet three separate motions for the Judge to sign. The first was a protective order designed, once again, to avoid producing the documents. As George droned on, he described that the Judge said he was, in no way, going to reverse his previous order allowing the Citizens access to the documents they needed. Then a second order was pulled from the sheath, which requested that the file, and all the documents in the file, be sealed and kept under lock and key. George related that the Judge had no problem with that. We all knew that the file contained only motions by the parties and copies of documents we had provided. There was certainly no harm in keeping those documents under seal, at least for a time. The Hospital Lawyer may not have realized that it was a harmless motion.

As George stood in front of my desk staring out the picture window into the lower parking area, and without missing the rhythm of his peanut munching, described: "I was then flabbergasted when the opposing lawyer pulled out his final motion. It was a motion to discontinue" George continued to stare out the window and munch and I asked, "Discontinue the case?" "Yes", he said. "Do you mean it's over?" "Yes", he said. We stood there silently for a bit before I said, "They really do not want those documents in the news." "No", he said, "they do not."

In a few days, George's final letter arrived expressing thanks for the way we had worked together and noted that the case had been dropped without the forfeiture of "one red cent."

The Judge's final order was signed that the case was discontinued, "with prejudice", which George explained meant that the Hospital was prevented from ever opening the suit against the Citizens again. The letter made clear that a lawyer who filed suit, conducted discovery, and then dropped the suit, was treading on very thin ice.

Chapter 16

> *"The law is a crude machine at best, and only spits out something approaching justice if its attendants are committed to justice. As lawyering has become less about doing right and more about doing what you can get away with, our standards of acceptable shenanigans-as-usual seem to be in a free fall."*
>
> — *The Wall Street Journal*

THE FEDERAL COURTS - THE TWELVE YEAR ODYSSEY

Ralph Smith and I became friends the first time we met. Ralph's family were well-known in Pittsburgh's North Side. His Dad had been a judge - the youngest in the history of Allegheny County's Common Pleas Court; but he had died at an early age, leaving Ralph to be the patriarch of the family. Ralph was devoted to his mother and two sisters and spent some difficult years looking after them while working as a clerk in the Prothonotary's office and studying Law at the University of Pittsburgh.

The Dean of Pitt's Law School was Judson Crane, a gruff, plain-spoken intellectual teacher. The Dean was a close friend of my Dad, and in the later years of Medical School, I would meet many of Ralph's Law School classmates. The Dean's students had great respect and regard for him; while Ralph and his friends seemed to be in a friendly battle to be the top of their class - and they all made it or came very close.

The Dean would be quoted at one time or another, in illustrating, that in our System, anyone can sue anyone. He would say, " You can sue the Pope in bastardy".

During those final years in school there would be the Law School parties and later, during internship and residency training, there would be the occasional dinner with the lawyers and the free-for-all discussions at the University Club.

The lawyers were in their earliest years of practice and the discussions would be around a large, circular table in the Club's ornate dining room. I not only enjoyed the discussions, but would have some misconceptions shattered. I recall my simple, naive belief that our Court System guaranteed justice; and I still recall the hilarious response from the group when I once expressed that thought.

More than philosophy, I was learning of the differences between lawyers and docs. We had all learned of the different personality types typically gravitating to the various medical and surgical specialities; surgeons were outgoing and bold; the orthopedists were rough and tough; while pediatricians were more apt to be a little timid and the psychiatrists a little nuts.

But, there was no doubt of the personality differences between those who selected the Law and those who chose Medicine. More and more it would be evident that the physicians, almost to a man, were overachievers - overachievers by necessity. The personalities often were fragile and overachievement was a means of maintaining self-esteem. Any threat to a physician's perceived self-image could lead to surprising reaction or overreaction and to lifetime enmity.

On the other hand, I was learning that the lawyers either by nature or nurture, could scrap with each other without restraint and then go out and share a pitcher of beer. Not surprisingly, lawyers, in addition, often have difficulty understanding why anyone would take an attack on credibility or truthfulness as "personal". "You shouldn't take it personally", is often a lawyer's advice after a courtroom testimony followed by an attack on cross-examination.

Personal though, to a lawyer, is his devotion to winning and to compensation. Some say that the present System, beginning in Law School, encourages winning at any cost. But compromise is still the mainstay of many law practices. The blend of aggression and principle in any lawyer will determine his ethics in any given situation. Thus, we have the broad spectrum between shyster and statesman as well as the spectrum between quack and physician.

A recent book review in the Pittsburgh Post Gazette, describes Law professor Paul Haskell's news publication entitled, "Why lawyers Behave as They Do". One of the professor's quotes hits home. He says, "Lawyers should abandon the hired gun approach and pursue whatever justice their clients are entitled to under the law, and nothing more. Period."

Ralph and some of his former Law School friends were struggling to make their new law firm a success, while I was struggling with the later years of training. I still recall giving young lawyers, on occasion, a tranquilizer before a venture into the courtroom for an important argument.

After a few years in practice, Ralph, following in his Dad's footsteps, became the youngest Judge in the history of the Court of Common Pleas of Allegheny County. At once, he gained a reputation for integrity. Over a period of many years, I never knew of that integrity to be compromised. We would get together on Wednesdays at the "U Club". Ralph liked Manhatans and I liked Martinis; but we would share Ralph's pack of those powerful Camel cigarettes over dinner. Our talk was of Law and Medicine; I think we were both learning. Never would information about a case before him be discussed, and I admit to trying to pry information about a celebrated case from time to time, but was never successful. I once learned, that, at one time, a messenger from a large Pittsburgh law firm had been shown into Ralph's chamber and had handed him an envelope containing a thousand dollars in cash, for the Judge's reelection campaign. Ralph called in a court reporter and his tipstaff and dictated his comments as he handed back the cash. We all know that returning money has not been a common practice.

Many of our discursive chats over dinner did inevitably focus on our professions. At the time, there was a fair amount of newspaper publicity reporting irregularities in the court systems. Anyone reading the papers would have to exert real effort to avoid becoming contemptuous of the whole legal system. Ralph would gradually come to the point of believing that the public, in general, held the judiciary in contempt. He loved the story of the judge who said to the young lawyer before him, "Sir, you have repeatedly attempted to show your contempt for this Court". Whereupon, the young man replied, "Quite the contrary, your Honor, I'm doing my best to conceal it".

Similarly, later, I unabashedly discussed some of the unusual personalities and some of the unusual behaviors of the people beginning to populate Indiana County's Health System. We would tend not to take those things too seriously and would chuckle at the doctor and spouse climbing a non-existent social ladder in a small town, the driller who was putting his name on a number of the town's buildings, the devious Hospital Administrator and the policy of allowing general practitioners the widest range of hospital privileges. The town's judges were not excluded. On occasion, Ralph would sympathetically advise that I was working with a "bunch of yo-yos".

Ralph and I drifted apart for awhile - until a fortuitous meeting. John DeMay and I were fighting our way through the State Court System and the Citizens Committee was battling the defamation suit that the Hospital had filed against them. It was a rainy evening and John and Ralph bumped into each other, under umbrellas, at the bus stop in front of Pittsburgh's City-County Building. They had been classmates and friends in Law School. It was there, that Ralph learned of the turmoil in Indiana County. I suppose Ralph was more than a little disturbed at what was occurring. DeMay had been distressed by the rigged hospital and court hearings in Indiana, and within those few minutes, conveyed his concern to Ralph. It was then on that dull, rainy Pittsburgh evening that the thought of a cause of action in the federal District Court to address the illegal activity of the Hospital bunch was first entertained.

It wasn't long after that, that a post card from Ralph and Clara arrived from a vacation spot. Clara asked me to call when they got home. I did; and the Wednesday evening dinners at the "Club" started again. Only now, there were no cigarettes on the menu. We would both laugh at giving up the strong, unfiltered Camels. I often remarked to Ralph's friends that I didn't know why he put up with me. We were certainly different in many ways - but probably very much alike in some of the things that count. We did share a fondness for a good laugh and an awareness of Shakespeare's observation, "What fools these mortals be".

I would ride Ralph unmercifully over some of our experiences. For awhile there was great interest in the news relating to the first really "dirty movie" to come to a Squirrel Hill theater. "Therese and Isabel" was a graphic depiction of the lives of two lesbian lovers. The movie had been threatened with closure somehow; and Ralph was in the position of conducting a "trial" for the movie. Of course, the longer the whole thing went on; the longer the lines at the theater. The Judge took his jury by bus out to Squirrel Hill to see the movie. I made the most of that, but had the most fun when I read a copy of his opinion. It was a little tricky for him to find the appropriate language to describe what they had all seen on the screen. I thought it was elegant literary skill when he described, "and then we saw Therese in juxtaposition with Isabel's pubic region".

Then, there was the time that I got into town a little early and strode into the Court in session. I quietly took a seat in the rear of the courtroom. Sitting before the Judge were two very attractive and heavily made up young ladies. Everyone was speaking softly and it took awhile to determine that they had been arrested doing their performance at a suburban night club. I was eager to hear what the girls had done - probably something pretty lewd. One was a tall, lanky, blonde and the other a really cute, petite, brunette. The smaller girl was answering questions quietly, but the blonde had a louder, husky voice. It turned out that it wasn't a husky voice. It was a man's voice. I began to notice a closely shaved face on the blonde but the little one could have fooled anybody. I was never sure why the female impersonaters had somehow gotten themselves arrested.

Another time, as I looked through the oval windows in the courtroom doors, I could see that the courtroom was darkened. A movie was being projected for the benefit of the jurors. It was apparently a porno flick from one of the infamous Liberty Avenue showplaces and the jury was to rule on whether to censor the film.

It didn't take long for the censorship fad to fade, but we would often reflect with good humor on how the standards had changed and how those courtroom dramas had faded into the past.

One of Ralph's decisions carried no humor at all for him. The University wanted to build its new field house on the bluff overlooking Pitt Stadium. The problem was a cemetery on the site. The University planned to exhume all the remains and move the cemetery. A group of relatives of the deceased had objected and had filed suit.

Ralph ruled in favor of the relatives, preventing the University from proceeding. He was overruled by Superior Court. In a word, he didn't like it one bit. I would have opportunity later to reaffirm that judges do not like to be overruled. Do you suppose they take it "personally'?

Our troublesome odyssey through the Pennsylvania courts was disappointingly coming to an end. Beginning with Dr. Goldfarb's in-the-pocket Judge Handler and nearing its close with that ridiculous three man panel of judges in the Superior Court, it appeared that the travesty afforded by the state courts would not be the final answer to our search for some form of justice.

For me, the Wednesday night chats were the beginning of a second education. Ralph was worldly and had had years of experience on the bench. But he would have difficulty in accepting that a community hospital, supported by public funds, could operate like a private kingdom with accountability to no one. He probably had more difficulty with knowing of the cover-up support by the likes of Earl Handler - President Judge of the Indiana County Court of Common Pleas. Handler's actions and rulings were the result of his friendship with my antagonist, Dr. Goldfarb.

It was becoming even more evident that there were unusual and firm interrelationships among some of the town's institutions. The Coal Company, the banks, the Hospital and the Court were jelled into the town's "Establishment". Boards of these institutions and their satellites were often populated by the same faces. They all seemed to be in lock-step. They were all dancing to the same tune being whistled by a selfish elite. It was the players, dancing to the common tune, that led to the town's reputation - not always complimentary. It was this reputation that would, at times, have litigants attempt to have their cases transferred to other counties.

We were at a favorite spot in North Carolina - the Orville-Wilbur Wright Lodge in Kill Devil Hills when I finally got around to listening to a cassette tape Ralph had given me. It was entitled, "Antitrust and Health Care".

Our good friends who owned the Lodge kept a set of rustic lawn chairs and a low circular table up on a large dune between the Lodge and the Atlantic. The sun was just peaking over the horizon as I listened to the speakers of a conference describe how the emerging law was including the health care industry in antitrust scrutiny. It was the first that I had heard my profession called an industry. We always considered ourselves professionals and had jealously protected that status.

At the state level, by law, hospitals were losing the charitable immunity that had sheltered hospitals and churches, from not only law suits, but also from taxation. Hospitals were increasingly being seen as businesses - big businesses.

At the federal level, health care had been protected from the antitrust laws by an exemption for the "learned professions". But this was changing. The law was beginning to recognize health care as an industry and anti-trust suits were being filed against hospitals and professionals who engaged in conduct designed to put their competitors out of business.

A District of Columbia Federal Judge, Gerhart Geisel - later to become known for his role in the Oliver North case - decided against the Hospital in a suit against Washington's Sibley Hospital. His opinion sent a warning that hospital boards would be held personally accountable for their negligent actions.

It was now being recognized that physicians and hospital boards were capable of joining into actions that were in direct violation of antitrust laws, opening the possibility of criminal penalties and extensive damages for illegal activities.

As I enjoyed that beautiful Outer Banks sunshine, I was learning from the cassette that the antitrust laws were created to protect America's free enterprise system - the system that had made the country the world's commercial giant.

In the late 1800's the system was threatened by John D. Rockefeller and others who were about to monopolize the nation's oil industry by the formation of a series of "trusts". In reality, the trusts were combinations of oil producers banding together and dealing only between themselves in producing and marketing oil; thereby eliminating competition. The threat was obvious. Such a cartel could control oil prices on a whim; therefore holding the nation hostage to their control of a vital commodity.

Congress reacted by enacting the first antitrust act in 1887, named for its sponsor - the Sherman Antitrust Act. The act was in two sections; making it illegal for a "combination" (two or more people) to conspire to create a monopoly or to restrain trade. The legislation was designed to protect businesses from "mom and pop" grocery stores to industrial giants from unfair efforts to put them out of business.

Early in the twentieth century, Congress saw the need to add civil penalties for violations of the law and passed the Clayton Act. Penalties for illegal, anti-competitive activities included triple damages which could be demonstrated at trial as a deterrent for anticompetitive activities.

Over the years, there had been some political tinkering with the law, such as exclusion of the insurance industry. But, on the whole, through surveillance by the Department of Justice and through scores of civil suits, the Law, to a great extent, had protected American businesses from unscrupulous practices.

In prominent decisions, the Supreme Court ruled that the American Medical Association was guilty of anticompetitive behavior against the chiropractic profession and a similar case in Arizona found against the Arizona Medical Society.

The courts were, indeed, increasingly recognizing that hospitals, medical societies, and the "professionals" were indeed business entities and were often involved in interstate commerce. Activities such as price fixing, boycott and division of territories were, under the law, violations and could expose anticompetitive activity to the onerous penalty of triple damages.

As I continued my seashore learning experience, I found myself comparing some of the Indiana Hospital activities to provisions of the law. There wasn't much doubt that the reckless behavior of the Hospital crowd could be seen as obvious antitrust violations.

It was a beautiful, warm sunny morning, and as I gazed out across the white caps, I began to reflect on the true nature of our community hospital. Early on, it had been a product of the Coal Company's need for its employees. But, as the town grew and became more cosmopolitan, there would be more townspeople using its services. As my thoughts wandered, it was becoming apparent, that in recent years, the institution had wandered farther and farther from its original humanitarian purpose. As I reflected, I was beginning to accept that there was a common denominator to the Hospital's perception of a threat from our multispecialty group practice and its willingness to allow a Kangaroo Court; not to mention its willingness, to ignore life-threatening problems. The answer was money! Why else would the Hospital crowd tolerate the outrageous tragedies of Lester Lazarus, Claude Clippins and others?

While the Hospital tolerated backwardness in medical care, it very likely was backward in its concept of the law. Perhaps it was time for a counterattack. Not only was I weary of being on the defensive, but I was seeing that if an antitrust action could be successful anywhere - all the elements for a successful outcome were in Indiana County.

As the messages from the cassette concluded, I began to see that the law applying to my profession was, indeed, a response to reality. It was becoming more difficult to ignore that a number of people, who were beginning to populate hospitals, and their boards, had one goal - the accumulation of wealth and status. These people would put little value on what I thought was paramount - excellence in the provision of health care.

As I sat there contemplating it all and gazing across the surf, my reverie was broken by a brilliant copperish glow coming from the sand just to the right of my rustic chair. The rays of the early morning sun, climbing over the horizon, had struck the edge of a brand new penny, all but covered by sand. As I uncovered it and brushed it off, I was certain that this was an omen - a glimpse of success ahead. Although I've never been one to be superstitious, the penny has been on my desk ever since.

A Saturday morning meeting with John Evans in his Frick Building office had been arranged. John Evans was the undisputed dean of Pittsburgh trial lawyers with a well deserved reputation for an outstanding record as a lawyer and gentleman.

The Frick Building was a gray, stone structure, just across Grant Street from the Courthouse and the City-County Building. The lobby was paneled in patterned white marble. There were two banks of heavy, brass elevator doors and heavy brass lighting fixtures hanging suspended on brass chains from the high vaulted ceilings. Footsteps and a few conversations echoed through the nearly deserted foyer. The elevator let us off on an upper floor, and the hallway, between the banks of elevators, led to an adjoining hall to the left. We passed a couple of law office doors with the firm's titles over them. Most announced the firm with large, ornate letters. As a contrast, the glass-panelled door into the Evans firm was modestly lettered in black; and the reception area of the firm lacked any modern flare. The plain beige walls of the reception area were covered with group photos of lawyers and justices; and, in a prominent spot, hung a photo portrait of the senior Evans who had founded the firm.

A highly polished mahogany chair-rail circled the room, matching the mahogany doors. A few bland leather sofas were flanked with brass table lamps. As we settled into the dark leather of a sofa, the receptionist offered coffee, and shortly later, ushered us into Mr. Evans' corner office looking out onto Grant Street and the City-County Building.

John Evans was of a solid, medium build for his age. His bright blue eyes, snow white hair and ruddy complexion were striking. But, more so, was his soft-spoken, confident manner. His firm hand shake and a pleasant smile couldn't help but put one at ease. He exuded both self confidence and humility. I knew that the initial pleasantries about the practice of Medicine and the Law and about Indiana, Pennsylvania and about our families, was his way of sizing me up. He already knew about the hearings at the Hospital and spoke about the "ridiculous charges". He knew about Handler's opinion from the local Court and of the "snap" opinion from the bench by Pennsylvania Superior Court Judge Sydney Hoffman.

We talked at length about possible claims to have my staff privileges restored and to collect damages for the exclusion from the Hospital. He knew of the Hospital Attorney and his behavior during the hospital hearings and knew of the bizarre rules under which Attorney Mattern conducted the hearings. At one point, he arose, walked to a window and stared at the Courthouse across the street. He said, "This will never stand".

As we left his office, I thanked him for his time and courtesy and remarked that the case represented problems within both of our professions that needed to be addressed. He agreed, and as we parted, he opened the door and said he would be in touch with me within a few days.

As we made our way down the marble-lined hallway and stood before the ornate brass elevator doors, we wondered what his decision would be.

In a few days, the call came from Mr. Evans himself. He was the respected head of a major Pittsburgh law firm; but dispensed with the petty little ploy of using a secretary to make a call. He had simply picked up the phone and told me it was John Evans. Mr. Evans said he thought of the case and of our conversation and was interested in talking further.

At our second meeting, he asked if I was requesting him to take the case; what I wanted to achieve, and if I expected the case to be taken on a contingency basis. I answered affirmatively to all the questions and we discussed my involvement in the case. I would be collecting documents and helping in the formulation of strategies. When we parted, Mr. Evans said that I would be receiving a contract by mail, and if satisfactory, it could be signed and returned. He would then get to work to compose the complaint which was to be filed in Federal District Court for Western Pennsylvania.

Before the complaint was completed, a call from Mr. Evans revealed that he favored talking with the Hospital Lawyer, the prosecutor for my hearings; who had now become the Hospital's Counsel. I agreed that the case could be settled at that point with my reinstatement to the Medical Staff. Mr. Evans' next call reported that he had walked down Grant Street to the Lawyer's firm in the U.S. Steel Building and had discussed the upcoming case with him. He had advised that there was "horrendous litigation" ahead and asked if this could be avoided. The Hospital Counsel admitted that a trial could be avoided if enough time would elapse for certain persons to leave or resign from the Hospital. He never identified those hardliners but they obviously included the Board Chairman, the Administrator and Doctors Goldfarb and Vader. I knew too well that John Evans was too wise to be taken in and delay upon that vague information.

Within days, the complaint, a thirty-seven page document, was filed in Federal Court. The complaint accused the Hospital Board, the Executive Committee of the Medical Staff and Claude Clippins, of violations of

Section I and Section II of the Sherman Act, violations of the Clayton Act, the Civil Rights laws and certain state antitrust laws.

Local constables were engaged to serve the complaints on each of the Defendants, a total of twenty-five. One of the Constables was a wiry, middle-aged retired policeman who seemed to enjoy being involved. After a day or two, he returned to our office with proofs of service for all twenty-five of the defendants. He wryly laughed as he described the Administrator's reluctance to accept the document until he conferred with the Hospital Counsel. Our office staff giggled at that, since they had always observed that the Administrator was a frightened, deceitful little rascal - not to be trusted, even though he was one of our patients, and always had profuse thanks for our care.

Our constable saved the best for last. Encouraged by the response to his Administrator story, he related his experience with the Goldfarbs. The girls, along with many of the townsfolk, knew of the Goldfarb's reputation for snobbery. Both of my girls had come from coal mining families and knew of Goldfarb's nastiness with his patients when he was a Company Doctor, in the little mining town of Lucernemines; that is, except for the important patients from Indiana. It was understandable that they saw the humor, as the Constable described visiting the Goldfarb's residence at suppertime. The Grand Lady (who liked to be called Fluffy) answered the door and informed the Constable that they couldn't be disturbed since the Doctor was "dining". The Constable related the rest of his tale with some restraint and obviously polished his syntax somewhat. But, it was apparent that he had advised the Madam that if the Good Doctor didn't interrupt his "dining" promptly he would be completing his "dining" in the local lock-up.

Joe's newspaper carried the headlines the next day: "Hospital Sued in Anti-trust Suit". Despite the front page spread, the story was cautiously worded to name only the Hospital, the Board of Directors and "certain members of the Hospital's Medical Staff". Still protecting "The Boys", the Paper was demonstrating its loyalty to the Establishment.

As I began work with John Evans, the reasons for his continuing respect among his peers was obvious. He was an ideal blend of toughness, intelligence and impeccable manners. Combine this with a man consumed with his work and you have either a formidable ally or a fearsome adversary. I was grateful that he was on my side and believed in our case. I learned, early on, that he would treat me as an equal. That's not necessarily a part of all lawyers' personalities. He would send a letter and a document each time he made a motion to the Court or spoke with the Hospital

Attorney. He also was a good listener and would consider suggestions for an effective strategy. Although nothing directly was ever spoken, he quickly learned not to trust the Hospital crowd. Nothing from the Lawyer was considered unless it was in writing, and then it was subject to serious question.

John Evans was a perfectionist in his writing. He had been a teacher prior to pursuing the Law and had a master's degree in English. It showed. He and I began work on the first phase of discovery; that is the phase in any civil action where each side, under the direction of the Court, seeks information from the other side. The information sought is usually that which would help in the evaluation of strengths and weaknesses of a legal action. During discovery, each side can give the other side written questions to be answered under oath, requests for written admission of certain matters of fact, requests for relative documents, and on occasion, to question members of the opposing side under oath. The rules of "discovery" were apparently forged to prevent the parties in legal actions from conducting trials "by ambush" - that is, each side would be warned in advance of the other's case.

The two of us began work on interrogatories (questions to be answered under oath). It was a tedious and lengthy chore to formulate questions related to the Hospital Defendants' individual roles in the Kangaroo Court and those activities surrounding that travesty. There were questions relating to interactions of the members of the Hospital Board of Directors with other physicians and the Administration. We were hoping to get honest answers linking people like Vader and Goldfarb to the Board Chairman and the Administrator in the conspiracy to eliminate our multispecialty practice - Indiana Medical Center. Any successful antitrust outcome, in order to show violations of the Sherman Act, must show a "combination or conspiracy", a "restraint of trade" and an "effect on interstate commerce".

Within a month or two, a stack of documents was delivered to the Hospital Lawyer at his office. The interrogatories to each defendant averaged forty or more pages with several questions on each page and with a space following the questions for a detailed answer. The request for admissions were answered within a few months, but the interrogatories were stacked, according to visitors, on the end table in the office of the Hospital Lawyer's assistant, an obvious understudy. We would learn that he had assumed the same aggressiveness as his mentor. It is no credit to the Legal System that the interrogatories sat there conspicuously for almost two years. The Lawyers were obviously orchestrating a delay.

In addition, the Hospital had been required to produce the documents kept in my personal file. The Hospital, of course, keeps a folder on each physician on staff and we had requested to see this file as well as any other documents that could be related to the alleged conspiracy by the Hospital actors. The Hospital had decided that rather than produce these documents at the Hospital, they would be copied and shipped to the Hosiptal's law firm in Pittsburgh. My lawyers would then be given access to review those documents.

A day was set for the lawyers to review the documents. A young lawyer from Mr. Evans' firm had been assigned to go to the Hospital Lawyer's offices and start the chore. But, it became apparent that it would be difficult for him to know the significance of many of the things that would be provided. He willingly agreed to take me along. I cancelled hours for the day and met him at his office.. To my surprise, Mr. Evans himself had decided to go along. It was his way of assuring that there wouldn't be any cheap tactics to stonewall our efforts, although he never said a word.

At the offices on one of the upper floors of the lawyer's building, we entered the reception area decorated in brilliant colors, with an unusual amount of gilded wall coverings behind the receptionist's desk. There were two or three over-dressed and heavily made-up young ladies vying for attention as we entered. One of them condescendingly advised us she would let someone know we were there. In a few minutes, a somewhat surprised Assistant Lawyer appeared in shirt sleeves and accompanied us to a long conference room with one wall of windows overlooking Grant Street and downtown Pittsburgh. A long mahogany conference table, surrounded by matching leather upholstered chairs, occupied most of the room. The Lawyer showed great deference to Mr. Evans and explained that the box of documents on the table were the first of several and that a legal assistant would be with us and would be stamping sequential numbers on each document prior to our seeing them. He explained that this was to maintain order, but it was obvious that we were not being trusted. He wanted to be certain that no documents would be purloined..

I brought out the old trusty tape recorder from my brief case and explained to Mr. Evans and his associate that I was going to record each document with a brief identification of each. The Assistant Hospital Lawyer's ploy of using serial numbers would help greatly. It occurred to me, that in his effort to prevent us from filching a document, he was locking himself in with the serial numbers. With my taped description of each corresponding page, there was no way to deny the existence of a particular document. It had become obvious that the gentleman was greatly surprised and concerned that I was to be part of the review team. He didn't have the courage to confront John Evans on the matter, and by my being there, I was able to quickly identify documents that may have been considered irrelevant if the Lawyers had been alone.

After we worked for an hour or so, Mr. Evans, seeing that things were going well, excused himself and departed. When the Assistant Lawyer came back later with the second box of papers he was not the same cordial self. He was obviously no more thrilled with my tape recorder than his supervisor had been during the Citizens Committee depositions.

The first box of documents were helpful, but not surprising. The box contained minutes of various Hospital committee meetings and letters relating to hospital administration. We concluded the day and agreed to return the next day. Early on that second day, we again met, and after a quick cup of coffee in the law office pantry, walked down Grant Street to the lawyer's building and crossed its ornate cavernous lobby. The lobby was criss-crossed from floor to ceiling with diagonal, highly polished , stainless steel beams and stainless steel escalators, advertising the beauty of polished steel. The polished steel doors opened and we were rushed upward to the firm's ornate reception area. This time we were ushered right into a small room where a paralegal was already busily stamping numbers on the documents in their lower right hand corners. After we introduced ourselves, I untangled my tape recorder and attached the remote control and we began our work.

We began working through papers that I had never expected to see. It was becoming apparent that the selection of documents had been delegated by the Hospital Administration and that the papers that we were beginning to see had never been screened before we were given access to them.

The Hospital Administrator's Secretary, a widow who needed her job, had always been resentful of the brutal way that the Hospital Board Chairman had fired her boss and my friend, the young Administrator who had begun to improve things at the Hospital. Had she seen to it that we got those documents?

After we had completed the listing of the top shelf of papers, I realized that something was very different. Page after page of memos and personal desk notes bore a characteristic set of initials - H.H.H. Characteristically, the initials were drawn with the vertical lines intersected with a horizontal cross hatch. The memos had apparently been collected over a period of years and were apparently a file collected by the Hospital Board Chairman himself. Included were typed phone messages recorded by the Hospital Secretary. One read, "I answered the phone and a deep male voice said, "Adolph Hitler is still alive"." There were a series of lists naming people who had been suspected to be members of the Citizens Committee, along with their addresses and a brief description of their personal work and their work supervisors. Had these people intended to interfere with someone's livelihood if they joined a committee?

One of the strangest things we found was a photostat of a post card I had sent to the operating room nurses from one of Pitt's bowl games in Florida. Why should the Administration or the Board Chairman save that card and put it in a file? Another shocker was a report with an inaccurate condensation of my practice in Pittsburgh and was apparently in the Chairman's handwriting. Another report authored by the Chairman contained strange comments such as , " Dr. Kellum despises Dr. Capizzi", and various comments that were attributed to a Dr. Lapsley. It is difficult to describe my reaction to those notes. Shocked is not an adequate word. It seemed that my mind just froze. The Chairman, running a local industry and serving as the head of the community Hospital, had been keeping a file on me for years. The man was deranged. The next document was a copy of a manilla folder and its contents. The contents included a brief article from the journal of the American Medical Association, entitled, "Paranoid Schizophrenia in The Medical Profession". It gave a description of unusual personality traits found in physicians who the author felt were schizophrenic. I was having trouble determining the significance of that when we looked at the file folder itself. The label had been typed, "Information concerning Dr. Miller given to the Administrator by Dr. Vader". There it was. There was the origin of the Administrator's gossip that Dr. Miller was "paranoid". It appeared that blind hatred was encouraging Vader to outdo himself.

My lawyer-associate was not grasping the significance of these documents, and as we hurried through them, I attempted to make my recording matter of fact. We did not want to alert the young lady across the table to something unusual; and similarly, we did not want to gain the attention of another lawyer who had been assigned to overlook our recording.

But then, I pulled from the box a sheaf of papers about an inch thick. I saw that it was photocopies of a large, legal sized manilla envelope with contents of about fifty pages. Once again, I couldn't believe what I was seeing. The envelope was filled with legal documents from our office that I had mailed to Judge Ralph Smith in Pittsburgh. The outer portion of the envelope was torn and the addressee had been removed from the envelope. Ralph had always claimed that he had never received this envelope; but there it was. It carried $1.20 postage made with the imprint and identification of our office postage meter and the date of cancellation, October 20th. I had mailed the envelope at our main post office and the postage had been canceled. But, rather than being delivered to its addressee; it fell into the Administrator's hands where it was opened and its contents copied, with the copies going to the Hospital Lawyers. As I looked at that pile of papers, I was unable to move. I wasn't even, once again, able to think. My companion couldn't guess what was happening and urged me to keep going. Again, not to tip my hand with the paralegal across the table and the lawyer in the room, I continued to dictate, but I couldn't believe what was obvious. The Hospital had intercepted my mail!

As I thought of the infrared spy detector on the roof of the hospital, the electronic burglar devices in the Administrator's office and now, this; I just couldn't avoid the irony of the Administrator confiding in people that Miller was "paranoid".

For the next taping session I went to the lawyer's office without company and was, as usual, met by steely silence from the Assistant Hospital Lawyer. He and the legal aides were obviously instructed not to talk and he was showing signs that the careless production of documents had been an error. As I plowed through the remaining Board of Directors minutes, I came across The Chairman's instructions to the Hospital Board to turn over all mail from Ralph Miller or the Citizens Committee to the Hospital office. Later, as I continued to review documents, I found copies of Citizens Committee mail which had been intercepted by the Hospital and copied with the copies sent to the Hospital Lawyers. The Hospital Administrator had confirmed the interceptions by writing the agencies whose letters had been intercepted. Copies of his letters to those agencies were also in the file. By the time the taping chore was completed, we had logged over sixteen hundred pages. There was little doubt that the Lawyer's ploy to number those pages had locked him in, and that they had been caught off guard by my being present to help interpret the files. The theft of my mail would lead to a two year investigation by the Postal Inspection Service.

On one of the following days of copying, one of the documents made reference to a correspondence file of the Medical Staff Executive Committee. As that file appeared, its contents began to reveal the mentality of the people who were rotating themselves through that Committee and the Medical Staff offices.

Until now, I had felt only awe at the documents as they appeared. I had been incredulous that Vader, the Administrator and the Board Chairman would keep such an ugly file filled with their petty fabrications. But now, as I held that letter to a Medical School Dean - the emotion was anger.

Clippins had come to town at about the same time I was being recruited by the Hospital Administration. He had been given a lesser staff appointment than the appointment I had been given by the Hospital Board. Over a period of years, I had, without much difficulty, ignored him. But his malicious gossip finally had reached the point that I had asked the Pennsylvania Medical Society to help with a warning that his behavior was unprofessional. Rather than quiet him, he had increased his whispering campaign telling anyone who would listen that I had tried to "lift" his license. Now I was holding a letter which reflected his behind-the-scenes malice in bold print. It was written to the Dean of the Pitt School of Medicine. I wanted to see the little rascal before a jury.

The minutes of the noontime Medical Staff meetings reflected on the cowardice of the group who did a great deal of the talking at those gatherings. On one occasion, Abdul Hankey complained that I hadn't used him to help resuscitate a patient and Vance Vader, on another occasion, advised his colleagues that if the medical staff didn't show some "backbone" towards those who opposed the preceptorship assessment, they were heading for "a lot of trouble". These were both meetings that I had chosen to miss. No one, absolutely no one, was ever discussed when they were in attendance. Both Abdul's and Claude's noontime complaints would be later transferred into charges at the Kangaroo Court.

In the Hospital Board Chairman's pile of notes, a letter to him appeared. It had been written by a young woman practitioner who had been disgusted with the Hospital atmosphere and was resigning. She called the Hospital an "intellectual desert" and wrote that she had never seen a Medical Staff meeting "brought to order".

One of the files contained letters of application from physicians applying for Hospital privileges as well as letters of resignation from physicians leaving town. A thoracic surgeon had written a letter, promising not to compete with anyone. His letter of resignation came after he had done one surgical procedure for an abdominal aneurism, with questionable technique, followed by death of the patient.

There were letters of resignation from three urologists who had come to town and then left.

Among the letters of recommendation (or lack of same) was a letter from an Altoona hospital commenting on a poor attitude and poor performance by a Doctor Kottabachchi who had worked there. The Doctor, nevertheless, was hired to a position in the Emergency Department of the Hospital.

After several long days of recording the boxes of documents, I found myself at the end of the chore. Rather than feeling a sense of relief, I was feeling only revulsion. The pieces of a contemptible conspiracy were falling into place. It had become strikingly understandable why the Hospital group were so vigorously relying on the "conspiracy of silence" as well as their lawyers to cover their tracks. The Board Chairman had kept a file on me for years and had announced the results of the Kangaroo Court weeks before it ever began. But still, he tried to convince all that he had "stayed out of this thing from beginning to end".

The records were beginning to document the behind-the-scenes activity of the active staff physicians.

Vader had begun the "paranoid" rumor with his clandestine passing of material to the Administrator for "my file". Yet, he had watched my patient die without helping. He had demanded payment in advance before he would see an emergency heart patient, and he had refused to respond to a call for help for one of his dying patients.

Goldfarb, the eye doctor, regularly refused to see emergency eye problems and viciously berated Hospital people trying to get his assistance.

The hopelessly inept Abdul Hankey, never allowing false modesty, kept pressuring for a "permanent" position for him on the Hospital Board.

Lester Lazarus was regularly making a mockery of decent behavior, let alone, professional behavior.

When, During the Kangaroo Court, while facing the absurd behavior of the Hospital Lawyers, John DeMay had whispered to me, "Get me to a judge, any judge". He and I had felt that no court would allow the findings of that obscene hearing to stand. Obviously, however, we hadn't counted on the likes of local Judge Handler brazenly replacing his former law partner, Judge Earley in the midst of our local court action.

It was beginning to appear that we had enough information for trial. Mr. Evans, my lawyer, had attended a status conference for the case before federal Judge Donald Ziegler. Ziegler informed the conference that he allowed the parties to conduct their discovery with either interrogatories or depositions - not both.

A new Judge was added to the court - Carol Mansman. The custom, we learned, was for the sitting Judges to give some of their cases to a newcomer to establish a reasonable work load. There was apparently no standard for which cases were to be transferred - resulting in the Judge's unloading some of their "dogs". Our case was considered a "dog" and Carol Mansman became our Judge. A "dog is apparently a case that would require a fair amount of work by a judge.

A status conference was scheduled before the new Judge. But, instead of a conference we experienced a tragedy. As I arrived in the law offices in the Frick Building, I learned that John Evans had been hospitalized. He died following a minor procedure two days later. There was no doubt that I had lost an indispensable ally who would have eventually brought about justice. The legal profession had also lost one of its greats.

The young lawyer who filled in for Mr. Evans was the bright and energetic son of my friend, Judge Ralph Smith. Ralph III was just as convinced in the worthiness of our case as Jack Evans had been. But the Evans' ability to move a case along toward trial was gone. We were destined to face delay after delay which was being engineered by the Hospital Defendants.

The status conference was rescheduled and Ralph and I were invited into Judge Mansman's chambers. The "chamber" was furnished with thick carpeting and beautiful walnut furniture. The Judge was a short, attractive woman with a straightforward and pleasant manner. She had known Ralph; she had served her clerkship with Ralph's father, the Judge. She advised us to have a seat as she sat in her robes behind her very large desk and advised that the Assistant Hospital Lawyer was delayed and that she would meet with him a little later. Ralph spoke well and outlined our case. He added that the Hospital group was advising that, if Miller came back, the entire Medical Staff would resign. She blurted out, "That's absurd!" When she asked if I had any comment I advised that Ralph was doing fine. She agreed with "Yes, isn't he?"

I've often wondered what an impression we made on the lady. I've wondered more about what effect the foul comments of the Assistant Hospital Lawyer would have. We bumped into him on the way back through the courtroom and Ralph talked with him briefly. Ralph related that the Assistant Lawyer advised Ralph that he had a "slimy client". He would later use the same description for my lawyers. In the coming months, I would hear him advise my counsel that they were "slimy" for not giving in to his demands.

Our destiny with Judge Mansmann lasted only a year or so, but she determined, after an early motion by the Defendants, that the civil rights portion of our case was not valid and dismissed that portion. But she retained that portion of our case citing the Hospital's alleged violations of the antitrust Laws.

We learned that the Judge's husband's law firm was representing Indiana Hospital on an unrelated matter. With our experience with the biased Judge Handler, and the behind-the-scenes activities of the Hospital people well in mind, we presented a motion for Her Honor to recuse - that is, remove herself from the case. In a petulant fit of pique, she fired off a reply that indicated that she and her hubby didn't discuss matters of mutual interest ... and besides, she was leaving the case by moving to a seat on the Third Circuit Court of Appeals.

Over the next months, citizens of Pittsburgh were treated to multiple reviews and front-cover likenesses of Judge Mansman as an outstanding citizen and woman jurist.

We learned that our case had been transferred to Judge Paul Simmons. Simmons had been highlighted by a series of stories in the Pittsburgh Post Gazette as one of the three most controversial of Pittsburgh's Federal Judges. The story outlined his career as a success story, beginning in Pennsylvania's Washington County. During his employment as a railroad worker, he had lost a leg as a result of an accident. He had acted as his own counsel in a successful suit against the railroad and then went on to Law School. We thought that this man would show a tolerance for the underdog in a dispute, but we were destined to be victims of unbelievable sloth for a period of years.

Months passed after the case was transferred to Simmons with absolutely nothing happening. By that time, Judd Crosby, had taken over my case. Judd was a remarkable, bright lawyer with an innate sense of decency and fairness. Judd was a gentleman and became an able and intelligent ally , as well as a friend. Over a period of weeks, he became familiar with our case and became as frustrated as I, with the failure of the Court to allow our case to proceed.

I was beginning to learn about Judge Simmons as lawyer friends learned that he had been assigned to our case. When I gave the news to one lawyer he gasped, "Oh, God! You now have a real problem". A lawyer related that Simmons had sat on one of his cases for four years. He had finally solicited help from the Court of Appeals to require Simmons to move. Another explained that Simmons would make statements and give instructions and then would later deny that he had said any such thing. As a result, the District Court had required that all conferences with judges have a court reporter present, recording a transcript.

I finally urged Judd to request a status conference. He wrote to Judge Simmons suggesting a meeting. Despite the experience with local Judge Handler in Indiana County and Sydney Hoffman's snap opinion in the state Superior Court, I continued to be optimistic of our chances for a fair trial. After all, we were in the Federal Court System.

I had been given a paperback describing the Federal Courts. It was entitled, "The Benchwarmers- The Private World of the Powerful Federal Judges". It was written by Joseph Goulden, a trial lawyer.

The book, I thought, was a balanced insight into the Federal Court System. While it describes the majority of federal judges as conscientious and reasonably diligent, the description of erratic behavior and outlandish decisions by some Federal Judges, is indeed, sobering. As a Chicago Sun-Times quote says it, "To be read with both fascination and horror". As the book's cover exclaims, "There are no guidelines for their selection - and virtually no limits to their power. They are the Federal Judges of the United States. Few of us know their names, yet all of us are vitally affected by their decisions. These men influence virtually every aspect of our lives and every facet of our society - yet they, most often, are chosen for purely political reasons and given practically total license to operate as supreme tyrants in the kingdom of the law".

A quote from the Chicago Sun-Times Bookweek reads: "The author tells about federal judges all over the country: Judges who are sots, senile judges, immature and ignorant ones, as well as learned ones, low-browed bullies and high-browed snobs, bigots and bores, greedy men, preoccupied with extracurricular activities, men incapable of cooperation and at war with themselves".

After reading Goulden's book, I couldn't say that I hadn't been forewarned. But, I had no concept of the abuse that lay ahead as the result of Judd's letter to Judge Simmons.

It was early afternoon. The conference was scheduled after the lunch hour. The Federal Building at the lower end of Grant Street was a soot-blackened, unadorned stone structure with unimpressive entrances from the street.

A few men in navy-blue jackets and ties had us empty our pockets and pass through metal detectors on our way through the small lobby. The courtrooms and the judges' chambers occupying an entire upper floor were entered from a hallway running the entire length of the building. The courtrooms were all empty and there was scarcely a sign of life as we looked for Judge Simmons' Court.

The courtroom itself was empty and quiet as a tomb as we made our way toward the front row in the spectator's section. Judd went on into the trial area and opened his brief case onto one of the conference tables. In a few minutes, the uncivil Assistant Hospital Lawyer came in and went through a similar routine at the other conference table. A middle-aged and well-dressed court reporter came in and set up his transcribing equipment and then recorded the lawyers' names and our case's title.

We were allowed to wait awhile for His Honor, but finally, a walnut panelled door to the right of the bench opened and Simmons appeared. He was a moderately built with an impeded gait - obviously from his impairment. As he shuffled past, I noted his thick lenses; but he never looked our way and headed for a seat between the conference tables. We were surprised at the way he slouched into a chair as though he was in a recliner. He was followed by a young fellow, who was apparently his Law Clerk.

I think we all became somewhat hardened to the realities of the court systems with our experiences with Indiana's Judge Handler and Superior Court's Sydney Hoffman. Handler had used his seniority to substitute himself for another judge and to dismiss the injunction against the Hospital. Hoffman, similarly, had given a snap opinion from the bench and had stuck with it.

Outside influences on people were becoming more evident by the day. But the behavior of Handler and Hoffman was a Sunday school outing compared to the fury we experienced from Simmons over the next ninety minutes. It is beyond comprehension that this Carter appointee would have such a flagrant contempt for his duty to apply the Law in an environment owned by the citizens of his country. His disgraceful behavior would demonstrate his total lack of sensible judgement and fair play. What influences led to this behavior?

In any event, the transcripts tell it all: The hospital lawyers had asked the Court for Summary Judgement - that is, they had produced a motion asking Simmons to dismiss our case based on two or three different arguments.

Simmons instructed the Assistant Hospital Lawyer to proceed. It was very, very difficult to sit quietly and hear that Lawyer twist previous happenings into a fabrication of my lack of competence; especially since the Senior Hospital Lawyer had gone on record previously admitting that my competence was <u>not</u> the issue. The Hospital Lawyer demonstrated his lack of respect for honesty. He and the Judge allowed his argument to proceed:

The Court: "Now, really, what it comes down to basically there could be a violation of the Antitrust Laws, but this Doctor's damages might be de-minimus. Do you understand what I mean?"

The Hospital: "The real harm here Your Honor, is that the relief he seeks is to get back onto the staff at the Hospital...the Court would be put in a position , Your Honor, of placing a physician on staff...who is potentially dangerous to the public...even though it has been determined that he is not qualified to be on staff".

The Court: "What he seeks and he is going to get and could get are two different things. He might show that it is a monopolistic activity if it is the only hospital in the whole area and they are barring him from using this facility to make a living, which is basically the situation here".

The Court: "But I can't see how it is part of his liability case, his inability to exercise a right. He has the right normally, but for the fact he is incompetent, they couldn't bar him".

The Court: "If it weren't for his incompetency he wouldn't be barred...I don't know what runs through Judge Mansman's mind, but she probably had a lot of serious inhibitions...nothing has been done on it (the case) for four years.

It was very, very difficult to sit and listen to the insults of these two, who were showing total disregard for the truth.

More than a year later, on a renewed hearing on the Summary Judgement Motion, the Judge obviously still hadn't reviewed the case. As he concluded that second meeting, the record reads:

The Court: "I have to look into all of this. As I say, I did not even know this stuff was here until a few minutes ago".

The "stuff" was my case.

Back to the initial hearing:

After the Hospital Counsel finished his argument with concurrence of the Judge and without interruption the Judge looked at Judd, my lawyer, and opened:

"Let me hear you address this: Are you just suing for the fun of it, or are you suing to obtain the objective of his practice? And another thing too, you are charging this Plaintiff money presumably for this representation. And if he can't obtain the right to practice, even though he wins the Antitrust Case...which is your role in this thing...I am positive from my experience in antitrust cases, which I had enough experience in, that I could tell you you are up against a hard road".

Judd addressed the Hospital Lawyer's fabrications of my incompetence, and found himself interrupted by the Judge each time he attempted to make his point:

Mr. Crosby: "My name is Judd Crosby, I represent Dr. Ralph Miller...the Plaintiff in this case."

The Court: "My point is assuming you win this case, how can you get this man back on staff if he is incompetent and it has been established that he is incompetent whether you win or lose the case; what is your motive? That is the point."

Judd attempted to advise the Court, that no one at no time had ever challenged my competence, in effect, showing the Hospital Lawyer's arguments as abject falsehoods. The Court wouldn't hear to it.

Mr. Crosby: "Your Honor, my challenge to Defense Counsel, or the Court, to anyone, would be to show me anywhere on the record of this case of Miller versus Indiana Hospital...".

The Court interrupted:

Again Judd tried:

Mr. Crosby: "My challenge to the Court and to counsel would be to show me, on the record of this case, where the Hospital has raised the incompetency of Ralph Miller to practice his profession".

The Court: "Now, wait a minute. You didn't listen at all to what I just finished. Stop dead in your tracks and listen to me".

After another fifteen minutes of tongue lashing, Judd tried for a third time:

Mr. Crosby: "What I urged the Court in my brief is not to accept the invitation of Defense Counsel to assume without some facts of record that Dr. Miller is incompetent".

The Court: "That has been established, hasn't it?"

Mr. Crosby: "I don't think so, your Honor. That is...".

Again the Court interrupted:

The Court: "What do you mean you don't think so?...Wait a minute. Let's not talk about foolishness now. Don't argue foolishness". Again:

The Court: "Don't argue against the obvious. I mean you are up against something that you can't win on. As far as his competency is concerned, that has been determined. So don't argue that question".

Mr. Crosby: "May I read from the Court what the admission was of the Hospital during those proceedings?"

The Court: "The admission? What do you mean admission?"

Mr. Crosby: "This is a statement in those proceedings that they want the Court to rely on for collateral estoppel. It admits that Dr. Miller is competent and qualified, perhaps one of the best urologists in the country".

The Court: "It doesn't say that. He doesn't admit anything here. You see we better read this into the record".

The judicial admission of the Hospital Lawyer, given in the Indiana Court proceedings, was then read into the record. The Hospital Lawyer had said:

"I think that I ought to point out at the outset of this proceedings and this summation what this is not — this for example, is not a contest or a fight or attack on Dr. Miller's right to practice medicine. Indeed it is not in any way an attack on his competency, his capability to practice in a highly specialized field of medicine - urology. Indeed, I don't think anyone who has known Dr. Miller for even a short period of time would question one or two facts: one, that he is intelligent, indeed brilliant; and, two, that he is capable, capable of practicing the finest type and standard of urological medicine in the country".

The Court: "Who is making this statement?

Mr. Crosby: "That was the attorney for the Hospital, the present counsel's supervisor."

The Court: "That attorney is not talking about what we are talking about. His capability to practice medicine in general and his capability of practicing in the context and confines of a hospital are two different things, you see, that is what you are confused about".

As we sat there and listened to that judicial tantrum we were all thinking, "Baby, you really do have us confused".

In effect, His Honor had steadfastly held to the Junior Hospital Lawyer's distortion that the State Courts had decided the competency issue. He deliberately misled the Court and the Court was just not able to understand that.

The Hospital Lawyers were attempting to use a legal argument called collateral estoppel which, in effect, states that an issue determined in one court can be used as a determination in another court. In attempting to use this argument the Hosital Lawyer lied; and the Court believed his lie. In effect, the Judge kept dancing around the fact that he just didn't know the facts of the case.

Judd attempted to state our case as the Judge moved on:

The Court: "Now let's don't argue, you know, a lot of fantasy here."

Wow! It was difficult to believe that I had to sit there and listen to that series of insults. I had to think of Dr. Berberian's advice on that Easter morning in Lancaster. He had said, "The toughest thing ahead for you is to retain your self-respect." I doubt that he would imagine that I would face a lying lawyer in front of a questionable Judge.

Another try:

Mr. Crosby: "Your Honor, if I may respond...".

The Court: "Yes you may".

Mr. Crosby: "The Plaintiff...".

Another brazen interruption:

The Court: "Let's be practical and intellectually honest. Don't argue fantasy. Remember you got a duty to your client not just to argue to hear yourself.

"...You might convince some other judge of that but you are not going to convince this judge because I have made up my mind on that point after hearing and reading what was going on here". (Even though His Honor would not even begin to read the case for more than another year) "Go ahead, but you have to come to grips with the reality of your client's cause and you owe a duty to your client to come to grips with the realities of his case. You have got a tough road here as far as his ultimate desire if he wants to practice medicine in light of these records in the State Court System".

Mr. Crosby: "Your Honor, I was going to simply point out that the Plaintiff disagrees with the position of the Hospital wherein the Hospital indicates that competency is a threshold question to any antitrust staff privilege case".

The Judge then continued to demonstrate that he didn't have the faintest inkling of what was transpiring under the antitrust laws.

The Court: "We are away from that already. I have already agreed with you on that. Why argue something I agree with you on? I agree with you on that. But that is irrelevant. That has nothing to do with this case. Think now. Use your head. Think. "...The fact that they, the Hospital Directors, or whoever runs that hospital, has not acted in this man's case in an arbitrary and capricious manner has been established".

Mr. Crosby: "It has not been established, Your Honor, that they acted in compliance with the antitrust laws. That's what our position is — ".

The Court: "Listen to me, you are not thinking. You are not using your head. And I am saying that advisedly not insultingly. I've already told you, and will tell you for the fifth and sixth time, I already mentioned to the Hospital Lawyer - I told him that there was not a fall-back position of the Seventh Circuit. It is not a fall-back. I'm trying to tell you that you could win the antitrust case but still not get this man into the Hospital as a practitioner. Can't you understand this?"

Mr. Crosby: "I understand the Court's position." Then:

Mr. Crosby: "What I am using is the antitrust laws, Your Honor".

The Court: "What you are not using is common sense. Now your common sense should tell you — I am being sincere now. I am very frank to tell you these are foolish arguments you are making now".

Mr. Crosby: "We have to analyze it from the point of view of the antitrust laws, not what we would like to socially impose".

The Court: "You have a conceptualistic problem. That is what your problem is. Your are mixing up oranges and apples. They are actually trying to solve a very, very difficult problem by not allowing people like, say, this Plaintiff in this case to use the antitrust laws vainly and foolishly and improvidently at no gain to the litigant at all just because he has a right to do this because, basically, even assuming that he wins the antitrust case, he still can't exercise any privileges."

"Now if a fellow who was a blacksmith would file an action like this he could succeed just as easily as Dr. Miller in establishing that this Hospital was a monopoly. But you wouldn't seriously argue, I am sure, because he succeeded that then he had a right to go in and practice medicine without any education, you see. So now think about it. Don't argue foolishness".

Mr. Crosby: "I am sure the Court is aware that Dr. Miller practiced urologic surgery in Indiana Hospital for nineteen years".

We were again treated to another obtuse, ten-minute lecture in complete contradiction of the antitrust laws. Then an unbelievable attack:

The Court: "That is why I'm saying you could have serious ethical problems. Now I am telling — you might not be able to understand it, but you will understand it if you have got to come before a disciplinary board and somebody is talking about lifting your license to practice law. I am saying this sincerely. I am trying to help you. You don't seem to want to take help. You have very, very grave ethical problems."

Mr. Crosby: "I appreciate the Court's comments".

The Court: "You have ethical, grave ethical problems".

It is almost beyond comprehension that our System would require that an ethical, gentlemanly and knowledgeable lawyer like Judd would have to take abuse like that from that man and with the likes of the Hospital's Junior Lawyer standing by.

Not satisfied, Simmons continued:

The Court: "That is what I am talking about. You don't have much experience in this area. You are talking to a judge who has, as a lawyer, litigated antitrust cases. I mean as a lawyer; I don't mean as a judge. And I could tell you I have had lots of involvement with antitrust cases. I am giving you the benefit of my experience. I am telling you that you could win this case theoretically...".

He went on and on repeatedly saying things, over and over. As we now look at the transcripts, the Court Reporters have been very kind. They have taken Simmons' slurred speech and have put it into reasonable prose.

I truly believed that lies propagated by the Hospital Lawyers will, at some time, have to be faced by them.

Judd patiently waited for repeated illustrations by the Judge that if the Antitrust Laws were applied we would have janitors and blacksmiths practicing hospital medicine. The Judge was repeatedly demonstrating that he was buying the Hospital's diversion. The case was being litigated under the antitrust laws and the Judge just didn't get it.

Judd then attempted to rebut the Hospital's lie.

It was becoming impossible to educate the Judge that violations of the antitrust laws carry with them triple damages as defined by the Sherman and Clayton Acts. Patiently, Judd attempted to have the Judge understand that his comments regarding the antitrust laws were simply not true.

Mr. Crosby: "What is the law on that, Your Honor? The law that indicates that if an individual establishes violations of the antitrust laws and establishes that there were damages as a result of those violations, what is the law that indicates he would only be entitled to nominal damages? I am not familiar with that and I will plead ignorance".

The Court: "The point is that the damages, only damages, he could get would be nominal damages. He is not losing any actual damage because for other reasons not associated with the antitrust laws."

Continuing the lecture with ridiculous examples, His Honor continued:

The Court: "Now if a fellow who was a blacksmith would file an action like this, he could succeed just as easily as Dr. Miller in establishing that the hospital was a monopoly. But you wouldn't seriously argue, I'm sure, because he succeeded, that then he had a right to go in and practice medicine without any education, you see. So now think about it. Don't argue foolishness".

For the final time, the Judge again stated His Honor's misconception of the Law as he referred to Judd's letter requesting a conference and the Hospital's reply:

Mr. Crosby: "With all due respect ,Your Honor, I don't believe the law is such as what you have just stated".

The Court: "What do you mean the Law isn't such? What do you think I said wrong? I don't know what you are talking about. What do you mean you don't believe the law is such?"

Mr. Crosby: "As you just stated".

His Honor then launched into yet another diatribe lasting another quarter-hour.

The Court: "I didn't state the Law. All I said was that I think that the issues are separate. I am not speaking about the Law. I said the issues of this man's right to practice Medicine at this Hospital, and the issues involved in the antitrust case are distinct, they are different, they are different.

Let me tell you something. I will give you an illustration. While I could give you a lot of illustrations today. But here again, I will talk about the blacksmith illustration which I have given you. The blacksmith would have brought this action just as easily as Dr. Miller, but he would never be given the right to practice Medicine merely because they found that that the Hospital was engaged in anticompetitive activities."

Mr. Crosby: "I think what the Court fails to do is grasp the full context of a conspiracy against Dr. Miller. In our brief, in our affidavit…"

The Court: "Tell me what the conspiracy is".

The Judge was demonstrating, time and again, that his arguments were being presented without his having the advantage of ever reading the pleadings of the case. Judd continued:

Mr. Crosby: "We laid out, Your Honor, in an affidavit, for example that the Administrator of the Hospital, in the early years, stated, "We are going to terminate the privileges of Dr. Miller at the Hospital". That is some five years before the termination came up".

The Court: "The point is—let me hold you just for a second because I don't want you just to go off on a tangent".

Mr. Crosby: "I didn't mean to do that".

The Court: "I am going to address the point you just made. All the things you say might be true. It also might be true that in the mental recesses of all these administrative heads they might have had vicious improper motives in what they did to Dr. Miller. But as to that issue, that issue is settled ,and it was settled against Dr. Miller and approved by the Court. That is the problem you have".

Mr. Crosby: "It is our position, Your Honor, that under antitrust law that conduct, even though it may be lawful, has to be evaluated under all the circumstances from the antitrust perspective. That is what the law is".

Even though he obviously didn't understand it, the Court responded:

The Court: "Stop your point right there. I agree with what you say on that".

Mr. Crosby: "O.K.".

The Court then continued:

The Court: "But you can't seem to get through your head—true, what you say might be true, and it might be true that under normal circumstances the hospital is guilty of violating the antitrust laws".

Mr. Crosby: "I am convinced of that, Your Honor".

The Court: "I can see that. But I am assuming that what you say is true. I am saying, yes, you might win on that point".

Mr. Crosby: "Right".

Despite that suggestion that the Court was beginning to have some rudimentary knowledge of the antitrust laws, he again embarked on a further dissertation of his previous point that there was no relationship between hospital privileges and the antitrust laws. After the Judge, with the Hospital Lawyer's help, had concluded that rendition, Mr. Crosby again tried to clarify the subject.

Mr. Crosby: "I want to make sure the Court doesn't get misled into thinking that this collateral estoppel issue regarding the state court proceedings has already been decided. The Defendants pursued that issue. Whether or not the state court's action collaterally estops this action, Judge Mansman ruled on that in her opinion and then subsequent to that the Defendants asked for reconsideration of that".

The Court: "Did she have an opinion on this?" Did she write a full opinion?"

Once again, the Judge was documenting the fact that he had never looked at our case.

Mr. Crosby: "Yes".

The Court: "I don't disagree with her opinion. I already told you that I don't think collateral estoppel estops this antitrust case".

Mr. Crosby: "Good, because I don't think so either, Your honor".

The Court: "All I'm trying to get through to you, if I could, and this is a (old) case that obviously has caused a lot of soul-searching or it wouldn't be this old—I don't have any—maybe I have one case that I inherited from some other judge. But this is an old case. Any time a case lingers in the Court for three or four years—I can see why it has been lingering in this Court, because Judge Mansman maybe, perhaps—I don't know as I can't read her mind—but I am just surmising that she felt this is like a study in frustration. Yes, you are going to force her or force me now to try a case like this..."

"And don't be proud as I say, and think carefully about these things. Go back and do some soul-searching. Don't just litigate tenaciously and doggedly to prove something that is not going to help your client. You have a duty to your client. You see, that is what the problem is. Your duty to your client is foremost and if the client is not misled, of course, that is something else. But your client might be out here sitting in the audience. If he is, I hope he has heard all the things I have said. If he does, he will go home and think a little bit too and sometimes clients ought to get second opinions as to what their lawyers are doing, you know, because the Courts are not just play things that we use to you know, to satisfy our ego unless we have extraordinarily greats amounts of money and a principle so dear, something like free speech or something on that order".

Mr. Crosby: "This is much more than free speech to my client, Your Honor. This is his living, his profession".

The Court: "You see, you said it again, his living and profession. His profession, it is not going to help him in his profession because of this prior litigation. That is the point I keep trying to tell you but you don't want to listen to it. Let me say that anything I have said here, based on the admitted facts, stipulated facts, I have not said anything here at all today that is not factually based, that based on the facts I see them, I have made all my statements which are undisputed facts, prior litigation, and so on. So I don't know exactly how to address this other than how I have done it. But the biggest problem is how to prevent this Plaintiff from wasting the resources of this Court—".

Mr. Crosby: "There is about a million and a half dollars in damages at this point that my client wouldn't mind obtaining".

The Court: "There is no damage. You are just pipe dreaming about damages. On the admitted facts of this case, you have got a dollar of damages at most coming even assuming you win the case. You got a peppercorn, twelve and a half cents. That is all you are going to get out of this if you win it. You are going to spend all that time to get a peppercorn. It is possible that you can win it, but it is not possible on this admitted facts that you are ever going to get any damages because — let me tell you no you ought to write this down. Get a pencil".

Mr. Crosby: "I will get a copy of the transcript, Your Honor".

Not only had Simmons not read the case at that point, but we would hear him admit that he had still not read the pleading more than a year later.

Several months after that conference, the "Court" handed down an opinion that seemed to go part way toward dismissing our case. But no decision was made until a notice came for a renewed hearing - more than a year after the first.

On that occasion we were ushered into the Judge's chambers. He sat behind an elegant walnut desk and beside him the court reporter set up his equipment. Judd flanked the Judge in an upholstered chair to the right and the Hospital Assistant Lawyer, similarly, to the left. We were allowed to observe from a sofa behind an ornate coffee table.

His Honor seemed more subdued than he had been a year earlier. His intellectual capacity, however, showed no observable change; even though there were suggestions during the two hour conference that he was grasping portions of the antitrust law that was being argued.

The Hospital argued that the opinion the Court had filed several months earlier had gone half way toward dismissing the case and that the Judge should now address the second half and grant Summary Judgement (dismissal of the case). The Hospital argued that one of the lowest legal standards (substantial evidence) be used to judge whether the Kangaroo Court at Indiana Hospital had been fair. The Hospital was asking the Court to rule, that if some evidence was presented by the Hospital, that it be accepted regardless of its truthfulness and without question. This time the Judge wasn't registering any understanding of his own arguments. This time, apparently without a clear understanding of the issues, he wasn't sure what should be done. If he accepted the Hospital's argument, he would grant Summary Judgement and dismiss the entire case. It was difficult to believe that any test of fairness would lead to a conclusion that the Kangaroo Court held at Indiana Hospital was fair- yet this is what the hospital Lawyer argued the "substantial evidence test" would do. All through his argument, the Hospital Lawyer kept alluding to my "incompetence".

Judd's job it appeared, was to attempt to help the "Court" to gain some understanding of what had taken place at Indiana Hospital before and during the Kangaroo Court. Again, the Judge obviously had not read the voluminous mound of evidence that had been collected, and there didn't appear to be much indication that he wanted to.

Judd gingerly approached the contents of the opinion that the Court had submitted some months earlier. On the subject of unequal treatment at the Hospital he described the number of affidavits that had been submitted into the record by witnesses who would later testify at trial, knowing that the Judge had not seen any of them. As an example, he said, "The Court may recall, we have an affidavit in this case, that a nurse had been assigned to use very special procedures for Dr. Miller, to try to gather information of him in the Hospital, in the Emergency Room. Instead of going through the normal channels used for other doctors, she was instructed to use special channels that applied to Dr. Miller only".

Judd continued:

"The Court may recall, one Administrator at the Hospital was requested by the Defendant Administrator to befriend Dr. Miller, so that he could get reports from Dr. Miller on the expansion of his medical holdings and then report back to the Defendant". "There were many cases that we put on the record here who were guilty of heinous conduct. (There was) one doctor who had prescribed a fraudulent drug protocol for patients, and in that case, the Hospital, after they discovered all this, put him on probation as opposed to terminating him from the staff".

For the first time, it appeared the Court was hearing of the "defective procedures" at Indiana Hospital: "The entire bringing of charges and the whole hearing process had been predetermined years earlier".

Judd continued: "...if the result of the hearing was predetermined and, further, if the reason for that predetermination was the result of anti-competitive activities, and there is a great deal of evidence in the record —".

The Court: "What is this competition you are talking about? Are you speaking of anti-competitive motives? What are these anti-competitive motives you have referred to?"

Mr. Crosby: "There are numerous affidavits filed by Plaintiff in this case, Your Honor, that indicate that the Defendants, the Administrators at the Hospital, were very much concerned about the expansion of Dr. Miller's health related holdings. The Court may recall that Dr. Miller had set up a medical center and the intent was that this medical center would provide all sorts of ambulatory care services, x-ray services, laboratory services, that would be in direct competition with the Hospital.

There are, at least four or five affidavits that indicate that the Administrators at the Hospital were going to get rid of Dr. Miller because of the competitive threat to the Hospital itself. I would urge the Court to take the time to read those affidavits...which indicate this whole nature of the hearing was just something that was a way that the Defendants in this case decided to use to get rid of Dr. Miller".

The Court, which had gone to great lengths to tell of his vast experience with antitrust litigation, asked a decidedly unusual series of questions.

The Court: "(what) is the relevancy of it? How does this bear on his case here?"

Mr. Crosby: "That is what the antitrust laws are all about".

The Court: "That is what you say. Saying it does not make it true".

Mr. Crosby: "There are really two things going on. One is that there was envisioned by Dr. Miller, a family practice approach to Medicine. He built a Center. He put his own office there. Then he had other doctors coming into the Center even from here in Pittsburgh. He had hired two pediatricians and the idea was that a family would come to the center for all of its care. The Center would include diagnostic testing, laboratory services -very similar to what the Hospital was offering on an outpatient basis.

"...the defendants well knew that if they could cut off Dr. Miller's means to earn a living as a urologist, and surgeon, they knew there would be no way he could continue any kind of practice in Indiana County.

Therefore, everything that he had started, everything he had envisioned and made known in terms of his plan would have to be driven out of the county with him. That is the reason."

"There is plenty of evidence in this record to indicate that is the reason the Defendants in this case started their proceedings against Dr. Miller. There is affidavit after affidavit, and these people, if Dr. Miller gets his day in court, these people are going to come to court and say that in so many words. That they were even told that that was the reason Dr. Miller was going to have charges filed against him."

"The Hospital, these Defendants, were sitting and waiting for something to happen. Fortunately, for them, this incident with (his elderly patient) —".

The Court: "Them meaning who?"

Mr. Crosby: "For the Defendants. They had this incident where a very old gentleman under Dr. Miller's care died".

The Judge, never having read the record, was hearing for the first time of Dr. Vance Vader's treachery, by allowing my patient to die without help and of the Hospital Lawyer's divorce client testifying that the patient's care had been below standard.

Mr. Crosby: "The Hospital seized on that opportunity (the death) not because there was any real indication that anything had been done wrong. They didn't even find this expert that the Junior Lawyer refers to until a couple of weeks before he testified. That one expert was never even revealed to Dr. Miller and his attorney back at the hearings. The expert was somebody (Dr. Sladen) who the Hospital Attorney was representing in Family Court. All of a sudden he says, Hey, you might be the man I can use up at the Hospital". They never gave notice to Dr. Miller about this guy who was going to be testifying. Not until the moment he came in there and the Hospital Attorney offered him as a witness."

Mr. Crosby: "...they had this one person to be able to say that what Dr. Miller did was not good practice. This is the only indication in this physician's entire life that he had ever been accused of anything wrong or incompetent. That is the only incident in nineteen years of practice at Indiana Hospital. What the Hospital was trying to do, on the basis of this one fellow's testimony, compared to the testimony of seven outstanding physicians who testified that what Dr. Miller did was proper, they are trying to say Dr. Miller is incompetent."

Judd had laid bare the Understudy Lawyer's accusation of incompetency. I looked at the Lawyer and he gave no indication that he was bothered by the revelation of his deception. There was also no indication that the Judge understood - or wanted to.

Judd continued:

"We submit, Your Honor, if a close scrutiny is made of this record, and it is looked at closely, regarding the incompetency question, if you can appreciate that this Dr. Sladen was someone who happened to be in an attorney's office on his divorce proceeding when they started to talk and said that maybe he can testify. He is the only guy who ever said Dr. Miller has ever done anything wrong."

"If you balance that against the evidence in this record from many, many witnesses who indicate that this hearing was a pretext, a subterfuge, to accomplish the goal of eliminating Dr. Miller as a competitor. I submit that if you look at that in those terms, Your Honor, the way they really exist on the record, you would have to let the case go to the jury."

"...and we have put many indications in this record of other physicians at Indiana Hospital who were accused of incompetency...and where they brought the Hospital in".

Hopefully, the Judge would know that Judd was referring to the malpractice suits filed against the Hospital and some of its physicians; never involving Dr. Miller.

Judd moved on to have the Court understand the nature of the Hospital Hearing Committee headed by my antagonist Claude Clippins..

Mr. Crosby: "You will recall Dr. Clippins. He was the physician who was named as the chairman of the Hearing Committee that sat in review of Dr. Miller ... before the hearings actually got started, Dr. Miller, through his counsel, objected to Dr. Clippins sitting on the Hearing Committee because Dr. Miller had filed certain charges concerning Dr. Clippins with the State Licensure Board...in addition, Dr. Clippins had made certain statements about Dr. Miller and had written hateful letters to him".

The Judge, for the first time, began to show some interest in Clippins and his letters.

The Court: "Did anyone except to this fellow Clippins sitting as the chairman?"

Judd replied: "Yes", and then told of a fellow named Vernozzi sitting on the panel who had been sued for malpractice by Dr. Miller's lawyer.

The Judge wondered where the record was including one of Claude Clippin's letters.

The Court: "Was this submitted upstairs to the clerk?"

The Hospital: "It has been delivered".

The Court: "The record upstairs for some reason is impounded. Which Judge impounded this?"

Mr. Crosby: "I do not know".

The Court: "I do not know where they are".

The Court: "Judge Ziegler had this case years ago. Why did he impound this? Are all the matters that were filed in clerk's office, were they impounded?"

Mr. Crosby: "The Defendants sought that, Your Honor. I am not sure why either".

The Hospital: "Because everything seemed to wind up in the newspapers, Your Honor, at Dr. Miller's behest and we were having all sorts of problems".

The Court: "I am wondering where all these papers are. Are you sure they weren't taken upstairs and impounded?"

Mr. Crosby: "I have no knowledge".

The Court: "I do not know where they are. Let me see if I can find them while they are here".

The Judge then asked about the Dr. Vernozzi that had sat on the Hearing Panel.

Mr. Crosby: "The attorney that was representing Dr. Miller at the Hearing...that attorney pointed out to the hospital that he had sued Dr. Vernozzi or his father who is also a physician up in Indiana. He stated he did not think Dr. Vernozzi should be sitting on the Hearing Committee".

The Court: "Because he would be prejudiced against Dr. Miller, you mean?"

Mr. Crosby: "Correct".

A middle-aged, plump, lady came into chambers carrying a moderate sized pasteboard box. She sat the box on an empty chair and someone blew dust from the top. As the box was opened, Judd reached into the box and produced one of Clippin's vitriolic letters.

Mr. Crosby: "This is the letter—".

The Court: "Speak to the reporter. He had to get this".

Mr. Crosby: "What I am referring to here, Your Honor, is items of this transcript, it is called Respondent's Exhibits and within the first five pages of this thick booklet is the letter I have read from that was authored by Claude Clippins, Chairman of the Hearing Committee that heard the charges against Dr. Miller".

The Judge then responded to the revelation:

The Court: "Let me see that".

Claude's two page letter to me was read into the record. Its multiple paragraphs attempting to indict anyone critical of his "preceptorship" plan or assessments reached the peak of its crecendo in one of the final paragraphs.

It read:

"...I consider your constant complaining, lack of cooperation, indifference to progressive programs, and destructive criticism as conduct unbecoming a person of your professional status. It is my considerate opinion that if any prizes are ever awarded to the one who has done the most to create an unpleasant hospital atmosphere you would have no problem becoming a winner." And the letter continued:

"You would do well to gather proper information and weigh it carefully before embarking upon any further such malevolent pursuits."

(It appeared, on first glance, that someone had helped Claude author his vehement letter. There were too many adjectives and unusual nouns for his vocabulary.)

Also in the packets of letters that Judd was presenting to the Judge was the letter from the counsel for the Pennsylvania Medical Society. In reference to Clippins, it said:

"Dear Doctor Miller:

I reviewed your letter to the State Board of Medical Education and Licensure. I think the letter is fine, although, if it has not yet been sent, I would suggest the addition of a paragraph which says that you believe that Dr. Clippins's actions are in violation of the Medical Practice Act and request that the Board undertake an investigation.

Sincerely,
Fred Speaker"

In describing Clippin's letter, Judd continued:

Mr. Crosby: "Now, the man who said that, Your Honor, you have to understand that, this is the man who sat as the Chairman of the Hearing Committee passing judgement on Dr. Miller."

"Now, I do not claim to be an expert in terms of what is fundamentally fair, Your Honor, but I know if my own professional credentials were being reviewed...I would not want the person who had already passed judgement on me and committed it to writing...to have been the person that was appointed Chairman of the Hearing Committee."

The Court: "Let me see that."

Mr. Crosby: "Again, it is our position that this does not sit right in terms of what is fundamentally fair. The other point I was going to make, Your Honor, was off the original thing in terms of substantially defective procedures."

The Court: "Read back what he just said." (whereupon, the last statement of Mr. Crosby was read)

The Court: "What is the other thing? I do not understand that English".

Judd explained that in current antitrust law there had been two criteria necessary. The first, he explained, was a substantial defective procedure (the Hospital hearing) and the finding as to whether the findings of the Hospital hearings were supported by substantial evidence. He continued to outline the antitrust principles and the case law that determined that there was sufficient doubt and issues created in the court records that our case should go the jury.

He continued:

Mr. Crosby: "I think it would be possible for a jury to find that when the Hospital gave all that weight to the one doctor (Sladen), who lied to the Hospital, and when we hear other people saying it was a sham hearing, we would find, in fact, that the Hospital violated the antitrust laws. That is a genuine issue of fact that a jury would have to decide".

It was doubtful that the Judge was following when he replied:

The Court: "I do not think that is true. Do not get into that now". Then:

The Court: "We have heard enough from you. What about you?"

The Hospital: "I will be real brief. We have heard a lot about how unfair the procedures were and how this guy was biased and that guy was biased — ".

The Court: "He had one good argument here. He argues all around one good argument, but it is a good argument. It is the fact that this fellow, who is presiding was openly antagonistic and hostile".

The Hospital: "I was about to respond to that specific argument".

It appeared that The Court was beginning to understand a small and simple portion of the entire equation. The Court: "You ought to. That is his basic argument. All this other stuff is chaff. That is a substantial argument. You have got a guy running a hearing who has condemned this man in advance". Also:

The Court: "But the problem is though, that you keep overlooking, we are also according to Judge Cohill, we are to check into the bonafides of the procedures involved".

The Assistant Hospital Lawyer made a final effort to have the Court simply expand upon its previous opinion and grant summary judgement to throw out the case without deciding on the fairness of the hearings held at the Hospital. But the Court, after seeing Clippin's vitriolic letter, continued:

The Court: "When I see letters like this, maybe I can rethink my position", and: "If I decide to reopen these other issues, I certainly can do it and will do it.

I have to look into all of this. As I say, <u>I did not even know this stuff was here until a few minutes ago.</u>"

He then, amazingly, after several years and not even knowing he had the record, gave great insight into the Federal Court System:

The Court: "Evidently it is a hot potato because I am the third judge that has it. It must have not been an easy thing or else it would have been disposed of a long time before I got it. I got it last year, about four or five years after we started, so a whole lot of other people fumbled over this case before I got it. I will have to look into it. Maybe I will have to re-examine these things in light of this record. I am not promising one way or the other. I do not know how this Court will hold, but we will look into it and see what we have to do. I can see why this case is where it is, in light of all this. We have to address these matters and it will take a long time to do it. That is the problem".

So — years after Judge Simmons was assigned our case, he was going to look into the record. That was our last head-to-head encounter with the Judge, but it was clear - he had little of any concept of antitrust law. But, he was now, apparently, aware of the likes of Claude Clippins sitting in judgement. He had to be aware of the Hospital's illegal ex parte communication to the Pennsylvania Department of Health and the Hospital Lawyer's divorce client's perjury during the hospital hearings.

No one doubted that the Hospital gang would have no hesitation to influence the Court - one way or another. We hadn't forgotten Indiana's Judge Earley's revelation of Dr. Goldfarb's blatant attempts to advise the Court on how to rule.

One comment Simmons made during the first hearing continued to echo and re-echo.

He had said, "If his objective is, which I believe it is, to practice Medicine according to the letters (Dr. Miller) wrote, and I read, then there is no way in the world that he is ever going to gain his objective".

What letters? Who gave the Judge letters when he hadn't even seen the record? Who was working behind the scenes this time?

About a year later, Judge Simmons handed down an opinion which granted the hospital's motion for summary judgement, thereby dismissing our case after about five years of litigation.

We immediately filed an appeal to the U.S. Court of Appeals for the Third Circuit. The Court sits in Philadelphia, and after several more months, the Court announced the date for verbal arguments on our appeal.

Philadelphia's Federal Building is not much different from the federal edifice in Pittsburgh. The train system to downtown Philadelphia from the airport is a fast thirty minute ride. We enjoyed the four or five block walk to the Federal Building among the early morning crowds rushing to work as we entered the building's large, marble-walled interior. A large directory to the right of the entrance listed the Court's judges in order of seniority. The Chief Judge, Delores Sloviter, was sitting on the three judge panel hearing our arguments.

The courtroom itself, on an upper floor, is more of an auditorium. Its modernistic design with mahogany paneled walls and its long, paneled bench, is indeed, impressive. Somewhat more impressive was the professionalism of the judges. As a contrast to the obtuse bullying we had seen with our encounters in Pittsburgh's Federal District Court and Judge Hoffman in the state's Superior Court, the judges were professional and courteous. At one point, Chief Judge Sloviter eluded to the lot in life of an appellate judge. She said that they were required to read, and read, and then read some more. It was good to hear a judge who felt some responsibility to her profession.

After the two cases before ours were argued, Judge Becker, another member of the panel, arose and did a few spinal flexions; explaining that his bad back was acting up again. His informality in that grandiose setting, was a refreshing relief.

The Hospital Counsel argued his opposition to our appeal in the ten minutes allotted and Judd followed. The Hospital's argument, of course, supported Judge Simmons' reasoning, which was to say the least, judicially bizarre. After Judd's argument, the opposing lawyer rose with a short rebuttal. Judge Sloviter invited Judd to respond. He rose, and quite appropriately, said, "There is no need for rebuttal, Your Honor, this is an antitrust case."

The flight back to Pittsburgh was uneventful. We just wondered how many more months it would take to hear from the Third Circuit.

Months later, Judd called. The Third Circuit panel had reversed Judge Simmons and had returned our case to Pittsburgh for "further proceedings".

Judd and I felt encouraged by the Third Circuit's action but didn't look forward to more litigation under the auspices of Simmons.

Simmons continued to get in hot water with the Third Circuit. The Post Gazette reported: "U.S. District Judge Paul A. Simmons, was ordered by the U.S. Third Circuit Court of Appeals to vacate (cancel) a series of his own orders." He had again insulted two lawyers and had dismissed them from a major case, "questioning their integrity."

The same Judge Becker who helped overrule Simmons' dismissal of our case, wrote that, "The appeals panel could find no justification for Simmons's disparaging remarks about the lawyers", and that he had exceeded his authority.

Simmons appealed to the U.S. Supreme Court and his appeal was rejected.

The Appeals Court also urged Simmons, according to the Post Gazette, "in light of the animosity that appears to have risen between himself and the two lawyers, to consider never again presiding over any matters involving their firms."

Out of the blue, as I opened the day's mail, there was an envelope from Judd. The single page inside was a court order with the full heading: U. S. District Court for the Western District of Pennsylvania. The order was signed by Simmons. I had to read the single sentence twice before I could believe it.

Simmons very simply announced that he was recusing himself from Miller v. Indiana Hospital, et al.

I thought I was prepared for most anything that this man would do or say, but this was truly phenomenal.

At the bottom of the order Judd had penned: "All good things come to him who waits". For awhile I forgot the years spent in waiting and began to think of going to trial under a competent, fair-minded judge. Little did we know we were going from the skillet into the fire.

Simmons' recusal, it turned out, was apparently based on a potential conflict of interest. He had taken a spill outside a downtown Pittsburgh tavern and had entered a law suit against the building's owners and several construction firms, claiming they had constructed a hazardous sidewalk. The suit apparently was causing the conflict.

With Simmons' previous sermons well in mind, the complaint he filed in the Court of Common Pleas, beginning his law suit, was quite a contrast.

It is well known that physicians become somewhat more sympathetic and understanding of their patients after they have had a personal hospital admission. Did something similar happen with Simmons?

Simmons' complaint was indeed interesting reading. It seemed implausible that the man who had threatened my lawyer and other lawyers with accusations of greed and unethical motives, would submit such a document into the public record.

The complaint averred that Paul A. Simmons, after leaving a downtown tavern, was "carefully and lawfully walking" from the building's exit and slipped on the wet surface of the sidewalk as his overshoe struck on the sidewalk causing him to fall. His complaint continued that, "by reasons of negligent acts and omissions, of the defendants, Simmons sustained the following injuries - all or some of which may be permanent in nature."

A. Internal injuries;
B. Contusions, abrasions, and lacerations to many parts of the body;
C. Severe shock to the nervous system resulting in digestive disturbances, insomnia, irritability, headaches and a complete change in personality;
D. Damage to the left leg;
E. Damage to the left hip;
F. Damage to the tendons of the left leg and hip;
G. Damage to the quadriceps tendons of the left knee;
H. Other injuries to be diagnosed."

When one reads the list, one wonders if this is the same person who, on the record, accused Pittsburgh lawyers of greed and lack of ethics. Was there indeed, "a complete change in personality"?

The judge who advised that we would likely win the antitrust case against Indiana Hospital, but would get "one dollar" or a "peppercorn" in damages, listed the following damages.

"A. The expending of large sums for medicine and medical attention (etc.);
B. Serious and permanent and great physical and mental pain and suffering;

C. Inability to perform normal and customary duties and activities;

D. Inability to perform normal and customary occupations with sustained loss of earnings and earning capacity;

E. Deprivation of the ordinary pleasures of life;

F. Embarrassment;

G. Loss of dignity;

H. Severe, great and permanent inconvenience;

I. Loss of general good health, strength and vitality;

J. Dependence upon others;

K. Other damages that may develop."

There was a similar list of damages for Mrs. Simmons (Gwendolyn).

The Pittsburgh newspapers continued to pick up on Judge Simmons' continuing escapades:

One headline read, "Judge Calls Lawyers Greedy". The two lawyers involved were quoted as saying, "The Judge has failed to focus on ... nine related cases for five years".

Another headline read: "Judge leaves...case, assails two attorneys."

It appeared, that after five years Simmons had discovered a conflict in that same case - his daughter worked for a bank which was a party in that case..

Despite his announced departure from the case, he continued to issue orders. The lawyers appealed the orders and the Third Circuit Court of Appeals reversed Simmons and dropped all of his improper orders.

Not limiting his evaluation of lawyers motives, Simmons, during a child custody conference, told the litigant that she was "greedy and vengeful" for filing the civil suit against her former spouse. As a result, the Pittsburgh Press reported that the "remarks to a woman in a civil case prompted the Allegheny Bar Association to file a complaint of misconduct and sexual bias, against him, with the Judicial Conference of the Third U. S. Circuit Court of Appeals".

Before long, the Pittsburgh Press headline announced: "Paul Simmons, First Black Federal Judge Here, To Retire."

There was no satisfaction in reading that announcement. The damage had been done. I was only one of those whose hope for a little legal justice had become sidetracked by this political appointee for a long, long five years.

The next headline was: "Judge Says the Pittsburgh Press treats Him Unfairly Because of His Race." The story read: "Senior U. S. District Judge

Paul Simmons accused the Pittsburgh Press of being racist by misusing its power to unfairly attack him and trying to force him from the Federal Bench".

The final word may have been the printing of a "Letter to the Editor" headed by "Biased Judges". It read: "With the announced retirement last week of U. S. District Judge Paul A. Simmons...citizens who believe in true justice may breathe a sigh of relief and hope that an era unprecedented for its judicial arrogance and persecution has finally ended".

In its investigative series, looking into the workings of Western Pennsylvania's District Court system, "Lords of the Court" was published by the Pittsburgh Post Gazette.

In its investigation, through interviews with lawyers, " time and again the names of three district judges surfaced." One of them was Simmons, of course.

But now, we learned that our case was transferred to the second member of that questionable triad, Judge Allan Bloch. The Post Gazette had published a long description of Bloch. According to the lawyers interviewed he was labeled "intemperate".

The Post Gazette repeated one description that Bloch was "in court a picture of propriety-calm, patient and polite. Many agree that he runs dignified and impartial proceedings". As one of his critics put it, "He's not a screamer, he's not a name-caller and he doesn't personalize things. The problem is what happens before trial. Judge Bloch thinks the case he has with you is the only case you have and everything else is expendable", a trial lawyer said. "I consider that arrogant", he concluded.

When I read that and the remainder of the story, I felt that we may very well have been assigned to a firm, fair jurist which should help us prevail. Once again, I would be found to be pitifully naive.

While the months and years were passing and while we waited for Judge Bloch to do something, more and more details about the Hospital crowd were surfacing.

Remembering the fateful day of February 12, some years earlier, it had been Dr. Lee Daugherty, our first Emergency Room physician, who had called for help with the eighty-one year old patient. The patient, three days later, had suddenly experienced a cardiac arrest and had died.

It had been Dr. Vader and supervising nurse Marshall who had gotten together after the death and who had fabricated the charges that led to the Hospital hearings.

Dr. Daugherty had resigned from the Hospital and had opened a family medicine practice in the little town of Tyrone. Before he left town we had asked him to testify at the hearings, but he declined, understandably not wanting to be involved.

I hadn't heard from Lee in the months after he had left for Tyrone. The hearings and the appeal to the Hospital Board were over and the Hospital was leaking to the media the news that I had been suspended from the Hospital.

At that time, we had just finished a quiet evening supper when the phone rang. It was Lee and he had been watching television and had heard the announcement of my dismissal. He was both angry and upset. Surprisingly, he was sorry he hadn't spoken up sooner and was now hoping in some way to help. He invited me to visit him and his wife, and within the week, I drove to Tyrone.

After the children went to bed, the Daughertys and I had a long conversation and I was beginning to learn how long the Hospital gang had been planning. Some of the revelations were frightening. Lee had rented a house in town from Dr. Hoffman, one of the Hospital Executive Committee members.. He was afraid of physical encounters with Hoffmann, and he described Hoffman as threatening. Both of the Daughertys had heard Hoffman describe Dr. Miller's Christmas Open House as an excursion into debauchery. Our Open House at the office had always been well-attended by business friends from town and Pittsburgh. We all had to smile as the Dipperys described Hoffman's tale of "naked women" running through the crowd of men.

It became apparent that Dr. Dippery's testimony would be valuable if and when we would take the small Hospital group to trial. I convinced the lawyers to take Lee's deposition and we planned a trip to Tyrone.

Lee's office was in a modest, converted house facing Tyrone's Main Street. The reception area was in the former living room and Lee greeted us in shirt sleeves. Young Ralph Smith was along and would conduct the questioning. After brief introductions, the young lady Court Reporter set up her equipment and the Junior Hospital Lawyer arrived and introduced himself around.

Ralph conducted the routine questioning quickly and promptly got into the meat of Lee's testimony. The questions and answers were as follows:

Q - "O.K. Doctor, we're here today concerning matters relating to Doctor Ralph Miller and Indiana Hospital. After you left Indiana Hospital did you have reason to contact Doctor Ralph Miller?"

A - "Yes, I did."

Q - "Could you tell me why you did that?"

A - "...It was approximately three months after I moved here. I was watching the evening news on our local Channel Ten television station here. And they, as a news item, they stated that Doctor Miller had been removed from the Staff of Indiana Hospital. And there was more to it than that, but that was the general substance of the announcement. And whenever I heard this - I had prior knowledge of the situation at Indiana Hospital. I was shocked at this. I was outraged when I heard this."

Q - "Could you tell me why you were outraged?"

A - "I felt that if Doctor Miller could be removed from the Staff at Indiana Hospital for reasons of which I was familiar with, that it could happen to anybody - to me or anyone else in the Medical Profession."

Q - "Doctor Daugherty, could you tell us the reasons behind your outrage?"

A - "There was an effort or movement by some of the physicians as a group at I.H. to try to limit Doctor Miller's privileges or - I will be frank about it, to ruin him".

The Hospital Lawyer: "I would object, unless the physicians are named".

Q - "Could you give us the names of the physicians whom you believe participated in this matter?"

A - "Doctor Abdul Hankey was one. Doctor Ewalt was one. Doctor Post, Doctor Goldfarb, Doctor Vance Vader, Doctor Hoffman, Doctor Hamilton Burger. I'm stating physicians who I believe were at a meeting concerning taking action against Doctor Miller."

Q - "Doctor Daugherty, you are currently referring to what were identified as Doctor Daugherty Deposition Exhibits, letters from you to Doctor Miller. Could you explain to us what these documents are you are looking at?"

A - "All right. Whenever I had heard the news item on T.V., I had called Doctor Miller - about two hours later. I had turned this thing over in my mind. And I was trying to decide whether I wanted to get involved in this matter at Indiana Hospital. I felt that - finally, you know about nine o'clock, I believe it was - the news was over about seven. I called Doctor Miller and discussed what I had heard on T. V. I felt it was a matter of conscience. And there had been no contact or anything between Doctor Miller and myself regarding this matter. And I was very reluctant to involve myself in any matters at Indiana Hospital. I would have liked Indiana to have become past history. But I did call him and talk to him about the news item on T. V. and how I felt about it. Doctor Miller asked me if I would put it in writing.

I procrastinated as I stated in my letter, but between January and March of the next year, I wrote those letters to Doctor Miller. I wrote it down so I could remember and not make any errors while it was still fresh in my mind."

The Medical Staff president, (Fazio), had testified at the Kangaroo Court that, at evening meetings, the Executive Committee, had "sat around and somebody would say, "remember the time he did this and then someone else would say, remember the time he did that". That was the way "The Boys" formulated their list of charges - none of which were investigated for truthfulness or accuracy.

As Dr. Dippery referred to his notes, he was detailing the evening meetings "The Boys" were holding where no records were kept. The deposition continued:

A - "O.K. According to my notes here, I made these statements: These morning staff room and hallway discussions ceased after about two weeks, but the discussions concerning Dr. Miller continued during or after evening meetings shortly thereafter. In the three to six months prior to the Miller-McGee case, I was present in the Staff Room when at least six meetings left out. As the meetings dismissed, at least some of the physicians attending the meetings came back up to the Staff Room to get their coats or other personal items. As the physicians came to the Staff Room to retrieve their coats or personal items, some of the physicians left immediately. But, other physicians were making remarks about Dr. Miller - apparently repeating remarks made during the discussions which had taken place at the meetings".

Q - "Would you say that your relationship was a personal relationship which stayed within the Hospital?"

A - "Strictly professional relationship. Dr. Miller also treated me as a patient for a urological problem also. So then that was a doctor-patient relationship".

Q - "Now, Doctor, in your letters you refer to a meeting with (the Hospital Administrator) when you first became employed at Indiana Hospital. Could you tell us a little bit about that?"

A - "May I read from my notes?"

Q - "If you prefer it that way".

A - "Well, on the first day that I came to work at Indiana Hospital in the Emergency Room - I couldn't have a meeting with the Administrator because I was called into the Emergency Room for a cardiac arrest case. So, on the second day that I was working in the E.R., employed by the Hospital, The Administrator called me back to his office and in - with the idea, as far as I understood, of having a general discussion about duties and, and so forth in the E.R. At that time, he seemed to be quite agitated and angry and launched into a discussion of Dr. Miller and another physician. And it - basically he described him as a trouble maker and somebody I should watch out for. The discussion, as a matter of fact was mostly - I mean the matter of which the Administrator talked to me about was mostly a discussion of Dr. Miller and another physician who he called paranoid".

A - "I basically understood that he felt that Dr. Miller would cause trouble basically somewhere in the near future for me - or somewhere down the line".

Q - "Did Dr. Miller ever cause you trouble while you were at Indiana Hospital?"

A - "No, we never had any trouble. In retrospect looking back that he was making an attempt to shape my opinion of Dr. Miller ahead of time".

Ralph Smith then questioned into matters that reflected on the Administrator's preparation for the Kangaroo Court.

Q - "Did you again have a meeting with the Administrator at any time while you were at Indiana Hospital?"

A - "Yes, shortly before I left".

Q - "Doctor, could you tell us what the meeting entailed?"

A - "I was called into the Administrator's office. The Administrator was present and two Hospital Attorneys. There was a woman attorney. And a male attorney (the subsequent Prosecutor and the Judge at the Kangaroo Court)".

A - "They got right to the point in this meeting. The Administrator asked me if I knew anything about the (elderly patient) case. And I stated that I knew about the case in that I had referred this patient to Doctor Miller as an Emergency Room physician when the patient came in with hematuria (urinary blood). And I was then asked by the Administrator if I had ever seen the Hospital chart. And I said, "No". And he asked me if I would take a look at the chart and handed the chart to me and then asked me what I thought about the management of the case, which I did - honestly did not feel that there was any problem in the management. I was asked specifically about sputum cultures and so forth - whether I would have gotten them and so forth. Most of the questioning seemed to revolve around sputum cultures. And stated that I would have gotten them for academic purposes, but that I would have gone ahead and treated before the results of the cultures were known".

Q - "Did you - ?"

A - This was the essential gist of the conversation".

Q - "Did you feel at that time that Dr. Miller had mismanaged the case?"

A - "No. I did not feel that he had mismanaged the case".

Then:

The Hospital Counsel put an objection in the record, based on his distortion of the rulings of the Pennsylvania Courts. He said: "It's clear from these depositions, if there was any doubt prior to these depositions, that we are retrying Dr. Miller's revocation".

Ralph Smith responded:

"Just let the record show that we are not here to retry the revocation proceedings. We are merely here to try and establish that a conspiracy existed, for some period of time, culminating in Dr. Miller's revocation, and further a refusal to deal with him thereafter". Then the questions to the witness continued:

Q -"Is there anything that struck you funny with that meeting in discussions with The Administrator and those two Hospital Attorneys?"

A - "The questions and the review of the chart and so forth - asking me to review it and so forth did not seem to be a logical thing to do. I felt that there was a definite attempt to lead me to a conclusion at that meeting that there was mismanagement. "

Q - "In your letter, Doctor, you made the following statement. "I felt when I left Mr. Smith's office that Dr. Miller had been judged by the Administrator and certain staff members before I was asked to be involved in The Administrator's office". Is that how you recall that today?"

A - "Yes".

As I listened to Lee's testimony, I couldn't help thinking about all the Administrator's actions while he was a patient of mine - such treachery, such deceit.

On questioning from the Hospital Attorney, the matter of the Directress of Nursing keeping files on certain physicians came up.

A - "I was asked if there could have been files on other physicians or whether I had reason to believe that there may have been and I answered, "Yes"."

A - "In this Emergency Room, O.K. the nurses reported to the Directress of Nursing anything of interest that happened during the day. Let's be frank, - particularly any dirt on any doctors."

Lee's evening telephone call was to be one of many that came after the news of my dismissal hit the television screens and the Pennsylvania newspapers. I had seriously underestimated the number of good friends I had in the Hospital and the Community.

As Dr. Berberian had said, "The toughest job ahead is for you to maintain your self esteem."

That was probably very right and my friends, in no small measure, helped in that regard. Let there be no doubt, the constant bombardment by the likes of "Abdul" and "Claude" over the years, could be easily deflected. But, now to hear the description of the deceitful two-faced Administrator entering into the chorus of fabricated lies, was annoying. The Hospital Lawyers, with the meter running, were obviously content to help spread the venom.

Some of the friends who had heard the Hospital Lawyer, in open court, describe nurses coming to him in tears, were more than a little annoyed with his carelessness with the truth. The Apprentice Hospital Lawyer's suggestion that the entire Medical Staff would resign if I returned was handled best by Judge Mansman's remark, "That's absurd".

Almost daily I would read Kipling's advice:

"If you can wait and not be tired by waiting, or being lied about, don't deal in lies, or being hated, and don't give way to hating, and yet don't look too good or talk too wise."

During this period of time, "The Boys", as well as the Administration, began to become uneasy with the revelation of detailed inside information that we had been collecting. The Administrator's electronic devices and his infrared scope on the roof never caught anyone and the flow of information never stopped. Watergate had its "Deep Throat" as did Indiana Hospital. No one ever learned who Indiana's "Deep Throat" was or were, and never will. But, much of the information coming to us was recorded in affidavits and would be backed by testimony at trial.

Some of the intemperate conversations of "The Boys" were relayed. One of The Boys, Ham Burger, told a confidant that he "was on a committee to get Dr. Miller out of town." All this was beginning to fall into a complete description of the conspiracy.

Another of the more surprising revelations came with an anonymous phone call during a late evening. The voice was obviously a young man who was also obviously very hesitant and nervous. The voice said that he had a great deal of information that would help with our case in Federal Court. He wanted assurances that his information be kept confidential. He volunteered that his local lawyer had advised the call. I couldn't do more than advise him to think it over and to talk with his trusted friends to decide if he could trust me.

A week or more later a call came to the office from a man who wouldn't give his name. I wasn't surprised, and when I took the call, the voice very quietly said, "You know who I am, don't you?" I told him I did, but his identity was safe. That call led to several meetings and the preparation of documents, which at trial, would show some unusual transactions of the Hospital Management and Board. His name has never surfaced but we agreed that he would be a witness at trial. His testimony would incriminate the Hospital's Board and some of the Medical Staff.

Another late evening call was even more surprising. It was a hospital Board member who had openly challenged The Board Chairman on more than one occasion. He had opposed some of the activities that most of the Hospital's rubber stamp Board had endorsed. He came to the office several times. We negotiated a settlement and he was dropped as a defendant in the antitrust suit. He added to the bulk of information we would use at trial.

It was certainly becoming evident to the Conspirators and their Lawyers what they would face at trial. How would they react?

Our adventure with Judge Bloch began with a status conference in the Judge's conference room. Each time we passed that long row of photos of Judges on the walls of that long corridor leading to the courtroom, I wondered how honest, how impartial and how learned each one was. On this trip I was more interested in what sort of man we were now facing. Bloch was another Carter appointee and he was said to have been a Committee Chairman for the political campaign of one of Pittsburgh's mayors.

I was hoping against hope that this man was not another in the parade of political hacks. I was just beginning to learn of the selection process for these judicial prima donnas and what I was learning was not reassuring. Appointment to the federal bench was predominately political with involvement of the American Bar Association which, in itself, was probably just as political. I wondered if the Founding Fathers had truly planned our Federal Court System as we were seeing it. They probably honestly believed that lifetime tenure for these people would free them from politics.

We waited for Bloch in the conference room across from his chambers. The standard large conference table dominated the room and several straight backed chairs surrounded it. I kept out of the way and settled into an upholstered chair. The Junior Hospital Lawyer and Judd, my lawyer, settled across from each other, leaving the head of the table for His Honor.

Surprisingly, the door opened and there was the Senior Hospital Counsel - my prosecutor. As always, he attempted a grand entrance. His first stop was me. With great enthusiasm he extended his hand for a friendly hand shake. By that time, I had seen just enough duplicity and deceit; it didn't make sense to be friendly. I, therefore, just looked at him. There was no handshake.

His Honor entered, took his spot at the end of the table and got right to business. I stood up respectfully as he passed between me and the conference table. I have since regretted that.

He began: "This is the date and time set for a status conference in the matter of Miller versus Indiana Hospital...which began a little bit before I was born."

While the Judge was obviously aware of the age of the case, the following exchange between him and my lawyer friend Judd gives a little insight into whether he was going to let our case go to trial.

The Court: "Defense Counsel raises an issue that was raised in a previous summary judgement and was not decided."

We didn't know how that issue had been raised. "Behind the scenes?"

The Judge was referring to an immunity issue that the Hospital Lawyers were using to try to immunize the Hospital Defendants. It was called the State Action Doctrine which granted immunity from damages for public officials and for certain activities that were performed "under color of law".

It was a bit of a stretch for hospitals to claim that they were operating as a governmental agency, but they had been getting away with claiming that immunity. That is - until the landmark case of Patrick v. Burget et al.

Tim Patrick was a successful general surgeon who had been a member of a group practice in Astoria, Oregon. Tim had left the group and had set up practice nearby. The remaining members of the group joined in attempting to have him dismissed by the local Hospital. They began to conduct a sham hearing to review some of his cases, in order to find him unqualified and to use that as a basis for dismissal. Tim walked out of their "Kangaroo Court" and resigned from the Hospital so that a "dismissal" would not appear on his record. It was reported that one of the clinic members served on the Oregon Board of Licensure and attempted to revoke Tim's medical license as retaliation.

Tim had then filed an antitrust suit in the local Court, and at trial the jury awarded him 2.2 million dollars in damages from the doctor-defendants who were found guilty of violations of the Antitrust Laws.

On appeal, the Ninth Circuit Court of Appeals reversed the decision and remanded the case back to the District Court for a new trial. Before that occurred, Tim and his lawyers appealed the Ninth Circuit decision to the United States Supreme Court.

The visit to the Supreme Court was indeed impressive. I decided to hear the arguments before that Court. My friend, Bill London, agreed to go along. The majesty of the building itself, atop that long flight of granite steps, inspires a sense of awe. The double line of visitors was forming from the metal detectors across the great marble lobby. The conversations were muted - it seemed that the place required a degree of reverence. One of the Justices walked by and gave a friendly "hello".

Before long, a few well-dressed men opened the large doors into the massive courtroom. Our trip through the metal detectors was not one which would be considered smooth. I emptied my pockets as required and moved through without much of a pause, but my friend Bill kept setting off the alarm. The line of people waiting were becoming a little restless - they probably wondered what type of cannon Bill was hiding. After an eternity, the foil on a stick of gum was found to be the culprit.

We were seated by ushers and took in the magnificence of the place. The elevated bench was backed by huge, hanging velvet curtains. The curtains finally parted and the justices entered and took their places on high-backed chairs. We heard two or three arguments before Tim's case. The lawyers were exceptionally skilled at argument. They had to be. The justices asked very pointed questions and presented a number of hypothetical scenarios based on the Law.

Tim's lawyer was friendly, as we chatted after the arguments, and he was interested in the progress of Miller versus Indiana Hospital. That was the beginning of a friendship with Tim who, by coincidence, moved to a small town not more than thirty miles from Indiana.

The Supreme Court ruled in favor of Tim. It was a landmark decision - ruling, in effect, that hospitals and their medical staffs are not immune from the Antitrust Laws and are, therefore, subject to triple damages for participating in "bad faith peer review".

This was the very issue Judge Bloch was talking about during that first conference before him. By then, the furor over the Supreme Court decision had reached most corners of the health industry. The ruling settled firmly the State Action issue and if Judge Bloch had known this, he ignored it.

He said: "Defense Counsel raises an issue that was raised in a previous summary judgement and was not decided by the District Court...and asks that we allow them to file a new motion concerning the issue. I think we will do that. Is there any objection or opposition to that?"

Mr. Crosby: "Yes, Your Honor".

The Court: "What is it?"

Mr. Crosby: "The problem is, we are going to end up back in the Circuit Court and back in the Supreme Court again. It will be another two to three years".

The Court: "If I decide the legal issues in their favor, it is a trial we may not have to go through. We can't concede we are going to make an error".

The Hospital: "If there is an immunity from suit, we shouldn't have to sit through a two or three week trial. That's very important from the doctor's and the hospital's viewpoint. That's why we believe it is the fairest way".

The Court: "I'm not worried about how fast you can brief it. We have 120 motions on our motions list and it's going to be a long time till we get to this motion - maybe a year".

Mr. Crosby: "That's very disconcerting, Your Honor".

The Court: "I might as well tell you, there is no reason why we would give you priority over other motions...although no case is as old as this case".

The Hospital Junior Lawyer then made a pitch to have the case handed down to a magistrate of the Court.

The Court then replied:

The Court: "That would, no doubt, hurry the processes".

The Court: "Okay. If you would agree to a trial before a magistrate, it would be sent to a magistrate immediately".

The Hospital: "I think we are prepared to agree to that".

Mr. Crosby: "I would prefer to wait until I could consult with my client".

Without looking my way, the Judge said: "Is this your client?", much as one would say "Is that a grasshopper on your shoulder?"

Judd answered: "Yes, this is Doctor Miller".

The Court: "Would you want to confer with him now?"

Mr. Crosby: "I would rather wait and inform the Court as to the decision on it".

It was not readily apparent, at the time, but this Judge was not even a little interested in giving us our day in Court. His chummy discussions with the Hospital Counsel were obviously motivated by his desire to get rid of our case. I can't help but recall Judge Simmons' observation: "This case must be a hot potato, because so many people have fumbled over it for so long".

The Judge concluded the meeting with : ...if I decide I am going to decide it in their favor (Hospital Defendants), I am not going to sit through a two or three week trial (the Hospital Lawyer's exact words) - just to make you happy".

Mr. Crosby: "I can understand that, although my happiness is unimportant".

The Court: "If I look at it and I think they deserve summary judgement I'm going to grant it".

Bloch again gave a final pitch to have the case transferred to a magistrate.

The Court: "...I can just hear this. More and more cases are being tried by our magistrates. We have excellent magistrates and I can't tell you which one you will go to".

We didn't agree to downgrade our case by having a magistrate decide the issues, but it would become apparent that we had been trampled by this judge.

So, after some months, Bloch did what he warned he would do. As he said, "If I decide the legal issues in their favor, it is a trial we may not have to go through. We can't concede we are going to make an error".

But, make an error he did. He again dismissed our case and again we appealed to the Court of Appeals. And again, the Appeals Court reversed Bloch and sent the case back for trial.

When it appeared that we were looking for an even break from a biased judge, I looked into Bloch's background. His biography would show that he had been a member of a Rule 11 (discipline) task force. This must have given him the gall to threaten my lawyer with discipline on a whim. But, more revealing, was his position on the Board of Directors of a Pittsburgh hospital. What were his biases? Was he showing preference to the Hospital Counsel?

Before the District Court (Bloch) decided the motion to, once again, drop our case, the Hospital Apprentice Attorney decided he wanted to take my deposition. He, therefore, submitted a motion to the Court called a "Motion to Compel".

The Courts usually grant a limited time in any case for the parties to conduct discovery, that is, seeking information by production of documents or Admissions of Fact, or submitting interrogatories (written questions and answers) and by deposition (questioning of the parties under oath). Discovery in our case had been closed for a period of several years. The Court ordered a hearing on the Hospital's Motion to Compel. At a hearing before Judge Bloch, the Assistant Hospital Lawyer attempted to get full leeway to take my deposition and tried to have the Court limit our discovery. He certainly wanted it both ways.

During that conference, Bloch agreed to all or nothing - either both sides would be allowed unlimited discovery or both sides would go to trial without further depositions or interrogatories. At that conference, the Assistant Hospital Lawyer said:

"Well the problem is, Your Honor, what I think is going on here is that Mr. Crosby has no intention or inclination to take these depositions. But now, because I want to take one, he is going to end up noticing twenty, and I would be forced with a choice of deciding whether I really want this one bad enough to permit the twenty". This fellow, more and more, was sounding like a tattling child, reporting a sibling to his mother.

Bloch, dutifully, followed up on the accusation:

The Court: "I think that is a bit of abuse of the process. If you can show me the process has been abused and you file a proper motion under Rule 11, we would deal with that".

Now Bloch had threatened my counsel unnecessarily on the Assistant Lawyer's accusation.

Rule 11 was a Court rule that allowed for the discipline of lawyers who had been accused of misconduct. There was no need for him to threaten Judd. It was becoming more obvious that he was giving the Hospital great latitude.

The transcripts tell the story; but being at those hearings would allow anyone to note the chumminess the Judge showed with the Hospital Lawyer, but none to my counsel. Would this affect his decision? Had he already made up his mind?

The Assistant Hospital Lawyer got his request approved for further discovery. Bloch had authorized a period of three months or more for both sides to continue discovery. The Hospital Lawyer scheduled my deposition for two days and Judd sent a set of interrogatories for each of the twenty four defendants and scheduled five depositions.

The depositions were scheduled, but before they were completed, The Junior Lawyer ran back to compliant Judge Bloch and now petitioned the Court for a "protective order". He had wanted to take my deposition but didn't want the Hospital Defendants to be asked any further questions. He wanted it both ways and he got what he wanted.

Bloch called for a conference where the Hospital Lawyer complained that Judd had submitted additional interrogatories to the Defendants. The Judge accommodated him by ruling that Judd could submit only one set of questions and again threatened him.

The Court: "It appears to me that your are using discovery to punish the defendants. That's what it appears to me that you are doing, and I'm telling you right now I'm cautioning you that if I find that to be the case, I intend to take Rule 11 action and see that you are properly disciplined".

Mr. Crosby: "I can assure the Court that there is no basis for the Court to conclude that".

The Court: "I know you're trying, but that's what it appears because there is no reason to file the kind of interrogatories that you're filing, asking questions about the actions of the Hospital from twenty four different individuals; and that is the first indication to me that you are using discovery as a weapon".

Mr. Crosby: "I can assure the Court—".

The Court: "Well, your assurances don't assure me".

The Hospital: "If I understand the Court's ruling, I should answer that set of interrogatories that is directed to Indiana Hospital—".

The Court: "Yes".
The Hospital: "—and that's all I have to answer".
The Court: "—Yes that's all".

The Judge was continuing to give the Hospital great leeway and to restrict our need for further discovery.

Judd tried to explain to the Court with: "This is the gist of this case -a conspiracy and Antitrust Case, in essence which involves a combination of two or more people". He attempted to explain that there were twenty four people involved in this particular conspiracy.

I appeared at the Hospital Lawyer's office in Pittsburgh for my deposition. The new offices were spread over two floors of the building. We were led down a flight of steps in that paneled interior and into a typical conference room for the deposition.

The Junior Hospital Lawyer sat opposite, across the conference table with Judd at one end and the Court Reporter at the other. He asked questions hour after hour with brief lapses while he ran his fingers through his hair or did one of his digital nasal checks. Through those long days of questioning, Judd never objected to any of the questions. He was showing a professionalism that made a great contrast with the tactics of the Hospital legal people. That team interrupted the questioning of their clients after nearly every question with long speeches designed to interrupt their opponents' concentration.

Judd, on one occasion, did sit with the morning paper held unfolded in front of him. There was no doubt that he was listening to every word, but his disrespect for the other Lawyer couldn't have been more apparent.

Early during the process on the first day, the Assistant Hospital Lawyer was asking about various members of the Hospital crowd. He asked if the Medical Staff Executive Committee was a separate group from the Joint Conference Committee - but he changed his question and asked if it was a discrete group. When I answered that I didn't know how discrete that group was, Judd let out a howl.

That was the only levity during those two days. The other lawyer's demeanor was difficult to abide. I had determined that he was just a nasty, aggressive personality, so his nasty comments were just shrugged off. But, I did admit annoyance when he began to threaten with again tattling to Bloch.. It became apparent that he felt secure that Bloch was on his side. At one point, he didn't approve of one of my answers and warned:

Q. - "You are going to have to answer it, Doctor Miller, because anyone reading this transcript, including Judge   Bloch, will conclude as I have that you haven't given me an answer to a very simple and somewhat innocent question".

Again, after I had answered:

A. - "I have answered that question in great detail."

He then replied: "I told you and I prefaced it Doctor Miller and we are very close to having to appear in front of Judge Bloch".

I asked, "Am I being threatened?"

I, of course, was to be terrified at the thought of appearing before Judge Bloch, but the only problem would have been that I would be at risk to tell him candidly what I thought of him and his Court System, even though I had been warned not to say "word one" to the man.

After I had spent two days answering the Hospital's questions, the Assistant Lawyer began to flex his muscles when he apparently knew he would be approved by the Judge. He demanded another two days for me to answer his questions. Judd resisted saying that he had never heard of a deposition lasting more than two days. It was at that point that the Assistant Lawyer told Judd that he was the "slimiest" lawyer he had ever worked with.

When I got the transcript, that comment had been deleted by the Court Reporter who was being hired by the Hospital. Nevertheless, I guess both Judd and I were doomed to be "slimy."

So, once again, the Assistant Lawyer ran to the Judge with the complaint that I wasn't cooperative.

Without the Court's knowledge, he had scheduled depositions for five members of the Citizens Committee as well as an additional two days for my deposition. He had told the Committee members that if they didn't cooperate, they would be arrested by federal marshals and transported to Court. Telling our Judge that I had never had notice of the Hospital's continuing deposition didn't seem to matter. He advised:

The Court: "You know, we've accommodated Doctor Miller as much as we can. He brought this suit, he has to expect some inconvenience with bringing law suits. He is going to appear tomorrow and the 25th. He is going to cancel his patients. And I'm going to sign the order now, and you tell him I ordered him to be there".

The Hospital: "Appreciate that".

With the appearance that he had the Judge safely in his pocket, The Assistant Lawyer continued: "Could we take two more minutes of your time on another matter since we're here?"

The Court: "Sure".

The Hospital: "We have a deposition scheduled for a Doctor Clippins. He's very sick. He has a serious heart condition. But we have agreed to make him available. However, he has asked, because of a long-standing animosity between himself and Doctor Miller, that Doctor Miller not actually be present in the room during the deposition. Doctor Clippin's physician has written me a letter. He originally said no deposition, and in fact, that's what it says in the letter, but Doctor Clippins nevertheless wants to appear at the deposition. He wants to get it over with. But this is the only copy I have of the letter I had saying that — short trip, it would kill him actually".

Finally, the record now contained the Hospital's admission of animosity with Clippins, and in direct conflict with his story at the Kangaroo Court, where he was appointed to sit in judgement of my career. Again, the Lawyer lied, and showed no regard for the truth. Clippins, rather than being "very sick" and in danger of dying, was engaged in a full time general practice. The character assassination was in full swing.

Bloch responded:

The Court: "Well, Doctor Miller seems so busy, so I don't imagine he would intend to attend the other depositions anyhow. He's too busy for his own deposition".

It was becoming very evident that this man wasn't going to give us the even break we had been looking for - an impartial court. He continued: "We don't certainly want to affect this man's health...if you want to have Doctor Miller standing by somewhere...have him available by telephone".

The delighted Hospital Lawyer responded: "We'll put it on a speakerphone of course so he can hear it".

Clippin's deposition took place in a lawyer's office in upstreet Indiana while I listened on an open telephone line. The Hospital Lawyer interrupted and made a speech after just about every question and Clippins answered most questions with "I don't know" or "I don't recall".

At the beginning, Clippins claimed to be "board certified" in family practice; but when asked if he ever had residency training in either family practice or obstetrics he answered, "No".

There was long series of questions about his role as the Chairman of the Hearing Committee during the Kangaroo Court. When asked about his role in the resuscitation efforts for my elderly patient who died, his answer was the following:

A. - "...I don't remember the details of what we did, but both of us worked on this gentleman in some manner attempting to restore his respiration or his cardiac function, whichever was involved or both were involved. I don't remember the details of exactly what each of us did, but we both were there and we both attempted to revive the man without success".

In the face of Claude's obvious lie, the next question was:

Q. - "I would like to show you a copy of a report from Doctor Vader regarding the patient".

The Vader report read in part: "...Doctor Clippins arrived almost simultaneous with me and when he observed that appropriate management had been effected, he questioned whether his services were needed. When informed that sufficient help was present, he departed".

Claude's memory suddenly improved but he would easily be refuted at trial.

A. - "Before I could answer that question, I will have to look at that pile of documents".

Now Claude was shown a letter he had published in Medical Economics The letter was headlined: "No More Medicaid Patients". Clippins' letter read:

"Deputy Assistant Secretary Karen Davis wrote to you from her ivory tower at the Department of Health and Human Services to reproach doctors for lack of compassion because they want to limit the number of Medicaid patients...In my twenty two years of private practice, I've seen regrettably that doctors who open their door to public-aid patients find their practices inundated and subject to the Medicaid program inequities. Treatment of Medicaid patients in my office will continue to be limited to life-threatening situations only. A cost analysis of my family practice shows that the actual cost for each patient visit is eleven dollars while my usual fee is fifteen dollars.

Clippins' letter continued:

"My state Medicaid program paid me a maximum of six dollars last year for a patient visit yet the government sponsored clinics were reimbursed twelve dollars. Is it any wonder that I want to retain the right to decide whom I wish to treat and how?

"It explains that it doesn't pay because, when it costs me eleven dollars per patient visit and they're paying me six there's not much point in seeing these patients".

Clippins' Kangaroo Court Committee had found our office guilty of asking welfare patients to pay a small token fee..

Another of Clippin's wild allegations was then exposed in one of his letters that was now shown to him. The letter had been part of the file that the Hospital had provided and it had been sent to the Dean of Pitt's School of Medicine. It was on hospital stationery with a blind copy to the Administrator. There was a very strange coincidence. The letter was dated one day before my elderly patient was allowed to die without adequate help, and Clippins had been sent from my patient's bedside.

Clippins's letter began:

"Dear Doctor Werner:"

"It has been reported that a member of the Medical Staff of Indiana Hospital contacted you recently regarding our Preceptorship Program at Indiana Hospital. This physician allegedly reported our program to be poorly conducted, mismanaged, and supervised by a group of second rate physicians practicing a poor quality of medical care."

"This physician, Dr. R. J. Miller, has been a dissident in our midst for the past seventeen years. We of the Medical Staff are very familiar with his tactics of freely spreading misinformation and derogatory statements about any successful program which he didn't happen to think of first."

Whether or not the reported discussion between you and Dr. R. J. Miller took place, I feel it is my duty as Chairman of the Preceptorship Committee to tell you about our program, and hopefully dispel any fear you may have about the manner in which it is conducted".

When Claude would be confronted with this letter at trial it would well document the mentality of the little group who were doing the Hospital's business. The vague beginnings of their letters would often be "it has been reported" or "it has come to our attention". In this case, the maliciousness of the group seemed to have no bounds. I had never heard of Doctor Werner. And he had never heard of me.

When Claude was asked:

Q. - "Do you have any information about any incidents—where a baby was decapitated during delivery?"

The Hospital Lawyer broke in with a speech and ended…"I'm going to instruct the witness not to answer. It's privileged. If it was investigated, there's peer review. The patient had a privilege. You name it."

Once again, we were documenting the Hospital's compulsion (through its lawyer) to hide the truth from public scrutiny. But, Clippins had previously admitted, under oath, that he had decapitated a baby during delivery.

At about this time in the course of the federal litigation, an interesting letter to the editor was printed by the Pittsburgh Press. It read:

"Voting for judges"

"No citizens of the United States can feel secure and comfortable in their homes with fuzzy-minded federal judges in their seats.

The newspapers of this country instead of writing editorials, should be leading the way to a long-needed adjustment to the U.S. Constitution. I speak, specifically of the election of federal judges.

Federal judges should be accountable to the public for exceptionally stupid decisions."

Leonard Jones

Penn Hills

At the time, the Chicago syndicated columnist, Mike Royko, published a story with a large headline
"The Fix As A Way of Life". With even greater cynicism, he began:

"CHICAGO-At a party attended by a lot of politicians, lawyers, judges and other Chicago folk creatures, I got into a conversation with an attorney.

He had had a few too many.

I asked him what kind of law he practiced.

"I fix," he said.

At first I wasn't sure if I had heard him correctly.

"You what?"

"Fix."

He said it so casually - the way a lawyer might have said he specialized in probate, personal injury or patent law - that I still wasn't sure what he meant.

"You fix cases?" I asked. "Judges?"

He nodded. When he saw the look of surprise on my face, he looked amused.

And he said if I quoted him by name, he would naturally deny it and sue the pants off me.

Now I wasn't surprised that a lawyer would be a fixer. I've known several and suspected a lot of others. Everybody knows that the city has fixers.

But his man was the first one who ever came right out and admitted it."

Later in the piece Royko wrote:

"Style, he explained, is important because even when a judge is being fixed for a sum of money, he wants to maintain his dignity.

You can't walk in and slap a wad of bills on his desk. Envelopes must be used, the contents never opened in the presence of both persons, and the transfer of the envelope must be done so casually that it could be a cigaret or a stick of chewing gum."

The story concluded with:

"During our conversation, the fixer wouldn't discuss specific judges or cases he had fixed. He didn't think that would be ethical."

Also, at about that time, Delores Sloviter, Chief Judge of the Third Circuit Court of Appeals in a Law Journal headline announced, **"United States Judicial system Sinking: "Future in Question"**.

The Chief Judge related that the threat to "the American System of Justice was related to Congressional reluctance to appropriate more funds to the System and to expansion of the Court's jurisdiction.

Did this influential judge truly believe that more money would insure integrity in her System?

HIRED GUN.

This physician is an expert witness, paid to testify in a medical malpractice suit. The verdict may be influenced as much by his courtroom presence and medical reputation as by the facts presented in the case.

In efforts to sway juries that have no medical knowledge, our legal system pits physician against physician in the courtroom and imposes ever-increasing litigation costs.

The AMA has consistently urged tort reform and has succeeded, through the support of our members, in getting a strong reform bill introduced in Congress. But while there is general agreement on the urgent need for professional liability reform, there has been no agreement on how to achieve it. In some states, traditional reform efforts have simply not worked.

The AMA/Specialty Society Medical Liability Project has proposed an innovative alternative to the current handling of medical liability claims. It's an alternative that would take liability cases out of the courts and reduce the time and expense involved in deciding these cases. It's an alternative that would rely on a rational process instead of hired guns. And it's just one of the ways the AMA is working on behalf of physicians everywhere.

For this Project—and all our other programs—to succeed, it's vital we have your support. In return, we'll stand up for your rights on every front. And we'll keep you up-to-date with information and assistance on all aspects of your practice.

Our members make a difference.
If you're already a member, we need your continued support. If you're not, JOIN TODAY.
Call 1-800-AMA-1452.

In most cases, medical association dues may be deductible as professional or business expenses.
Dues and other contributions to the AMA are not deductible as charitable contributions for Federal income tax purposes.

Advertisement printed in Pennsylvania Medicine *by the American Medical Association during the period when Miller v. Indiana Hospital was in litigation in the Federal Courts.*

Chapter 17

> *"False words are not only evil in themselves,*
> *but they infect the soul with evil."*
> — Plato

THE DEPOSITIONS

Over the months that we waited for the decision on the Hospital's unusual third attempt to have the Antitrust action dismissed - another motion for summary judgement - we were constructing a highly detailed picture of the incredible atmosphere of Indiana Hospital, its leading actors and its lawyers. Parties to a legal action are generally limited to one Summary Judgement Motion. But, not this Court.

When the Hospital Lawyer convinced Judge Bloch to reopen discovery in order to take my deposition, we established our own schedule to take a series of depositions - much to the exasperation of the of Hospital personalities and their lawyers. We had certainly learned that the defendants were prepared for answering questions under oath with a court reporter making a record of all testimony; but it was obvious that the preparations of these witnesses included advice for "memory lapses", whereby many of our questions would be answered with the comment, "I don't recall".

The Court of Appeals, in their latest opinion, had opened the door for us to show the Hospital's unequal treatment of physicians, depending on who they were, and the Hospital was making frantic efforts to keep the news of its mishaps from the public. Both the State Court records and the Federal Records had been sealed from public view at the Hospital's request and the players in that shabby drama were far less than enthusiastic about being questioned under oath.

The depositions - questions answered under oath by the Hospital Defendants - extending over several months, ran the entire gamut of possible responses from the defendants being questioned.

Obviously, for us to show that there was a "combination" or "conspiracy" to eliminate me and the Indiana Medical Center from the scene, in violation of the Antitrust Laws, we needed to demonstrate conclusively that the Hospital group worked together in the events that led up to, and included the Kangaroo Court.

Much of that had already been accomplished by affidavits from the numbers of people who had come forward and who had offered help. There were sworn statements from two former Hospital Chief Financial Officers who told of being recruited by the Administrator and the Board Chairman to "gain Doctor Miller's confidence and report back on his plans". There was a sworn statement from a laboratory technician who was told by Dr. Burger that he was on a committee to "get Doctor Miller out of town". There was an affidavit from a nurse describing Dr. Vader's refusal to help one of his patients who died without help. Another nurse affidavit described Vader refusing to see an emergency heart patient unless he was met at the emergency department door and was paid his thirty dollar fee in advance. A former Hospital Administrator provided a notarized statement that he had been warned by the Board Chairman not to associate with the Millers and, of course, there was the affidavit from the Postal Inspector describing the theft of my mail and Citizens Committee mail by the Administrator and the Board Chairman. Another nurse had been instructed to keep a particular watch on me when in the Emergency Department and to report anything unusual directly to the Nursing Director.

Probably the foulest behavior documented was the description of Dr. Goldfarb telling people that I had put my wife in the home for battered women.

The Citizens Committee records detailed one tragic episode after another - two babies decapitated during delivery, the Health Department report of an emergency room patient bleeding to death in the Emergency Department after surgeons refused to help. There was the description of two women being blinded by misuse of a new operating instrument for eye surgery. There were descriptions of the ophthalmologist berating Emergency Room nurses for calling him at night or for calling him at the local golf course. Of course, the crown jewel of dastardly behavior were the details of Dr. Vader refusing a colleague's help and then standing by and watching my patient die without providing help. The record, of course, confirmed that, within hours of that death, Vader had written his report asking for my dismissal and then never testifying at the Kangaroo Court. No one could illustrate shabby behavior better than Lester Lazarus. So, our first deponent was Lester. Lester's blend of unusual behavior and unusual medical practice was, indeed, bizarre, but he was accepted, if not emulated, by "The Boys." He made an unsuccessful attempt to charge five hundred dollars an hour for his testimony.

Typically, a deposition begins with establishment of the deponent's name, address, family status, and so forth, by the questioning lawyer.

Lester was first asked to describe his marriages and he did so with a flare:

"Q: Could you give me your wive's names going backwards in order and dates of your marriages?"

"A: Well, my first marriage was in 1958".

"Q: When did that marriage end?"

"A: That ended in 1975".

"Q: Your second wife would be next".

"A: ...that marriage only lasted about three months - yes in 1976".

"Q: Three marriages?"

"A: Four. And the one before this was 1977, and that was another short one. That lasted only a few weeks".

Lester could confirm that the Hospital rules allowed the general practitioners to admit and care for all types of patients regardless of their qualifications.

"Q: And in what areas did you have privileges?"

"A: ...When I applied for privileges we really didn't have to spell out what we wanted to do. I had privileges in the Department of Medicine and then subsequently got privileges in the Department of Obstetrics and the Department of Pediatrics".

Lester, continuing with unusual frankness, described our meeting when he came to town. He opened a chapter which he probably would have wanted to forget.

The question was:

"How long have you known Doctor Ralph Miller?"

"A: When I first came to Indiana, Ralph Miller was introduced to me, and I have known him since then". (At that time) I would say that he and I had a brief social friendship. In fact he was the first person I took a drink with in Indiana, and the first time I played golf in Indiana, I played with him and his father".

Of course, the next question would be why the friendship was brief. The answer would be evasive - and with good reason. But Lester would describe graphically the atmosphere in the medical community.

As I recall, the friendship with Lester seemed to abruptly end after a Saturday dance at the unpretentious, old Country Club on the hill. Those affairs were the place to let off a little steam where everyone knew everyone else. On this occasion, someone took me by the arm and asked if I'd look after a sick colleague in the men's locker room. The place was deserted except for Lester, stretched out on one of the benches between the lockers. He was not what one would describe as fully alert, so I half dragged, half carried him, to the car. His place was only a mile or so from the Club, but as we headed down the long hill to town, he gasped that he was sick and before I could completely stop, he had opened the passenger side door and fallen out onto the roadside.

Poor Lester was unhurt, but was a real mess - covered with debris and most of his evening meal. He kept mumbling that he had disgraced himself. I eventually got him back into the car, and at his house on Oak Street, I hoisted him onto a shoulder and carried him straight up to a bedroom and tucked him in for the night. His spouse was a nice girl and I could imagine what she was thinking. I made, what I guess, was a clumsy attempt to reassure her that people got sick at the Club all the time and that no one ever paid much attention to it.

That probably was accurate because later on, Lester became the Country Club President for a time. But, all chances for a continuing friendship seemed to have vanished with what I thought had been an act of kindness. I was finding that any threat to a fragile, self-esteem could trigger unusual and profound reactions.

Lester continued his answers with unusual candor and gave some insight into the devious Doctor McGee's stay with our Medical Center.

He said: "McGee subsequently told us that he came and worked with Dr. Miller for a year at a low salary because he was getting a divorce when he came to Indiana and wanted his divorce settlement based on that low salary, and that made sense to me because about that time I was paying a lot of alimony and getting ready to pay more".

Lester continued:

"Well, in regards to Dr. Miller, I wasn't in Indiana very long when particular people had seen me with him at the Country Club and I got a few phone calls and people wanted to know what camp I was in. Well, I didn't know what they were talking about".

"So there was a pathologist at the Hospital by the name of Dr. Householder, and he called me one Sunday and wanted to see me, so I went over to his house and I got a long list of reasons why — the Hospital was divided into two camps. There were the older people, the Bees the Logans, the Ellises, the Dills, and then there was the other crowd, Greene, Mills, Post and Miller, and these, the older people wanted to know who I was siding up with".

"Well, I was younger than all these guys and so it made me wonder why they would do that, and Dr. Householder, for some reason he disliked Post and Miller so much that , I mean, it was, I never heard such language on a Sunday. I mean I never will forget it".

(This was the pathologist who would be seen wandering through the operating suite in street clothes and who had heckled at operating room doors.)

"He had lots of incidences and lots of things that I didn't know whether he was lying or not, but at least it made me wonder just who I was making friends with, and as a matter of fact, it was that same Sunday that I told my wife I didn't know if I was going to stay in Indiana a year, even though Peter Post and I had an agreement".

A further description of the unusual Hospital atmosphere came with another answer:

"Q: ...Was that what you meant by these two camps?"

"A: Yes, for example Logan was the chief of O.B, he couldn't stand John Marsh, the sight of him because, you know, Logan had been the chief of obstetrics, and John Marsh came, and I guess there was some criticism. So Logan's group of doctors, you know, they would speak to these guys in the Hospital but, you know, no Christmas cards".

Kipling had said ... "On being hated and not give way to hating". I have no doubts that the hating by Logan, Vader, Goldfarb and a few others was so intense as to be self-destructive. It was reported that Logan's end came as a result of a suicide by a self-inflicted shotgun blast to the head.

Lester's observation of those raucous years came out as follows:

"A: The staff you talk about, you know, a split down the middle, if you went to a staff meeting, you knew how this bunch was going to vote...and that was very important for any new person, each camp to know which side they were on. Well my decision was, hell, I'm not going to be in any camp. I'm not going to get into this. You know I'm too damned busy to have this on my mind".

Lester continued with his view of the Hospital world with:

"...Why the division was there, I was never quite sure. If Householder were alive - he could answer it - he kept records on everybody. I don't know where those records are now, but he could tell you what everybody had done wrong or questionable since he had been there when the pathologist should know that".

Lester was confirming that, in addition to the Administrator keeping files and the Nursing Director keeping files on the doctors, our nutty pathologist was also in the record business.

Lester was certainly giving his views without restraint. I don't know whether his deposition was after a two martini lunch or not, but he blabbed on. I had sensed, early on, that this fellow just had thought processes that were a little different from the norm. I had to advise him, on occasion, not to change the medications on my patients and one of the surgeons considered him a real lunatic when he wrote on a patient's order sheet, Have Doctor_____ do an appendectomy". Physicians just do not tell nurses to have a surgeon do a major surgical procedure.

Without much prompting, our deponent described his role in the resignation of the young woman doctor who got into an argument with the Nursing Director. Rather than appear before that learned tribunal, the Medical Staff Executive Committee, she resigned with the letter identifying the Hospital as: "an intellectual desert where meetings were never brought to order". Lester's description of the episode was as follows:

"A: Well I was on the Executive Committee and President and we had to suspend her. Now, that was for the way she talked to nurses, made rounds in a mini skirt and, used language very unbecoming to a lady.

But there was nothing there that you would, you know, that you could say was poor technique or poor medical practice".

If it weren't pathetic it would have been humorous that Lester and "The Boys" were sitting in judgement of appropriate speech. Lester himself, had a very loud, guttural voice with a Norfolk flavor and could be heard from one end of the Hospital to the other. In fact, Lester seemed to be so unaware of his own image that he was becoming a substantial witness to the entire Hospital scene.

He then talked of his review of Hospital charts for Blue Shield to identify improper treatment. He continued: "And we had a case once in

Indiana where, you know, we reviewed all the normal appendices that were taken out, and we had one appendix that was taken out when the admitting diagnosis on the chart was that the child had been stung by a bee, so that obviously it brought some question. Blue Shield didn't pay for it".

Lester never related whether anyone had ever reviewed his B-12 injection line, his prescriptions for many, many drugs for his patients or his dispensing of drugs from his office. Nor, did anyone ever challenge his hospital admissions for everything from childhood illnesses to psychiatric disease or ask about his orders for inappropriate x-rays.

The following questions to Lester could very likely be termed "loaded".

"Q: So have you formulated an opinion with regard to any Hospital Staff Physician that their care and treatment of a patient fell below established acceptable medical standards?"

"A: Probably lots of times, but I never expressed it...and I never would (conspiracy of silence) but I think, by and large, our doctors were, for what we are and what we had to work with, were pretty damn good".

Lester then, rather honestly, discussed the Hospital's malpractice cases, including one when he and a urologist were sued for failure to diagnose a testicular cancer; one against a surgeon following treatment for a leg injury leading to an amputation; one against a surgeon for resecting a lower bowel for cancer when no cancer was found in the operative specimen, and suits against two other surgeons.

Lester was then asked a series of questions related to his arrest for reckless endangerment. He had gone to trial and was placed on an Accelerated Rehabilitation Program for a year. There had been descriptions of his firing a shotgun at people on a Country Club fairway.

"Q: ...Have you become aware of any Medical Staff Physician being arrested or convicted of a crime?"

"A: Arrested or convicted of a crime? What are you talking about? Well, I'm probably the only one that I know of".

"I came home from the Country Club one night - my house used to be right by the Country Club...I saw somebody running...and took a shot at him...I wasn't arrested and I wasn't convicted...and this has all been since expunged, but I was charged with recklessly endangering someone. I had been drinking, in fact, I was drinking with the Sheriff ".

"Q: And were you found guilty or not guilty?"

"A: I don't remember whether I was guilty or not. There was an arrangement worked out, what do you call that ARD?...and I had to go up at that thing in Kittanning for counseling for alcoholism and then I was on probation for a year. I was ordered not to drink for a year".

"Q: Did anybody sustain any injuries or property damage?"

"A: I had a few pellets in the roof of the car. I think that was all".

"Q: Did the Administration of the Hospital become aware of that arrest?"

"A: Oh, I'm sure they did...".

"Q: Did you receive any sanction of any nature from the administration in Indiana Hospital?"

"A: No".

"Q: Have you ever become aware of any Medical Staff member at the Hospital...who refused to treat a patient because of the patient's inability to pay?"

"A: Yes, there's several doctors that won't take Medicaid...but then, a lot of the doctors will turn around after they take care of them in the hospital, they won't see the patients back in their office".

"Q: Are you aware of any physician ever in Indiana County being penalized by Indiana Hospital - or sanctioned in any way for refusal to take Medicaid patients?"

"A: No".

One of the charges at the Kangaroo Court made the accusation that my office charged an indigent patient a token fee.

Lawyers often, even routinely, leave the difficult questions till the end of a deposition - for very obvious reasons. Until now, Lester had been talking about others - now the questions were beginning to involve his own practice.

"Q: Do you recall, back at any point, when you were on the staff of Indiana Hospital, of any Staff Member admitting patients to the Hospital when the reason for the admission was not within that particular staff member's field of expertise?"

"A: Well, what's field of expertise?" I have admitted people with low back pain; I have admitted people with kidney stones; - I have never done any surgery, but that's, you know, from my personal standpoint".

The questions relating to some of Lester's personal tragedies followed:

"Q: To your mind, Doctor, have you yourself ever made any professional mistakes in the care and treatment of your patients over the years?"

"A: Have I ever done what?"

"Q: Made any professional mistakes in the care and treatment of your patients?"

"A: I'm not able to recall any".

"Q: Do you recall ever...making errors as part of your obstetrical practice?"

"A: I had a patient once have a ruptured uterus and died after the baby was born, and that had nothing to do with my decision to give up O.B.".

"Q: Did that situation perhaps involve an overdose of Pitocin?"

"A: I don't think it was an overdose. I think it may have been a bad reaction to it".

"Q: If I understand your earlier testimony, nothing ever came of that with regard to your staff privileges at the Hospital; is that correct?"

"A: Right".

Lester continued to outline the Hospital's policy of allowing its general practitioners great latitude regardless of training and experience:

"Q: Do you recall, Doctor, having ever admitted anyone to the Hospital outside your particular field of expertise?"

"A: What is your field of expertise when you do family medicine? So you know, I have admitted urologic cases, orthopedic cases, never any fractures or anything like that, but low back problems".

Lester was outlining the previous Hospital policy of allowing the General Practitioners to admit patients with most any diagnosis and to then have medical or surgical specialists manage the case - resulting in the double billing scheme.

Some of us didn't care to engage in that kind of dishonesty. Regardless of Lester's explanations of his referral patterns, the underlying principle of Lester's practice was MONEY. He had announced on arriving in town that he would make a million his first year; and he probably did.

The County Commissioners had told of the admission of a young man with a family who was taken to the Hospital "depressed and agitated". Lester responded to questions about that admission to his care:

"Q: Do you recall having ever admitted any patient with the initial impression of being a psychiatric problem?"

"A: Oh, (he) is the guy who hanged himself? I was just talking about that the other day; yes, we admitted him. He had lost his job and he had come to Indiana with the promise of a job and he didn't get it, and he was very depressed, and we admitted him and found him hanging in the shower the next morning".

"Q: Do you know if there was an investigation by Indiana Hospital as a result of that suicide by hanging?"

"A: I don't think there was an investigation".

At the time, the Coroner had advised that he never knew of the case until he accidentally learned of it from Hospital gossip. Yet, the following colloquy continued:

"Q: Did you report the hanging yourself to the State Police?"

"A: I think the Charge Nurse did".

"Q: Do you know who that was?"

"A: I don't remember".

"Q: Did you call the Coroner about that incident?"

"A: I don't recall that either".

"Q: Do you know if anybody called the Coroner about the incident?"

"A: I don't know that they did".

Whether Lester belonged to one group or another, his deposition graphically described the Hospital's atmosphere and its standards - if any. After he reported that he would make a million his first year, he further advised that Indiana was a G.P. town. He was probably right on both accounts. More to the point, though, his unusual behavior (including rousting elderly nursing home and Hospital patients on rounds in the wee hours) was tolerated. His description of the Hospital is, indeed, the description of a G.P. hospital. His candid descriptions of medical misadventures and the Hospital atmosphere would substantially help prove "unequal treatment of physicians" for us at trial. His graphic descriptions were also helping pave the way for our additional upcoming depositions.

Missing from Lester's candid description was any understanding of the motives of some of the physicians and their spouses. There was the description by the spouse of one of the surgeons. She described the end of referrals to her husband from one of the physicians when they built a beautiful house near him. When a Hospital Board member came to our office he remarked, "You have built a beautiful office, but you have lost all your friends." I doubted that at the time, but he turned out to be right.

Doctor Burger and spouse were early on our list for questioning. Both Burger and the Mrs. made numerous phone calls to the pediatricians we were recruiting for the Medical Center. I had been amazed at the gall of this pair but was more dumbfounded when our bright recruits would pay any attention to them. To read the transcript of their depositions one would think that this pair were the patron saints of Indiana County. We were beginning to see that an oath to tell the truth meant so little to some of these people that they probably began to believe their own fabrications.

Burger's deposition was taken in the small conference room in my lawyer's offices. Burger brought along his local lawyer as well as one of the Hospital lawyers. They all occupied the opposite side of the long conference table and Burger squeezed his bulk into an arm chair. His expressionless features were unrevealing, but he glanced right and left without any motion of his head. We were to find that he had been thoroughly coached. He knew he would be questioned about the calls to our pediatric recruits - aiming to discourage them from joining the Medical Center.

Early in Burger's deposition the following question was asked:

"Q: ...Have you ever been interested in recruiting other physicians to Indiana County?"

"A: I sure tried...and I sure made a lot of expensive phone calls". He then admitted that he had no success with his "recruitment". Amy Price had been our first pediatrician. Burger was asked:

"Q: Did you have anything to do with Dr. Price coming to Indiana County?"

"A: No, Sir".

On the next answer I expected to see Burger's nose begin to grow.

"Q: ...that you were pleased that she came to Indiana?"

"A: I was delighted that she came to Indiana".

It had been reported that Burger had been involved in walking through the Hospital's operating suite in street clothing while he had actually been the Chairman of the Infection Control Committee. One of the surgeons had reported that Burger had improperly written orders on the chart of someone elses patient and had been involved in a physical altercation in the Hospital parking lot. He was asked:

"Q: Doctor, have you, as an individual staff physician, ever been required to appear before the Executive Committee of the Medical Staff for any reason?"

"A: Yes".

"Q: What was the substance or what was the basis of that?"

The deposition was then stopped by the Hospital Lawyer and the witness had an off-the-record discussion out of the room with the Hospital

Attorney who then continued the interruption with the following:

The Hospital: " As I have learned from speaking with Dr. (Burger) the appearance before the Executive Committee did involve a peer review investigation, peer review situations if you will, a matter covered by peer review privilege. Therefore, we are objecting and I'm instructing him not to answer any questions about the substance of that appearance".

"Q: Were there any sanctions of any type resulting from that appearance before the Executive Committee?"

"A: I don't believe so".

Burger, without knowing it, had taken a substantial step toward demonstrating the Hospital's unequal treatment of physicians. The questions were becoming difficult for Burger. He had previously been accused of caring for pediatric surgical patients beyond his expertise. The next question related to that.

"Q: Doctor, have you ever been warned or had raised with you the matter of your accepting patients under your care at Indiana Hospital when the problems did not fall within your field of practice - pediatrics?"

The Hospital Lawyer again interrupted the deposition, as he had, time and time again.

The Hospital: "Again, I'm gong to instruct the witness not to answer.

His staff privileges are not on trial here. That information is privileged".

Mr. Crosby: "Just so the record is clear the staff privileges of every physician that has ever gone through Indiana Hospital are on trial here, because the gist of what the Third Circuit has said has to be addressed in an Antitrust medical staff privilege decision".

When the doctor was asked if it was proper under the Hospital rules to "walk into that Hospital and go into any patient that you want to and enter orders on that patient's chart", the witness answered:

The Witness: "The only time you can do that would be in a life threatening situation".

Burger, nonetheless, did just that, on occasion.

Burger was one of "The Boys" and his erratic behavior was generally overlooked by his cronies. The following question would shed some light on that:

"Q: Have you ever been treated for any emotional or psychological problem?"

The Hospital: "I'm going to instruct the witness not to answer that".
Again:
"Q: Let me ask the question that I was interrupted on. Have you ever been a patient of a hospital or similar institution for the care and treatment of any emotional or psychological problem or any nature whatsoever?"
The Hospital: "I'm going to instruct him not to answer that question".
Then:
"Q: Are you aware of your tenure at Indiana Hospital that a physician who has been treated for the use or abuse of alcohol or drugs report that to any individual at the Hospital?"
The Hospital: "It's just a yes or no question".
The Witness: " Off hand I don't know the policy right now".
Then, another question and interruption:
"Q: During your tenure, ...what did you do if anything, as President of the Medical Staff when you determined that one of the Staff Physicians had been accused of making a mistake in the care and treatment of a patient?"
The Hospital: "...I'm going to object and instruct the witness not to answer about what went on in those meetings".
In relation to Burger's contamination of the operating suite the following was asked:
"Q: Do you recall Dr. Burger when you entered the Operating Room in street clothing?"
The Witness: "Yes, I do".
"Q: Was an operation in progress when you entered the room - on that date?"
The Hospital: "So that the record is clear, some of these breaks are occasioned because I do not want the witness to inadvertently declare privileged information and that is why I am questioning the witness in the hallway before (we answer)".
Relating to Burger's role as chairman of the Hospital's Infection Control Committee:
"Q: ...Do you recall whether or not there was an issue within the Infection Control Committee - of casual observers entering the Operating Rooms in the hospital?"
"A: I couldn't recall".

Burger had ascended to the Presidency of the Indiana County Medical Society and had been able to change the Society's bylaws. Therefore:

"Q: During your tenure as president of the Medical Society, were the bylaws of the Society revised?"

"A: Yes, Sir".

"Q: Was that pretty much at your direction?"

"A: Yes".

"Q: Were you aware of any physician in Indiana County whose staff privileges had been taken away?"

The Hospital: "Other than Miller?"

"A: No sir".

Burger's new bylaws were then quoted: "The loss or restriction of Hospital privileges for disciplinary reasons shall automatically result in an investigation by the Board of Sensors as specified by Section Six of these bylaws".

"Q: ...The only person that these bylaws would apply to was Ralph Miller; is that correct?"

"A: Yes".

Burger obviously was going to attempt to conduct another hearing for me which never occurred. He may well have begun to see that there could be consequences to his reckless behavior.

When asked about his phone calls to pediatricians that were being recruited by our Medical Center, the answer was: "I not only called. I was excited".

But, the people Burger called described his attempts to discourage them. The truth gained little respect from him.

In response to further questions regarding his phone calls to a Pediatrician recruited by our Center, the following ensued:

"Q: Did he say anything else to you?"

"A: Yes he said he had been recruited by Dr. Miller".

"Q: Did you say anything to him in response to that ?"

"A: I says, wonderful, great, please come".

The Pediatrician quoted was, in fact, discouraged and decided to open practice in Eastern Pennsylvania.

When the Doctor was asked, "Have you ever taken any period of time away from your practice of medicine for any reason other than vacations?", Burger's personal lawyer, who had been sitting there without a whimper, in response to that question said to Burger: "Let's go chat".

With that, the two left the room for a "chat" in the hallway.

In a grand finale, Burger described the Hospital atmosphere and The Boys' character assassination:

"Q: Do you recall talking to Dr. Vance Vader, your social buddy, and one time partner?"

"A: Well, I don't know who I talked to about it (Kangaroo Court) but it was all over the Hospital. And, over the years, and I personally have not been involved fortunately in most of these things, there has always been a Ralph Miller incident story going on. How much of these were truths, half truths, heresay, this constant swirl was always going on, and it was sad".

He went on to say that the Staff Room would be "buzzing."

Sadder yet was this tale. But, he had unintentionally uncovered the behavior of the small, unprofessional group. I had pretty much been able to ignore this band of gossips, while enjoying a better than average success. I believe a lot of it was due to my belief in the Kipling admonition: "On being lied about, don't deal in lies, or being hated, don't give way to hating".

After the remarks about "buzzing", the witness was asked about the little boy who died of a head injury after being examined and sent home by one of the Hospital Physicians:

"Q: Have you heard from any source whatsoever, about any details involving the patient and the malpractice action filed against the Hospital?"

"A: Not really".

"Q: So, there was nothing buzzing around the physicians lounge about the death of the little boy?"

"A: Not really, I don't recall".

When questioned about an obstetrical mishap involving Dr. Fazio, leading to a malpractice action, the answer was:

"A: I gave a deposition involving a malpractice suit that involved one of the obstetricians at the Hospital".

"Q: Had you given the baby a transfusion that was involved with Dr. Fazio?"

The answer was positive.

Mrs. Burger also was later questioned about her role in the telephone calls to our recruits and her role in the furor created by a local woman's club when the Medical Center's pediatrician broke his contract with the Center. She repeated the party line that she and her husband made phone calls only to encourage our recruits. She claimed she had no role in the woman's organization which presented petitions to the local Court and published letters in the local paper and who packed the local courtroom in support of the pediatrician who broke his contract. But, she described attending the Hospital hearings for the pediatrician, along with Burger's office staff.

She demonstrated a full knowledge of Burger's activities - leaving little doubt that she was involved in most everything he did.

During her deposition, she continued:

"Q: ...From the time since you moved into Indiana County, has your husband been treated for any psychological or psychiatric problems or illnesses?"

The Hospital: "Again, I'm going to object, although I will talk to the witness about this...and that if he was ever at any time in his life under the care of a psychologist, it is simply not relevant to this case."

The people undergoing deposition had previously answered in interrogatories (written questions and answers) and had attempted to avoid giving incriminating answers. Many of the answers were "I don't know, or I don't recall". Now, deceitfulness had become more evident.

After the Dr. Burger deposition, my lawyer friend and I walked down the long, quiet, upper floor hallway without a word. As we waited for the elevator, he broke the silence: "Can you imagine anyone trusting their children to someone like that?"

I answered, "No".

The earlier depositions had shown the ability of the Hospital Defendants to limit the amount of information they would supply. Through "I don't recall" answers, the unprofessional interruptions by the Hospital Lawyer and out and out, bald-faced lies, it was a chore to extract information from the hostile defendant-witnesses. There was a distinct contrast when our witnesses testified.

The Hospital Administrator and the Hospital Board Chairman had brutally fired employees on twenty minute notice and had sometimes attempted to blackball them from other regional hospitals. Two of the former assistant Administrators - chief financial officers of the Hospital - were more than willing to testify for us. One had risen to be a the CEO of a west coast hospital and would testify by telephone from California. The other served as an accountant for a regional hospital and would testify at the Hospital Lawyer's office. The depositions were requested by the Hospital to determine how much damaging evidence these two witnesses would present at trial.

These two former management employees would give similar accounts of their time working for the Administrator and the Board Chairman. Both had been instructed to use their friendships with me to gain information on my plans and to report back to the Administrator and the Chairman. The Hospital Lawyer was first surprised when one of these witnesses gave an unusual response following a question regarding the Hospital's Administrator.

The Hospital: "You said...he referred you to Dr. Miller and I take it described him as a good urologist; that was your words?"

"A: Described him as the best in town and that he was a patient of Dr. Miller. I had been doctoring with a Urologist in Kittanning and the Administrator suggested that Dr. Miller was the best around".

Continuing, the witness was asked about the Hospital Administration's spying activities.

"Q: When do you recall that The Administrator first made a negative comment to you about Dr. Miller?"

"A: Primarily after the former Assistant Administrator left, when I became directly reportable to the Administrator".

"Q: And what do you recall the first negative comment being?"

"A: Right before I was promoted, he said he wanted me to be friends with Dr. Miller, and find out what he was doing and sort of keep an eye on him".

"Q: Did you ask him why he wanted you to do that?"

"A: Well, he said Dr. Miller was trying to get doctors in and he wanted to run the Hospital and he was not going to let him run the Hospital and he was getting physicians in to his Medical Center and trying to change the way the Hospital was run and so I should try to find out what his plans were and let him know in advance".

The continuing spying was illustrated by the following exchange:

"Q: ...I would think that might cause you some trepidation".

"A: Well that was one of the reasons The Administrator had asked me to do that plus he told me that the (former Assistant Administrator) had been doing that for him".

"Q: What did you find out about Dr. Miller in this period?"

"A: I found out that Dr. Miller was a very capable and competent urologist".

Later the witness's response was as follows:

"A: He (The Administrator) was concerned about the Medical Center...he was concerned that Dr. Miller would get physicians on the Staff and, to use his words, he would "pack the Medical Staff". He was concerned economically that possibly this would take business away from the Hospital. I never really saw his reasoning, because I saw it as a supplement to the Hospital rather than taking business away from the Hospital".

The Junior Hospital Lawyer, indeed was getting an earful ; how were they going to handle this kind of testimony at trial? The Board Chairman would finally be deposed and he had continued to say over and over, "Remember, I was out of this thing from beginning to end." But, when the Hospital Lawyer asked the witness who had been recruited as a spy, the next exchange was:

"Q: ...Did he (the Administrator), at any time, indicate to you in any way that he had been asked by the Board of Directors to ask you to keep an eye on Miller?"

"A: ...When he asked me to keep an eye on Dr. Miller, a month or so later...he, - the Board Chairman, was in the Administrator's office, and I was with the Administrator, and he says,(to the Chairman) "He has agreed to keep an eye on Dr. Miller like(the former assistant CEO) did. That said in front of me to the Board Chairman".

The Hospital was beginning to see what they would face in front of a jury at trial.

Another deposition was scheduled for the following day and the witness was the earlier Assistant administrator who was going to be asked to confirm or deny the Hospital Administrator's espionage system. We met in The Hospital Lawyer's conference room and the conference call was put into the west coast.

The Hospital Lawyer cautiously worded the question:

"Q: Were you ever asked to in any way spy on Dr. Miller, collect information on Dr. Miller by anyone in the administration or on the Board of Directors?"

"A: I was asked by the Administrator to, in my friendship with Dr. Miller, if I heard or became aware of anything that he was doing with relation to his business that would have anything to do with the Hospital that they would appreciate it if I would pass any information on to them.

His instructions related to the fact that Dr. Miller was planning on building a clinic, which was considered by him anyway, like a mini hospital kind of setting. He was concerned about that and requested that if I heard anything about that or the status of that part of Dr. Miller's practice that I related that back to him…and I believe in particular the Board chairman, would be very much interested in being kept informed on the status of that project of Dr. Miller…he led me to believe that he and the members of the Board were concerned about the potential competition that the clinic would cause the Hospital and potential revenue at the Hospital".

"Q: Is there anyone other than the Chairman on the Board who you believe shared the Administrator's concerns?"

"A: Yes, I would believe that the majority if not all of the Executive Committee". (of the Hospital Board)

"Q: Well then what is the basis of your conclusion that they shared the concern?"

"A: They would have conversations among themselves when I was present at meetings".

"Q: What concerns were expressed during these conversations?"

"A: The conversations made be believe that they were concerned that if Dr. Miller were to complete his plans, opening basically a clinic, that would compete with the Hospital, that it would have a financial impact on the Hospital that would be detrimental".

"Q: Well, what was their understanding of what his plans were?"

"A: In essence, he was opening what they believed was a mini hospital and would offer services such as laboratory, radiology, minor surgery, pharmacy, areas that they believed were in competition with the Hospital".

"Q: Do you recall whether those concerns were expressed very early in your tenure or did they develop later?"

"A: I believe it was later in my tenure and intensified up until the point I left".

"Q: I am just a little bit puzzled as to if it was only in the planning stages how the members of the Board knew about it already. Can you shed any light on that?"

"A: …They were aware of meetings that were conducted by Dr. Miller with certain groups. He also was going through the process of recruiting physicians for that clinic and the Board was aware of that".

The Assistant Hospital Lawyer continued:

"Q: I am a little bit puzzled as to why you would so willingly agree to spy if Dr. Miller was your friend. Why did you agree to do that for the Administrator?"

"A: Well there are basically two components to the answer; one, of course, the Administrator was my immediate supervisor. However, the primary reason is that I never got the impression from Dr. Miller that his plans were some big secret. I never felt I was divulging anything to the Administrator or the Board that they might not have gotten if they had asked Dr. Miller themselves".

"A: There seemed to be some concern in the Administrator's mind that they were a little bit troubled that Dr. Miller was attempting to gain a little bit more control within the Hospital operation than they would appreciate".

"Q: Did he ever make in your presence any negative comments about Dr. Miller? You know, disparaging comments about him personally?"

"A: ...He made those remarks; he was psychotic, that kind of thing. However, it is difficult for me to determine whether he meant that in a serious vein or not".

"Q: You mention certain specific people in your affidavit...Here you are specific. First of all as I understand it to be members of the Board Executive Committee. How was it then that these particular individuals were chosen to be named? Did you overhear these people talking?"

"A: That is correct".

"Q: Your affidavit states "numerous times I heard statements especially from the Board Chairman that Dr. Miller and his plans for a competing health center separate from the Hospital had to be stopped".

"A: He made statements such as that infrequently during breaks or prior to meetings when the Executive Committee met".

"Q: You say (in your affidavit) that separate steps were taken to discredit Dr. Miller. Can you tell me what those specific steps were?"

"A: When Dr. Miller was attempting to recruit physicians, there seemed to be a strategy developed that would interfere with recruitment...there was a strategy developed, I believe, to interfere with his recruitment effort".

"Q: What was the nature of the strategy?"

"A: The only specific incident that I can remember in this case was that they attempted to recruit a physician of their own at that time".

"Q: Who was that? Was it (Urologist)?"

"A: I believe it was. He was an Oriental urologist".

My lawyer then asked the deponent:

"Q: If you could answer the question, as to whether Dr. Vance Vader was one of those others".

"A: Yes, Dr. Vader was at the meetings. I don't recall how many. The Administrator used Vader as an advisor".

"Q: Do you have any knowledge as to whether the type of statements that the Administrator made about Dr. Miller's mental capacity were part of those subjects to discredit Dr. Miller? Were those comments regarding Dr. Miller's mental state ever discussed?"

"A: The comments would have been made during those meetings, yes".

Those two depositions, two days in a row, put an entirely new spin on what the Hospital Lawyers would face at trial. Here were two high level management employees of the Hospital who would describe conversations between the major conspirators on plans to run me from town - and in violation of the Antitrust Laws. The named were The Administrator, The Board Chairman, two lawyers on the Hospital Board and the little politician-Assistant Chairman, and of course, Dr. Vance Vader.

When I first heard those descriptions of treachery, I had more than a little difficulty in believing that this type of behavior could occur in a hospital setting. Most of these people or members of their family were patients of our office. I still have difficulty absorbing the thought of such deceit. How many people would trust themselves to a physician's care and, at the same time, be making plans to run him from town?

Particularly revealing was the previous testimony tying Dr. Vader into the plans of the Administrator and the Hospital Board. He had recruited the Oriental urologist which was thought somehow to hinder the Medical Center. There was no doubt that Vader had ingratiated himself with the Hospital Management, but it was beyond comprehension to think that he would stand by and let a patient die without helping in order to create an excuse for the revocation of my Hospital privileges.

It was indeed a surprise to learn that these people had been engaged in this subversion for so long without me knowing. But, on the other hand, how could this crowd be so obtuse to think that they could hide the truth forever? There is only one answer - the protection of numbers. There wasn't one of those people who had the stomach for a one-on-one encounter. Their mindset was indeed something akin to the psychology of a lynch mob.

Some of us were able to see the irony as more and more friends came forward with revelations of the group's deception. A favorite was the description of the Administrator running around telling people that Miller was paranoid, and at the same time, having the night scope on the roof of the Hospital and having his office wired. He was, indeed, showing an abnormal preoccupation with what I was doing.

It was revealed, with the testimony of one of the management people, that the Administrator's obsession led him to "drive by Dr. Miller's and see maybe four or five cars at the Medical Center and then say, "He's got four or five cars", then "I wonder what he's doing today", and things of that nature".

The evidence against the Hospital crowd - the Board, the Administrator, the Executive Committee of the Medical Staff, was becoming more and more conclusive. We would later supply the Court with a list of over one hundred and fifty possible witnesses.

The witnesses who had supplied affidavits and testimony at deposition had firmly involved The Administrator, The Board Chairman and Doctor Vader as working closely together in their attempt to destroy the Medical Center.

The details of conspiracy were so well established, in preparation for trial, that additional information was probably not needed. The documents, the affidavits, the deposition testimony documented an effort beginning much earlier than I would have expected and it unmistakably coincided with the ascension of the Board Chairman to the control of the Hospital Board. It will be remembered that one of his legacies was the closure of the local instrument manufacturing plant, where he was manager. In the same period he would fire, on twenty minutes notice, the bright young administrator who went on to success with Project Hope. Consecutively, the two Chief Financial Officers and his ex-son-in-law would be dismissed on very short notice.

The Monday firings at the instrument plant had earlier been dubbed by some sources as "the Monday morning massacres". The same fearful atmosphere permeated the Hospital. The mass of documentation, that had been gathered for trial firmly established that the Hospital atmosphere and its clandestine activities were not only tolerated but originated at the top - with the Chairman of the Hospital Board.

Here was another of the unusual personalities that populated the Hospital. This very strange, singular man made great efforts, through church and neighborhood civic involvement ,to be seen as a kind, benevolent figure, while attempting to destroy lives. He was, of course, aided in his fantasy by frequent coverage of his activities in the local news. With the closure of his local industry, and the inevitable revelation of his hypocracy, he would leave town quietly and not return. That is, until he was required to return for a deposition.

As one of the defendants in the Antitrust suit, the former Chairman was flown back for a day-long deposition. He had flown in from Connecticut a day earlier and had been schooled with appropriate answers for the deposition by the Assistant Hospital Lawyer.

On the next day, listening to this personality during the hours of deposition was frightening. It was the portrait of a tyrant who had been able to maintain a hold on a community resource - its Hospital - for a number of years. The new Hospital wing, obviously intended to be a memorial to this man, had escalated from a nine million dollar project to over twenty-four million during his reign.

But the true cost of his unholy reign cannot be measured in dollars.

The deposition was to give an unusual insight into an unusual persona despite the Hospital Lawyer's efforts to interrupt the questioning and obscure the truth.

The Junior Hospital Lawyer picked us up in his firm's paneled lobby. I had been glancing at several Who's-Who volumes that were conspicuously left on an end table as self-promotions for some of the firm's members. The Hospital Lawyer, as usual, in shirt sleeves, led us down a flight of carpeted steps and through a paneled passageway to a conference room. The former Chairman was already seated and gave perfunctory hellos to both of us as Judd identified himself.

The court reporter at one end of the conference table recorded those present and swore the witness to tell the truth. His disregard for that oath was obvious at once.

Judd began:

"Q: During your tenure as President and/or Chairman of the Board, did you personally, ever conclude that Ralph Miller was unfit to serve on the medical staff of the hospital?"

"A: That was in the hands of the medical staff, not me".

"Q: You never personally made that conclusion yourself?"

"A: That is right".

and;

"Q: Other than your signature on this letter (termination of privileges), was there anything that you did either toward retaining Ralph Miller on the medical Staff or having him removed from the medical staff?"

"A: No".

then;

"Q: At any time did you become aware of any physician on the hospital staff that desired to terminate or revoke Dr. Miller's privileges?"

The deposition was interrupted:

The Hospital Lawyer: "I am, of course, free to object to any question, which I deem unfair, misleading, a mischaracterization of earlier testimony, duplicative, going into attorney-client matters. Although relevancy is preserved, if it is completely out of left field and has nothing to do with this law suit at all, I can also instruct the witness not to answer those questions".

then;

Mr. Crosby: Let the record reflect that the Defense Attorney had indicated that he will explain to the witness what the last question that the Court Reporter was about to read back was, as opposed to having the court reporter read back the question. Let the record further reflect an objection that the Defense Attorney is explaining the question in private without my being able to hear. So, I have no idea what the explanation is".

The question relating to what physicians were involved was then answered:

"A: Dr. Vader and a number of others, I specifically wouldn't want to name any particular ones, but a number of others".

From an individual who had held great responsibilities, there were some very strange answers. In response to a question of my being a "disruptive" person, the witness answered:

"A: I think he was just a disruptive individual".

"Q: Can you think of any specific incident indicating him in your mind to be a disruptive individual?"

"A: I think I can remember specifically that he and other physicians would block the aisles so that the Administrator could not get through without really going around them. I witnessed that on several occasions".

Even though we had all heard the nations' hospital hierarchies describe "disruptive physicians", this was the first indication that some of us could be disruptive by just standing in a hallway. The witness then answered the following question:

"Q: In the 1960's on several occasions?"

"A: I would say so. I don't know.

The former chairman answered questions about some of his firings with candor but with questionable truthfulness:

"Q: Do you know who William Paxton is?"

"A: Yes, he was Administrator".

"Q: What would it be based upon if you think he might have ill will toward you?"

"A: I was unfortunately the man who had to terminate him".

"Q: What was the reason that you terminated William Paxton?"

"A: He was simply not a hospital administrator".

"Q: Was that the same reason - you terminated the more recent?" Administrator?

"A: No".

"Q: What was the reason you terminated him?"

"A: I think he had reached the point of burn-out. He was completely frustrated".

The Hospital, through the local newspaper, had described the Administrator's "resignation" and appointment as a "consultant."

Bill Paxton went on to success as the Administrator of the Hospital Ship Hope. His "termination" had come after a later evening secret meeting of the Hospital Board at the Board Chairman's house as reported by some of those present.

The next Administrator had been terminated when called into a lawyer-board member's office at night in the presence of three lawyers.

The Chairman's deposition continued when he was read an affidavit from William Paxton, the "terminated" administrator stating that the Chairman had referred to Miller's office building as part of Miller's "grandiose plans".

The former Chairman then denied by saying:

"A: I seriously doubt that I ever talked about Miller's plans".

Following that:

"Q: Do you recall having expressed displeasure to William Paxyon of his having been a guest in Miller's home?"

"A: I don't recall it, but now that it is there, I don't know how to look at that".

"Q: Did you ever recall indicating to William Paxton that your concerns or dislikes of Ralph Miller were based on his tendency to expand his health care holdings in Indiana County?"

"A: No".

"Q: Do you recall ever referring to Ralph Miller as a nut?"

"A: No, I don't".

The witness was attempting to retain his self-image of benevolence by denying things that we all knew had occurred.

The matter of nepotism at the Hospital was a major issue with the Citizens Committee with both the Chairman, Dr. Vader and the Directress of Nursing hiring relatives over other qualified people. The next questions related to that:

"Q: Do you know who Richard Bancroft is?"

"A: He is my ex-son-in-law".

"Q: And you got Mr. Bancroft a job at Indiana Hospital?"

"A: Yes".

After the divorce from the Chairman's daughter, Bancroft was fired as Purchasing Director for the Hospital, again on twenty minutes notice, and escorted from the building by a security guard. Now, once again , the witness's character traits were expressing themselves.

"Q: What were the reasons that you are aware of from any source for his termination from employment?"

The Witness: "After my daughter's divorce I made it clear to the administrator and everyone I wanted no part of it, no discussion. I had no discussion about it, nothing. I didn't know what went on. That is one thing I stayed out of".

"Q: Is it your impression that, but for your having gone to bat for Richard Bancroft, that he would never had gotten his job at the Hospital?"

"A: Absolutely".

The Chairman had previously testified on more than one occasion that he had "stayed out of this thing from beginning to end". Now he was being shown affidavits wherein people had sworn to his involvement with interception of my mail, the Administrator's spying activity and the events leading to the Kangaroo Court.

He still did not know that his ex son-in-law was waiting in the wings to testify that the Chairman would repeatedly discuss Dr. Miller during weekly Sunday dinners and that he felt the Chairman had directed the entire vendetta against Miller's competition to the Hospital. The Chairman also had not been told that we had the Board of Directors minutes describing his announcement of the Kangaroo Court guilty verdict before those hearings ever began.

To establish the Chairman's involvement with the Hospital hearings, he was asked:

"Q: As you are here today, do you recall having appointed Clara Mattern (hospital lawyer) to serve as the presiding officer at Ralph Miller's revocation of staff privileges?"

"A: Yes".

The Hospital Lawyer was disturbed by the answer and interrupted - then:Mr. Crosby: "Let the record reflect that the Board chairman and his attorney have now left the room to confer in this response", then:The Hospital Lawyer: "Let the record reflect the Chairman and I conferred outside. What we talked about is none of Mr. Crosby's business".

In an attempt to have the answer changed, the Hospital Lawyer then said: "This was in the hands of the Medical Staff and they appointed her. We did not appoint Mattern to preside over that staff meeting". The Chairman denied that he or his Board had anything to do appointing the Hospital Lawyer, Clara Mattern, and denied that her sitting as Hearing Officer had ever been challenged.

The Chairman was then shown the letter challenging Mattern's bias and then he altered his response:

"Q: I want to show you a letter. It is a letter addressed to the Chairman of the Hospital Board, and ask if you recall receiving the letter".

The Chairman's distinctive initials were on the letter which had challenged the fairness of the "Hearing Judge", Ms. Mattern.

"A: I received it. There are my initials".

Then:

"Q: Following receipt of the letter, did you do anything to investigate the propriety of Ms. Mattern sitting as the presiding officer at Dr. Miller's revocation hearings?"

The Witness: "No, I didn't do anything".

The Hospital Lawyer, now concerned with the questions related to the fairness of Mattern's role in the conspiracy continued:

The Hospital Assistant Lawyer: "He has already answered that he did not appoint Clara Mattern. I wish you would stop repeating incorrectly his answers. I am warning you I will stop this deposition if you continue to do that".

Then:

Mr. Crosby: " You agree with your attorney, under oath, that there is no doubt in your mind that you never appointed Clara Mattern to preside at the hearing; is that right?"

The Witness: "That is right".

In the face of the changing answers, the question was again asked:

"Q: There is no question in your mind about that?"

The Hospital Lawyer interrupted: "For the fourth time, asked and answered. That is enough. I would instruct him not to answer. Mr. Crosby,

I am warning you that this deposition is about to end".

Judd replied: "You are not warning me about anything".

The Chairman was then shown a letter which he had written and which confirmed his role in the staging of the Kangaroo Court, including the appointment of Hospital lawyer, Clara Mattern, to be the hearing officer.

Then:

"Q: In light of that letter, do you wish to change any of your earlier testimony that you have given in the deposition?"

"A: It seems I have to. It seems that the Medical Staff did not appoint Clara Mattern, but apparently I did".

Then:

The Hospital Lawyer exclaimed: "There is no problem. This issue has already been described. Counsel is having fun with it".

The Witness: "I know. I think he's having a good time".

Mr. Crosby: " I am just trying to get the truth here, Mr. Chairman".

The Chairman, then red-faced and furious at having his duplicity revealed, despite his lawyer's efforts to hide the truth, said: "It would have been much easier to just show me this. I think the whole thing is too cute, if you want to know what I think, too damn cute".

The lawyers decided to take a short lunch break and Judd and I walked through the building's plaza after a quick sandwich from the building's's cafeteria. It was a beautiful November day and there was little conversation. We were just content to be out of the tension of that conference room. It was apparent though that we were beginning to show convincingly the interplay between the Hospital's Board Chairman, the Administrator, Dr. Vader, Dr. Goldfarb and the Hospital lawyer, Mattern. It appeared that no one was going to take responsibility for appointing the hostile Claude Clippins to sit in judgement at the Kangaroo Court.

The Chairman was then asked: "Do you have any recollection of Ralph Miller having reported Claude Clippins to the state Board of Licensure for any alleged misconduct?" The Chairman answered: "Vaguely. Seems to me I have read that somewhere".

And then: "Was it ever suggested to you personally that Claude Clippins perhaps might not be an appropriate person to serve on the Hearing Committee and specifically as Chairman of the Hearing Committee prior to the time that the hearings began?"

"A: I don't remember anything like that".

And, then:

"Q: Do you personally ever recall doing any type of investigation into the appropriateness of the individuals that were appointed to serve on the hearing committee?"

"A: No".

It had been evident, from the beginning, that no one, absolutely no one, had looked into the validity of all those accusations made at the Kangaroo Court.

It had been documented by the Postal Inspection Service that the Administrator and the Chairman had kept and copied mail that I had posted in the local post office and mail that had been addressed to me - with copies sent to the Hospital Lawyers.

The following question asked:

"Q: Do you recall, ever instructing the persons in attendance at the Board of Directors' meeting that if they were to come in possession of any mail with regards to Ralph Miller or the Concerned Citizens Committee, that they forward or direct their mail to the Hospital Lawyers?"

"A: Yes".

And then:

"Q: Was it your decision that the Board members should give mail addressed from Dr. Ralph Miller to the attorneys?

The Hospital Lawyer: "If it was on the advice of counsel, don't answer".

"A: It was on the advice of counsel".

It appeared that the brazen arrogance of the Hospital Lawyers would certainly suggest that they harbored no qualms about interfering with the delivery of the U.S. mail.

Questions further related to the interception of my mail followed:

"Q: Do you recall whether you personally ever possessed mail that had been addressed from Dr. Miller to anyone other than yourself - originals?"

"A: I probably did. I don't know. I can't remember, and I remember seeing mail from the Citizens Committee in there".

It appeared that the Chairman was unaware that he had plead guilty to a federal felony.

In regard to Hospital finances the following questions and responses:

"Q: Did the shortening of the average length of stay of patients at Indiana Hospital create economic problems for the hospital?"

"A: It did not."

The following excerpt from Hospital committee minutes was read:

"The Board President reported that the Hospital's patient statistics for the past three months of operation are far below the figures of Hospital budget projections. The decision in the length of stay together with other factors will be investigated in depth as this has a profound effect on the resources of the Hospital."

It was becoming evident that the Chairman had been thoroughly coached to lie or to claim memory loss. Here was the man who, through his Board of Directors, or through the Hospital's Medical Staff, would set the moral tone for the entire institution.

Being annoyed with his deception revealed, the Chairman exclaimed: "I don't know whether I am being tricked here." Mr. Crosby answered, "You are not being tricked". His lawyer then advised: "You are being tricked, but you answer to the best of your knowledge".

The witness then added: "You asked me a question. Then you pull a document when you have it in front of you. I resent that. I don't like it."

The Chairman was asked for the validity of a document mailed by him to citizens of the community. He answered with: "Read the thing. Well, come on now. Let's not be cute. Read the damn thing. I'm getting a little sore about this thing. There is a document that is trying to improve the operations of the Hospital. It says exactly what it is there. Don't ask me the purpose. It is in there." He then added: "I don't remember, how in the hell could I remember way back then?"

The Chairman was then asked the ultimate question: Judd asked: "Now my question is: Prior to the commencement of the actual hearing, did you have any reason to believe that the Medical Staff would ultimately recommend the revocation of Dr. Miller's Staff privileges?" He answered: "I didn't believe they would do it. I did not believe they would recommend the revocation. When it started, I didn't believe it." This was from the man who had been the clandestine power behind the "Bad Faith Peer Review."

This had to be the ultimate in deceit. A passage from the Board of Directors minutes recorded weeks before the hearings read: "The Chairman then advised the Board that the Medical Staff is in the process of revoking Dr. Miller's privileges and the matter will be presented to the Board in a few months. "

Witnesses would later describe at trial, the Chairman's behind-the-scenes efforts to have his Board concur with the results of the Kangaroo Court.

As the day and the deposition was drawing to a close, Judd presented a document that had been found in the Hospital files. It presented an insight into another unusual personality. The one page document, which was part of many that had been stored at the Chairman's house, was <u>some sort of detailed log of the Chariman's whereabouts for the three days following his letter revoking my Hospital privileges</u>. The Chairman's initials were in the upper left corner dated October 7th. and October 8th.

The log for October 7th. began:

"At home, 10:45 A.M. to 1:45 P.M." with an entry to the right of that note:"(wife) at home", then, "1:45 P.M. to 2:00 P.M. - travel to town",followed by: "Travel to Dr. 2:00-2:15. At Dr. 2:15-3:05" and, "Travel to home 3:45-4:00 P.M.", with the additional note: "No one at home" to the right of the original column.

Then:

"4:00-5:15 (Chairman's spouse) at home" followed by: "to IUP 5:15-7:45" and "7:15 on (spouse) at home" and 7:15-12:00 (Chairman) - home".

Near the middle of the page, the log for October 8th. began and appeared as follows:

"Sat. 10/8
 Both home all day to 2:30 P.M.
 Out 7:30 A.M. to 4:30 P.M.
 Both home 4:30 P.M. on"

For October 9th., the following:

"Mrs. London and daughter here 10/9 from 2:30 P.M. to approx. 3:15 P.M.

 Both out 3:30 P.M. to 8:30 P.M.
 Both home 8:30 P.M. on
 This letter received 10/10 - 10:56 A.M."

In an effort to learn what this strange recording of the chairman's whereabouts for three days, the following exchanges occurred. It was obviously not a coincidence that this strange record was started the day I got the Chairman's letter discharging me from the Hospital Staff:

"Q: It appears to me, from this document, that is exhibit No. 8, that it is a chronological by time indication of what you were doing."

"A: That is right, what I was doing. I can't tell you why I made this. I really don't know, but there was a reason why I seemed to attach importance to where I was at the various times."

"A: I don't know what the reason for it was at this time."

"Q: I know you don't know the specific reason. Would it be fair to say the reason for this somehow related to the revocation of Dr. Miller's staff privileges?"

Hospital Lawyer: "Object and instruct him not to answer."

"Q: Do you have any reason to give us why this document showed up as part of papers that had been sent to the attorneys for the Hospital?"

The witness answered that it was "at the bottom of the cardboard box at the Hospital, I can assure you. I know damn well I wouldn't have sent that sort of thing to anybody."

"Q: Prior to your voluntary retirement, are you aware of anybody raising any questions about your fitness to serve?"

"A: Oh, yes."

The Chairman then turned to the Hospital Lawyer and asked: "You want me to answer first?"

Hospital Lawyer: "No. If you are concerned about answering this, let's talk about it outside."

When the pair returned to the table, the witness was asked:

"Q: Do you remember the question?"

"A: Yes, Roger Randall. He didn't think I was fit to do anything. He was disruptive, difficult at meetings. He just didn't — he was just bad, bad news even though I was the fellow that supported to put him on the Board."

"Q: Do you know what his objections were to your fitness to serve?"

"A: He's just a younger, smarter man than I am. He and I did not agree on what he thought was right and wrong and that was it."

The Chairman opened up and continued: "To just keep you along with this, he made a special trip to see (the Hospital Lawyer). He told the lawyer about it. The Hospital Lawyer said, "I think you should know that I'm going to tell (the Board Chairman) about this". That is all I knew about it. He knew about it." Finally (Randall) resigned from the Hospital Board.

Randall became a friend. He had called late one evening and asked if we could meet, and his first visit at the office was friendly and more than a little informative. He was not the first to resign from that Board when he, in good conscience, could not be one of The Chairman's rubber-stamp marionettes.

His description of the Hospital Lawyer's office was interesting. He described walking around bar bells and weight lifting equipment in the office. The Lawyer had explained that, in place of lunch, he lifted weights. In all fairness, I don't think I'm able to put that in proper perspective.

It seemed that both the Chairman and his Hospital Lawyers had forgotten that the Chairman had given a deposition when the Hospital had sued the Citizens Committee for defamation. The current responses were not matching his previous answers.

The next question and its answer was obviously false. The question was:

"Mr. Chairman, do you recall having a meeting at any point in time with a representative from the U.S. Postal Service, by the name of Omar?"

"A: No, I don't."

The theft of mail by the Administrator and the Chairman was obviously something they didn't care to talk about. But, this issue would certainly not just disappear.

As the deposition was coming to a close, the Chairman was asked:

"Q: In a question posed to you in interrogatories, you were asked whether you ever told anyone, that as long as you live, Dr. Ralph Miller will never get on the staff at Indiana Hospital. Did you ever make such a statement?"

"A: I'm sure I didn't."

Surprisingly, during that explanation I became aware that the Chairman, believe it or not, was becoming concerned. In place of answering questions, the Chairman was looking across the table and was speaking to me. He apparently fearfully thought that we could be convinced that he had no part in this - one of his many hurtful dismissals from that Hospital.

The Chairman continued with: "...I tried to explain that this was an action of peers, the physicians and has been done by the procedure and bylaws and rules and regulations of the Hospital, and I was the chap that signed the document."

As he looked across the table at me, he continued: "I have told that story to a number of people. You should know that, and that story has been twisted around from time to time where I have said it. I can assure you that I have never believed that I could personally stop you, and I never tried to."

As I sat and listened to that series of lies, I couldn't grasp how this tyrant could expect people to believe this cowardly ruse. Didn't he know that a former member of his own family had described the Chairman's discussing his role in the conspiracy during Sunday dinners? Didn't his lawyer tell him of the number of witnesses who had given affidavits describing his clandestine role in the Hospital firings and the Hospital's punitive atmosphere?

As I looked at that emotional, pitiful performance, I couldn't help but reflect on the nature of all the bullies we encounter through life. From school yard bullies to the courtroom bullies, they will all whimper excuses when directly confronted. The Chairman's deposition had laid the foundation for the deposition of two of the Medical Staff bullies and that of the Administrator.

The Administrator was more of a pathetic figure at the time of his deposition than a menacing administrator. He had been hired by the Chairman and had dutifully served as the Chairman's puppet, only to be suddenly fired by the Chairman and the Hospital Lawyers. He had been serving as a real estate agent and would be seen strolling through the Indiana malls from time to time. There was little doubt that he had wilfully served as the Chairman's hatchet man and had, on occasion, done the firings and had followed up with attempts to blackball people at other regional hospitals.

Judd, as the inquiring attorney at depositions, was not predictable and was adept at fending off the Hospital Lawyer's delaying tactics. As I had watched that Assistant Lawyer's antics during those depositions, I had inwardly smiled as I reflected that in Indiana County, the Hospital Lawyer may well have been considered "disruptive".

Next was the deposition of the former Hospital Administrator.

Judd quickly dispensed with the standard opening questions used to identify the witness, then quickly asked:

Q: "Mr. Administrator, on Tuesday, June 6th., as a part of legal proceedings in the case of Ralph Miller v. Indiana Hospital in the Court of Common Pleas of Indiana County, the Hospital Attorney made the following statement:

"One of the things I ought to point out at the outset of this proceeding and this summation what this is not; this for example is not a contest or a fight or an attack on Dr. Miller's right to practice Medicine. Indeed, it is not in any way an attack on his competency, his capability to practice in a highly specialized field of medicine, Urology. Indeed, I don't think anyone who has known Dr. Miller for even a short period of time would question one or two facts; one, that he is intelligent, indeed brilliant, and two, that he is capable, capable of practicing the finest type and standard of Urological Medicine in the country". Do you agree with that?"

The Administrator answered:

A: "Essentially, yes."

And then:

Q: "At any time after that, did you ever revise your opinion that Dr. Miller was capable of practicing the finest type and standard of Urological Medicine in the country?"

A: "No."

The next series of questions were designed to have the Administrator detail numerous facts that would confirm, for trial, the Hospital's "relevant market", which is essential in Antitrust litigation.

Contrary to the testimony of two former Chief Financial Officers of the Hospital, the Administrator answered the following:

Q: "As the Chief Executive Officer at Indiana Hospital, do you recall having any concerns that there were doctors at Indiana Medical Center employed by another doctor?"

A: "None whatsoever."

Q: "When did you first visit Dr. Miller's office?"

A: "As far as I can recall, when I became a patient of Dr. Miller."

Q: "Do you recall if you reviewed an affidavit from a Dr. Daugherty?"

A: "No."

Q: "In Dr. Daugherty's affidavit, he indicates that he worked in the Emergency Department of Indiana Hospital. He makes a statement that the Administrator, referring to you , "His tirade and hostility toward Dr. Miller culminated in a warning to me regarding Dr. Miller". Do you recall holding any hostility toward Dr. Miller?"

A: "I don't' recall any such event; none whatsoever."

Q: "Without regard to the event, do you recall holding any hostility toward Dr. Miller?"

The Hospital Lawyer interrupted with: "At any time to today whether he has ever had a hostile thought about Dr. Miller? Who hasn't?"

Mr. Crosby then asked: "Did you just insult the Plaintiff by commenting who hasn't had a hostile thought of Dr. Miller, knowing Dr. Miller is sitting here?"

The Assistant Hospital Lawyer: "If you want to read back in the record, you can construe what I say any way you choose. You're asking him at any time did he have a hostile thought, you're asking him to tell Dr. Miller who is sitting across from him that he is hostile to him and if he's ever been hostile to him, but yet you're upset when I make a comment."

Mr. Crosby: "Yes."

The Assistant Hospital Lawyer: "So what!"

Mr. Crosby: "You don't want to say anything else at this point in the record in light of your comment?"

The Assistant Hospital Lawyer: "My comment was simply designed to show that your question was irrelevant. There were a lot of people who I'm sure that Dr. Miller was hostile to and I'm sure that there are a lot of people that were hostile to Dr. Miller.

Mr. Crosby: " And you don't want to indicate anything else in the record?"

The Assistant Hospital Lawyer: "No. The only thing I will indicate on the record is that I meant no offense, and if counsel took it, then I don't know why he took it as an offense, but I certainly meant no offense. I meant to point out that the question was irrelevant, that was my only intent."

Q: "Please read the affidavit."

Mr. Crosby: "My question is, do you recall ever feeling hostility toward Dr. Miller?"

A: "Personal hostility?"

Q: "Yes."

A: "No."

Q: "Do you recall ever expressing your belief that Dr. Miller was going to be a problem to the Hospital at any point in time?"

A: "No."

Q: "Do you recall whether or not you reviewed the affidavit of the Hospital's former Chief Financial Officer?"

A: "Yes."

Q: "The financial officer indicates that, over a period of five years, you, and others were attempting to have Dr. Ralph Miller removed from the Medical Staff of Indiana Hospital. Were you doing so?"

A: "No."

Q: "He further indicates that you and others, were concerned that Dr. Miller's medical holdings such as the Medical Center, posed a threat to the Hospital. Did you ever perceive that the Indiana Medical Center posed any threat to the Hospital?"

A: "Never."

Q: "Would you deny the allegations in the affidavit?"

A: "I would deny any part of the statement there, that I had anything to do with it."

Q: "The affidavit further states that, under oath, that you worked to resist Dr. Miller's increased influence with the Medical Staff in Indiana Hospital. Do you deny that?"

A: "Yes."

With the Assistant Hospital Lawyer's next objection, he instructed the witness not to answer the question and then expressed the following:

"I would like the record to reflect that counsel, after my legitimate objection, and after I instructed the witness not to answer, whether he agrees with the objection or not, made a face, shook his head, had his lips go side to side and basically acted childishly."

Mr. Crosby: "I apologize. There was coffee coming down my lip and I was trying to catch it before it hit my shirt."

Before that exchange, I may have had some doubt about the Hospital Lawyer's ability to make an ass of himself in front of a jury - now, any doubt was dissipated.

The following was asked in relation to the hiring of the Board Chairman's son-inlaw as the Purchasing Director of the Hospital even though the young man had no experience in that field.

Q: "Whose decision was it to hire the son-in-law?"

A: "Mine."

The Administrator then described his help to the Hospital Prosecutor before and during the Kangaroo Court:

The Witness: "As the hearings progressed, our lawyer had certain things that he wanted to be provided with, and I would do that. I would see to it that he was provided information from the Medical Records Department" and, "during the hearings, I remained accessible to him, in the event that he needed any additional services of any kind."

I would help him load his car up with all the documents he brought with him or was taking with him as late as midnight or one o'clock in the morning." and, in regard to the hiring of the Hospital Prosecutor:

"He was engaged by the Board of the Hospital to represent the Hearing Committee of the Medical Staff."

and then:

Mr. Crosby: "As part of your role with the hospital, were you asked by anyone, prior to the commencement of the hearings or during the course of the hearings to contact any persons who, did in fact, become witnesses at the hearings?"

A: "Yes."

Q: "By whom?"

A: "A lady who is the Director of Volunteers at the Hospital appearedone morning and thought I should call a Mrs. (relative of my elderlypatient)."

Q: "Who was the volunteer?"

A: "Her first name was Marge."

Q: "Did you understand at that time that it involved the Miller hearings?"

A: "All I know was she wanted me to contact a Mrs. (daughter-in-law of elderly patient)."

Marge, one of the town's busybodies, had found that the family of my patient who had been allowed to die without proper help, were angry that the Hospital was using their father's death as a means for Dr. Vader to bring the charges leading to the Kangaroo Court.

(The daughter-in-law)) did testify for us at the Hospital hearings that their eighty-one-year-old father had been in poor health for some years and had neglected getting medical care. She further testified that the Administrator and Dr. Vader had called her the previous evening and tried to have her change her upcoming testimony.

The Assistant Hospital Lawyer, attempting to block this damaging testimony, interrupted and tried to bully a change of subject. He said:

"I'm getting a little annoyed because these questions have all been asked, not in the exact words, but I'm going to have to stop it soon. And, I may have to go to Judge Bloch soon because we're not supposed to be doing this, we both know it."

But, the cat was out of the bag - both the Administrator and the Board Chairman had been attempting to claim no involvement with the Hospital hearings. It was interesting to watch them be under oath contradicting each other as well as themselves.

The Administrator had called the Pennsylvania Department of Transportation and had recruited a witness for the hearings who had testified to one of the phony charges compiled by the Hospital Prosecutor and the Medical Staff Executive Committee.

Mr. Crosby asked: "Do you recall calling anybody involved in any way with the Department of Transportation, in regard to anything to do with the Miller hearings?"

A: "Not in connection with the hearings; I don't believe, no."

Once again, the Hospital Lawyer, after an objection to a question and a speech, advised the witness:

"I'm going to instruct him not to answer the question." He wanted to keep his objection off the record but Judd said:

"No, I want it on the record. I find when you interrupt before the witness answers my question and then repeat something to the extent he doesn't remember, when he hasn't even indicated he doesn't remember that really what you're doing is telling the witness what to say when you ultimately do let him answer my question."

The Administrator was then asked about two physicians that were admitted to the Hospital staff despite poor recommendations. The names were Fezzi Kattahachchi and Wijepala Akcay. In response to questions regarding the qualifications of physicians applying for the Medical Staff, the Administrator answered after the Hospital Lawyer interrupted:

"I do not recall, no. I can't recall specifically, no."

Judd, recalling that one of the charges leveled against me at the Kangaroo Court was failure to complete medical records on time asked:

"And in the case of Indiana Hospital, during your tenure as CEO, would it be fair to say that was a very common practice of staff physicians, that is, failure to complete their medical records in a timely fashion?"

The former Administrator answered: "It's a common problem at all hospitals."

When asked about mail that was intercepted by him and the Board Chairman, the following was asked and answered:

Q: "Was there a hospital policy with regard to mail which involved Dr. Ralph Miller or the Concerned Citizens Committee?"

A: "No, no policy specifically regarding that group, none whatsoever. I don't recall any."

The next question asked about the large envelope that was mailed by Dr. Miller to Judge Smith in Pittsburgh but intercepted by the Administrator and the Board Chairman, and was copied and given to the Hospital Lawyers.

Q: "Did you receive instructions with regard to that piece of mail from the Board Chairman?"

A: "I think I did, yes."

Q: "What were (his) instructions?"

A: "File it."

Q: "Did he tell you where to file it?"

A: "No. I think he just said, "File it"."

Q: "Do you recall whether or not you copied the materials that were in the envelope?"

A: "I don't recall."

Q: "Do you recall whether or not you instructed (your Secretary) to copy the documents?"

A: "I don't recall."

When he was asked about his interceptions of Citizens Committee mail, the Hospital Lawyer interrupted with: "Are we almost done with this area? I would like to get this deposition over with."

That remark was followed by the following:

Mr. Crosby: "Shoosh."

The Assistant Hospital Lawyer: "Hey, Judd, please remember you are a professional."

Mr. Crosby: "I know."

The Hospital Lawyer: "I would appreciate if you would treat me like a professional. If we don't move on, I am going to stop the questioning."

We had determined over a period of time that the Hospital Management and the Medical Staff politicians had little, if any, regard for the truth. The Kangaroo Court was an extreme example of deception by the Hospital. But, the final minutes of the Administrator's deposition would show the disregard these people had for each other. As I listened to those final minutes of testimony, the questions and answers were giving new meaning to the phrase, "No honor among thieves". See if you can believe the following colloquy:

Q: "Did you not voluntarily leave the Hospital as Chief Executive Officer?"

The Hospital Lawyer: "Instruct the witness not to answer. The question has been asked and answered."

A: "No."

Q: "While you were not given any reasons, what was your perception as the reason that you were forced out as the Chief Executive Officer of the Hospital?"

A: "It came as a surprise."

Q: "Could you give me what your beliefs have been by way of speculation?"

The Witness: "I believe the Chairman of the Board decided that I should leave, and that, after a period of time, he accomplished his goal, period."

Q: "Do you have any idea how long, it took him to accomplish his goal?"

A: "I recall he was creating circumstances toward that end about three months before, three, three and a half months before it happened, yes. He was setting the stage."

Q: "I believe you indicated that the Hospital Board Chairman began "setting things up" and I was asking what did he do?"

A: "During a routine annual recommendation, we were making recommendations to the Board for salary increases, wage and salary increases. All were accepted except about a certain number of department heads, key department heads. I was told that the recommended percentage for everyone was not to be granted for this group. Further, I was told that it was my duty to inform these people that it was my idea not to recommend an increase."

Q: "Was it the Chairman who told you not to tell them that?"

A: "Yes."

Q: "Was it, in fact, your idea not to recommend an increase?"

A: "No, I was recommending one thing and he told me the Executive Committee of the Board decided not to accept that recommendation."

Q: "It's my understanding that the Chairman gave you orders to represent something to the Staff at the Hospital that wasn't true. Did (he) instruct you to lie to other employees of the Hospital?"

The Hospital Lawyer: "I'm instructing the witness not to answer."

The former administrator didn't need to answer. He had described, with finality, the viciously punitive Hospital atmosphere. The stage was set for us to document the spread of that corruption to the Medical Staff politicians who had been encouraged by the Administration. The documentation would be through the depositions of Dr. Vance Vader and Dr. Nathan Goldfarb - coming up soon.

It was certainly no secret that Vader and Goldfarb were the outspoken advocates in the Medical Staff that, very often, the other members of the staff followed. I would, with some regularity, find myself all alone in not going along with their self-appointed authority. It had become evident that the nasty atmosphere would likely deter truly high quality medical and surgical specialists from coming to town. One surgeon, who did come to town, claimed that he had been aware of the atmosphere before he could get both feet past the front door. He and his spouse later described the Vader family as frequently and anxiously looking over their shoulders.

Vader and Goldfarb, in addition to influencing the Medical Staff, had ingratiated themselves with the Hospital Administration and the Board. Vader and the Administrator were seen with their heads together conversing in hushed tones almost daily. Meanwhile, Goldfarb and spouse pushed their social agenda to include the local judges and the Hospital Board members.

I had admittedly underestimated the effectiveness of this pair, Vader and Goldfarb. But, their uncontrolled animus was their common trait, if not their driving life force. The venom they spewed was becoming frightening to watch. It appeared to me that this pair could not have a normal existence and vigor while harboring such self- destructive hatred. I had truly never seen either of this pair smile - never. I had often reflected that they may very well be leading a very unhappy, unrewarding existence.

With Vader it had begun when I turned down his suggestion for his own office building next to ours. With Goldfarb it had begun when I began to question some of his activities, rather than let his sly, behind-the-scenes activities go unchallenged.

Goldfarb's deposition was taken on the second floor of a turn-of-the-century house that housed a law firm in downtown Indiana. While we were still climbing the steps to the second floor, the Assistant Hospital Lawyer shouted chastisement over the upper railing for our slightly late arrival. The pompous Goldfarb just stared at us. We were led into a small bedroom facing the front street which was apparently now serving as a conference room. The Court Reporter swore the witness to tell the truth. That was the first and last time, during that encounter, that truth was given much significance.

When one of the pediatricians at the Medical Center had broken his contract, with the urging of "The Boys", Goldfarb led the charge by attending the court hearings with a number of the Medical Staff in the local Court, obviously in support of the pediatrician. He had also signed derogatory letters published in the Local Blab.

One of the early questions and its answers were as follows:

Q: "Do you recall anyone submitting a statement to the Media or the Court with respect to the law suit between Dr. McGee and Dr. Miller that read as follows? "We the undersigned physicians oppose and deplore the action by Ralph J. Miller and confirmed in the Indiana Court legally forbidding a well qualified and capable pediatrician from practicing within a twenty-five mile radius of Indiana for the next two years"."

A: "I would say it sounds like something I would agree to. O.K., Yep. It looks like I did. I'm delighted to have signed this."

The published letter carried the signatures of several of the Hospital Medical staff with Nathan Goldfarb's signature right at the top.

During the litigation between the Hospital and the Citizens Committee, Goldfarb had written a long letter, printed in Joe Donnelly's newspaper. In the letter was the statement: "Only one physician has had his privileges permanently revoked and, in this case, it was the judgement of the Medical Staff and the Board of Directors that quality care in the Hospital would be sacrificed if this physician were allowed to remain on the staff."

This led to the following questions and answers:

Q: "I ask you on what basis you used the term "permanently revoked"?

I take it this refers to Dr. Miller."

A: "I would assume."

Q: "Well, what do you mean by "permanently revoked"?"

A: "It didn't mean anything other than what the word says. Permanent means permanent."

When asked about his influence with the local paper, the question was:

"Did you make any recommendations or requests that Mr. Donnelly do anything in regard through his position as Publisher of the Gazette?"

A: "I wouldn't do that. I wouldn't pressure from a friendship to do that."

But then the question was: "Did you ever have any discussions with Mr. Donnelly about the media coverage of the revocation of Dr. Miller's privileges and the McGee law suit and any other law suits involving Dr. Miller in the Hospital?"

A: "I'm sure, that at some point in time, I voiced my opinion to Editor Joe Donnelly. I felt this Committee for Concerned Citizens was getting entirely too much play because they were doing and did terrible harm to the Hospital through unjustified accusation."

Goldfarb, in his righteous indignation, probably allowed himself to believe that he and Dr. Vader had not been the real source of the "terrible harm to the Hospital". I had come to believe that he and his spouse considered themselves on a plane above mere mortals. They obviously considered themselves royalty here on earth, infallible and here to reign.

The next question relating to Goldfarb's attempts to influence judges was:

"Dr. Goldfarb, in your answers to interrogatories, you have stated that you urged only one person to attend the McGee law suit hearing. Was that your wife?"

A: "That sounds like it."

Q: "The question and answers indicate that the reason you urged her to attend was because you thought it was "interesting".

A: "Well, it was of general interest - forcing a pediatrician..trying to force a pediatrician out of town. My wife, along with me, have been involved in the medical community for years and I still say it was interesting because we never had anything like that before; had anything like that since. I hope we will never or do during my time here."

Q: "Was urging your wife to attend intended to show or indicate support for Dr. McGee?"

A: "Oh, not especially."

The glib suggestion that a pediatrician was being forced from town was contrary to the fact that the pediatrician was encouraged to stay in town and honor his contract.

The skillful sophistry had been echoed by "The Boys" of the Medical Staff to the media and anyone who would listen. In a search for the motive, the following questions were asked:

Q: "Could you describe what your feelings were toward him (Dr. Miller) prior to the Hospital hearings?"

A: "Personally he was awfully hard to like, always has been. And I didn't like him. You know, after I got to know him I didn't like him. And I make no bones about that at all, but professionally I had nothing against him."

And:

A: "On a few occasions we socialized and, at those times I found him friendly and nice in those early days. As I said, after I got to know him, his disruptive behavior and trouble-making penchant just turned me off completely and he just has always been a troublemaker. And that's the reason."

Q: "Did this disruptive behavior that you're talking about be in regard to Hospital affairs?"

A: "Yeah, that too. I don't recall specific incidents, I just recall the general deportment and so forth, his actions and so forth."

As I sat there and listened to those remarks and after reading the transcripts, I was beginning to think that maybe this fellow really didn't like me.

It became known that if a nurse would call Goldfarb for help at night or at the golf course, she could expect a barrage of verbal abuse even though he would happily castigate anyone else, not in his good graces for anything similar. With this in mind, and knowing that nurses had given affidavits describing this, Goldfarb was asked: "At any time did you advise the Emergency Room personnel that you did not wish to receive any emergency call after eleven o'clock in the evening?"

The answer reflected that the Doctor was establishing his own rules - no one else and not the Hospital.

His Answer: "At numerous times I had requested that the Emergency Department that I not be called during the night for things that could be taken care of the next day. So, I had guidelines as to what I wanted to be called for because it was very difficult practicing all day and being bothered at night, extraneous, unnecessary calls."

Nurses at the Hospital had described Goldfarb telling them that Dr. Miller had put his wife in the local home for battered women. This is rotten, unprincipled behavior for anyone, but for a physician to be so blinded by hatred that he would lower himself that far was difficult to comprehend. Bill London and I would often have coffee together on Sunday mornings. At the time, I repeated the nurses' report of Goldfarb's fabrication during that next Sunday's coffee. Bill was a soft-spoken gentleman, but on that occasion he said, "That son-of-a-bitch".

The obvious question was asked:

Q: "Dr. Goldfarb, did you ever engage in a conversation or hear a conversation regarding Dr. Miller's wife having been in a home for battered women?"

A: "I had heard by the grapevine—I don't remember where or how, it's a small town. Things get around. I remember hearing somewhere along the line that Dr. Miller's wife had been treated at the Alice Paul House. That was all I ever heard about it."

Q: "Did you ever question anybody about that or relate that alleged incident to anyone?"

A: "I never did. I never did."

I had had a fair amount of practice fending off wild tales that originated from the little Hospital Group, but this was the grandaddy of nastiness. I was truly annoyed but again had to remind myself of the admonition: "On being hated, don't give way to hating, or being lied about don't deal in lies". I remember countering Goldfarb's tale with a little humor; by telling people that I had never had to raise a hand against Joan, except in self-defense.

Goldfarb's close relationship with President Judge Handler came to the fore when Handler dismissed Judge Earley from our case in the State

Court and then dissolved the injunction that Earley had imposed on the Hospital. It was all too obvious, particularly since Judge Earley had told me that Goldfarb had called him at least twice, attempting to influence his rulings.

The questions relating to Goldfarb's attempts to influence judicial decisions were as follows:

Q: "Did you and your wife know Judge Earley personally?"

A: "Sure, we've known Judge Earley for many years."

Q: "Did you or your wife ever have any discussions with Judge Earley or Judge Handler about the McGee situation?"

A: "Never to my recollection, and I would also add that I would deem it the height of impropriety for me to contact a judge. I'd be afraid I'd be held in contempt of court or something. It was—no, I never approached a judge. In fact, it never even entered my mind to do that."

Someone was demonstrating unusual skill at prevarication - and it wasn't Judge Earley. Judge Earley had unequivocally described Goldfarb's calls to him, trying to influence his decisions.

Goldfarb had undoubtedly been the spark plug of the Executive Committee group dedicated to getting me out of the Hospital and probably out of town. He was asked if he favored revocation of my hospital privileges:

A: "It would not have been my place to recommend revocation. I wasn't on the Board. Frankly, I would have been just as happy if he would have picked up and gone some place else, but I had nothing to say about revoking his privileges or even suggesting that he be revoked because you don't do that to people."

Then:

Q: "You were on the Committee at the time that it recommended that his staff privileges be revoked."

A: "I believe I was."

Q: "And would you have cast a vote to recommend revocation of privileges?"

A: "Probably."

As a matter of record, this gentleman made the motion to revoke my privileges.

The surgical department meetings were always something less than organized.

As the young lady doctor who resigned from the Staff had said, she, "never saw a staff meeting brought to order". Goldfarb and his crew had staged the coup with a nasty telephone campaign replacing the Surgical Department Head because he had attempted to attain reasonable standards for the operating suite. At one of the meetings after Goldfarb had taken over the Department Chairmanship, he made a pitch for everyone to be generous with donations for the Board Chairman's new Hospital wing.

Someone asked if there were any reasons that we shouldn't give generously to the new project.

I took the bait at that meeting and gave a number of reasons: the vindictive Hospital atmosphere, the recent nasty political climate and the standards of mediocrity that ruled the entire place.

The next day, we found copies of the minutes of that meeting - prepared by Goldfarb himself. The fourth paragraph of the two page report read:

"Dr. Miller then launched into a long and familiar harangue about the ills of the Indiana Hospital in general and the evils of the not-so-wonderful Medical Staff in particular, as he viewed them. In typical selfrighteous and pontifical manner, he defended the former Chief of Surgery, listed his ideas what a doctor should be and quoted unconfirmed statements from supposedly disgruntled previous staff members and lashed out at the targets of his wrath".

Goldfarb then distributed his "minutes" widely. The writings of the Chairman-Secretary seemed to have lifted a few passages from the Old Testament and had the effect of documenting the response when challenged with constructive criticism.

I had attempted, for some time, to have a department Secretary and to have the meetings conducted in accord with Robert's Rules. That set of "minutes" seemed to have its effect. At the next meeting, I again made a motion for an elected Secretary. The motion passed and, surprisingly, I was nominated for the post. I had recently resigned as Editor of the very modest County Medical Society Journal and, at this point, again cited a busy schedule as an excuse for declining. But, we at last, had a Secretary who would deliver objective minutes without the lavish personalized descriptions of the Department's skirmishes.

During this deposition, these voluminous minutes were shown to Goldfarb to confirm his creation and then they were entered into the record.

One of Goldfarb's operating room mishaps had been investigated by the Pennsylvania Department of Health. He was asked: "Do you know if any physicians on the Staff of Indiana Hospital were investigated by the Department of Health for any reason?"

A: "No, I don't recall anything like that."

Q: "You still don't recall any investigation by the Department of Health?"

A: "I just don't recall offhand."

In light of my "disruptive" behavior, we tried to find what Goldfarb considered disruptive. Minutes of a Surgical Department meeting were entered into the record and a passage from those minutes was read:

Q: "There is a statement in the middle of this paragraph here which says, "a heated discussion followed". Take as much time as you want to read it. Did you consider that "heated discussion "to be disruptive or any one involved?"

A: "I think there were differences of opinion. And general surgeons have generally some very strong opinions as to how things should be run in the hospital. I don't consider this particular thing disruptive, it was more discussive than it was disruptive."

Q: "And when you say heated, does that mean voices were raised?"

A: "It could have been, yes. I would say voices were raised because some of these people raised their voices rather routinely."

Also entered into the record was the successful conclusion of that meeting which Goldfarb had entered into that meeting's minutes. It read:

"Dr. Miller then moved that the Department Head submit, in writing, to the Board of the Hospital, through the Chief Executive Officer, a request for relief anesthesiology when the anesthesiologist is away. The motion was seconded and passed unanimously."

Later, the deposition of Dr. Vance Vader was, indeed, the climax of our series of depositions. The long-term intrigue involving the Board Chairman, the Administrator, Goldfarb and Vader, with their lawyers, had already been solidly documented, allowing an optimistic view of the chances for our case before a federal jury. Dr.Vance Vader had been implicated in the planning leading to the Kangaroo Court, but had shown that he was masterfully adept at agitating others to take the lead in the unhappy Hospital machinations. This time, though, he had uncharacteristically dictated a savage report a few hours after he had stood by and watched my elderly patient die - the report that began the entire chain of events leading to the Kangaroo Court.

After I had had that first meeting with the Medical Staff Executive Committee and I was accused of refusing to discuss the matters with them, they found that they had violated Hospital bylaws. Vader then dictated a back-dated memo to the Administrator's Secretary asking for my dismissal. His initial report began: "Pursuant to Medical Staff rules and Regulations, Section I, paragraph four, the following report is submitted for your information and consideration of the Executive Committee."

Vader, always walking in the shadows, looking over his shoulder or huddled in his little Hospital office, was obviously confident of his support from the Administration and the Board Chairman. In fact, in his hatred and in his gratification at being the CEO's advisor, he was probably oblivious to the obvious - both he and the Administrator were becoming pawns in the Board Chairman's blueprint for immortality.

Vader's "report" was a recitation of the electrocardiographic findings that he noted as he stood by and watched my elderly patient die.

Amazingly, he dismissed help to care for the patient. The report read: "Dr. (Clippins) arrived almost simultaneously with me, and when he observed that appropriate management had been effected he questioned whether his services were needed. When informed that sufficient help was present he departed."

As Vader's report continued, the notion that only practitioners such as Lester Lazarus were qualified to treat medical problems was revealed with the following:

Vader had written: "The clinical record reveals that the patient with a primary diagnosis of respiratory disease and only a secondary diagnosis of microscopic hematuria was admitted to the service of Dr. R. J. Miller, a physician with hospital privileges limited to Urologic Surgery."

He continued:

"I was astonished that this physician would attempt to initiate and continue management in a patient with primary cardio-pulmonary symptomatology and, additionally, medical consultation should have been obtained since management of this patient is beyond the approved hospital practice privileges of this physician."

The final distortion came with:

"Finally, when the patient presented an acute circulatory arrest, the attending physician did not come to assist in resuscitation efforts or really express any concern over the condition of the patient."

Knowing that to be a fabrication, Vader remained in the shadows and never testified while seven Hospital Department Heads throughout the Northeastern United States refuted Vader's wild charges at the Kangaroo Court. In addition, the patient's family joined in our actions against the

Hospital's charges. Our efforts to have the appearance of Vader stepping from the shadows to testify before a court reporter at the Kangaroo Court was, indeed, not successful.

At Vader's deposition, as the Hospital Lawyer, once again, led us down the carpeted steps to his firm's conference room; I found myself wondering how Vader would appear. He was seated at the conference table and was motionless - almost rigid - and stared straight ahead as we entered giving no sign of recognition. His thick lenses set in those black, tortoise-shell frames hid those eyes; those eyes that had projected hatred, beyond belief.

As I sat down opposite him, I recalled a Labor Day evening, the worst night of my life. After those life-saving transfusions for Dad, some years earlier, he had developed progressive liver disease. It was hepatitis - a truly horrible disease - leading to a series of hospitalizations, each more terrifying than the one before. We were becoming helpless to manage the ravages of that infection. I was nearing exhaustion from a night and day vigil, and on that Labor Day evening, left the Hospital for a brief rest and dinner at home. No sooner in the door, the phone rang. It was the Emergency Room. Dr. Vader had instructed me to insert a catheter in a patient he was admitting. The nurses knew it was a terrible time for our family and didn't mind asking Vader if he would pass the catheter. He refused and I left the dinner table and headed for the Emergency Room. Unfortunately, Vader was headed down the back steps to the parking lot as I started up. With a big grin he gave out a bitter, sarcastic, "Working tonight, Dr. Miller?"

The callousness and malice of that despicable goading was shrugged off for the moment - I was already hurting so badly that a little more didn't matter. But, I never will forget the look in those eyes with the realization at that point that this was more than a professional dislike. I was dealing with a pathologic personality. Dad died a few hours later.

As the deposition was about to get under way and as I looked at that rigid stare through the thick lenses, I wondered how such a grotesque personality could survive in a hospital environment unless the environment itself was grotesque. This was the person who advised the duplicitous Administrator.

In that environment, Goldfarb and Vader were indeed sufficiently influential with the Medical Staff and had managed to become the Medical Staff spokespeople with the Hospital Board. It may very well have been that their biases were presenting a very distorted picture to the Governing Body.

For instance, this pair espoused a firm set of ethical and professional standards for the Medical Staff and an entirely different set for themselves.

At the time of Vader's deposition, we had valid affidavits from Hospital people describing Vader's difficulty with off-hour calls for help. There was a description of his refusal to help a patient whose swollen tongue progressively caused the patient to die a horrible death. Later, his demand for an advance payment before he would see an Emergency Department heart patient was revealed in another affidavit.

The questions relating to those events began the deposition as follows:

Q: "Are you aware (Dr. Vader), in your entire tenure at Indiana Hospital of any physician refusing to see a patient in the Hospital unless they received payment for their services from the patient?"

The crafty answer was: "I vaguely recall that there was concern with Dr. Miller in regard to his acceptance of Medical Assistance patients (patients on welfare)."

Q: "Now, in addition to Dr. Miller, are you aware of anyone else that has ever refused to see a patient at the Emergency Room of Indiana Hospital unless they received payment from the patient first before providing services?"

A: "I recall no physician who did that. I don't recall one."

Q: "To your knowledge: if a physician did in fact refuse to see a patient in the E.R. of the Hospital unless they first received payment for their services would there be no misconduct or wrongful conduct as far as the Hospital is concerned?"

I think the witness, in his own mind, quite likely felt that the truth was anything he uttered, without any relevance to his own conduct.

His Answer:

" I think it would be misconduct. I think that would be abusing a patient who might need care. If you have to have the money before you are going to treat the poor person, I think that is inconceivable."

The Hospital Lawyer, at one point described that he had "coached" Vader the previous day when they had reviewed a number of documents. As Vader continued his rigid recital of his coached answers, sprinkled with an adjustable memory, he was becoming pleased that his answers were fending off the potentially damaging questions. In reality, he was systematically boxing himself in when he would be confronted with testimony and documents at trial.

Vader described that he had stopped referring patients to me shortly before he left private practice and became a Hospital employee (and advisor to the Administrator). He began a series of fabrications which seemed to encourage him to continue with each tale a little wilder than the preceding. Judd skillfully allowed him to rage on.

The question was asked:

Q: "Can you think of any way, that if I wanted to obtain the records or the chart on which you formulated your opinion that you could be specific enough so that I could get those records?"

A: "I would have no record of that patient's name or hospital number anywhere."

And then:

Q: "Can you think of other specific incidents, Dr. (Vader) and I'll refresh you back to the original question talking about Dr. Miller's professional abilities and professional competency?"

A: "Yes."

Q: "Please continue."

Vader then gave his version of my elderly patient's death when he had simply just watched the patient die. When the Hospital Lawyer attempted to stop that line of questioning, and after Vader had admitted that no emergency medications had been given to my patient, he objected to the following questions and advised Vader not to answer, resulting in the following comment from Attorney Crosby:

"Just so you know again, it is our position that Dr. (Vader) filed his report concerning Dr. Miller, trying to cover his own mistakes in resuscitative efforts of the patient. I am free to ask him anything in terms of his involvement."

Vader was encouraged to continue: and he did.

The Witness: "Well, I have always considered the care of patients as much an art as science, and I think it has a great deal to do with the success of the practitioner. Ethics are involved. We have to consider these things."

This was a strange lecture for a practitioner who had given up regular contact with patients to become a Hospital employee after only a few years of practice.

He continued with his tale: "I remember one of my first meetings with Dr. Miller.

Dr. Miller called me aside in a hallway and said, I expect when you admit patients to this Hospital, that if they have any sort of a urinary diagnosis that you will be putting them on my service; won't you Doctor! As a young practitioner, I was quite intimidated by that reference."

This line of questions and answers was uncovering the source of some of the malignant blather that I had managed to ignore for so long. As I listened to those pathetic fabrications, I couldn't help reflect on the thoughts of some of the professionals who left town for friendlier surroundings. One surgeon who left, expressed his disgust by calling the Medical Staff "sick" and an exiting Emergency Room physician described the Medical Staff as "sicker than their patients.

The witness, despite his rigid stare straight ahead, seemed to be energizing himself and we were, at long last, uncovering the source of some very strange tales that probably had been circulated around the Hospital and the town. We had obtained from the Hospital file that the Administrator had kept, a folder with the typed heading - "Material given to (The Administrator) by Dr. (Vader) relating to Dr. R. J. Miller". Inside was an article on paranoid schizophrenia that Vader had provided. It was obviously the genesis of Smith's frequent comments that Miller was "paranoid".

Now the questions to Vader:

Q: "Did you ever come to the conclusion Dr. Miller suffered from any type of psychiatric or psychological impairment?"

A: "I think it has been mentioned by people that Dr. Miller may have some psychological problems, personality disorders."

Q: "Did you ever come to a conclusion yourself?"

A: "No, I was never qualified in psychiatry."

Q: "Do you recall ever giving articles with regard to psychiatrically impaired physicians to any hospital administrator at any point in time?"

A: "I don't recall giving such."

There had been an occasional physical confrontation between staff physicians - usually disregarded. But the response to a question relating to that was interesting:

Q: "Doctor, have you ever become aware from any source whatsoever of physical confrontations between staff Physicians on Hospital premises?"

A: "I have only heard about them."

Q: "How many have you heard about?"

A: "Well, physical confrontations, I heard one, been involved in one."

Q: "You were involved in one?"

A: "Oh, yes."

Q: "Tell me about that and when was that?"

A: "I think Dr. Miller was mad at me one time. He swerved his automobile very close to me, caused me to jump back between a couple of cars in the parking lot, scared me half to death and then raised his fist."

Q: "Was there any contact between you two?"

A: "No. I tore my trousers on another car; other than that, there was no contact with his vehicle."

Q: "Did you ever talk to Dr. Miller about that?"

A: "No, I didn't talk to Dr. Miller about that."

We have all heard exaggerations that greatly stretch the truth, but this story by Vader was a pure hallucination.

The depositions had been effective in helping plan our case at trial, but in addition they were exposing some of the squalid mentalities who had become the Hospital's ruling faction.

I was now hearing the tales - probably first handed - "My wife in the home for battered women", "patient mistreatment leading to death", suggestions of a "paranoid psychosis" in my hospital file, "attempts to run down a physician in a parking lot". These people were sick and we had just deposed one of the sickest.

The climactic moment of the deposition occurred when Judd asked:

Q: "Are you aware of anybody other than Ralph Miller who has had their privileges at Indiana Hospital revoked or terminated?"

A: "No."

Q: "Of all the physicians that you have become aware of at Indiana Hospital during your entire tenure, would you hold the opinion, Dr. (Vader), that Ralph Miller is the least well qualified professionally of all the physicians that have ever practiced at Indiana Hospital?"

Then:

The Assistant Hospital Lawyer: "I am going to object to this. That is really kind of silly. I am not sure there is a purpose to this, what relevance this has, where he ranks him on a list of Doctors he knows. I am going to instruct him not to answer."

Mr. Crosby: "I am going to state on the record, and you can do whatever you want. This witness instigated the entire proceedings against Ralph Miller with regard to treatment that Dr. Miller rendered in the (elderly patient) case."

The Assistant Hospital Lawyer continued to filibuster and the witness began to get redder and redder until the veins in his neck appeared ready to pop. He ignored his instructions and blurted:

"The least qualified, that is the end of your question; wasn't it? Was he the least qualified to practice? I am going to say yes in my opinion."

During the deposition, Vader had been skillfully required to date each of his fantasies. At trial he would again be asked to recall all my transgressions.

He would again repeat his testimony that I was the "least qualified " of all the physicians on the Hospital Medical Staff. It was established, during this deposition, that all of those transgressions took place before he left private practice to become a Hospital employee.

At trial, I would then take the stand and testify that Vader called me one evening, shortly before he left private practice, flatteringly saying he wanted the "best urologist in Western Pennsylvania" for a patient he was admitting from a northern Pennsylvania hamlet. We would then present to the Court and Jury that patient's Hospital and Office records:

<u>IT WAS VADER'S FATHER!</u>

Chapter 18

"The American people are very generous people and will forgive almost any weakness, with the possible exception of stupidity."

— *Will Rogers*

THE POSTAL INSPECTION SERVICE

How many times have we heard, "Don't fool with the mail - that's a federal offense?"

At this point in time, I think some folks <u>can</u> fool with the mail and get away with it. Here's why:

During that first period of discovery in the federal antitrust action against the Hospital, Ralph Smith, (the lawyer son of the Judge), and I had been going through and recording Hospital documents that had been sent to the Hospital Lawyer's office. I had come across a document that I didn't believe - a document I couldn't believe. It was a photocopy of a large manilla envelope with a row of canceled stamps. I knew at once that it was the envelope that I had mailed to Judge Smith in Pittsburgh - an envelope that had never been delivered. For some reason, the addressee had been torn away. Ralph didn't understand why I was just sitting there staring at the sheet and urged me to keep moving with our chore of recording each document in that pile. Any explanation to him would have tipped our hand with the two paralegals who sat there watching, while I dictated into the tape recorder, a description of each Hospital document we uncovered. I didn't want to risk having a crucial document disappear from that file.

As I resumed uncovering documents in that file, it was obvious that the next forty-five or so pages had been the contents of that large envelope.

How did my mail get from the post office into the Hospital files? With my mind racing, I was finding it difficult to concentrate on the remaining documents.

When we finally took a break, I explained to Ralph. He just looked. I don't think he thought what I was telling him was possible. We were, however, making a list of those documents we would request as part of the discovery process. Once again, I had to smile at the Hospital Lawyer's instruction for all of those several thousand documents to be serially numbered. We couldn't see any way he could now refuse to supply a document requested by number.

When we returned to our chore we came across letters from The Hospital Administrator to government agencies admitting that he had intercepted letters from them addressed to the Citizens Committee for Hospital Improvement and admitting that he was returning those letters to them rather than giving them to the Committee. He said he didn't know the names of the Committee members, even though the Hospital had hired an investigator to identify the members.

To no one's surprise, the Hospital Lawyers waited several weeks to send us copies of that bizarre collection of Hospital documents that would, not only document the interception and copying of my mail and the Citizens Committee mail, but would reveal some of the peculiar activities of the Hospital group.

Another Hospital Lawyer - Clara Mattern - who had been the self-appointed hearing officer at the Kangaroo Court, had also reacted to the intercepted mail with a letter to the accreditation organization of hospitals, basing a series of complaints on information she found in the purloined mail. We found a copy of her letter in the Hospital file.

In the face of the serious nature of the theft, we decided to wait, for a time, until we could determine the extent of the crime before reporting to the Postal Service.

During that period, both the Administrator, the Board Chairman and the Administrator's Secretary underwent deposition as part of the defamation suit that the Hospital had brought against me and the Citizens Committee. As part of the day-long responses to questioning, both the Board Chairman and the Administrator admitted to receipt of the mail, as well as copying and retention of the mail with copies sent to the Hospital

Lawyers. They admitted the return of intercepted Citizens Committee mail to the original senders with a cover letter dictated by the Administrator.

At first they denied knowing members of the Citizens Committee who would accept delivery of the mail but eventually the Administrator said, under oath: "I think that the identity...from the articles in the local press, ...I think they were known...I think some of the names were known to us, yes". He also said..." (it was) directed by the Postal Authorities to the Hospital and inadvertently opened in my office; not only opened, but the letter was exposed and shown to us - to my secretary and myself." He was apparently detailing the Board Chairman himself opening someone else's mail.

As to the large manilla envelope with its forty-five documents, the Administrator later denied ever seeing it. But, when interviewed by the Postal Inspector, at a later date, he advised that it was addressed to a judge in Pittsburgh. How did he know that, if he denied seeing the large envelope with its addressee torn away?

The four plus years with the Postal Inspection Service, was during the time that we were heavily involved with the antitrust litigation. It was not until those years were ending that we finally obtained internal Postal Inspection Service documents which, in themselves, tell the unusual story.

During a period of several months, we were watching our mail carefully and would occasionally find an envelope which had been carefully opened and resealed. I finally mailed a complaint to the Postal Service on a May 7th. and, thereby, opened the four-year saga with the United States Postal Inspectors.

After a few weeks - probably a pretty fair time for a federal agency - the call came. It was from Postal Inspector Charles O'Marr, who was calling from Harrisburg. In a businesslike tone, he advised that he was calling to arrange an appointment to discuss my complaint.

O'Marr came to the office on the following June 18th., as we were finishing office hours. The Inspector was a nice looking fellow in casual dress and had an equally casual manner. After a friendly handshake, he slipped off his zippered jacket and comfortably sat across from me at my desk and advised that he would be taking a few notes.

During that first, almost three-hour meeting, I gave the Inspector additional copies of the intercepted mail that had been retrieved from the Hospital files: copies of diverted Citizens Committee mail, the Administrator's cover letters and the photocopies of the large manilla envelope and its forty-five enclosed pages. O'Marr was intrigued by those copies and wondered out loud why anyone would tear the address off the envelope after it had fallen into their hands. He noted that the Hospital Lawyers had serially numbered the photocopies with 1144 stamped on the large envelope and the enclosed forty-five pages of numbers starting with 1145.

The Inspector reviewed our postage meter contract and noted that the serial number of our postage meter matched the cancellation on the envelope and that the amount of postage on the envelope corresponded to the weight of those forty-five pages of documents. The cancellation of the stamps by the Indiana Post Office noted that the envelope had been posted on October 30. It appeared that, after diversion of the envelope, someone had pasted a small square label on the envelope with the typed date, "Nov. 5" - six days after the postmark. The typing on the small label resembled the typing of the Hospital Secretary's typewriter. The Inspector also took with him a copy of the transcript of the Administrator's deposition which included the Administrator's admission of receipt of the intercepted letters.

Before leaving, O'Marr advised that the matters discussed were violations of the United States Postal Code and that there were possible "additional violations" related to fraud if members of the Hospital Governing Body had profited or if their activities had "increased the cost of health care to the public." He advised that he would be seeking advice from an Assistant U.S. Attorney in Pittsburgh, as to whether to confront The Administrator and his Secretary directly or have them appear before a grand jury.

On leaving, O'Marr advised that there was no "statute of limitation" on the crimes discussed but he, nevertheless, would be back in touch in a few days. He advised that I go to Pittsburgh and ask Judge Smith for the contents of that manilla envelope. He was assuming that the envelope had been finally delivered after the Hospital people had opened and copied its contents.

To confirm the Inspector's advice, we obtained a copy of the relevant law, which contradicted the Inspector's advice and we learned: "Except as expressly provided by law, no person shall be prosecuted, tried or punished for any offense, not capital, unless the indictment is found or the information is instituted within five years next after which an offense shall have been committed."

So, indeed - unless the indictment was handed down within five years of the crime - the offenders would be scot-free.

The Postal Code, sec. 1702 states: "Whoever takes any letter, postal card, or package out of any post office or any authorized depository for mail matter, or from any letter or mail carrier, or which has been in any post office or authorized depository, or in the custody of any letter or mail carrier, before it has been delivered to the person to whom it was directed, with design to obstruct the correspondence, or to pry into the business or secrets of another, or opens, secretes, embezzles, or destroys the same, shall be fined not more than $2,000.00 or imprisoned not more than five years or both."

Another section: Sec. 1708 - refers to the copying of another person's mail as... (anyone who) "abstracts or removes from any such letter, package, bag, or mail any article or thing contained therein...shall be fined not more than $2,000.00 or imprisoned not more than five years or both".

After a little more than two weeks -on July 2nd. - O'Marr and a young trainee appeared at the office near the end of the day. O'Marr described that he had interviewed the Administrator for more than an hour at the local Holiday Inn. He described that the Administrator contradicted his earlier testimony under oath and now said that the letters were opened when he got them.

O'Marr's notes were finally acquired through the Freedom of Information Act. One note was dated July 3. The Administrator , according to that note, in addition to claiming that the letters had been opened when he got them, claimed that he had been advised by the Board Chairman to return Citizens Committee mail, which had been intercepted, to the senders rather than to the Committee to whom they were mailed.

Another of O'Marr's handwritten reports described interviews with the Administrator on August 1st. and August 8th. The notes state: "The Administrator states that if his prints are on the packet or not, he does not remember seeing the packet" and, "the letter (packet) was written to a judge by Doctor Miller".

I recall, at the time, asking O'Marr how the Administrator knew that a judge in Pittsburgh was the addressee if he hadn't seen the packet. The Inspector's notes for those dates include the comment: "Only friend that the Administrator knows, that Miller has in Pittsburgh, is Judge Ralph Smith", and the Hospital Secretary stated that the Administrator subsequently dictated a cover letter for each of the two letters that were returned to the senders".

O'Marr's file included handwritten "reports of contact". One dated July 5 was from the Hospital Lawyer "at the request of The Board Chairman".

The Inspector's note reads: "The Hospital Lawyer admitted Hospital copied contents of incoming mail for Concerned Citizens".

The Hospital Lawyer then forwarded to the Inspector an envelope that he claimed had held the forty-five pages of documents found in the Hospital file. It was a standard size envelope that had been mailed to the Hospital relative to another matter. The Lawyer was attempting to have the Inspector believe that forty-five pages could be stuffed into an ordinary envelope.

The Inspector's note of July 9, after another telephone conversation, described the Lawyer's explanation as an "unlikely story." At that time, the Inspector advised that he would shortly be ready to present the case to the U. S. Attorney and again asked that I attempt to obtain the originals of the large manilla envelope and its contents in Pittsburgh.

He was still believing that the envelope and contents had been forwarded after copying. There was no success in finding the originals in Pittsburgh. Judge Smith had never gotten the envelope.

Then, out-of-the-blue, the Hospital Lawyer surrendered to the Postal Inspector the entire original packet of documents and the manilla envelope.

On July 13, the Inspector called our office and advised that he would be in Indiana on the 16th. to fingerprint the Administrator and his Secretary as well as the Board Chairman. He dropped into the office, after hours, and gave us additional copies of the purloined documents with the Hospital Lawyer's serial numbering in the lower right-hand corner.

On August 30th., during a telephone conversation, O'Marr advised that there was the possibility of other pieces of our mail in the Hospital files and that this would be investigated.

Inspector O'Marr again appeared in Indiana on October 31st. and appeared at the office shortly after calling that he was in town. He proudly showed us the original large manilla envelope he had gotten from the Hospital Lawyers and it was an exact original of the copies which showed that the addressee had been torn away, the postage and cancellation intact and the small label reading, "Nov. 5" which matched the Hospital typewriter. The Inspector then told us that the Hospital Lawyers had no explanation for the large manilla envelope and contents being in the Hospital's possession.

The Inspector's files, which we reviewed later, had another unusual note. It described the Administrator as saying, "Someone could have planted the file in the Hospital records."

At that time, the Inspector advised that the case concerning the interception and copying of the Citizens Committee mail was complete, since these acts were confessed by the cover letters of the Administrator, as well as the copies of the letters intercepted, and a direct reference to the contents of the stolen letters by a letter signed by Hospital Lawyer Mattern.

During one of the later visits from the Inspector, there was a profound change in attitude. All of a sudden, he expressed doubts about his ability to prove the facts he intended to present to a Grand Jury. I had trouble following his logic. It just didn't make sense. The evidence was still irrefutable and I was at a loss when he left. It was nearly lunch hour and, as I was leaving our building, I noticed the Inspector sitting in the front seat of his car facing the other way in our parking lot. As I looked in his side window - there he was, with several wads of high denomination bills in his lap. I never figured out what the money was for, but when I mentioned it to some of the postal authorities they said it was "for another case".

During one of the conversations with the Postal Inspector, he mentioned that he had received a complaint from the "Director of Security" at the Hospital. The "Director" had complained of receiving threatening letters in the mail. I was unable to give the Postal Inspector any information about the man. I did manage to contact him and arrange a meeting with him and one of my lawyers.

During our meeting, we heard from him an outstanding description of Hospital activities. My lawyer prepared an affidavit carefully wording the document to judiciously reflect the man's words.

The affidavit read as follows:

"I was Director of Security for Indiana Hospital for two and a half years from September 15, until January 6, as well as the Safety Officer from April until January.

My immediate supervisor was Geryl Gates, Director of Personnel, and after the first year, I was accountable to the Management Committee composed of Mr. Gates, Mr. L. Marshall, Leona Shank and Dr. Larry Kachik.

Based on my experience at the Hospital I became convinced that there was a conspiracy to get rid of Dr. Ralph Miller from the Medical Staff and to keep him from practicing at the Hospital. Based on statements made, it was apparent the reason for this conspiracy was economic considerations and fears of Dr. Miller.

When I first started to work, I was involved in a conversation with Drs. Hoffman and Georges. After Dr. Georges had made a disparaging and derogatory remark about Dr. Miller, I inquired as to who Dr. Miller was. Dr. Hoffman responded by saying he was some doctor who tried to take over the Hospital, but "We took care of him."

The affidavit continued:

"On another occasion in September that year, I was involved in a conversation with two members of the hospital management team, Larry Marshall, the Head of Fiscal Affairs; and, Dr. Kachik. Dr. Kachik indicated that he had heard that Dr. Miller killed one of his patients at the Hospital, to which Larry Marshall replied that that was only what some people thought. When I asked what Mr. Marshall meant by that statement, he replied that Miller "wanted more than his share of the pie."

"These are examples of the types of comments heard leading me to my knowledge of the conspiracy."

"In my capacity with the Hospital I was asked by my supervisor whether there was any way in the event someone like Dr. Miller called the Hospital we could tape or record his conversations and whether this was legal."

Later, I was directed by Mr. Valentine (the new Administrator) to screen all mail going out of the Hospital, to intercept any mail addressed to certain addresses, including the post office box number for the Concerned Citizens Committee. The management at the Hospital considered this group to be a committee of one person, namely, Dr. Miller. My instructions were to turn over all such mail to the Administrator's office and I did this for a period of seven (7) months as ordered."

"I frequently heard derogatory remarks made concerning Dr. Miller, including statements from Drs. Hoffman, Georges and Kachik, Mr. Gates and Leona Shank. Whenever the slightest thing went wrong at the Hospital, the Hospital management always believed that somehow Dr. Miller was the cause of it, although, of course this wasn't true on closer investigation."

"I have read the above statement and certify that it is true and correct."

The Security Chief came back to the office some days later and presented a plan for security of our building. He seemed to think that we were at some risk. But he balked at signing his affidavit. It was, quite frankly, no surprise. I recalled his earlier contact with the Postal Inspector after he claimed receipt of threatening letters and could understand reluctance at admitting that he had helped divert mail for seven months. He was anxious, to say the least, and said he was leaving town in two days to accept a security job at an eastern Pennsylvania hospital.

Before he left, he confided that the hospital management was becoming most apprehensive of "inside information" finding its way into the hands of the Citizens Committee. He was summoned, by the Hospital management during that period, and was given the documents of the Indiana Hospital Coal Company to deliver to the office of an attorney-hospital-board member, for safekeeping.

For almost a year, there was no word from the Postal Inspector and no indication of progress in the investigation. I was finally able to reach him by telephone the following August. He advised that a desk clerk at the Indiana Post Office, apparently a relative of a Hospital Board member, had retired from the postal service and that there was an effort to "get (the Postmaster) out". He described receiving instructions from the U.S. Attorney to administer polygraph testing to the postal employees and the Postmaster.

A few weeks later, by telephone, the Inspector advised that he planned to be in town the following week. His visit was delayed for a week or two, but when he did arrive he assured again that he was about to "present the whole bundle of evidence to Assistant U. S. Attorney Curry for possible prosecution". He was planning to administer polygraph testing to the Postmaster, two postal employees, the Hospital Administrator and Secretary and the Hospital Board Chairman. He said that he would request the Hospital group to appear before a grand jury. Then, a year and a half after O'Marr began his investigation, a letter arrived from the Office of the Inspector in Charge, Harrisburg, Pa. It was from O'Marr, advising that the "investigation" was over.

The letter stated:

"The Inspection Service has completed its investigation. Our investigation failed to disclose any evidence which would indicate a conspiracy by employees of the Indiana, Pa. Post Office to intercept your mail and/or divert it to individual(s) employed at the Indiana Hospital, Indiana, Pa. and; ...the investigation did not establish any reason other than human error for the misdelivery, and; ...in the view of the U. S. Attorney, Western district of Pennsylvania, the subsequent handling by Hospital employees was lacking in criminal intent and would not be a violation of federal law."

The Inspector concluded his letter referring to the large manilla envelope he had retrieved from the Hospital Lawyer saying: "The envelope was missing. Therefore, the investigation could not independently verify the mailing and subsequent diversion of the packet to the hospital."

I simply could not believe that I was expected to swallow that cover-up.

It was becoming evident that the postal "investigation" was farcical at best. I was more than a little annoyed at the irresponsible functioning of a government agency. Inspector O'Marr had told me that the Postal Inspection Service was a totally independent agency with its own laboratory and with no oversight by Congress or an Inspector General. Nevertheless, I contacted our Congressman and he had his staff begin to look into the "investigation".

The Congressman's staff began their inquiry with the U. S. Attorney's office in Pittsburgh. We were working with the Congressman's top aide - Sam Siple. Sam visited our office and began to restore our faith in government. He was a tall, lanky, friendly and intelligent young man. He honestly and shockingly told us that his contact with the Assistant U. S. Attorney in Pittsburgh had revealed that the U. S. Attorney's office had no information about the Indiana Hospital case and had had no communication with Postal Inspector O'Marr. The U. S. Attorney's office had advised him that nothing was uncovered in a subsequent thorough examination of records except for a parking ticket on federal property issued to my older son while he was at the Pittsburgh Veteran's Hospital.

Sam was disturbed by the deception that had been occurring and collected copies of the documents that the Inspector said "nailed down the case".

The Congressman became personally involved and invited us to Washington to meet with Postal Department officials. My younger son Mark and I drove to Bethesda the night before the meeting, and the next morning travelled the Metro's cavernous route to the Capitol.

The Cannon House Office Building - one of the older buildings at the Capitol - was a dreary series of hallways leading into anterooms and Congressmens' inner offices. We made a near-complete tour of those hallways until we found the Congressman's name on a gold-lettered sign to the right of his entrance.

One of the Congressman's staff ushered us into a large, panelled office to the left and advised that the Congressman would join us shortly. The hallways we had left and a large room to the right were a beehive of activity. People were milling about and chatting with each other.

The Congressman was a big, gregarious guy. He filled a substantial portion of the doorway when he entered and his handshake was, at the very least, very firm. He seated himself behind his huge walnut desk and the three of us casually reviewed the rough details of the matter of intercepted mail. He advised that the Postal People would be arriving shortly and, without a warning, picked up his clicker and turned on a T.V. set in the far corner. There were some highly publicized Congressional hearings in progress and the Congressman had an obvious interest as he clicked from one network to another.

The large, paneled door swung inward and the "Postal People" came in - two gents and a lady. The lady introduced herself to Mark and me and acknowledged that we had corresponded for a time. She mentioned that she was the spokesperson for the United States Postal Service. Likewise, the two gentlemen shook hands and identified themselves as an attorney for the Postal Service and an Assistant Chief Postal Inspector. We were then introduced to two other young men who were members of the Congressman's staff.

The Congressman opened the meeting with an opinion that there were severe problems to be addressed and that he hoped that the officials there would bring about a satisfactory solution as quickly as possible. He asked me to give a summary of the case - which I did ; while he sat behind his desk jabbing the air with his clicker to get instant updates on the Congressional hearings.

The Postal People were knowledgeable and attentive and asked some appropriate questions as I gave a history of the case.

The Congressman then entered the discussion which was taking an hour or more. Betty Bryant, the spokesperson, finally said, "The Postal Inspector is stonewalling and you should make an effort to find out why he is stonewalling".

The well-spoken lawyer for the Postal Inspection Service spoke for a few minutes and concluded that he was going to advise reopening of the case.

The Congressman took us to lunch in the House dining room. He was a gracious host and the conversation during lunch never lagged. Despite all we read about the Congressional opulence, the House Dining

Room and the food and service were below average. That didn't affect our appreciation of the Congressman one bit. The Congressman then gave us a tour of the entire Capitol and I remember him looking up at the high dome of the rotunda and expressing the pride he experienced in being part of it all.

Mark and I found our car where we had parked it in the parking lot of the Bethesda Naval Hospital. As we headed north for home, I described the first time that I had traveled to that Hospital on the first hospital train with casualties from France shortly after D-Day.

One of the Congressman's assistants made a follow-up call to Betty Bryant after we had met in the Congressman's office. Ms. Bryant revealed that she had finally found the case involving Indiana Hospital and indicated that there was enough evidence collected for prosecution.

She advised that she would be calling him back with the name of the U. S. Attorney who would be prosecuting the case. This was the conversation when Ms. Bryant again advised that the Postal Inspector had been "stonewalling" and "needed to be moved along". This was when she advised that we find out why the Inspector was "stonewalling".

In a later conversation with the Congressman's aide, she changed her story and said that, "The chances of prosecution were zero."

Who or what was influencing these people not to prosecute the case or to present the evidence to a grand jury?

After that meeting in Washington, we were expecting some serious activity from the Inspector. But, nothing happened for about two months.

On September 23, I phoned Attorney Birch who was the Postal Inspection lawyer who had been at the meeting in the Congressman's office. He had, indeed, recommended reopening of the investigation but had been overruled by his superior, a C. W. Lawrence, of the Postal Inspection Service. It appeared that Lawrence had phoned an assistant U. S. Attorney, Mead, in Pittsburgh and had gotten assurances from Mead that the Hospital Group would not be prosecuted, even if new and additional evidence was forthcoming.

Later records would reveal that Inspector O'Marr had also phoned the Assistant U. S. Attorney, claiming a lack of evidence that would justify prosecution. At the time, the Pittsburgh Post Gazette ran a story under the headline, "Postmaster Indicted". The story read: "Assistant U. S. Attorney John J. Mead on Wednesday asked the Court Clerk to issue a summons for Lana G. Lear to appear on October 7 to post bond which he recommended be set at $5000.00." There was no connection with our case except for the appearance of Mead in both cases.

Scarcely weeks later the same newspaper ran another headline: "Postal Clerk is Convicted". The final paragraph of the story read: "The judge ordered the prosecutor, Assistant U. S. Attorney John J. Mead to present briefs on the constitutionality of the statute that sets a mandatory twenty-five year sentence for a postal robbery". It was another appearance for Mead.

There was enough question about all these machinations that the Congressman wrote the U. S. Attorney and didn't mince words. The letter was headed by: "Thomas A. Daley, Chief, Criminal Division, U. S. Attorney's Office". The letter began with:

"Dear Mr. Daley:

I am writing to you regarding a despicable incident with my constituent, Dr. Ralph J. Miller."

His letter advised that his request was directed toward seeing that "justice was done." He must have been keenly aware of the difficulties citizens encounter when seeking justice.

Sam, the Congressman's top aide, then made an appointment to meet with the U. S. Attorney and his assistant at the Federal Building in Pittsburgh.

Sam and I met in the small lobby off Grant Street leading into the blackened stone Federal Building. We went through a rather rigorous electronic examination for firearms before we were allowed to approach the bank of large brass elevator doors to the right of the entrance foyer.

The sixth floor hallway was quiet as a tomb; and not a soul was in sight, until we found the U. S. Attorney's Office, half way down and to the left of that silent hallway. As we stepped into an anteroom, an attractive blonde, middle-aged secretary asked our names with a pleasant manner and invited us to take a seat.

There was only a short wait until a tall, well-dressed man entered and greeted the secretary by name - Bernadette. He was told to go on into Mr. Daley's office. He had hardly entered the inner office to the left when he returned and invited us in. He introduced himself as Assistant U. S. Attorney Curry and reluctantly shook hands. He lacked Bernadette's charm but he was certainly outdone in coolness by the U. S. Attorney Daley, himself. Daley was a small, bespectacled man hunched behind a huge, ornate desk. There was no movement as we introduced ourselves; he just sat and stared.

Finally, he advised that his time was short and that we should limit ourselves to presenting only new information, gained since the Postal Inspector's final report closing the case. Sam explained that, in addition to new information, such as more recent letters which had been opened and resealed, there was a need to review the unlikely conclusions of the Inspector.

Curry bluntly advised Sam that he knew the contents of the entire file and that we were to limit ourselves to "new evidence". Sam invited me to proceed and I began, as I did in the Congressman's Washington office, to summarize the case. Daley began interrupting and telling me that my disclosures "weren't new". He wouldn't acknowledge the multiple examples of interviews and procedures that had never been completed by the Inspector.

Somehow, we finally convinced these two gentlemen that there may have been serious deficiencies in the handling of the investigation and serious questions regarding the people who somehow entered into what appeared to be a choreographed cover-up.

Grudgingly, those two finally advised that they would not oppose a reopening of the investigation by the Postal Inspection Service which had been promised in the meeting in Washington.

As Sam and I parted, we shared our doubts about the sincerity of those two public servants we had just left.

As we stepped from the building, I said to Sam, "We have seen a masterful cover-up. It must have originated at a high level."

Sam said, "Without a doubt."

After Sam and I had met with the U.S. Attorneys, there was a flood of correspondence between the Congressman's office and various Postal dignitaries. In addition to the "stonewalling" of the Postal Inspector, we were getting the same treatment from the U. S. Attorneys and the Government Accounting Office which had entered into the case. These people were all "passing the buck" - all claiming that the other agencies were responsible for the decisions.

It had been soon after the Postal Inspector had done his about-face, that we had begun efforts to get his notes, guaranteed through the Freedom of Information Act.

When the notes were finally received, they were more than just enlightening.

Through the Congressman's efforts, another meeting was arranged with the Postal People in the Congressman's Beaver Falls office. The office was in a former retail space fronting on the town's Main Street. My son, Mark, and I met Sam in the front portion of that office where two secretaries were busily typing. One made friendly remarks to Sam as he guided us to the rear of the office through two doorways - the last leading into a small room with a conference table surrounded with plain folding wooden chairs.

The three of us took places around the table and I sat the trusty old tape recorder in front of me. In order to have this meeting take place, the Chief Postal Inspector in Washington required that I provide him with a list of "new evidence" that had been collected since the investigation had been closed. I had provided a list of twelve issues that had never been addressed by the Inspection Service, knowing that the Postal People would argue that none of those items were "new evidence".

The door opened and two gentlemen and a woman entered and introduced themselves as Nick Cook, Chris Mocho and Gary Claytor, all in supervisory positions with the Service in the northeastern region of the country.

Sam began by recounting the Washington meeting: He said, "Coming out of that meeting, the U.S. Attorney's office had no objection to the Postal Inspector continuing the investigation, so that's when we pursued having another meeting." Sam continued: "Going through the steps, through the Congressional Liason's office, we were getting bogged down and feeling like we were treading water. That's when we went directly to the Chief Postal Inspector Clauson's office to get this meeting set up."

Sam was reflecting the twists and turns anyone had to endure while working with the Washington bureaucracy.

Any hopes we had for a legitimate reopening of the investigation were dashed when Mr. Cook took over and announced:

"Before Dr. .Miller begins, let me tell you what I perceive to be our role here today. And I have some knowledge concerning the case, and I followed it and I'm aware of the correspondence that has passed between Dr. Miller and the Congressman and the Chief Inspector's Office. And, <u>in accordance with the Chief's wishes</u>, I see my role here today to listen to Dr. Miller, to see if there's new evidence that has not been presented to the United States Attorney for consideration up until this point.

To listen to what he has to say with respect to that new evidence and then to consider it. Is that your understanding Dr. Miller?"

It was evident that Mr. Cook had his instructions that came directly from the Chief Postal Inspector.

I began by reminding that the interception of my mail was an act intertwined with the ongoing antitrust litigation with the Hospital. I couldn't resist telling the group, that on that very day, the United States Supreme Court had denied the Hospital's petition to have the high court hear the Hospital arguments to overturn our victory with the Third Circuit Court of Appeals.

I briefly ran through a description of what had occurred in Washington where we were told that the investigation would be reopened and we would be allowed to review all the evidence before it was presented to the U. S. Attorney.

I asked my first question, directing it to Mr. Cook: "What happens now?"

Cook was making every effort to be articulate and to control the meeting. He said:

"I'm not here today to review what's happened in the past. I'm here today to consider any new evidence that has been considered up until now. I'm here to hear that. I'm willing to go through your list of items that you presented and discuss them."

I then asked, "You're not prepared to answer my question?" Cook replied, "No, Sir."

Although Cook had advised us in feigned politeness, it was more than evident that he would discuss nothing. It was a continuation of what Betty Bryant, the Postal Service spokesperson called, "stonewalling".

I decided to put the details of four years effort with the Inspection Service into the record for whatever it was worth. I began a narrative of the details of all the misinformation we had been given over the four year period. It was difficult. Cook kept interrupting and kept repeating that he knew all this - he was "familiar with the file".

A little later he again interrupted with: "Again, Dr. Miller, we're aware of this."

Once again, his interruption was: "Again, O.K., it may be helpful to skip over some of these things that are clear from the record."

When I explained that I wanted this information on the record, he advised: "Well

O.K., but I'll listen to you for some time, but I think at some point in time I'm going to have to restrict you to the items that are on this letter."

I decided to complete the record and ignore the interruptions.

Cook kept interrupting and I kept recording. At one point, Cook interrupted with:

"I appreciate your comments, Dr. Miller, but I have to go back to the facts. I have been an Inspector for twenty years and I know what needs to be done here."

The four years of frustration with this outfit finally led to the following exchange.

The transcript reads:

DR. MILLER: "I would like to make one comment, Mr. Cook. It's rather personal. You say you've worked for the Postal Inspection Service for twenty years. For those twenty years, I'm one of the people who have paid your way. I'm not apologizing for inconveniencing you for fifteen or twenty minutes here."

COOK:: "I'm not talking about inconvenience I'm talking about covering ground which has been covered before."

DR. MILLER: "You've sat there and done nothing but obstruct."

COOK: "I'm sorry Dr. Miller, but I don't see it that way. I see it as doing my job."

When I resumed recording the history of the case, the complexion of the meeting suddenly changed. I came to the statement of the former Security Chief at Indiana Hospital which described that he had been instructed to intercept mail to or from the Citizens Committee or to or from me and to take it to the Administrator's office. He had also told us that he suspected a window clerk at the post office who was related to a Hospital Board member. Inspector Claytor, who had been silent, now asked for a copy of the former security chief's statement. Claytor was showing interest with what we saw as a terribly incriminating bit of testimony from a former security head at the Hospital.

After the next interruption by Cook, I asked: "Well, have you predetermined the outcome of this meeting today?"

He answered: "Absolutely not."

Young Mark had sat quietly through all this dialogue and probably couldn't believe what he was hearing. He looked at Cook and said:

"Sir, do you determine the validity of any of this right now?" Cook quickly replied: "That is not a question I'm going to answer."

He continued: "We're here today to gather facts about new evidence that has been presented. And, up to this point, and we're well into this meeting by forty-five minutes, all Dr. Miller has done is talk about things that are already documented."

I think Mark, with his youthful idealism, was truly stunned by the behavior of an intelligent, responsible person who would attempt to gloss over what he knew to be overwhelming evidence of a felony.

He looked directly at Cook and said:

"Given this situation and given your position it is evident that you are following your instructions. But, everything in this case has to be considered. I don't think there is anyone in this room who is going to say that this mail has been inadvertently intercepted and that this was an accident. I don't think you believe that Sir, and I don't' believe anyone in your Inspection Service believes that. The fact, that you can come here and say, "Well, we can't listen to that right now", is not basically going to get to the bottom of this. We have a citizen here who has been denied some basic rights. That is the problem - not the technicalities you use to stifle a valid complaint. This is all right here in front of us. If you were sitting here on the other end of this table, I don't think you'd want to say, "Well, okay, let's forget about all this."

I was certainly proud of that little speech - it came directly to the point. If Mark's mind could come to that conclusion and express it so well, it seemed to add credibility to our pursuit of a little justice in the face of obvious behind-the-scenes activity.

I presented the group a small envelope with a hand-written note inside which entered a complaint about the Hospital. It had been mailed to the Citizens Committee and had been opened and carefully resealed. It was part of the "new evidence" that Cook wanted. I showed it to Cook and he again said he was familiar with that letter. I then told him that that was certainly interesting since we had never given the envelope to the Inspection Service nor to anyone else. I gave the envelope and the Hospital Security Chief's statement to Inspector Claytor.

Inspector Claytor asked, "Is there anything else you want to add?" He seemed to be truly interested, so I explained that we knew of two or more phone calls from an assistant to the Chief Inspector in Washington to the U. S. Attorney's office in Pittsburgh. These calls were obviously the factor in dropping the postal inspection. I asked if we could have a record of those phone calls.

We were now getting to the heart of the matter and Cook said, "Can you tell me who gave you that information?" I told him that if he wanted to reopen the investigation I would gladly supply all information.

Everyone in that room knew that there wasn't a chance of the investigation being reopened. The fix had been put in at a high level.

We all shook hands and the postal trio departed. Sam was truly amazed that the System functioned so poorly. We decided all we could do was to try to document the Washington to Pittsburgh telephone calls that had apparently "called the tune".

The Congressman's efforts didn't stop. It appeared that the Chief Postal Inspector himself was now attempting to keep a lid on internal information. The Congressman's letter to the Chief Inspector said:

"I would ask if you could send this information (all records that are available under the Freedom of Information Act) immediately; we have been waiting well over three months to hear from your department. I believe the request is being unnecessarily detained and is not receiving proper attention."

In a letter to the general counsel of the United States Postal Service, the Congressman wrote:

"We expect to obtain the records of the Inspection Service for activities leading up to and following the meeting in my Washington office. We would like all the records that are available under the Freedom of Information Act."

The Chief Postal Inspector first wrote, "There will be a delay in responding to your request due to the time involved in retrieving the records in question from another Postal Service facility."

Over two years later, his letter ended with: "There will be a delay in responding to your latest request due to the time involved in preparing the material for release."

Some time after the Congressman's last letter, a large, brown envelope arrived from the United States Postal Service, Washington, D. C.

We now had the Inspector's notes. The notes confirmed some of the Inspector's activities. He had actually fingerprinted the local Postmaster and a Post Office counter employee. Most of the names in the Inspector's notes were obliterated with a black highlighting pen, but it was not difficult to guess who the subjects were. The notes confirmed that the "investigation" had suddenly halted. But the phone call from Washington and from the Postal Inspector to the United States Attorney were never recorded. Of course not.

Miracle of miracles: A recent communication with the U.S. Postal Service produced a copy of a "Memorandum of Understanding" between the U. S. Postal Service Inspector General and the U. S. Chief Post Inspector. The memorandum reads:

"Public Law 104-208 ("the Postal IG Law") established a new Inspector General in the U. S. Postal Service who has the authority and responsibilities set out in the Inspector General Act of 1978, as amended ("The 1978 Act"), relating to detecting, reporting and preventing fraud, waste and abuse in the programs and operations of the U. S. Postal Service. <u>The new Inspector General is taking over this role as delineated in the Postal IG Law from the Chief Postal Inspector who has performed the Inspector General function since 1988.</u>

Can we possibly believe that cover-up may now be more difficult?

We all know too well the frustration of hitting a "stonewall" when we attempt to have our public servants do what's right. Yet, the future of our system probably depends on the few who persist; and, our faith is restored when our efforts produce some results.

Our experience with the Postal Inspection service may not have been an isolated incident, but may also have been "one of the straws on the camel's back."

Chapter 19

"Judge me by the enemies I have made."

— *Franklin Delano Roosevelt*

THE TRIAL THAT NEVER WAS

After the twelve years of legal skirmishing with the hospital lawyers, Judge Bloch finally scheduled a pre-trial conference. Presumably, this is a meeting between the Judge and the opposing lawyers to resolve loose ends and set the date for trial, along with establishing the Court's rules.

We were indeed encouraged that we were to finally get our day in court. The lawyers had filed pre-trial statements which would essentially outline the plaintiffs' and defendants' cases - the legal people like to refer to this as the "case-in-chief". Included with the outline of the case were lists of witnesses and copies of documents which would be presented at trial. Our case was strong and we had submitted to the court our list of 197 witnesses and 212 documents.

The Judge had moved into more elegant quarters, following the earlier conference with him and we were ushered into a larger conference room with a larger conference table and with a wall lined with legal volumes. The young woman guiding us advised that His Honor would join us in a few minutes. The Assistant Hospital Lawyer arrived a few minutes later and sat on the opposite side of the table without a greeting and began a conversation on a few points that the lawyers had agreed upon. It was apparently a rule that lawyers attempt agreement on witness lists and documents that would be presented at trial.

After a half-hour, the Judge entered with the young lady clerk and the lawyers reverently chorused: "Good afternoon, Your Honor". We all rose, of course. I felt a little uncomfortable with this routine deference. There was no doubt that His Honor would continue to smart from the Appeals Court opinion overturning his previous ruling which had attempted to throw our case out of Court.

Nevertheless, he began, "This is the date and time set for a pre-trial conference in the matter of Miller v. Indiana Hospital, filed at Civil No. 81-1091."

He continued: "Plaintiffs have filed a pre-trial statement listing 197 liability witnesses. There's a large number, I won't go through all these names where there are no addresses." He then looked at the Hospital Counsel and asked: "Does that cause you any problem?" The Hospital Lawyer then said something unusual: "That doesn't. <u>As you know,</u> I have another problem with a lot of them, but the addresses, no."

I looked at the Judge - <u>how did he know?</u> We had seen the Judge's familiarity and deference to this fellow in the past and I had wondered what the influencing factors were. I began to wonder if the Assistant Hospital Lawyer had talked to His Honor directly or if the communication was through his law clerk - something that lawyers admit happens regularly.

The Hospital Lawyer whined a bit about our witness list and the Judge, dutifully, attacked our list claiming that all our witnesses should have been submitted with previous answers to interrogatories (questions submitted by the hospital) earlier.

He said, "That's the problem we're dealing with, is that you are now listing individuals who you didn't list in your answers to interrogatories. And you don't seem to have any satisfactory explanation for why you didn't do this."

Here was a blatant double standard. We had great trouble getting answers from our interrogatories directed to the Hospital Defendants. They had sat unanswered in the Hospital Lawyer's office for two years. Now, in a case that had been successfully delayed for twelve years, he was applying a stringent standard to us.

I thought of a recent Pittsburgh newspaper story in which a lawyer questioned the integrity of a judge in the investigation of the Martin Luther King assassination. The Appeals Court had said: "A judge is a fair and impartial adjudicator. Not an investigator. In this regard we find that Judge Joseph D. Brown, Jr., has crossed the line. We are disturbed by the trial judge's handling of these procedures."

I was more than a little skeptical when the Judge said, "Let's put it this way, I rule at this time that none of these additional people that weren't listed in answers to interrogatories can testify." His Honor was demonstrating how a judge can influence or cripple a citizen's case before it ever gets to a jury.

Then began the big deception: We were being instructed on how to prepare for trial that was imminent. The conference was a sham.

The transcript reads:

The Court: "We have this listed for jury trial. Would like to get some trial estimate time-wise - your case-in-chief plaintiff, how long do you think it's going to take?"

Our Answer: "I would say three weeks."

The Court: "O.K. I take it — do you know we only try four days a week? We don't try on Fridays, so does that still apply? Are you talking about twelve days of trial?"

Our Answer: "I was thinking fifteen, but I don't know that we can guarantee..."

The Court: " In the area of twelve to fifteen days, plaintiff's case?"

Our Answer: "That would be fine."

Then he commented to the Hospital Counsel::

The Court: "Defense, your case-in-chief."

Hospital Counsel: "It's hard to estimate, only because some of the issues that we had raised to strike..." (the Hospital Laywer was hoping, or perhaps knowing, that some of our case would not be allowed by this judge).

The Court: "We understand it's an estimate."

Hospital Counsel: "If everything would go in, it would take, I think about eleven days - would be my guestimate."

We remembered the Judge's invitation to submit yet another Summary Judgement Motion at an earlier hearing. IIe had said, "Although I certainly hope we aren't going to have any more Summary Judgement motions, but if you have that in mind, this would be filed within fourteen days after the close of discovery accompanied by any supporting documents and a brief."

The Hospital, of course, had taken that open invitation and filed the third motion to throw out our case - a very unusual accommodation by His Honor.

In spite of that, the charade continued with the caveat:

The Court: "<u>O.K. We're not going to put you on the trial list now until the Summary Judgement motion is decided.</u>" (The third attempt by the Hospital to throw out the case)

His Honor then went on to give instructions on voir dire (jury selection). I wondered why they never just said, "jury selection" - maybe it was something similar to the use of Latin for prescriptions.

At any rate, the instructions for the trial to be would be was continued:

The Court: "Two weeks after you receive our opinion on the Summary Judgement motion, we're ordering that you submit any requests for voir dire beyond our standard - and I'm going to pass out our standard voir dire questions to you. So, two weeks after you receive our opinion on the Motion for Summary Judgement, any requests for additional voir dire are due. Points for charge, with case authority for each point, are due at that same time and, I'm going to pass out to you instructions for trial."

And:

"O.K. There is your instructions for trial, and the clerk will get you our standard civil voir dire before you leave." "You should be aware of a couple of things. Number one, you know that the rules have changed. In civil cases we no longer have alternate jurors who now — they're not called alternates anymore, and who are not discharged at the end of the evidence. They now stay and take part in the deliberations. So, with a case of this length, we will probably have four — I hesitate to refer to them as alternates any longer. So, we'll go with a jury of ten is what I'm saying. Now, that — the case can go on with as few as six. So, if we leave four, the case would still go on. If we still have ten, or somewhere in between six and ten, everybody who is left takes part in the deliberations. Those are the changes that took place the first of the year on the Civil Rules." "The only thing I'll tell you, we are now using wireless microphones for the lawyers in the courtroom because of the acoustics. Now, they're handheld, they're very light and once you get used to them you'll forget you even have them in your hand. But you have to be holding them at all times, and that would include during your arguments, as well as everything else. There's no wires, so you can walk anywhere you want with them, and the sound is good. We just started using them this week and they're working very well. The acoustics in these large courtrooms are not very good and that's the reason we got them."

His Honor then addressed the clerk: "Where in the Summary Judgement motion list is this case? How far, do you have any idea?"

The Clerk: "It's about two-thirds of the way down. It's recent. It's pretty new."

The Court: "It will be awhile before that's decided. You won't be called to trial until then."

With all that, we began to think about and prepare for trial. I began to visualize the coming course of the trial. I began to see in detail each event of the trial. Even though it was a daydream it was becoming very real.

The Defense, as they had done in the state court arguments, would paint me as a disruptive doctor - a truly despicable character who made nurses cry and who made life miserable for the Hospital Administrators. They would argue that my "disruption" kept the hospital from functioning and was a direct threat to the hospital's quality of care.

It would begin on Day One - with jury selection. We would hope for an intelligent jury who would be able to understand the significance of the Antitrust Laws and understand the Hospital's actions designed to put a competitor out of business.

As I imagined, the first day of trial would begin with an overcast sky and, after a light snow, the drive to downtown Pittsburgh would be a little treacherous. I certainly would be preoccupied and paying little attention to the traffic signals and would almost step out into traffic in downtown Pittsburgh.

The security check in the dingy lobby of the Federal Building would be a little smoother than usual. We had learned that even a pocketed car key would set off the alarm. As I would step off the elevator on the eighth floor, there would be more activity than seen on earlier trips down that long hallway. The alcoves leading into the courtrooms would be occupied now with people waiting for Court to resume. Some of the people would wear paper badges marked "juror". These folks weren't supposed to talk with anyone. Something might influence an opinion. Heavens, what a thought! I would have one of those instant thoughts that come and go in a flash - wouldn't it be nice if the judges wore one of those badges?

Our courtroom was at the far end of the hall. The lawyers would already be at the counsel tables, inside the rail separating the spectators from the "arena". The lawyers would be reviewing their voir dire questionnaires that the potential jurors had completed and they would show little interest in the people now filing into the jury box on the right. I would begin to imagine who these people were - housewives, teachers, office clerks, steel workers or whatever. The ladies would all be neatly dressed and the men would be dressed casually except for one or two who would wear suits. The tipstaff would be quietly advising the potential jurors until they would all be seated. He would then walk across the arena and knock on the paneled door to the left of the judge's bench. He would disappear beyond the door for a minute or two and then lead the judge into the courtroom with a loud: "All Rise" and we would rise. The judge, in his robes would sit down on his high back throne which, due to substantial carpentry, put him well above the rest of us.

As my vision of the trial continued, the judge would advise the people in the jury box to answer the lawyers' questions honestly and without embellishment. He would assure them that if they would be dismissed, that it in no way reflected on their character. They were to raise a hand when their name was called. The lawyers would huddle with the group's questionnaires. Most of their conversation would be too garbled to understand but, every once in awhile one of the jury panel would be asked a question, and would softly answer. After much back-and-forth activity and numerous trips to the bench to confer with the Judge, the Judge would order the tipstaff to read the names of the ten panelists selected for the jury. There was no sign of response as the names were read. The judge would then thank the people who were to be dismissed for doing their civic duty and advised them to report back to the jury room downstairs. He would then advise the ten jurors that the trial proceedings would begin at 10:00 A.M. the following day and would ask all to report by 9:00 A.M. He would advise that the jurors were not to discuss the case with anyone or among themselves. He would smack the desk in front of him with a gavel and proclaim that the Court was in adjournment. He would then leave his perch and disappear through the door on the left.

The courtroom would empty quickly and I speculated that we would sit in the front row of seats behind the railing and discuss the issues to be presented in our opening statement the next morning. On the drive back to Indiana I would keep going over and over the points for the jury. We hoped to make a favorable impression and hoped the revelation of hospital activities would sour the jurists' view of the Defendants.

That's the way the system works. Juries frequently base decisions on emotions and we knew that we had to simplify the Antitrust Law involved in our case in order not to lose the jury.

That evening, I would have gone to bed early and would have spent most of the night rehashing our arguments. It would be almost a relief to get up, do my morning jog for a mile, and get started for the city. We would go over a few questionable points at the law offices and then would head up Grant Street.

The judge would be seated and call for the jury right on schedule. As the jury would file in and be seated, there would be an air of expectation. The jury would appear to be keenly interested. So would I. I would sit there in anticipation of finally having the truth told, despite the Hospital's efforts to seal records and have its actions hushed. My vision of the trial anticipated our opening statement. My lawyer would make a professional and articulate appearance.

When the judge would ask if the plaintiff was ready for opening statements and, after a "Yes, Your Honor" answer, my lawyer would begin:

"Ladies and gentlemen, you are about to hear of a most dramatic and frightening series of events by a group in control of a community hospital. You will hear of events designed to run a successful surgeon from town. That surgeon has fought for the last twelve years in the Federal Courts to be reinstated to the Hospital's Medical Staff. You will hear that his dismissal from the Medical Staff was based on a series of petty and false charges. You must certainly believe that a physician who perseveres with the Federal Court System for twelve years knows that he is in the right and that his dismissal from the Hospital Staff had nothing to do with professional ability. You will hear testimony that the physician was perceived as a threat because he had formed a competing medical center which was thought to be a threat to the Hospital's profits - its bottom line."

"We all grew up in era when hospitals were considered charitable. They were certainly non-profit organizations and were due certain protections under the law. But one would have to be hard-pressed now to consider hospitals charitable, non-profit or above the law. Hospitals are big, big business, and more and more hospitals are merging, making them huge conglomerates. Big hospitals now hire expensive lawyers to protect their turf and their bottom line."

"In the past, hospitals, as well as houses of worship, were immune from legal liability for any transgressions. But, some years ago, the Pennsylvania Legislature, as well as other state legislatures, declared that hospitals no longer deserved immunity from the law. That is, if hospital managements broke the law, their transgressions were open to challenge in our courts."

"This case, before this Court, is based on our national Antitrust Laws which are in place to protect small businesses from unfair practices by larger businesses which attempt to put the little fellow out of business. How can a Mom and Pop grocery store survive if the big chain market down the street makes an exclusive deal with distributors to buy its products and sell them at a fixed price and cheaper than Mom and Pop? This is price fixing and it's illegal. It is also illegal for a business to conspire and take action to destroy its competition. This is known as restraint of trade. How can a physician, opening a fledgling medical center designed to provide quality, low cost outpatient medical care survive, if a sixty million dollar a year hospital, like Indiana Hospital, with an annual profit of two million dollars, decides to dismiss him from its Staff and orchestrates a campaign to ruin his reputation? Ladies and gentlemen, it isn't easy. That's why we ask today that you look at the witnesses and the documents we present and judge whether the Hospital's actions in this case were in any way reasonable, or in any way fair or, indeed, were the Hospital's actions illegal?"

"This action brought by Dr. Miller is based on the Hospital's anti-competitive activity judged by the federal Clayton Act, along with the earlier Sherman Antitrust Act. These acts were enacted as law by Congress to protect the little guy from unfair practices by the big guys - in this case, a community hospital. The Antitrust acts were passed late in the nineteenth century and early in this century. The acts were passed, in part, due to John D. Rockefeller, who was forming combinations of oil producers who would join together and who would eliminate competition, fix oil prices and be an obvious threat to the American Free Enterprise System. The laws ban unfair practices: First, the law declares illegal those acts by conspirators who use unfair practices to destroy competition and thereby restrain trade, again leading to higher prices.

Secondly, the laws ban combinations of people illegally to conspire to create or to perpetuate a monopoly.

Section I of the Sherman Act states:

"Every contract, combination in the form of trust or otherwise, or conspiracy, in restraint of trade or commerce among the several States, or with foreign nations, is hereby declared to be illegal. Every person who shall make any contract or engage in any combination or conspiracy hereby declared to be illegal shall be deemed guilty of a felony, and, in conviction thereof, shall be punished by fine not exceeding $10,000,000.00, if a corporation, or, if any other person, $350,000.00, or both by imprisonment not exceeding three years, or by both said punishments, in the discretion of the court".

And Section II of the Sherman Act states:

"Every person who shall monopolize, or attempt to monopolize, or combine or conspire with any other person or persons, to monopolize any part of the trade or commerce among the several States, or with foreign nations, shall be deemed guilty of a felony, and on conviction thereof, shall be punished by fine not exceeding $10,000,000.00 if a corporation, or , if any other person, $350,000.00, or by imprisonment not exceeding three years, or by both said punishments, in the discretion of the Court".

"What this means, in everyday language, is that if two or more people or two or more companies join together in unfair and illegal practices to put a competitor out of business or to restrain his competition they shall be deemed guilty of a felony and are subject to fine and imprisonment."

"The same conditions are met if a monopoly of a product or a monopoly of a service is formed or if two or more persons conspire to monopolize, they are subject to the same conditions of fine and imprisonment."

"The law is just this simple although it has been complicated by court ruling over the years. "

"You will hear testimony on the relative market of Indiana Hospital, the only general hospital in the county which may be contradictory or even confusing. But, your charge is to determine whether Indiana Hospital, one of the largest businesses in Indiana County, enjoys a monopoly of position and whether the Hospital actors joined together to illegally force a competitor from the health care market."

"As we present our evidence, you will ask yourself where a successful surgeon can go if a big business hospital decides to put him out of business."

"More recently, Congress enacted the Clayton Act, which mandates civil penalties for violations of the Sherman Act. The financial penalties for illegal behavior are designed to compensate the victims of illegal activities which have harmed or destroyed their livelihood."

"This is the law by which you are being asked to judge the Hospital people who ended the surgical career of a physician who was just reaching the peak of his skills."

"Dr. Miller first attempted to have his privileges restored by the Indiana Court of Common Pleas. In the argument before that court, the Hospital Lawyer said: "One of the things I think that I ought to point out at the outset of this proceedings and this summation that this is not - this, for example, is not a contest or a fight or attack on Dr. Miller's right to practice Medicine. Indeed, it is not in any way an attack on his competency, his capability to practice in a highly specialized field of Medicine, Urology. Indeed, I don't think anyone who has known Dr. Miller for even a short period of time would question one or two facts: One, that he is intelligent, indeed brilliant; and Two, that he is capable, capable of practicing the finest type and standard of Urological Medicine in the country."

The people in that courtroom who heard that from the Hospital Lawyer who had prosecuted the doctor in a sham hospital hearing, then asked, "Why was that Hospital Lawyer prosecuting a successful surgeon on frivolous charges?"

My lawyer would continue:

"Today we will begin to document a tale of unbelievable nastiness and intrigue which has been documented over the years that Indiana Hospital and its lawyers were able to delay this trial.

The Hospital will tell you that it just tolerated Dr. Miller's antics for nineteen years until he just got too much to bear. But, we will present witnesses - the Hospital's former Administrator (its Chief Executive Officer), Hospital governing body members and physicians whose families were under Dr. Miller's care. Their testimony will cause the hospital's assertions of disruptive behavior to ring hollow. Dr. Miller held the top staff ranking for a period of nineteen years. He held several Committee Chairmanships and was elected Vice President of the Medical Staff. He had been a member of the Medical Staff Executive Committee for a term during this period of nineteen years. Does this sound like a disruptive physician? "

The opening statement would continue:

"As Chairman of the Hospital's Infection Control Committee, he began to document the large number of hospital acquired infections. This is when the Hospital paranoia began. Dr. Miller's opening of a small medical center and the recruitment of primary care physicians and specialists for the center increased the fear of competition and triggered the hate campaign. There were many tales circulated by the small group of physicians and the Hospital Administration. Although many of these people were patients of the Doctor, they circulated tales that Miller was paranoid. You will hear testimony from a physician who gave the Hospital Administration a medical article entitled, "<u>Paranoid Schizophrenia In The Medical Profession</u>", to be placed in Dr. Miller's file. You will hear the same physician admit that he and the Administrator called a witness and attempted to have her give false testimony at the Hospital hearing (subornation of perjury), which was held to bring frivolous charges against Dr. Miller. You will hear testimony of a nursing supervisor admitting that she altered Hospital records. But, most egregious of all here, will be the testimony of the physician who spread the false tale that Dr. Miller had put his wife in the Home for Battered Women. Ladies and gentlemen and the Court, you are expected to be shocked.

The Hospital Lawyer who was prosecuting Dr. Miller in the Hospital hearing, provided his own witness - a recovery room physician from Montefiore Hospital who perjured himself and was helped in his perjury by the Hospital Lawyer. He denied any real relationship with the lawyer but we will present the documents which will show that the perjuring witness was a divorce client of the Hospital Lawyer at the time of the hearing.

We will present witnesses who will graphically establish that the conspiracy to eliminate the competition of Dr. Miller began several years before the hearing and that this conspiracy began at the very top with the President of the Hospital Board of Directors."

Continuing, my lawyer would say:

"The conspirators' plan was executed when, on a Wednesday evening, the conspirators got the chance they had been waiting for. An 81 year old patient of Dr. Miller, who had been in ill health for years, suddenly went into respiratory arrest on a hospital ward. He stopped breathing. A hospital employed physician, Dr. Vance Vader, assumed control of an unsuccessful resuscitation He dismissed another physician who had offered help and then stood at the patient's bedside and watched the patient die. There were no emergency drugs given and no intravenous line started. The standard procedures for a resuscitation were not followed. The patient was dead in fourteen minutes. When Dr. Miller was called, he stayed on the line until he was certain that the patient was provided for. Instead, he was told that the patient had died. "

"Dr. Vance Vader then engaged the help of a nursing supervisor who provided a copy of the patient's chart. Within hours, he dictated a report which began the series of events which led to Dr. Miller's dismissal from the Hospital's Medical Staff.

We will put into the record Dr. Vader's report. It reflects Vader's arrival at the patient's bedside. It says: " When I arrived, Dr. Clippins arrived almost simultaneously with me and, when he observed that appropriate management had been effected, he questioned whether his services were needed. When informed that sufficient help was present he departed."

"We will show, through witnesses and documents, that this vicious series of lies in Dr. Vader's report was a result of a pathologic hatred and a desire to aid in the elimination of Dr. Miller's competition."

"The report by Dr. Vader was the basis of a letter to Dr. Miller from the Medical Staff Executive Committee, reporting that there had been serious mishandling of case number 320,120 and case number 322,193. The letter ordered that Dr. Miller report to an informal meeting with the Committee in two days."

"Dr. Miller met with the Committee and was presented the report we have just read. It was the first he had seen it. He was then given the second report written by the nursing supervisor present at the resuscitation attempt. It alleged a vague claim based on several frivolous nursing notes from the chart of another patient.

Ladies and gentlemen, we will present a witness and documents which demonstrate that the nursing supervisor and four of her nurses, took a full page from a patient's chart and completely rewrote the page with altered information. "

"Dr. Miller's meeting with the Medical Staff Executive Committee was disorganized and, when the Committee prepared its own minutes, they described that Dr. Miller suddenly left the meeting without answering the Committee's inquiries. We will dispute this through Dr. Miller's testimony. Dr. Miller demanded a full hearing, knowing that he had done nothing wrong. That hearing was an unbelievable travesty of due process. One of the Hospital Lawyers appointed herself to be the hearing Judge and she hired another lawyer to prosecute Dr. Miller. The hearing was marred by the Hospital's engagement in perjury, falsification of medical records, witness tampering and a set of rules established by the self-appointed Judge, that unbelievably, mock the basic rules of fair play and American Justice."

"We will present our witness, an expert on American jurisprudence who will present to you in chapter and verse the despicable charade that the Hospital would have you believe was a fair hearing. We will present a witness who will be a window into the operations of a corrupt hospital group. He is the judge who ordered a temporary injunction against the Hospital which, in turn, allowed Dr. Miller to practice there for several months after the hearing. He will tell you how a physician-Hospital Executive Committee member (Dr. Goldfarb) attempted to influence the rulings of that Judge in the Indiana Court of Common Pleas with behind-the-scenes telephone calls."

"In the twelve years since this suit was first filed, it has been dismissed twice and has been reinstated twice by the Third Circuit Court of Appeals. In the Court's opinion on the second reversal of this Court's dismissal, the Appeals Court very firmly ordered that a core issue of this case is the need to show disparate treatment - that is, are all doctors on the Medical Staff of this Hospital equally treated or are certain doctors selected for harsher treatment than others? In essence, it is our burden to show disparate treatment in this case. This we will do with witnesses and documents that will show anything but equal treatment or fair play in this case. We will show some horrifying examples of incompetence of other physicians when the Hospital took no action and looked the other way. In short, ladies and gentlemen, we will show you with unmistakable clarity, the details of corrupt Hospital actions to eliminate a successful surgeon that it considered a threat to the hospital's bottom line - all in violation of the Law."

As I envisioned that scene, my lawyer would carefully walk to his place at the conference table and be seated following his opening statement. The jury would have to be transfixed by the suggestion of the sheer weight and volume of the incredible evidence we were about to present. Would our witnesses and documents convince the jury that these things really happened?

His Honor would ask if the defense was ready for its opening. There would be little doubt about the content of the Hospital's argument. We had heard it all before - both at the Hospital hearing and in the local Court when the Hospital Lawyer argued to dissolve the injunction the Court had imposed on the Hospital. At both hearings the Hospital Lawyer had paraded before his audience forcefully pushing his nose toward his forehead - claiming that I had done that to a nurse- something that never happened. The opening argument by the Hospital Lawyer would be very similar to his argument in the Indiana Court. The transcript of that argument in Indiana with its obvious flattery reads as follows:

"Your Honor, Judge Handler, counsel and parties, if I might be permitted at the outset I would like to express my appreciation and I am sure that say this on behalf of Attorney DeMay as well for the manner in which this Court has paid respect and hospitality to counsel who come in from out of county; and I am always very conscious of that kind of treatment and it is deeply appreciated."

"And, in addition, I would like to, because this case is not yet determined and its final result is yet before Your Honor for decision and even though it may foreclose certain arguments on the record in some other day by the conduct of this hearing before Your Honor so be it, because I think that Mr. DeMay also would join with me in saying that in Mr. DeMay's long experience, certainly longer than mine, and in my sixteen years or so of trial practice which has brought me before Courts in many states, not just Pennsylvania, and practicing in the large county of Allegheny I have an opportunity to observe some forty judges and I can say without a doubt and I think it ought to be put on this record that the consciousness, the objectivity, the, indeed, not only having read a very extensive record, and I tell you that it is my experience that frequently if not most frequently judges not only don't have a good recollection of the facts they have rarely read the record below and it is obvious that the Court has done so and I think of us and Mr. DeMay I know will join with me in expressing this rare opportunity to observe and particularly say when we are coming from out of the county up here to a strange county the county of Indiana."

I can recall that when I heard that opening statement when we were in the Indiana County Court, I recognized that it was typical of what used to be printed in psychiatric texts as an example of "flight of ideas".

And then the Hospital Lawyer would probably come out with one of his marathon sentences which would have to be a world record. The transcript from Indiana, believe it or not, with its extravagant flattery continued with:

"I might say on that point it is going to be something that I'm going to miss in terms of coming to Indiana County, I find it one of the more pleasant things in my practice to get away from the city and come up here. You have a beautiful courthouse and I believe you should be proud of your judges."

Now that we were in the Federal Court system, we were certainly hoping that the Hospital Lawyers' bountiful self-praise would surface during his opening remarks. It would uncover the insincerity of this person.

The flatulent ramblings in the Indiana Court had continued with:

"I would like to say, Your Honor, at the outset if I might that this case has given me great pain. I think the record indicates that my practice ninety five percent of the time is in representation of doctors. I represent doctors who are charged with malpractice and I have gotten to know doctors and have gotten to hold a deep amount of respect for every single physician who has ever been licensed. There are good ones, no question about that; some are better than others. But no matter how many problems or defects any physician might have, and they are human and they have in them, there is much good in every single one of them. They work hard. In my experience most of them are very conscientious and very dedicated and deserve and still deserve in our count a great deal of respect."

The orator hopefully then would continue as he did in the Indiana Court when he opened the door to a core issue in our case - the medical professions's policing of itself - the process called Peer Review. As he continued, in the Indiana Court he had said:

"It is also true in the last ten to fifteen years that primarily only in the last five that physicians have begun to recognize even among themselves the great need to try to police themselves rather than have an outsider come in and do it, to set up procedures whereby they can honestly judge themselves in a peer review type of proceedings in the interest of good medicine and in the interest of the public and in the interest of themselves.

Such a proceedings is here before us, a peer-review proceedings that has gone on before this court ever became involved or even aware, I suppose of this entire matter but one of the things, Your Honor, that present review procedure requires is to recognize that there are peers because without that, it will surely fail."

What the Hospital orator would not say was that laws had been passed which protected physicians from liability if they participated in Good Faith Peer Review. There was no way that the hearings at Indiana Hospital could qualify for "good faith peer-review". The Hospital hearings were part of a national hospital scandal which was becoming known as "Bad Faith Peer Review". We had been in touch with the Semmelweis Society - a group of physicians who were fighting bad faith peer-review wherever they found it. The Society had agreed to enter our case and would present an Amicus Brief (friend of the Court) to the Court on our behalf. The brief would read:

"INTEREST OF AMICUS CURIAE"

"The Semmelweis Society is a non-profit corporation whose physician members throughout the United States share a common commitment to the fair treatment of doctors in hospital peer review and privilege matters. The Society takes its name from the 19th. century Hungarian physician, Ignaz Semmelweis, who was vilified by his colleagues and superiors in the medical profession because of his strongly held belief that physicians should wash their hands and use clean instruments before delivering babies and performing surgery. His life ended in disgrace for advocating views which ultimately led to the breakthroughs of Lister and Pasteur."

"Semmelweis is remembered in history as the classic victim of abuse of power by fellow medical professionals to the detriment of society. The Semmelweis Society is dedicated to seeing that the peer review process in the United States is not used to drive competent doctors from practicing in the professional field and geographic area of their choice by the denial or revocation of their hospital privileges for reasons that have nothing to do with the improvement of the quality of medical care. The use of the peer review system - so prevalent in the health care industry - for anti-competitive purposes has been a long-standing concern of the Society. As a result of this concern, the Society has previously appeared before the United States Supreme Court as an amicus curiae in a brief supporting Dr. Timothy Patrick in the landmark antitrust case of Patrick v. Burget, 486 U.S. 94 (1988)."

"ARGUMENT"

"While the legal and factual issues particular to this case have been thoroughly addressed, the magnitude of the problem of bad faith peer review - a problem so detrimental to the societal good and to the rights of patients to have access to the best and most affordable health care - has not been made clear. Accordingly, and because the Courts' decisions in this case will have a dramatic impact upon peer review and the physicians and patients affected thereby, the Semmelweis Society respectfully submits this brief asking this Honorable Court to review the potentially far-reaching decisions of the lower courts in the light of the persuasive and meritorious arguments set forth in Dr. Miller's pleadings."

"The members of the Semmelweis Society assert that quality as well as price fairness to the paying consumer of health care services is best achieved through vigorous competition. Through personal experience, the members of the Society know only too well that the health care market has been dominated for many years by practices which are anti-competitive and, which, consequently, have denied market entry to skilled practitioners, stifled innovation and alternative methods of health care delivery, and destroyed operations designed to allow prices to be dependent upon competitive forces of the marketplace.

Many of the anti-competitive ills of the health care marketplace emanate from peer review processes such as that found in the case now before this Court."

"The Semmelweis Society strongly believes that the facts of this case serve to underscore the destructive and insidious nature of <u>Bad Faith Peer Review</u> decisions. For it is within the peer review setting, where competitors review the services of other competitors, that decisions are routinely made in hospitals across the United States which drastically affect the practices and livelihoods of physicians and which unfortunately but frequently emanate from anti-competitive motives. In this case, moreover, the conduct of the Respondents is so outrageous and flagrantly anti-competitive that this Court should afford Dr. Miller's suit the degree of careful consideration commensurate with society's obvious interest in preventing and curing such professional and judicial injustices. Indeed, this Court should demonstrate a healthy skepticism toward the entry of summary judgement in any antitrust case in which the evidence of anti-competitive motive and effect is as blatant as in the case now before the Court."

"Peer review is the cutting tool for economic control in the medical profession. It allows for the creation and maintenance of monopolies. The painful truth is that many within the health care marketplace have been ready and willing to utilize this tool for anti-competitive ends. Data collected and analyzed by the Semmelweis Society indicates that as much as 80% of peer review decisions are dictated by economic concerns. In such an environment, the ideal of competitive health care practices with resultant cost containment and quality improvement can barely be expected to survive, let alone flourish. Conduct such as that of the Defendants in this case, and judicial decisions such as those of the lower courts in this case, can only serve to perpetuate this stifling environment. Accordingly, this Honorable Court should intervene.

As Edmund Burke once stated, "The only thing necessary for the triumph of evil is for good men to do nothing."

Playing to the audience in the Indiana Court when a number of my patients were in the audience the Hospital Lawyer had attempted to cover the fact that he had brought in his own divorce client (Dr. Arnold Sladen) as a witness at the Hospital hearing, and had aided that witness to commit perjury at the hospital hearing. We hoped that he would continue the deception in the Federal Court trial. In his opening statement he would then say as he had in the Indiana County Court:

"And I might say to you that what occurred basically, Dr. Arnold Sladen and I absolutely thought he had nothing pertinent to the situation being heard, and having heard that Dr. Sladen, he brought the case before, the two cases before he testified and he was brought in because I had heard seven doctors were to come to the stand just in connection with the charge, the elderly patient charge and out of that charge there was testimony by the doctors and the testimony by these seven doctors was such that anyone, absolutely anyone of you would have to say to yourself:

"My heavens to Betsy, we don't believe that", and I'm going to go just briefly into the evidence."

He would continue:

"Dr. Sladen came in and took time away from his very busy practice and he does not testify as an expert witness - no big fees paid; that is, the fees paid the expert witnesses for Dr. Miller; and he came in and reviewed and testified such elemental things for him to come in for in terms of treating someone, not as a Urologist but coming in to medicine. Nothing more than a bad pneumoconiosis. We can talk about that; this can't, doesn't involve malpractice, Your Honor. Your Honor is correct about that, it does not involve malpractice. The issue here is much larger than malpractice."

One takes a risk to interpret that lengthy bit of rambling, but apparently it was designed to smooth over the fact that the Hospital Lawyer and his divorce client-witness had committed perjury and that it had never been reported to the Courts.

I imagined that, when he finished his opening statement, the Hospital Lawyer would again take his seat at the opposite table next to co-counsel.

The Judge would likely then advise that the court would take a lunch break and reconvene at 1:30 P.M. He would advise that the plaintiff would present their witnesses at that time.

Our strategy was to present strong evidence first, to get the attention of the jury. After the lunch break - there was no lunch - we just walked around downtown Pittsburgh and spoke very little. After the break we would again go through the "All Rise" routine and the judge would advise us to proceed.

I imagined that my Lawyer would rise and say in a confident voice, "We call to the stand Mr. William Paxton." Our witness would testify that he had been the Hospital Administrator some years earlier. He had been dismissed on twenty minutes notice by the Chairman of the Hospital

Board. He would testify that he had given us an affidavit stating that he and our family had been friends and that he had been warned by the Board Chairman not to associate with the Millers. He was given no reason for that warning and no reason for his dismissal.

He would then testify that he had gone on to a highly successful career with Project Hope and had been one of the top administration officers of the Good Ship Hope - taking medical care to the underprivileged around the globe.

As I imagined his testimony, I couldn't imagine what the cross examination would be. He would be the lead-off witness in our demonstration of bias and unequal treatment by the hospital originating at the very top of Hospital management.

We then would call to the stand, Mr. Robert Kingsley. We were familiar with what he would testify since he had undergone deposition at the request of the Hospital Lawyers. As with all witnesses, he would acknowledge that he had given us an affidavit and he would reveal, as the affidavit stated, that he had been the Chief Financial Officer of the Hospital for several years and would frequently have a cup of coffee with Dr. Miller in the Hospital cafeteria. He would testify that he considered Dr. Miller a friend and would go on to testify that he was asked by the Hospital Administrator to use his friendship to learn of Dr. Miller's plans and report back. He would say that the Hospital was afraid of Dr. Miller's competition as an economic threat to the Hospital. As a climax to this testimony, he would describe conversations between the Board Chairman and board members-lawyers, making plans to dismiss Dr. Miller from the Hospital. He would describe these men as saying that, "Dr. Miller has to be stopped."

On cross examination he would be asked by the Hospital Lawyer why, if he were a friend of Dr. Miller, why he would spy and report back to the Administrator. As he had said during deposition, he didn't consider he was spying, since Dr. Miller was making no secret of his plans and would have discussed them directly with the Administration if he had been asked. Kingsley would testify that he had also been fired on short notice by the Board Chairman and the Administrator because the Board Chairman had used his position at a local bank to review Kingsley's financial records and claim that Kingsley was demonstrating too high a life style. Kingsley would advise the jury that he was now the successful administrator of a California hospital.

We would then call to the stand Mr. Don Gable. As stated in his affidavit, Mr. Gable would testify that he became the Hospital Chief Financial Officer after Robert Kingsley was dismissed. He would testify that the Administrator, who was a patient of Dr. Miller, recommended Dr. Miller to take over the care of his only child - a seriously handicapped daughter. He would also say that the Administrator told him Miller was "paranoid". He would testify that he was advised also by the Administrator with the Board Chairman present, to spy on Miller and report back. He would state that the Administration was afraid that Dr. Miller's fledgling medical center was an economic threat to the Hospital's finances, and he was told, early on, that the Hospital was going to try not to renew Dr. Miller's staff appointment. He would reveal that he and his family had, indeed, become friends of Dr. Miller and that the professional relationship with his daughter was continuing over the years. He would then describe the hateful continuing pattern of hospital tyranny. He was also fired on short notice a few days before Christmas and would testify that the Administrator attempted to have him blackballed at other regional hospitals. He would describe though, that he continued to be a successful accountant.

    In my vision of the trial to come, I believed that if these three witnesses hadn't established an illegal conspiracy nothing would. It was now our chore to show unequal treatment of physicians by the Hospital as the Court of Appeals had directed.

    We would then call to the stand Dr. Lester Lazarus. After the swearing-in, the questions and answers would very likely follow closely the questions and answers that occurred when the witness underwent deposition some time earlier.

    But, we would avoid embarrassing the witness with any of the personal revelations from his deposition. He was simply a prime witness to describe that some horrendous problems were overlooked by the Hospital, while other petty infractions (or accusations) were pursued with vigor. The testimony would show what the courts describe as "disparate treatment of physicians."

    The questions and answers would proceed as follows:
    Q: "Did anyone at the Hospital keep records of medical mishaps?"
    A: "The Pathologist had lots of incidences and lots of things that I didn't know whether he was lying or not, but at least it made me wonder just who I was making friends with, and as a matter of fact, I told my wife I didn't know if I was going to stay in Indiana a year, even though Peter Post and I had an agreement."

    In describing the Hospital's Medical Staff he would continue:

"The Staff, you talk about, you know, a split down the middle. If you went to a Staff meeting, you knew how this bunch was going to vote and how they were going to vote, and that was why it was very important to know which side they were on."

Q: "And you never in terms of all your years were able to formulate an impression of what distinguished one camp from the other?"

A: "Why the division was there, I was never quite sure. If the Pathologist were alive, he could - he kept records on everybody." And then in relation to unequal treatment of physicians Lester was asked:

Q: "Doctor, did you ever become aware of any staff privileged physician at the hospital making any professional mistakes in the care and treatment of their patients at any time?"

Lester would answer: "Well when I was on the Executive Committee and President, we had to suspend (the young lady physician). Now that was because the way she talked to nurses, made rounds in a mini skirt and, you know used language unbecoming a lady."

Instead of taking a two week suspension, the lady resigned.

And, Lester would continue:

"We had to suspend (a surgeon). We had a female pathologist and he got into an argument with her. They were swearing and I think he actually pushed her a little bit so we gave him a couple of weeks off."

Lester was certainly helping to show unequal treatment of physicians at the Hospital. There was never any discipline other than short suspensions.

Again, Lester would continue:

"Early on I was a Blue Shield investigator. We had a case once in Indiana. We were reviewing appendectomies where normal appendices were taken out. In that case, a normal appendix was taken out. The child had been admitted for a bee sting."

The next question had been:

Q: "Have you ever formulated an opinion with regard to any staff physicians that their care and treatment of a patient fell below acceptable medical standards?"

A: "Probably lots of times, but I never expressed it." (conspiracy of silence)

Q: "Have you ever become aware of any medical malpractice cases filed against Indiana Hospital Staff members?"

A: "I have had one. G.H. was in a suit. K. H. was in a suit which he won. F. D. has had some suits against him. The new surgeon just had a suit which he won. Yes, we have had our share of malpractice suits. There's a couple of suits against the Emergency Room physicians."

Q: "Did the Hospital have a policy with regards to sanctions or penalty against staff members with medical malpractice cases against them?"

A: "No."

Q: "Would there be any requirement by the Hospital that you report medical malpractice suits to the hospital, the Credentials Committee, to anybody at the hospital?"

A: "No."

Lester was continuing to be very helpful in uncovering the hospital's unequal treatment of physicians.

Lester would continue:

"There's a surgeon who lost a case." He then described that the patient had his colon removed despite no evidence of malignancy. Lester said: "They took a colon out, and they settled out of court."

When asked if any Medical Staff physician ever was arrested or convicted of a crime Lester had answered: "Well, I am probably the only one that I know of. I was charged with recklessly endangering someone. I had been drinking. In fact, I was drinking with the Sheriff. I saw somebody running and took a shot at him."

Q: "Were you found guilty or not guilty?"

A: "I don't remember whether I was guilty or not. There was an arrangement worked out, what do you call that - accelerated rehabilitation. I was ordered not to drive for a year."

Q: "Did you actually fire a gun and were there property damages?"

A: "I had a few pellets in the roof of the car."

Q: "Did the Administration of the Hospital become aware of the arrest and the disposition that you have given us?"

A: "Oh, I'm sure they did."

Q: "Did you receive any sanction of any nature from the Administration at Indiana Hospital?"

A: "No."

Q: "Other than Ralph Miller, are you aware of anybody else at the hospital having had their staff privileges revoked?"

A: "No, I am not aware of it".

and then:

Q: "Are you aware of any physician ever being penalized by Indiana Hospital or sanctioned in any way for refusal to take Medicaid patients?"

A: "No."

Vance Vader in his infamous report following the death of my elderly patient, claimed that a surgeon's privileges at the Hospital didn't allow them to treat medical problems such as pneumonia.

Lester would describe his unlimited privileges despite his limited education.

Q: "Do you recall back at any point when you were on the Staff of Indiana Hospital of any staff members admitting patients to the Hospital when the reason for the admission was not within that particular staff member's field of expertise?"

A: "Well, what's field of expertise? I have admitted people with low back pain, I have admitted people with kidney stones, I have admitted people — I have never done any surgery, but that's, you know, from my personal standpoint."

And then the question would be:

Q: "Do you recall having concluded that you had made any errors as part of your obstetrical practice?"

A: "I had a patient once have a ruptured uterus and died after the baby was born and that had nothing to do with my decision to give up O.B."

Q: "If I understand your earlier testimony, nothing ever came of that with regard to your staff privileges at the hospital: is that right?"

A: "Right."

Continuing with evidence that the Hospital's general practitioners were admitting all sorts of problems, perhaps beyond their expertise, the following questions and answers would result:

Q: "Do you recall, Dr. Lazarus, having ever admitted anyone to the hospital outside your own particular field of expertise?

A: "What is your filed of expertise when you do family medicine? So, you know, I have admitted urological cases, otrhopedic cases, never any fractures or anything like that, but low back problems."

Q: "Do you recall having admitted any patient with the initial impression being a psychiatric problem?"

A: "Oh, (young depressed man) is the guy that hanged himself."

Q: "Did you consider that the depression that you described as being within your field of expertise or outside your field of expertise?"

A: "Depression is the most common diagnosis in primary care practices. We treat depression, all people in primary care treat depression."

Q: "Do you know if there was an investigation by the Indiana Hospital as a result of that suicide by hanging?
A: "I don't think there was an investigation."
Q: "Do you remember talking to the Coroner about that incident?"
A: "I don't remember."
We would then call to the stand the Coroner of Indiana County. After questions establishing his position, he would testify that, following the hanging death, no one at the Hospital reported the death to him. He learned of the death only through "the grape vine".

He would be asked if this was part of the Hospital's veil of secrecy. He might very well say he didn't know.

We would then announce: "We call to the stand, Dr. Harold Cooperman". Dr. Cooperman had agreed that he would tell the truth and testify that when he was the Hospital Pathologist, during the relevant period , that he had received the bodies of two infants which had been decapitated by obstetrical forceps during delivery. He would identify the physicians responsible as Clippins and Ewalt, both members of that "Executive Committee" that had initiated the Kangaroo Court. It was difficult to imagine an effective cross examination for this revelation. It was also unlikely that the Defense could have the jury dismiss such a revelation.

We would then call to the stand Dr. Claude Clippins. We would show Dr. Clippins the transcript of his deposition when he was asked: "Doctor, have you ever heard of babies being decapitated at birth?"
ANSWER: "Sure."
QUESTION: "Have you ever had a complication like that?"
ANSWER: "Sure."
QUESTION: "Did you ever have any complications such as this when you delivered a baby?"
ANSWER: "Certainly."
QUESTION: "In what year?
ANSWER: "I have no idea."
QUESTION: "Is it on record at the hospital?"
ANSWER: "Certainly."
QUESTION: "Doctor, you previously testified that you had had post graduate training. Have you ever had any residency training?"
ANSWER: "No."
QUESTION: "Have you ever had residency training in obstetrics?"
ANSWER: "No."

QUESTION: "Did you have any limitations on your obstetrical privileges at Indiana Hospital?"
ANSWER: "No."
QUESTION: "After the decapitation tragedy what action did the Hospital take?"
ANSWER: "There was no action."
QUESTION: "Who appointed you to be Chairman of the committee that was to sit in judgement of Dr. Miller's future?"
ANSWER: "I don't recall."
QUESTION: "Doctor, have you ever had any trouble with Dr. Miller?"
ANSWER: "Yes."
QUESTION: "What was the trouble?"
ANSWER: "He tried to have the state lift my license."
QUESTION: "Why?"
ANSWER: "He said I was making false statements about him."
QUESTION: "Isn't it true, Doctor, that Dr. Miller only had the State Society warn you?"
ANSWER: "Possibly."
QUESTION: "And you added to that that he was trying to lift your license?"
ANSWER: "Yes."
QUESTION: "And yet, you were appointed to be an impartial head of the hearing committee - the committee that ended Dr. Miller's surgical career?"
No answer.
QUESTION: "I ask you again, who appointed you to be chairman of the hearing committee?"
ANSWER: "I don't recall."
QUESTION: "Doctor, before your last deposition you produced a doctor's statement which said that you were in poor health and the Assistant Hospital Lawyer told the Court that if Dr. Miller were to attend your deposition, it would "quite frankly kill you"." Did the Court know that you were practicing medicine full time at the time?"
ANSWER: "I don't know."
QUESTION: "Do you think you're qualified to judge Dr. Miller?"
The answer during his deposition was: "_I think I am qualified to do anything I want._"

445

A letter would be shown. It had been written by Clippins to Dr. Miller accusing Miller of "creating an unpleasant Hospital atmosphere". The letter reads:

"It is my considerate opinion that if any prizes are ever awarded to the one who has done the most to create an unpleasant hospital atmosphere, you would have no problem becoming a winner."

QUESTION: "Dr. Clippins, I show you a copy of another letter you wrote and dated February 15 - one day before the death of Dr.Miller's elderly patient. Do you recognize it?" And your previous letter?

ANSWER: "Yeah."

QUESTION: "The second letter is to Dr. Gerhard Werner, Dean of the University of Pittsburgh School of Medicine. In the first paragraph you state:

"It has been reported that a member of the Medical Staff of Indiana Hospital contacted you recently regarding our Preceptorship Program at Indiana Hospital. This physician allegedly reported our program to be poorly conducted, mismanaged, and supervised by a group of second rate physicians practicing a poor quality of medical care." and in the second paragraph you state:

"This physician, Dr. R. J. Miller, has been a dissident in our midst for the past seventeen years. We of the Medical Staff are very familiar with his tactics of freely spreading misinformation and derogatory statements about any successful program which he didn't happen to think of first." and in the third paragraph you state to Dr. Werner:

"Whether or not the reported discussion between you and Dr. R. J. Miller took place, I feel it my duty as Chairman of the Preceptorship Program to tell you about our program, and hopefully dispel any fear you may have about the manner in which it is conducted.".

QUESTION: "Dr. Clippins, do you now realize that Dr. Werner and Dr. Miller never heard of each other?"

ANSWER: "I don't know."

QUESTION: "In your letter, you then go on to blame the difficulties of your program. You say: "This student (fourth year medical student) resulted in the demise of our Preceptorship Program. His record at the Medical School will explain why." Is that correct?"

ANSWER: "Yes."

QUESTION: "Dr. Miller really didn't have anything to do with the failure of your program, did he?"

ANSWER: "No."

As a final question: "Doctor Clippins, once again, who appointed you to be Chairman of a committee sitting in judgement of Dr. Miller?"

ANSWER: "I don't recall."

QUESTION: "And do you still claim that you are qualified to sit in judgement of Dr. Miller?"

ANSWER: "Certainly".

The Hospital Lawyer's cross examination and the answers in this case were predictable and would attempt to refute the damaging testimony.

It would seem that the Court day was drawing to a close. The Judge would announce that the Court was in adjournment. He would caution the Jurors not to discuss the case and that the Court would resume the following morning.

I had felt that the testimony of Vance Vader would be the most damming of all. I imagined the courtroom would be buzzing as we entered the next morning. The visitor's section would be nearly full and I would slip into the last seat just behind the rail. The lawyers would be at their posts and the tipstaff would open the door to the right of the jury box and have the Jury file in and take their places. With the hushed conversations quieted, the tipstaff would disappear again into the door into the Judge's chamber. He would emerge with his now familiar "All Rise" and the Judge would enter without looking around. He would give a few instructions to the lawyers and then advise that the plaintiff could proceed. There would certainly be an air of expectation. The Jury would look tense as my Lawyer would rise and very deliberately announce, "We call to the stand, Dr. Vance Vader." Vader would walk briskly to the jury box, and standing before the box, would follow the Court's instructions. With hand raised, he would speak firmly, "I do", when asked if he would tell the truth, the whole truth, and nothing but the truth.

Vader would take the stand stiffly and would look at his questioner with a fixed gaze through the lenses of those tortoise shell glasses. He would describe that he had left private practice and was a Hospital employee. After the statement of his name and occupation he would be told: "Doctor Vader, I would like to take you through the years and your relationship with Dr. Miller."

We had taken Vader's deposition and could judge, to some degree, his answers and his reactions.

The first question: "When did you first know Dr. Miller?"

Vader would advise that we met when he first came to town and that during that period we would occasionally refer patients to each other. Then:

QUESTION: "Now, Dr. Vader, did you ever go to Dr. Miller's office and make a request to join him at his Center?"

ANSWER: "At one time I was looking around to purchase property to build an office. I may have stopped at Dr. Miller's office briefly."

QUESTION: "Isn't it true that you were sharing an office with Dr. Peter Post and had a parting of the ways with him, and that you were urgently attempting to break ties with him and build an office building next to Dr. Miller?"

ANSWER: "No, I was just looking around at a number of locations."

QUESTION: "And isn't it true that you were incensed that Dr. Miller didn't accept your offer and that the next day you told him to forget your request and that you never wanted to be associated with him?"

ANSWER: "Absolutely not."

QUESTION: "What was your relationship with Dr. Miller after that?"

ANSWER: "We were never that friendly. We would refer patients from time to time."

QUESTION: "When the Executive Committee of the medical staff brought charges against Dr. Miller you were a member of that Committee, weren't you?"

ANSWER: "Yes."

QUESTION: "And one of the charges was that he failed to hold enough meetings of the Infection Control Committee. Is that true?"

ANSWER: "Yes."

QUESTION: "And who suggested that charge?"

ANSWER: "The Committee did."

QUESTION: "Isn't it true that you, as President of the Medical Staff, dismissed Dr. Miller from that chairmanship?"

ANSWER: "Yes, he wasn't reporting often enough to the Executive Committee."

QUESTION: "Dr. Vader, did you know, that at the hearings for Dr. Miller, which you were responsible for, the Head of the Hospital Surgical Department testified that Dr. Miller was the best Infection Control Chairman the Hospital ever had?"

ANSWER: "No."

QUESTION: "Doctor, weren't you just venting your growing malice?"

ANSWER: "That is absolutely not true. He didn't hold enough meetings."

QUESTION: "Dr. Vader, I have here a photostat of a file jacket that was in Dr. Miller's file in the hospital administrator's office. It was provided to us by the Hospital under the rules of discovery. Now, at your deposition you testified that you had never given anyone material to put in Dr. Miller's file. Would you look at the typewritten label of that jacket? Now, would you read the label on that jacket?"

ANSWER: "Material about Dr. Miller given to (the Administrator) by Dr. Vader."

QUESTION: "Dr. Vader, would you care to change your previous testi mony?"

ANSWER: "No."

QUESTION: "Here is an article from the Journal of the American Medical Association. It was found inside the jacket you just saw. Do you recognize it?"

ANSWER: "No."

QUESTION: "Dr. Vader, the article inside the jacket that describes your putting material in Dr. Miller's file is entitled, "Paranoid Schizophrenia In The Medical Profession". That's a very serious accusation, Dr. Vader. Do you deny giving this to (the Administrator) for Dr. Miller's file?"

ANSWER: "Yes, I never saw that before."

QUESTION: "Dr. Vader, you filed the report that led to Dr. Miller's demand for a full hearing and eventually led to Dr. Miller's dismissal from the Hospital's Medical Staff. I'm showing you a copy of your report. Would you carefully look at this copy of the report and tell us if you recognize it?"

ANSWER: "Yes, it's a copy."

QUESTION: "In that report you state that Dr. Miller was treating a patient for pneumonitis and that that was beyond his Hospital privileges. Where do you have the authority for that?"

ANSWER: "It is official Hospital policy."

QUESTION: "Can you tell us where it is stated anywhere?"

ANSWER: "It is in accordance with annual appointments."

QUESTION: "Do the Hospital regulations anywhere state that the Surgical Staff does not have privileges to treat pneumonitis?"

ANSWER: "No."

QUESTION: "Doctor, you may have heard Doctor Lazarus' testimony that there were no restrictions on his practice at the Hospital. He could admit and treat any type of illness or injury. Why would you say that a surgical specialist was unqualified to treat an uncomplicated case of pneumonitis?"

ANSWER: "These people should get consultations on medical problems."

QUESTION: "In your answers to interrogatories you stated that the people qualified to give consultations in a case like this were Hospital general practitioners and internists. What residency training do these people have?"

ANSWER: "There are now residency programs that train family physicians."

QUESTION: "What residency training would Dr. Clippins have had?"

ANSWER: "I suspect that he didn't have formal residency training."

QUESTION: "Isn't it true, Doctor, that the surgical specialists have attained a status before surgical residency that qualifies them to enter general practice?"

ANSWER: "Yes."

QUESTION: "And you still contend that Dr. Miller was unqualified to treat one of his patients with pneumonitis?"

ANSWER: "Yes, he was unqualified and he didn't have Hospital privileges to do that."

QUESTION: "And you believe that the general practitioners at the hospital, like Dr. Clippins, were qualified?"

ANSWER: "Yes."

QUESTION: "In your report which led to the Hospital hearings relating to the elderly patient who died in your presence, and which ended Dr. Miller's surgical career, you state that Dr. Miller never even talked with the deceased patient's family. Do you wish to correct that statement now?"

ANSWER: "No."

QUESTION: "Dr. Vader, in your report, you state:

"Finally, when the patient presented in acute circulatory arrest, the attending physician did not come to assist in the resuscitation efforts or really express any concern over the condition of his patient."

Isn't it true that the patient expired in fourteen minutes while Dr. Miller was still on the telephone?"

ANSWER: "He may have."

QUESTION: "How do you know that Dr. Miller didn't really express any concern over the condition of his patient?"

ANSWER: "I was told by the nursing supervisor."

QUESTION: "Did you know that Dr. Miller immediately phoned the patient's family?"

ANSWER: "No."

My lawyer would then show the witness an affidavit from the patient's oldest son.

He would say, "Have you ever seen this before?"

ANSWER: "No."

It reads:

"I, ____, son of (elderly patient), want to express my complete satisfaction with Dr. Miller concerning the medical care given to my father during his hospitalization." The affidavit continued:

"My father has been in poor health for quite a long while and had refused medical care for a long time before he was admitted to Indiana Hospital. I was the closest person to my father during his illness, and I visited him every day and I felt that he was receiving the best of care from Dr. Miller. At this time I also want to express my anger with Indiana Hospital for using my father's name in this case without my permission. I was also very upset when, the Hospital Administrator, who I feel should have remained neutral in this case, phoned my wife the evening before she testified at the hearing and tried to influence her against Dr. Miller."

"I would be pleased and willing to testify for Dr. Miller."

QUESTION: "Doctor, in your report, you go to great lengths in describing what you observed on the cardiac monitor, while you watched the patient die. You describe elevation of the S-T segment, a pattern of the dying heart with progressive slowing of the rate, idioventricular rhythm and gradual bizarre broadening of the QRS. Now, as laymen, who don't know the fine points of electrocardiography, we have to rely on physicians for the truth. Do you know that the seven distinguished physicians who testified at Dr. Miller's hearing, disagreed with you - unanimously? They testIfied that the patient had suffered an unpreventable pulmonary thrombosis related to longstanding pulmonary disease. Did you know that?"

ANSWER: "No."

QUESTION: "In your report, you state that you were appalled in themanagement of the patient in the days preceding his demise. Testifying for Dr. Miller during the Hospital hearing was the Hospital's Chief of

Surgery, the Chairman of the Department of Urology from the University of Pennsylvania, the Chairman of the National Medical Advisory Service from Washington, D. C., an internist from Johnstown, the Chief Pathologist from the Western Pennsylvania Hospital, another internist from the Western Pennsylvania Hospital and a urologist from Greensburg. All these physicians disputed your diagnosis of a coronary heart attack. Are they all wrong?"

ANSWER: "Yes."

QUESTION: "Those physicians from academic and teaching hospitals took strong exception to your claim that urologists are not qualified to treat pneumonitis. Are they all wrong?"

ANSWER: "Yes."

QUESTION: "Doctor, are you aware that the patient's family testified at the hospital hearing that their eighty-one-year-old father had been in ill health for a number of years and had refused medical care?"

ANSWER: "No."

QUESTION: "Are you aware that the deceased patient's family condemned the hospital for using their father's death to bring charges against his physician?"

ANSWER: "No."

QUESTION: "Did you know that the patient's family filed an amicus brief to the Court in support of Dr. Miller?"

ANSWER: "I may have heard something along that line."

And then:

QUESTION: "Were you with the Administrator when he called the patient's family and attempted to have them change their upcoming testimony at the Hospital hearings?

ANSWER: "Yes."

QUESTION: "Doctor, you took charge of the attempted resuscitation of Dr. Miller's patient and dismissed Dr. Clippins who offered help. Your report states that he wasn't needed. Is that correct?"

ANSWER: "Yes."

QUESTION: "Did you know that your Executive Committee filed a charge against Dr. Miller for not using him and Dr. Hankey in a previous resuscitation effort?"

ANSWER: "Yes."

QUESTION: "Doesn't that show different standards for different physicians?"

ANSWER: "Possibly."

QUESTION: "I show you now the resuscitation record from the so-called resuscitation that you took charge of - leading to your "report". Do you recall seeing this record?"

ANSWER: "I may have seen it some time ago."

QUESTION: "Would you tell us what emergency drugs were given?" After a period of silence, the answer would come.

ANSWER: "There were no drugs given."

QUESTION: "Would you please look at the record and tell us what intravenous fluids were given?"

ANSWER: "We were unable to start an intravenous line."

QUESTION: "During the time of resuscitation, what did you do after Dr. Clippins left?"

ANSWER: "I was watching the cardiac monitor."

QUESTION: "Did you attempt to give any drugs?"

ANSWER: "No."

QUESTION: "Did you help start an intravenous line?"

ANSWER: "No, other people were attempting to do that."

QUESTION: "So, while the patient was dying with you in charge, you stood there and watched the electrocardiograph of a dying heart?"

There was no answer.

The Judge would very likely say, "We will continue this testimony after a fifteen minute break."

Vader would be redder than ususal and would walk out of the courtroom without a word and without a glance at anyone.

My friend and lawyer wouldn't look at me or speak during the recess. He wouldn't want to break his train of thought or be sidetracked. I had learned to know him. He was a coiled spring at this point and he knew that probably the most important testimony of the entire trial was just minutes away.

When Court resumed the Judge would remind the witness that he was still under oath and we would be told to proceed.

The first question would be:

QUESTION: "Now, Dr. Vader, before we recessed, you were describing how you had stood and watched a cardiac monitor while Dr. Miller's patient died. After the patient's death, did you ask the Nursing Supervisor, Velma Marshall, to get you a copy of the patient's chart?"

ANSWER: "Yes."

QUESTION: "Why did you request that?"

ANSWER: "It appeared that the patient did not have proper medical care."

QUESTION: "Did you know that, at the Hospital hearing, seven distinguished physicians, mainly department heads, testified that Dr. Miller's care had been appropriate?"

ANSWER: "I may have read that."

QUESTION: "I'm now going to show you the transcript on the deposition you gave some time ago. At the center of page 139 you are asked the question: "Doctor, with regard to all the physicians that you have known over the years, since you first got to Indiana Hospital, and to the extent that you are aware of their perspective practices, do you have an opinion as to whether or not Ralph Miller was the least well-qualified to practice at Indiana Hospital?" Your answer was: "I'm going to say yes."

QUESTION: "Now we ask, was that opinion based on your experiences with Dr. Miller during the period when you were in private practice?"

ANSWER: "Yes, mainly so."

QUESTION: "So, during that period, Dr. Miller was practicing with privileges in urology and in your opinion was the worst physician on the Hospital Staff?"

ANSWER: "Yes."

My lawyer and everyone else in that courtroom would sense that something was about to happen. You would have been able to hear a very small pin drop. The next question would be:

QUESTION: "Do you know a Clayton Vader?"

The witness would clench his jaw and would redden with that large vein in his neck almost popping and would answer:

ANSWER: "He's my father."

QUESTION: "Dr. Vader, I show you the admission record at Indiana Hospital for Clayton Vader. Please look at the date. It is during the period when you say Dr. Miller was the worst physician at the Hospital. Would you please read the name of the admitting physician?"

ANSWER: "I was the admitting physician."

QUESTION: "And would you read the name of the physician to whom you were entrusting the care of your father?"

ANSWER: "It was Dr. R. J. Miller."

The questioner would then slowly turn around, glance at the Judge, and would very quietly say, "Doctor, can we believe anything you say?"

There would undoubtedly be a strenuous objection from the Hospital Lawyers.

My lawyer would then say, "I have no further questions for this person."

The courtroom would remain quiet. It could be anticipated that the Hospital Lawyers would attempt to revive this witness. The Hospital Lawyer would rise and ask a series of questions designed to show the witness as an outstanding and influential member of the Hospital's Medical Staff in a fine community hospital.

Would they be able to succeed?

I would imagine that, After Vader's testimony, we would call Dr. Lee Daugherty, who was the Emergency Department physician who admitted the elderly patient to Dr. Miller's care. He would contradict Vader's malicious report and its accusations. He would describe being called into the Hospital Administrator's office where two Hospital Lawyers, Mattern and the Hospital Prosecutor, were attempting to create a case for improper care of the elderly patient. He refused to testify against me and shortly resigned from the Emergency Room Staff to enter private practice. He would tell the story of being one of my patients and of calling me and offering help after seeing the report of my dismissal on television.

The Court would likely then be recessed for the day and we would be in preparation for the fourth day and the testimony of Nathan Goldfarb. The opening by the Judge and tipstaff would become a little more routine. There still would be no empty seats in the audience as the jury again filed in.

We would call Goldfarb on that fourth morning and he would give his usual self-assured appearance as he would raise his hand and swear to tell the truth. The questioning would pretty much revolve around Goldfarb's testimony under oath when he underwent questioning at deposition.

After he had identified himself as a member of the Hospital's "Executive Committee," the first of those questions would be:

QUESTION: "Doctor, we have evidence that you told various people at the Hospital - as part of a hate campaign - that Dr. Miller had put his wife in the Home for Battered Women. Would you care to respond to that?"

ANSWER: "I had heard by the grapevine, I don't remember where or how. It's a small town. Things get around. I remember hearing somewhere along the line that Dr. Miller's wife had been treated at the Alice Paul House. That's all I ever heard about it."

QUESTION: "Did you ever question anybody about that or relate that alleged incident to anyone?"

ANSWER: "I never did. I never did."

QUESTION: "Would it change your testimony if we produced people who say they heard you repeat that story?"

ANSWER: "No."

QUESTION: "Did your or your wife ever have conversations with Judge Earley or Judge Handler about the hearings in the Indiana County Court of Common Pleas?"

ANSWER: "No."

QUESTION: "I'm now going to show you a statement under oath that describes that Judge Earley related that you called him twice and attempted to persuade him against Dr. Miller in the litigation in the local court. Is that true or is Judge Earley in error?"

ANSWER: "Never to my recollection and I would also add that I would deem it the height of impropriety for me to contact a judge. I'd be afraid I'd be held in contempt of Court or something. It was — no, I never approached a judge. In fact, it never entered my mind to do that."

QUESTION: "Do you know of any information that another doctor contacted Judge Earley?"

ANSWER: "Why don't you ask the other doctor?"

QUESTION: "If Judge Earley testifies that you did, in fact call him, and if we produce a witness - a clergyman - who will testify that he overheard you and Judge Handler in a heated discussion, would you change your testimony?"

ANSWER: "Certainly not."

QUESTION: "During your deposition, you were asked your feelings about Dr. Miller. You answered: "Personally, he was awfully hard to like. You know, after I got to know him, I didn't like him and I make no bones about that at all. But, professionally I had nothing against him."

"On a few occasions we socialized and, at that time, I found him friendly and nice in the early days. As I said, after I got to know him, his disruptive behavior and troublemaking penchant just turned me off completely."

QUESTION: "Doctor, isn't it true that your dissatisfaction with Dr. Miller came after you took over the chairmanship of the Hospital's Surgical

Department in an irregular fashion? Isn't it true that he felt you were not qualified to be the Department Head?"

ANSWER: "No, I disliked him before that."

QUESTION: "Isn't it true that what you call "disruption" was really discontent with the political activity that had forced the previous Surgical Department Chairman out of office because he had tried to improve conditions in the operating room?"

ANSWER: "That is unlikely."

QUESTION: "Doctor, isn't it true that, when you took over the Chairmanship of the Department, that you began writing your own minutes of the meetings?'

ANSWER: "Yes. Both positions were held by the same person."

QUESTION: "In looking at what you call disruptive behavior please look at this set of minutes. Did you author these minutes?"

ANSWER: "It appears that I did."

QUESTION: "On the second page of your minutes, you state: 'Dr. Miller objected to the presentation of any physicians' cases when that physician was not in attendance and stated that this formed a Kangaroo Court and would not be condoned by him.' Wasn't Dr. Miller upholding a basic principle of fairness by not wanting a surgeon to be investigated in absentia?"

The minutes of that meeting read:

"Dr. Goldfarb informed Dr. Miller that the matter was brought up, not to castigate any physician, but to formulate an opinion as to the best treatment in such cases."

As Chairman at that meeting, you then went on to say:

'None of the other members of the surgical department present indicated support for Dr. Miller's position. However, so that no misunderstanding might ensue, the Department members were asked to keep their comments on any case reviewed non-specific.' The question then is, "Was this part of Dr. Miller's disruptive behavior?"

ANSWER: "Yes."

QUESTION: "Doctor, I show you another set of your minutes. In the middle of the second paragraph recording this meeting it reads:

'A heated discussion followed.' One of the surgeons said that he refused to be any part of a system which is discriminatory and which punishes the general surgeons.' Did you, at any time, feel that the participants in the "heated discussion" were disruptive?"

ANSWER: "No."

Then we would ask Goldfarb:

QUESTION: "Thank you, you have helped us illustrate the unequal treatment of medical staff physicians. Now, at the beginning of the final paragraph of your minutes we read: 'Dr. Miller then launched into a long and familiar harangue about the ills of the Indiana Hospital in general and the evils of the not-so-wonderful medical staff in particular as he viewed them.' You then say: 'In typical self-righteous and pontifical manner, he defended the previous Department Chairman and listed his ideas of what a doctor should be, quoting unconfirmed statements from supposedly disgruntled previous staff members.' Doctor, our only question is: Did you indeed compose these minutes?"

ANSWER: "Yes, but you're taking all this out of context."

QUESTION: "Again, we thank you. You have helped demonstrate disparate treatment in the surgical department. One group in a heated discussion, are immune from your literary efforts and another is described as 'launching into a long and familiar harangue'. You really don't like Dr. Miller do you?"

ANSWER: "I do not."

QUESTION: "Doctor, you testified at the Hospital hearings that led to the revocation of Dr. Miller's medical staff appointment, that the feeling toward Dr. Miller by the entire surgical department was the same as yours. Is that correct?"

ANSWER: "Yes."

QUESTION: 'How could you possibly know that?"

There would be no answer.

QUESTION: "You have painted a totally negative picture of Dr. Miller and have accused him of putting his wife in a home for battered women. Please look at this record. It is one of your Surgical Department minutes.Is that correct?"

ANSWER: "Yes."

We would then read in the very same minutes that stated that "Dr. Miller moved that the Department recommend that a relief anesthesiologist be hired to serve the surgical department when the regular anesthesiologist was away." The minutes read that the" motion was seconded and passed unanimously."

QUESTION: "Is that correct?"

ANSWER: "Yes."

QUESTION: "Please identify this additional set of your minutes. These minutes of yours were written while Dr. Miller was Chairman of the Infection Control Committee. He was asking those present to help control the infection rate in the Hospital operating rooms. Is that correct?"

ANSWER: "Yes."

QUESTION: "Finally, after your minutes describing Dr. Miller as entering into a 'long and familiar harangue', at the same meeting Dr. Miller made a motion that the Department elect a Secretary to replace you to write the Department's minutes. What was the outcome of that motion?"

ANSWER: "A secretary was elected."

QUESTION: "Wasn't it true that Dr. Miller declined after he was nominated for that post?"

ANSWER: "I don't recall."

QUESTION: "Do you still testify that all those in the Surgical Department shared your feelings toward Dr. Miller?"

ANSWER: "Yes."

QUESTION: "After Dr. Miller's dismissal from the Medical Staff, you continued your campaign. Is this your writing published in the Indiana newspaper?"

ANSWER: "Yes."

QUESTION: "In your letter published in the newspaper you wrote: 'No qualified physician has ever been denied Hospital privileges if he, in fact, requested them. Only one physician has had his privileges permanently revoked, and, in this case it was the judgement of the Medical Staff and Board of Directors that quality care in the Hospital would be sacrificed if this physician were allowed to remain on the staff'." I imagined we would then continue with:

QUESTION: "Doctor, you refused to state at your deposition how you knew that Dr. Miller's privileges were 'permanently revoked'."

The questioning would then probably take a tack, not pursued during Goldfarb's previous deposition.

QUESTION: "Doctor, have you ever had complications occurring during surgery?"

ANSWER: "Occasionally."

QUESTION: "Tell us your experience with the Phaco Emulsifier purchased for you by the Hospital."

ANSWER: "We found that this type of equipment was not suited to our work."

QUESTION: "On how many occasions was the equipment used?"
ANSWER: "I believe twice."
QUESTION: "And what was the result of that use?"
ANSWER: "The equipment didn't function properly."
QUESTION: "And what were the results?"
ANSWER: "The surgery on those occasions was terminated."
QUESTION: "Was there damage to the patients' eyes on those occasions?"
ANSWER: "Some."
QUESTION: "Were the patients blinded on these occasions?"
ANSWER: "Not totally."
QUESTION: "Isn't it true that the equipment was purchased by the hospital for your sole use at a cost of about $35,000.00 and that after you used it twice it sat idle for a year or more?"
ANSWER: "Yes, it was of no use to me."
QUESTION: "And isn't it true that the equipment was sold to a Pittsburgh hospital where it was successfully used?"
ANSWER: "I'm not certain of that."
QUESTION: "Doctor, have you ever had a complication during eye surgery which required you to send the patient by ambulance to Pittsburgh?"
ANSWER: "One."
QUESTION: "During your deposition, you testified that you had never been investigated by the Pennsylvania Department of Health. I show you this report marked Exhibit 22. Take your time and read it. Is it not a report from the Pennsylvania Department of Health after they investigated another operating room mishap?"
ANSWER: "I guess so."
QUESTION: "Now, in face of these mishaps, what action did the Hospital take?"
ANSWER: "None that I know of."
QUESTION: "Were you ever suspended for a time?"
ANSWER: "No."
QUESTION: "Were your privileges ever suspended or revoked?"
ANSWER: "No."
QUESTION: "But you wanted to revoke Dr. Miller's privileges?"
ANSWER: "He had repeatedly criticized the Medical Staff Officers and the Administration. He was insulting and uncooperative."

QUESTION: "The Hospital Lawyer in the Indiana County Court said that Dr. Miller made the nurses cry. Have you ever made the nurses cry?"

ANSWER: "Certainly not."

QUESTION: "Have you ever told the Emergency Department of the hospital not to call you after eleven o'clock or when you were on the golf course?"

The reply would be the same as that given at deposition.

ANSWER: "At numerous times I had requested the Emergency Department that I not be called during the night for things that could be taken care of the next day or some minor thing like conjunctivitis or pink eye. I got many calls in the middle of the night that somebody had a pink eye or conjunctivitis for three or four days and they come in the Emergency Room at that time. Those are the calls I didn't want to get, but at the same time, I specified strictly that anything of a potentially serious nature, I was called for, or any corneal foreign body in a one-eyed patient I was to be called for. So, I had guidelines as to what I wanted to be called for because it was very difficult practicing all day and being bothered at night. Extraneous, unnecessary calls."

QUESTION: "Do you recall anybody ever complaining about those instructions you gave the Emergency Room personnel?"

ANSWER: "They may have."

QUESTION: "Do you have any recollection of an incident involving Dr. _____who went to the Emergency Room?"

ANSWER: "Very well."

At that point, the Hospital Lawyer would interrupt as he had during Goldfarb's deposition. He would say: "I assume this goes to the unequal treatment argument somehow by some stretch of your imagination. If you want to discuss the incident, Doctor, as long as my objection is noted for the record that this is truly silly. I will let you briefly describe it."

ANSWER: "I have no objection to answering that because I have nothing to hide in that —. When you're the only opthalmologist at an area as Indiana, you can't be on call twenty four hours a day, seven days a week.

But, before the time of beepers, I would call the Hospital periodically to see if they needed anything. I think that may have been one of the instances when I had a beeper then, I don't recall. I do recall, for whatever reason, and it must have been a beeper, that I was en route to Pittsburgh, stopped. I remember exactly the gas station where I stopped and called and they told me the incident, that Dr. _____ had been struck in the eye when this gun exploded and so forth, and they described the incident to me and I knew that I would not be taking care of that at Indiana Hospital. So I made plans with them or told them to send him to the Emergency Room at Eye and Ear Hospital. Dr. _____ subsequently lost that eye and if I had been standing right there when he came in, I would have done exactly the same thing. So I admit to no negligence in the treatment at that time."

QUESTION: "Were you ever disciplined by the hospital for not being available for hospital emergencies?'

ANSWER: "Never."

As I imagined the presentation of our witnesses, our lawyer would ask to approach the bench and would approach the Judge with the two Hospital Lawyers. He would ask: "Your Honor, our next witnesses have testimony which bears strongly on the credibility of our last two hostile witnesses. Because of the sensitive nature of the upcoming testimony and its direct relationship to our claim of disparate treatment, we ask that the affidavits of the witnesses - nurses from the Hospital - be read with only the Court and Counsel aware of the witnesses identities. We believe that the witnesses employment would be in jeopardy if they are identified."

We would remind the Court that Dr. Miller was not allowed to attend Dr. Claude Clippins deposition because Clippins had a letter from a physician asking that Dr. Miller be excluded for the deposition. The Hospital lawyer had said that if Dr. Miller were present it would "kill Clippins". We would ask for similar latitude.

The Hospital Lawyers would object strenuously. They had already seen such incriminating evidence and they would be desperate to stem the tide.

The Judge would call for a recess and, when the proceedings resumed, he would announce that the affidavits could be read and he would warn that if the course of the trial changed, these witnesses would be called and identified.

The Jury had heard the testimony of both Goldfarb and Vader. It would be apparent to the jury that both of them were indeed a force - perhaps the major force behind the Medical Staff's Executive Committee. The affidavits would be revealing. My counsel would take the affidavits and face the jury.

The first would read:

"Within weeks of graduating from nursing school, we were assigned to night shift for the experience. Sometime around 2:00 A.M., a new admisssion came over to the med/surg floor from E.R.(Emergency Room), and the E.R. nurse included in her verbal report on the patient that the doctor (Dr. Vance Vader) had been called (on rotation) but had refused to come in and would see the patient whenever he came in for morning rounds. We tried to make the patient comfortable, but he was having significant breathing difficulty. Though in an upright position in bed with additional propping, and with O2 at 7.1, the respiratory distress increased steadily, and within forty-five minutes of arrival to the ward, not only did the patient's color change markedly, but his anxiety level became quite concerning. We noted that his tongue was swelling, and he had trouble swallowing, and his eyes were becoming more wide and frightened. Vital signs were changing and also cause for increasing concern. The charge nurse went to the desk to call the doctor, and as a student there to gain experience, she took me with her in order to observe her report to the doctor as well as hear (on the other phone) his response and/or orders. After telling the doctor of the patient's deteriorating status and the rapidity with which it was happening, Dr. Vader became irritated and said he had already asked the E.R. nurse and R.N. supervisor if the patient was anyone important or related to anyone important in town, and since they had said no, he would see him in the morning. In the meantime, his orders would cover/stand ... and anyway, the patient was an old man. The patient remained fully aware and increasingly panicked as his tongue became so swollen it protruded from his mouth as his throat continued to swell shut and his questioning eyes bulged in terror and disbelief as we stood by unable to do anything to help ... until mercifully, he finally passed beyond the need for oxygen or for Dr. Vader."

As I imagined the sequence of events, a second affidavit relating to Dr. Vader would be read. The nurse's affidavit would read:

"When called to consult on a heart patient in E. R. (around 8:30-9:30 P.M.) Dr. Vader at first refused. But when reminded that the doctor of the day would be notified, he finally stated he would come, but <u>only</u> if the family or someone met him at the E. R. door with a thirty dollar consult fee. If it was not in his hand at the door, he would not come through the door. (He had also asked before initial refusal who the patient was, who did he work for, where did he live,did he have insurance.) Patient's family subsequently met him just outside the E. R. door, gave him his fee, and he saw the patient and admitted him. (In the short distance between where he parked his car and E. R., he used a breath atomizer as he walked toward E. R.)"

My lawyer would then face the jury and explain: "You have heard affidavits from responsible nursing personnel from Indiana Hospital's nursing department which show a pattern of unequal treatment of physicians at Indiana Hospital. If there is indeed no penalty, in fact, no investigation of a physician who would not assist an elderly patient who, unfortunately wasn't important, we certainly can't have equal treatment. What does it take to have action that also applies to physicians on the Medical Staff Executive Committee? The same physician is the one who brought charges against Dr. Miller after he had stood by and allowed Dr. Miller's patient to die."

He would continue:

"We will now hear from a third affidavit, the behavior of a second Executive Committee member (Dr. Goldfarb) who had had a series of operating room mishaps and never had any semblance of a Hospital investigation. You will now hear sworn testimony from a nurse relating to the second Executive Committee member which gives more insight into the unequal standards of the hospital's Executive Committee. The affidavit reads:

"On a summer Saturday afternoon, a twelve-year-old boy was brought to E. R. with a small stick protruding from one eye. Dr. Goldfarb was located on the golf course. At first he refused to come back to the club house to take the phone, but after insistence from E. R. via a repeat approach by club house personnel who again went out to whatever hole he was playing, he finally called the E. R. back after a lengthy wait. To say he was lividly furious would be a gross understatement!! Not only did he yell, berate and swear over the phone at the E. R. Nurse and the Supervisor, he stated he was not leaving his golf game because of some stupid kid who couldn't watch where he was going, and to ship the patient off to Pittsburgh Eye and Ear. When Supervisor reminded him that we could not transfer patient without being seen, he again said he wasn't coming and don't <u>ever</u> call him on the golf course again and hung up. Dr. of the day was notified and came to the E. R., saw patient, and signed off to transfer him to Pittsburgh. We later learned that the boy lost a large percentage of sight in the eye and that doctors in Pittsburgh had acknowledged that had he been seen and treated more promptly and appropriately in Indiana, vision loss would have been minimal if not negligible."

My lawyer would then again face the jury and say: "We have now heard of the behavior of a second member of that Executive Committee who had had a series of operating room mishaps and never had any semblance of a Hospital investigation." These affidavits outlined graphically the unequal standards of members of the Hospital's Medical Staff Executive Committee as compared to other members of the Medical Staff.

We had agreed early on, that it would be an advantage to our suit to allow the jury to see and hear some of the members of that Hospital "Executive Committee". Most Jurors would probably have an image of a medical staff Executive Committee as a group of distinguished, articulate gentlemen. Seeing these people would either erase or confirm those images.

We would call to the stand Dr. Bruno Hoffman. Hoffman was one of the disgruntled group of Army people. He had been helped to arrive in Indiana by Hank Bailey, the first of the Army people. Hoffman had just appeared. There were no niceties, such as the usual meeting with the Surgical Staff of the Hospital or the courtesy call to the surgeons in his specialty. Hoffman promptly began demonstrating martial prowess. There would be discussions of his vicious dogs, a firearm collection, and the hanging wall trophies. About that time, Hoffman would be featured in the Roto Section of the local paper as a karate devote'. His friend Hank would later describe that the wildlife trophies were actually his kills and that he had given the trophies to Hoffman. Hoffman, early on, kept a muscular frame in shape, but after a bit began to fill in a little. With the residual crew cut and an uncharacteristic suit and tie, he would take the stand and swear to tell the truth.

The opening questions would establish the witness as a member of the medical staff Executive Committee and then:

QUESTION: "Have you attained Board Certification in your specialty?"

ANSWER: "No, but I'm Board "eligible"."

There had been questions over the first few years of practice, relating to the number of surgical procedures that had been performed on children. Questions would then relate to the number of surgical procedures that would be performed in an average week and an average month.

Then:

QUESTION: "Dr. Hoffman, I show you an affidavit fully notarized, by your friend, Dr. Bailey (who helped you come to Indiana). Do you recognize the signature?"

ANSWER: "Yes."

QUESTION: "I'm entering this document into the record and will then ask you to respond.

The document reads:

"In the physicians' lounge at Indiana Hospital there was a discussion of the hearings concerning the suspension of Dr. Ralph Miller's privileges at Indiana Hospital between myself and Dr. Bruno Hoffman, who was a member of the Executive Committee of the Medical Staff. This discussion occurred approximately three weeks prior to Dr. Miller's hearings at the hospital.

"Dr. Hoffman asked me if I knew about Dr. Miller's suspension. I replied that I preferred not to know about it. Dr. Hoffman stated that 'they had finally gotten Miller and that he wasn't going to get away this time because the Board members had enough money behind them to make it stick.' Dr. Hoffman stated that the family ought to sue Dr. Miller for malpractice and hang his ass."

Dr. Bailey's affidavit continued:

"Approximately three to four months after Dr. Miller's suspension, a discussion with Dr. Hoffman took place in the physicians' lounge in the operating room. Dr. Hoffman asked me if I saw what happened to Dr. Miller. Dr. Hoffman stated that, 'We finally got rid of that bad apple. At least now we are going to have some peace at the Surgical Staff meetings.' Dr. Hoffman stated that Dr. Miller was probably going to be suing the hospital and all of us like a damn fool, but with all the money behind us he won't get anywhere."

Dr. Bailey's affidavit then stated:

"After I had been temporarily suspended from Indiana Hospital due to illness, I indicated to Dr. Hoffman that I was considering suing the Hospital. Dr. Hoffman stated," 'You saw what we did to Miller, didn't you? Do you want to look like a fool like Miller and get your name dragged through the mud in the newspaper?'

The affidavit continued:

"In that summer, Dr. Hoffman asked me if I was going to reapply for Hospital privileges. I stated that I did not know. Dr. Hoffman stated that he had 'finally seen the last of Miller, that he hadn't heard anything about or seen him for some time.'

The final statement of the affidavit would be read:

"On a number of occasions, Dr. Hoffman described to me killing an individual in Philadelphia, Pa., and the method of his killing which was breaking the victim's neck. Dr. Hoffman stated that he could hear the neck break and the guy fell over dead. This incident was apparently a fight with someone in Philadelphia, Pa."

It would be very difficult to predict the rebuttal from this witness. But, it would be unlikely that anyone would believe that Dr. Bailey would fabricate a tale and then have the story notarized.

There would be one final question:

QUESTION: "Dr. Hoffman, have you ever told anyone that one of the nurse's husbands was a 'state trooper who packed a gun and that Dr. Miller had better watch out'?"

ANSWER: "No, I never said anything like that."

Hoffman would be excused and we would give the jury the opportunity to see Abdul Hankey. It would be a contrast to first see the bulk of witness Hoffman and then Abdul. Abdul was a small fellow and at this time, would not have that stethoscope dangling.

After a few identifying questions, he would be asked about his training. He would describe medical school and internship. When asked if he had any specialty training or residency training, he would answer, "No."

Abdul would then be asked how he became appointed to the Hospital Board of Directors and the board of a local bank. It may be revealed that he had a large amount of stock in that bank with the interrelationship with the Hospital.

Abdul had been a Hospital Executive Committee member and had attended the unscheduled evening meetings of the Medical Staff Executive Committee while the group compiled charges against me. He had provided one of the charges. The charge was that I had bumped him in the medical staff coatroom six years earlier. He had testified at the Hospital hearing and had an almost comical time trying to demonstrate how he had been bumped six years earlier. We hoped that he would repeat that performance.

Dr. Burger would be called to testify. His appearance on the stand would give the Jury the opportunity to see the type of physician who had been a part of the conspiracy. Burger would be quizzed about the long telephone calls that he and his spouse had made in attempts to interfere with our recruitment of pediatricians. He, of course, would testify that he and spouse were only trying to encourage the young pediatricians to come to town - a tale not likely to be believed.

We would next call James Lieber, a law school professor, who would testify that he had reviewed the transcript of the Hospital's Kangaroo Court. He would confirm his credentials as an "expert" qualified to judge administrative procedures such as "peer review" hearings. When asked to give an opinion on the fairness of the Hospital hearing he would confirm that, in his years as a legal "expert", he had never seen such an abuse of "due process of law" such as occurred during the hearings at Indiana Hospital. He would scorn the self-appointed Hospital Lawyer as "Judge", the biased hearing panel and all the obscene rulings by the "Judge" and her obscene bylaws.

I imagined that we would then conclude what the lawyers called the liability portion of our case, with three witnesses with the following opening to the jury:

"Ladies and gentlemen of the jury, you have, undoubtedly seen that there was an intentional campaign, as part of the illegal acts of the conspiracy to destroy Dr. Miller's professional reputation and to destroy his perceived competition to the Hospital. Please listen to our final three witnesses and decide whether you can believe that Dr. Miller was the hospital tyrant that the Executive Committee members would have you believe."

We would call to the stand Mrs. Mary Shimps. Mary would testify that she had been the cleaning lady at the Hospital's Men's Ward for a number of years and that Dr. Miller was always kind to her. As a matter of fact, she would describe that she always left a gift for the Doctor in the Medical Staff Room on his birthday and at Christmas.

One of the operating room nurses would then testify that she worked frequently and harmoniously with Dr. Miller and that there was always a birthday cake for him in the operating room nurses' lounge. She would describe that a group of operating room nurses went to the Miller home and caroled on the first Christmas Eve that Dr. Miller was gone from the Hospital. We would then ask if that would have been done for a hospital tyrant.

Our final witness would be Annette, my secretary. She would read an affidavit that she had prepared after an Antitrust Conference in Pittsburgh. The affidavit would read:

"The undersigned hereby deposes and states as follows:

1. My name is Annette H. Loshelder of Blairsville, Pa. I am secretary to Dr Ralph J. Miller.

2. I accompanied Dr. Miller to the conference on Antitrust Law and Health Care in Pittsburgh, Pa., on February 28.

3. During the lunch break, Dr. Miller and I were at the buffet table and Dr. Miller was approached by the Counsel for Indiana Hospital.

4. After inquiring about Dr. Miller's family and about the status of former Indiana Hospital Board Chairman, (the Hospital Lawyer) told Dr. Miller that over the years he had advocated that Dr. Miller was correct on a number of things that he was attempting to do to improve Indiana Hospital.

5. (The Hospital Lawyer) then asked Dr. Miller if he (Miller) knew that he (Miller) had been responsible for a number of significant improvements over the past few years.

6. (The Hospital Lawyer) concluded by asking Dr. Miller if he would be willing to join with them (hospital authorities) and help correct the remaining problems at Indiana Hospital.

Signed, Annette H. Loshelder"

Following our final witnesses, we would announce to the Court that our presentation of the liability portion of the trial had been completed.

We would expect the Hospital Lawyers to make a motion for dismissal of the case claiming that we failed to present a valid claim. Despite our doubts about the integrity of the Court, it would be unlikely that, even this Court, would dismiss the case in the face of the amount of evidence we had presented.

The Hospital would present their "expert" who would claim that the hospital did not hold a monopoly in the County and would present figures showing large numbers of patients leaving the area to enter other regional hospitals.

We would similarly present an "expert" who, also with statistics would show that the Hospital holds a commanding monopoly position as the only general hospital in the County.

These experts would give detailed statistics to demonstrate the Hospital's geographic and product markets. It is quite likely that the jury would be bored to tears during this testimony, but would probably see all the illegal activities of the Hospital people that had occurred as a significant "restraint of trade".

The Court would be expected to advise us to proceed with the second phase of the trial to show damages. I would very likely be called to testify to the effect the negative publicity and loss of hospital privileges had on my reputation as a threat to my livelihood.

We would be required to have another expert testify as to the losses that the Hospital's actions had caused.

My pipe dreams of a trial where the truth would emerge, came to a sudden sickening halt. If we had assumed, all along, that the Court had no intention of giving us our day in Court, we would not have been so shocked that our case was thrown out of Court for the third time.

In a Catch 22 move, Judge Bloch ruled that one of our experts was not qualified and then granted the hospital motion for "summary judgement", claiming that we lacked expert testimony. The climate of that Grant Street temple was becoming more and more odorous.

Once again, for the third time, we appealed to the Third Circuit Court of Appeals to overturn Bloch's ridiculous ruling. It seemed so obvious that, in a case running for a period of twelve years, that something was very basically wrong for a judge to dismiss a case "on the eve of trial" after he had gone through a fantasy "pretrial conference". How compliant, how stupid do these courtroom denizens believe the public to be?

After another few months, our appeal to the Court of Appeals was answered by a one page faxed statement from sunny Santa Barbara. The opinion was written by a person named Aldisert and confirmed that our Judge Bloch had not exceeded his authority and that his dismissal of the case stood.

We would learn through a call to the clerk of the Court of Appeals in Philadellphia that this Aldisert was a "senior judge" who had retired and was almost never seen in Philadelphia. We are all apparently paying for this guy and his office in California to fax one page opinions affecting the lives of Pennsylvania citizens.

Our appeal to the United States Supreme Court was joined by the family of my deceased elderly patient and by the Semmelweis Society. Both submitted "friend of the court" briefs to the high court.

Our highest court approved the submitted amicus briefs but declined to hear the case.

Can anyone have respect for a Court System that allows a retired Judge, three thousand miles from Pennsylvania, to dismiss a major suit after twelve years, and thousands of pages of pleadings and testimony?

This is the file of documents generated by twelve years of litigation in the Federal Courts. (Miller v. Indiana Hospital 81-1091) The case was dismissed by a "retired judge" Aldisert with a one-page faxed opinion from Santa Barbara.

Chapter 20

"*The truth shall make you free.*"

— Gospel of St. John

THE AFTERMATH

It had been a pleasantly slow day at the office and our last patient was leaving as the former Hospital Administrator came into the reception room. We had seen each other in the local malls from time to time, and I think he was repeatedly stunned that I would stop and chat for a minute. He had been a patient of ours until the deceitful atmosphere surrounding him and the Hospital conspirators made a professional relationship with him impossible. He had been right in the thick of the Hospital Lawyers' Bad Faith Peer Review. Despite all, it was a little depressing to see him aimlessly wandering through the mall hallways after a career of worshiping false gods.

    He had cast his lot as a pawn for the Hospital Board Chairman and had energetically entered into the atmosphere of deceit using the morals and advice of Dr. Vance Vader in forming his policies and choosing his allies.

    My good friend, Bill London, was always supportive in the troublesome days following the Hospital hearings. He would often reflect on the instability of any group that appeared to enjoy harming others. We often reflected on the personality of a physician who would stand by and watch a patient die without helping; or refusing to attend to an elderly dying man or to demand his fee before he would attend a heart patient in the Emergency Room, and who would bring false charges against a colleague. It had been disturbing that the Hospital Administrator would allow such a personality to chart his course. The instability of such a Hospital group was in mind when Bill would observe, "There is no honor among thieves". When he would hear some of the wildly malicious tales of the Hospital's character assassination, he would repeat, "Time wounds all heels". In a lighter vein we frequently enjoyed a good laugh, such as when we heard that the macho Bruno Hoffman was telling folks that we had "naked ladies" at our annual office open house. Bill wryly observed that he must have gone home too early. He didn't though, see any humor in Goldfarb's Home for Battered Women tale.

I invited the former Administrator into my office, and despite all that had happened, I couldn't help feeling a little sorry for him. I tried to put him at ease, but was only partially successful. It seemed that he believed that I could tell him why he had been dismissed by the Hospital Board Chairman and the Lawyers. This was understandable since this was the fellow who had installed electronic equipment in his office to trap Dr. Miller. He truly believed that all the Hospital's secrets that had surfaced were from his office. He apparently felt that I knew more about his dismissal than he did.

He quite candidly told of his late evening severance from the Hospital. This openness was possible for him, knowing that the Hospital's hate campaign had not produced the same emotion on my part. This didn't mean that I wasn't prepared to fight, and fight hard; and as a Hospital colleague had advised, "When dealing with rats, you use rat poison".

It was almost pitiful, as he sat across from me, to hear of the tale of the Hospital crowd beginning to turn on each other. It apparently began with a call from the Board Chairman asking for an evening meeting with the Administrator. The meeting was set for late evening so that the Administrator could attend a Rotary dinner. He related that when he entered the conference room in the office of one of the Hospital Board members - a lawyer - he was surprised to see a total of three lawyers. Apparently, without much explanation, he was given two batches of papers to sign - essentially having him promise to leave his post quietly. There was apparently little conversation and the papers promising a payment of two thousand dollars a month for two years were signed. He claimed that there was no explanation or a reason for the dismissal and he would continue to brood over reasons for this group to turn on him.

A Board member described that one of the lawyers went to the room's book shelves, pulled out a volume and advised that they were holding an illegal meeting.

We would eventually take the deposition of the Hospital Board Chairman who would testify that the Administrator was completely "burned out" and "had to be replaced".

The local paper ran a tiny notice with a heading: "(Administrator) Named Consultant at Hospital". The notice read: "The Board of Directors of Indiana Hospital announced today that (the Administrator) has been appointed Consultant to the Board at the Hospital. The appointment was effective today. He formerly served as Administrator and President."

At the same time, the Hospital Board announced that "(a local pediatrician) will serve as interim administrator." It was certainly a contrast with the headline pasting I had taken from the paper a few years earlier. As he sat across from me, the Administrator now advised that he had never been called to "consult".

So, it seems that the record for the Hospital's twenty minute dismissals had been broken. Years later, we opened the paper to see a photo of the former Administrator's family receiving an award honoring him in gratitude for his years of service. Was this an unkind hoax or were we burying old skeletons? Were we seeing an expression of guilt?

Dr. Goldfarb had carefully cultivated the Board Chairman; so it was a surprise to learn from members of a small, exclusive club, that members Goldfarb and the Board Chairman had stopped speaking. Is it possible that their hate just had to have somewhere to go and that it afflicted those who had harbored it?

It will be remembered that an affidavit from a former Chief of Hospital Security described that, after the Kangaroo Court and Dr. Miller left the Hospital, "every little thing that went wrong was attributed to Doctor Miller." As one of my lawyers, George Weis, had said, "They're seeing Ralph Miller behind every bush."

As document after document had reached the Citizens Committee, there was obvious humor at some of the petty ramblings that were entered into Hospital records.

One of my favorite quotes comes from the record of a Hospital Medical Staff quarterly business meeting. It reads:

"Topic" "Dr. Miller's Concerned Citizen Group"

"Dr. Kachik noted that Dr. Miller's Concerned Citizens report of physicians' fees had been accurate to the cent. Apparently there is free access to past income tax returns. There is some feeling that Dr. Miller may be attempting to organize the Hospital employees. Further communication with these employees via Hospital routes is to be considered."

Among the less pleasant past memories, is the excoriating surgical staff minutes composed by Dr. Goldfarb and his testimony at the Kangaroo Court that I was disruptive at Surgical Department meetings. (I had called attention to the oppressive Hospital atmosphere, some of the problems with medical staff politics and the Nursing Director's "secret" incident reports.)

After I left the Hospital Medical Staff, it was regularly assumed that the Hospital atmosphere would undergo a metamorphosis to glorious tranquility.

But, is seems that not too long after the Kangaroo Court, friction between the Hospital Board Chairman and the Hospital Medical Staff surfaced. Were "The Boys" feeling their oats after their successful Kangaroo Court?

The physicians demanded a meeting with the Hospital Board to air complaints. The Board refused and issued a "statement". It reads as follows:

POLICY STATEMENT
BY
THE BOARD OF DIRECTORS OF INDIANA HOSPITAL

"This statement is intended to improve harmony at our Hospital. Some of the Medical Staff have complained of deteriorating morale among the nurses. Many nurses have complained of a great amount of harassment from the Medical Staff that has been increasing, stressing that it comes from a small minority of the physicians. The Administrator and Trustees have been aggravated by numerous disrupting acts of misbehavior."

"Final responsibility rests upon the Governing Board and its decisions are these:

"1. Expressed concern by physicians concerning personal "dossiers": There are no such things."

"2. Of greatest importance is the matter of the harassment of nurses by some members of the Medical Staff. We demand that such behavior must stop at once. Every professional person must act as a professional person in the future. We will require the reporting of incidents and strict disciplinary steps will be taken, if necessary."

"3. The Board stands squarely behind the Administration as well as the Nursing Staff and expresses the hope that all aggravating occurrences will come to an end. Hospital privileges granted to physicians carry with them the responsibility for supportive conduct."

"It is hoped that disciplinary measures will prove unnecessary and that a friendly team spirit will evolve."

At the Kangaroo Court, we had shown that nurses secret "incident reports" had been uncovered. Now here was the Hospital, still denying that the Nursing Director was keeping "dossiers" on physicians yet threatening to " report" incidents involving physicians.

Facing an open revolt, the Hospital Board Chairman then issued a "Resolution" stating: ..."The Board of Directors of Indiana Hospital rescinds its policy statement..."

Then, the Medical Staff President - an associate of Dr. Vader - issued an "Executive Committee Report" to the Medical Staff. Most of the nine typewritten pages held a series of petty complaints. A few notations weren't so petty. Excerpts from that report read:

"...'incident reports' - examples of incidents involving patients...not presented to the physician involved and were at times inaccurate and totally misrepresented." (Hadn't anyone learned from the revelation at the Kangaroo Court of nursing note alteration?)

"...Hospital employee concerns - hospital staff had complained about poor morale and poor working conditions in the Hospital. Such complaints came from all levels of employment, from clerk-typists to Department Chiefs to Assistant Head Nurses."

"...The Board Chairman was told that many middle management personnel were fearful of losing their jobs if they expressed themselves openly."

"...and to impress upon Board Chairman by the number of complaints that there was a serious morale problem within the Hospital."

Another report of a meeting between the Hospital Board and two members of the Medical Staff stated:

"...it was emphasized that Hospital morale was felt to be at an extremely low ebb and that it had already adversely affected the following areas:

1. Nursing Department
2. Other hospital departments
3. Medical Staff
4. Hospital-Community relations"

Continuing, the report of that meeting described: "individual contacts with staff nurses and assistant head nurses who complained of poor staffing, poor morale, lack of effective input and total frustration with their jobs."

Reminiscent of the findings of the Citizens Committee, the report continued:

"Emergency department physicians are being hired on a "rapid fire" fashion prior to proper credentialing."

In addition to those "reports", Dr. Vader's associate, as the President of the Medical Staff, issued a statement to the Hospital's physicians with "items for discussion" for an upcoming meeting with the Hospital Board."

Interesting was the suggestion that : "Reorganization of the Hospital Board of Directors should take place on a periodic basis with some provision for limitation of tenure of office. This is felt to be especially important since in the opinion of the Medical Staff there are some Board members that are distinctly anti-physician in their views."

Where had we heard that before?

Included in the memo to the Medical Staff by the Staff President were "items for discussion" at the upcoming meeting with the Hospital Board.

The Staff President ended his "items for discussion" with:

"Finally, it is suggested that while Medical Staff members are talking that there should be considerable "head-nodding" in agreement with even spontaneous exclamations of support during these statements."

It is probably true that the Hospital's physicians had never gained total respect from the Board of Directors, but what did the Medical Staff President think the Board's reaction would be when they confronted a group nodding their heads and giving "spontaneous exclamations" like a flock of chickens?

At about that point in time, the middle management employees of the Hospital were speaking for themselves. In a letter to the Administrator, their grievances read:

"1. Demoralization of middle management

2. Question of job security

3. Disappointment that the contribution to the organization is not recognized

4. Concern for recruitment and retention of competent middle management personnel

5. Frustration and embarrassment as the news spreads throughout Western Pennsylvania

6. Confusion about the value of our loyalty and team effort"

As an added thought, the letter signed by eighteen management employees noted: "...while Board members are knowledgeable and respected members of Indiana businesses and industries, they are not inherently familiar with personnel issues in the health care institution."

It would seem that the issues brought to light in the Kangaroo Court were now being accepted as reality. <u>The Hospital environment was stifling.</u>

The old saying, "When one door closes, another opens" has been prophetic. A number of doors have opened.

The earlier experiences with lawyers had been principally adversarial - but the opportunity arose to enter into rewarding experiences with lawyers.

It began with a call from a Pittsburgh surgeon who asked if I would review a case of alleged medical negligence for a lawyer who was a family member. I agreed, and after a thorough review of medical and hospital records, advised that there was no evidence of care below the applicable standard. The potential malpractice suit was dropped and I began to see that honest physicians can prevent wasteful and troublesome litigation. Rather than participating in the "conspiracy of silence", thoughtful and upright relationships with lawyers can indeed help prevent frivolous suits and also uncover those few who create a major portion of medical negligence litigation. I had also begun to see that the threat of lawyers and malpractice suits could be a significant force in quality control. That is, the threat of malpractice litigation can help deter reckless behavior.

The calls from out-of-town and out-of-state lawyers began slowly, but rapidly increased and I found that, in the overwhelming majority of cases, the advice to a lawyer would be that the evidence presented was not sufficient to enter a negligence suit. There is widespread opinion in Medicine that physicians who aid lawyers in legal actions are traitors to the profession. This just isn't so. Most of the lawyers I encountered wanted absolute candor. They often would be grateful for help which would prevent them from investing in a suit with ill-founded advice. Of the dozens and dozens of cases reviewed, it was necessary to testify in Court only twice and each of those appearances was quite an experience.

The lawyer was from Wayne County, Michigan. An elderly man had undergone prostate surgery and had died on the operating table. The patient's family and their lawyer suspected that something negligent could have led to the death. Would I review the record and, would I testify if necessary? I gave a cautious "yes" and waited for the hospital records to arrive.

The large packet was delivered ,and over a period of two weeks or more, and as time permitted, I began a careful review of the case and kept meticulous notes. The operative report for the deceased patient's surgery was found to hold the answer.

Urologists doing this type of surgery know of the syndrome that occurs when irrigating solution passes from the instrument used, into the patient's bloodstream. Early recognition of this complication, during surgery, can allow quick and effective treatment. But, in the case under review, neither the surgeon nor the anesthesiologist had recognized the telltale signs of trouble. One anesthesiologist had been relieved during the surgery and the second anesthesiologist had noted pulse and blood pressure changes and had responded with the wrong treatment which, in effect, caused the patient's demise.

My several page report detailed the course of events and stated that the applicable standard of care had not been met.

Weeks and months passed. Finally, a call from Detroit - the Hospital Defense Lawyers had demanded my deposition, which is routine for defense lawyers. The Wayne County Court agreed to allow a video deposition which would be played back to the jury at trial. On the appointed day, the Plaintiff's Lawyer arrived at the office early and we reviewed the facts of the case. We set up an easel and chalkboard which we would use to acquaint the jury with the anatomy involved and the sequence of those operating room events. I think the Lawyer wanted to put forth a strong case for the opposing lawyers - probably to encourage a settlement rather than going to trial.

Right on time, three well-dressed young men appeared. They introduced themselves with perfunctory handshakes and then huddled with the Plaintiff's Lawyer asking to chat with me without the conversation being put into the record. He agreed. While the Court Reporter was setting up her camera and audio equipment, we were not making a record.

Rather than a chat, the three lawyers pounced. I was sitting behind a large desk and I thought they were going to come right across. The Plaintiff's Lawyer finally recognized his mistake and put a halt to the grilling. He advised that, from that point on, we would be making a film that would be shown to the jury. The plaintiff's lawyer asked me to present the case, and with the help of the chalkboard, I presented the evidence which had been found with the careful review of the records. I felt the case was compelling. I wouldn't have testified if I thought the findings were marginal. The three lawyers representing the Physician, the Hospital and an insurance company then took turns attempting to discredit the testimony. Their questions began slowly but graphically became anything but civil. This was not the first time that I had experienced the aggressive tactics of defense lawyers, but this group, despite their gentlemanly appearances, was out for a kill. They were going to save their clients from responsibility. I was happy to see them leave. If anything, their browbeating left me a little ashamed that I hadn't effectively defended the case. I felt that I had lost the encounter.

Many weeks passed and I had forgotten the episode when a call came from Detroit. The plaintiff's lawyer was in a bind. The case was scheduled for trial to begin and the Trial Judge had disallowed the video testimony. The plaintiff's lawyer was left without expert testimony. Would I come to Detroit and testify?

My first thought was of subjecting myself to a gang fight in front of a courtroom audience. It would have been simple enough to decline, but the Lawyer was a decent guy and the case was bonafide. I had seen enough of the "conspiracy of silence" protecting charlatans and quacks. And, besides, it didn't seem right for those three lawyers to bully their way to an undeserved victory.

One of the plaintiff's junior lawyers met me at the airport and we discussed the case to date. My testimony was scheduled for the next morning. It seems that the three defense lawyers had intimidated the witnesses who had appeared; and the expert testimony, to date, had not established a cause of death. The more we chatted on the ride to town, the more it became apparent that there was a real tussle ahead.

We waited at the Lawyer's office until the Senior Lawyer came back from trial. He looked tired and suggested an early dinner. He said we needed to review the case again before morning. There was a leisurely dinner at an Italian restaurant and I was invited to stay at his home overnight.

His house was elegant. It sat in a grove of towering oaks and was flanked by a beautiful pool. He showed a great deal of pride, as we entered his trophy room. The room was filled with lighted glass cases filled with elegant ancient bronze figurines and artifacts. The room compared with most museums. My host explained that the value of the artwork was astronomical and was protected by a sophisticated alarm system.

We sat at his circular bar in his luxurious living room and reviewed the case over and over. My host was attempting to be certain of every detail. We worked until the wee hours and I finally suggested that we call it quits for the day. I got the impression that the three defense lawyers were getting the best of the trial and had been a little brutal in cross examining the plaintiff's witnesses. I was determined not to be again bullied.

The Courthouse in downtown Detroit was just an average courthouse - there was nothing unique about the building, but the courtroom itself was a little smaller than average. The judge's bench and the room furnishings were lifeless -not new and not ancient.

I took a seat a few rows back from the trial area and watched the tipstaff adjust the easel and blackboard sitting before the jury box. The Plaintiff's Lawyer spread his documents on a conference table and his notes on the lectern. He had advised that he didn't have a great deal of trial experience, but that he had taken the case at the request of a friend. The door leading to the judge's chambers to the left of the bench was opening and closing with clerks running in and out. The courtroom began to fill and a young dark-haired gentleman and a middle-aged woman sat in the front row. They were the son and spouse of the deceased patient. The Defendant Doctor came in and sat with the three lawyers at the second conference table, with a few nervous looks around the room.

The judge, a thin attractive woman, came in informally and advised the lawyers to proceed. The first witness called was a pathologist who testified as to the findings at autopsy. The three defense lawyers each took their turns on cross examination. There was no argument and the witness readily agreed with the lawyers' suggestions that there was no evidence of substandard care in the autopsy findings.

My turn was next and I can't say I wasn't apprehensive, but I wanted to make a favorable impression with the jury. They appeared to be an average group of people and appeared to show great interest in the proceedings. An attractive young woman sat in the front row of witnesses and I learned later that she was the foreman.

I had stashed my brief case at my feet, and as I was called, I reached down and took a large plastic bottle of distilled water from the case. It was the type of irrigation fluid used in the type of surgery which had claimed the patient's life.

As I walked past the conference table, I carefully set the plastic bottle on a corner of the table nearest the jury. I think that, not only the jury, but everyone in the Court wondered what was going on. I was expecting the judge to ask. She didn't. For the moment, the jurors' eyes were riveted on the bottle.

I took the stand and quietly said "hello" to the judge. The Plaintiff's Lawyer explained that we would like to use the chalk board and asked permission for me to step down and face the jury.

They were attentive as I drew a diagram of the urinary system and explained the surgery that had been performed. I explained the mechanism of fluid entering the blood stream during surgery and the need for the surgeon and the anesthesia people to recognize the early signs of the syndrome that can lead to death if not recognized. I answered a few questions from the floor and then the judge told me to get back into the witness box. I did so and the fun started.

The first of the defense lawyers loudly questioned my "theory" of the surgical death and kept asking whether some other factors were really the cause of the death. He finally became exasperated and sat down.

The second of the defense team was a tall, nice looking and gentlemanly fellow. He had been the least aggressive at the video deposition. He simply rose and said he had no questions.

The third member of the team was chomping at the bit. He was dying to get into it. He was medium in height and a little heavy. He gave a barrel-chested appearance and this apparently led to an effortless volume of voice. He had a tendency to interrupt while I was answering questions. During the earlier testimony he had jumped up several times with a loud "objection", and had lectured that I was to stop talking when he objected. This time I just kept on with answering his questions until the Judge finally said, "Let him finish."

The poor guy was becoming livid and, for some reason, walked toward the rear of the courtroom shouting his questions. We had no trouble hearing him. In his exasperation he became insulting. He asked something to the effect of "How could you expect any intelligent person to believe fluid caused this death?"

I had hesitated being blunt with these people, but this fellow was apparently trying to bully another witness to change testimony. I shot back at him, "Because your clients pumped into their patient, the equivalent of four times the fluid in that plastic bottle on the table. The patient was a small man and weighed nine pounds more at autopsy than when he entered the hospital. Your clients drowned the poor man."

The Lawyer exploded. He wasn't acting. He was truly getting out of control. I don't remember what he was yelling; but the judge interrupted and warned she was going to find him in contempt. There were one or two quieter questions and the Lawyer sat down.

The Judge declared a two hour lunch break. On the way through the spacious lobby of the Courthouse, the family of the deceased thanked us for the help. We sat around a table in a downtown restaurant and discussed the morning's events. There was concern as to how the jury was going to react to the day's testimony.

A week or so later, we got a call from Detroit. The Plaintiff's Lawyer advised that the jury had ruled in favor of the Plaintiff. The Junior Lawyer had talked with the woman foreman, and she had said that the fellow with the plastic bottle had helped them decide.

Another door that opened was the appointment as a Consultant in the Social Security Disability Program. I had never realized how many citizens were collecting benefits due to a "disability". Eligibility for benefits is determined by adjudicators who are educated people who rule on disability qualifications in accord with regulations known as "listings of impairments". It was quite an education working with these people and in the decision-making process. The cases covered the entire gamut of human disease states.

In the earlier years of the Program, the adjudicators had wide latitude in their decisions. Some of the adjudicators were known to be very liberal in their decisions, while others were more conservative. But, over time, the regulations have been tightened, so that usually, only truly disabled persons are given help.

The applicants for disability benefits are often examined by physicians who honestly give opinions on the degree of impairment. But, there are physicians who liberally dole out taxpayers' funds - it is exceptionally good for their personal public relations. This appeared to be the case with Dr. Lester Lazarus.

While I was working at the Social Security Office, a call came in from Dr. Vader, protesting my appointment. On another occasion, a similar call came from Lester Lazarus. The Manager of the office had become a patient of ours, and he understandably wondered what type of medical community populated Indiana.

All those who occasionally examine these applicants know that it is sometimes very difficult to determine if the person looking for benefits is malingering. At other times, it his not so difficult. My favorite was the woman who was applying for benefits due to a neck problem. Quite by accident, I had glanced out an office window into the parking lot. There she was, opening the rear door of her car, lifting out a cervical collar and putting it on before appearing for her exam.

The second opportunity to tussle with defense lawyers came with a call from Philadelphia County. A well-cultured, articulate voice asked for a review of a record. The case was obviously a complicated one by the description. The package arrived and held a pile of records from three Philadelphia hospitals. It seems that a patient had developed a tuberculous infection of the lower urinary tract following prostate surgery. The infection had been treated over a period of time by two or three urologists. Finally, a Philadelphia urologist found that, in the center of a severe inflammatory reaction in the prostatic area, was a piece of rubber. The fragment of rubber had been sent for analysis, and the Hospital Pathologist described that the rubber had a "ribbed" surface - a dead giveaway that the rubber was a portion of a catheter that had not been completely removed.

A careful review of the record uncovered an obscure nursing note that described the removal of a catheter by an orderly. The records from a total of three hospitals revealed that catheters had been inserted on three occasions and removed on three occasions. Could it be shown which catheter had been negligently removed? By combining all hospital records and a little deduction, it could be shown which catheter had been incompletely removed.

After several months, the call came from the Philadelphia lawyer; would I testify? Once again, I accepted with reluctance. The drive to Philadelphia allowed time for the mental gymnastics of preparing for the ordeal of courtroom testimony.

The Lawyer arranged for me to stay at the Bellview Stratford, the hotel that had been the scene of the American Legion's infamous epidemic of infection that became known as the Legionaire's Disease. The lower floors had been converted into commercial offices and the upper floors were still for guests. The rooms were still luxurious.

My Lawyer friend suggested dinner at the hotel dining room on the top floor. It is certainly an elegant place to dine. The ladies were in long gowns and there was a pianist at the baby grand. There was a commanding view of the city and the elegant high vaulted ceilings. I was enjoying the ambiance until the maitre d' in a tuxedo went through an exaggerated routine with an obviously exaggerated French accent. We ordered a drink, and when he left, we unkindly discussed the phony accent. It sort of broke the ice and led to some humor during the upcoming trial and thereafter. The menus came, and it took only a glance to see the outrageous prices. I assumed my friend was perfectly comfortable with the scene; but I limited my supper and retired a little hungry. It wasn't until the next day that we both confessed we didn't require French cooking or service. Some months later, during a telephone discussion with my Lawyer friend, I learned that the maitre d' had eloped with an heiress who apparently enjoyed French cuisine.

The next day provided another courtroom challenge. The courtrooms in the Philadelphia County Courthouse are on an upper floor. The hallway and courtrooms are modernistic - paneled with light brown mahogany. There are low railings separating the audience from the trial areas. The judge's benches are not quite as high as the average. We left our coats on a rack just inside the double doors and I took a seat in the second row of chairs. In a few minutes, a professional looking young fellow came in and began unwrapping some large, pasteboard exhibits. He was obviously one of the defense lawyers We exchanged a few comments about the ice storm that was making driving treacherous on the expressway.

My lawyer friend joined me and I casually remarked that the Defense Lawyer seemed like a nice fellow. His reply left me a little confounded. He said, "Don't even talk to them, they are the enemy - <u>this is war!</u> This mild mannered gentleman was describing the tenor of things to come. I should have been grateful for the warning. The Judge entered from an inconspicuous door to the right of the bench. He was the notorious Judge Sabo. He was short and balding and spoke rather quietly. He had been involved in a much publicized murder trial and sentencing involving a well known radio personality. Some newspaper accounts had referred to him as the "Hanging Judge". He called for the jury to be seated.

My Lawyer called his first witness. It was a urologist who had briefly treated the plaintiff. He spoke with a German accent and agreed that the piece of ribbed rubber found in the urethra of his patient had been the source of the lingering infection.

There were three defense lawyers, two young men and a young woman representing the physician, the insurance companies and the named hospital. Their cross- examination produced little controversy. The witness agreed to several theories that the lawyers produced, which tended to confuse any judgement as to what surgeon or what hospital was responsible for the foreign body and the resulting infection.

I was next and took my place beside the Judge. So far, he hadn't had much to say. He just sat there with a sour expression. The plaintiff and his wife were sitting near the front row and facing the witness box, while the jury was to the side of the witness box.

I was led through a careful questioning of the known facts of the case and then was asked to step down and use a large display to explain the relevant anatomy to the jury.

I had tried to imagine what the various jurors were thinking and couldn't come to any conclusion. It took almost an hour to describe, in detail, the anatomy and the mechanism of the foreign piece of rubber being left after the final catheter was removed. Judge Sabo announced a lunch break and advised that cross- examination would take place after the break. My Lawyer observed that the jury had been riveted to the diagrams during the anatomy lesson. He seemed to think it was a hopeful sign. The Judge's tipstaff was a pleasant, outgoing and authoritative fellow. He followed some of us into the restroom and loudly announced that we were not to speak to each other.

The young Lawyer I had chatted with, began the cross-examination and began slowly but gradually became louder and more forceful trying, I think, to confuse both me and the jury. He had the original patient record from one of the hospitals and kept shouting at me, trying to evoke a reaction. He finally got one when I noticed a difference between the record he was showing and the one I had reviewed. I observed that some of the laboratory studies appeared to have been changed. He finally backed off and the Judge dismissed Court for the day. My Lawyer was perplexed that the defense's delaying tactics were extending the trial. I had certainly hoped to start the drive back home, but there were two lawyers to go.

My Lawyer friend advised that his case would go down the drain if we didn't allow the remaining cross-examinations. So - another night in Philly. We engaged a local watering hole and restaurant and joked abut the contrast with the elegant French cuisine of the evening before.

The next morning, the Judge announced that the cross-examination of the witness would resume. The second defense lawyer approached and began. He was a very muscular fellow and he had a very muscular voice. His raspy amplitude was enough to be heard a block away.

His questioning, although forceful, was a bit of a repeat of the questions of the previous day. He made one mistake. He was obviously going to attack the credibility of the witness. He asked, "Why is it that you have to be brought here from the other end of the state? Why aren't Philadelphia physicians here to testify?" I countered that "everyone in the courtroom knew the answer to that; It was called the "conspiracy of silence".

He didn't hesitate a moment. He went over to his conference table and picked up a sheath of papers. He thundered: "You have already told us of your problems with a hospital but you have certainly glossed over the fact." He began then to read off the four pages of those phony charges from the Kangaroo Court. He paused very briefly and ended with: "Were you found guilty of those charges?" I answered, "Yes." He said: "That's all, Your Honor." I have often wondered what effect that attack had on the jury.

The young woman lawyer then had her turn. She advised that she was representing the Hospital and asked a few bland questions. She ended with, "You understand that Mr. Griffith was just doing his job, don't you?" I agreed; but with 20-20 hindsight, I should have noted that that was also what Hitler was doing.

The Court announced a break and I was looking forward to getting out of that place. As I stood by the bank of elevators my Lawyer and an attractive lady from his staff and the plaintiff and his wife came over and gave sincere thanks. They each wished me well and advised that I shouldn't take the attack "personally". I advised them that I did take it "personally".

Now, I wonder who gave that lawyer that list of charges?

More recently, the Philadelphia paper announced that the Pennsylvania Supreme Court had required Judge Sabo to retire.

The headline read: "**King of Death Row**" Forced From Bench - Pa. Jurist who has sentenced 31 to die is ordered to retire." Under his photo - the caption: "Sabo:

The Philadelphia jurist was called "a prosecutor in robes."

The majority of us don't believe that Bad Faith Peer Review should be protected by the sealing of court records or by the "conspiracy of silence." The records of Miller v. Indiana Hospital had been impounded from the outset ; first, in the Indiana County Court and then in the Federal Court - all at the request of Hospital Lawyers. It appeared that the record of Bad Faith Peer Review was to be kept from public view.

My lawyers had sent a motion to Judge Bloch to unseal the federal record. The Judge refused.

I had always believed that there was as strong element of truth in the old adage that, "anyone who served as his own lawyer had a fool for a client." Nevertheless, I was not prepared to see a community hospital, owned by the County citizens and largely supported by public funds, conceal its activities with impoundment of public records; and therefore, decided to represent myself to the Court of Appeals.

The preparation of the necessary papers to request an appeal of Judge Bloch's impoundment was not difficult. It was pretty much a matter of reviewing previous appeals by the lawyers and following the format. In place of a lawyer's name, one simply inserts "pro se" (by oneself).

After many weeks, I was pleased to see an envelope from the Third Circuit Court of Appeals in Philadelphia. It was an order from the Chief Judge of the Court of Appeals directing Judge Bloch to unseal the record. Enclosed was the opinion of the Chief Judge.

Reflecting her annoyance with Bloch's high-handed denial of access to the record, she began:

"In this case, the District Court denied appellant's Motion to Lift Seal which in effect denied him access to the court records of his own lawsuit. Because we can find no justification for the initial closure of the record, nor for the order on appeal, we will reverse."

Chief Judge Sloviter included in her opinion the full text of the Hospital Lawyer's original "Motion to Impound the Record." The Hospital's motion had read:

"Defendants (the Hospital) request this Court, for the following reasons, to enter an Order impounding the record in the within action and forbidding any individuals other than counsel of record and/or their designated and authorized representatives from viewing any pleadings, depositions, or court papers filed of record with the Clerk of Courts (sic) for the United States District Court for the Western District of Pennsylvania:"

In response to Judge Bloch's attempt to keep the record sealed, the Chief Judge of the Appeals Court continued her admonition:

"On February 8, without a hearing or even a response from Miller, the Court entered an order directing the Clerk of the Court to "seal and secure all Court papers filed of record and to allow access to any such papers only by counsel of record and/or their authorized representatives.

Access to the same records by any other person is prohibited and shall be allowed only by further Order of Court and upon good cause shown."

In reversing Bloch's decision, the Chief Judge added:

"This Court has made it clear that our "strong presumption" of openness does not permit the routine closing of judicial records to the public. The party seeking to seal any part of a judicial record bears the heavy burden of showing that "the material is the kind of information that courts will protect" and that "disclosure will work a clearly defined and serious injury to the party seeking closure." A party who seeks to seal an *entire* record faces an even heavier burden."

She concluded with another notation related to the Court's previous refusal to allow a well-known medical publication to print the story of "Bad Faith Peer Review":

"We note from the docket in the District Court that, on November 3, the journal, <u>Medical Economics</u> petitioned for access to the record impounded in this case and that no action on that motion is reported."

With the Chief Judge's order, the Federal Record was now open to public scrutiny.

And, with that effort in hand, I prepared a similar motion to the Indiana County Court of Common Pleas. Those records also were promptly unsealed by Judge William Martin.

A recurring phenomenon of recent history is that the corrupt dealings of people or organizations comes to light only after inept, bungling cover-up attempts.

Webster's defines arrogance as "full of or due to unwarranted pride and self-importance."

Deceit is defined as "deliberate misrepresentation of facts by words, actions, etc. generally to further one's ends."

And, cover-up is defined as "something used for hiding one's real activities and intentions."

Former Senator Howard Baker recently, on reflecting on the national tragedy of "Watergate", advised that. "Cover-up never works."

It was obviously a combination of all three (deceit, arrogance, and cover-up) for the Hospital Conspirators to believe that they were immune from any accountability for their actions over a period of years. It's true that hired lawyers can cover for awhile, but not forever.

Honorable people just don't call judges to influence decisions, don't alter hospital records, don't lie under oath, don't intercede with editors to kill truthful stories, don't intercept another's mail and don't attempt to have witnesses change their testimony.

Honorable physicians don't refuse help to dying patients.

One has to marvel at the cover-up that took place over many months during the efforts of the Citizens Committee.

While the Hospital crowd's behind-the-scenes activity had been suspected for some time, it was the candid revelation by local Judge Earley that truly broke the ice. It was when he described that Dr. Goldfarb had called him on at least two occasions, attempting to sway his opinions in the Hospital litigation.

It didn't take much imagination to suspect other such calls. After all, if Goldfarb, with great self-importance could "endorse" local politicians during medical meetings, he would certainly feel called upon to attempt to influence the workings of the Courts.

The next revelation came from the Hospital Board Chairman, who admitted, under oath, that he and the local Newspaper Publisher - the Hospital Board member Donnelly - had traveled to Pittsburgh and had effectively quashed an investigative story about the Hospital scheduled for printing in the Pittsburgh Press, by their meeting with the Editor, John Troan.

It was interesting to follow the minutes of the Hospital meetings when they were made part of the public record. With all the clandestine activity, these people were all counting on their minutes never seeing the light of day. Their arrogance is reflected in the Hospital's Board of Directors' minutes describing the excursion to Pittsburgh to kill the investigative story.

The minutes read:

"The (Hospital Board) Chairman reviewed the latest developments on the matter of an article on the Indiana Hospital which possibly might be published by Joseph Grata, an editor for the Pittsburgh Press. He understood from Mr. Grata, that before the article is published in the Sunday edition, our legal counsel would get a call by Thursday of the week of publication. The Chairman then remarked on the appointment he had with Mr. Troan during which he reviewed the matter of publication of the article." The Board minutes then read:

"The Chairman indicated that he would <u>like to keep within the Board members, the matter of his audience with Mr. Troan.</u>"

The parade of cover-ups probably first became apparent when the Administrator locked the copy machine and the record office to prevent any leak of records of patients acquiring infections after entering the Hospital.

The camouflage had originally begun with the Hospital Board's secret meeting at the Chairman's house leading to the dismissal of the young Administrator and continuing with the late evening meetings of the

Medical Staff politicos when no records were kept and the Kangaroo Court held out-of-sight in the nursing home basement.

Then there was the absence of the accuser, Vance Vader, to testify.

The efforts to stifle news coverage was successful for awhile, but the obscene defamation suit against county citizens was not. The hospital hadn't considered that entering a libel suit would greatly increase the flow of information and arouse public interest.

Sealing court records was also successful for awhile, but it is frightening to know that a group controlling a community hospital can engender secrecy of a public-funded institution by our courts, by our Health Department and by our Postal Inspection Service.

Of all the botched cover-ups, that of the Pennsylvania Department of Health was among the most outlandish.

The clandestine activities of the Hospital actors had been uncovered, over time; but a few documents later surfaced that revealed the anatomy of the Health Department's operations.

As a result of the Citizen Committee's efforts, the Health Department had made repeated visits to Indiana.

It was reported that the Department's surveyor, Nurse Sandra Jill Coffman, at one meeting with the Hospital's Medical Staff, announced that the Staff "had better clean up their act." She was "tired of coming to Indiana", according to those present.

She advised that no notes be taken and any already taken be destroyed.

Ms. Coffman again visited, in response to "Substantial Allegation, Complaint #229". Citizens visited Ms. Coffman's small office in the State Office Building in Pittsburgh's Golden Triangle for a copy of a report of that complaint. She refused, and with great authority, advised that Health Department investigations were always "confidential."

We would later see why. When a copy of the report of Complaint #229 finally surfaced from other sources, we read:

"Problem"
"Patient bled to death in Emergency Room
(Substantial allegation submitted by Medicare)"
"Methodology"
"1. Unannounced survey
2. Review of hospital record
3. Interview of Medical Staff members

    4. Special meeting with Executive Committee of Governing Body and Medical Staff
    5. Interview of Administration Committee"
  The report continued:
  "On call surgeon was called at 1:35 A.M. for the patient regarding rigid abdomen, arrived at 1:55 A.M."
  "The surgeon called for an assistant at 2"15 A.M. - He was under the weather"
  "Next surgeon was called at 2:25 A.M. - and refused to come"
  "Life Flight contacted by surgeon at 2:40 A.M. Refused to accept patient in unstable condition. The on call surgeon refused to take the patient to the Operating Room without an assistant since he didn't know what he would find"
  "The Director of the Emergency Room was notified of the problem. He in turn called the Chairman of the Department of Surgery. No assistant was gong to be provided for surgery. Only supportive care would be given to the patient. At 6"43 A.M. the patient died."
  "Conclusion"
  "Knowing the results of the autopsy, the patient would have died inspite (sic) of exploratory surgery..."
  "Deficiencies"
  "At this time, there are no deficiencies to be cited."
  "Recommendation"
  "As the surveyor for this facility, I don't feel that Dr. Ralph Miller, alias Concerned Citizens Committee should dictate the functions of the Department of Health, Division of Hospitals."
  The final comment had been obliterated with "white-out", but a little solvent revealed the surveyor's comment which was never intended to see the light of day.
  About a month later, the Director of the Health Department's Division of Hospitals wrote to a "certification specialist" at the federal Health Care Financing Administration.
  The letter read:
  "The report submitted to you during my absence contained several conclusions drawn by our surveyor that actually reflected her private opinion and in no way should reflect the opinion of the Pennsylvania Department of Health and the Division of Hospitals. We are submitting a corrected copy of the record for your files."

The cover-up was complete!

Another surfacing letter was to the Department of Health during its investigation of the Hospital. It was written by the Hospital Board Chairman to the Pennsylvania Secretary of Health.

One of the paragraphs reads:

"The last item of concern is that we believe Dr. H. Shue Hammon (one of the Health Department investigators) went beyond the scope of the investigation when he suggested that Dr. Miller be reinstated. The doctors were deeply troubled that such a suggestion was even considered..." - this from the Board Chairman who "had stayed out of this thing from beginning to end."

So much for the influence of the Pennsylvania Department of Health.

It has often been said, "Follow the money." The Citizens Committee had looked into Hospital finances and had documented that $16,500.00 each had been paid to two Lawyer Hospital-Board members for services on a bond issue and then each were paid another $11,000.00 when the bonds were reissued. Another Hospital Board member had drilled gas wells on Hospital property. A source reported to the Citizens Committee that, after revelation of these activities, certain monies were returned to the Hospital both by one of the lawyers and the driller. The Committee had learned that large sums were deposited interest-free in a local bank. The Hospital Board Chairman was a Director of that bank.

In response to the Citizens Committee obtaining copies of financial audits of the Hospital, the Hospital Lawyer wrote to the Director of the Pennsylvania Bureau of State-Aided Audits: The Hospital Lawyer's letter reads:

"Dear Mr. Ross,

We serve as legal counsel to the Indiana Hospital and we have noted your letter to the so-called Committee of Concerned Citizens for Hospital Improvement, with which letter you have enclosed copies of the most recent financial reports which have been submitted by Indiana Hospital to the Auditor General's office. While these financial statements are statements of which anyhospital could be proud, I think you would agree that the financial statements of any individual or institution are items which ought not to be distributed in any manner not consistent with need and propriety."

Signed, (The Hospital Lawyer)

Over the past few years, one has been led to ponder what could have been done differently, now knowing what occurs in our state and federal courts. The answer is, probably not much. But, when one considers the mentality of a gang, there is always the possibility of separating a few of the ringleaders. These personalities will seldom take on a fair tussle - they usually lose all motivation unless they are surrounded by their fellow members. Perhaps an attempt to bring the ringleaders to trial would have been successful. As it was, the conspirators were being protected by lawyers paid from Hospital insurance funds.

The moment of decision had come when I was summoned to meet with the Medical Staff "Executive Committee." The muddled confusion of that group was a reflection of limited intellects, mixed with a generous portion of hatred and envy. It is very unlikely that any self-respecting physician would subject himself to judgement by such a group.

The entire course of events was made possible because of my firm belief in the integrity of the people serving on the Hospital Board and the integrity of the Courts. Such folly! Hopefully others will be better informed and will avoid the pitfalls. Hopefully the professions will, at some point, control the evil in their ranks.

As the Hospital Lawyer advised in a brief encounter after the Kangaroo Court, "You must understand that you have been responsible for some significant changes at Indiana Hospital."

One of those changes that followed as a result of the obscene Kangaroo Court was a complete overhaul of the Hospital bylaws that would make outrageous hospital hearings less likely; the dramatic changes read:

*Prior to a disciplinary hearing there must be an informal discussion between any accused and the appropriate department chairman.

*When a hearing is scheduled the accused and his counsel must be provided documentation of any charges against him <u>before</u> the hearing.

*The accuser (such as Vader) is precluded from being present at a hearing and in participating in decisions related to the hearing.

*Reasons for any changes must be provided to the accused in time for preparation of a rebuttal.

*Names of witnesses must be provided prior to a hearing (contrary to the unannounced appearance of the Hospital Lawyer's witness Dr. Sladen at the Kangaroo Court.)

*The hearing officer must not be an advocate of either side (as opposed to the bias of the self-appointed Ms. Mattern as the hearing officer at the Kangaroo Court.).

*Intimidation not allowed at any hearings.

*After a request for revocation of hospital privileges, charges must be investigated (contrary to the Kangaroo Court when those wild charges were never investigated.)

*Individuals with conflicts of interest are expressly excluded from hearings (as opposed to Claude Clippins and the other members of the hearing panel at the Kangaroo Court.)

*Laypersons may be appointed to any hearing committee.

*Nothing shall prevent a physician whose privileges have been revoked from reapplying after a period of two years.

Not only will Indiana County physicians benefit from these required rules hopefully leading to "due process", but awareness of the scourge of Bad Faith Peer Review will perhaps not easily be kept from public view at state and national levels.

As the Semmelweis Society reported to the United States Supreme Court - "80% of the nation's peer review activities are economically driven and have nothing to do with quality of care."

It is quite possible that obscene hospital bylaws and egregious indifference to fair play and due process will continue to be more difficult to defend. It will, perhaps, be more difficult for a hospital lawyer to compose an outrageous set of bylaws and then be self-appointed to conduct a "trial"; using those corrupt standards, and to arrange the hire of a prosecutor, surrounded by secrecy.

Not to be overlooked, is that it has been demonstrated that effective medical care can be efficiently and safely provided in physicians' offices - even for surgical specialties. Not all patients require excessive testing or probing of their cavities with hollow tubes. Some of those who have been part of a line-up undergoing probing or who have even consented to a deforming procedure angrily reflect on their ignorance when they learn that they could have been treated with a surgeon's office management.

<u>Doctor in Jeopardy</u> evolved over a period of several years. Its creation has necessitated management of an number of obstacles - not the least of which involved the attempts by the Courts to keep records sealed.

But, never did the story face greater hazard than when the airline lost the baggage which held the only copy of the manuscript. After three months, the baggage turned up in Tampa and was delivered very late at night by a special courier.

Shortly before going to press, a copy of the manuscript was stolen from the back seat of a Pittsburgh lawyer's car. Things may still be getting stranger and stranger.

As we remember the past years, one would hope that it would become more unlikely that a hospital management enter into a defamation suit against citizens who do nothing more than expose the truth.

Above all, it would be hoped that hospital governing bodies would be loath to pursue a thorny path that has been shown to benefit no one.

Fate has not been kind to the conspirators. The Administrator was dismissed. The Hospital Board Chairman quietly left town, as have others. A woman Board member ran for public office and was handily defeated. The former Vice Chairman of the Board has seldom been heard from and is living out his dotage in a neighboring town. The Head Nurse was dismissed - apparently with rancor. Another Board member ended his life with gunshot in a shower stall. A former Board member describes that a consulting firm advised removal of the Board Chairman, the Vice Chairman, and the Lawyers from the Hospital Board. But, Vance Vader continues to lurk in the shadows.

Of that infamous Medical Staff "Executive Committee", some have passed on (some prematurely), some have decided on doing something else rather than practice Medicine, or have left town. One more Hospital Administrator was encouraged to serve a hospital somewhere else.

There isn't much doubt that the Hospital crowd was capable of retaliating against anyone who would dare to break ranks.

After one of our victories in the Court of Appeals, the Hospital and its lawyer called a meeting of the Hospital Defendants and their wives. One of the Hospital Board members who attended, berated the Hospital lawyer for not attempting to settle the antitrust suit.

Those present described that this provoked an outburst from three of the Defendants - Goldfarb, Hankey and Burger ; Vader, typically, stayed in the shadows. It was said that the Board member was called everything from "traitor" to "back-stabber."

There was possibly one positive outcome of that gathering - the wives saw first-hand how Medical Staff business was conducted.

Not so positive was the changed status of the dissenting Board member. There appeared to be a retaliatory loss of special status for a Board member who would, of course, ordinarily, have a V.I.P. next to his name or that of a family member.

The Board member resigned; his affidavit tells the story. It reads:

"8:35 P.M. I received a call from a postal employee that my father was in his car in front of the post office and appeared to be very sick. I arrived approximately five minutes later and found that Dad had been vomiting and I asked him if he felt any numbness and he said he did not. I also asked him if he felt strong enough to get into the back seat and he said he felt he could (I was trying to determine whether he needed an ambulance or not.) Before he got out of the car he noticed the vomit on the street and he said that he wanted to back the car up so as not to step in it. He then started the car put it in reverse and backed it three feet and then put the car back into park. Dad then got out of the car with my help (he appeared to be very weak) and largely on his own power got into to the back seat. I drove immediately to the Emergency Department. On the way Did told me very clearly that he felt he had had a stroke. (I thought he had the flu). Dad was then helped out of the back seat. Once again he did this pretty much on his own power and was then placed into an adjacent wheel chair and taken to the hospital emergency ward. How he got in the hospital bed I do not know because at the time I was in the process of admitting him.

His condition was evaluated by the emergency room physician. Upon completion of that evaluation which was some time after 9:00 the emergency room physician informed me that he felt Dad had had a stroke. With that information I told the emergency room doctor I would need (Dr. Garrels) to come out and attend to him. I then called (Dr. Jamie Garrels.) I told Jamie that Dad was in the Emergency room and had been hospitalized and it had been determined that he had had a stroke. Jamie told me that he was sorry to hear that but that he was not on call. I reiterated that my father appeared to be quite ill and had a stroke and I needed him there immediately. He told me the second time that he was not on call and that (Dr. Peter Post) was covering for him. I told Jamie Garrels that Peter Post was a total _ _ _ _ _ _ _ and incompetent and that I would not have him treat a sick dog. Apparently the emergency room physician heard me and requested a Dr. (J.E.A.) Who came in shortly after and reaffirmed the emergency room diagnosis and asked a lot of medical questions that Garrels would have known automatically and then admitted Dad to the hospital.

I told Dr. J.E.A. that I wanted my father moved immediately to Allegheny General Hospital. Dr. J.E.A. asked me not to do this and tried to convince me that the staff at the Indiana Hospital was every bit as good and competent as Allegheny General Hospital. I am not exactly sure what I said to him but it did not in any way confirm his conclusion. I do not think Dad saw another doctor until Garrels visited him at 7:30. At 8:30 when I went in to visit Dad after demanding that he be moved to Allegheny General I noticed a severe deterioration in his condition. He barely recognized me. His left hand was almost claw-like and it was obvious that his vision had become impaired.

At 11:30 AM we moved Dad to Allegheny General Hospital.

P.S. the conversation with Dr. Garrels was witnessed and overheard by my brother-in-law.

As a small subnote: When I appeared at Indiana Hospital on Friday morning I ran into Dr. Peter Post who quipped, "I see your Dad's in the hospital. What did he do, slit his throat?" I called him a _ _ _ _ _ _ _ _ _ _ _ _ _ _ (which he is!)"

Jamie Garrels and Peter Post were members of the Medical Staff Executive Committee which brought about the Kangaroo Court.

<u>Doctor in Jeopardy</u> has been a historical account of the clandestine activities that were part of a highly publicized legal battle involving a community hospital. There has been no effort to learn, nor interest, for that matter, in the present status of affairs at that institution. However, mindful of the admonition "he who ignores history is doomed to repeat its mistakes", one has to wonder.

Did anyone learn from the events of years past or would the Hospital continue to pursue a course of secrecy? The answer would come in spades.

After the Citizens Committee brought about a state and federal review of the Hospital, the Hospital Board was required to observe the law requiring hospitals to involve their communities by hosting at least one annual Board meeting with participation by the community.

The first of those meetings by the Hospital was probably the last. That meeting resulted in one more episode of contempt for the County's citizens.

It was an early summer evening and few of the Citizens Committee and their lawyer entered the ground floor of the new wing of the Hospital from the parking lot.

Our group took seats in the front row of the meeting area facing a series of folding tables for the Hospital's Board.

The audience was filling the room's seats and the Hospital Board, one by one, filtered in and took places around the folding tables. One had to wonder how qualified these people were to set standards for our community hospital.

As soon as we were seated, two large fellows, apparently security people in plain clothes, sat directly behind us. It must have been felt that we were there to cause a disturbance.

Without apology or explanation, I couldn't help feel repugnance as Abdul took his place at the table, followed by the busy Marge, who had initiated the former Administrator's witness tampering. The sick feeling wasn't helped when Abdul asked for a round of applause for Marge, for some reason. As the Board politely applauded, the audience sat mute and just stared at the charade. The ultimate in contempt for the audience followed, when the Board Chairman, a local bank president named Duggan, announced that there would be no questions from the audience.

So much for the Hospital involving its owners, the community, in its management.

Over time, there has been a fascination to watch matters go full circle. Not long ago, a caller asked if I would address a group of Health Care Lawyers of the Allegheny County Bar Association; the subject to be Miller v. Indiana Hospital. I did, and the irony of the invitation hasn't been lost. Some would think that my hobnobbing with Hospital Lawyers would be akin to Daniel in the lions den. Rather than that, it served as a beginning for people to learn the truth.

During that talk, the audience sat in silence as they learned of the Kangaroo Court and the following adventures in the state and federal court systems. Where they embarrassed? Surprised? Or, indifferent? One can only guess.

There are those who point to human behavior as a lesson that mankind is in its infancy; and most of us haven't earned doctorates in history. But we know that, in one way or another, we have paid a price, directly or indirectly, for the tyrants of the world who have induced others to follow them in their quests for power. It takes not only those demented ambitions with no regard for others, but a gullible following whose need to belong to a group overshadows any serious questioning of the "leaders."

A syndicated columnist recently lifted the description of a "psychopath" from a psychological text and paraphrased a psychological description of some of our nations leaders.

He wrote:

"These Trust Bandits (psychopaths) are everywhere. Most don't murder. A few become powerful figures in the world, politicians or corporate presidents. Since they are not controlled by accepted norms and do not have consciences, the usual rules do not apply. This can give some psychopaths a so called edge. But the mistake would be that the murderers are the only ones who can hurt us. Nothing is further from the truth. It is what most people don't know about these people that is so dangerous. At the core of the unattached is a deep-seated rage, far beyond normal anger. This rage is suppressed in their psyche. These bondless men, women and children see those around them as objects, targets, stepping stones. Most lie, steal and cheat without conscience, and they feel no remorse for their actions. If the suppressed rage even surfaces, they are capable of much more than a con."

It is unlikely that a serious reader confronting the unvarnished truths of <u>Doctor in Jeopardy</u>, after the varnish remover has been applied, would argue that the Health Care System and the Legal System are immune from those defective human beings, skilled at manipulating other people to achieve their goals.

Equally unlikely would be an argument denying the potential for tragic harm at the hand of these people.

As a Pittsburgh hospital advertises: "Choose your hospital as if your life depended upon it."

For physicians it would be prudent to "choose your hospital as if your career depended upon it."

The enlightened will usually set aside blind faith and deliberately ask, "Who do I want to deliver my baby, incise my body or order my drugs?" Who do I trust not to advise something unnecessary?"

With care, they will find one of the majority of competent physicians of integrity.

They will learn where to find the good doctors.

In the interim, as Shakespeare observed, "The evil men do lives after them; the good is oft interred with their bones.

So be it.

Epilogue

The earliest conviction that we were witnessing the beginning of what would become an astounding, almost unbelievable, series of events involving physicians and lawyers, came during the "Kangaroo Court", held at a Pennsylvania hospital.

After a series of incredible rulings by the biased hired "judge" at that trial, a comment to my lawyer friend was that the unfolding drama simply had to be told. His answer advised that the title had to be <u>Doctor in Jeopardy.</u>

Events that followed were to eclipse even that fetid scene of illegal behavior.

Perhaps we have become so hardened to the constant drumbeat of scandal and violence that we are resigned to the indifference of our institutions and our courts. We no longer dunk witches nor stone unfaithful women, but we do tolerate the secrecy of some of our hospitals and medical lynchings are common. They will remain common so long as we allow them to be held in secret.

While the story of <u>Doctor in Jeopardy</u> unfolds in a single Pennsylvania county, it is probable that none of our nation's counties, nor their community hospitals, are immune from the threats of Bad Faith Peer Review and the Conspiracy of Silence.

The stakes are too high when the veil of secrecy exists.

It is the belief that the light of publicity will help eliminate the menace of Bad Faith Peer Review affecting responsible physicians, throughout the nation, that has prompted the story to be written. It is written to inform health care professionals, as well as their patients, of some of the hazards that await the uninformed.

This is the story of one of those physicians dubbed "disruptive" for refusing to "go along to get along."

Frank Sinatra said it best when he sang:

> "The record shows,
> I took the blows, . . and
> did it my way."

The Author

Sources

Court Records - Indiana County Court of Common Pleas
    Miller v. McKown
    Miller v. Indiana Hospital
    Indiana Hospital v. The Committee of Concerned Citizens for Hospital Improvement
    Indiana Hospital v. Ralph J. Miller, M. D.
Court Records - Pennsylvania Superior Court
Court Records - Pennsylvania Supreme Court
Court Records - District Court for the Western District of Pennsylvania — Miller v. Indiana Hospital 81-1091
Court Records - Court of Appeals for the Third Circuit
Court Records - The United States Supreme Court
Documents, Pleadings - The Semmelweis Society
Amicus Briefs - United States Supreme Court
Citizen Affidavits
Publications - Indiana Hospital
Publications - Savings & Trust Bank
Communications:
    Joint Commission on Accreditation of Health Care Organizations
    University of Pittsburgh School of Medicine
    Pennsylvania Department of Health
    U. S. Department of Health and Human Services
    American Medical Association
    Pennsylvania Medical Society
    Indiana County Medical Society
    U. S. Federal Trade Commission
    Pennsylvania Bureau of State-Aided Audits
    U. S. Internal Revenue Service
    Allegheny County Bar Association
    The Pittsburgh Press
    The Pittsburgh Post Gazette
    The Indiana Gazette
    Johnstown Tribune Democrat
    Greensburg Tribune Review
    The Pennsylvania Medical Journal
    Medical Economics
    United States Postal Service
    United States Postal Inspection Service
    Records - Pennsylvania State Police
    Allegheny County Bar Association et. al.

ORDER FORM

POSTAL ORDERS:

AESCULAPIUS PUBLISHING
P.O. BOX 427
INDIANA, PA 15701-1

PAYMENT ☐ CHECK ☐ MONEY ORDER
NO. COPIES @17.75 - SHIPPING INCLUDED ☐
PA RESIDENTS ADD 6% SALES TAX
($1.07 — TOTAL $18.82)

ORDER FORM

POSTAL ORDERS:

AESCULAPIUS PUBLISHING
P.O. BOX 427
INDIANA, PA 15701-1

PAYMENT ☐ CHECK ☐ MONEY ORDER
NO. COPIES @17.75 - SHIPPING INCLUDED ☐
PA RESIDENTS ADD 6% SALES TAX
($1.07 — TOTAL $18.82)